THE ONTARIO HISTORICAL STUDIES SERIES

The Ontario Historical Studies Series is a comprehensive history of Ontario from 1791 to the present, which will include several biographies of former premiers, numerous volumes on the economic, social, political, and cultural development of the province, and a general history incorporating the insights and conclusions of the other works in the series. The purpose of the series is to enable general readers and scholars to understand better the distinctive features of Ontario as one of the principal regions within Canada.

THE BIOGRAPHIES OF THE PREMIERS

J.M.S. Careless, ed., *The Pre-Confederation Premiers: Ontario Government Leaders, 1841–1867*

Charles W. Humphries, *'Honest Enough to Be Bold': The Life and Times of Sir James Pliny Whitney* (Premier, 1905–1914)

Charles M. Johnston, *E.C. Drury: Agrarian Idealist* (Premier, 1919–1923)

Peter Oliver, *G. Howard Ferguson: Ontario Tory* (Premier, 1923–1930)

John T. Saywell, *'Just call me Mitch': The Life of Mitchell F. Hepburn* (Premier, 1934–1942)

Roger Graham, *Old Man Ontario: Leslie M. Frost* (Premier, 1949–1961)

A.K. McDougall, *John P. Robarts: His Life and Government* (Premier, 1961–1971)

FORTHCOMING

A. Margaret Evans, SIR OLIVER MOWAT (Premier, 1872–1896)
Robert J.D. Page, SIR GEORGE W. ROSS (Premier, 1899–1905)

W9-BPN-288

Mitchell Hepburn, 1934

JOHN T. SAYWELL

'Just call me Mitch': The Life of Mitchell F. Hepburn

Published by University of Toronto Press
Toronto Buffalo London
for The Ontario Historical Studies Series

ISBN 0-8020-3467-5 (cloth)
ISBN 0-8020-3468-3 (paper)

Printed on acid-free paper

Canadian Cataloguing in Publication Data

Saywell, John, 1929–
  Just call me Mitch

(Ontario historical studies series, ISSN 0380-9188)

Includes bibliographical references and index.
ISBN 0-8020-3467-5 (bound) – ISBN 0-8020-3468-3 (pbk.)

1. Hepburn, Mitchell Frederick, 1896–1953.
2. Prime ministers – Ontario – Biography.
3. Ontario – Politics and government – 1923–1943.*
4. Liberal Party in Ontario – History.
I. Title. II. Series.

FC3075.I.H46S3 1991   971.3'04'092   C91-094871-2
FI058.H46S3 1991

This book has been published with funds provided by the Government
of Ontario through the Ministry of Culture and Communications.

FOR ALL MY CHILDREN

Contents

Illustrations following pages 132 and 356

The Ontario Historical Studies Series

For many years the principal theme in English-Canadian historical writing has been the emergence and the consolidation of the Canadian nation. This theme has been developed in uneasy awareness of the persistence and importance of regional interests and identities, but because of the central role of Ontario in the growth of Canada, Ontario has not been seen as a region. Almost unconsciously, historians have equated the history of the province with that of the nation and have depicted the interests of other regions as obstacles to the unity and welfare of Canada.

The creation of the province of Ontario in 1867 was the visible embodiment of a formidable reality, the existence at the core of the new nation of a powerful if disjointed society whose traditions and characteristics differed in many respects from those of the other British North American colonies. The intervening century has not witnessed the assimilation of Ontario to the other regions in Canada; on the contrary it has become a more clearly articulated entity. Within the formal geographical and institutional framework defined so assiduously by Ontario's political leaders, an increasingly intricate web of economic and social interests has been woven and shaped by the dynamic interplay between Toronto and its hinterland. The character of this regional community has been formed in the tension between a rapid adaptation to the processes of modernization and industrialization in modern Western society and a reluctance to modify or discard traditional attitudes and values. Not surprisingly, the Ontario outlook is a compound of aggressiveness, conservatism, and the conviction that its values should be the model for the rest of Canada.

From the outset the objective of the Board of Trustees of the series has been to describe and analyse the historical development of Ontario as a distinct region with Canada. The series as planned will include thirty-one volumes covering many aspects of the life and work of the province from its original establishment in 1791 as Upper Canada to our own time. Among these will be biographies of several premiers, numerous works on the growth of the provincial economy, educational institutions, minority groups, and the arts, and a synthesis of the history of Ontario, based upon the contributions of the biographies and thematic studies.

In planning this project, the Editors and the Board have endeavoured to maintain a reasonable balance between different kinds and areas of historical research, and to appoint authors ready to ask new questions about the past and to answer them in accordance with the canons of contemporary scholarship. Nine biographies have been commissioned, because through biography the past comes alive most readily for the general reader as well as for the historian.

'Just call me Mitch': The Life of Mitchell F. Hepburn is the seventh biography to be published. It is a vivid, scholarly account of the career of a premier who enjoyed life to the full, and often in scandalous ways. An Elgin County farmer, Hepburn rose through the House of Commons to become leader of the moribund Ontario Liberals, and in 1934 the first Liberal premier since 1905. He governed the province vigorously but erratically, and resigned in 1942, leaving his party in a coma from which it did not emerge until the 1980s.

John Saywell has used an immense range of written and oral sources in constructing a masterful and illuminating interpretation of the motives and actions of a politician liked by all who knew him, and whose contradictions baffled his party and his province.

The Editors and the Board of Trustees are grateful to Professor Saywell for undertaking this task.

Goldwin French
Peter Oliver
Jeanne Beck
Maurice Careless, Chairman of the Board of Trustees

Toronto
28 June 1991

Preface

This book has been far too long in the writing. Administrative chores got in the way: Africa and Japan beckoned. Without a rich central spine of Hepburn papers, no sources could be overlooked, however low their prospective yield. I know the editors and directors of the OHSS despaired of ever seeing a completed manuscript, and I am deeply grateful to Goldwin French, Peter Oliver, and Jeanne Beck for their infinite patience and generous research support. Without York University's policy of supporting graduate students with research assistantships, many sources would have remained unexamined. Many York graduates will see the results of their labour in the text and the endnotes; I thank them all. To single out a few does not minimize the contribution of others, but I must name Jock Bryce, David Coombs, David Moore, George Vegh, and Greg Johnson, as well as Jane Harrison and Michael Wiebe who did not attend York. My administrative colleagues at York – Susan Merry, Lillian Kindree, and Diane Jenner – provided invaluable assistance.

In St Thomas, George Thorman, Don Cosens, and Bill Tapsell were invaluable local guides. John Ricker, my close friend and co-author in many endeavours, did his best to improve the quality of the prose and the clarity of the exposition. Without his work on a draft, Diane Mew of the University of Toronto Press would have had an even more formidable task of editing the manuscript for publication. Jack Granatstein has been a constant source of encouragement and sound advice – and when necessary a burr under the saddle. I have learned much over the years from the quiet wisdom and sure historical touch of Blair Neatby, whose friendship goes back to the day we first met at the old archives in the spring of 1953. Over the years – indeed, since 1961 when I did a TV documentary on Hepburn – I have talked to many of Hepburn's contemporaries: Elgin farmers, friends and relatives, politicians and journalists, Queen's Park bureaucrats and secretaries. That experience has left me with serious reservations about the value of oral history, unless the testimony is consonant with other evidence, for many of the recollections are self-serving and factually incorrect. There were some who spoke to me without attribution and I am particularly grateful to two of them.

'Whoever turns biographer commits himself to lies, to concealment, to hypocrisy, to embellishments, and even to dissembling his own lack of understanding,' Sigmund Freud insisted, 'for biographical truth is not to be had and, even if one had it, one could not use it.'[1] That absolute biographical (or historical) truth is not to be had is undeniable, but by basing the life of Mitchell Hepburn on the solid footing of contemporary evidence and letting his life unfold in the context of his time, not mine, I hope the reader will agree that something approaching biographical truth can be had and can be used.

'JUST CALL ME MITCH': THE LIFE OF MITCHELL F. HEPBURN

1

'Into the Promised Land'

It was cold and clear in St Thomas on 7 January 1953. Men and women shivered and blew into their hands as they greeted each other on Wellington Street. Slowly they filed into Knox Presbyterian Church. Moving to the front pews were Leslie Frost, the premier of Ontario, and three ex-premiers: George Henry, Harry Nixon, and George Drew. Behind them sat those who had served their time in the House of Commons and the Legislative Assembly at Queen's Park, and some who were still there. Weather-beaten farmers from all over Elgin County and southwestern Ontario shifted uncomfortably in the starched collars and dress suits reserved for weddings and funerals. They had come to the church, as they had in happier days to the Masonic Temple, Pinafore Park, and the birthday parties at Bannockburn Farm, to be with Mitch Hepburn.

'You met him, you shook hands with him, you were warmed by his famous smile and you heard him say "I'm Mitch Hepburn" and in a few minutes you were calling him Mitch and you liked it and you knew he liked it and you felt you had always known him ... He offered you his greatest gift – his friendship. It was yours to accept. It was as simple as that.' The man in the simple wooden casket had not spent many mornings in church, but the Reverend Harry Rodney had captured these essential qualities. Among the mourners there were those who felt that Mitch Hepburn could do no wrong. There were others who believed that in the end he had betrayed the boys in the back concessions, that he had been too much the sinner and too little the saint.

But that afternoon they agreed with Rodney that time should determine his place in history. They were there because of 'our affection, for not the leader, the statesman, the orator, the successful farmer, but the man. His warm personality, his buoyant spirit, his love of life and people, his friendliness – these are the things that endeared him to the people who knew him best, both in public and private life.' As the casket was lowered into the ground near the resting place of old Mitch and his mother, Les Frost murmured quietly to a friend, 'No one could dislike Mitch, not if you really knew him.'

Les Frost had known Mitch for more than twenty years, and remembered only too well that day in June 1934 when the Hepburn mania that swept the province forced him to practice law in Lindsay for another three years. There were reporters at the funeral who remembered when Hepburn came to Queen's Park to form the first Liberal government in almost thirty years. 'Do you want to be called Mitchell Frederick Hepburn or Mitchell F. Hepburn?' one asked. The young man smiled: 'Just call me Mitch.' And 'Mitch' he has remained.

There have been no other Mitches – before or since. Even the modern practice of an early and easy first name familiarity did not bridge the private space between Les and John and Bill and David and their public. 'Old Man Ontario' has usually played it safe, preferring university graduates to kids who walked out of school at sixteen. Ontario has chosen cool and cautious men, whose ambitions, however unbridled, were cloaked in assumed modesty, whose public words were deferential to the traditional values and institutions of their community, and whose private life, however incontinent, was clothed in the dress of virtue and shielded from public view through some covenant with the opposition and the press.

Mitch Hepburn was unique. Hot and impulsive, incapable of imposing restraint on his private life, and hyperbolic in speech and behaviour, he lived on the edge of his physical and emotional resources. Ontario has preferred leaders who had a firm grip on the tiller or, some would say, who used the brake more than the accelerator. Mitch Hepburn held the tiller of his public and private life with a light hand, and his foot sped from brake to accelerator with a seemingly carefree and sometimes dizzying abandon.

As a boy he was called 'Mitchie' or 'Little Mitch' to distinguish him from his grandfather after whom he was named. Old Mitch had come to Yarmouth in Elgin County in the fall of 1843, at nine the youngest in a party of fifteen led by Andrew Hepburn who had left Newborough in Fifeshire for the shores of Lake Erie in Canada West. Although there were rumours that he was both Andrew's son and grandson by his own daughter Margaret, the truth is less incestuous. Left behind in the Parochial Register in Newborough was an entry recording that on 21 July 1834, Margaret, then twenty-four, had given birth to a son. The father was Michael Broom, a hand-loom weaver, and the boy was, the entry baldly stated, 'Born in Fornication.' He carried the name Michael Broom to Canada, but as time passed he became known as Mitchell Hepburn and Michael Broom disappeared.[1]

The west end of Yarmouth gradually became Hepburn country. The girls married into the neighbouring families, and the men became substantial landowners and members of the political élite. But none prospered more than Old Mitch. He lived with his grandfather until he died in 1850 and left the sixteen-year-old £50 and a yoke of oxen. By 1863 Old Mitch had saved enough to buy land in the fourth concession north of Union. It is still Hepburn land today. Six foot three and well proportioned, he was as shrewd as he was strong and hard-working. In 1888 when he added one hundred acres across the road from his homestead – now the site of Bannockburn Farm – he was prosperous enough to be in the mortgage business. By the turn of the century, with six hundred acres, Old Mitch was one of the largest landowners in Yarmouth.[2]

But Old Mitch's personal life was tragic. In 1865 he had married Elizabeth Johnson, daughter of a prominent Yarmouth settler. Mitch and Eliza had four children, but two lived only nine months and the other two died of scarlet fever in 1875. About 1873 they inherited a baby boy who, it was said, had been left on the doorstep. Although never legally adopted, the boy was named William Frederick Hepburn. His mother almost certainly was Annie Mustard, a buxom young girl who had come from Michigan to work on the farm. There were many who believed that Old Mitch was the father, but the more likely culprit was a young buck named Luton.[3]

Will grew up as the son and heir, hard-working enough to satisfy old Mitch and 'ever kind and obliging' to Eliza. But Will was not cut of the old man's cloth. He was too restless, too fond of good clothes, good times, and the company of women. Will married Maggie, the daughter of James Fulton, one of five brothers who had left northern Ireland in 1836 and settled in Southwold Township. Old Mitch gave Will, in trust, a hundred acres across Fruit Ridge Road from his home, and helped the young couple build a small but stately brick house. The first child, Irene, arrived in August 1895. A year later, on 12 August 1896, Mitchell Frederick Hepburn was born in the second-floor bedroom.[4]

Farm and family could not absorb Will's restless energy. The dashing young man with his bowler at a rakish angle, and the belle of Southwold with the full figure and the upswept hair, were a popular couple. Will enjoyed his trips to town with a stop along the way at Charlie Miner's farm to take a glass or two, play a bit of euchre, or even toss the dice. For a popular young man carrying the Hepburn name, politics did not seem too much of a gamble and Will was easily elected councillor in 1901. A year later he moved to St Thomas to try his hand at selling agricultural implements. From their rented house on Queen Street young Mitchell walked the short distance to Wellington Street School to begin grade one under the watchful eye of Miss Allie Pye. But in May 1904 Will moved the family back to the farm.[5]

When Sir Wilfrid Laurier went to the people in the fall of 1904, Will Hepburn seemed the ideal choice for the Liberals to capture the Tory stronghold of East Elgin. A good speaker with a good organization, Will ran a strong campaign but the Tories held the seat by a narrow margin. Whispers of increased Tory support among Yarmouth farmers were only to be expected. Even if Will was not the 'whiskey barrel' the Tories claimed, he was known to take a drink now and again and had too sharp an eye for the ladies.

Mitchie was eight when his father ran in 1904. The next two years were as idyllic as any he would know as a child. When the family moved back to the farm he walked or rode his pony the mile south to the one-room school at Union, often stopping for a visit with Grandpa Mitch. He was a good student, seldom at a loss for words, with a reputation for playfulness, and an abundance of enthusiasm if not talent on the playground. But his life was dramatically altered when his father contested a federal by-election in 1906. Despite a whispering campaign that Will's personal life would not bear inspection and that he had profited personally from some government contracts, victory seemed almost certain when suddenly he withdrew. Rumours of his involvement with two women of 'bad character' during the campaign, he told his supporters, threatened to 'destroy my home life.'

Although the whole truth was never known because the political and personal feuds in Elgin went much deeper than the fear of perjury or libel, Mitch and Maggie lived for years under the long shadows cast by Will's excesses. What actually happened, according to Will, was that after a long day campaigning he had arrived at the Orwell Hotel on the Aylmer road about 6:30. After dinner he wrote some letters and went to bed. But according to the proprietor, David Butler, and other witnesses whose testimony the Tories secured over the next three years, Bessie Gilroy, a waitress in an Aylmer hotel,

and Anna Stinger, a piano seller, with her fifteen-year-old son, were
also at the hotel. Will ordered a few rounds of drinks and, Anna
recalled in an affidavit, retired with Bessie to his bedroom until after
midnight when they all hitched up a rig and took Bessie home. After
a few drinks the others returned to the Orwell. Anna insisted she
had retired with her son; Butler said she slept with Will.

Despite Hepburn's claim that it was a wicked Tory conspiracy,
Magistrate Hunt accepted Butler's tale and found him guilty of
keeping a disorderly house. Later that fall Judge Colter, re-exam-
ining the evidence, concluded that Bessie and Anna had come to the
Orwell 'to entrap' Hepburn and that the whole affair was, as Will
claimed, 'a foul and most wicked conspiracy.' By then Butler had
disappeared, Bessie had left town with $25 of Will's money in her
purse, and Anna had found the $100 that had come her way to leave
the country more immediately rewarding than selling pianos. But it
was Bessie and Anna's written testimony, sent from a distance three
year later, that persuaded a commissioner appointed by the provincial Conservatives to conclude that there could be 'no reasonable
doubt that Hepburn was the victim of his own indiscretion rather
than any conspiracy against him.' To the Elgin Grits it was still a
conspiracy, however, for the Tories knew only too well that with
booze and women Will was bound to be indiscreet.[6]

Like the others, Will Hepburn had not lingered in St Thomas to
hear the outcome of the Colter hearing, but had found it convenient
to visit relatives in St Paul, Minnesota. When school was over, Maggie and the children joined Will in St Paul, where they stayed for a
year before moving to Winnipeg. The fortune Will hoped to make in
real estate eluded him; he lost money on a contract to harvest telephone poles; and Maggie vainly hoped that once his fishing boat
was working 'we will have lots of money coming in.' Moreover, the
Winnipeg papers picked up the Orwell Hotel story during the 1909
inquiry. As Maggie sadly reported to her brother, 'Well Sam Will
came home to-night nearly Broken hearted ... he is worried to death
to think it is in the paper out here it is so terrible to think they will
swear to such lies when Will cannot be there to deni them Poor Will
he is worried terrible they will kill him yet with that old thing Stirring it up for ever.' Indeed, Will was so worried he had 'them cold
sweats again.'[7]

Maggie and the children lived in Winnipeg for two years. Mitch
enjoyed school. He stood first in his class, with a 90 in history, but
complained about the lack of hills for sleighing and worried all the
time about the animals on his farm. He wrote his high school

entrance exams before an increasingly homesick Maggie moved the children back to St Thomas in the summer of 1910. She rented a house about ten minutes walk from the St Thomas Collegiate Institute where Mitch registered in grade nine. He stood third much of the year and was best in history and composition, although he missed most of May and June with typhoid fever. George Gray, his grade ten history teacher, gave Mitch 100 and said he 'was one of those students a teacher rejoices in,' a student with a lively mind who liked to read and discuss, who not only answered questions but asked them. Mitch's performance in other subjects was less impressive. His average fell from 74 to 66 and he stood tenth in the class.

Mitch registered for grade eleven in September 1912, but his education was soon cut short. On Monday, 7 October, the students were let out to go over to Alex Anderson's farm on the outskirts of town to watch the latest electric circus promoted by Adam Beck, the father of Ontario Hydro. Talbot Street had become the Great White Way in March 1911 when Beck had turned on Hydro, and now he was back to demonstrate the miracle of rural electrification and such labour-saving devices as automatic milkers. There were the inevitable speeches, and to one restless teenager perched in an apple tree the combination of an apple and Beck's bowler was irresistible. The crowd laughed as Beck recovered his bowler, and although the local reporters overlooked the incident, V.K. Greer, one of his teachers, pointed the accusing finger at Mitch. Denying that he had thrown the apple, Mitch refused to apologize or name the culprit, gathered up his books, and stormed out of school. A few days later he got a job in the Merchants Bank and in November transferred to the Bank of Commerce. Mitch never said so, but he probably seized on the opportunity to bring his formal education to an abrupt end.[8]

Maggie yielded to Will's appeals to come west again in the summer of 1913 and in the fall Mitch secured a transfer to a bank in Winnipeg. In the summer of 1914 he joined the recently organized Fort Garry Horse. He was eight days from his eighteenth birthday when war broke out on 4 August. When the Fort Garry's were mobilized, Mitch drilled with C squadron for a week. But when the order came to proceed to Valcartier, Mitch was still a few days under age and Will and Maggie refused their consent. 'Hepburn was paraded in and in view of his parents' statements,' the Commanding Officer wrote, 'the enlistment was cancelled.'[9]

Maggie may have leaned on a son very close to his mother, for she knew that the Winnipeg reunion could not last. They returned to St Thomas, where Mitch was soon transferred to the sub-branch of the bank in Port Stanley. He joined the Bachelors Club, a group of fourteen young men-about-town who enlivened the long winters with dances at the town hall. As spring moved on to summer, life picked up for the bachelor who lived above the bank. The Port was a resort town and the boardwalk, the beach, and the dance floor at Hopkins' Casino attracted the young and the beautiful from all over the county and as far away as London.

Many of the young men on the boardwalk in the summer of 1915 were in uniform, and Mitch was anxious to join them. From Winnipeg, where she was trying another reconciliation with Will, Maggie wrote Uncle Sam Fulton to try and stop him: 'He is her only boy so you can't blame her,' Sam explained to his girl friend Clara. Mitch went on the rolls of the 25th Regiment, the local militia unit in St Thomas, and on 8 December was listed as a provisional lieutenant. A week later he took six weeks' leave from the bank for military training, and on 24 January resigned to undertake 'full-time military duty.' After a short officer training course with the 91st Overseas Battalion in London he qualified as a lieutenant. But his attempt to become an officer on the 91st's establishment failed, according to Major Frank Palmer, because 'it was easier for a camel to get through the eye of a needle than a Grit to get an appointment to a commission in one of Sam Hughes' battalions.'

Mitch apparently had no desire to enlist as a private and joined his elderly grandfather on the farm. Old Mitch had been married again in 1915 – just a week before his eightieth birthday – to Elva Waite, a spry spinster of forty-seven. In December he repossessed Will's farm and gave Mitch the land, subject to a life lease to Maggie. The life of a farmer, however, did not interfere too much with Mitch's social life and by May 1917 there were a number of women in his life, as Uncle Sam self-righteously reported to Clara:

Mitch is going with a Miss Fraser and also is going with Eva Burton for he thinks she is far ahead of Grace G. I do not think so but he said Eva Burton never went with anyone yet and was so smart and a real girl that she suited him everyway. He met her at the Coon Road School dance ... Burton has four girls so he can have a choice. He has not been with Grace for a month I hope they make it up for I think she is a sweet little girl and he has kept steady company for four years.

There was also a new Ford that became a familiar sight on the gravel road between St Thomas and Port Stanley.[10]

But in October 1917, with the proclamation of the Military Service Act, Mitch's days as a civilian were numbered and he was ordered to report for duty in London on 21 May 1918. Two weeks later he was released to join the Royal Air Force and was posted as an air mechanic third class to Deseronto where he joined his good friends George Ponsford, a flying instructor, and George Loney, another banker from Port Stanley.[11] Soon afterwards the three men were driving home for the July 1 weekend in Mitch's Ford when, with Mitch taking a break from the wheel, the car hit some loose gravel and overturned near Woodstock. The three were badly shaken up and Mitch spent some time in hospital with internal injuries. The doctors diagnosed the pain around his kidney as a faulty appendix – which they promptly removed. Not until late in August was he posted back to the base, and then as a hospital orderly.[12]

During his recovery Mitch had seen even more of Eva Burton, one of the daughters of John Burton, a Fingal farmer who had won 180 votes as a Socialist candidate in the 1905 provincial election. A weekend of haying with Uncle Sam early in September put him to bed, but he was well enough on Sunday night to take the Burton girls to the Port. Eva was going to London the next day to find a boarding-house while she attended normal school. 'Let's forget normal school,' said Mitch impulsively, 'and you and I get married.' Three days later they were married at Knox Presbyterian Church in a ceremony so small that even Uncle Sam was not invited. 'We just up and got married,' Mitch explained. 'Didn't say anything to anybody.' Mitch was back in Deseronto when he was struck by a severe attack of influenza later in the fall. It was a slow recovery, his weight dropped from 149 to 118 pounds, and the war was over before he was discharged as medically unfit on 2 January 1919.[13]

At twenty-four Mitch Hepburn looked forward to life as an Elgin County farmer. He and Eva settled in the brick house where he was born. The two hundred acres of good farm land Old Mitch had given him was not a bad start for a young man, and he also helped supervise the farm hands on the more than three hundred acres the old man still worked. Maggie and Mitch grew even closer to Old Mitch and with each successive change in his will from 1920 until his death he became increasingly generous. In his last codicil four months before he died on 15 October 1922, he gave Maggie the $10,000 once intended for Will, and Mitch $1,000. Once all his cash bequests had been made, Elva, Maggie, Will, Mitch, and his old friend Andrew Grant were to split the rest of the estate equally.

The estate was valued at $156,000 with $28,500 in land, $10,000 in stocks, bonds, and cash, and the rest in mortgages. Mitch spent much of the next two years winding up the estate. He could not hold the original homestead, but he was determined to retain the two-hundred-acre Yorke farm which Old Mitch had bought in 1892. With Maggie's help and the use of Will's share he bought it for $11,000 and took out a $4,900 mortgage. By Elgin County standards Mitch was prosperous. He owned almost four hundred acres of land, with a good house, barns and stables, silos and a granary, and up-to-date equipment. Maggie too was more than comfortable. Once the estate was settled she bought a home at 59 Gladstone Street in St Thomas and left the farming to her son.[14]

Although Mitch boasted that he was a good farmer, many of his neighbours said he was too erratic and men who worked with him described him as a gentleman farmer, a man close to the land but never of it. His resources allowed him to be progressive, and his farm was one of the first in Yarmouth to be completely electrified. Like most dairy farmers he kept a large number of hogs and, with considerable pasture, some sheep. Although he had a tractor, he preferred to work the farm with fourteen horses. By the time he was thirty, Mitch had one of the largest farms in the township.[15]

Like Old Mitch, however, his private life was tragic. Eva's first child arrived stillborn in June 1921. Three years later, on 9 October 1923, she bore a son whom they named William Burton. He lived only three months and a day. Mitch and Eva were to have no surviving children of their own.

Mitch had grown up in an intensely political family and, despite his father's indiscretions, it was natural that he too would be drawn into politics. Old Mitch had been an ardent Grit, and the young boy papered his room with pictures of Laurier. He had driven voters to the polls in the family rig in 1911 in a losing cause in Elgin, and worked for the provincial Liberals in 1914 and the Laurier Liberals three years later. Keenly interested in public affairs, Mitch was much in demand as a speaker. In church basements and local halls he dealt with the post-war upheaval which had produced the farmers' movement that had swept Ontario and the west, and the new militancy in the labour movement. His views were influenced by the socialist views of his father-in-law, by long talks with his friend Albert Rogers, a local socialist, and by the laments of Elgin farmers about the cost-price squeeze and the costly effects of the tariff.

Personally, Mitch concluded that some form of political action was essential to 'combat the economic injustice which the influence of big interests was inflicting on the people.'[16]

Mitch voted for the United Farmers of Ontario in the 1919 provincial election when both Elgin ridings sent UFO members to Queen's Park, where E.C. Drury formed a farmer-labour government. He had been one of the founding members of the East Elgin UFO and by the 1923 election was secretary of the association when the UFO ran a poor third in both ridings and Howard Ferguson and the Tories returned triumphantly to office. Although the UFO officially withdrew from politics at the December convention, the disillusioned delegates agreed that 'since political action is necessary to the full attainment of our aspirations and ideals we will not oppose the formation of a political party which shall embody these principles.' To many, Mitch among them, that party was the Progressive Party, and by 1925 he was widely regarded as 'the leading progressive of the district.'[17]

By 1925, however, Mitch was working for the Liberals in the federal election. He had become convinced, wrote his elderly friend Alex Darrach, 'that a narrow organization like the UFO was only dividing those of the electorate who should be acting together and that it was necessary for all of us to pull together or go down to defeat at the hands of a compact enemy whose financial strength made cohesion natural and whose ownership of the newspapers, the banks and other great sources of influence made it easy to enlarge their army by attracting the unthinking masses.' Mitch was a familiar figure during the campaign as his car churned up the dust on the gravel roads and he leaned over the fence to persuade his neighbours to vote for Sloggett, the Liberal candidate, and Mackenzie King, the prime minister. His speeches made the headlines in the local Tory paper: 'MITCH ASKS WHERE MONEY COMES FROM'; 'HEPBURN STIRRING UP DUNWICH PROGRS.'; 'SPEAKER AT LIBERAL GATHERING HOLDS OWN WITH HECKLERS.'

Mitch was completely at home on the Elgin hustings. With a few notes on a sheet of paper, he combined a rapid-fire delivery, flashes of wit, dashes of left-wing rhetoric, and doses of traditional Liberal free trade economics to woo the Elgin farmers. At Crinan he dramatically held up large advertisements which at $1,000 each had cost the Tories a total of $40,000 a day. 'If Mr. McKillop is elected and it comes to a vote in the House, will he do his duty to his constituents or will he fulfil his obligations to the source of these funds?' At Eagle he warned the farmers not to repeat the error of 1911.

'Through the medium of the tariff each class seeks by legislation to boost the price of his product,' he lectured. 'Thus the great law of supply and demand is trampled underfoot by selfish interests in their mad scrambling to take more out of the market than they are willing to put into it.' Everywhere he portrayed Arthur Meighen, the Tory leader, as the pawn of those selfish interests, supporting high tariffs and the vicious combines that flourished under their protective shadow. But Mitch could not stem the Tory tide. McKillop won comfortably in Elgin. All five of King's Ontario ministers and the prime minister himself suffered crushing defeats. With only ninety-nine of the 245 seats in the Commons, King nevertheless clung onto power, hoping that the twenty-four Progressives would support him rather than Meighen.[18]

Less than a year later, however, Mitch was on the hustings again when the governor general refused King's request for a dissolution and gave Arthur Meighen the opportunity to form a government and appeal to the people. There were many Elgin Liberals who believed that Mitch Hepburn had demonstrated his ability to stimulate the party and arouse the voters, but as Alex Darrach said, 'Milton spoke for West Elgin Grits when he said there [are] those who would "rather rule in hell than serve in heaven".' Factions in the east and west end of the riding battled for control, while John Elliott, the MP from neighbouring Middlesex West, intrigued with friends and relatives in Elgin. The chaotic state of the party organization was starkly revealed when, after three hours of tortured and sometimes angry discussion, none of the eleven men nominated agreed to stand. In the end, the executive persuaded William Tolmie, the 'Bean King of Aldborough,' to run.

Tolmie had carried the Liberal flag nobly to defeat in three federal elections, and was not the man to win Elgin. The executive visited Mitch at the farm on two successive days and tried to persuade him to run. The obstacle was less Mitch than his mother, who felt that Mitch's indifferent health could not stand the strain of a political career. Perhaps she also reflected on her own life with Will, and already saw in the son too much of the father. Finally she relented. On 12 August, his thirtieth birthday, Mitch Hepburn's name was the only one put forward when the Liberals met again at the Masonic Temple.

Mitch astutely insisted on running as an Independent Liberal. Free of any formal attachment to the Liberal party, he could appeal to the old Progressives, many of whom had returned to the Tory fold, as well as to the Tory railwaymen in St Thomas. Accepting the nomination, Mitch asked for the support of all Elgin farmers and workers, regardless of their party loyalties, and promised 'to subscribe to no party policy that made him vote against his own convictions.' Mitch Hepburn would obey his constituents, not the party whip. But non-partisanship had its limits, for it was the Tories 'standing behind the exploiting classes who would make dromedaries of the masses' and who in 1837 had taken 'men from South Yarmouth to London and hung them because they stood for responsible government.' And it was the scandal-ridden Tories in Ottawa and Queen's Park who reminded him of 'the old negro at a camp meeting who confessed to chicken stealing, bribery and a dozen other offences but thanked the Lord that he "never lost his religion". It would appear,' he shouted over the laughter, 'that as long as these Tories don't lose their Toryism, they can do no wrong.' As for Hugh McKillop, he had only been awake in the Commons long enough to vote against lower automobile prices, a lower income tax, and freer trade. 'That's a damned lie,' the three-hundred-pound slow-spoken lumberman retorted, 'I was too busy to sleep.'

Mitch promised a vigorous campaign. For a month he packed town halls and country schools, drove unannounced into countless farms to sit around the kitchen table or walk behind teams in the field, greeted old friends in Port Stanley, and with carefully chosen friends visited the local bootleggers. The arguments were always the same: the King government had already reduced the tariff on agricultural implements, reduced taxes, and cut the letter rate from three to two cents. The Liberals stood for freer trade, lower freight rates, and the end of tariff-protected combines. The country needed the abolition of the Senate, that pasture for the exploiting classes, and Elgin needed an active spokesman free from the evils of partyism.

Mitch could expect to gain some votes in the rural townships and the small towns. But to win Elgin he had to crack St Thomas which contained 15,500 of the 40,500 people in the riding and which had given McKillop all but two hundred of his eighteen hundred majority. The key was to cut into the votes of the three thousand railwaymen, who had voted Tory since the days of John A., and their newly enfranchised wives. His friends among the young railwaymen worked the east end of the city, and in their enthusiasm broke not only the election laws but also the provincial liquor law. Prominent left-wingers, such as Albert Roberts, endorsed his denunciation of Toryism and partyism. From Toronto came Arthur Roebuck, a 1911 Liberal who had run as a Lib-Lab in 1917 and for the UFO/Labour alliance in 1923. A well-known labour lawyer, Roebuck had worked for the Brotherhood of Railway Trainmen, a very large union in St Thomas. Mitch later said that he owed a great deal to Roebuck, who 'seemed to be the connecting link between progressive, labour and liberal parties.'

There was no help from Ottawa, and appeals to the 'highlites' of the party brought 'snubs instead of assistance.' Elgin was not a riding the Liberals expected to win. There was no cabinet minister who could draw a crowd, no organization, and little money. However, the record of the government before its demise in June did help, particularly Finance Minister James Robb's retroactive reduction in the income tax. 'Just about election time the lads were receiving forty dollar cheques in the way of refund,' said one railway worker after the election. 'A man would stick his cheque in his pocket and say, "It's no josh about the Grit government saving us money".' Robb had also lowered the duty on agricultural implements in 1924 and in April 1926 slashed the duty on lower-priced cars from 35 to 20 per cent.

It probably cost about $10,000 to fight the election. Most was found locally, largely in St Thomas, and Mitch also dug deeply into his own pocket. On the whole it was a clean campaign. Mitch laughed off rumours about his private life with the comment that if he had done everything the Tories whispered he was indeed an active man for one they also claimed was in such poor health.

Mitch and Eva waited for the results in the office of the *Times-Journal*. The early returns from St Thomas showed that the Tory vote had dropped sharply in the east end. By the end of the night McKillop's majority in the city had fallen from sixteen hundred to six hundred. The returns from every township but South Dorchester gave Mitch a majority. In the traditionally Tory towns men looked suspiciously at each other as only Dutton and Port Stanley remained loyal, and even there Mitch had cut deeply into McKillop's majority. The Liberals had asked that the 'boy from Yarmouth' be given a chance and by a margin of 178 votes Elgin sent the first Liberal member to Ottawa in the century.

Mitch spoke to the jubilant crowd from the window of the *Times-Journal*, lavishing praise on the party organizers, the women, the railway and harbour workers, and the independent farmers of Elgin. Even for his opponents there was some consolation, as Mitch promised to represent everyone in Elgin and make 'you who voted for me and you who didn't vote for me proud of me.' And then it was into the night and a procession along Talbot Street behind a thousand flaming brooms. The next day, despite the rain, there was a tumultuous auto parade out to the farm where the ladies ate ice cream and cakes and many of the men frequently disappeared to the hundreds of cars and trucks that were parked along R.R. 4 to toast their new member with something more fitting.

The *Times-Journal* felt the victory was the result of Mitch's dynamism, sense of humour, and great personal appeal, and joked that his 'whirlwind oratory' would 'make him the terror of the Hansard men in Ottawa.' In Ottawa, Mackenzie King was pleased with the upset that had unexpectedly sent him eight new Liberals from western Ontario. From old Donald McNish, who had been fighting in the Liberal trenches since the days of Macdonald, he heard about the man who had engineered the biggest upset of them all. 'What do you think of West Elgin? To my mind it is one of the greatest victories in the whole Dominion. For 30 years we were in the wilderness until we chose the youthful Moses to lead us into the Promised Land.'[19]

2

'Let the rafters ring'

Mitch waited three months for Mackenzie King to return from the 1926 Imperial Conference and summon Parliament. He had been reluctant to see King attend the conference. Like most isolationists, he was deeply suspicious of British motives. He believed Downing Street hoped to get Canada 'to subscribe to some scheme of Imperial defence' and he opposed a policy of 'in time of peace prepare for war.' He enjoyed his new celebrity status and was besieged by friends already tasting the fruits of victory. He met with the three other new members from neighbouring ridings – Billy Taylor from Norfolk-Elgin and Tom Cayley and Hugh Allan from the Oxfords – to plan their role in Ottawa as spokesmen for the western Ontario farmer. The others were worried about where to stay, what to wear, and the complicated rules in the Commons. Mitch kept any doubts he might have had carefully hidden from his friends.

The session opened on 9 December, and Mitch took a room in the Chateau Laurier. When he went up the hill to the House there was a letter from the boys back home encouraging him to let the 'Rafters of the House of Commons Ring with the voice of the Boy from Elgin.' That afternoon from his seat in the far corner of the Commons Mitch surveyed the Liberal front bench. The members of the cabinet King had assembled from Ontario were not particularly impressive. Peter Heenan, the genial Lib-Lab member for Kenora, had the Labour portfolio and had replaced old Charles Murphy as spokesman for the Irish Catholics. The other three came from western Ontario: William Euler, the dour Kitchener businessman, underlined his stubbornness by calling himself an independent Liberal; James Malcolm, a wealthy Kincardine manufacturer, was rewarded with the Customs portfolio; and John Elliott, the bachelor barrister from London, controlled much of the patronage from the

Ministry of Public Works. If a young member thought of advancement, there seemed little except time to stand in the way. Certainly none of those men spoke for the farmers of Ontario.

But that afternoon the rafters rang with applause for Mackenzie King. At a short caucus he told the back-benchers that the session was to be over as quickly as possible, Mitch wrote, and 'any member who tries to display his eloquence at this early stage is likely to be ejected by the hook route.' But when the time came, Mitch promised, 'I will try to do my stuff for the satisfaction of the boys back home.'[1]

During the four days before the recess Mitch explained to the Liberal whip that unless he could have a seat where he could see and hear he would prefer to sit on the cross-benches with the Progressives. King was upset at the new member's audacity. He reminded the Elgin Liberal executive that the seating arrangements reflected seniority and 'new Members, no matter how brilliant they may be had to be given seats less advantageous than some others who may be inferior in debating strength and ability.' A move to the cross-benches, he warned, 'would be completely misconstrued both in Parliament and the country ... No matter how loyal his support to the Government might be, he would prejudice his own interests in the eyes of all Members of the Party, and he would gain no thanks from those who are his political foes.' After the slight flick with the stick came the hint of a carrot as King promised to meet Hepburn and 'to further in every way a career which is so full of promise.'

Mitch met his riding executive several times during the holidays. He agreed to keep his seat in the corner and made all the arrangements for a bean growers' meeting in February. There was also much to do on the farm. His tobacco had to be shipped the first week in February, and there were several carloads of cattle to be sent to the United States. By the end of January he was sick in bed, but recovered in time to be in his seat when the session resumed on 9 February.[2]

For the next two months King and the Liberal whips wondered whether Mitch really did belong on the cross-benches, for he was singularly unimpressed with the need for party unity. On five of the eight divisions when he was in the House, Mitch voted with the Progressives against the government, including the division on J.S. Woodsworth's amendment to exclude incomes over $10,000 from a 10 per cent reduction in the income tax. This independence may have been on King's mind when he asked Mitch to see him late in March. The young back-bencher was not impressed. The prime minister was 'certainly a man of outstanding ability,' he wrote, 'but the severe strain of the last two years is beginning to tell' and it was 'fortunate indeed that he has such able lieutenants as Lapointe & Dunning.'

The encounter did not bring Mitch to heel. He was among the back-benchers who made it clear to King at the 13 April caucus that they 'were not in the happiest frame of mind. They complained that they had not seen enough of the Ministers during the Session, that the caucus had been too few, that the Govt had not taken them sufficiently into their confidence on many measures.' That afternoon Mitch voted against King's attempt to hurry through the session by limiting debate on private members' bills.[3]

The clearest evidence that his radicalism and independence ran deeper than the rhetoric needed to woo the railway workers or the Progressives was his bellicose attack on Sun Life. The giant in the insurance industry, Sun Life, under T.B. Macaulay, had long required constant vigilance by the Superintendent of Insurance. In 1927 the company undertook a financial reorganization, which involved an increase in the capital stock from $1.5 million to $4 million. Charles Cahan, a Conservative MP and lobbyist for the Montreal financial community, sponsored the necessary private bill. In the three months before he introduced the bill, Sun Life stock rose a spectacular 500 points and was listed at $1,000 a share.

As a Sun Life policy-holder, Mitch was interested in the bill. He dared Macaulay's wrath by intervening at the hearings before the Banking and Commerce Committee of which he was a member. When the bill reached the Commons, Mitch and his Progressive friends were not prepared to let it pass without a fight, and he and William Irvine talked it out. As he wrote one of the boys back home who were behind him, he found it 'hard to understand how the government can support such a measure sponsored by a notorious Tory like Cahan of Montreal. Of course, you can readily understand that the Sun Life Insurance Company is able to employ an army of lobbyists, and sometimes their work is very effective.' The cabinet redeemed itself, however, when Finance Minister Robb and Euler supported an amendment to limit dividends to 15 per cent. Cahan angrily withdrew the bill.[4]

Rebuffed in 1927, Sun Life marshalled its lobbyists for the 1928 session. Although Mitch, like others, had been visited by Liberal friends of the bill, he continued his opposition. Opponents of the bill selected Mitch to lead off the debate in 1928, and in a carefully researched and documented speech he charged that the proposed increase in capital was nothing but stock watering and market manipulation in the interests of the 259 shareholders – sixty-five of whom owned fifteen of the twenty thousand issued shares. To issue another twenty thousand shares at $100, when the stock was selling at $1,000, was simply a gift to the shareholders while the dividends would come out of profits that should benefit the policy-holders. 'We often hear references made in vague and indefinite terms to the influence of the big interests on the governing body in the Dominion' and perhaps 'the enthusiastic support' given the bill in the Banking Committee reflected the recent appointments of men such as Premier Taschereau to Sun's board. To Mitch much more was at stake than Sun Life. As a result of 'stock-manipulation and stock-watering' by industrialists and financiers, 'the Canadian public is weighed down today paying interest on tremendous capitalization of this kind, built up by the manipulations and profits taken from the people themselves.'[5]

Although the cabinet supported the bill, Mackenzie King was clearly unhappy about the opposition of the western Progressives and other Liberals less outspoken than Mitch. T.B. Macaulay held out the spectre of an American takeover – it was rumoured that he had sold stock to Americans – and told King that despite 'the opposition of a handful of extremists, I am convinced that approximately 90 per cent of the members of the House favour the measure. All that is needed is that the Bill be brought to a vote.' King was sympathetic, but explained that it was government policy to allow ample time to debate private bills. This time Edward Garland, the United Farmers of Alberta member for Bow River, prevented third reading. In 1929 Sun removed the recapitalization provision, and Mitch boasted that 'Those of us who have opposed this bill can justify our position now in letting it go through. At the same time, however, I want to pay tribute to those who have taken an active part in opposing the bill.'[6]

Although Mitch's attack on Sun Life had attracted considerable attention among the farmers of Ontario, it was his all-out war against J.J. Morrison and the clique that ran the United Farmers of Ontario which made his name a household word in the back concessions. Despite the formal withdrawal of the UFO from politics in 1923, Morrison was determined to remain a political force and insisted the the Progressives stay exclusively a farmers' movement. The Morrison wing persuaded the 1925 UFO convention to establish a political committee to coordinate 'the political activities of the various constituency organizations.' In February 1926 the executive extended the authority of the committee to determine the ideological acceptability of both issues and candidates. The political committee itself also concluded that implicit in the 1925 convention resolution was its authority not 'to recognize as a U.F.O. candidate, anyone nominated at a joint convention of the U.F.O. with any political party whatsoever, but will recognize as U.F.O. candidates only those nominated at a convention called by the U.F.O. constituency organization.' In one astute move Morrison and his allies had regained control of the political activities of the UFO, a move that threatened not only Liberal attempts to bring the Progressives into camp but also Mitch's appeal for non-partisan farmer support.[7]

The federal by-election in North Huron on 12 September 1927 starkly revealed the threat to the Liberals. J.H. King had held the riding since 1921 as a Progressive, and the Liberals had agreed not to contest the riding in 1925 and 1926. Liberal organizers believed that with the waning of the Progressives the time had come to run a candidate nominated by a joint Liberal-Progressive convention. But the UFO claimed the riding 'by virtue of inheritance' and nominated Sheldon Bricker.

During the campaign, E.C. Drury, the one-time UFO premier who had become a Liberal Progressive, urged the farmers to vote Liberal not only to endorse low tariffs but also because the UFO had become a Morrison 'family compact' and his advocacy of group government was a 'morass that will make the farmers of the province ridiculous, futile and lead to their destruction as a political force.' Despite a vigorous campaign by the Liberals, which included a personal visit from Mackenzie King, the farm vote went decisively to Bricker and the Liberals lost the election.[8]

The North Huron tacticians had also brought Mitch into the riding, and word got back to St Thomas that he had attributed the decline in UFO membership to its political activity. That at least was the burden of Carl Jones's attack on Mitch at the West Elgin convention of the UFO in October. Mitch immediately invited Jones, a member of the UFO provincial executive, to debate the whole question with him 'any day and you can have anyone you want to assist you' – a clear invitation to bring Morrison to Elgin.

Mitch chose Dutton to launch his counter-attack. The Community Hall was jammed long before he arrived. Reporters from the Toronto and London papers were there; Jones and Morrison were not. Mitch wasted little time. Since the formation of the Drury government in 1919 Morrison had been the Judas in the farmers' camp.

'Cool, calculating and cunning,' he had destroyed the Drury government, and then 'became dictator of the U.F.O.' In the end, a 'truly democratic political and co-operative movement' had become a Morrison tyranny.

'Mr. Morrison has control absolutely of the UFO Co-operative Company, the UFO political machine, and the *Farmers' Sun* editorial policy. The head office of the UFO is run by the Morrison Family Compact.' Dramatically waving a sheaf of papers, Mitch listed members of the Compact employed by the UFO. These included Morrison himself, his son, son-in-law, daughter, cousin and his cousin's son. 'All together the clan is drawing about $20,000 a year from the farmers of Ontario; yet many times we have heard Mr. Morrison with sanctimonious complacency condemn political patronage and all the evils of using position to help a friend.' It was a performance long remembered, and one that got headlines across the province.

Contacted by the press in Toronto, Morrison answered in kind. 'Mr Hepburn's unprovoked and cowardly attack upon myself reminds one of the stealthy assassin ... Mr. Hepburn did not prepare his lingo. It has been in preparation for weeks by one whom we very well know – a man who would not say it himself. He uses Hepburn and hides behind him.' The charge was true. Before the Dutton meeting Mitch had talked to Drury who provided the details on the compact 'on the understanding,' Mitch later said, 'that it was to be made public.' But three days before the Dutton meeting Drury had written Mitch that 'I anticipate an attempt on the part of J.J. to prevent me getting a hearing at the Convention and I would like to hold this in reserve to compel J.J. to see that I get one.' To Mitch the admission that blackmail was necessary to get fair play in the UFO was a 'complete acknowledgement of the Morrison dictatorship' and 'showed such an unhealthy state of affairs that I felt I would be untrue to the United Farmers of Ontario if I was party to covering up the facts for Mr. Drury, Mr. Morrison or anyone else.'[9]

Mitch Hepburn and his 'damned lies' became the agenda of the December UFO convention in Toronto. Morrison and Drury traded insults, and Agnes Macphail charged that the attack on Morrison was a Liberal plot, 'planned by very clever men...to capture the U.F.O.' The convention was also forced to reconsider its political role. After heated debates that threatened, as one delegate said, to drive the last nail into the coffin of the farmers' movement, the UFO finally backed away from politics. Mitch had deliberately forced the issue, and as the *Farmers' Sun* commented, his 'ears must have burned even if they did not blister' during the three day convention.[10]

Mitch had become a celebrity. A few days later he was the guest speaker at luncheon of the Toronto Young Men's Liberal Club. He obviously enjoyed it, and it was their first opportunity to see Mitch in action:

Picture Mr. Morrison cloaking himself in the robes of righteousness, pointing an accusing finger of scorn at ex-Premier Drury and shouting 'You did it.' Then, overcome with relief and a sense of being cleared of the charge by so cleverly tracing to its lair the demon who spilled the beans, Mr. Morrison sat down with an air of egotistical complacency that you could not put a dent in with a pick-axe.

Mr. Drury, guilty, but honest, like little George Washington, said: 'Yes, Daddy Morrison, I got the information but Hepburn is the bad boy. I got your relatives salary list to scare you a little, and if it worked, I would put the figures back and tell no one. Hepburn was the bad boy. He talked out loud. Honest he did!'

Since the convention was so badly divided between the Drury and Morrison factions, he continued, the only face saving device was to turn on him: 'To make me the goat was the only dignified way out for the pious and august assembly. So I was denounced as an assassin, a coward, a snake in the grass and one good lady even said that I should have my head examined.' The real snake in the grass had always been Morrison. 'For years I was a great admirer of J.J. Morrison. I believed that he had a vision for a better and happier rural people.' But in the end, said Mitch, group government, or an exclusively farmers' movement, had become a theoretical cover for more sinister and practical motives: 'to render a great favour to the Tory machine by encouraging three-cornered contests in rural Ontario.'[11]

While many Ontario farmers enthusiastically supported him in the battle against Sun Life and the Family Compact, Mitch knew that far more important to his political future than these skirmishes would be his role as the spokesman for western Ontario farmers. Western Ontario was farming country, and the smaller cities and towns were agricultural in their interests and outlook. The counties along the northern shore of Lake Erie specialized in cash crops. Dairying was the staple of Oxford, Perth, and the western section of Elgin and Middlesex. To the north in Huron, Bruce, and Grey, beef and dairy cattle, hogs and poultry, and mixed farming provided the livelihood for the rural communities which in many ridings represented between 50 and 70 per cent of the population.

In Elgin West the population was almost evenly split between rural and urban, but the five thousand who lived in the towns and villages were very much part of the agricultural community, as were many in St Thomas. The value of livestock in Elgin County was $4 million about half of which was in cattle and the rest in sheep, hogs, and horses. Many farmers, including Mitch, made part of their living from dairy farming. Field crops – wheat, oats, fodder corn, clover, and mixed grains – returned well over $3 million annually. By 1927 tobacco was becoming increasingly important in Elgin and the neighbouring counties of Essex, Kent, and Norfolk. Field beans were an important cash crop from Lake Erie north to Huron County.

Mitch was a natural spokesman for the southwestern farming community. Of the two dozen mainly agricultural ridings, the Liberals had won fifteen and the Progressives two. But of the fifteen Liberal members, only two others were farmers. Billy Taylor from Norfolk was a quiet, self-effacing man, a few years older than Mitch, a good worker and a conscientious member. But he lacked Mitch's charm, energy, and platform ability. Thomas McMillan, a well-liked retired farmer of limited talent from Huron South, was old enough to have voted in Macdonald's last two elections. Only Mitch Hepburn could hold his own with the likes of Burt Fansher and Agnes Macphail, the Progressives from Lambton East and Grey Southeast, or even Eccles Gott, the Conservative high-tariff fanatic from Essex South.

By the late 1920s his opponents were supporting the cry for more protection for the bean growers and tobacco farmers of southwestern Ontario, who blamed cheap imports for low prices and poor markets. The short-lived Meighen government had implemented anti-dumping provisions for beans by order-in-council in 1926 and the farmers were concerned that the low-tariff Liberals would remove them. Mitch persuaded William Motherwell, the minister of agriculture, to send a representative to a meeting of bean growers at Rodney in February 1927.

Opening the well-attended meeting, Mitch urged the farmers to express their views clearly and strongly. For three hours the farmers described their plight in the face of mounting costs of production and cheap imports. Many argued that a general tariff would protect the industry, but the 'overwhelming opinion of those in attendance,' said Mitch, undoubtedly reflecting his own view, was that the industry only needed protection against countries with a lower standard of living and depreciated currencies. The Japanese and Hungarians could pay the anti-dumping duty and still sell in Canada for $1.73 a bushel, he pointed out, while the Department of Agriculture estimated the cost of production in Canada at $2.22. With beans selling at between $2.10 and $2.35, the Ontario farmer was selling at a loss. The departmental report was sympathetic, even if it did not endorse the view that a grower's price of $3.00 a bushel should be protected. The government took no action, but did not, for the time being, rescind the order-in-council."

Mitch was delighted with the meeting. Within a few months he had brought Ottawa to Elgin and shown that he was a man of action. An ardent free trader, he was distressed by demands for protection, which he believed would always hurt the primary producer in the long run by increasing the costs of production. To his good friend Walter Rodgers of St Thomas, he wrote, 'I agree with you that the only hope for this country is in the way of lower tariffs and lower cost production. In the meantime with the recovery of agricultural production in European and Asiatic countries I can see hard times ahead for the farmers of Canada.'¹³

The tobacco farmers were also up in arms. When the British put tobacco on the preferential list in 1925, southwestern Ontario farmers moved into tobacco with a vengeance. Production increased from twelve million pounds in 1924 to thirty-five million pounds three years later. Many of the new farms were large plantations with absentee owners in Canada and the United States, as a rule professionally managed and often with firm contracts from manufacturers. But many inexperienced farmers, including Mitch himself, had quickly added tobacco to their cash crops, and concentrated on the easily grown burley and dark tobacco rather than the higher-quality and higher-priced flue-cured variety used in cigarettes and better cigars. When the market opened for the large 1927 harvest, burley tobacco dropped from twenty-five to fifteen cents a pound. Mitch laid the blame on the large buyers who monopolized the market and manipulated the prices downward. Hepburn the farmer got out of tobacco but urged the farmers to organize and set an example by forming the Elgin County Growers' Association. Mitch Hepburn the politician took the train to Ottawa to see his friend the minister of agriculture.

The result was a meeting in Chatham in December 1927 unlike anything western Ontario had ever seen, exclaimed the *Times-Journal* reporter as he described the scene that Saturday afternoon.

A great army invaded this city, Saturday, an army at least five thousand strong ... From east and west, north and south they came, young men, middle-aged men and old men – men who have the blood of pioneer Canadian settlers in their veins, men whose voices carry the drawl of the American South, men but recently arrived from Middle Europe limited in the knowledge of the English tongue, French Canadians from the western frontier and staid Scotsmen from West Elgin and Middlesex, tobacco growers all, and all congregated here in a common cause – the safe-guarding of the future of the industry.

Long before two o'clock the thousand-seat Griffin Theatre was full, and when the Armouries were opened for the overflow, over three thousand rushed in until there was no room to stand. When the doors closed there were still over a thousand lining the sidewalk outside.

The growers heard Motherwell, a pioneer in cooperative marketing in Saskatchewan, and Ontario Agriculture Minister John Martin urge them to form a marketing pool. They applauded Eddie Odette, the MP for Essex East, when he suggested that one look at Imperial Tobacco's profits revealed the culprit, and cheered Eccles Gott when he demanded that the tariff be increased from forty cents to a dollar a pound to keep out the fourteen million pounds of tobacco pouring in from the United States each year. But the hero of the day was Mitch Hepburn. He admitted that a higher tariff might help, but warned of the dangers. Since Canada did not produce all the types of tobacco necessary to make cigarettes and cigars, too high a tariff would increase the price, and the boats and trucks of the rum-runners would return to Canada laden with American cigarettes. The real enemy was not the low tariff, but the monopoly buyers who used 'a little system' of offering a low price and if you don't take it you 'are going to be penalized on the second round' when the offer will be even lower. The true solution was concerted action by the farmers, aided by the government, to organize a production and marketing pool that could combat the interests which exploited them. The cheers were deafening. 'He aroused those tobacco farmers to enthusiasm, time after time, with his concise, straight-from-the-shoulder remarks, and his challenge for unity and initiative,' wrote the *Times-Journal* reporter.

There were few cheers when Motherwell's commission on the industry concluded that the problem was the overproduction of the wrong kind of tobacco and the growers' inexperience in harvesting and marketing. There was no evidence of a combine among manufacturers to control prices, but there was already ample evidence of large-scale organized smuggling that would become worse with any increase in the tariff. Mitch did help the farmers organize a pool, but it accomplished little. The growers could not resolve the problem of production, burley and flue farmers pursued their own interests, the banks were reluctant to loan money to the pool, and the buyers for Imperial and Macdonald's continued to play one farmer against the next. Nevertheless, Mitch had gained immeasurably in stature and credibility as the farmers' champion. As J.E. Hancock of Leamington wrote, 'I trust every farmer in south western Ontario will get behind you hook, line and sinker, irrespective of race, creed, or political connection. Opportunity knocked at your door and you were at home and in my mind have the greatest chance to make a name for yourself and at the same time protect the tobacco growers of any member of Parliament in the last decade.'[14]

Two weeks after the Chatham meeting Mitch was back in Ottawa for the opening of the session. It was fitting that Mitch should have been selected to speak in the debate on Robb's budget, for it was a dull budget – another surplus, cuts in income and sales taxes, and modest tariff reductions – and a dull session.

He acknowledged that Ontario farmers were crying for more protection, and argued that if protection were justifiable the primary producers rather than the manufacturers should enjoy it. Unfortunately, however, the industrial structure was now far too complicated to dismantle the National Policy; only the Progressives were naïve enough to believe it could be done. Since free trade was impossible, the Liberals at least had found a way 'to draw the line of demarcation between tariffs that were used for exploitation and tariffs that are really and truly protecting a legitimate industry in the country.' Yet the country was still suffering from the suicidal Tory anti-Americanism. Canada needed American investment, American markets, and American tourists. As for this budget, Mitch confessed that 'I am not so partisan as to say that I swallow the budget in its entirety. I do not think any budget could be brought down that would suit any party or any ten members.' In particular, he opposed Robb's intention ultimately to abolish personal income taxes. There were too many millionaires who 'sprang up like mushrooms' during the war and more of their ill-gotten gains should be recovered. But one had to be for the budget or against it. Mitch was for it.

It was an impressive performance, and Mitch became a regular speaker during debates on the budget and tariff. His direct, aggressive, and hyperbolic style aroused the Tory front benches and provoked incessant heckling from the back benchers. While his attacks were sharp and often personal, they were usually friendly and often witty. John Dafoe was not alone in concluding that Mitch was 'one of the most original, industrious and persistent men who have entered Parliament in the last decade.'[15]

Mitch was a reasonably industrious and conscientious member. His work on the special committee on veterans' pensions in 1928 and 1929 earned him the commendation of the Canadian Legion and made a friend of its chairman, Charles 'Chubby' Power, the bibulous bon vivant MP from Quebec South. His support of Woodsworth and the Progressives on many issues placed him well to the left of the Liberal front benches, and he described the old age pension as the 'most humanitarian bit of legislation that has been attempted.' Mitch's constituents were never far from his mind. He questioned the government about the reduction in the repair work done in St Thomas by American railways and their refusal to pay pensions to Canadian workers. He persuaded his friend Peter Heenan, the minister of labour, to support a bill encouraging the use of union labels. Lake Erie fishermen knew he had attempted to get fishing regulations relaxed, and he often intervened with immigration officials on behalf of his farmer constituents to process visas for agricultural labourers from central Europe.

Mitch was also sensitive to the views of the wives of his farmer constituents. The people of Elgin County were overwhelmingly Protestant and, however promiscuous some of their private lives, most lived by the Book. Although Mitch was willing to forward divorce petitions from the riding, he was always conveniently absent when the bills came before the House. In the 1930 session he not only opposed a bill easing divorce requirements in Ontario, but voted for an amendment that viewed 'with alarm the spread and increase of divorce and divorce applications in Canada, and instead of providing additional means of obtaining divorce the House would favour the encouragement and carrying on of a campaign of education for the purpose of impressing upon the hearts and minds of Canadians the sacredness of the matrimonial tie and the permanent stability of the Canadian home.' That might end the wagging of mischievous tongues in Elgin.[16]

Nor did Mitch overlook the business community. He lobbied intensively with the Dominion Fuel Board to license a coking plant in Port Stanley, and encouraged American and British capitalists to invest in it after persuading the government to spend almost half a million dollars on harbour improvements. He found Americans to build a brewery in St Thomas. The shell of the building was finished when the depression struck and was still standing years later when the end of prohibition in the States made it irrelevant.[17]

Patronage was the stuff of which Elgin politics was made and, in power at last, Elgin Grits were determined to feast at the trough. But the novice with the nose for politics knew that patronage was a double-edged sword, and Mitch often decided that while he wanted to bestow the gift he did not want to select the recipient. When the Dutton post office was vacant he told local Liberals that it 'would be a very poor policy to get involved in any way in making a choice, and it would relieve me a great deal if the boys could select their own man.' They did, but when the Civil Service Commission seemed reluctant to appoint old William Tolmie, Mitch happily carried a declaration of war from Elgin Liberals to Ottawa: 'This meeting views the situation as having come to the pass where the government must either insist on its Commission dealing fairly with Mr. Hepburn or the election of Mr. Hepburn or any other supporter of the government will be an impossibility. Let the government choose.'[18]

Mitch not only had to do battle with the government and the bureaucracy, but often with his own supporters who, being closer to the ground, did not share his more non-partisan views. Mitch had been looking for a good Liberal, 'rather a rare specimen in these parts,' to take over the Port Stanley customs office. When he learned that the incumbent was a very popular Tory in that Tory town, he unsuccessfully urged Euler not to force his retirement at seventy: 'Turning him out against his wishes, is going to antagonize the great host of his friends, and will be of no benefit to me, especially in view of the fact that I must have considerable conservative support if I hope to hold this riding.' In St Thomas, too, he told the local organizers on the eve of the 1930 election that a 'fair portion,' perhaps even half, of the polling officials should be Conservatives: 'I do not think we would lose any votes by playing the game in this manner and it would give the conservatives a certain degree of confidence.'

With considerable justice, Mitch could state in his 1930 election advertisements: 'Vote for the man who when elected was big enough to know that in transactions between his constituents and the Government, he represented ALL the people, not only a party. Conservatives will testify that they always got a square deal from Mitch Hepburn.' Even the Tory *Times-Journal* admitted that 'we have yet to hear that he shows discrimination or lack of interest because the man or woman he is asked to help ... opposes him politically.' There were many in Elgin like G.B. Blakelock, an old Southwold

Tory, who told Mitch he was sick and had no money to buy seed, but confessed that he had never voted Liberal. Mitch loaned him $35 and made a convert: 'shour my hart run cold when I started your letter in that kind way you spoke you will never have to worry over me and my wife if we are living when the day Comes in Regards to our vote.'[19]

Mitch was equally non-partisan when it came to sports, which was just as well in a sports-crazed town like St Thomas, where the baseball and rugby teams were perennial provincial finalists and often champions. He was often at the ball park and frequently accompanied the teams when they travelled. When the junior rugby team went to Ottawa in 1929 to play for the provincial championship, Mitch went with them. On a snowy field before fifteen hundred partisan spectators, St Thomas built up a commanding lead when the Ottawa bench and then the stands emptied to protest an Ottawa penalty. The referee was knocked unconscious and the assault moved to the visitors, many of whom were savagely kicked and beaten as they fought their way to the bus. Mitch tried to carry an injured St Thomas player to the bus but the boy was ripped from his arms and Mitch himself got what he described as a 'good trouncing.' A week later he went to Moose Jaw where the St Thomas team won the national championship. Charles Dunning, King's minister of finance, came over from Regina to make it an all Grit affair.[20]

Mitch liked the rough and tumble in the House and the day-to-day work of nourishing his riding. 'I find this parliamentary life very exacting and one hasn't a great deal of time for anything but work,' he told George Ponsford soon after his arrival in Ottawa. At first he shared a flat with Mac Lang, the MP from Temiskaming who had been born in Elgin, but during the 1929 session when Eva came to Ottawa they rented a small house. He had good friends among the back-benchers. There were his neighbours – Billy Taylor, his deskmate, Jim Rutherford, the paternal doctor from Chatham, and Eddie Odette, a drinking buddy from Tilbury. His western Liberal friends included Jack Vallance from Onward, who had married a St Thomas girl, and Fred Totske from Humboldt. He was on good terms with Chubby Power and Jean-François Pouliot, the eccentric but engaging member for Rivière-du-Loup. There was a great camaraderie among the boys on Dynamite Alley, as they called their seats up in the gods. During the Easter recess in 1928 Mitch and Eddie Odette took forty western MPs on a rollicking tour across Ontario to Windsor and back through St Thomas and Niagara Falls, on coaches provided by the Michigan Central and refreshments from

Hiram Walker. And after returning from a Florida vacation, he wrote that while he missed the Florida sunshine and the 'moonshine ... the boys have been celebrating a little over my return – tried to make things pleasant for me and prevent me from getting a cold.'

Despite his lament about the hard work, there was always time to spend with congenial companions. Friends from Elgin often dropped by for 'a chat over the flowing bowl,' as his friend L.M. Bradley put it. But Mitch had no taste for the dress-up functions held by Viscount Willingdon at Rideau Hall. In the Commons he repeatedly mocked Agnes Macphail who criticized the expenditure on Government House yet never missed an opportunity to attend. And he made the farmers of Elgin aware of her inconsistency:

Following the big state banquets, they tell me that considerable silverware and other articles were missing; hence it is necessary to replace them by voting money through the Commons. We even have to pay for the orchestra that furnishes the music for Miss Macphail, the champion of the common people and of democracy while she trips the light fantastic with the Governor General himself ... Personally I have no use for the caste system or anything which perpetuates snobbishness or class distinction in this country. I have never attended any social event at Rideau Hall and in my present frame of mind I do not think I ever shall.

Mitch much preferred Hull which then, as later, seemed to be the favoured spot for rest and relaxation. With increasing frequency he found his way across the river, often accompanied by out-of-town friends whom he introduced to his watering holes. Most seemed as appreciative as C.D. Browne, the manager of Castrol Motor Oils, who wrote that he 'enjoyed every minute of the time I was with you. Your "sparring partners" were exceptional, and I believe they appreciated your work ... I hope you arrived safely back in Ottawa, and that your "colleague" was there to greet you.'

For Mitch life in Ottawa was anything but dull. Even before he faced his constituents again in 1930 some of his more staid friends like Billy Taylor and Doc Rutherford were concerned about his health, if not his morals. Beneath his levity, there was a serious touch when Doc advised Mitch to 'Keep your head cool and your feet warm; say your prayers faithfully every night for good men are scarce and Heaven's full.'[21]

The election of Herbert Hoover in November 1928 suddenly intensified Mitch's problems with the Ontario farmers, for the new American president had promised the American farmers all the protection they needed. Although Mackenzie King cautiously decided to tread water in the 1 March 1929 budget, the Tories were determined to make the tariff the critical issue in the next election and demanded that Parliament 'deal in a red-blooded Canadian manner' with the Yankees. On 9 April, in a speech Mitch described as a masterpiece, King called for a 'cool-headed attitude.' It was a reasonably cool-headed speech that Mitch made later in the day. Without minimizing the damage of higher American tariffs, he warned that retaliation would be ruinous. He countered the blast of Eccles Gott, the high-tariff Tory from Amherstburg, with a sure-handed mastery of the figures – whether on corn, potatoes or dairy products – and enough humour to keep the members in their seats.

When he moved from feed corn and butter to tobacco, Mitch first accused Gott of helping to destroy the tobacco pool by insisting that only protection would save the grower. Indeed, the reverse was true. Since Canadian cigarettes were made with a mixture of local and American tobacco, an increase in the cost of American tobacco would simply lower the price the manufacturers paid for Canadian. And if the price of the finished product were raised, the increase in what was already a multi-million dollar smuggling racket would further reduce demand. Turning to his own front bench, Mitch said, 'I have a word of criticism against my hon. friend the Minister of Finance. There is only one way in which the government can help the tobacco industry in southern Ontario ... and that is to lower the excise tax on manufactured tobacco' which in turn would reduce smuggling, encourage consumption, and increase the market. And that he was confident would be done in the next 'tax reducing budget.'[22]

Eccles Gott had not been in the House when Mitch ridiculed him for planting a story in the Windsor press that his speech on the budget had been so brilliant that even the Speaker had left his chair to congratulate him. But the ridicule provoked Gott to challenge Mitch to a public debate, and at the St Thomas Masonic Temple, with hundreds turned away, the debate won a headline in the *Mail and Empire*: 'MITCH AND ECC WAGE WORDY WAR.' In every way it was an unequal contest. Gott was as slow-spoken as Mitch was quick, as weak on facts and figures as Mitch was solid. Mitch's simplified lecture on comparative advantage, seasonality, retaliation, and cost of production was perhaps less memorable than his story of the pirates on the Island of Tariffa. For years the pirates plundered 'to their hearts content. Finally they discovered that they were ruining their own business and so they decide to be merciful and to take only a portion of the goods from the captured vessel. Thus an agreement was consummated ... whereby the pirates would take all the traffic could bear and felt that he was a real good fellow to leave the others enough goods and boats to do business so they could pay a further tax to the pirates. Down through the ages the pirates disappeared but not the principle.'

Gott countered with stories of potatoes and beans, cabbages and cucumbers rotting in the ground and American strawberries driving Canadians out of business. Gott knew that history and common sense proved that more protection would increase production. Asked what price growers had received for their crop at various times, Gott replied, 'I can't tell you; perhaps Mitch can.' Indeed, Mitch could and in his fifteen-minute rebuttal produced figures not only on tobacco but on all the tariff-protected goods the farmers had to buy and concluded with a peroration of which Adam Smith would have been proud:

In the natural course of trading, which is a test of modern civilization, our northern hard wheat is traded for Southern grown fruits which we cannot produce; our daily produce of Ontario pays for our coal requirements from Pennsylvania and Virginia; ... and thus it follows all along the line, and that is the way it should be. That is the way the Maker intended it to be; but along come the high tariff advocates to build the tariff walls to block the avenue of trade whenever possible ... Instead of having it God's way, they want to have it Gott's way.

As the reporters from Toronto, Windsor and London raced to file their front page stories, there was no doubt that Mitch had won the debate. Robert Deachman, an ardent free trader and sometime researcher on economic questions for the Liberals, informed Senator Andrew Haydon, Liberal party organizer and bagman, that he had gone to St Thomas 'to catch the affect [sic] on the audience – an Ontario audience in a supposedly protectionist district and see if I could form some opinion as to how these people stood.' The protectionist arguments could be answered, he continued, 'providing Liberal representatives and Liberal speakers are willing to face the issue as Hepburn has faced it – manfully and squarely, meet the enemy in the open and it is not hard to put him to flight.' As for the gladiator himself, 'He proved himself in the contest an exceedingly able man and with a little bit of training, I would imagine that in the course of a year or so, young Hepburn may be one of the strongest debaters in Ontario. He has a very bright sense of humour and literally brought the house down on one or two occasions.'

Haydon sent a copy of the letter to King and every member of the cabinet, but he was less optimistic than Deachman. 'The economic theory and economic policies are very hard for the ordinary man to understand,' he replied, 'and they are harder still for the general member to so get into his head that he can make them easy for his listeners. That's what Hepburn has done, but he has the enthusiasm of youth and personal conviction and he is willing to work hard at the subject he undertakes to investigate … I would think it difficult to have Hepburn's performance very freely duplicated within the Liberal Party.' After Gott's Way, Mitch was a man marked by the Liberals for advancement, by the Tories for defeat.[23]

As the months passed it would be impossible for Mitch to duplicate his success, for the farmers were in no mood for stories of the pirates of Tariffa. Already they were demanding cancellation of a preferential treaty with New Zealand which had increased butter imports from $4.6 to $12.7 million between 1927 and 1929. In the United States the pirates were out in full force in 1929 as Congress raised tariffs to their highest levels in history. By November, details of the Smoot-Hawley tariff that would be approved in June 1930 were revealed, and to many Canadian farmers they spelled disaster. The multi-million dollar market for dairy products was closed when the tariff was doubled or tripled. A 50 per cent increase in the tariff on cattle on the hoof threatened that export and doubling the tariff prohibited the export of beef. Hog breeders faced a punitive 400 per cent increase and chicken farmers could not compete when the tariff jumped from three to eight cents a pound.

The American tariff hit an industry already in the first stages of a recession. Farm prices had remained more or less stable as the cost of production had risen in the late 1920s. Farmers had increased their acreage in response to the high prices in 1928, only to see prices fall in 1929. Mitch had sold his beans in 1928 for $3.50 a bushel, but by February 1930 the price had dropped to $2.55 and plummeted to $1.36 by the summer. The wholesale prices of onions, hides, steers, fresh milk, and cheese were in a free fall, and the value of Ontario's tobacco crop fell from $35 million in 1928 to less than $21 million a year later. In Oxford, farms were being thrown on the market; in Kent many farmers looked elsewhere for their income; in Essex, commented the agricultural representative, there was a 'policy of retrenchment'; and in Elgin the farmer was spending 'most of his milk cheque in feeding his cattle.' As conditions continued to deteriorate the cry for protection was deafening.[24]

With an election approaching, the signs were ominous for a low-tariff Grit. To placate the tobacco growers, Mitch arranged another meeting with Motherwell, but with the bean growers knocking on the door of the federal Tariff Board demanding higher tariffs, Mitch knew there was no place to hide. As usual he did his research. Before large crowds of growers at Rodney and Chatham in March, Mitch had the facts to support his argument that the reason for low prices was largely overproduction and poor quality; the answer was not tariff protection but standardization, reduced freight rates, and collective protection against the dealers. Mitch said that he would support any decision reached by the Tariff Board, but that he could not honestly advocate a policy that, in his judgment, would lead to a fall not a rise in price.[25]

Butter, not beans, dominated the session that opened on 20 February 1930. After a hard-hitting high-tariff speech by H.H. Stevens in the Commons on 11 March, Mitch was asked to respond on very short notice. Mitch denied that the dairy industry as a whole was suffering. Exports had fallen because the growing home market paid the best prices. The number of milch cows had fallen because farmers had improved the quality of their herds and sold cows, as he had, at a good profit to American buyers. And what was there to be learned from the United States where the industrialists had seized the opportunity to fasten astronomical tariffs on the people and Hoover was paying the farmers millions to keep butter off the market? As for Mitch, he was 'going to ask this government to stand pat on their tariff policy, despite the protectionist propaganda that is coming through all the papers of this country.'

Mackenzie King admitted that Mitch had made a 'good speech,' but the *Globe* was less restrained: 'Mr. Hepburn's admittedly brilliant speech precipitated the entirely unusual scene of a major party rising from its seats to cheer a private member's oratorical effort. The cheers ... started the moment he took his seat and were continued out in the Liberal lobby for many minutes after the House had emptied.' The Toronto *Star* reporter wrote that it was a 'more sustained effort' than most of Mitch's speeches. There was 'the same driving force of logic, the trip hammer blows of fact following fact in convincing succession.'[26]

Mitch knew that he was risking his political career, and warned Deachman that 'the farmers are determined to get an increase in the tariff.' As he told the *Star*, however, he would not change his position. 'They may crucify me, but I cannot betray them. These are the people I have grown up among. These are my friends. Am I to lead them up a blind alley? Never. I shall go back to the farm – far, far better to be a good farmer than a dishonest politician.' Mackenzie King and Charles Dunning had no desire to go back to the farm. King canvassed the views of the back-benchers, spending an afternoon with Rutherford, Odette, and Mitch. With all of southwestern Ontario threatened, it was time to retreat. However opposed in principle, Mitch the politician was not unhappy with the budget Dunning brought down on 1 May.

The budget was a masterpiece for it united the Liberal party. Dunning reported another surplus and gave the people lower taxes and cheaper tea. He called for an increase in British preferences and threatened – and in some cases implemented – tariff increases on American goods. For some fruit and vegetable growers there was immediate protection, including the bean growers who got the $1.20 a bushel they had been demanding. For the dairy farmer there was an immediate increase in the duty on butter, and the promise to modify the concessions made to New Zealand. For others there was the promise of countervailing duties on eggs, meat, and grains.

Selected to defend the budget before Ontario farmers, Mitch somehow had to square the circle. The modest changes in the tariff, which helped 'settle the unrest among the farmers,' were not really a return to protectionism or a 'brick for brick' response to Smoot-Hawley. In fact, the idea of countervailing duties was really a form of reciprocity. 'The latch key is in the door, and if our American friends want to give us access to their markets and gain access to ours, they have it within their power to do so. As one who believes in reciprocity I believe we should leave that key right where it is.' Cheaper tea, cheaper homes, lower taxes, a budget surplus, protection for the farmer without really raising the tariff were all in the interests of the Canadian consumer and he, for one, was prepared to take the issue to the people. For just as the King's government went on forever, so would that of Mackenzie King.[27]

Mitch found swallowing some of his convictions on the budget much easier than supporting King's decision to end the practice of clearing vessels carrying liquor to the United States. The tariff changes at least would hold some votes, but the end of rum-running not only threatened the livelihood of a good many folk in south-western Ontario but smacked of prohibition – a cause detested in the Border Cities and the east end of St Thomas. Mackenzie King had known for years that organized gangs of smugglers in league with brewers and distillers made a mockery of the laws of both countries. By the fall of 1929 he had convinced himself that he was engaged in a titanic battle between good and evil and 'would go out of office if need be before being dictated to by liquor interests.'

King faced bitter opposition from Ontario. Senator James Spence told King that at a meeting of the Ontario Liberal Association the 'whole committee voted in favour of allowing clearances with the exception of Sanderson and myself.' When Fred Sanderson, the Ontario whip, told Ontario MPs assembled for an emergency session in Toronto in mid-January that King would dissolve on the issue if necessary, Mitch and others put pressure on the government to withhold any announcement until the caucus had met. Personally he had no choice but to oppose the decision, he warned, and to vote against the government.

At the first caucus, King made an impassioned appeal for abolition and, as usual, felt that the caucus was behind him. But even King admitted that the opposition was vocal: 'Power said he would oppose the party. Hepburn too was quite strong, also Wellington Hay (tho he was ready to support).' The reason often given was that it would raise the familiar Tory charge that the Liberals were bowing to the dictates of Washington. But as Alex Darrach, a total abstainer, explained to King, there was more to it in Elgin, a county without a brewery or a distillery:

Yet I feel sure that so strong is the feeling against the temperance people on account of their treachery and on account of another class (mostly railway people who love their bottle) that if Mr. Hepburn supports your bill I'm afraid it will defeat him. We cannot afford to have him defeated and the poor boy has worked so hard, has spent his time and energy tirelessly, in the interests of the country and the party, that it would be too bad if a whip were needlessly put into the cruel and unscrupulous hands of enemies to bring about his defeat.

While the Liberal organization would support Mitch, whatever the decision, said Darrach, that 'will not be true of hundreds of beer drinking Englishmen whose cross on the ballot paper counts for as much as that made by the really intelligent.' King was determined, however, and on 14 March, with the whips out, only eleven members, Chubby Power among them, voted nay. Mitch voted with the ayes. King wrote at once to Darrach that while the vote proved that Hepburn had been wrong, 'I must say, however, that he played the game very well, and, I believe, will be strengthened as a consequence, rather than weakened, in his constituency.'[28]

Mitch was soon to find out. Before returning to Ottawa for the session on 20 February 1930 he and his riding association had set the election machinery in motion. During the Easter recess he had held a three-riding rally, with entertainment by his close friend Ned Sparks, the famous Hollywood comedian who hailed from St Thomas. He also spoke to the founding meeting of the London branch of the 20th Century Liberal Women's Club which was graced by the presence of Odette Lapointe, the daughter of King's Quebec lieutenant, and his close friend Lucette Valin from Ottawa. But his political career almost ended like his father's when a plain clothes officer saw two men and two women drinking illegally in a broker's office on the ground floor of the Hotel Richmond. By the time the police got in, the two girls had skipped out; but Mitch and his finance manager Chester Smith were charged. Mitch paid his fine, but persuaded the police to leave his name off the record and the only conviction recorded was Chet's. It was a close call.

King dissolved the House on 30 May and within days the Liberal Club rooms in Elgin were open. The Dunning budget led Mitch to be optimistic, and initially he believed the election would be 'somewhat in the nature of a Liberal sweep.' But his optimism was short-lived as he sampled opinion in Elgin. 'I am having a good stiff fight,' he told Bob Deachman, 'but am still hopeful of the results. I find the worst trouble is with liberal farmers who have gone tariff mad.' The tariff madness was understandable as prices continued their steep, seemingly irreversible decline. Late in June the farmers felt the full impact of the Smoot-Hawley tariff, which virtually closed the border to milk and dairy products. There were not many farmers who shared the philosophical view of the Oxford agricultural agent: 'And so we pass through the ordeal, and emerge stronger from it.' In Elgin, the increase in farm mortgages better reflected the farmers' response to the ordeal of 1930.[29]

While the tariff dominated the campaign in the townships, in St Thomas, Mitch told Percy Parker, the Ontario campaign manager, he was 'handicapped by the most serious unemployment we have ever had.' Employment fell 20 per cent in 1930. The American railways that ran through town were laying off more men every week. Two weeks before the election the New York Central closed its shops and several hundred men were unemployed. Added to real unemployment was the threat of unemployment. The Nursery Shoe Company told its worried employees that a Bennett government would lower the tariff on hides and raise it on shoes. The Monarch Knitting Company intimated that the company could not survive a Liberal victory. The Tories broadcast reports that factories else-where in Ontario were firing workers and closing their doors as proof of Liberal bankruptcy. Local factories were only open to Conservative election workers in a campaign of intimidation.

In St Thomas and Port Stanley, Mitch argued that unemployment was beyond the control of any single government. It was the result of mechanization, of the decline in international trade, of false economic ideas like Bennett's belief in protection. At least old age pensions, lower taxes, and balanced budgets – all gifts of a Liberal government – would help to ease the impact. Restricted immigration during the slump and some form of unemployment insurance would help the unemployed. Mitch urged the investors in the coking plant and brewery to show signs of life, but the Tories joked about the few men 'fiddling away at Port Stanley,' where it looked as if the weed inspector had forced the coking company to clear the weeds from the proposed site. Mitch hounded the Department of Public Works to let the contracts for the latest $160,000 harbour and port improvements he had been able to secure, and wrote in exasperation to Parker that he was 'thoroughly disgusted and rightly so' by the inability of the bureaucrats to move quickly and the apparent unwillingness of their political masters to make them.[30]

Mitch received no help from Ottawa. The Liberal party in Ontario was weak and disorganized. Fitful attempts throughout the 1920s to create a strong organization were repeatedly frustrated by the seemingly terminal illness of the provincial party, personal and historical feuds, lazy or incompetent ministers, and the total ineffectiveness of King's sporadic interventions. The semblance of an organization had been put in place in the spring of 1929, but its impotence was revealed when Howard Ferguson swept the provincial Tories back into power in October. The cabinet ministers gave little support and no direction. John Elliott and James Malcolm appeared once, but as Chubby Power reported, 'Billy Euler refuses to move out of Kitchener. He says he has a difficult election and sees no reason why others should not help themselves. Naturally he is not popular. Jack Elliott also thinks it is of excessive importance that he be returned ... He has not very much time to go outside and besides I am informed his services are not often required.' Ernest Lapointe refused a small patronage favour despite Mitch's plea that it would 'be of great assistance to me locally,' and Mackenzie King turned down his request to visit Elgin. However, his friend Chubby Power came to Elgin to appeal for the veterans' vote and Charles Dunning joined Mitch on the platform. As in

1926, Arthur Roebuck campaigned among the railway workers and Harry Nixon, the Progressive MLA from Brant, stood beside Mitch to praise him and the Dunning budget.

Mitch was never too busy to lend a hand outside Elgin. He spoke for his friends in almost every riding in western Ontario, appeared in Toronto and Hamilton, and moved as far east as Northumberland and Hastings. Mitch seemed to be the one man who could match invective with Howard Ferguson. As Ferguson told Sir Robert Borden, Ontario would be 'the cockpit of the fight' and 'I felt from the beginning that the budget was designed to capture this Province and realized that we had to make a desperate effort to combat the appeal to British sentiment.' Ferguson threw the provincial machine into the battle and declared on the radio and at rallies across the province that King, not the tariff, was the central issue. Privately, King called Ferguson a 'skunk' but in public he argued ponderously that the alliance of federal and provincial Tory governments would be a monopoly of power that threatened democracy.[31]

Mitch went for the jugular. During the 1929 provincial campaign he had traded blows with Ferguson, mocking the spurious imperialism that prompted him to name Ontario roads the 'King's Highway.' He welcomed Ferguson's entrance in the campaign with the promise to take him out to the back yard and spank him. Ferguson's 'righteousness and egotistical complacency' was out of place for one who demanded money from Ottawa for unemployment relief, but refused to share with the municipalities, who bore the burden, the revenues from liquor and gasoline taxes, charged them 20 per cent of the old age pensions, and reprimanded 'with tongue in cheek' a cabinet minister who tied mothers' allowances to Tory votes. Provincially, if the liquor question could be removed from Ontario politics, Mitch predicted, the Liberals would soon 'put this man Ferguson out.' The electorate seemed to enjoy Mitch's spankings more than King's sombre warnings of a threat to democracy.

The Tories made a dead set against Mitch Hepburn, clearly the leading Liberal in tariff-crazed western Ontario. If he could not be defeated, at least he could be kept busy at home. Ferguson ordered the two Elgin MLAs and their machines into action. From Ottawa came Robert Manion, Senator Gideon Robertson, Earl Rowe, the rising Tory star from Northumberland, and in the last week of the campaign Bennett held his major rally in western Ontario in Port Stanley. Tory speakers mocked Mitch's so-called 'independence' of the whips and sneered at the contradiction between Liberal billboards which proclaimed BUILD CANADA AND EMPIRE TRADE and

Mitch's anti-imperialism. 'How long is it since Mr. Hepburn acquired his sudden warm affection for the British Empire?' asked Andy Ingram who had sat for East Elgin for fifteen years before the war. Titles had been proudly born even by Liberals such as Mowat and Laurier, 'whose names are imperishably written in the history of the British Empire,' and it was contemptible that Elgin should now witness this 'ungrateful son insulting his mother' and hypocritically waving the imperial flag over the Dunning budget. Not only in Elgin but across the west Mitch was singled out as the low-tariff exponent, the enemy featured in pamphlets such as *Eight Years Too Late for the Bean Grower*.

Arthur Ford, the Tory editor of the London *Free Press*, believed that in Jonathan Dowler the Elgin Tories had a 'winner.' He seemed to have all the markings of a loser. A hopeless platform speaker, a man who had left the farm to become a prosperous merchant fond of wearing the imported clothes he sold in his men's store, Dowler was the perfect foil for Mitch's wit. Few ever forgot the debate at the joint nominating convention in the Masonic Temple – the only time Dowler dared face Mitch on the platform. 'Jonathan, a protectionist!' laughed Mitch, then verbally stripping off his collar, tie, jacket, shirt, trousers, and socks he joked that the only thing Canadian on the almost naked Dowler was the leather in his shoes. The crowd loved it, and Dowler could only reply feebly that while his wardrobe was imported, at least 'I earned the money myself to buy it – I didn't inherit it.' Always provoked by the silver spoon suggestion, Mitch retorted that he was not 'in the enviable position of being a retired merchant able to live on the profits I made from the community in which I live.'

Although Dowler could not defeat Mitch, the tariff might. To combat the tariff and the Tory machine, Mitch had to rely on the appeal of a charming personality, the advantage of knowing half the people in the county by their first name, and the gratitude of the George Blakelocks who remembered his kindness. The West Lorne voters knew that he had made a new community hall possible when he persuaded the government to lease space for a post office. The residents of Dutton were grateful for the improved rural postal delivery on the eve of the election. Improved harbour facilities in Port Stanley were a tangible sign of his industry. Dairy farmers welcomed the news that the Carnation milk factory would soon place an order for a million dollars' worth of milk – an order that seemed to evaporate after the election. There were many St Thomas voters who seemed to prefer Mitch's brand of whiskey to Dowler's, for although the official Liberal organization ran a clean campaign, Alex Darrach told King, the same could not be said of the 'bunch of useless tools' surrounding Mitch 'whose principal claim to his approval lay in their flattery and the way they could pull his leg for money.' If the Tories had the facts and filed a protest, 'he would not have lasted an hour and disqualification would have followed as surely as day follows night.'[32]

Mitch declared election expenses of only $3,800, though he later admitted privately that he had spent $14,000, while the Tories had started with $25,000. Even legitimate expenses were heavy. Scrutineers in the polling stations expected four dollars, and there were 250 in St Thomas alone. There were some volunteers, but even in the townships most expected to be paid, and among 'those railway people who love their bottle' neither Liberals nor Tories could quench their thirst to have the issues explained. Chet Smith, Mitch's financial manager, disliked the 'chisellers' whose Liberalism was in their pockets, but elections, he knew, were not won by prayers. Chet raised some of the money locally, and some may have come by way of Percy Parker in Toronto. But according to Colin Campbell, Mitch's close friend and driver during the campaign, Mitch dug deep into his own pockets and by the end was left only with the bonds he had inherited from Grandpa Mitch.

'The Election in West Elgin became the focal point in Western Ontario,' wrote John Dafoe. 'What about Mitch Hepburn? was a constant question among both Liberals and Conservatives.' The answer was clear soon after the votes were counted on the night of 28 July. Mitch had 'Hepburnized' Elgin County. His majority had jumped to 1,437 as he swept the rural townships and, with the exception of West Lorne and St Thomas, had carried every town and village. Even in St Thomas the Tory margin had fallen from 600 to 198. But elsewhere in western Ontario Liberal majorities fell and the Tories gained five seats. Despite Ferguson's promise to keep 'the pot boiling' and deliver seventy seats, the Tories won only six additional seats in the province for a total of fifty-nine. But with the Maritimes solidly Tory and Quebec sending a contingent of twenty-four Conservatives to Ottawa, R.B. Bennett had a comfortable majority. The jubilation that night along Talbot Street and out at the farm was perhaps a little restrained. Mitch Hepburn would not grace the Liberal front benches as minister of agriculture, as some had expected, but faced the dreary prospect of four or five years in opposition.[33]

3

'A Joshua who will really do the trick'

When Mitch Hepburn arrived in Ottawa on 8 September for Bennett's special session he was no longer the unknown back-bencher from Elgin. His performance as a freshman MP had been impressive. He had more than held his own against the combined efforts of Bennett and Ferguson among the tariff-mad farmers of Elgin and the traditional Tories of St Thomas. And many Liberals attributed their narrow victory to his intervention or the spillover from Elgin. So impressed was W.D. Gregory, whose battles for Liberalism went back to the days of Edward Blake, that in speculating about possible successors to King, he told John Dafoe of the *Winnipeg Free Press* to keep his 'eye on Mitchell Hepburn, member for West Elgin. He is a Canada first man, has good judgement and what so many of our men lack – unfailing courage.'

Mitch's performance during the short session called by the new Conservative government to deal with unemployment relief and the tariff confirmed Chubby Power's view that he was one of the men on whom King could rely to take the war to the enemy. Mitch had moved from the crossbenches and sat in the fourth row directly behind King and Lapointe. He was an obvious choice to speak during the short debate on Bennett's emergency measures. While King was cautious and defensive, Mitch was cocky and belligerent. Boasting of his increased majority in the face of Ferguson's machinations and Bennett's 'ballyhoo,' he labelled Tory promises as hypocritical and the tariff changes fraudulent. In the best Tory tradition, Bennett had 'enslaved the Canadian people,' delivering them through the tariff into the hands of the big business interests. Was it not appropriate, he wondered, that a man who had promised to find magical cures or 'perish in the attempt' should have as his chief whip 'a gentleman who, I understand, has been an undertaker.'[1]

During the session the Ontario members brooded over the plight of their party federally and, even more important, provincially, for the federal party was weakened by the lack of a strong provincial base. The long and glorious history of Liberalism in Ontario had ended with Sir Oliver Mowat's departure for Ottawa in 1896. The party had never recovered from its defeat in 1905. The wounds left by the wrenching debate over union government in 1917 were still raw and the farmers' entry into politics and the prohibition crusade tested Liberal leadership and found it wanting. Defeat followed defeat, and after the 1929 election Premier Ferguson and his ninety-one followers looked across the floor at Queen's Park at a forlorn band of thirteen Liberals. It was little consolation that the federal Liberals had not won a majority in Ontario since 1874, or that they had not been serious contenders in more than a few dozen, largely rural and northern, ridings since the disaster of 1911. Ontario was Tory.[2]

There were Liberals in Ontario, but it was difficult to find a Liberal party. Unlike the Tories, the Liberals had not split their national and provincial organizations, and in theory the Ontario Liberal Association was responsible for both federal and provincial organization. With over a thousand members, however, the OLA was unwieldy and seldom met, while the smaller Management Committee met infrequently. For all practical purposes the OLA was largely financed by Senator Arthur Hardy, the wealthy barrister-businessman from Brockville, and run by an informal consultative executive committee of Hardy, his fellow senators James Spence and W.H. McGuire, a few other leading Toronto Liberals, and King's lethargic Ontario ministers. By the mid-twenties Hardy had installed Duncan Marshall in the Reford Building on Bay Street as organizer. Marshall was as lazy as he was uncouth and offended genteel Liberals by his barnyard language and sometimes spirited behaviour. Party workers quipped that Marshall would give one speech in a riding and declare it '*organized.*'

Since even the limited activity in the Reford Building was largely in the interests of the federal party, by the mid-twenties the provincial members had established their own office on King Street. Nelson Parliament, a six-year veteran of Queen's Park, acted as secretary and organizer. Like Marshall, he worried about overdue rent and unpaid salaries. Although Parliament also worked for federal candidates, the two offices viewed each other with a suspicion bordering on hostility.

In the spring of 1929 the Ottawa Liberals had moved abruptly to improve the organization and hired Harry Johnson as secretary of the OLA and in charge of the Reford office. A thirty-seven year-old journalist who had worked for both the *Globe* and the *Star*, Johnson was to be responsible to Fred Sanderson, the Ontario whip, who had replaced Marshall as Ontario organizer. Johnson's appointment outraged Parliament, and many others in the Liberal establishment. C.M. Bowman, the head of Mutual Life, who had assumed some responsibility for party organization and finance, wrote angrily to King that those who knew Johnson 'state that in their opinion he does not possess one qualification to fit him as an organizer' and that not even King's 'bitterest political enemy' could have devised a scheme more certain to bring political disaster at the next election. But after his usual disclaimers of responsibility, King held firm. Six months later Senator Haydon told him that Johnson 'seems to be an excellent man and for the first time in years there is some hope of doing something in Ontario.'[3]

The causes of the seemingly terminal illness of the provincial party were many, but none were more important than the lack of leadership and the fanatical determination of many Liberals to keep the province dry. The caucus had selected W.E. Sinclair as acting leader in 1923. After leading the party to two disastrous defeats he was 'acting' leader still, for the OLA had never confirmed his selection. Bill Sinclair was a man of undoubted integrity whose mind was locked in his principles and in the past, a man without curiosity, generosity, or imagination. There were no signs of a sense of humour in public and no one observed it in private, and he carried with him the dour presence of an unrelenting Presbyterianism. With Sinclair everything was dogma. Proclaiming the old-fashioned rural values of Whitby Township where he had been born in 1873, he had no sympathy with the new mood of urban Ontario, if indeed he understood it. Sinclair believed in the worth of what he liked to call the better class of people, a grouping that probably excluded French Canadians, Jews, and other minorities, and undoubtedly Mitch Hepburn and his friends.

Above all, Bill Sinclair believed in a dry Ontario. That the people of Ontario had made a mockery of prohibition, that doctors had fattened on medicinal prescriptions and druggists become licensed bootleggers, that livers were destroyed and minds deranged by 'hootch,' and that law enforcement had become an expensive joke did not alter his view that prohibition was the touchstone by which men should be judged. Backed by the equally fanatical Joe Atkinson of the *Star* and Colonel W.G. Jaffray of the *Globe*, he battled against 'Fergie's Foam,' the 4.4 per cent beer that quenched the thirst but did little for the spirit. In 1926 he had opposed the sale of liquor in government stores and was crushed. And his refusal to let prohibition rest assured his defeat in 1929.

There were no French Canadians and only one member from an urban riding among the thirteen Liberal MLAs elected in 1929. And there was some truth in the comment of Martin Quinn, a leading Catholic layman, that the party had become 'a haven for every quack and crank in the country.' Much of the blame rested square-ly on Bill Sinclair's shoulders, and when the Tories were thinking of running a strong candidate against him, Premier Ferguson exclaimed, 'You damn fools, if you do that the Liberals may elect a leader who may want to get into power.'[4]

For years Senator Hardy and his associates in the OLA had want-ed to remove Sinclair, but feared that the attempt would irrepara-bly split the party and drive its rural dry supporters into the arms of the Progressives. Although Sinclair had offered a way out when he expressed an interest in running federally in 1926, the federal Lib-erals had no desire to be tarred with the prohibition brush or to offend the Progressives they were so assiduously wooing. And two years later, vainly pressing King for an appointment to the Senate, Sinclair candidly admitted that his appointment would 'solve some of the Ontario difficulties provincially and place the party in a posi-tion where it could say which way it wanted to go.' Despite the obvious truth in Sinclair's admission, King had different priorities. Yet there was no hope for success under Sinclair, and an appeal for federal funds to assist in the 1929 election led to King's admission that 'My own feeling is that Sinclair will make little or no headway, may even be worse off & it seems a shame to exhaust what resources we have.' His defeat and King's made a leadership con-vention inevitable.[5]

Many Liberals, including King and Hardy, were reluctant to hold a convention because there was no obvious – indeed, no aspiring – successor. But during the session Alex Young, Mitch's friend from Saskatoon, found that many members pointed to Mitch Hepburn as the man who might get the Ontario Liberals 'out of the slough of despond.' That possibility had also been raised by others, probably the triumvirate of senators that dominated the OLA. Inviting Mitch to stop off in Northbrooke and relax over a few drinks after the ses-sion, Colin Campbell added 'I was pleased to hear what you had to say about the Ontario situation but don't be in too much of a hurry until they assure you off [sic] all arrangements.' On his return from Oxford in September, Paul Martin found his friend Bob Deachman suggesting that Mitch's ability on the platform, low-tariff views, boundless energy, charming personality, and engaging wife made him an attractive candidate. Soon after the Management Committee finally bit the bullet late in September and called a leadership and policy convention for 16 December, a Toronto *Star* reporter observed that 'in some quarters ... a quiet book is going on in favour of M.F. Hepburn' whose backers stressed that he was 'young and vigorous, a good speaker and likely to capture the imagination of the people.' It was a prospect that made Joe Atkinson shudder.[6]

Mitch was clearly interested in the leadership of the moribund party. Speaking to the West Elgin Liberals when they met to elect delegates to the convention, he spent much of his time attacking the record of the Ferguson government and very deliberately distanced himself from Sinclair. 'Prohibition should not be a political question,' he stated categorically. 'I maintain that it is unfair and absurd to talk as if all Liberals are prohibitionist and all Conservatives are the opposite.'

It was his speech to the Toronto Men's Liberal Club on 30 October, however, that made him a front runner. Many of the eighty leading Toronto Liberals who met at Hunt's at Yonge and Bloor had not heard Mitch before. The speech was classic Hepburn. He mixed a little tariff talk with attacks on Bennett for his impertinence at the imperial conference in lecturing the British on trade policy, while Ferguson, 'the title seeker' accompanied him to London to 'listen at keyholes.' His quip that Ferguson and the King of Abyssinia were the only absolute monarchs in the world was more memorable than his slashing attack on government policy. During the recent campaign, Mitch recalled, Fergie had laughed when one of his henchmen had innocently asked where Mackenzie King had been during the war: 'Well he wasn't acquiring the Eddy millions as Mr. Bennett was and it took a Royal Commission to find out where Howard Ferguson himself was.' Prolonged cheers followed when he declared that prohibition was no longer a political issue: 'I thank God prohibition is no longer a question because that means the next time we are going to be able to get out in the open and fight Ferguson on his record which I think is the most damnable ever written.' The Liberal party had to shed its past, to 'humanize itself,' and in its policies 'get right down and interpret the sentiment of the overwhelming majority of the people of Ontario. Then we will beat Ferguson.'

The audience of well-dressed lawyers and businessmen, senators and Liberal activists reacted enthusiastically, 'lustily cheering and applauding' his attack on Liberal dryness, reported the *Mail and Empire*. 'He created something akin to a sensation,' Percy Parker reported to King, 'and after the Dinner was over expressions were heard on every hand that this was the man for Leader.' Frank O'Connor, the wealthy owner of Laura Secord candies and a prominent Catholic layman, heard Mitch for the first time at Hunt's and was 'greatly impressed.'[7]

On that October weekend there were many hurried consultations in Toronto among Liberals of different views and others on the fringes of the party. Percy Parker sent King a long letter reviewing the situation. Knowing his reader well, Parker emphasized that the road to power in Ottawa could pass through Queen's Park, a not impossible task since Ferguson was vulnerable to attack on so many fronts. But success depended upon finding a new dynamic leader and casting off the albatross of prohibition. Private conversations with leading drys such as Newton Rowell, a former leader of the Liberal opposition at Queen's Park, and Joe Atkinson, and with Harry Nixon, the Progressive leader, revealed that they were prepared to live with the government sale of liquor, now endorsed in two elections. New leadership posed more of a problem, for with the possible exception of Sidney Tweed, the president of a Waterloo life insurance company, who had been first elected in 1929, there were none of leadership calibre among the members of the legislature.

The three men most frequently mentioned, Parker continued, were W.H. Moore, James Malcolm, and Mitch Hepburn. Billy Moore was a fifty-eight-year-old lawyer, businessman, farmer, and lobbyist, who had shared the task of fund-raising with Percy Parker in 1926 and ran successfully in 1930. Although Parker did not mention it, both Moore and Sinclair were close friends. Moreover, Parker observed, King would not like to lose Moore or Malcolm, neither of whom seemed interested in the position. However, 'Hepburn is in a different position, and I believe he would accept if certain arrangements were made for him, and if he is willing to stand at the Convention I trust this will secure your approval. For myself I would favour his selection as Leader of the Party, with Tweed as House Leader.'

King had received Parker's letter hours before he met Dunning, Haydon, Moore, and McGuire to discuss his plans for a new national Liberal organization. Coincidentally, Mitch was in Ottawa and King invited him to the lunch at Laurier House. When the luncheon conversation inevitably turned to the convention, all agreed that a new leader must be found. 'Quite clearly Hepburn is flattered by the approaches made to him,' King noted, 'and would like to be given the leadership. We pointed out the dangers, no seat in the Legislature, no funds for organization, Tory attacks in Fed. & Prov. House, riding two horses & falling between, the affront to Sinclair etc. etc. I was frank in saying we did not want to lose him from the Federal House.' After Mitch had left, the others discussed 'his danger of drinking & getting mixed up with women, at his young age this wd be fatal to success.' King privately doubted 'if he is sufficiently broad gauged.'[8]

After the meeting at Laurier House, Mitch returned to Toronto and then St Thomas. A few days later he left for Florida with Eva and his mother. He had not recovered from the exertions of the campaign, and his doctor had ordered him to get some rest and avoid his usual winter bouts with bronchitis and influenza. But as Mitch basked in the Florida sun his thoughts were never far from the drama that was unfolding in Ottawa and Toronto.

It would have been uncharacteristic of Mitch not to be drawn to the leadership. He loved the roar of the crowd, and the immediacy of the provincial crown was far more enticing than the long-run possibility of a seat on the Liberal front benches in Ottawa. Was there even a future for him in Ottawa? King had made it clear he did not want Mitch to run and force a federal by-election in Elgin, but he had never mentioned a future portfolio as a reason for staying in Ottawa. Moreover, King had not been particularly discreet in talking to McGuire about Mitch's weaknesses, and had told that earnest young Catholic Paul Martin, among others, that he disapproved of Hepburn's drinking, his fondness for women, and his friends. Mitch may have suspected that there would be little room in a King cabinet for a man who so openly and enthusiastically embraced temptation.[9]

Mitch did not underestimate the opposition. Sinclair, who seemed determined to run, would have the support of most of the caucus and the dry wing of the party. Colonel Jaffray of the *Globe*, who thought more of heaven than the Liberal party, was certain to oppose a leader 'too wet to burn.' Although Atkinson of the *Star* had reluctantly accepted the will of the people on the liquor question, he would also be opposed to a wet candidate when all the signs pointed to the sale of beer and wine by the glass, at least in hotels and restaurants, as the next step in the delivery of Ontario to Satan. It was no secret that Atkinson disliked everything about

Mitch: his life style, his lack of moral earnestness and religious convictions, and an apparent flippancy and irresponsibility which suggested unsound judgment. Atkinson was not alone in questioning
Mitch's capacity to lead the party, for even many of his friends
believed that he would have to grow into the role.

The opposition seemed particularly intense among many of the
older generation of Toronto Liberals. Like Atkinson, they had been
raised when Mowat's writ ran across the province and they distrusted the Elgin maverick as well as the crowd around the Reford
Building who were pushing him forward. Yet it would have been
uncharacteristic of Mitch to accept their criticisms or back down
in the face of their opposition. After all, the *Star* and the *Globe*, the
Sinclairs and the drys, had never won an election, and probably
never would. Mitch had unlimited self-confidence, and he relished
the prospect of an assault on Queen's Park. He did not underestimate the difficulties, for he was a realist. But a man who lived so
recklessly was not deterred by difficulties.

However, Mitch faced other problems closer to home. He was a
farmer, and farming was a full-time job. Although he was not a
poor man, he had a mortgage on the farm and he had just invested in a new herd of good dairy cattle. His income had dropped with
the slump in agricultural prices, and the summer election had been
expensive. His $4,000 salary for a few months in Ottawa was attrac-
tive. And a decision to remain in Ottawa might also appease Mackenzie King. As leader of the provincial party he would have his
own expenses and would need the support of an office staff capable of handling organization and publicity. Before he left for Florida, Mitch had discussed a financial package with Parker, McGuire,
Spence, and others, but he knew that the party was chronically
short of funds and promises were easier made than kept.

While Mitch relaxed under the Florida sun his Toronto friends
were enlisting support. Late in November came the welcome news
that Arthur Roebuck, often mentioned as a candidate, would not
stand in his way. Roebuck's advanced views on social policy, industrial relations, and civil liberties appealed to many Liberal reformers,
including Wilson Southam of the Ottawa *Citizen* and Joe Atkinson.
He had run as a dry UFO-Labour candidate in East York in 1923,
and helped organize the dry coalition in 1926. But he also believed
that the Liberals should not be a prohibition party, and that somehow the issue should be removed from the political agenda.

Despite the differences in their lifestyles and age, Mitch and Roebuck were good friends and he had often sought the assistance and

advice of the fifty-two-year-old lawyer. He wrote at once to thank Roebuck, and confessed that he was 'very much perplexed and quite at a loss to make a definite decision.' Roebuck replied at once. He stated bluntly, as he had to others, that 'by training and natural aptitude, I am fitted for the work this position involves' and the party 'is sadly in need of the inspiration and idealism which I think I possess.' On the other hand, the task of winning a seat and organizing the province, with probably minimal support from the party, was not an inviting prospect for a practising lawyer with a family to support, particularly one without government patronage or corporate clients.

Mitch would likely hold his seat in the next election, however, and if the Liberals won there would be a 'fair chance' of entering the cabinet. Was it not also a fact, asked Roebuck, 'that by both interest and training your political thought is largely federal?' As provincial leader, Mitch would face the expensive and unpredictable task of finding a seat and then the formidable task of defeating the entrenched Tories. 'Generals who have lost battles, even through no fault of their own,' he warned, 'have never slept on beds of roses.' Perhaps, he concluded, neither should run:

I am trying to keep an open mind. I am not a candidate for the position. Were it offered to me, I would of course apply myself to the problem of seeing whether it could be handled. This is so unlikely, I mean such an offer, as to need no present consideration. Should you, in disregard of what I think are your best interests, determine to go after the job, you may count on my friendship, notwithstanding my disapproval, which is purely personal. So far as the public is concerned, and the Liberal Party, I think you would fill the position with credit to yourself and with benefit to the Party ... I have said so before, and I say it again, that you have as a candidate, greater powers of leadership than any other man in the Province. If you are chosen leader at this convention you may be assured of my continued friendship and support, and of every effort within my reach.

With Roebuck behind him Mitch could count on the support of many reformers and perhaps the opposition of the moderate drys could be defused.[10]

The opposition of Mackenzie King could not be so easily defused. For two months King twisted and turned, trying one problematic tactic after another. His argument that he did not want a by-election in Elgin became increasingly transparent and his tortured prose disguised neither his sophistry nor his hypocrisy. King first tried to find a candidate outside the Commons who might undercut Mitch's support, and his selection of Percy Parker revealed his desperation. Parker had known King for many years, and was one of the few to call him Rex. A wealthy fifty-nine-year-old lawyer and businessman, Parker was vice-president of de Havilland and had extensive interests in northern mines. His country estate in Erindale was one of the finest in the province, and he kept a city apartment at Bloor and St George. Parker had never run for office, but had served King as Ontario organizer and fund-raiser in 1926 and 1930. Like Sinclair, his hopes for a seat in the Senate had been dashed, partly because King distrusted him 'as dangerous in talking too much when *full*.' In principle, as well as in practice, Parker was wet, and many attributed his fierce opposition to the abolition of liquor clearances and a new interest in provincial politics to his close connections with the distillers.

However, King not only promised Parker a transfer to Ottawa if the Liberals won federally, but also pressed Spence, McGuire, and Harry Johnson to support Parker rather than Hepburn. After a suitable delay Parker declined the invitation, and wrote King that the 'younger element seemed to be very strong for Hepburn, and, all things considered, I favour him myself. If he were selected I believe sufficient financial backing would be provided to give him a free hand.' Although he had been repeatedly warned that if Sinclair were retained, there would be 'a tremendous defection from our ranks. which we will never regain either provincially or federally,' King countered with the absurd proposal that if Hepburn could be considered as 'an ultimate leader' then the question could be postponed until after the next provincial election. At that moment, however, Sinclair shattered any possibility that Ontario Liberals would endure his leadership for another three years when he lashed out viciously at his detractors on the OLA who were determined to impose a new – presumably wet – leader on the party. It was the party, not the leader, which had failed: 'Where were the recognized leaders of Liberalism in the 1926 and 1929 campaigns?'[11]

While A.J. Young, former president of the OLA, brooded over his reply – that stopped just short of calling Sinclair a liar and pointed an accusing finger at 'the vociferous, unreasoning and at times fanatical crusade' of Sinclair's prohibitionist allies – Harry Johnson sent King the Reford Building's reading of the situation:

We are now at the point where Hepburn seems the only possible choice. I am afraid that Sinclair's recent statement makes it impossible to carry a

Resolution leaving the decision open for even a year. So incensed are some of our supporters by the attack on Senator Hardy and the Association that they will gladly help the younger men to raise the necessary amount to get Hepburn's consent to stand. There is, I gather, a general feeling that the Convention must produce a young man of colourful personality, outstanding platform ability, decision and courage, who can also as leader appeal to our rural people. Hepburn, they are convinced, meets these requirements and in addition they seem certain that he will devote his whole time to the position and continue attacks from all angles on the Queen's Park Administration until it is overthrown.

Confirming Johnson's report, Parker admitted that King's determined opposition to Hepburn placed him in a dilemma. 'As you know I have felt that he would be the best man who is really available, and have so told him. He is at the present time resting up in Florida, but will be back shortly, and today I received word from a mutual friend that Hepburn would like me to nominate him.'[12]

Unwilling to admit defeat, King replied to Parker with yet another inventive proposal. With Ferguson's appointment to London as high commissioner there would be a change in the Conservative leadership, 'and this could well be made a reason for postponing the selection of a Liberal leader and placing the affairs of the Party in the hands of a committee of management for the time being. Of this committee Hepburn, yourself, and others might well be made members. It would then be apparent to the public that no leader had been officially appointed, and the appointment could then be made at any time, once something in the nature of general agreement had been reached.' He assured Johnson that while he would be the last 'to stand in the way of Hepburn's advancement,' the opening of Elgin would undoubtedly arouse resentment among his colleagues in the Commons and would 'be construed by the country generally as an evidence of lack of faith on the part of our members in our future.' Moreover, King warned, both the federal and provincial Tory governments would not allow Mitch to win a by-election, and with a seat in neither House, 'his political career would be jeopardized in the extreme.'

King's proposal was dismissed over dinner at Percy Parker's, and Johnson informed King that delegates to the convention could never be persuaded to accept such a proposal. Moreover, he continued, 'Steps have been taken which have resulted in Hepburn's deciding to be a Candidate for the leadership and I understand he will be in Canada shortly, if he has not already arrived.' The Toronto wisdom was that Sinclair could not get more than 30 per cent of the vote and Hepburn was the only man who could get a majority without creating a split in the party. Johnson added that while Tweed had been considered, 'it is doubted as to whether at the decisive moment he would allow his name to stand with Mr. Sinclair in nomination.' There was some consolation, however, for those 'behind Hepburn feel that he should not resign his Federal seat before another Session, and perhaps not even until the Provincial Election is called.'

King was usually content to wait upon the future, and a provincial election could be three, maybe four, years away. But he seemed determined that Mitch Hepburn should either withdraw or be defeated – whatever the consequences. He told Johnson that if the question should come up he wished it to be known that, while he wished the delegates to have a 'free hand,' he would 'greatly deplore any action the convention might take which would have the effect of creating a vacancy in the Commons, before another federal appeal is made to the country.' Rather than suggesting any 'dictation on the part of Ottawa,' King assured Johnson, it was simply a statement of what 'the interests of the party in the federal arena demand. The convention, of course, must decide whether it regards the claims of the Liberal party in the province, everything considered, as superior to the claims of the party in the federal field.'

King's penultimate ploy was an attempt to persuade Sinclair to retire in favour of Tweed, who seemed to be the only compromise candidate capable of blocking Mitch. If he could no longer offer the coveted seat in the Senate, King could at least offer advice to his old friend from college days. The fact that Sinclair had never received the support and recognition he deserved, wrote King, was perhaps even more reason for stating that 'you desire, both as respects the leadership and policies to be adopted, that the convention have a perfectly free hand. It seems to me that this is the only wise, as well as dignified course for you to pursue.' Victory would bring unity, and defeat no dishonour. 'The only real terms on which a man can hold a position of any real leadership' continued King in what could be read as an appeal for something other than an open convention, 'is to let it be known that, once disloyalty or dissatisfaction assumes any proportions, the party cannot too soon find someone else to undertake the thankless task it has imposed.' There was nothing further King could do, and he knew that he had probably failed: 'I am afraid a mistake will be made and that possibly Hepburn will be chosen. The one saving possibility would be the selection of Tweed, which may follow if Sinclair accepts the advice

I have given him, but Tweed is far from the kind of man to have at the head of a province like Ontario.'[13]

King's opposition to Mitch may have been rational; it was not political. Only King could believe that Bennett would be forced into an early election, that the loss of Elgin would be certain or disastrous, or that the country would see in Mitch's resignation a lack of confidence in King and the federal Liberals. Some Liberals knew that King's relentless pressure was based on much more than a rudimentary and wrong-headed political calculus. They agreed with King that Mitch was young, impetuous, sometimes irresponsible, and lacking in judgment. They also knew that he had enormous personal and political appeal and hoped that he had the capacity to grow. They understood King's concern about Mitch's private life, yet a fondness for the bottle had not seemed to disqualify Percy Parker and King had men about him whose spirited exploits with women were notorious.

Perhaps King himself was unaware of the nature and depth of his own feeling towards Mitch. A man controlled, almost pathologically, by his suspicious and envious mind, he resented the self-assured and impudent back-bencher who had so quickly emerged from obscurity and been promoted by others to the front ranks of the party. He envied Mitch's easy camaraderie, his effortless way with a crowd, the enthusiastic response to his spirited interventions in the Commons, the style that in his view masked the lack of real substance. Afraid of his own weaknesses, which he had disciplined, King may have envied as much as he disliked Mitch's carefree immorality, his apparent success with the scarlet women King possessed only in his dreams. Closeted in his own respectability, ruled by convention, King distrusted men who rejected respectability, who ostentatiously defied convention. Mitch Hepburn simply was not the sort of man Mackenzie King liked. King did not want Mitch Hepburn to be leader of the Liberal Party in Ontario and he faced that prospect with an irrational anxiety.

Mitch returned from Florida at noon on 10 December, and went almost at once to meet the Elgin Liberals at the Grand Central Hotel in St Thomas. The ghost at the party was Mackenzie King who had urged his Elgin friends 'to assist' Mitch in resisting the pressure to run. For over two hours they urged Mitch not to leave Elgin. His interests lay in the broad field of national economic policy and his future in Ottawa as an MP and cabinet minister was much more certain than at Queen's Park, if indeed he ever reached there. Albert Rogers reported to King that the attempt had failed: 'As Emerson (and even one greater than he observed) flattery is a most subtle and deadly weapon. I am afraid that the Agents of "big interests" are preparing a political grave for one who they wish to bury and are employing a most effective instrument for the digging.'

In Toronto the next day Mitch was briefed on the most recent developments. Many Toronto Liberals, obsessed as Sinclair had been with the power of the press, were becoming apprehensive. Thirty-five of them had met at Hart House a few days before and concluded that the convention should not elect a permanent leader, for if the party left the dry platform they would lose the *Globe* and if they elected Hepburn, Joe Atkinson promised they would lose the *Star*. They urged King to make it known that 'Ottawa' had not consented to Mitch's election. King needed no urging, and his heavy-handed insistence remained the only obstacle to Mitch's coronation.

James Malcolm personally brought King's command to a meeting with Mitch, Spence and McGuire, Parker and Johnson. Convinced it would destroy the party, they rejected King's proposed management committee or any other scheme that would leave Sinclair as leader. But bowing to King's pressure, they reluctantly canvassed the prospect of Tweed's candidacy. The consensus, Parker told King, was that 'Hepburn should not be called upon to give any decision one way or the other until Sinclair had definitely been eliminated,' in which case they could support Tweed. Malcolm located Bill Dryden, Sinclair's close friend and campaign manager, and bluntly told him that unless Sinclair dropped out he would denounce him on the convention floor. While Sinclair did not respond officially, he told Dryden that he 'would not clear out of the way for Tweed or anybody else and was going to the mat with Hepburn.'[14]

The convention opened at the King Edward Hotel on 16 December. Liberals were apprehensive and the Tory press patronizing. 'After wandering for twenty-six years in the arid wilderness of opposition, the Liberals of Ontario are further away from the Promised Land than ever before,' gloated the Tory *Mail and Empire* on the eve of the convention. 'Moses after Moses had arisen to show the way, but none had succeeded in getting anywhere. One of the avowed objects of the present gathering is to select a Joshua who will really do the trick.' Mitch had arrived the night before, and stayed in a room rented by Colin Campbell at the Prince George. The early edition of the *Star* stated categorically that Mitch would announce his irrevocable decision to remain in Ottawa, where he expected a cabinet position. The press also reported that the Liberal caucus had met the night before and unanimously endorsed Sinclair, and it was unlikely he would withdraw.

The rural rump in the legislature contrasted sharply with the Ontario that was represented by the 607 delegates to the convention. Of the 112 ridings, only Dundas had failed to send a delegate and most had elected their quota of four. The cities were well represented, Toronto and the Yorks sent over a one-fifth of the delegates; there were large contingents from Windsor, Hamilton, Ottawa, and other urban ridings. There were many French Canadians, Roman Catholics, and some Jews. Reporters estimated that one-third of the delegates had yet to reach middle age, and perhaps one in ten was a woman. Most of the federal MPs and senators were there, as were a high percentage of defeated federal and provincial candidates, officials of the OLA and the Twentieth Century Clubs, Liberal editors, and party elders.

That morning the small delegation from northern Ontario caucused and made no secret of its determination to dump Sinclair and the dry platform, a decision reached earlier by delegates from Windsor and Essex and riding associations in Toronto and Hamilton. A few hours later a meeting of the eastern delegation erupted into an attack on Sinclair. Sinclair's support would have to come from central and western Ontario, a region stretching from Peterborough around York and west to Lake Huron, which had sent only 30 per cent of the delegates, many of whom spoke for urban wets.

The selection of a new leader and a resolution on liquor dominated every discussion at the convention. Both were closely connected with the determination of many Liberals to chart a new course for the party. A platform committee had been at work for several months drafting policy resolutions for the convention. Broadly representative of the party as a whole, the committee was dominated by reformers centred around Toronto.

Joseph Atkinson had opened the pages of the *Star* to spokesmen for the reformers. Colonel A.T. Hunter, an Atkinson protégé, had insisted that Liberals were 'tired of picking splinters of moral victories out of our seats.' Let the Tories boast of 'their millionaire leaders and the splendid establishments of their plutocracy,' he wrote, while the 'rest of the city that keeps up this swollen grandeur is all slum and ghetto.' The future of the Liberals was in urban Ontario, which had voted Tory by overwhelming margins, and Liberalism had to appeal to the industrial workers: 'It is here and now for the Liberal party to put on its workman's overalls, step out in front and step first.' Roebuck also had used the *Star* to appeal for a platform based on the principles of social and economic justice: 'This is the Liberal party's function in this generation, but the Liberal party avoids the issue and has left the debate to the Tories on the one hand, and to the Communists and Socialists with their socialistic programs on the other.'[15]

The reformers encountered considerable resistance. The *Farmers' Sun* spoke for the rural bloc when it warned that city delegates would control the convention and 'seek to influence the adoption of socialistic policies.' The platform committee was aware that farmers often viewed any measures of benefit to the urban worker as an additional burden on agriculture. Some committee members argued strenuously that the party should make few commitments and confine itself to a few slogans and an attack on the Tories. 'Such a position of negation met with considerable support from those who consider themselves politically wise,' Roebuck informed Wilson Southam of the Ottawa *Citizen*. 'The convention will push such thinking aside, but it shows how little assistance the rank and file may expect from those who have been in control.' Among the politically wise was James Malcolm, whose close association with Mackenzie King had reinforced an instinctive caution. 'His position in the party entitled him to take a very prominent part, which he did,' Harry Sifton, a Toronto reformer, reported, 'but the result of it was that he threw out all the resolutions, finding something wrong with all of them.' As chairman of the committee, Sifton called another meeting, 'leaving out those who appeared too reactionary in the first one.'[16]

The platform finally presented to the convention was as advanced as any in the country. Peter Heenan had put forward resolutions promising free public employment offices, cooperation with Ottawa to provide unemployment and health insurance, enforced minimum wage legislation, the eight-hour day and six-day week, improved mother's allowances and maternity benefits, the equitable treatment of male and female workers, and freedom of association for all employees. For the farmers and rural Ontario the resolutions promised relief from excessive and unequal taxation, equalized hydro rates, local autonomy in education, lower interest rates on farm loans, government assistance in cooperative buying and marketing, and, in a tactfully worded resolution, a reduction in the price spread between producer and consumer. A long resolution committed the party to a rational and honest approach to northern development, including more assistance to settlers, controlled timber leasing, and assistance to the mining industry. Most of the resolutions were passed enthusiastically without debate. However, Harry Sifton's condemnation of the Ferguson government for buying hydro-electricity from Quebec and promising cooperation in the construction of the St Lawrence Seaway and power project aroused some concern because it could embarrass the federal Liberals.[17]

Mitch and Sinclair had spent the afternoon greeting old friends. Mitch was not yet a candidate, nor had he confirmed the *Star's* prediction that he would announce his decision to stay in Ottawa. He had agreed to propose the toast to the party at the evening banquet and, tanned and relaxed, obviously enjoyed the opportunity to lambaste the Tories. First, there was Ferguson who had gone to London to combat socialism and revive the spirit of pride in the old country, sacrificing himself for Canada, the empire, and $85,000 a year. And then Bennett who had gone to the imperial conference with empty hands and come back with empty pockets. 'I have heard it said that you can tell a Scotsman by his complexion and an Irishman by the twinkle in his eye – but you can't tell an Englishman anything'; he went on amid the cheers and laughter, 'Nonetheless, it is true we have produced a superman, who has gone to tell 40,000,000 Englishmen what to do.' Mitch also scathingly condemned Tory corruption and scandals, extravagance and debt, the endless legacies of Tory misrule. Such conditions would not last much longer, for the Liberal party 'will ally with the thinking elements in the social and business community in this province, and when that body of thought formulates and crystallizes, these men will disappear like snow. Ladies and Gentlemen, I give you the toast. "The Liberal Party – may its shadow never grow less!"'

The audience leaped to its feet. The ballroom echoed with thunderous applause. W. Rupert Davies, the enlightened publisher of the *Kingston Whig-Standard*, saw the raw political appeal of a man who had 'the thousand guests alternately laughing and cheering for thirty minutes, something which no provincial leader of the party has had the ability to do for two decades.'

After the banquet Mitch escaped the throng of well-wishers, and went to Jack Elliott's suite for a drink and to talk about the next morning when nomination papers had to be filed. Downstairs, Patrick Donnelly, a Toronto Liberal, was passing the word around that those who wished Mitch to run should go to the Yellow Room which he had rented for just that purpose. Within an hour there were several hundred delegates in the room. Reporters gathered outside could hear only animated conversation punctuated by frequent cheers and bursts of applause. Donnelly finally responded to the demand 'Go get him' and told Mitch to come down: the election was his if he wanted it. Mitch and his friends entered the room to thunderous applause, and there was no doubt in the *Globe* reporter's mind when he left at 12:30 to file his story that Mitch would run. But the debate continued, as the Elgin Grits and a few King loyalists battled the contagious enthusiasm. Finally, after Peter Heenan exclaimed that if Mitch ran, together they would 'set the heather on fire,' Mitch declared that as a good Liberal it was clear that he had to stand. 'Jesus, Mitch,' said Coly Campbell as they went back to the room to celebrate until five, 'Jesus, it's in the bag.'[18]

When nomination papers were filed the next day there was no doubt about Mitch's strength. Twenty-three of the fifty-four signatures were from Toronto and York, six from Windsor/Essex, three from Ottawa, and eleven from the north. There was support from the OLA establishment, radicals and reformers, French Canadians and Roman Catholics, women and Jews. Two of his colleagues in the Commons, Fraser of Northumberland and Blair of Wellington, dared King's wrath and supported Mitch, and after he had lost the battle in the Yellow Room, Wilson Mills of Elgin was not to be left out. The most prominent names on Sinclair's papers were those of four members of his caucus, and most were from rural and small-town central and western Ontario. None were wet.[19]

On the morning of 17 December the convention faced the controversial task of defining the party platform on booze. Although Liberals would have liked to adopt an advanced policy including the sale of beer and wine by the glass, it was clear that the result could be the formation of a dry party. The Reverend A.J. Irwin of the Political Action Committee of the Prohibition Union had told the Liberals that the creation of a dry party had been considered after the last provincial election, but a decision had been deferred until after the Liberal convention. 'Temperance people will be deeply interested in the policy it may adopt and even more deeply interested in the character of the leader it may select as constituting a real guarantee of fair treatment of the temperance issue,' he warned three weeks before the convention. On the other hand, even realistic prohibitionists, such as Atkinson and Roebuck, realized that as long as the party remained tied to the principle of prohibition it was sacrificing any hope of gaining power.

The platform committee had tried for weeks to find an acceptable compromise before the drys reluctantly accepted a resolution stating that 'prohibition should not be regarded as a partisan political issue' and the wets agreed that the party should go on record as supporting an educational program on 'the benefits of temperance.' However, the drys insisted that the door to salvation be left open. Roebuck explained his position to a sympathetic Tweed:

It seems to me that all we have to do is to see that neither the 'wets' nor the 'drys' have just cause for complaint. In matters of perplexity, one usually takes refuge in principles. Our principles have always been those of democratic control, and I would be in favour of saying we will administer this Act until it has been altered or abolished by referendum. The 'wets' seem very much opposed to the mention of a referendum, and I am willing to concede the mention, but nothing more. It seems to me we must leave this to public opinion, however expressed. Those who take serious objection to that proposition, should be in the other party.

In another statement to the press on the eve of the convention, Irwin lent his powerful support to the Roebuck position. The Prohibition Union would accept the principle that the issue be removed from politics, he said, if a 'fitting opportunity be given for the people to declare in a definite non-partisan way their wish on various aspects of the liquor problem should they desire.' The refusal of the Liberals to accept that proposition, he warned, 'will, we fear, give rise to suspicions that the liquor forces are entrenching themselves within another political party.'

No agreement had been reached when the convention opened, and the committee met again after the banquet. There was still no agreement when the meeting broke up at 6:15 in the morning. Three hours later the committee met again and at 10:20 the wets won with Sifton, the chairman, casting the deciding vote. The final resolution placed before the convention said simply 'That the Liberal Party undertakes to keep the administration of the Liquor Control Act out of politics and to administer the same by a Commission of an entirely non-political nature.'

The debate then moved to the convention floor where for two hours the drys fought to add some reference to the possibility of a referendum. Support for the resolution was wisely left to speakers long associated with the temperance movement, including J.C. McRuer and E.C. Drury. Delegates loudly applauded John Newlands of Hamilton when he observed that he had always voted Liberal, never voted wet, and never voted for a winner. When the issue was put to a vote only eight hands were counted in opposition to the resolution and with 'spontaneous and enduring cheers' the Liberals abandoned prohibition.[20]

Mitch spent the morning working on his nomination speech, while Colin Campbell went over to Elliott's suite to discuss the promised financial guarantees. Percy Parker, William Mulock of North York, and George Fulford, a wealthy Brockville business-man still in his twenties and Senator Hardy's brother-in-law, signed a letter of intent, while others, including Hardy, who felt it would be indiscreet to put their names on paper, promised their support. Campbell returned to find Mitch still concerned about Sinclair, but just as they were leaving the room Bill Dryden phoned to ask Mitch to come secretly to a floor in the King Edward when he was taken to meet Sinclair. After promising to say nothing, Mitch was told that Sinclair would withdraw on the floor of the convention. The last-minute decision was undoubtedly influenced by the vote a few hours earlier on the liquor platform. It may also have been influenced by the failure of Charles Collins, one of Sinclair's nominators, to get the convention chairman to accept a motion stating that no permanent leader be appointed 'but that the members of the legislature appoint a House leader until the next annual meeting of the convention.' Clearly, for whatever reason, Bill Sinclair was not going to hand the crown to Sydney Tweed.

As the delegates massed in the ballroom for the convention finale there was an atmosphere of uncertainty. A London *Free Press* reporter thought Heenan, Malcolm, and Elliott showed visible signs of anxiety. There was one report that Mitch would withdraw in favour of Tweed, another that Tweed had told the convention chairman in the morning he would not allow his name to go forward if Sinclair was on the ballot. Before taking his seat Sinclair stopped to chat with Joe Atkinson, a Tweed supporter, and assured him he was still in the race. Six men were nominated, but W.K. Murphy, a Toronto lawyer, Roebuck, and Heenan all declined. Elmore Philpott, the crippled war hero and radical journalist who had resigned from the *Globe*, delivered an enlightened appeal for social and economic reform. The delegates then greeted Mitch with an enthusiasm which his painfully laboured recitation of Tory sins would not deserve. But his promise to 'supply the pep and ginger and you people put on the brakes when we get to Queen's Park' aroused another outburst.

Sinclair who had sat motionless, his unlit pipe clamped in his jaw and his book of ballots a convenient note pad, was the last to speak. 'I am sure that I see here today a good majority if I contested the leadership,' he began, but victory would not end the criticism, or bring unity to the party. And so, waving aside the 'No No's' from his friends, he would 'call the bluff' of the two young men who were offering themselves to the party and 'stand aside in the hope and with the conviction that a new start will make things better in Ontario ... At least if it is not I shall know that I have not stood in the way.' Even his bitterest critics stood to applaud as he stepped unsteadily from the platform and pushed his way quickly down the aisle and out of the room. Tears in her eyes, Mrs Sinclair followed as the chairman called for the vote.

The book had ten ballots, but the delegates used only one as Mitch swept to an easy 427 to 97 victory. Every section of the province, even Sinclair's stronghold in central Ontario, gave him an overwhelming majority. Amid the tumult when the results were announced, Philpott moved to make it unanimous. But the only MLA to join Mitch on the platform was Tom Murray, the Renfrew Catholic, who said that although he would have voted for Sinclair, his own baseball team had lost the championship because he left the pitcher in too long: 'We may have been doing that with the Liberal Party.'[21]

4

'Rise dead men and fight'

Mitch received an abundance of gratuitous advice after his election. Because it suited his temperament, he found that of Rupert Davies the most congenial. 'For years the Provincial Liberal Party seems to have been suffering from sterility,' wrote the publisher of the *Kingston Whig-Standard*, 'and this is what will happen to it again if all the bald and grey-headed old wiseacres in the party persist in worrying the brilliant young leader with advice. If young "Mitch" Hepburn is wise he will pay no attention to these gratuitous advisers. He has reached his present position by being himself. If he tries to be anything else, he is done.' One piece of advice from the old wiseacres was to let the Tories take two February by-elections by acclamation rather than begin his new career with two humiliating defeats. Mitch preferred the spirited command of the French general at Verdun: 'Rise dead men and fight.'

Mitch knew, as Sinclair complained, that the party was 'dead in the ridings.' There was no provincial organization and no money to lubricate whatever machinery might be created. Mitch also knew that despite his victory the party was far from united, and that he had little support in the caucus. There were threats that with the Liberals wet the farmers would return to the political arena and disgruntled Liberals would find a new home in a dry coalition. When he paid a courtesy call on Joe Atkinson, he had received an 'extremely frosty' reception, and Colonel Jaffray's *Globe* had no love for a drinking man. Even among Mitch's friends there were many who felt that he was too young and inexperienced, that his judgment was often flawed and his outbursts irresponsible.

Mackenzie King was an uncertain ally. Despite his effusive congratulatory telegram and his sudden pleasure that Mitch had chosen to run, only through his actions could King demonstrate his acceptance of the convention's decision. King's refusal to attend the non-partisan victory celebrations in St Thomas, on the specious grounds that it would not be appropriate to make a political speech until Parliament met, was not reassuring. Mitch would not have been surprised by the entry in King's diary the night of his election: 'I doubt if he will succeed, tho' he has many qualities. He is a leader of young people, but hardly the qualities for a premier. It will be fortunate if his habits do not undermine him, with the temptations there are in public life.'[1]

Aware of the doubts and the opposition within his own party, Mitch was convinced that he must fight the by-elections. A spirited battle would maintain the momentum of the convention, and hopefully arouse a dormant party. It would also provide an opportunity to test, or display, his leadership on the hustings and begin to set the tone and agenda of his political crusade.

The outlook was undoubtedly more promising with 'Boss' Ferguson gone to his reward as high commissioner in London and George Henry in charge at Queen's Park. The Illustrious Potentate of Ramses Temple and a staunch Methodist, George Henry lacked the personality, political ability, and commanding presence of Ferguson. A graduate of Upper Canada College and the University of Toronto, where he mingled with King, Arthur Meighen, and Bill Sinclair, Henry took law before purchasing part of the family farm from an uncle. It was not difficult to make a good living with a three-hundred acre dairy farm on the northern fringe of Toronto. By organizing the Farmers' Dairy and cutting out the middlemen, Henry assured a maximum return to himself and his producer associates. He began his career as squire of East York at Queen's Park in 1913 and joined Ferguson's cabinet as minister of public works and highways in 1923. He was soon Ferguson's most trusted colleague. In December 1930 Ferguson easily imposed Henry on a docile caucus.

Henry was instinctively a Tory, a man who did nothing on impulse and if possible preferred to do nothing at all. He was incapable of bold argument or impassioned rhetoric. Often blunt and impatient, he had once been gently reprimanded by Ferguson for using 'bare knuckles' rather than 'padded gloves.' Henry admitted that when unreasonable demands were made he had 'a tendency to tell them to go to hell.' A down-to-earth man of affairs, the businessman-farmer saw little point in endless talk. 'I quite appreciate the difficulties the farmers are in,' he once wrote, 'but I doubt very much whether it is of any real value to them or anybody else that we should accentuate the matter by making speeches about it.'²

George Henry had no doubt about the outcome of the by-elections in Grenville and Hamilton West. Grenville had never sent a Liberal to Queen's Park, and the party had never put up a candidate since it had become Ferguson's fiefdom in 1905. There were no Liberal volunteers to combat the Ferguson legend and the Tory machine, but Mitch finally persuaded a Spencerville miller whom he had known in Elgin to run. Mitch was the real candidate, however, and from his first speech in Prescott to his last he made Ferguson the issue, believing with John Dafoe that with their 'best love' gone, the people would realize 'like the character in Midsummer Night's Dream that they have been hugging a jackass.' The Ferguson legacy, he charged, was a record of reckless extravagance and maladministration, of skyrocketing debt and increased taxes, with the treasury an open trough for the Tory party and the civil service 'an army of political parasites who feed on the people and whose sole object is to do the bidding of the Government.' Hydro's purchase of power from Quebec was a scandalous sell-out to the private power barons, and Price's failure to police the mining brokers demanded if not a public hanging at least his dismissal and restitution of the millions lost by innocent investors. Even the Tory press in Toronto carried Mitch's assault on the front page.

A stockbrokers scandal was the focal point of the campaign in Hamilton West. The urban riding had not elected a Liberal since 1894. After voting Labour in 1919, it returned to its Tory allegiance in 1923 and in the last two elections the Liberal candidates had lost their deposits. With Mitch's approval, Elmore Philpott decided to run 'as a public acceptance' of Price's challenge to make his administration of the stock market the issue. Philpott was an excellent choice. As a prohibitionist who had nevertheless accepted the decision of the convention, Philpott might be able to keep the dry wing within the party. A radical, he had made an excellent impression at the convention. With more than two thousand families on relief in Hamilton his slogan of 'Unemployment Insurance Now and the 8 Hour Day' had a natural appeal. Mitch opened the campaign with Philpott and, although the crippled war veteran with the inspired tongue was more than capable of holding his own before large and exuberant audiences, Mitch spent several days each week in Hamilton. The attack on the Ferguson legacy was similar to that in Grenville, but the charges against Price in the Solloway and Mills case seemed the most devastating and were fully reported in the press.

Isaac Solloway and Harvey Mills were the most celebrated of the mining brokers who had practised what the courts called 'gaming in stocks' at the expense of the investors. The Liberals charged that Price had been negligent in monitoring market practices and took action only after Solloway and Mills had been tried and convicted in Calgary. Even when Price was forced to launch a suit, he was content with a fine of $250,000, while other brokers similarly charged were sent to jail. Did campaign contributions explain his leniency? Would the government return the millions lost by innocent investors because of the apathy or corruption of the Ferguson-Henry-Price administration? Would Price dare to debate the issue?

The Tories spent more time attacking their opponents than defending their record. Price campaigned in both ridings, portraying Mitch as 'deliberate issuer of false information' and Philpott as a man who 'prostituted the press, prostituted principle to ambition' when he joined a 'dripping wet' leader. But he refused to meet Philpott on the platform. Leo Macaulay, the young Bay Street lawyer who could equal Mitch in invective, was sent from the cabinet to debate with Mitch at the Grenville nomination meeting. Would the voters of Grenville support a man who 'tries to assassinate the reputation of Ferguson, Grenville's greatest son?' Would they not prefer to end the political career of a man so 'reckless and irresponsible ... a disseminator of slander, abuse and vilification ... an undesirable element in the politics of Ontario'? There was no doubt, retorted Mitch, that both Ferguson and Price should have been jailed, as should Tory ward heelers like Grenville's Gordon Sheppard who received handsome commissions from the distillers for getting their brands listed with the Liquor Board. One of the first to be dismissed when the Liberals took office, he promised, would be Sir Henry Drayton, the knight who ran that arm of the Tory party for $20,000 a year.

The results were better than Mitch could have expected. Although Grenville could not be won, the popular vote increased, and it all seemed to go Liberal. In Hamilton West, despite the best efforts of William Clysdale, the 'ruthlessly Tammany Hall politician' who ran Tory campaigns, the Conservative majority fell from 4,763 to 443 votes. The Liberals were elated. King assured Mitch that he had won 'a real victory' and 'aroused the greatest possible enthusiasm on the part of our friends ... How wise you were to fight these by-elections. I hope that you will continue to adopt that policy towards every vacancy that crops up, even to one in Toronto should a vacancy occur.' Arthur Roebuck was ecstatic: 'It seems to me that you have not only dealt the government a blow but you have absolutely established yourself as leader by right of leading as well as election. You have brought the provincial party to life again.' In six weeks Mitch had altered the agenda and changed the tone of political debate. The Tories, it seemed, were vulnerable and there were many like Philpott who promised 'to continue wading through the mud, just so long as it is necessary to win our objective.'

Mitch was exhausted. After the celebrations in Hamilton he returned to St Thomas with bronchitis that developed into pneumonia. As soon as he was well enough to travel he returned to Florida for a month in the sun.

Tanned and rested, though still feeling listless, Mitch was back in the Commons within days of his return. King had given the task of organizing the Liberal assault forces in the House to Chubby Power. The front bench was so weak, Power told King, that they would have to depend on the back-benchers, particularly 'Hepburn and Co.' But although Mitch was effective when he intervened, he was seldom in the House. He was seen more often around the Liberal office in the Reford Building in Toronto than on Parliament Hill and when in Ottawa spent more time organizing the eastern Ontario ridings than in the Commons. Although his new eminence was suitably respected by his colleagues, it did not endear him to Mackenzie King. When the federal Liberals held a testimonial dinner for Mitch late in April, King praised Mitch for his 'great gift of humour, his tremendous power of invective, and his skill as a leader,' but felt compelled to advise him to learn endurance and patience and to restrain his joy in victory. King found Mitch's impromptu speech 'pretty poor stuff, the first fifteen minutes were stories, jokes of one kind or another,' but the 'solid part of his speech was an attempt to grapple with the economic problems of today, to which he was clearly not equal ... I could see the reception to Hepburn's speech was none too good. There appears to be a general feeling that he is not going to last long as leader.' Among the few who shared King's view of Mitch's future were Billy Sinclair and his supporters.[3]

Mitch had no illusions about Sinclair's loyalty. On the night of his victory, Mitch had spent two hours with Sinclair and five members of the caucus. He explained that he would retain his seat in the Commons. While keeping in touch with the caucus, he would speak on his own as Liberal leader. Sinclair agreed to continue as House leader, and did not dissent immediately from Mitch's view that the caucus must remain loyal to the leader and the Liberal Association. Although he brushed off reporters' questions with 'You'll have to ask Mitch – he's the boss now', Sinclair's comment the next day that the House leader was selected by the caucus not the party suggested a different view of their relationship.

It was no secret that Sinclair detested Mitch. An appeal from King for party unity provoked an unequivocal and bitter reply:

You suggest that I aid Hepburn. I do not see how I can be of much assistance. His friends are not my friends. Whatever faults I may have, I know he is of a much inferior type of mind to my own. His personal habits do not appeal to me. We have nothing in common. I am prominent in my profession and he has no training. His chief qualification consists in making rabid speeches, one sentence of which at any time may be his undoing. If he does not make a rabid speech, he makes no speech at all. He makes no thoughtful analysis of any subject in his speeches. He is not and never has been a strong party man.

The feeling after the convention, Sinclair continued, was that the party was a 'mess' and that he had been 'treated most unfairly after years of hard work. This feeling will grow as time passes and Liberals learn exactly what was done at the Convention to force me out, and the parties by whom this was done. To overcome all this is the present work of those in the Party, who have created the present situation.' Sinclair was even more forthright with Howard Ferguson, who informed Henry that Sinclair hoped that 'the conduct of the new leaders will disgust the party generally and that they will turn to him again. I assured him in a private letter that in my judgement if he played his hand carefully that this would be the inevitable result.'

Sinclair did not hide his refusal to accept Mitch as his leader. When the session began he refused to attend caucus if Mitch was present, and responded to Hepburn's request that the members be aggressive in their attack on the government with the comment that it was 'not time for political manoeuvring.' The Tory front bench and press encouraged his rebellion. The *Mail and Empire* reported authoritatively that the Liberal caucus believed 'that the machinations of the federal junta' had set the party back a decade and that only Mitch's demise, by political or natural causes, could 'possibly cure the situation.' Sinclair agreed completely. Although some of the caucus were more obstreperous, he made no attempt to attack Henry during the session and seized an opportunity in the summer to embarrass Mitch and his friends.[4]

By the summer of 1931 the government's hydro-electric policy once again had become a major political issue. The smell of scandal hung over contracts Ferguson had negotiated with Quebec power companies, and Mitch believed that the Tories were vulnerable if only the facts could be unearthed. Even before the death in 1925 of Sir Adam Beck, the father of Hydro, it had become clear that Ontario's insatiable appetite for power was rapidly absorbing the available supply. By the mid-twenties Hydro engineers were forecasting a shortfall of 600,000 horsepower by 1933. The obvious new sources were the Ottawa and the St Lawrence, but the development of both rivers was caught up in the conflict with Ottawa over the respective power and navigation rights and interests of the provinces and the federal government. Harnessing the St Lawrence would involve lengthy negotiations between Ottawa, the United States and the province on an international power and seaway agreement.

There were rivers with enormous potential in Quebec, however, including the St Lawrence. Quebec was as committed to private power as Ontario was to public. The private power interests in Quebec were allied by interest and interlocking directors with the giant Niagara Hudson consortium that held a stranglehold on the American side. Like their American counterparts, they had long fought a guerrilla war not only against public development of the St Lawrence and other rivers with enormous potential, but also against Ontario Hydro, the most successful public utility in North America. However, the Quebec government had consistently refused to allow power to be exported, since cheap power was seen as one of the dynamics of Quebec's industrialization.[5]

But principle had to yield to necessity. Premier Taschereau and the extraordinarily powerful Quebec power interests, whose tentacles reached into almost every sector of the economy, were determined to prevent the development of the St Lawrence under federal auspices. By 1926 Taschereau had agreed to the export of power to Ontario in the expectation, or with the guarantee, that Ferguson would restrain his advocacy of the Seaway project and that both would combat any federal attempts to control power developments on the Ottawa and St Lawrence as an adjunct to federal control over navigation. In 1926 Ontario Hydro signed a contract with A.R. Graustein's Gatineau Power Company, a subsidiary of the giant International Paper Company, for 260,000 horsepower to be fed into the Niagara system between 1928 and 1931. Ferguson fulfilled his part of the bargain a year later when the Conservative convention in Winnipeg adopted his resolution favouring the construction of an 'all-Canadian' seaway 'as and when conditions warrant' and recognizing the 'sovereign rights' of the provinces to all the water power. The St Lawrence had ceased to be a critical priority in Ontario's immediate hydro-electric strategy.

Despite the contract with Gatineau, the need for more power remained critical. By 1928 the government was negotiating three more large contracts with Quebec companies and arranging to purchase property on the Madawaska River and the plants of the Dominion Transmission Company in Hamilton. At Chat's Falls on the Ottawa, Ontario Hydro agreed to buy all the 192,000 horsepower generated by a joint development with the Ottawa Valley Power Company, which was controlled by Isaac Killam of Royal Securities who had recently bought the Tory *Mail and Empire*. Hydro also signed a contract with MacLaren Quebec Power for 125,000 horsepower. In each case the company prospectus boasted that the Hydro purchase alone guaranteed annual earnings more than double the bond interest.[6]

In November 1929 Hydro signed the largest and most controversial contract with Beauharnois Power for 250,000 horsepower. Beauharnois was the creation of R.O. Sweezey, engineer, promoter, and head of Newman, Sweezey and Company, investment dealers. Sweezey had long been interested in developing the enormous potential of the Soulanges section of the St Lawrence in Quebec and by 1927 had launched the scheme which promised staggering profits for the promoters. The Taschereau government approved a lease. The syndicate then asked the King government to approve the diversion of 40,000 cubic feet per second which would permit the development of 500,000 horsepower. King faced strong opposition from his Ontario ministers who, as advocates of public power, resisted complicity in a private project of such scope that it could doom the development of the St Lawrence in Ontario. But the pressure on King from Taschereau and the Montreal financial community, from influential Liberals strategically placed on the Beauharnois board, and from hired lobbyists such as Senator Spence was compelling.

Sweezey had also ensured that Ferguson would lend his support. From the outset, it was critical to Sweezey's plan to sell power to Ontario. In November 1928 the syndicate was able to send King a copy of a letter in which Ferguson thanked Taschereau for his offer to allow the export of Beauharnois power, for 'Beauharnois would seem to me a very convenient and favourable point from which to procure our requirement.' King persuaded the cabinet to approve the necessary order-in-council. Hydro secretly reached an agreement with Beauharnois in the spring, but Ferguson did not sign it until November, a month after the provincial election. Already Hydro

Chairman Charles McGrath, a Beauharnois enthusiast, had warned Ferguson that with all the new contracts Hydro could have a short-term surplus, and Ferguson privately secured Taschereau's consent that Ontario could export Beauharnois power surplus to its needs. In 1927 Ontario Hydro had distributed about one million horsepower. By 1930 it had undertaken to buy an additional 800,000 from private power companies in Quebec, and had discussed options for more.[7]

Months before the contract with Beauharnois was officially signed the company's prospectus for a $30 million bond issue had boasted that the Hydro contract alone guaranteed success. The company's prospectus also implied that it was its intention to divert the full flow of the St Lawrence and develop over two million horsepower. And it was Beauharnois's audacious request for a further diversion that led Robert Gardiner, the Progressive leader, to demand a parliamentary investigation into what his colleague, Edward Garland, termed a shocking tale of 'political brigandage.' Bennett agreed to appoint a special select committee of the Commons, which began its hearings in June 1931.[8]

In April, when Gardiner began to raise questions about Beauharnois, William Sinclair issued a press statement denouncing Beauharnois and insisting that any further development would ensure that the 'financial and political interests' of Montreal would 'doom Ontario and its lake ports to remain inland' for ever. Sinclair asked Bennett to conduct a thorough investigation of Beauharnois, including the contract with Hydro. 'The opportunity is available, and if Ontario is to be protected, it should be held, no matter whom it affects,' he argued. 'Mr. M.F. Hepburn, M.P., Ontario Liberal leader has an opportunity which he will no doubt embrace, to demand such an inquiry from his place in the House of Commons.'[9]

Sinclair undoubtedly had the interests of Ontario at heart, but his unilateral statement also seemed designed to embarrass Mitch and the federal Liberals who had agreed to the diversion. As Senator Hardy angrily informed King, 'I have heard in several places that our friends interested in Quebec corporations are feeling decidedly sore over Sinclair's ridiculous statement that he would break these contracts with Quebec power producers,' one of whom, J.R MacLaren, had run as a Liberal in Leeds in 1930. The conspiratorial Senator Charles Murphy praised Sinclair's initiative. He informed him that it had been Senator Spence and Percy Parker who had agreed to underwrite Mitch's expenses. 'While a member of the firm of Starr & Spence, the Solicitors for the Dominion Securities Corporation, the financial backers of the Beauharnois grab, is Mr. Hepburn's paymaster, or is in a position to control what Hepburn is paid, you will, I am convinced look in vain for the starting of an investigation by Mr. Hepburn.' Sinclair replied that it 'will certainly be interesting to watch his manoeuvres.'[10]

In fact, Mitch had been attacking the Ferguson-Henry hydro policy for months. The Liberal convention had condemned the Quebec contracts, and Mitch had invited Harry Sifton, the author of the resolutions, to campaign with him in Grenville where the future of the St Lawrence could be of critical importance in that depressed county. He continued the attack in the few speeches he made after his return from Florida, and in the Commons on 19 May supported Robert Gardiner's request for an investigation into Beauharnois. However, Mitch's attack on Hydro was not well informed. Denied essential information by Hydro, he resorted to innuendo. Was it not Ferguson who in 1927 had deliberately delayed the St Lawrence power and seaway project, a project bitterly opposed by the power barons of Quebec? Had not Hydro repudiated the principles of public ownership and become dependent on its most bitter critics, the private power interests in Quebec? Did Isaac Killam's ownership of the *Mail and Empire* influence the Chat's Falls contract? Was not the $21 million paid to the Nesbitt Thomson interests for the antiquated plants of Dominion Transmission more in the interests of the company than the province?

The theme was always the same: public power had become political power. At Milton on 21 May, Mitch cited figures to show that public power under the Tories had become more expensive to produce than private power in the United States. Was the government attempting to undermine public ownership and 'to place Hydro on the auction block to satisfy the designs of a Yankee electric power ring'? W.D. Gregory, the Liberal who had headed a royal commission on Hydro in 1923, wrote Mitch at once to warn him that his figures had come from 'what is called the American Power Trust, a most unscrupulous organization, and no doubt an effort will be made to identify your arguments with those that have been advanced by these people. You should I feel avoid the danger of being associated with them.' But it was too late. The figures given to Mitch by his staff had come directly from a propaganda pamphlet – some paragraphs in fact were in quotation marks – produced by the Utilities Publication Company in Chicago whose aim was nothing less than to destroy the reputation of Ontario Hydro in the interests of that Yankee power ring. Was it not Mitchell Hepburn, the Tories asked, who was determined to destroy the reputation of Hydro?[11]

Mitch's speech at Milton was not one of his best, and it was the last he made for many months. After his return from Florida he complained increasingly of the abdominal discomfort he had felt first during the by-elections. Throughout the spring he was constantly tired and irritable. Early in May Dr Holbrook of Hamilton found a large stone on the left kidney. Mitch fulfilled his last speaking engagements, rested for a few days at the farm, and entered the Memorial Hospital in St Thomas. On 12 June his good friend Doc Rutherford successfully removed the kidney. Mackenzie King sent a basket of flowers, and thanking him Eva said that Doc Rutherford predicted Mitch would be in better shape than in many years. But King had already made his own diagnosis. 'The little fellow has been very plucky about the whole affair,' he wrote to Malcolm a few hours after the operation, but 'it is just questionable whether he will ever be sufficiently strong to continue in the position of leadership.' Should Mitch decide to resign, he continued, 'his retreat will be wholly honourable and easily understood, but I imagine he has wished many times that he had accepted the counsel of his older friends and not allowed himself to be too quickly precipitated into the task which he assumed, the duties of which, we all agree, he has met with considerable ability, courage and fortitude.'

As Mitch was about to leave the hospital, he developed pleurisy, and although he went home in mid-July, it was not until August that the doctors allowed him to see his friends. When he was well enough to travel he rested at a camp on the Magnetawan River for ten days, and by the end of August was ready to try to restore some unity to a party that had been badly shattered by the events of the summer.[12]

Mitch followed the proceedings of the select committee of the Commons inquiring into Beauharnois from his bed. From the moment the committee began its hearings on 15 June the country was shocked by an incredible tale of the fortunes made in the exploitation of Canada's natural resources, of shares and properties worth nothing one day and millions the next, of the incestuous relations between business and government, and the open and calculated purchase of political influence. 'The lid is off,' Lapointe exclaimed to King on 17 July when R.O. Sweezey calmly told the committee that operating on the principle that 'Gratefulness was always regarded as an important factor in dealing with democratic governments,' he had given the Liberal Party 'somewhere around $600,000 or $700,000' during the 1930 election. And the Ontario Liberal party? 'Oh, trifling amounts,' he replied. 'I do not recall exactly; it may have been $1,000 or $2,000 or $3,000.' The donation was made to Percy Parker who admitted at once that on 10 February 1931, with the party 'hard up,' he had happily accepted $2,000 from Sweezey, a man of Liberal leanings who was thinking of running for Parliament.

It was then the Liberals' turn. Had he made any contributions to the Conservative party? It had been suggested that $200,000 would be an appropriate donation, Sweezey replied, but apparently Bennett had overruled his bagman. However, in addition to smaller contributions to Tory candidates and organizers, Sweezey continued, 'I know we made a contribution to someone who represented himself as standing for a Ontario fund of this kind.' The $125,000 in cash and bonds to John Aird, Jr, the son of Sir John Aird, president of the Canadian Bank of Commerce, seemed eminently reasonable, for Beauharnois would 'probably be having a lot more dealings with the Ontario people.' In his testimony, Aird flippantly admitted that he had received the $125,000 but insisted it was for his offer to assist in securing the contract with Hydro. It was not his fault if Sweezey assumed that his offer, never acted upon, was a discreet way of collecting campaign funds. Aird added that he had also received $50,000 from Ontario Hydro for assisting in the Madawaska purchase. Premier Henry and Hydro denied any knowledge of the $125,000 but admitted that Aird had been paid $50,000 for professional services, although it was not exactly clear what those services had been.[13]

In Oshawa, Sinclair immediately wired all the Liberal MLAs not to attend a luncheon hosted by Parker to avoid any contamination from 'any of those who have been identified with the unsavoury facts brought out in the recent inquiry.' Early in August he went further and publicly demanded a full-scale investigation into the politics of Beauharnois. Reached at the farm by a persistent Toronto *Star* reporter, Mitch refused any comment: 'Right now my motto is "let the rest of the world go by".' Senator Hardy was not prepared to accept Sinclair's continual criticism of the party, however, and issued a blistering statement to the press:

Time apparently has not softened the rage of Mr. Sinclair against his rejected leadership and his desire for revenge against the Liberal convention last December ...

Our young leader, Mr. Hepburn, has suffered a grievous illness – one which carried him nigh unto the gates of that veil from which there is no returning. Taking advantage of that situation Mr. Sinclair has indulged in what is nothing more or less than an attempt to place himself in the limelight, apparently in the dream that he may make a return to the leadership of the party ... The political history of Ontario presents no such cowardly, shameful attempt at the betrayal of a leader, as this.

The question of an investigation into Hydro electric affairs in Ontario will be taken up without any doubt whatever, at the proper time and in the proper manner by the Liberal party through its accredited leader but not by a repudiated aspirant for its leadership. If such an investigation would be carried on by Mr. Sinclair with no more success than his leadership for seven years then indeed it will be better that no inquiry be held at all. No wonder is it he received so many kind words from the Conservative party during the last session of the legislature![14]

Sinclair's open attack on the OLA seemed even more sinister because it coincided with the formation of a new organization of some of the federal members with W.H. Moore as president and Nelson Parliament as organizer. The *Globe* reported that the federal Liberals planned to sever all connections with the OLA. Hardy and Parker at once informed King that they would resign, and Parker was convinced that 'the activities of Moore and Sinclair are linked together to the detriment of Hepburn.' To clear the air Hardy called a meeting of the Management Committee when Moore and Fred Sanderson explained that the members were simply attempting to improve their own riding organizations with no thought of leaving the OLA. There was no doubt that Sinclair would continue to create dissension, A.J. Young informed King, but 'Hepburn is back on his feet again and as the official leader of the provincial party will be able to smooth out many of the difficulties and bring some of the conflicting elements into closer harmony.' However, after discussions with McGuire and other Liberals, Floyd Chalmers of the *Financial Post* concluded that the party could 'split wide open. W.H. Moore is the man who is pulling the strings attached to Sinclair's arms and legs, but the bigger Liberal crowd including McGuire, Senator Hardy and those who would ordinarily control the finances of the party, if there were any, are on the other side.'[15]

Mitch was under no illusions about the possibility of a reconciliation with Sinclair. 'My own opinion is that it is best to let Mr. Sinclair have all the rope he wants,' he informed a supporter. 'He certainly is showing himself up in a bad light and I think that before

long the Provincial Members themselves will be heartily sick of him.'
In the meantime, the tensions between the OLA and the federal members could perhaps be lessened and, as soon as he was back on his
feet, Mitch visited Kingsmere. King was delighted to see Mitch
'looking so well & I formed a higher opinion of him in our talk
together. He has picked up wonderfully & seems to be taking a
more sober view of things & to be keen and in earnest.' The four-
hour discussion with King covered a wide range of provincial and
federal issues, presumably including the need for party unity and
improved organization.[16]

Later in September Mitch met with Sinclair and members of the
provincial caucus. Some members·were dismayed by 'the apparent
efforts of the Reford crowd to discredit us, a very important part
of the Liberal party,' but others, particularly most of those first
elected in 1929, had no desire to continue Sinclair's vendetta against
Hepburn, the OLA, or the wets. Six MLAs were on the platform with
Mitch three days later when he gave his first speech after his illness
and several others sent telegrams. Sinclair was not among them.

The plot against Mitch and the Reford crowd thickened as the
1931 convention of the OLA approached. During a trip to Toronto
Senator Murphy learned that Moore was actively canvassing dissident Liberals, one of whom explained that 'a mistake had been
made in Hepburn's selection' and that it was necessary to get rid
of him 'at the first opportunity.' Murphy warned Fred Sanderson
not to get involved in 'any of the innumerable stupid schemes,' for
if given enough rope they would 'all hang themselves.' The scheme,
it seemed, was to 'rip the roof off' at the London convention, presumably by electing an anti-Hepburn slate to the Management
Committee and forcing his resignation.

Mitch was aware of the plotting, though not perhaps of its intricacies. In a speech at Dutton, he went out of his way to attack
Moore's (and Sinclair's) appeal for a non-partisan approach to public issues. 'Anyone who submits to the present Bennett autocracy
in Ottawa and the Tory administration in Toronto,' he thundered,
'is a traitor to his fellow citizens.' B.H. McCreath, an old guard
Toronto Liberal, read his morning *Globe* and immediately wired
King: 'Toronto Liberals are astonished at Mitchell Hepburn's attack
on W.H. Moore. J.E. Atkinson and many of your influential friends
have been assisting Mr. Moore in endeavouring to strengthen your
organization in Ontario. Many are of the opinion that you should
find it impossible to attend London meeting.' King too believed the
attack on Moore was a mistake and further proof that Mitch 'has

poor judgement & lacks discretion & no wisdom.' But he refused to give up the opportunity to lay the blame for Beauharnois on the apathy of the Liberal rank and file, and told McCreath he would speak on party organization not politics.[17]

Although King's apologia for Beauharnois won the headlines, the real battle at London was for control of the provincial Liberal party. Four men were reported to be candidates for Hardy's position as president: W.H. Moore, who had the support of some federal and provincial members; Albert Matthews, a wealthy Toronto investment dealer and party fund-raiser; G.N. Gordon, a prominent Peterborough lawyer who had sat briefly in King's cabinet; and William Mulock of North York who was most closely associated with the Hepburn wing. The decision was not made on the floor of the convention, but in secret conferences that went on most of the night. When the weary delegates assembled the next morning Senator Hardy announced that to prevent a rupture in the party and out of loyalty to Mitch Hepburn he would remain as president for another year. 'There isn't a particle of doubt that the great ovation they gave me ... was ninety-nine percent your own,' Hardy later assured Mitch, 'and an endeavour to show openly that the convention approved of you – my part being only an agent of yourself.' With the election of Tom McQuesten, a prominent Hamilton Liberal, as vice-president, Percy Parker as chairman of the Management Committee, and most regional organizations in the hands of good friends, Mitch's victory seemed complete.[18]

The late luncheon to wind up the convention was anticlimactic. The speech Mitch had intended to give the night before or earlier that morning remained in his pocket. The depression, he had written, called for a radical reorientation of political thought. 'My position as an opponent of reactionary Toryism is one of no compromise. Let those who are Tory by conviction and do not choose at this time to champion the cause of Liberalism go to the Tory Party.' Mackenzie King had advised him that endurance was a leader's chief asset and endurance in the face of 'Tory shafts' was a 'curse I have to bear and I do not complain or beg for mercy':

The Tory papers have filled their columns with reports of dissatisfaction amongst the Liberal members of the Legislature over my Leadership. This propaganda ... has assumed such magnitude that I have decided to clear the air once and for all and I am now going to frankly tell the delegates and party heads here assembled the unfortunate state of affairs in our ranks ... Of the fourteen Liberal members of the Legislature I have the good will, support and absolute co-operation of ten of them. Included amongst that number is Mr. Tweed ... Two of the members I would classify as being neutral and I feel that in the course of time they will stand by the convention platform and the leader. Dr. McQuibban, while not opposed to me for personal reasons is, I believe, definitely a supporter of Mr. Sinclair. From Mr. Sinclair I have not had the slightest degree of co-operation nor do I expect it now. I do not know the strength of the so-called Sinclair forces at this convention, but I am quite prepared to give Mr. Sinclair a chance to test his strength. If he can carry the majority vote of this convention then I , as a good Liberal, will cheerfully step aside.

It had been Moore and Sinclair who had appealed for a political truce, and it was Moore who 'in an endeavour to oust me from the leadership' was seeking the presidency of the OLA. It was time for a decision: Moore should allow his name to stand and 'if he is elected as president I shall be pleased to hand him my immediate resignation.'

Senator Hardy and others had persuaded Mitch to keep that speech in his pocket. Yet even with the insurrection quelled, he used his brief luncheon speech to raise the same issue and suggest that 'those men who have failed to give me the support which I should expect of them ... will fall in line now, I am sure' and 'destroy that source of destructive propaganda the Tory papers have at the present time.' The prolonged standing ovation suggested that, for the moment at least, his position was secure. Hardy congratulated Mitch for leaving the speech in his pocket: 'When you see how well things worked out without it you must be pleased yourself. Just keep this incident in mind when you want to slam somebody else some time – and don't do the slamming.'[19]

Since early October Mitch had maintained a feverish pace and Doc Rutherford urged him to 'ease up a bit ... and do not kill yourself on the first lap.' But after an absence of three months, Mitch wanted to restore some of the lost momentum. There had been no economic recovery during the summer, and he believed that Henry could be defeated if the Liberals adopted 'advanced policies applicable to the present situation.' He confessed to Arthur Roebuck, however, that he was perplexed about the course he should follow.

As always, Roebuck was ready with advice. He questioned whether Ontario was 'ready politically for any advanced programme of social reform' and argued against revealing proposals of a constructive nature before a general election. Mitch should simply adopt the 'well-worn and established tactics of the office-seeker,' his speeches moderate and thoughtful, his manner ingratiating, his criticism restrained, and his jibes friendly. Resist the urge to make 'hot speeches' and let 'others turn the sausage machine or drive the manure spreader.' Minimize the losses by avoiding issues, and focus on hard times, the extravagance at Queen's Park, and the undermining of Hydro. 'A *few* stories, wise cracks and spicy illustrations will make up all you require,' for even Macdonald's 'stump speeches consisted of a few sentences of good, serious material and the balance was jolly. We have made some progress since then, but not overmuch.' It was a good script. But Mitch was too impulsive, too sensitive to criticism, too combative, and increasingly too angry not to turn the sausage machine or drive the manure spreader.[20]

Every seat in Bernhardt's Hall in Preston was taken and the aisles and halls jammed when Mitch made his first speech in the fall. The problem facing Canada, he began, was not overproduction but underconsumption because unemployed workers and farmers, faced with falling prices and glutted markets, lacked purchasing power. Yet manufacturers maintained prices and profits behind the tariff, and the Henry government yielded to the bankers' pressure and lowered interest rates in Provincial Savings Banks while borrowing from the same bankers at excessively high rates of interest. The politicians refused to discuss the concentration of wealth in the hands of very few, wealth that was often acquired through corrupt covenants between government and business. A Liberal government, he promised, would not only oppose special privilege but within its limited jurisdiction would adopt 'a system of taxation that will place the burden upon those most able to pay.' While the Tories had driven the province to the brink of insolvency, the Liberals were 'prepared to put on the brakes' and follow a policy of retrenchment, of debt reduction and lower taxation. The Liberals would also conduct a thorough investigation of Hydro, now little more than an adjunct of the Tory machine and a distributing system for the power barons of Quebec. It was an impressive performance, although, as always with Mitch, style both reinforced and was a substitute for content. As the audience came to its feet it was clear that Mitch had recovered.

A few days after the Preston speech, he was at Dutton to accept the Liberal nomination for West Elgin in the next provincial election. He charged that Bennett's tariff policy lowered farm prices and increased the farmer's costs, and was only one of many examples of special interests feasting at the public trough. The result of such inequalities, he declared, would be the 'greatest political evolution that has taken place in this generation at least. I look for a National Government at Ottawa in the near future and a complete realignment of political thought.' Liberals who were Tory by conviction would drift to the Tories, but the great body of Conservatives would join the ranks of 'a true Liberal Party,' a party that would be engaged 'in the political struggle in which the masses are striving to rid the country of the special privileges enjoyed by the few.'[21]

With the approach of an 18 November provincial by-election in Wellington South, the Tories had to respond to Mitch's assault. Despite their overwhelming majority in the House, they were determined to retain the riding and dampen the prospects for a Liberal revival. William Clysdale organized the Tory campaign with his usual quiet efficiency. Hugh Guthrie, the local MP and minister of justice, came from Ottawa with the promise of a $150,000 post office for Guelph. To do battle with Mitch on the hustings, the Tories selected Karl Homuth, a powerful speaker who had sat in the legislature as a Labour member and then a Conservative from 1919 to 1930. Most of Homuth's campaign was a personal attack on Mitch. Who were those members pledged to a dry Ontario but found on the platform with a dripping wet leader? Who was this 'boy leader' so very liberal in his abuse of public men but whose own private life should, of course, not be an issue? And just how much of Sweezey's $700,000 had found its way to Elgin in 1930? By voting Tory the electors of Wellington South had a golden opportunity to end the political career of this menace, Mitch Hepburn.

Homuth intended to provoke Mitch into some indiscreet outburst, and he succeeded. Mitch responded to the charge that he was tainted with Beauharnois money with the statement that if Senator McDougald, who had been deeply involved in the scandal, were an Ontario Liberal he would 'drum him out of the party without consideration.' Clearly the boy from Yarmouth still had much to learn. Senator Hardy warned him that McDougald 'has for fifteen years or thereabouts, been very close in touch with all the financial operations of the party and heaven alone knows how much he knows.' And in Ottawa the embittered senator replied to King's suggestion that he retire gracefully that 'if Hepburn and fellows like that kept up he would not, but wd. shew them up.' The McDougald indiscretion should be a warning, wrote Hardy, 'not to let your impulsive nature run away with you on occasion. They will do everything they can in this election to try and draw you. Don't let them do it and absolutely ignore all personal attacks or slights unless you want to laugh at them.'[22]

Mitch was in the riding almost constantly, spending much of his time driving around the rural townships and making short speeches in village schools and town halls. He also persuaded Harry Nixon, the Progressive leader and a prohibitionist, to campaign for the Liberals. With a population of twenty-one thousand, Guelph dominated the riding, and with over a quarter of the men unemployed the Liberals hoped to cut into the traditional Tory majority. Harry Johnson was in the riding for three weeks, and worked closely with Mitch and the Liberal candidate, Paul Munroe, the popular alderman from the working-class ward of St Patrick. Johnson and Munroe conducted a door-to-door campaign which a rejuvenated Liberal organization 'brought down to the level of the people.' Although the Liberal vote fell sharply in the dry rural polls, a dramatic drop of 1,200 votes in the Tory majority in Guelph gave the Liberals the victory by 291 votes. 'In South Wellington we won through the aid of the young people of both sexes, the Italians, the Jews, the Armenians and the men and women who liked a good fellow,' Johnson wrote Chubby Power. 'We may not at all times have been dignified, but on election night we sure were popular.' Senator Hardy found the victory 'astonishing' and McGuire assured Mitch that the victory not only confirmed his leadership, but also the position of the controversial Harry Johnson. To Johnson himself the moral was clear: 'If we can keep Hepburn going around the province making friends as the main job and speeches as a side line, Henry and Price will only increase the size of the landslide against them by cuts of millions in expenditures and cuts in government salaries.'[23]

Yet the results in the rural townships revealed a potential, perhaps fatal, weakness. Liberal strength was concentrated in rural and dry Ontario, and in 1929 over two-thirds of the voters in the forty-five rural ridings had cast their votes against the government. But agrarian distress had revived the interest in a farmers' party, and when the Liberals left the dry platform and selected a wet leader there was talk of a new agrarian-dry party. Joe Atkinson endorsed the logic of such a move, and Sinclair spoke menacingly of some of his colleagues seeking new alliances. However, if farmers and liquor could be kept out of politics, and the prohibitionists returned to their old allegiances, a united opposition could win as many as twenty more rural seats, and virtually blanket the ridings around Georgian Bay and in western Ontario.

Mitch believed the key was in fashioning an alliance with Harry

Nixon, the St George farmer who had become leader of the Progressives when the UFO left politics in 1924. Five years older than Mitch, prohibitionist Nixon was a pragmatist who had little patience with the Morrison ideologies or the single-issue fanatics in the UFO. Mitch had known Nixon since his UFO days in the early twenties, and Nixon had been impressed by Mitch's work for the farmers as an MP. Nixon had worked in Elgin during the 1930 election, and had slipped almost unnoticed into the London convention as an independent delegate from Brant. Undoubtedly Mitch assured Nixon that he had no intention of jumping on the wet bandwagon and Nixon in turn retained his freedom of action on the liquor question.

South Wellington was the beginning of a formal alliance. 'Had a conference yesterday with members at Toronto,' wrote Nixon. 'They entirely approved of our action in S. Wellington. Had it been otherwise I would have handed them my resignation.' Mitch may have written or talked to some of the caucus and consulted Senator Hardy who advised him to 'join up with him to the limit ... Dangle a portfolio before him and I think we can have the whole crowd and he is well worth it.' At Mount Brydges on 11 December, much to Sinclair's surprise, Mitch announced that the Liberals and Progressives would cooperate in the legislature. Four days later at Paris, at Nixon's request, Mitch joined him on the platform: 'If I am called upon to form a cabinet,' he promised, 'I intend to surround myself with men of independent views, not only those subservient to myself.' The Liberals would not 'swallow' the Progressives, he said reassuringly, but with 'two schools of thought, one moving along the line of progress, the other reactionary, it is felt those favouring reform policies should cooperate to the greatest degree.' Mitch believed that the alliance was a major triumph, and that Liberal fortunes rested on its stability.[24]

'I swing to the left'

Mitch was not a poor man, but he had a much deeper personal experience of the Depression than either King or Bennett closeted in Ottawa. Mitch was a working farmer, who spent much of his time among Elgin farmers and St Thomas railwaymen. When not at home or in the Commons, he was on the road organizing the party, speaking in mining and mill towns, talking and drinking with local Liberals until the early hours of the morning. And as he lamented in the spring of 1932, the 'suffering and privation one witnesses now in travelling throughout this land of ours would bring tears to the eyes of a Pharo [sic].'[1]

In that spring of 1932 it was difficult to imagine that the worst was yet to come. The captains of industry and finance no longer spoke of interruptions and dislocations. Sir Herbert Holt's assurance that 'it is darkest just before dawn' may have comforted his Royal Bank shareholders, who received their customary dividend without the customary bonus, but it was of little consolation to the thousands without power because of unpaid hydro bills. The promised recovery in the summer of 1931, when 18 per cent of all wage earners in Ontario were unemployed, had not materialized. The ranks of the unemployed increased sharply over the winter, and by April trade unions reported that one-quarter of their members were unemployed, while many with jobs worked short shifts. Wages had held up reasonably well, but they too began to fall early in 1932.[2]

Some parts of the province suffered more than others. In April only one Torontonian in ten was on relief, but in the suburbs that had mushroomed during the 1920s the figure was one in five. In Oshawa and the Border Cities the automobile industry ran at one-sixth capacity. Three thousand people had fled Oshawa since 1929,

and in East Windsor almost 40 per cent of the people were on relief.
Much of northern Ontario was a wasteland. Falling commodity
prices had closed many mines. Export markets and domestic consumption declined drastically and work in the logging camps came
to a halt. Abitibi, typical of the troubled pulp and paper industry,
closed half its mills. Single-industry towns were devastated. In the
summer of 1931 two-thirds of the men in Sudbury had registered
with the unemployment office and in the winter almost no one had
a job in Sturgeon Falls. Transients moved restlessly from city to
city, living in shack towns or squatter colonies like those in Toronto's Don Valley, where the men moved out of the ravines to pan-
handle in Rosedale or along the Danforth when the racoons
returned from their night-time marauding.

Sporadic strikes produced few gains. Unionized or not, workers
had little choice but to accept wage cuts or face unemployment.
Organizing the unemployed became the special mission of the
Workers' Unity League, an instrument of the Communist party,
under the direction of Tom McEwen. Street demonstrations by the
WUL led inevitably to confrontations with the police. Brigadier General Draper, chief of the Toronto city police and Major General
Williams of the Ontario Provincial Police were not alone in their
crusade to sweep the demonstrators from the streets. In August 1931
Attorney General Price, encouraged by the federal minister of justice, ordered the arrest of McEwen, Tim Buck, and seven other
communists. A compliant jury found them guilty under section 98
of the Criminal Code of being members of an unlawful association
and of engaging in a seditious conspiracy. All received jail terms.

The players on Bay Street did not escape the ravages of the
depression. Corporate profits slipped and the stock market continued its precipitous decline after the great crash of October 1929. By
May 1932 it had fallen to 16 per cent of its 1929 peak and the paper
value of fifty leading stocks had dropped from $6.2 billion to $880
million. There were fortunes to be made as Distillers Seagrams went
begging at $3.50 and Imperial Oil at under $5.00. There were some
with money to buy. Real wages of those who kept their job – civil
servants, university professors, railway workers – improved as the
cost of living fell 20 per cent between 1930 and 1932. The most fortunate were those with fixed-interest investments, the real value of
which leaped 20 per cent. Life for many was not difficult, and life
for the rich at the Hunt Club and the Royal Winter Fair, in Musko-
ka and Bermuda, went on much as before. Table talk about the

newest colt or the pregnant maid, the troublesome headmistress at Bishop Strachan or the manliness of a Ridley master, tended to ignore the social misery on the other side of town.[3]

While the urban unemployed were the most visible and vocal casualties, Ontario farmers were also bleeding. Even with record farm incomes in 1928 and 1929 – in part because of them – many farmers were overextended as the cost of new land, mechanization, and electrification was piled on old mortgages, and taxes rose faster than prices. Bountiful harvests in 1930 and 1931 were more than offset by falling prices. In Elgin wheat fell from $1.29 a bushel in 1929 to 50 cents in 1931; in 1932 Mitch got 48 cents for a bushel of beans that had brought $3.04 three years earlier. County agricultural agents monotonously reported prices below the cost of production, idle farms with food rotting in the ground, tractors left in barns as horses ploughed the fields, and many farmers unable to pay either their taxes or mortgage interest. By the end of 1931 the Henry government was forced to announce there would be no foreclosures on the $35 million farm mortgages held by the government.[4]

Mitch may have been in a quandary about how to solve the depression or relieve its acute distress, but he had no difficulty identifying those who suffered and those who did not. Those who did not certainly included the bankers, brokers, and bondholders who financed Henry's deficits at usurious interest rates; the oil companies who, behind Bennett's tariff, inflated the cost of crude to their Canadian subsidiaries, fixed prices, and exported their excessive profits to their American head offices; the tariff-protected manufacturers who cut wages to maintain profits; the middlemen who, as always, preserved an unconscionable price spread between producer and consumer; and the Tories, allies of all the exploiters, who showed little sympathy for the disinherited and used section 98 to sweep dissent from the street.

The Tories were an inviting target. During the 1930 campaign Bennett had attacked King for refusing to accept responsibility for the unemployed. Promising to end the dole, Bennett provided $20 million for provincial and municipal relief works and $4 million for direct relief, with the provinces and municipalities paying two-thirds of the cost. By the spring of 1932 the works program was an admitted failure as the costs far outweighed the benefits. Direct relief, however degrading, was financially ten times as efficient, and in 1932 grants to the provinces to pay for the dole became Bennett's answer to unemployment. In May 35,000 heads of families, their 110,000 dependants, and 5,000 single men and women in Ontario were dependent on direct relief. One year later they would number more than half a million.[5]

Mitch's criticism of reckless expenditures and irresponsible budgeting under Ferguson and Henry hit home when both local and provincial governments insisted they could not shoulder more of the financial burden of direct relief or public works projects. Ferguson had deliberately delegated more responsibilities to the local governments, and equally deliberately had denied them access to a broader tax base. Free of provincial control, municipal expenditures had soared beyond increases in the taxable assessment. Even before the Depression struck, many cities and towns had found the debt charges unbearable and were borrowing to meet current expenditures. As tax collections fell off leaving many municipalities on the verge of defaulting, in December 1931 Henry gave the Ontario Municipal Board power to declare a moratorium on debt repayment and in effect to act as trustees for insolvent municipalities. While the Border Cities were the first to go under, all the Toronto suburban governments, most of the northern resource towns, and even some of the older cities of central Ontario soon followed.[6]

As Mitch charged, the province also had borrowed heavily against the future. By 1930 Ontario's debt was the highest in the country as a percentage of revenue. Since Ferguson and Henry had charged public works and relief expenditures to the capital account, the debt soared. By 1931 the debt charges absorbed 21 per cent of total revenue and the bankers were insisting that the government control expenditure, make some provision for debt retirement, and increase taxes. Although the province had the lowest revenue as a percentage of income in the country, Henry was reluctant to do little more than levy modest increases on gasoline, liquor, and the minuscule corporation tax. Mitch promised that with the Liberals in office the rich would not get off so lightly.[7]

As the Depression deepened there was less humour and more anger in Mitch's attacks on the managers and defenders of the status quo. His friends noticed a new truculence when the session began in February 1932. Within a few days he had demanded the repeal of section 98 and asked whether the troops, stationed on Parliament Hill to defend it against a march of the unemployed, had orders to shoot. He attacked Bennett for giving the oil companies a tariff behind which they raked in excess profits of $20 million and pressed successfully to have the Banking and Commerce Committee, on which he sat, investigate the price of gasoline. Nor was he in any mood to put King's constitutional niceties above the interests of

Canadian farmers when Bennett proposed to provide emergency seed grain under the lapsed 1931 Unemployment and Relief Act before it was passed again. King was determined to oppose the measure, and was angered by the opposition in caucus. 'It is surprising how short-sighted some of the best men are, they want the "immediate" thing, they see the need for seed grain, for relief in their constituencies & wd. jettison all Liberalism has fought & stood for to meet an immediate situation. I was surprised a little at Brown and Vallance – disgusted with Elliott and felt Hepburn was not big enough for a leader when all favoured not opposing the Govt. making grants under a "dead statute".'[8]

When the bill came up for renewal, however, Mitch was one of the most effective opposition speakers. While King attacked form, he attacked substance: Bennett had used the act to give the banks a $29 million guarantee against losses on loans to the western wheat pool; to permit insurance companies to make a retroactive evaluation of their common stock assets; and to enable the cabinet to increase appropriations for the RCMP, buy riot bombs, and hire a secret service. In fact, Bennett had used the act 'to give the glad hand to the big interests and the mailed fist to the unemployed.' The back-benchers loved it; King admitted it was 'a fighting speech' but described it as 'claptrap.'[9]

Mitch had already upset the establishment with another attack on Sun Life. Unlike most of its competitors, Sun had invested aggressively in common stocks and by 1930, despite repeated warnings from the superintendent of insurance that such a heavy investment 'might at some time cause embarrassment to the company if not loss to the insuring public,' had half its assets in stocks. As the market continued its steep decline in 1931 the company became increasingly vulnerable and, following another sudden plunge in September, G.D. Finlayson, the superintendent of insurance, informed Bennett that Sun's assets had fallen at least $15 million below its liabilities. Sun rejected Finlayson's request not to issue its usual dividend, and instead successfully appealed to Bennett to use an order-in-council under the Unemployment and Relief Act to permit insurance companies to value their stock retroactively as of 1 June 1931. Citing the real value of Sun's assets, J.J. Harpell charged in his *Journal of Commerce* that Sun was close to insolvency but had added $3 million to the shareholders' account at the expense of the policy holders. He enlisted Mitch's support to bring it before the Commons.[10]

Bennett was convinced the attack on Sun would shake the precarious foundations of Canadian finance and undermine the financial stability of the country. Britain had gone off the gold standard in September; the Canadian dollar had fallen as hundreds of millions of Canadian obligations were due to mature in New York; many securities firms were teetering on the edge; and several banks were severely overextended in the West Indies and South America. In October 1931 Bennett had called in the press on several occasions to discuss the perilous financial situation and plead for moderation. When Harpell's article was published in December, Bennett wired Howard Ferguson to see Harpell, then in London, and urge him 'in the national interest' to stop the attack on Sun Life, 'which may result in a run upon all companies for cash surrender of policies, with consequent liquidation at forced sale of Canadian bonds and complete demoralization of financial structure of the Dominion.' Harpell replied bluntly that a return to a 'sound industrial system' demanded the denunciation of 'robbers' such as Wood, Gundy and T.B. Macaulay. When Bennett later warned him of the danger of a libel suit, Harpell said, 'I prefer to go to jail.'[11]

Michael Luchovitch, the UFA member for Vegreville, first raised the matter in the Commons, and Bennett solemnly asked the House to dispose of the resolution quickly and quietly so that no damage would be done to the company, 'the men, women and children in every part of the world' who had Sun policies, or to the credit of the country. But Mitch was unwilling to let the resolution die quietly. In a long and angry speech, frequently interrupted by Bennett and the Sun Life lobbyist, Charles Cahan, he denounced Macaulay for Sun's 'wild orgy of speculation' and attacked Bennett for saving the company from insolvency. Asked if he held a Sun Life policy, Mitch replied that he did, but 'I am cashing in my policy in Sun Life because I sincerely believe that the assets of the company are seriously impaired, and I do not like the management.'[12]

The response was immediate and inflamed, even among his Liberal colleagues. Percy Parker warned Mitch that 'there has been a lot of unfavourable criticism of your attack, but of course chiefly among financial people,' and from Windsor his friend Ellison Young of the *Border Cities Star* complained that the speech would 'further impair the general public confidence that unfortunately is none too strong at this time.' Even Elmore Philpott, now back at the *Globe*, termed his threat to cash in his policy a 'colossal blunder' which 'might have easily started a run on the Company equally as disastrous as a run on a bank,' a concern perhaps influenced by the fact that most of Philpott's savings were in a Sun policy. 'Your attack may appeal to the "back concessions" and to the irresponsible in the cities,' wrote one-time radical Patrick Donnelly, 'but these two classes are of little assistance at election time.'

Win him support on the back concessions it did, perhaps more for its daring than its substance. 'It's congratulations on your scrap about Sun Life,' wrote Malcolm Macdonald, the sage of Springfield, who boasted that his political education had begun with 'Sir John Aigh' and ended with 'Laurie Aigh.' 'Still and all, if you were my boy, I'd spank you for gipping yourself. No votes in it, I mean ... They're going to hang you for disturbing our sleeping Finance-thing. Wrecker they say. Better to let the burglars burgle than to alarm the neighbourhood.' Of course, Mitch was right, he concluded, but 'being right is how folks get hung.'[13] But Mitch would not back down. 'Some of our right-wing Liberals feel that I have gone quite a way in criticising the capitalistic system and the great financial people known as Sun Life,' he replied to Macdonald. 'However, I told them that if at any time they feel like kicking me out for not telling the truth that is their privilege.'

As the Liberals feared, the Tories hoped to hang Mitch over Sun Life and sent William Finlayson, the tough minister of lands and forests, to St Thomas with the rope. It was clear that Hepburn was too young and irresponsible to be trusted with the leadership of a party, he warned a politely bipartisan crowd, perhaps even with a seat in the Commons. 'These are serious times and you don't want a joker and a wise-cracker who is attacking financial institutions. You want a man of sobriety, of business experience and a man of steadiness.' Liberals prayed that Mitch would be steady and sober enough to ignore Finlayson's personal attack, and Senator Hardy begged him to follow King's commendable example of maintaining 'absolute silence under the bitterest of attacks.'[14]

Before an expectant crowd of over a thousand in St Thomas, Mitch struck back. Sun Life was a scandal, a scandal that exposed the unethical behaviour of big business and high finance, aided and abetted by Tory governments. And little could be expected of liberally inspired investigations, such as the one he had secured on the multinationals' control of gasoline prices, for the reformers were 'up against a subsidized press. If the situation became unpleasant for the protected interests, $200,000 or $300,000 was released and distributed among newspapers for advertising.' Right in St Thomas was it not fear of losing Sun advertising that led the *Times-Journal* to ignore his speech in the Commons? Commanding the reporters to report his statement accurately, Mitch stated that 'If elected I would apply a capital levy to take the ill-gotten gains from the multi-millionaires of this country.' The crowd loved it, and Gordon Reid, a prominent Tory who had driven from London to hear Mitch, reported to Bennett that 'This bird is a bad actor but is making ground.'

Albert Rogers, the left-wing Elgin Liberal, told King that 'Mitch was at his best in a bold and daring broadside, the discretion of which is not for me to say,' and 'evidently shares the opinion of a growing multitude, namely, that the hour has struck for action – that capitalism is on its death bed, and is lingering by virtue of "hypos" and "blood transfusions" such as "Hoover" has so drastically injected into an emaciated impotency.' In politics, matters even up in the long run, King replied, forgetting Rogers's radicalism. 'Mitch may be and is extreme in many things he says and this brings on his head much in the way of criticism and attack which he would otherwise escape. It is out of the pummelling of this kind that profounder judgements are evolved.' Over time Mitch would become more moderate and, meanwhile, in 'dealing with the forces that control at Queen's Park, he will perhaps gain more than he will lose by inclining, as he does, more to the left, than some, even of his close friends, may feel he should.'[15]

Mitch's inclination was to move even further left during the West York by-election in May 1932. The riding ran north from Lake Ontario on both sides of the Humber River, and with the exception of that part of Etobicoke north of Dundas Street, was almost completely urban. It was also very heavily working class. Only Lambton Mills, now the fashionable Kingsway and Swansea area, was the preserve of the well-to-do. The other communities were populated by railwaymen and the lunch-bucket workers in the dozens of small industries in Weston and along the lakeshore. Over half the voters in West York were blue collar, and one in ten a farmer.

West York had voted Conservative since the turn of the century, and since 1907 had been owned by Dr Forbes Godfrey. With Godfrey gone, Liberal strategists believed they could win West York. It was an angry community. Along the lakeshore a quarter of the families were on direct relief, unemployment ran as high as 40 per cent, and most workers had experienced wage cuts and layoffs. Relief administrators asked to be allowed to keep guns. Some of the local governments made no effort to collect taxes, most could not pay their share of relief costs, and all were on the verge of defaulting.

The Liberal convention gave William Gardhouse, a popular reeve and cattle-breeder from Thistletown, a narrow victory over W.A.

Edwards, a one-time mayor of Mimico who had strong labour support. And the Liberal chances of electing Gardhouse were immediately threatened by the decision of James Buckley, since 1929 the secretary of the Toronto and District Trades and Labour Council, to run as a Labour candidate. Buckley refused Harry Johnson's appeal to withdraw, and rejected Mitch's offer of a joint convention to nominate a Lib-Lab. Harry Price, the young Lambton businessman who ran for the Tories, faced a divided opposition.[16]

Mitch opened the campaign on Saturday night, 14 May, in Long Branch. Just two weeks earlier an epidemic of 'Bolshephobia' led police across Ontario to move in force against May Day demonstrators. The Saturday morning newspapers reported a crisis, with relief vouchers and charges against a meat-packers' combine in the Commons. That night, outside Sir Adam Beck School, communist handouts urged the working class to take up arms against the capitalists. Inside, Mitch, with Arthur Roebuck, his constant companion during the campaign, and Bill Gardhouse, faced the largest crowd ever seen in West York, and probably the most unruly. Roebuck could hardly be heard above the heckling and when Gardhouse spoke one-third of the crowd followed two pugilists outside.[17]

But when Mitch took the platform, the battlers and their entourages returned. He ran over the well-worn arguments about the tariff, over-production and under-consumption, inequitable taxes and corrupt extravagance. Mitch insisted that his position on the political spectrum was unequivocal, but 'there is one question which I fear will split even the Liberal party. There are men in Liberal ranks who are Tory at heart; there are men in Tory ranks who are reform at heart. I have met disapproval from Liberals when I said I wanted to see a definite decision in the matter of placing taxation on the shoulders where it belongs and not on the backs of the masses. I am not a Communist, but I go the whole way as a reformer.' When the cheers died down, Mitch fielded questions from the floor. Asked if he supported J.S. Woodsworth, Mitch replied that he supported him fully in the attack on section 98. Asked if he favoured an alliance of Liberal and Labour forces, he replied:

I favor and have advocated calling together the leaders of the Liberal and Progressive and Labor groups to pool our interests and see wherein we may follow a common road. Let me repeat that I swing well to the left where some Grits do not tread. If it is necessary to travel alone there, I will. One of the first things I will do if I form a government in this province will be to call together the best men of Labor, Progressives and

Liberals and seek their advice. I hope to see a realignment of political thought in this country.

The 'swing to the left' became the focus of the campaign. Everywhere Mitch's message was the same: 'The increasing concentration of wealth in the hands of the few is our biggest problem today, and no man in public life seems to have the courage to come out and say so. If someone dares to boldly put his finger on the evil he draws upon his head the wrath of the capitalist class.' At the Veterans' Hall in Earlscourt on the edge of the riding, he was praised as a radical and a socialist, and he promised to lead the fight against the money lenders who, 'like Alexander the Great have acquired so much that they have no more worlds to conquer – if you fellows support me.'

Mitch also injected a new note into the campaign. By the spring of 1932 talk of inflation was in the air. In April, King found it difficult to persuade the western members of his caucus not to support a Progressive amendment calling for government control of the financial system and an expansion of the money supply. Roebuck had urged Mitch to jump on the bandwagon, for 'it is on such popular measures that parties are swept into office and early reading of the public pulse is what constitutes political genius.' During a 24 May speech Mitch accused the government and the money-lenders of collusion to keep interest rates high. He suggested that 'inflation of currency might work here, though I do not advocate it at present, but something can be done to force down interest rates that increase the toll we pay to the money lenders who exploit us. The masses cannot struggle any longer under this burden of debt that has been laid on them.'[18]

After their unexpected loss in South Wellington, the Tories were determined to win West York. Rumours that they indirectly helped to finance the Buckley campaign were probably well founded. Premier Henry promised to take over the cost of relief from the insolvent municipalities and improve the food relief system. Half the cabinet entered the riding to warn that Hepburn's restraint program would mean cuts in relief payments, old age pensions, and mother's allowances. Above all, Tory strategy centred on Mitch personally and his swing to the left. Health Minister Robb demanded to know exactly where Mitch stood: 'Does Mitchell Hepburn mean he has communistic leanings when he talks of swinging to the left? Does he mean that he is condemning Canadian institutions that have stood the test of time? Does he mean that he does not believe in British institutions?'

The prize for invective went, as usual, to Leo Macaulay, who ministered to the needs of adjoining York South from his fashionable home on Humewood Drive. Hepburn was wild and reckless, his campaign 'mass production in political bribery on the grandest scale yet attempted in Canada by anybody. It is trafficking in the suffering of the afflicted, the poor and unemployed.' Macaulay mocked Mitch's promise to 'disgorge' the millionaires when among his closest friends and supporters were millionaires Hardy, Parker, and George Fulford. Mitch was 'their creature and he must be winking and nodding to them in the wings as the Liberal party goes on the Ontario stage: either that or there is an unscrupulous conspiracy ... that they will hoodwink the people, the credulous working man with his wife and family – in the demagogic appeal – and double-cross them if, and when, they get into power.'

George Henry ventured into West York on the last day of the campaign and could seldom be heard above the bedlam in New Toronto's Capitol Theatre. But finally he subdued the hecklers with a savage attack on Hepburn: his cowardly refusal to enter the legislature; his sell-out to American power interests whose propaganda he peddled; his promise to cut spending in times of social distress; and his dangerous swing to the left. The people of Ontario and Canada were measuring the calibre of West York voters. Would they tolerate a leader who swung well to the left? Would they desert their traditions and threaten their institutions?

Although Price defeated Gardhouse by 844 votes in a record turnout, the answer was ambiguous. The Liberals won easily in the rural areas, where Harry Nixon had campaigned. But Buckley ran second in most of the urban polls and won 23 per cent of the vote with a committee, he said, 'largely composed of the unemployed, on Relief, with not a postage stamp between them.' Seven out of ten working-class voters had cast their ballots against the Henry government. As *Saturday Night* commented and Mitch knew only too well, labour had become 'a political entity that must be reckoned with by all political leaders.'[19]

Exhausted by the campaign and even more by the winding down that went on into the early morning hours, Mitch returned home. The farm needed his attention, and there was much to think about. The alliance with Nixon seemed secure, but West York clearly revealed the danger of opposition on the left that might again deliver Ontario to the Tories. Some Liberals, such as Tom McQuesten, supported his proposed working arrangement with labour, and even Senator Hardy agreed that the Liberals had to have 'a program radical enough to catch the radical third party ... and take it into camp.' But he warned that even the moderate statements in West York had caused 'a good deal of talk about your "Swinging to the Left" and you talked a good deal about making the rich man pay.' That tactic might work in some ridings, 'but I don't think it will get you anywhere. The rich man is paying as much as he is going to pay and still remain rich and that means remain with the party that takes from him more than he thinks it should.' To drive the point home Hardy reminded Mitch that he had already experienced 'the difficulty of getting away money from people who have it and also getting the support of those people.' Generous as always, Hardy enclosed a cheque and begged Mitch not to burn the candle at both ends.[20]

But Mitch believed that the swing to the left had to be consummated by some alliance with labour. Speaking at Colin Campbell's nomination as the federal Liberal candidate in Frontenac-Addington, he expressed the hope that the November OLA convention in Ottawa would establish a committee to work out the details of an alliance. 'There will be no submergence of the identity of the Liberal Party,' he assured the rural Grits, 'but I believe labour should be given a definite allocation of seats to contest in the next election and I am of the opinion that a labour section in the opposition ranks would be of benefit.' Personally he was willing 'to forget factional differences and go into camp with the Progressives or the Labour people,' he told the Peterborough Liberals and, if they preferred, he would be prepared to step down for another leader.[21]

Mitch had already scheduled a meeting in Toronto to discuss an alliance with labour. Labour was represented by his friend Irwin Proctor, who believed the swing to the left 'started in West York will quickly sweep this country from coast to coast,' James Connors, secretary of the Toronto Labour party, and James Henderson. Mitch was accompanied by Roebuck, Nixon, Harry Johnson, and Colonel Hunter, the radical Toronto Liberal who had warned the London convention that the party must move to the left or die. The meeting was long, the rhetoric inspired. Discussion focused on the principles to be followed in allocating ridings and on the need for Mitch not only to define the swing to the left in policy terms but also to make it, in Hunter's words, 'definite, drastic and irrevocable.'

Proctor pressed Mitch to seize the initiative and earn his place in history. 'Napoleon alone carved up the whole of Europe,' he wrote him later. '*All history* demonstrates that in time of crisis, strong, even arbitrary, individual leadership is imperative.' The time had come for Mitch to act, for if not, 'some demagogue will assuredly arise and get the ear of an exasperated people ... An absolute and immediate break with the reactionary elements of your party, not only in fact, but avowed and apparent, is the only thing under Heaven that can now forestall a Fascist or Communist dictatorship in this Country.'[22]

Arthur Roebuck, the self-styled 'mummy at the feast', was far less enthusiastic. He questioned whether the riding associations would bow to the dictates of the leader and doubted the wisdom of formal manifestos that went beyond generalities. The Nixon alliance posed few problems because the Progressives were essentially agrarian Liberals, he argued, but labour was split among trade unionists and unorganized workers, moderate Lib-Labs and fire-breathing Marxists. 'No one will hold it against you for hitching organized labor to the hub of your chariot,' Roebuck cautioned, 'but they will not march with you if you let the labour leaders become your charioteer.'[23]

Mitch discovered that Roebuck was right when he canvassed the possibilities of allocating ridings or selecting joint candidates. He found it difficult, and sometimes impossible, to carry the local associations with him. Even in Windsor, where David Croll, the popular left-wing mayor, was willing to run as a Lib-Lab, there were rumblings among the Liberals. Yet Mitch remained convinced that some formal statement was essential to cement the association and, as Harry Johnson informed Norman Lambert, hoped that the Ottawa convention would pass a resolution to 'cover extent to which Hepburn may deal with Farmers and/or Labour.'[24]

Although the Progressive alliance was more manageable, it often took months of patient negotiations to persuade local Liberals or Progressives either to withdraw or to accept a joint nominating convention. Sometimes it was impossible. The advantages were demonstrated in the October federal by-election in South Huron necessitated by the death of Thomas McMillan, who had been elected as a Progressive in 1925 and as a Liberal the next year. The Progressives were particularly determined to reclaim the riding, because the provincial Liberals seemed certain to oppose William Medd, the Progressive MLA. Asking Mitch to enter the fray, King agreed to any course he wished to adopt for 'there is nothing which matters quite as much as winning that particular contest.' Hepburn and Nixon finally persuaded the Progressive candidate to withdraw with the promise that Medd would not be opposed in the next provincial election. To King, the subsequent capture of the seat by the Liberals was a personal triumph. To Mitch, it was a convincing demonstration of the need for a united opposition, and he hastened to thank Medd for his cooperation. But he also shared in the general Liberal enthusiasm and wrote his congenial drinking companion Larry McGuinness that the 'Grits have their heads up and their tails over the dashboards since the wonderful victory in South Huron.'[25]

Mitch had continued to hammer away at the hydro contracts in every public address, and by the fall of 1931 had Henry on the defensive. The cabinet had decided to hold a public inquiry after the South Wellington by-election but, following the totally unexpected defeat, Henry changed his mind. After Ferguson promised him there was nothing to hide, and the government-appointed accountants assured him the deals would bear public scrutiny, Henry reluctantly decided on a short inquiry. Mitch charged that the one-man commission under Mr Justice Middleton was an 'affront to the province.' The inquiry was restricted to the Dominion Transmission and the Madawaska deals and the sole counsel was W.N. Tilley, who had never pretended to be politically independent. After two days of hearings Middleton fell ill and the inquiry was adjourned, but not before Aird admitted that some of the Madawaska documents were missing and the press confirmed reports that they had been offered for sale.[26]

Before the Ontario inquiry resumed, Senator Haydon had told a Senate committee looking into Beauharnois that Sweezey had told him that Ferguson would not sign the Beauharnois contract 'until he gets $200,000.' Even the Tories agreed that after Haydon's statement Henry's inquiry was not 'worth a hoot' and when it resumed under Mr Justice Orde, the terms of reference had been extended to include Beauharnois. Sweezey testified again. He denied Haydon's story as well as the statement of George Kurdydyk and George Hyde of Winnipeg, passed on to Mitch by John Dafoe, that Sweezey had told them with some elation in November 1929 that he had got his contract but that '—— —— Ferguson had just stuck him for $325,000.' Sweezey stuck to his story that he 'assumed' Aird was the Tory collector 'properly constituted with authority' and while he did not think the payment was necessary to secure the contract, he believed it 'would keep friendly relations between ourselves and the powers that be in Ontario.' Sweezey knew that political parties did look for contributions and that 'sooner or later we would get a request in some form from Ontario, and this had the appearance of it.' Ferguson had raced back from Endland to testify at both inquiries. Under intense and disbelieving interrogation by Arthur Slaght, the brilliant counsel for the Liberals, he denied any knowledge of the $125,000 – or indeed of campaign funds at all – and even implied it might have gone to the Liberals since the Airds were regarded as a Liberal family.

In the end Slaght could produce no hard evidence to tie the $125,000 to the Tories. Indeed, an independent investigation proved that Aird had the bonds in his possession in May, and while his devious method of cashing the coupons and paying the milkman and the children's nurse with $50 bills was unusual, there was little about John Aird Jr that was not. Released in October, the report completely exonerated the government: the price paid for Dominion was reasonable; the 'propriety' of the $50,000 Madawaska payment was unquestioned; and the $125,000 had 'no relation' to the Beauharnois contract. But Henry's inept handling of the inquiry and the implausibility of so much of the testimony had more impact on a suspicious public than the earnest testimony of Hydro engineers or government-appointed accountants.[27]

Even before the final report appeared, the collapse of Abitibi sowed the seeds of another scandal that rocked the Henry government. The Abitibi deal was another of Ferguson's legacies, and the facts were as obscure as they seemed shady. In 1926, without consultation with Hydro, Ferguson had leased the Abitibi Canyon, the largest waterpower source in northern Ontario, to an Abitibi subsidiary. But the new Hydro chairman, Charles McGrath, advocated a policy of the rational development of northern power under Hydro and on the eve of the 1929 election persuaded a reluctant Ferguson to announce a policy of public development. Soon after the election, when INCO inquired about the possibility of securing 16,000 horsepower at Sudbury, Hydro engineers recommended harnessing the Mississagi River. However, there was persistent pressure from Alexander Smith, the president of Abitibi, to develop the canyon, and the Hydro commissioners finally turned the question over to the premier.[28]

A few months later Hydro engineers were forced to put their name to a report that they had neither written nor approved, and Hydro signed a contract with Abitibi for a 240,000 horsepower development on the canyon. Although there was little demand for power in the north, the government forced Hydro to buy back 100,000 horsepower from Abitibi. The agreement was so distasteful that the Hydro Commission demanded an order-in-council to protect it against any losses. Abitibi created the Ontario Power Service Corporation to carry out the contract, and as the company's prospectus made clear, the Hydro purchase was enough to cover the cost, including the interest of a $20 million bond issue, and leave the company with 100,000 horsepower as profit.

Strachan Johnson, one of Ferguson's close friends, negotiated the contract for the government. Ferguson's friend J. Homer Black became vice-president of Abitibi in charge of Ontario Power. Later he became head of Dominion Construction when it secured the construction contract. Coincidentally, Black's son-in-law was Hugh Aird of the Aird, McLeod brokerage firm and John Aird Jr's brother. As Ferguson admitted to Henry, it was a deal the 'ordinary man' would find difficult to understand.[29]

The government was reluctant to divulge the details of the contract, either to Mitch and the Liberals or to inquiring *Financial Post* reporters. But late in February 1932 the agreement began to unravel. Alexander Smith told Henry that the OPSC did not have enough money to finish the project and that Abitibi itself could not borrow without government backing. Henry agreed to support Abitibi, but it soon became apparent it was going under as well. Sick in bed for much of March and April, Henry set a trusted team of Tory lawyers, accountants, and brokers to work out a solution. The negotiations dragged into June, when Arthur Meighen, who had become a Hydro commissioner in 1931, with broker J.H. Gundy and E.G. Long, visited Queen's Park. The premier was in the north, and Meighen, meeting alone with William Price, appealed to him to reach an early decision in the interests of the widows and orphans who were suffering as the bonds dropped to fire-sale prices. Another visitor was A.J. Nesbitt of the Power Corporation, which owned Northern Ontario Power, whose offer to finish the project on undisclosed terms was not accepted. Late in June the cabinet approved an agreement with the bondholders and instructed Hydro to exchange $18 million in government guaranteed bonds for the $20 million in OPSC bonds.

Mitch and the Liberals denounced the agreement as outrageous, another even more convincing demonstration of the corrupt relationship between the Tories and the financiers. What else could explain offering $90 for bonds that had been selling as low as $30 in June? Although the government replied that the real value of the bonds was much higher, the *Financial Post* concluded that the agreement was excessively generous and 'based on considerations for bondholders and not on value ... and every new fact brought to light indicates that the rights of taxpayers have been grossly overlooked.' Mitch joined the *Post* in demanding an investigation. It was not long before the Liberals were hinting at corruption, not collusion.[30]

The Hydro revelations had done nothing to convince Mitch that his attack on the corrupt relationship between government and big business was unwarranted. When he returned to Ottawa for the fall session in October, Sun Life was again on his agenda, with the evidence more damning than before. In 1929 and 1930 Sun Life had become deeply involved in the financial affairs of the Insull financial and utility empire in the United States and Ivar Kreuger's Swedish match conglomerate. By the fall of 1932 the Insull empire was in receivership. Martin Insull had fled to Canada and his brother Samuel to Greece, and both were fighting extradition as the drama in a Chicago courtroom disclosed the involvement of T.B. Macaulay and other Sun executives with the Insulls. Kreuger had also gone bankrupt, and in March 1932 committed suicide in Paris. J.J. Harpell had continued his attack on 'The World's Greatest Crook' and attempted to have Macaulay arrested for defrauding Sun policy-holders. Macaulay countered by charging Harpell with libel.[31]

When Mitch reached Ottawa, Harpell gave him a copy of the indictment he intended to use in court which, supported by a stinging rebuke of Sun from the superintendent of insurance, Mitch planned to use in the Commons. Aware of the seriousness of the charges, however, Mitch first consulted King, Hardy and other leading Liberals. All agreed that the crash of Sun could be imminent. King said he 'tried to keep Hepburn from going too far, in precipitating a crisis thro' exposure in prlt. – until Govt. has had a chance to deal with Sun Life matters.'[32]

The opportunity to implicate Bennett soon overcame King's concern for the financial stability of the country:

Hepburn tells me Bennett sold his common stock in the Eddy Match Co. to the Swedish Match Trust for $3,000,000 when he became leader of his party. That Macaulay of Sun Life too[k] Swedish Match Trust stock in that amt. to give the Trust money to pay Bennett for his stock. This has all been lost by Kreuger collapse. Bennett & Macaulay had preference stock between them. Bennett is said to have sold a lot of his poor stock to Macaulay, unloaded on him. – It is now gone. The Sun Co. shareholders' money is in Bennett's possession. Bennett and Macaulay are mixed up in the Insul [*sic*] Co. transactions, the Sun having acquired much of that stock – What collapse in important Co's may come once all this is public, I hesitate to predict. – It should be the end of R.B. & a very fitting end, if it be true.

Senator Hardy was convinced that a renewed attack on Sun Life would mean defeat in the next provincial election, for a run on the company would 'mean bankruptcy for thousands of people including possibly one or two of our banks' and urged Mitch to proceed with 'the utmost caution.' Percy Parker phoned from Toronto to beg him to let others take the initiative. Arthur Roebuck wrote that 'if Sun Life is ruined as these figures indicate, it will fall over or be absorbed, but if you push it over the anger of those who lose will be divided between yourself and those who actually wrecked it.' The losers could be not just the 'high financiers,' he warned, but thousands of ordinary people. Moreover, 'I am satisfied that there are dangers lurking all through this resolution, dangers which a courageous man should not, perhaps, fear to face, but which it may be are quite unnecessary to face. Libel actions are extremely costly. Personally I would feel greatly relieved if you handed over this job to someone else who is perhaps not carrying as you are conflicting responsibilities and whose personal fortunes in a dog fight of this kind are less important.'[33]

Although King was prepared to let Hepburn bring a resolution before the House, the criticism in caucus infuriated Mitch. 'Hepburn was much annoyed at the way Malcolm spoke,' King noted, 're Liberals in Toronto seeking to prevent him from speaking out and said he would resign the leadership – his real problem is the financial one – no help from the political bosses, Parker et al.' Mitch's attempt to raise the matter as a question of urgent public importance was ruled out of order by the Speaker, and Mitch was outraged when a number of Liberals, Fraser and Moore among them, voted to sustain the chair. But as King confessed, the arbitrary ruling, on which he did not vote, 'really helped us all to meet Hepburn's situation and our own attitude. Only the very serious condition of Canada's financial institutions would justify the failure to clear up the Sun Life situation regardless of all else.'

Deserted but undaunted, Mitch then secured the Speaker's assurance that he could bring the matter before the House as a notice of motion, but two days later when it was still not on the order paper he belligerently asked, 'Is some official of this house exceeding his authority or is there some powerful influence at work to conceal from the people of Canada the true situation in connection with Sun Life?' The question was too important to be left to the Speaker, and Bennett was immediately on his feet to denounce Hepburn as Harpell's accomplice and state that since Harpell was being sued for libel in a Montreal court, Sun Life could not be discussed in Parliament.

Balked at every turn, Mitch angrily said he was 'through,' a decision happily relayed to A.B. Wood, the vice-president of Sun, by Jim Malcolm. But Mitch was incensed by the pressure from his own party. 'Needless to say I was very much surprised to get your letter,' he wrote to Arthur Roebuck:

In my humble opinion the financial racketeers of this country have so disregarded the laws covering bribery and the manipulation of watered stocks and promotion schemes that there is an acṭual danger of our whole monitory [*sic*] system being destroyed.

In this particular case there is no doubt that the life savings of people have been dissipated by trustees who benefitted personally in the transaction. The Liberal Party is either for or against that kind of business and cannot occupy a neutral position, and for my part I do not wish to be a puppet of St. James Street.

If the 'hush, hush' advice I have been getting represents the majority opinion of the Liberal Party then I feel completely out of tune, and I believe that the matter should be discussed frankly at the coming annual meeting in Ottawa. When I made the statement in West York that I was swinging to the left I meant every word of it, and am more determined than ever to fight class legislation and special privileges.

In Montreal, Chief Justice Greenshields refused to let Mitch testify on Harpell's behalf and a well-instructed jury took only an hour-and-a-half to find Harpell guilty of libel. Despite the recommendation for clemency, Greenshields sentenced Harpell to three months in jail.[34]

For the year following his recovery in the fall of 1931, Mitch maintained a feverish pace that would have taxed a man in good health. With the House in session he spent his weekends in eastern and central ridings wooing the Franco-Ontarians back into the fold, encouraging local organizations, resolving personal squabbles, and seeking potential candidates. There had been time for a trip to Sudbury with Ian Mackenzie, his good friend and fellow MP from Vancouver, and regular visits to Toronto to help oversee the assault on Queen's Park. Even in St Thomas, where he spent part of the summer, there were countless visitors, political meetings in southern and western ridings, and endless correspondence. Yet, despite all his accomplishments, he still faced the implacable hostility of Sinclair and his friends, continual sniping from the *Globe* and the *Star*, and underground threats to his leadership.

In the spring of 1932 Mitch promised Bill Fraser, the MP for Northumberland, that he would hold a joint meeting of the federal and provincial members to discuss party organization and attempt a Hepburn-Sinclair reconciliation. But Mitch changed his mind, and earned a stinging four-page rebuke from Fraser, who warned that 'noisy demonstrations of a certain class of people' would never bring the Liberals to power. Mitch's role was to unite the Liberal party, to realize that 'suspicion breeds suspicion,' and that a politician's 'greatest assets are diplomacy and tolerance, and the ability to stoop to conquer. These abstracts, commodities or virtues, you refuse to recognize.' The rank and file were concerned not with the Hepburn-Sinclair feud, he maintained, but with victory, and unless Mitch was prepared to find some accommodation with Sinclair and his followers in the caucus 'for your own good, you should resign as Leader of the Ontario Party.'[35]

Mitch may have respected the bluntness, but certainly not the content. As far as he was concerned, it was Sinclair who refused to put the party ahead of his own personal antagonisms. Although he disliked and distrusted Sinclair, he had repeatedly held out the olive branch, only to have it sullenly rejected. Sinclair, he believed, was perverse if not malicious, small-minded and stubborn, convinced that the party would some day realize its mistake and cast aside a man he detested. Billy Sinclair imagined himself to be a man of principle. But loyalty to the elected leader was not one of them. As far as Mitch was concerned, why should he 'stoop to conquer'? Why should he resign because Sinclair and his small group of ardently dry followers refused to accept the will of the convention and endorse its leader and its platform?

Mitch also wondered whether Fraser could be trusted. Bill Fraser was a decade older than Mitch, a wealthy Trenton fruit-grower and businessman with real estate investments in Toronto and memberships in the Granite Club and the Royal Canadian Yacht Club. Mitch had campaigned for him in 1930, and Fraser had supported him for the leadership. But there were those who knew that he had been working behind the scenes against him at London. Moreover, late in 1931 Fraser had been closely associated with Moore and Sinclair in the organization of the Central Ontario Liberal Association, and despite Fraser's reassurances that the new body would strengthen both the federal and provincial parties, no attempt had been made to bring it under the Ontario Liberal Association umbrella. Fraser had made it clear that he had no use for the OLA office, for

Harry Johnson and 'your other henchmen in Toronto' who 'purely and simply for their own selfish ends, feel they should run the
Liberal Party in Ontario and are endeavouring to do this through
the Liberal leader.' And it was this 'self appointed and selected advisory group,' he believed, who were responsible for Mitch's refusal
to stoop to conquer. At best, Billy Fraser was a question mark.[36]

Fraser was not alone in his hostility towards Johnson and the OLA
office. Some of the old guard complained that control of the party
seemed to be in the hands of their former Progressive enemies like
Nixon and Roebuck, while others resented the new prominence of
Frank O'Connor, Senator McGuire, and Percy Parker. Joe Atkinson refused to associate with Hepburn or the office, and even
refused to serve on King's new National Liberal Federation because
of its link with the OLA. And Hardy had been astute enough not to
recommend any active members of the OLA executive or Management Committee to King, to 'eliminate any possibility of a charge
that we are looking after ourselves.' The Management Committee
had added a number of prominent Toronto financiers and businessmen – Albert Matthews, J.F. McKay and P.J. Mulqueen – in
January 1932, but the criticism that the office was in the hands of
a small clique persisted. Even Hardy warned Mitch on one occasion to consult some friends, '*but not those from Toronto.*' So disliked was Johnson that many of the MLAs refused to answer his
letters, and the Central Ontario Association executive pointedly
refused to invite him to the inaugural banquet. Johnson took the
slight philosophically, and joked to Mitch that 'If anything happens
to you, this Office and I part company, *quick.*'[37]

By the fall of 1932 there were rumours that Mitch's leadership
would be challenged at the November OLA convention. Ambrose
O'Connor of Oshawa warned Mitch of a conspiracy, with Fraser
supplying the money and Moore the brains, to support Moore for
the leadership. The arguments used, he wrote, were that 'you are not
proper leader, you are federal MP, elected by Beauharnois crowd.'
They plan to go to Ottawa 'solidly against you and further I know
that they have a bunch of really good fellows convinced that while
you are an awfully nice chap you are not managing as you should.'

But it was Sinclair who most visibly symbolized the threat to
Mitch, and there were many Liberals who agreed with Patrick Donnelly that the party should 'face the inevitable' and force Sinclair
to resign as House leader. As always, Mitch was reluctant to make
any move that might irreparably split the party, but Tom
McQuesten argued that the issue had to be faced. While the OLA

convention could not deal with the leadership, he suggested that a strong vote of confidence 'might strengthen you in dealing with the Members. I feel that your position is even now strong enough to lay down the law to the members and read out of the party those who will not obey ... I believe you have one-half the members and it would be better to lose the rest than to trifle with the situation.' Whatever the outcome, the issue had to be faced for the 'average voter, particularly the one who has not strong party affiliations simply will not believe that Sinclair as House Leader does not represent and speak for the Liberal Party in Ontario.'[38]

For a while in the fall of 1932 it looked as if the Ottawa convention would have to deal with the leadership, for Mitch spoke often and openly of resigning. The blistering pace he had maintained for a year had taken its toll. He had never fully recovered from his operation and its aftermath, and during the summer his health got worse. He was exhausted, perspiring heavily and unable to sleep at night, and unwilling to relax during the day. He lost seven pounds and by October his weight had fallen to 165 pounds. As usual when he was worn out, he got bronchitis, and was afraid that he had tuberculosis. And all the party did, it seemed, was to carp and criticize, while making more and more demands on his time and energy.[39]

To make matters worse, the promised financial support had not materialized. Of the five who promised to contribute, two had reneged by the fall of 1931, Hardy told Pat Donnelly, and 'two of us have paid in a couple of thousand dollars each. I can't go any further and it would not be fair to ask young Mr. Fulford to do so either.' By the summer of 1931 the office rent and Johnson's salary were overdue, and Parker complained that 'Most people are so hard up that we have been at our wits end and have had to go into our own pockets.' The rent had apparently been guaranteed by Senator Spence, but some bad business deals had pushed him close to bankruptcy and he was 'worrying everybody sick' by the end of the year. 'He's determined someone shall take it off his hands,' Hardy told King, 'so I gave him a good sharp letter to-day asking him why anybody should especially Percy Parker whom he's been urging to do so. I told him he had received a Senatorship and that he'd better pay for it like the rest of us. The old rascal has never put up a dollar for anything.'[40]

In the Beauharnois fallout, an apologetic Percy Parker had suggested at the 1931 convention that each riding contribute $100 a year to the provincial office and that a dime a year from three hundred thousand Liberals would handily cover the costs. Later, the

Management Committee accepted Arthur Roebuck's proposal that two thousand Liberals contribute five dollars each to a maintenance fund. Although this 'begging scheme' was mocked by more cynical Liberals, Roebuck had raised $7,000 by November 1932 and the OLA debt had been cut in half. But it was far from enough. Rents and salaries were behind, Mitch had no staff except Eleanor Parker, his House of Commons secretary, and was covering most of his own expenses. In October he simply threw up his hands, and said the OLA executive would have to decide 'whether they consider it advisable to try and carry the load much further' or close the Toronto office. At the same time Mitch wrote angrily to William Mulock that 'I am not prepared to lose any more of my time and sessional indemnity running around the province like a greyhound ... As you are fully aware, the party has not lived up to any of its obligations. So far as I am concerned, I have done everything humanly possible to carry out my responsibilities. There is a limit to everything, and I have just about reached mine.'

Soon after he reached Ottawa in October, Mitch told King he was sufficiently fed up to consider resigning as leader. 'Between 6 & 7 I had a good talk with Mitch Hepburn and cleared up his mind on many things,' King wrote. 'He sees he has made a mistake in taking the Ontario leadership, he would like to get out, I advised him to stay. I would give him no assurance of a cabinet post – nor did he ask it though he mentioned the subject & told him events wd. decide whether or not it was best for him to remain in the federal or provincial fields – we wd. see which election came on first.'[41]

However, there was no suggestion of frustration in Mitch's speech to the Twentieth Century Club banquet on 12 November. Mitch spoke with a gusto that belied his fatigue, and he brought the crowd to its feet time and time again as he leavened his anger with humour and sarcasm. Mitch did not back away from his swing to the left, but the tone was muted, the language restrained. He had been called a socialist and a communist because he dared to discuss conditions as they were. But his solutions were not revolutionary, for the evils of special privilege and industrial oppression could be removed by democratic means if there were 'a fusion of all the forces that oppose Toryism.' As far as he was concerned, he declared, a little more cautiously than before, 'We are willing to extend a reasonable measure of support to other groups. We wish to remain close to our good friend, Harry Nixon ... We extend the hand of fellowship to Labour. (Cheers) We are not far apart in matters political.' The Liberal party was a 'virile fighting force ready for the fray. I want to say to Premier Henry, let him take his appeal to the people. We will be ready. We are ready now.' The standing ovation should have removed any doubts about his future.[42]

Not even the Tory press could report an imminent revolt as the six hundred delegates gathered in Ottawa a week later. There was no discussion of an alliance with labour, but the unanimous approval of Paul Martin's resolution that 'the curtailment of socialistic and communistic thought by methods of direct coercion is ill-advised, and with a view of arriving at political and social truth, a free and unrestricted discussion of these and other questions is desirable' placed the party well to the left of the Tories. Mackenzie King praised Mitch and lectured the dissident. The time was approaching when Mitch would be assessing cabinet potential and aspiring candidates would have to 'reveal their talents to the people.' It was already time, King added, for 'older men, who are somewhat critical because Mr. Hepburn is more radical than they,' to still their criticism and get into the fight.

Mitch rose to thunderous applause and boisterous singing, and his speech was constantly punctuated with applause and laughter. King thought Mitch was 'light & discursive – a little too much "my friends" – & jumped about – but the sort of thing the crowd likes.' The crowd certainly liked it, and was on its feet when Mitch promised that in the election expected in 1933 'we shall neither give nor take quarter.' The new slate of officers confirmed Mitch's position. Tom McQuesten, the progressive Hamilton bachelor lawyer, was a loyal if distant colleague. Bay Street and the old guard may have been appeased when Albert Matthews accepted the vice-presidency. Percy Parker chaired the influential Management Committee and Frank O'Connor, who was becoming one of Mitch's close friends, became treasurer. Arthur Slaght joined the executive officially as the head of the Toronto and Yorks regional association. The victory seemed complete.[43]

After the convention Mitch went on a twice-postponed northern jaunt from North Bay to Kenora with Peter Heenan. The trip was an unqualified success, and Mitch returned triumphantly to Toronto for a giant Liberal rally in Massey Hall on 15 December, the largest it was said since the days of Laurier. At the white tie banquet, Mackenzie King pictured Mitch as a 'political knight errant' and the next premier of Ontario. In an unusually serious speech, Mitch promised cuts in expenditure, a review of taxation, a study of overlapping federal and provincial services, and the honest and efficient development of northern resources. Like King, he discussed the growing threat from the newly formed left-wing political party, the Co-operative Commonwealth Federation, and stressed not his radicalism but his moderation. Swinging to the left did not mean that he was out 'to destroy capitalism,' he assured the well-dressed audience. 'If I thought for a moment the founding of a new order were necessary, I would not hesitate to join it for my first consideration is the welfare of the people. I believe in the capitalist system but I condemn in no uncertain terms the abuse of the capitalist system under the Tory administrations. I have long since learned that there is no Santa Claus, no pot of gold at the foot of the rainbow. I do not believe in sending people up a blind alley when we have the machinery for a sane democracy.'[44]

Mitch went home for a much-deserved rest amid praise from all sides. Both McQuesten and Hardy saw a great improvement in the recent speeches, and Hardy added that he was 'very glad to see certain people at the Toronto meeting and hope you can begin to chip away at the edges of that place before too long.' Harry Johnson was euphoric. The speeches 'have revealed you to the City man as a person of brains and common sense ideas on how to better conditions in the province. Old friends like J.F. McKay and Albert Matthews are delighted at the address you delivered and the effect they have had on business men generally.' From 'where I sit, I see you a natural born poker player, with four aces and a king from the dealer.' 'An expert with a hand like that needs no advice from anyone,' he added. 'All you need is a Doctor to tell you to keep your feet warm and your head cool.' Senator Hardy agreed, and warned Mitch to cut down on the after-dinner meetings: 'You have your feet in the saddle now and we can't afford even a slight or temporary breakdown.'

But to the *Farmers' Sun* it seemed that Mitch had abandoned his swing to the left and the attempt to rally farmers and labour under a progressive banner. His policy would be dictated by the interests of the federal Liberals and the *Globe*, 'that senile old lady whose mind is so failed that she has forgotten her noble past.' And at the Toronto Club, Leo Macaulay asked sardonically where was the man who would disgorge the millionaires of their 'ill-gotten gains? The muffler on the exhaust has now become a silencer.'[45]

'The Tories on the run'

'Just a few lines to wish you a Merry Christmas and a very Happy New Year with perhaps a Premiership dropped in as a plum somewhere near the end of it,' wrote Senator Hardy enclosing his usual cheque. Mitch also expected an election in 1933, and enthusiastic crowds at his rallies across the province suggested that Hardy might be right. The Depression showed no signs of lifting, and for most of Ontario the early months of 1933 were the worst on record. Unemployment reached a peak between January and March when more than half a million were on direct relief. The well-to-do slept more easily with thousands of single men, the potential shock troops of an urban revolution, removed from the subversive influence of the Workers' Unity League. The 'Royal Twenty-Centers' worked for twenty cents a day in General McNaughton's National Defence Camps clearing land for airstrips along the line of the proposed Trans-Canada Highway and improving the facilities at Petawawa and other military bases. Others worked on northern highways, guests of the Henry government in the dozens of board camps that stretched from the Manitoba border to the Ottawa River. For most farmers it was an austere Christmas, as prices and incomes hit rock bottom in December.[1]

George Henry would be an easy target for any opposition leader. But there were persistent rumours of a coup, and many among the Tory faithful prayed ardently for the second coming of Howard Ferguson. Moreover, it was not only the brewers and hotel-keepers who thirsted for a glass of beer, and Mitch knew that he would not be premier if the Liberals were again tagged with a temperance label. The thought of booze was a painful reminder that at Queen's Park the wilful and caustic Bill Sinclair still had the capacity and, in Mitch's judgment, the determination to do harm. The plum would not drop easily from the Tory tree.

The Depression was a powerful ally, but it might be fickle in its allegiance. By the end of 1932 Mitch was concerned that the CCF would reap its bitter harvest. During the fall and winter CCF organizers had secured the support of many labour and socialist organizations, and the CCF clubs hoped to attract others who leaned to the left. More disturbing were the large crowds of farmers who turned out to hear William Irvine and Agnes Macphail, eloquent members of the United Farmers, when they stumped the province appealing for support for the CCF. The UFO convention in November had not only voted overwhelmingly for conditional affiliation with the new party, but had also approved a radical manifesto endorsing a national economic planning council, inflationary monetary policies, and measures to prevent the 'exploitation of the new masses by the privileged few.'[2]

Although Mitch found time to unwind over the holidays, he spent many hours in sober and animated discussion about the CCF. His friend Huntley Sinclair, a Canadian economist at Washington University in St Louis, was visiting for the holidays, and Mitch invited Irwin Proctor, his radical Liberal friend from Toronto, to spend a few days at the farm. Proctor insisted that the CCF would sweep the Liberals aside unless Mitch broke sharply with the old guard, including Mackenzie King, and adopted a radical social and economic policy. Sinclair agreed that Mitch should 'lead the charge full tilt against the forces of reaction and inaction,' but warned his impetuous friend that 'if you take the jump you have been contemplating and land boldly on the platform of the C.C.F., or something approximate to it, there will be no turning back.' The three men agreed that there must be sharply increased income and inheritance taxes to hit the rich and break up the large accumulations of wealth, but once again Sinclair advised a realistic policy of social reform that would carry the party with him. Mitch had already moved well to the left of most Liberals, he warned, and while the platform should be 'in advance of the electorate ... let us not delude ourselves too much into thinking that we can make political capital out of ultra-radical ideas at the present time.'[3]

Much to Proctor's dismay, Sinclair also cautioned Mitch against any radical inflationary policies. In one guise or another, inflation had become the panacea of most reformers. Mitch was no exception. He had skirted around inflation during the West York by-election, but his frequent demands for measures to increase purchasing power drastically were so implicitly inflationary that his friends warned him to be careful. He had hoped to tap the wisdom of some

Queen's economists the previous June, but found that, like all good academics, they had vacated the campus for the summer. Without the benefit of their advice he had supported George Coote, the UFA member for McLeod, who introduced a motion in the Commons in November calling for inflationary policies. While many Liberals vanished behind the curtains, Mitch and his friends Tom Cayley and Billy Taylor from the neighbouring farm ridings had voted with Coote. There was no longer any doubt that Mitch Hepburn was a dangerous inflationist, trumpeted the Toronto *Evening Telegram* the next day.[4]

Proctor urged Mitch to go much further and advocate a massive inflation of the currency not only to increase purchasing power but as the first step towards reconstructing the social order. Sinclair countered with some basic textbook economics. While a moderate national inflationary policy could stimulate the economy and undo some of the grave injustices caused by the fall in prices, Proctor's massive and uncontrolled inflation would simply substitute one injustice for another. Did Mitch really want to reward those who had foreclosed on mortgages or bought property and stock at fire sale prices? Much better to increase government spending, argued Sinclair, bravely lecturing Mitch on the virtues of unbalanced budgets and deficit financing.

Mitch clearly preferred the simplicity of a bold inflationary policy to Sinclair's enlightened pre-Keynesian heresies. 'I thoroughly agree with you that it is not a panacea for all our troubles,' he told Sinclair apologetically, 'but at least it is the best expedient that I know of at the moment. We have reached the point in Canada where we must have some measure of inflation or repudiation, on a wholesale scale.' In his first speech of the new year he advocated major currency inflation and lower taxes, and praised the Australians who had cut government expenditures by 20 per cent, sharply reduced the interest rate on bank deposits and the internally owned national debt, and devalued and expanded the currency. Inflation would be the critical issue when Parliament met, he said, and 'I look to see a complete realignment in the Dominion Parliament when this issue comes up. Those who stand for the money lords and the exploiting classes will be in one camp, and those who stand for the common people will be in the other camp.'[5]

Bennett was clearly in the camp of the money lords. In a hard-hitting speech to the Toronto Board of Trade a few days later, he declared that with Canada paying 'a million dollars a day every day except Sunday' to the United States, inflation, devaluation and other nostrums were 'absurd.' What inflation means, 'nine people out of ten cannot tell you, except that you will have two dollars where now you have one.' Mitch made no attempt to explain the mysteries of inflation to the expectant overflow crowd at the Newmarket Town Hall the following week. But he did assure them that the depression was man made and not 'a visitation from the Almighty ... The Lord has been good to us, but in the midst of plenty we have privation.' Inflation was clearly one man-made answer to exploitation and under-consumption, and yet 'Mr. Bennett is against inflation and he is against departing from the gold standard. As far as I know there are only three countries on the gold standard: France, the United States – and Mr. Bennett.'6

When Mitch arrived in Ottawa for the opening of the session on 30 January 1933 he found that Mackenzie King had also become a student of monetary policy. King had been able to find a Queen's economist, C.A. Curtis, who explained that a central bank could provide social control of credit and, given the mounting political pressure, was essential to 'avoid the disasters of uncontrolled inflation and the perils of nominal control which is solely political in character.' Although King raised the question of a central bank at the first caucus, his desire to escape a divisive discussion of policy was thwarted by Woodsworth's motion in the Commons calling for the creation of a 'co-operative commonwealth.' Before King could speak to the motion the Liberals had to define their position on economic and monetary policy.

Mitch hoped that a new statement of Liberal policy would be sufficiently radical to counter the growing appeal of the CCF, and he probably urged that course on King when the two met after the evening session on 3 February. But King was so offended by the smell of liquor on Mitch that he neglected to report the substance of their discussion in his diary. The policy debate continued in caucus where, according to King, there was a 'first class discussion on currency, credit and banking, during which from all sides men were much more moderate than they have previously been.' But a usually well-informed reporter for the *Mail and Empire* wrote that the arguments in caucus were long and heated, with Mitch's friend and soul-mate, Ian Mackenzie, leading the radical attack and 'carrying out with enthusiasm the policy laid down by Mitchell Hepburn.'

As usual King had his way in the end. Caucus approved the creation of a central bank to manipulate the money supply on the basis of 'public need' and the 'domestic social and industrial requirements of the people.' Filling out his interminable speech on Woodsworth's motion, King promised a Liberal government would establish a national relief commission, reduce price spreads, cut expenditures, balance the budget and, of course, lower the tariff. As Frank Underhill commented, the speech might have been lifted from King's undergraduate lecture notes, for 'in this fourth year of widespread popular suffering the Liberal policy amounts to only a few plaintive vegetarian bleatings in the midst of a carnivorous jungle.' As far as undercutting the CCF was concerned Mitch was on his own.[7]

An ally with impeccable credentials but uncertain motives appeared in February when Elmore Philpott dramatically resigned from the *Globe* to begin his self-appointed mission of securing 'full and friendly team-play between the Liberal Party and the C.C.F.' While Philpott had promised Mitch to throw his 'whole weight behind Mr. King and yourself,' there were many Liberals who believed that he was an unprincipled and egotistical opportunist with designs on the leadership. All agreed that he was a powerful, but unpredictable and possibly dangerous, presence. McQuesten urged Mitch and Norman Lambert to 'hold on to him' but if possible get him out of Ontario. As Philpott's evangelical crusade gathered momentum, Mitch even considered some public recognition of his role as a Liberal spokesman to keep him in the Liberal camp.[8]

Even before Philpott began his passionate attack on the establishment, Mitch's strident advocacy of inflation and the sins of the money barons had alarmed his friends. Senator Hardy warned him that the mere mention of inflation would turn three-quarters of urban Liberals against him, with no appreciable gains in rural Ontario. A Windsor supporter begged him to secure the public support of bankers and businessmen to prove that 'while some of your views may be radical ... that such men have confidence in your leadership.' Harry Johnson tried to explain to an unhappy Colonel Jaffray that Mitch had to sound radical to keep his left wing, but Floyd Chalmers assured his boss at the *Financial Post* that although many Liberals were moving to the right, Hepburn, Philpott, and the *Star* were 'trying to swing the party towards socialism to undermine the C.C.F. movement.'[9]

Mitch was not a socialist. Yet he could not fight the CCF because he shared many of their criticisms of the social and economic system. Since the growing strength of the CCF threatened the Liberal revival, the obvious solution was to remain radical enough to hold left-wing Liberals and try to enter into some working agreement with the new party, as he had with the Progressives. From St Louis, Huntley Sinclair urged Proctor to bring his CCF friends, including

Woodsworth, to meet with Mitch. He also assured Harry Cassidy, a member of the League for Social Reconstruction, that Mitch would meet the CCF 'a little more than half-way both in coopera- tion for election purposes and in incorporating planks in their plat- form in the policy of the party. Mitch Hepburn is convinced that the defeat of the forces of reaction is much more important than party ends or party loyalties and where the leader goes there the other Liberals go also.' Cassidy replied that he was certain the CCF would be willing to avoid splitting the anti-Tory vote, 'if they get a certain amount of cooperation from the Liberals,' and Mitch could 'rely on the assistance of the L.S.R. group – that we will do what we can to assist Hepburn rather than Henry.'[10]

Mitch would have put it a little differently, but at that moment he was in fact discussing the possibilities of just such an arrange- ment with Graham Spry. The young Spry was a restless romantic, eager to make his way in Ottawa and have influence, if not power. Failing to become the director of the National Liberal Federation, he cast his eyes towards the ailing *Farmers' Sun*. His immodest ambition, he told a friend, was to work with the farmers' movement and 'to ride with it ... to drive farm opinion towards one or the other result, a Liberal party that is liberal, or a third party.' With some borrowed money Spry bought the *Farmers' Sun*. By March 1933, he lamented that while his prophecy of a third party and a farm movement in Ontario that is 'socialistic' had come true, the 'old idea of a left-wing Liberal party, so freely promised in private conversation by Liberal leaders, has not been created: on the con- trary, the Liberal party is either rightward or centrist or backward. The speeches of Mr. Massey and Mr. King having totally dismissed economic planning, inevitably dismiss me.' Already involved with the League for Social Reconstruction, Spry became an open sup- porter of the CCF.[11]

However, although the Quebec-based federal Liberals were reac- tionary, Spry believed there was a possibility of some alliance with Mitch in Ontario. Mitch and Spry had met for the first time late in 1931 at a birthday party for Odette Lapointe given by Lucette Valin, the beautiful young daughter of a prominent Ottawa doctor. When a slightly exuberant Ottawa socialite, Andy Drummond-Hay, began an argument about free trade, Mitch, though engaged in the arduous task of holding a drink and balancing Lucette on his knee, 'led Andy into contradictory positions and slew him agreeably.' Spry was impressed with both Mitch's taste in women and his economics: 'H. is better on a chair than on a platform, so far as appearances go, but I liked his incisiveness and the sincerity of his convictions. There is more to him than his newspaper reports would reveal.'

Late in March, at Spry's request, they spent a Sunday afternoon in Ottawa discussing the political situation, and talked again early in April. Mitch was confident he would have the 'whole-hearted support' of the *Sun*, and told Harry Nixon that Spry was 'very anxious to have a conference with us Apparently he is prepared to do everything he can to eliminate three-cornered fights.'[12]

But Spry's proposition went much further than the elimination of three-cornered fights. In a front-page editorial on 6 April, he proposed nothing less than the creation of a new party in Ontario. 'That is the clear course. The Progressives, the U.F.O., the labour elements, and the C.C.F. Clubs must work together. They must constitute the official opposition. And they must absorb the Liberals.' Mitch Hepburn was clearly the 'outstanding leader among the opposition parties,' but to defeat the Tories he 'should abandon the reactionary, introverted, office-seeking federal Liberal fold and proclaim himself an independent ... and work with the farmer, labour and C.C.F. groups ... The opposition groups must hang together or they will hang separately.' That had been precisely Mitch's point.[13]

The critical meeting took place the next weekend in a Toronto hotel room. Mitch came quickly to the point: would the CCF consider some coalition or working arrangement with the Liberals to create a united opposition front in Ontario? Donat LeBourdais, the CCF Club organizer, replied that while he had no authority to speak for the party he believed that any compromise of the CCF position as an independent party was unlikely. The meeting was over, and so was Mitch's attempt to reach any formal agreement with the CCF.[14] Philpott immediately broke his tenuous link with the Liberals and joined the CCF, and a few weeks later became president of the association of CCF Clubs. Mitch was convinced that Philpott's radical evangelical eloquence made his left flank far more vulnerable.[15]

Mitch could find some comfort, however, in the disarray in the Tory ranks at Queen's Park. Early in the year, Ed Carty, his friend from London, exclaimed that nothing 'short of a miracle' could prevent Mitch from becoming the next premier for 'he has the Tories on the run, and they hate him like poison – always crying what a shame it is to have a man of Hepburn's type leading a great party ... what embarrassing questions he asks and how he can say the things the Tories hate and the people like.' Mitch and his friends did have the Tories on the run. From England an angry and frustrated Howard

Ferguson boasted that he could put Arthur Slaght 'out of business' with one 'punch in the solar plexus' and 'choke off' his old friend Harry Nixon in the first week of the session. But George Henry was not Ferguson, and in the spring of 1933 he was more concerned with keeping his own precarious crown than administering the coup de grâce to his Liberal opponents.[16]

There were many rumours of plots against George Henry. If there had been an obvious successor few would have fought to keep him. As the session approached, there were rumours that some tycoons meeting at the Albany Club, the cathedral of high Toryism, had agreed to put up half a million dollars to finance a 'big business non-political coalition' to keep Mitch out of the office. Bill Sinclair would replace Henry and would agree to the sale of beer and wine with meals. Although it sounded implausible, Harry Johnson and others were not prepared to dismiss the possibility. The opposition to Henry rested on more than rumours, but Pat Donnelly assured Mitch that if the plotters 'believe that Henry will meekly submit to be set aside, I think they are greatly mistaken. In my opinion, Henry will go down fighting. He is too dumb to fully realize how hopeless is his cause.'[17]

The rumour was another reminder that Sinclair sat firmly in the seat of the leader of the opposition in the legislature. His speech at the opening of the session in February seemed designed to embarrass Mitch, not Henry. He not only denounced the inflationists, but he also maintained that 'to a certain point all people should support Governments of the day in these stressful times when law and order must be maintained and pernicious doctrines find favour.' Most members of the Liberal caucus were disgusted, and Tom Blakelock insisted that if Mitch came to caucus only three members would follow Sinclair if he walked out. Mitch checked into his rooms in the King Eddy. After a weekend of consultations, he declared that there would be 'no cooperation, no truce, no quarter. Mr. Henry's only hope is in securing the support of the Opposition groups under pretence of offering non-political government. He will not get it.' He and Nixon would continue 'to solidify the anti-government sentiment, to ally Liberal and independent thought,' and Harry Nixon would be the spokesman for an aggressive and united opposition at Queen's Park.[18]

For weeks there was little to attack. Premier Henry was felled by a duodenal ulcer. For several weeks his bedroom was the cabinet chamber, while at Queen's Park the members met for only a few minutes in the afternoon and never at night. By 23 March the premier was well enough to present his uninspiring budget which, despite cuts of almost $4 million, forecast a deficit of $3 million. The debt had jumped $33 million, and debt charges consumed over one-third of the provincial revenue. Civil servants faced another salary cut and the rich a 10 per cent surtax on succession duties, while the MLAs grudgingly cut a hundred dollars from their sessional indemnity of two thousand dollars. All Henry had to offer the ordinary taxpayer was further protection against foreclosures, a measure no longer opposed by the loan and mortgage companies for, although many had fallen below the acceptable liquidity level, the market was flooded with unsold farms and homes.[19]

A week later a committee began work on the details of Henry's redistribution bill. Twenty-two seats were to disappear as an economy measure, and the committee was instructed that the minimum population base should be 25,000 for rural and 50,000 for completely urban ridings. There were the inevitable charges of Tory gerrymandering, and Henry did confess that moving two Grit townships from Elgin to Kent and adding Tory townships to Elgin was not 'supposed to have improved the chances of Mr. Hepburn.' Although eight Liberal ridings were altered – and two merged or abolished – the largest screams came from the Tories, who claimed that Henry was committing political suicide in reducing the number of seats in solidly Tory eastern and northern Ontario.[20]

When the session opened the Liberals continued to probe the deal with Abitibi and the purchase of Ontario Power. On 15 March, the Hydro chairman, J.R. Cooke, finally replied that the government did not know the names of the Ontario Power bondholders. However, Parker and Slaght had discovered with little difficulty that Arthur Meighen, a Hydro commissioner since 1931, and George Henry were directors of companies which had been large bondholders. And late in March, after a long evening session with Mitch and Slaght, Harry Nixon asked if the premier, any cabinet minister, or any Hydro Commissioner had owned OPSC bonds.

Just four days earlier George Henry had told a thunderstruck cabinet that he had owned $25,000 in OPSC bonds. As he explained to his colleagues – and later to caucus, the legislature, and friends on each occasion with a differing emphasis and frequently confused chronology – it was all perfectly clear and reasonable. When he sold his substantial interest in the Farmers' Dairy in 1929 he was determined to keep his money in Canada. The bonds seemed to be a 'gilt-edged proposition and a matter of straight investment' and he bought them the day after the Abitibi agreement. Henry told Ferguson that he 'overlooked the fact of my holding them' when he became premier and 'certainly never would have bought them if I had been in this Chair at the time.'

Eighteen months later Abitibi was in trouble. Alex Smith was at his door and 'almost before I knew it,' he wrote a close friend, 'I found myself in possession of private information that would make it unfair of me to sell the bonds and get some innocent purchaser involved in a situation in which the future was very doubtful.' Or, as he told Sir Joseph Flavelle, 'I could at that time have given the bonds to some charity and been free and avoided all criticism, but I became so immersed in the intricacies of the whole proposition that I put behind any thought of personal interest in the matter, thinking only of the opportunity that was offered to the province to regain control of this very valuable development.' From the out-set he had pressed 'as strongly as possible for the very best terms for the province' and the same concern for the interests of the province led him not to inform the cabinet so that his colleagues could 'grapple with the problem with entirely free and open minds.' Moreover, had they known, his colleagues might have forced him to withdraw from the negotiations. 'I do not know what would have been the result if I had,' he told Ferguson, 'because I had to carry along some who were not very enthusiastic in agreeing to what was ultimately decided upon.'[21]

The revelation came when Henry was fighting for his political life. His illness had served as a cover for those Tories who believed that Henry had to retire before the election. Henry had never consid-ered retirement, and to resign over the bonds would have been an admission not only of the political ineptness of which he was guilty but of the dishonesty with which he was charged. When the cabi-net, however reluctantly, decided to fight it out, a tribal unity was imposed on the party. On the morning of 5 April, amid leaks of the scandal and rumours that he would resign, Henry took his story to the Tory caucus, where not a voice was raised against him. That afternoon, with the galleries crowded and hundreds standing out-side, he faced a tougher audience as he laboriously and defiantly read through a long speech written for him by Charles Foster, his secretary, and Strachan Johnson. To applause from the government benches, he assured the House and the press gallery that his only interest throughout had been the interests of his province. 'Mr. Speaker, I elected to be a farmer, and on the farm I learned to plough a straight and clean furrow.'

Information finally tabled in the House revealed that North

American Life, of which Henry was a director, owned $200,000 of the bonds. Companies of which Arthur Meighen was president or chairman of the board held $213,000, and Meighen personally had owned $3,000. The Toronto General Trusts, with the Conservative MLA Charles McCrea on the board, owned $104,000, and Royal Trust, with W.N. Tilley on the board – whose partner Strachan Johnson had acted for the government in the OPSC negotiations – owned a paltry $18,500. Although the party stood behind Henry, the Tory press did not. The Ottawa *Journal* stated bluntly that Henry should 'be faithful to the best traditions of the English-speaking public service' and resign. The Toronto *Evening Telegram* caustically commented that while posterity might conclude it was the best deal possible for the province, 'posterity will not vote at the next election.'

However, the Liberals wisely decided to concentrate their invective not on Henry, but on Arthur Meighen and the corporate world he represented. It was difficult not to believe George Henry, for there was nothing cunning or manipulative about him. In fact, Arthur Slaght suggested, Henry had been a 'pretty good sport' in taking responsibility for the decision. And it was Slaght, the brilliant courtroom lawyer whose eloquence had often swayed jurors, judges, and even hardened crown prosecutors, who played to the jurors of the province. Night after night that summer, sweat glistening on his forehead, hands punctuating every point, Slaght roused his audience to cheers, boos and foot-stamping denunciation: 'Is the Premier asleep when the interests of the province are at stake? Is the Attorney General asleep? Are the interests of the people of this province to bow down and worship at the feet of the directors of Meighen-controlled companies?' It may have been a little unfair, but fairness was the last thing on their minds as Mitch and Arthur walked out of countless halls to standing ovations and into the night to unwind with congenial companions and a bottle of Dewars.[22]

The bond scandal persuaded many Tories that so perilous was the state of the party that only by endorsing the Moderation League's campaign for the sale of beer by the glass and wine with meals could they survive the next election. Founder of the league was R. Home Smith, the bachelor playboy who had made one of several fortunes developing three thousand acres across the Humber River around his Old Mill estate. When not engaged with his real estate, railways, or mining interests, Home Smith had found time to become a leading Tory financier and organizer. Since 1923 his 'party within a party,' as he described the league, had become a well-organized and well-oiled lobby for the brewing and liquor interests. With their plants running at 20 per cent capacity, Ontario brewers were determined to end a system that allowed the holders of 150,000 home brew permits to make fourteen million gallons a year. They looked enviously at Quebec where the taps were open and pointed to the south where Roosevelt's inauguration heralded the end of prohibition.[23]

George Henry was a major obstacle to the work of the Moderation League, with its incessant propaganda and straw votes proving that 90 per cent of workers wanted beer by the glass. Since 1931 Henry had been pressured by both the league and the Prohibition Union. His equivocation had pleased neither. Short-tempered as usual, he had told Home Smith in the summer of 1932 that his public pressure was 'very ill-timed.' The public were only too well aware 'where the funds are coming from to carry on this campaign, and the selfish interests of the brewers are of little interest to the people of the Province.' As the movement to get rid of Henry grew in the spring of 1933, there seemed little doubt that Home Smith and the 'publicans and sinners' with whom he associated were solidly behind it. While there were reports that Charles McCrea, the cultivated and debonair minister of mines from Sudbury, would take over or that Howard Ferguson would return to keep the promised land for the faithful, no calculations could ignore the powerful presence of Attorney General William Price, who claimed to have the support of 95 per cent of the party and whose ambition, Henry dryly noted, 'sometimes gets the better of him.' As the Tory press boomed beer and Price, the *Globe* observed that 'Colonel Price is the camel on which the Moderation League hopes to ride to a still wetter oasis.'[24]

The Liberals believed that the Tories would wind up the session, select a new leader, endorse a beer and wine policy, and call a quick election. Percy Parker wrote Mitch in Ottawa that 'we must not be caught napping and must be ready to take a determined position at a moment's notice.' Mitch agreed and hoped to get to Toronto to discuss strategy. However, when the league's solicitor told Parker that a beer and wine resolution on the order paper could soon come to a vote, Parker hurriedly invited a few members of the Management Committee to a Sunday afternoon meeting at the Royal York.

Parker argued that in the interests of temperance the Liberals should condemn a policy that encouraged drinking hard liquor, 'produced revelry in hotel bedrooms, fostered secret drinking and turned the home into a bar room' and endorse the sale of Ontario-made wine and beer in hotels, restaurants, and private clubs under the supervision of the Liquor Control Board. Increased sales and a differential price for domestic spirits would give an enormous boost to the economy, increased taxes would make other tax cuts possible, and Ontario's annual $100 million American tourist trade would not be threatened. Slaght, William Mulock, and Senator McGuire needed no persuasion on principle, but Parker was surprised to find Roebuck, J.C. McRuer, and Albert Matthews, 'former strong prohibitionists ... among the strongest in their support of the beer and wine policy. Matthews stated that he knew "scads" of prohibitionists and had talked with many of them and not one of them would have the slightest objection to our adopting the policy.'[25]

But Mitch could not be pushed towards any premature declaration of Liberal policy. Although he had promised Nixon to keep the liquor question out of politics by not talking about it, Mitch bluntly told him that prohibition was 'a lost cause.' If the Tories chose to run on a beer and wine platform, he said privately as early as the spring of 1932, the best Liberal 'strategy would be to accept any change in the Liquor Control Act and insist on fighting the issues of taxation and hydro.' When they dined at the Chateau Laurier late in 1932, Mitch may have even gone further than simply assuring Harry Pritchard of the Moderation League that he would not oppose Tory legislation. At the same time he refused to bend to the incessant pressure from his wet friends in Toronto, the north, the border cities, and the French Canadians to move beyond the 1930 platform, because any Liberal statement would simply 'take the fire off the tories.' Mitch made no secret of his personal predilections: 'I have a little Scotch in me,' he would say with a grin, 'sometimes more, sometimes less.'[26]

There was still the danger of a Tory coup d'état and a late spring election when the Liberal Management Committee met on 5 May. The wet contingent was well prepared and out in force. Mitch had also insisted that all the MLAs attend to ensure that the dry wing from rural Ontario was heard. Behind closed doors at the King Eddy Slaght introduced Parker's proposal, but the burden of the argument was left to moderates like Massey and drys like Roebuck, whose presentation of the political futility (and therefore moral irrelevance) of hanging on to the vestiges of prohibition was impressive. The meeting was tumultuous. William Newman, the dry MLA from Lorneville, knew that Ontario was wet and prohibition a lost cause. But he also knew that he and many other members would be fight-

ing a lost cause if the party adopted a beer and wine policy before
the Tories. His angry 'I'll tell you, Roebuck' crashed through the
walls of the room like 'the bark of a gun' as he tried to stem the
tide. He later reassured one of his dry constituents that Mitch Hepburn
was a man to be trusted:

If you know as I know how much pressure has been brought to bear on
him, to declare himself wet: Well, you would admire his steadfast firmness,
in what he pledges himself to stay by.

   Last fall there was a set plan to get him to accept. A broadcast was
arranged, the country's ears were made ready to have him go ahead of
Hon. Geo. Henry, in announcing a beer and wine policy ... I told in a very
few minutes, that the Conservative Party would be the best pleased of all
Ontario when it was done. They would then be the less wet and the more
dry party. It would be giving over the election to them and I would not
be a candidate. I was done. The fight was on. With a big bunch of big bellied
men in the back of the room. The late Fred Elliott who died this week,
and the rest of the dry members of the Legislature said if this was carried
we were done.

   Mitch remained silent throughout the stormy debate. He was
obviously pleased by the stalemate. When finally asked for his opinion
he said that he preferred not to commit himself and believed,
with the deep fissures in the party, that it would be politically
unwise for the party to declare its position. Mitch knew there was
nothing to be gained and much to be lost by not playing a waiting
game. That night he said nothing about beer and wine in his broadcast
over CFRB. Though never intended, Mitch had won a moral victory.
If the Liberals had endorsed beer and wine, Newman said,
'then Mitch would not lack for money. It is ready lots of it. Mitch
is doing his best to keep clean.' Mackenzie King had been afraid
that Mitch would 'yield to the pressure of the liquor interests and
their own sense of need for campaign funds from that source which
is one of the very few sources left' and was delighted to hear of
Slaght's defeat: 'He is not a good type – immoral. I should think
not to be trusted with liquor interests, etc.' The *Globe* was also
pleased with the result, but warned the Liberals that if they ever
believed they could win 'political kudos by beating Mr. Price to Mr.
Home Smith's door, they are not reckoning on the astuteness of the
Laird of the Humber, who has never yet elevated a Grit – humble
or ambitious – to so distinguished a position as the Premiership.'[27]

Even more was to be gained by refusing to be drawn out on the controversial Roman Catholic school question that once again had bubbled to the surface. The facts were clear enough. The cost of a separate school education was about half that in a public school while residential taxes for separate school supporters were double. Although the law permitted corporations to split school taxes in proportion to the number of Catholic-owned shares, few did. Catholic schools were effectively denied access to corporation taxes in many cities where half of the taxable property was owned by corporations and utilities. The quality of education for the one hundred thousand separate school students – 17 per cent of the elementary school population – inevitably suffered. Catholics were also refused permission to establish publicly supported high schools, and by the mid-1920s some seventeen schools were ignoring government prohibitions and offering high school classes in elementary schools.

For several years the Catholic hierarchy had cautiously groped for some way to bring political pressure on Ferguson and Henry. But bishops have seldom made good politicians, and it was not until Martin Quinn, a Toronto businessman, failed to get taxes on a block of his stock paid to the Catholic schools that the issue found an outraged and uncompromising champion. With the approval of Archbishop McNeil, Quinn formed the Catholic Taxpayers' Association and soon had organized both clergy and laity as an effective lobby. By the summer of 1932 he could inform all parish priests that the movement was 'making splendid progress. There is no doubt about the deep concern of the Politicians of every political shade. They appear to recognize that for the first time we mean business.' Although Quinn was a well-known Grit, his initial objective was to secure redress from the Henry government. However, if that failed, he told an Ottawa audience late in 1932, 'we will be forced to go to the polls with a feeling of sadness and futility rather than one of malice, and to cast our votes in favour of a more fair-minded body.'[28]

Mitch was acutely aware of the enormous political importance of the issue. More than one-quarter of Ontario was Roman Catholic. In about a dozen ridings in the north and in the Ottawa valley the majority were Catholic, largely francophone. In another dozen in the north, east, and Essex more than one in four was a Catholic. With substantial concentrations of Catholics in some urban industrial ridings, an organized Catholic vote could be crucial in one seat in three. On the other hand, the province as a whole was overwhelmingly Protestant, not simply in numbers but in sentiment. Politicians still dreaded the power of the Orange Order and the capacity of one wing of the Protestant clergy to inflame the populace against the servants of the Pope of Rome.

Despite his upbringing in southwestern Ontario, Mitch did not share the religious biases of many of his neighbours, any more than he shared their view of the demon rum. Indeed, he could have said that many of his best friends – including girl friends – were Catholics, even French-Canadian Catholics. Mitch had discussed the school question with Senator McGuire and other leading Catholics as early as the spring of 1932, and by the end of the year was intimating privately that he supported some form of remedial action. After a two-hour conversation, the editor of *Le Droit* promised Mitch his support. Robert Burns of the London *Catholic Record* had become 'very friendly' and told Mitch that 'while the paper does not take sides politically he could give us lots of publicity which would help.' McGuire had also assured Quinn that Mitch was 'entirely in sympathy with the position we take and may be counted upon to support any legislation that the Government may initiate.' But Quinn asked Mitch for more tangible and 'personal assurance of sympathetic co-operation.' For the record – and to Quinn's dismay – Mitch replied that he was waiting for a statement of government policy and then 'of necessity, the Liberal Party will make its position known in the matter.'[29]

Mitch was trapped. Leading Catholics had warned the hierarchy that it was politically impossible for Henry to introduce remedial legislation unless Mitch informed Henry that it would have his support. Senator George Lynch-Staunton urged Archbishop McNeil of Toronto to see Senator McGuire and if he 'tells you that though Hepburn is in full sympathy but will not commit himself in writing you should tell him that you suspect his sincerity, and that the Catholic Liberals should tell him plainly that they will not give the Catholic support in the coming election unless he gives the assurance to the Government we require.'

Mitch refused to let Henry off the hook, but in another meeting with Quinn and McGuire he did promise that if Henry introduced the required legislation, the Liberals would not oppose it. If Henry did not and the Liberals were returned, they would introduce remedial legislation during the first session. 'Personally, I have no doubt at all as to what the Liberals will do,' Quinn later assured a sceptical colleague, 'and I feel that they have been tied up as tight as it is humanly possible to tie them.' Among Catholics, at least, Mitch was privately unequivocal in his commitment to remedial action. When he dropped by the Catholic Cartys in London over Christmas, the talk turned to the school question:

He told us among important things that the first thing he will do when he is premier of Ontario ... will be to right the wrong against Catholics and give Separate Schools their rightful share of the taxes of joint stock companies, all of which now go to the public schools. We warned him to be careful and not fall into a trap as the Tories would like to be able to say that Hepburn had sold out to the Catholics. But he said he is advised by Peter Heenan ... and also by McGuire of Toronto. Arthur Roebuck, Hepburn said, has agreed to join him and throw the labor party vote with him to help Separate Schools ... He also said the Premier Geo. S. Henry had written to him advising him to put it in writing that he is going to help Separate schools but 'Mitch' was too foxy for that. He told Henry to go ahead with legislation to satisfy the Catholics and the Liberals would not make an issue of it, but Henry has done nothing.

In the summer and fall of 1933, small cheques were reaching the Liberals from Catholic laymen. But publicly Mitch refused to be drawn out and again waited patiently for George Henry to make the first move.[30]

Late in April, Mitch began a four-month campaign that took him into every corner of the province in expectation of a fall or even a summer election. Local organizers had as little difficulty filling a country schoolroom or a local hall as did Mitch in captivating his audience. Without the hindrance of a prepared text, he was a master of reading the congregation. Words came easily, sometimes too easily if he had been drinking, and any audience, large or small, started the adrenalin flowing. Mitch was a natural politician: Instantly recalling a name or a face and sealing a new friendship with a generous smile, a firm handshake, and a 'Hi, how are you, I'm Mitch Hepburn,' he not only spoke to the people of Ontario, he met them. Reporters observed the symbiotic relationship, but could never explain it: so much was in the eyes, the gesture, the knowing nuance or inside joke that welded Mitch to his audience. Above all, perhaps, were the piercing faint-blue eyes that, once fixed, held an audience or an individual in their grip.

Much of the work of rebuilding the Liberal party went on in country kitchens, hotel bedrooms, and at the local bootleggers. Mitch had a firm grasp of the alcoholic topography of most ridings, and usually had time for relaxation, requesting only that he be delivered 'safely to the station some time Sunday night.' Some of his friends feared there was too much congenial relaxation and too many late-night sessions for the good of his health or that of the Liberal party.

Unlike King's laboriously written two-hour monologues, Mitch's speeches were short and crisp, the wit unbridled, the images apt. He varied the content to suit the audience but always included an attack on Hydro's Quebec contracts and the bail-out of the OPSC bondholders. He ridiculed Henry's straight furrow and denounced Meighen's greed. On occasion Mitch recited figures on government expenditure and the escalating debt with carefree abandon. A Hepburn government would cut administrative costs in half by abolishing useless boards and commissions, scrapping or amalgamating departments, firing all the Tory ward-heelers 'whose heads were so deep in the trough that only their ears stuck out,' and make certain that no cabinet ministers raced around the province in limousines bought by the taxpayer. The doors would be locked at Chorley Park, the lieutenant-governor's palatial Rosedale residence, until there was no unemployment in Ontario, and with Ottawa's concurrence the vice-regal functions would be performed by the chief justice. No audience was allowed to forget that the Liquor Board was simply an arm of the Tory party, and the tolls paid to have brands listed lined Tory pockets and filled the Tory campaign chest. In short, the government of Ontario operated to serve not the people but the Conservative party.

Mitch also shed much of his radical image. There was the occasional reference to the 'money barons and the exploiting classes,' but more frequently there was a milder insistence on lower interest rates, debt reduction, progressive taxation, and protection of consumers and producers. Mitch saved his strongest language to attack Henry and Price for using section 98 of the Criminal Code to harass, arrest, jail, and deport left-wing critics and effectively abolish freedom of speech in Ontario. By the end of the summer there were some who wanted Mitch to put more substance in his speeches, but for the moment he heeded Roebuck's earlier advice 'to avoid every debatable topic possible, with the exception of pure politics.' And as pure politics, his campaign was brilliant. Down in Aylmer, a friend reported, four men 'who never drew a Grit breath in their lives' had become Hepburn Liberals and 'I would not be surprised any time to hear that his Satanic Majesty had turned grit, after what I heard in Aylmer.' While hard times had helped, Parker assured

King that it was Mitch's 'destructive criticisms' that had 'set the heather on fire.'[31]

Mitch was convinced that the party could make major gains in the twenty ridings that ran in a great arc across the north from Kenora and Rainy River to the Ottawa and down to the St Lawrence. With their large French and Catholic populations many had been traditionally Liberal, until Sinclair's inept liquor and language policies had driven away all but the most dogmatic. Mitch promised in March that there would be a French Canadian in the cabinet, and the word certainly spread that he was a friend of the Catholics, French or Irish, and their schools. Travelling throughout the north with his good Catholic friend Peter Heenan, Mitch proved by word and deed that the Liberals were no longer dry. The Irish-born locomotive engineer from Kenora, who had sat in the provincial and federal houses since 1919 and had held the Labour portfolio in King's cabinet, was a tower of strength. Though twenty years older than Mitch, the two had become good friends in the Commons and it was not hard to believe that if Hepburn ruled at Queen's Park, Peter Heenan would have an office down the hall. Important too in an area devastated by the Depression was Mitch's spirited attack on Tory mismanagement of northern resources and the promise of a development policy that would bring the timber barons to heel and put men back to work. Mitch went north three times during the summer and spent ten days in the small towns and villages along the Ottawa and the lower St Lawrence.

Mitch's 1929 Dodge was a familiar sight in much of southern Ontario, except in dry ridings where his presence was not requested. Nixon often joined him, and the two spent much of their time persuading local Liberals and Progressives to hold joint conventions or find some suitable accommodation. Brantford Liberals had to agree not to run a candidate against the Independent Labour candidate MacBride and Oxford Liberals had to accept a Catholic candidate. Windsor and Essex needed special attention, for the obstreperous wets were always troublesome. In Windsor, the young labour mayor, David Croll, who many complained had 'the faculty of not being able to keep his mouth shut,' was demanding a cabinet post as the price of his candidacy and had the support of W.F. Herman's influential Tory *Border Cities Star*.[32]

Mitch frequently travelled with Arthur Slaght, who had become a close friend and ally. While practising law as a young man in Cobalt and Haileybury before the war, Slaght had become involved with Harry Oakes in the Macassa mine and made a small fortune.

Slaght was a relative newcomer to the party. Distrusted by the old guard, Slaght, like Percy Parker, was linked with the mining and liquor interests that had been Tory for so long. On the platform, as in the courtroom, he was eloquent, incisive, witty, and brilliantly manipulative. Later known as the Beau Brummell of the Commons, Slaght's passion for fine clothes was more than matched by his enthusiasm for a good time. Some Liberals felt that Slaght would make a better leader than Mitch, but Mitch never doubted his friend's loyalty, and Slaght insisted that the leader lead and be followed. To those who criticized Mitch's periodic swings to the left, Slaght replied that among Liberals 'there must be pioneers to clear the way – also men to watch the rear. Some may always be in advance – others may occasionally lag behind. But the only thing we have to demand is that nobody should stand still.' If Slaght would not be leader, many Liberals shared Percy Parker's view that he should be Mitch's attorney general.[33]

However, when Mitch announced at Arthur Roebuck's nomination that the candidate in Bellwoods would be the next attorney general, there was little surprise. Mitch and Roebuck had been political friends long before the leadership convention, and although Roebuck was never quite 'the power behind the throne' that he and his friends imagined, he was a key figure in the Liberal organization. He was a permanent fixture in the offices of the OLA where his major concern was the Management Fund he had started in the wake of Beauharnois. He also found time to write two highly effective pamphlets denouncing the Tory government. Ten thousand copies of *The Wreck of the Hydro* were published in the summer of 1933 and *The Forest Fiasco*, the tale of the timber barons and pulpwood pirates, followed in November.

The fifty-five-year old Roebuck helped the Liberals maintain a consistent radical image, while often urging Mitch to take a softer line. He supported advanced social legislation, including unemployment insurance, and was as biting as Woodsworth in his attack on the Tory use and abuse of section 98. Roebuck's left-wing rhetoric – with 'a multi-millionaire at the head of our country and a gang of financiers with a grip on the finances Canadians were being crucified on a cross of gold' – helped to counter the appeal of Philpott and the CCF. Indeed, there were some Liberals who urged Roebuck to follow them over to the CCF. The new commonwealth was 'claptrap for the emotional,' he replied, and 'I think if I am to leave a footprint it must be in the sands which I am now travelling. There are signs which seem to indicate that I may put a nick in the hide of privilege, which is our common aim, though perhaps not a gash which you envisage.' With portfolios for Roebuck and Nixon, Mitch was re-creating the old farmer and Lib-Lab alliance.[34]

There seemed to be no such logic behind his promise at Duncan Marshall's nomination in Peel that he would be the next minister of agriculture. Dunc Marshall was a man of extensive but dubious credentials. Born in Bruce County in 1872, he had been active in the Patrons of Industry before moving west in 1905. Elected to the Alberta legislature in 1909, he was minister of agriculture until the Liberal defeat in 1921. He returned to Ontario, where he worked as an organizer for the federal Liberals and then joined the Cock-field Brown advertising agency as an agricultural expert. With some effort, Marshall could be suave, but in general he was bombastic and crude, and addicted to off-colour jokes. Mitch's promise left many Liberals incredulous. There was no doubt that he was a powerful platform speaker, and the commitment may have been essential to persuade him to take on Brigadier Thomas Kennedy, the Dixie fruit-farmer who had owned Peel since 1919 and sat in Henry's cabinet as minister of agriculture.

Mitch resisted the pressure to make a cabinet commitment that would strengthen and confirm his links with the Toronto business and financial community. Many of the establishment along Bay and King Streets were openly Liberal federally, but had not given the provincial party the same allegiance and support. Deeply suspicious of the new leader and the gang around him, they continued to hope, if not plot, that the succession would soon pass to one of their own. But by 1933, as the once moribund party showed signs of revival, some of the old guard returned and even sat on the Management Committee.[35]

More promising was the stirring of Liberalism among the younger Toronto business community. Soon after his November 1932 speech to the Twentieth Century Club, Mitch heard from Harry Johnson that a 'number of the live-wire young men, most of whom have had Tory leanings in the past, planned to form a Reform Club in order to get their own group together to work for you. They feel that Queen's Park is run by a bunch of high-binders and racketeers and they desire to clean out the bunch there.' Percy Parker invited some of them for a Sunday talk at his Erindale estate and later had twenty to a lunch attended by Arthur Slaght. The outcome was the creation of the Centurions, limited to one hundred members elected by ballot. Initially there were about forty Centurions, all of whom, wrote Parker, were among the 'best known young men in the business and social circles.' The membership was impressive: Colonel Watson, the son of W.G. Watson, manager of Toronto General Trusts; Charles and Latham Burns of Burns Brothers, brokers; Joseph Clarke of Cockfield Brown; James Gundy of Wood Gundy; Geoffrey Summers who married Parker's daughter and Charles Fell who married Albert Matthews's only daughter; and George McCullagh, a vice-president and director of two companies headed by Percy Parker.[36]

Throughout the spring of 1933 Mitch's attacks went unanswered and rumours of a fall election abated as the Tories wrestled with internal problems, particularly that of Henry's leadership. On 28 June, however, rested after an Atlantic City vacation, Henry fired the first shots in what looked suspiciously like an election campaign. Flanked by cabinet ministers, MLAs and the local MP, Henry assured the Perth faithful that the torch entrusted to him was firmly held. Most of his unusually vigorous speech was an attack on Hepburn and revealed the thrust of the Tory campaign. The Liberals insisted they were the friends of Hydro – 'Yes, friends, with a knife behind their back.' Mitch Hepburn, the puppet of the private power barons, was the real enemy of Hydro and public power. His promise to cut expenditures in half would mean cuts in mothers' allowances or the abolition of the Department of Agriculture or the dismissal of sixteen hundred civil servants. The election of Mitch Hepburn, who supported the CCF and the communists in the attack on section 98, would destroy the foundations of law and order in Ontario. George Henry would go to the people 'not under any red flag of Communism or any other hybrid flag' but under the Union Jack.[37]

The Hydro Commission also entered the political arena. In a pamphlet, *Misleading Assertions that have been made relating to the power situation in the Province of Ontario EXAMINED AND CORRECTED*, the commission disputed Mitch's charge that the Quebec contracts left Hydro saddled with over a million surplus horsepower that cost the province $15 million. According to Hydro the surplus was due to a decline in demand and was less than 300,000 horsepower. 'A man with less desire for personal probity than Mr. Hepburn might be tempted to let his statement stand, but ... no doubt he will hasten to make the necessary public correction.'

The *Globe* gave Mitch's public correction a front page headline: 'Hepburn Charges Hydro Assists Power Barons' 'Reckless Buying of Huge Surplus Again is Alleged.' Before seven thousand cheering Liberals at Woodbridge, Mitch recited again the figures in Roebuck's *Wreck of the Hydro* and insisted that Hydro had a surplus of more than 600,000 horsepower, at a cost of over $9 million, and that by 1937 the surplus and the cost would triple. The commission's reply that with the expected recovery Ontario would need even more power than projected drew the response from Mitch that he stood by every charge, if not the 'exact accuracy of every statement attributed to me.' Mitch had been carefree with the facts, but Ontario did have a costly power surplus which cynics could easily assume had something to do with the fact that the Hydro contracts alone paid for the cost of the Quebec power developments.[38]

There were other signs of an approaching election: over a million dollars in highway contracts in June; rumours of a more generous relief policy; a flood of straw votes (organized by the Moderation League) proving that urban Ontario wanted beer by the glass; and innumerable hints from Henry and other Tories that the league's polls might be answered. In mid-August the Liberals heard from sources close to Price that unless Henry left there would be no election until after the 1934 session. But while Senator Hardy urged Mitch to slow the pace a little, he agreed that Henry and Ferguson could not be trusted 'around a corner and it might be only bluff to put you off guard.'

Mitch was tired and he did cut the pace a little in August. Eva and his farm manager, Billy Tapsell, saw a lot more of him, as did the farmers in the Tory townships that had been added to the east end of the riding. Mitch's birthday party, always a gala event in Elgin, was the largest ever. Postponed because of a torrential rain storm on 11 August, it was held three days later when four thousand cars jammed the roads and fields and twenty thousand people came from all over southern Ontario to shake hands with Mitch. A sprained ankle later in the month gave him the opportunity to rest for a few days at Percy Parker's in Erindale.

Weeks passed without any decision about an election. Finally, after a northern tour, Henry announced on 25 September that an election in 1933 would be an unnecessary interference with the economic recovery he had seen all across Ontario. 'I had all along been keeping the question of an election more or less in doubt,' he told Ferguson, 'as I felt we should keep the Opposition leader wondering.' But the leading Tory organizers and fund-raisers had never been in doubt. The party was not ready for an election in the fall of 1933, and there were still those who believed that George Henry had to be removed.[39]

Although the delay gave Mitch time to improve the party's central organization, he was afraid it would favour the Tories and the CCF. There were signs that Ontario was coming out of the worst of the Depression. Men and women were going back to work, or working longer hours. The number of families on direct relief had fallen from a high of 506,000 in April to 339,000 in August. Despite bad weather in the summer, farmers welcomed the first increase in crop prices since 1928. There was also good news on Bay Street, where stocks had doubled from their May 1932 low to reach 35 per cent of the 1929 bull market value in July. As Henry hoped, and Mitch feared, continued recovery could take some of the edge off political unrest.

More immediately disturbing was the surprising growth of the CCF. The summer and fall were proving to be halcyon days for the new party. The Regina Manifesto, adopted in July, gave a sharper ideological edge to the humanitarian image of the CCF, and the large crowds that turned out to hear Philpott, Woodsworth, and Agnes Macphail rivalled the Liberal rallies. It was little consolation to know that the CCF was also cutting into the traditional Tory working-class vote. Moreover, despite the uneasiness of the United Farmers' delegates at Regina with the socialism of the Manifesto, many UFO members were joining the party and local organizations seemed less inclined to support the Liberal-Progressive coalition. Mitch admitted he was 'thoroughly alarmed,' for it appeared that the CCF would run in most ridings and Tory strategists were openly counting on three-cornered fights to hand them another victory.[40]

While Mitch refused to attack the policy of the CCF, he had to offset its appeal. Clearly the time had come for another swing to the left.[41] The time seemed opportune, for on the morning of 27 September sixty men of the Royal Canadian Regiment with rifles and Lewis machine-guns had poured off the train at Stratford. In the afternoon, four Carden-Lloyd machine-gun carriers from the barracks in London lumbered into town on their noisy tracks. At the request of the city council, Attorney General Price had ordered the occupation of Stratford to keep the peace in a city torn by strikes in the furniture factories, which had been organized by Fred Collins and Izzy Minster of the Workers' Unity League in Toronto.[41]

Mitch spoke at Highgate in East Kent, where he expected Henry to call a by-election, the day after the army occupied Stratford. To his usual attack on the reactionary incompetence of the Henry government he now added the reactionary ruthlessness of a cabinet that sent 'artillery, machine guns and troops to Stratford because the cit-

A ten-year-old touched by 'a foul and most wicked conspiracy'

With Barney and King

'Why am I in politics when I have all this?'

Bannockburn

Winter on Lake Laurier with Eva, Peter and Patsy, and friends

Leaders of the Liberal oppositions: Mitch and King at Massey Hall,
15 December 1932

Arthur Slaght (left) and Frank O'Connor, 24 April 1934: men who seem
to 'have been prepared for the purpose'

The road to victory 1934:
'I have a little Scotch in me –
sometimes more,
sometimes less.'

Sketches of a premier, 17 July 1934

Arthur Roebuck gives his version of Hydro supply and demand,
27 February 1935. 'He was drawing the picture not me,' commented
a Hydro engineer. 'I knew it did not give a true picture.'

With David Croll (left), Roebuck, and children of the
'Unemployed Under Dog,' 25 April 1935

Croll (left), Dr Dafoe (centre), and the Quints. 'He was scared of the babies and hardly knew what to do,' said nurse Yvonne Leroux.

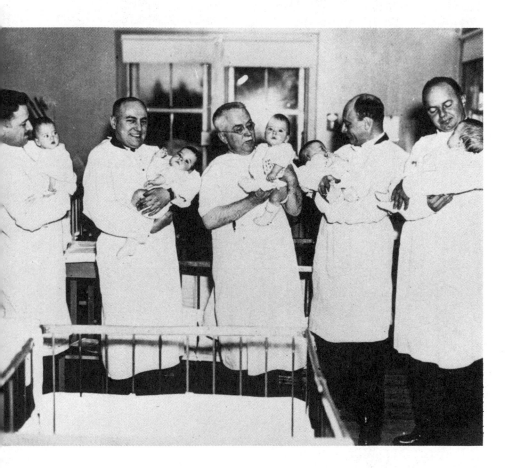

izens are objecting to the treatment given them by wealthy manufacturers who have the highest tariff in the country's history. They
take all they can from the people and give as little as they can to
the workers'. Mitch was praised in left-wing circles. But in Leeds
some of the farmers were 'kicking up their heels' and Senator Hardy
reported that his remarks about what looked to him like a 'Communist inspired' strike had caused a good deal of annoyance among
important Liberals. Mitch made no apologies and bluntly warned
Hardy that with the increasing strength of the CCF in western
Ontario, 'unless the Liberal party stirs itself into further activity, I
have very serious doubts in regard to our political future.'[42]

Two weeks later in a luncheon address to Liberal ladies in
Chatham, Mitch replied to his critics within the party. Much more
subdued than usual, he declared that his speech would mark a turning point in the campaign. The Liberals had earned the right to lead
the battle for reform, and his task was to achieve the 'solidarity of
the forces that are interested in suffering humanity and opposed to
Conservatism.' But the party could not 'remain in a neutral position' and had to become the real 'medium of expression for those
who are suffering from circumstances beyond their own control.'
Mitch appealed specifically to affluent Liberals 'to take a more tol-
erant attitude toward those of us who are forming the policy of the
party today,' and warned them publicly that 'if a re-alignment in
the Liberal party is necessary ... I am prepared to bring about that
re-alignment.' At the root of the problem was the burden of the
public debt and the ordinary taxpayer's lack of purchasing power,
both of which he claimed were the result of privilege and exploitation. The solution was to overhaul the tax system and use succession duties to 'deprive the progeny of the present money barons of
their power to exact an unfair interest carrying charge from the people.' Three days later, before the largest crowd ever to assemble in
Staffordville, he explained that 'I am not advocating confiscation
but only that the people get back what belongs to them.'[43]

The *Globe* and *Mail and Empire* carried only a short item on the
Chatham speech, but as Harry Johnson wrote, that was enough to
upset some of the affluent Liberals: 'Oh Boy! Is my face red from
your Succession Duty proposal? I did not know we had so many
people who would leave estates.' The sharpest public criticism came
from the editor of the *Border Cities Star* whose owner, W.F. Herman, wanted to pass on the paper to his family, as did Joe Atkinson of the *Star*. Mitch it seemed had 'out-lefted' himself, and in an

attempt to 'please the C.C.F. crowd' had advocated the 'confiscation of all fortunes as their owners pass on.' Of course, Mitch would 'turn over his own property to the State ... in order to be consistent, for we understand the costly farm he owns came to him from his grandfather,' otherwise 'he might not be in a financial position to gratify his taste for a political career.'

Mitch complained privately that he had been misunderstood, and had not used the word confiscation. But Ellison Young, the editor of the *Border Cities Star*, replied that Mitch was really making 'a distinction without a difference' and warned him that he was 'bound to alienate many Liberals if he persisted in leaning 'so sharply to the Left as one involving a serious increase in the present system of partial confiscation of private monies.' Five per cent of the people might indeed own 95 per cent of the wealth, added Young, but 'No matter what public orators may say all men are not equal and if you redistributed wealth equally in a few years it would be back where it was.'⁴⁴

There were Liberals who shared Mitch's liberalism and his concern about the CCF and urged him to make 'it evident that Liberals under your banner are a fighting group determined to do something positive, practical and thoroughly advanced to right existing economic wrongs.' Mitch replied sadly that while a constructive reform statement was desirable, 'as soon as we start a lean to the left we find ourselves in conflict with a lot of the re-actionary Liberals.' However, the obvious occasion for such a statement would be the banquet of the Twentieth Century Liberals in Toronto on 18 November, and Mitch planned to consult beforehand with some of the 'Party Heads.'⁴⁵

His advisers were obviously opposed to another swing to the left. Perhaps they agreed with Percy Parker that although the Liberals might be 'asleep at the switch,' it seemed clear that not only would 'the unemployed and mass of disconnected people with no stake in the country' vote CCF regardless of the Liberal platform, but also that CCF strength would come from the traditionally Tory working class. Should Liberal strategy not be to press the CCF to define their socialist policies for Ontario, in which case 'all people with any stake in the country would become speedily alarmed'? Others pointed to the many signs of growing uneasiness among the farmers not only about the socialism of the CCF but also the emerging conflict between the Communists and the Christians. Whatever the arguments in the OLA offices or the King Eddy, Mitch's spirited speech to the young Liberals was the familiar recitation of Tory sins, and in reply to Lucette Valin's toast he would only promise that the party would win every French-Canadian riding. The new swing to the left had been short-lived.[46]

Although Mitch had set the heather on fire, the Liberal party was not ready to fight an election in the summer of 1933. Under Harry Johnson's management the Ontario Liberal Association office ran smoothly and efficiently, but there was no central committee capable of running an election. Small contributions were dribbling in, but there was no war chest to finance an election in ninety ridings. Moreover, the party was still deeply divided. Sinclair's anomalous position as 'leader of the opposition' was an embarrassment and could be dangerous. More important was the continuing suspicion and tension between the federal Liberals and the new provincial organization centred around Mitch.

The OLA office was the focal point of the Hepburn Liberals. Harry Johnson was tireless, efficient, and completely loyal to Mitch. Although there was never enough money for an adequate staff, the office mailed over eighty thousand pieces of literature in 1933, maintained a reasonable clipping system, and helped to schedule Mitch's two hundred speeches as well as the one hundred and sixty given by members of the Speaker's Bureau. Most bills were paid from the Maintenance Fund which in 1933 raised $11,251.80 in donations from seventeen hundred members. With Mitch infrequently in Toronto, the OLA office served as a clearing house for the Toronto strategists and a link with the legislative group loyal to Mitch. The restructuring of the OLA planned at the December 1930 convention had not been completely carried out. Three regional organizations had been formed – in central, eastern, and western Ontario, the last in February 1933 – but since the central and western organizations owed much to the federal Liberals they were regarded with some suspicion in the OLA office.[47]

Mitch had a much greater appeal among the young of both sexes and the women than his federal counterpart. The Twentieth Century Liberal Association, whose membership was limited to those under thirty, had its inaugural meeting in Ottawa in March 1930, and formed a men's and women's branch. The president of the National Women's Association was his friend Odette Lapointe. Prominent in the Ontario branch was his close friend Lucette Valin, who served as French-language secretary. The young Liberals were to the left of the party and they found Mitch's youthful enthusiasm and unrestrained hyperbole a refreshing change from the sober and restrained performance of the old guard. Mitch gave the Ontario branch his full support, and repeatedly urged local organizers to get young Liberals – even high school students – out to meetings. Mitch also worked hard to stimulate the moribund Ontario Women's Liberal Association at the provincial and riding level. He frequently spoke to women's organizations, and urged his local hosts to secure a large female turnout at his rallies. By the summer of 1933 there were three deputy chairwomen in each Toronto constituency to assist the local organization.[48]

The critical area was the relationship, personal and structural, between the federal and provincial parties. The conflicts and rivalries among Ontario Liberals that had bedevilled the party since the 1920s had not been erased. Although Mitch was a federal MP, his election as provincial leader had not led to a union of federal and provincial forces, and King's creation of the National Liberal Federation in 1932 tended to confuse organizational lines and heighten suspicions. In June, Hardy complained to King that the 'complete boycott' of the provincial party by the federal Liberals was a source of weakness. King replied that a complete boycott was certainly not desirable, but just 'how far to go is a question that must be decided in relation to each situation as it exists, and in this matter, as in all else, the avoidance of extremes either way would appear to be the only sensible attitude.' Little could be expected from Kingsmere.[49]

Mitch was not interested in the details of party organization; his talents lay elsewhere. But he was determined to keep the Ontario party under his control and had no desire to see it captured by the federal Liberals, whose ineptness he knew only too well. While he was on his northern trip in June, Vincent Massey, the president of the National Liberal Federation, held a lunch at the Ontario Club for Parker, Matthews, Fred Sanderson, and Bill Fraser. The outcome was that the five men decided they would form 'an inside committee' to handle Mitch's campaign. Mitch did not openly reject the idea, yet three weeks later Fraser complained that the committee had not met and Mitch was still 'working along pretty much with one or two chaps. I am anxious to get a close committee working with him,' he explained to King, 'in order to eliminate mistakes and if possible establish some definite line of action and policy.' A month later Fraser complained again that he had 'made several trips to Toronto to discuss matters with Messrs. Parker, Massey, Matthews and etc., as well as to meet our mutual friend the "Chief", but up to the present time we have not been able to get anybody down to a definite program.' As leader of the party, Fraser lectured Mitch, he was 'soon going to have to insist on some person or a committee of three or four to get on this end of your campaign, and it is absolutely necessary that we keep in constant touch with the Ridings, if we are going to be at least partly prepared for the next election.'[50]

Mitch was not prepared to take orders from Fraser. As Vincent Massey scoured the province for funds for the National Liberal Federation he roused the ire of provincial organizers, also engaged in some modest fund-raising. Before too many blunders irreparably ruptured the party, Massey persuaded King to intervene. King spent the first day at the York Club with the élite of the federal wing, and the next morning Massey took him to the OLA office to meet Parker, McGuire and Spence, Marshall, Roebuck, and Harry Johnson. The discussion centred on the relations between the two wings of the party, and King 'spoke of the need of the Federal Ontario Liberals doing something in the way of organizing and suggested letting [Nelson] Parliament act for them – they to find the funds but to report to NLF on where monies were collected from (this being the suggestion of Massey etc.) Marshall and Roebuck were very down on Parliament as a traitor, etc. Marshall's whole manner was dour and hard and sinister, his gold teeth shining out like tusks on either side of his mouth.'

The next day, thirteen of the twenty-two Liberal MPs met at the King Eddy. The conference the day before, Massey reported to King, 'in which you helped the cause of conciliation, was very useful when it came to the question of Nelson Parliament and the issues which bear on it.' The MPs decided to employ and pay Parliament as a field organizer, but agreed that he could only operate under the direction of the OLA office. 'This attitude of co-operation with the Ontario Liberal Association office,' Massey wrote, 'represents a tremendous advance.' King was proud of his modest accomplishment and hoped, as he wrote Johnson, that 'fusion will take the place of faction in everything that pertains to the affairs of our party, both for the Dominion and the province.'[51]

Mitch had deliberately remained in St Thomas during the negotiations, but the time had come to move. On 13 November he sent a wire to all the members except Sinclair, insisting that they meet him and members of the Management Committee in his rooms at the King Edward on 16 November to discuss 'a matter of vital and immediate importance to the party.' The group agreed, however reluctantly, to accept Parliament as an official organizer for Ontario and formed an Organization Committee. Mitch was chairman,

Frank O'Connor was treasurer, Dr McQuibban represented the caucus, and Fred Sanderson and J.J. Duffus, the western and central Liberal associations. Fraser informed King that 'one very gratifying result of the Toronto meeting was the voluntary declaration on behalf of all Members that they were behind Hepburn. Individually this decision was arrived at through conviction and will be much more lasting and helpful than any previous possibility through persuasion.' Mitch was happy with the outcome, but less certain that unity had been achieved. He remained deeply suspicious of Parliament; Roebuck continued to be puzzled by 'the diffidence' of the federal Liberals in using the OLA office; and Sanderson ordered Johnson to stay out of the forthcoming federal by-election in South Oxford. But Mitch was slowly taking control of the Liberal party in Ontario.[52]

After spending a few days in Ottawa at the National Liberal Federation meeting, Mitch returned to St Thomas to carry on the campaign in East Kent. Mitch was certain he could win East Kent with the popular Liberal-Progressive farmer Douglas Campbell. The seat had been vacant since August, and Mitch and Nixon had been even exploring legal action to force Henry to call the election. Henry finally called a by-election for 3 January. But when the day came, Campbell was unopposed. East Kent, Mitch exclaimed, simply confirmed again that George Henry was afraid to face the people. Mitch relaxed at Bannockburn for another two weeks before leaving for his rooms in the King Edward to plan the 1934 campaign.

7

'Go out and slay the Assyrians'

Mitch would be thirty-eight in August 1934, and the thought must
have crossed his mind that if George Henry went to the people as
expected in June, he could be the youngest premier in Ontario's history, a few months younger than that earlier Liberal prodigy,
Edward Blake. Unquestionably the Depression had given the Liberals the opportunity, but Senator Hardy exaggerated only a little
when he said that Mitch was '98%' of the Liberal party. Mitch had
not brought the party to within sight of victory on his own, but the
party that was poised to fight the 1934 election was very much his.[1]

If victory were in sight, it was not certain. Mitch never underestimated the power of the Tory machine that Ferguson had be-
queathed to George Henry, a machine that found any distinction
between government and party naïve, if not incomprehensible. He
also realized that there were still those Liberals who found his personality and style distasteful, questioned his experience and stability, and suspected his convictions. An astute move by Henry on the
beer and wine question would test both the unity of the party and
his own leadership, while his public silence on the separate school
question could prove difficult to maintain.

The Liberal ship could also founder on rocks less obtrusive than
the province's thirst or its faiths, for not even the prospect of power
could curb Mitch's enthusiasms.Campaigning across the province
and relaxing in the King Eddy after their political ordeals, Mitch
and Arthur Slaght lived on the edge of scandal. Indeed, Harry Johnson felt compelled to tell Norman Lambert that 'if you hear anything break regarding Hepburn and women you will know it's
probably true.' The opposition hoped that Mitch's private life would
endanger his public career or, as Home Smith, a man who shared
one of his addictions, said, 'On the platform, Mitch Hepburn is

practically the whole of the Opposition forces and when he gets tight again he will probably pull off some pretty good stuff for us.' All friends and foes could do was wait.[2]

George Henry could not wait. The 1934 session would be the last before he had to appeal to the people. The Liberal strategists were determined to keep Henry on the defensive during the session, and the first step was to remove Sinclair as House leader. Informed that George McQuibban had called a meeting of the caucus for 6 January, Sinclair replied 'If there is anything to it it is being done behind my back. I have no intention of relinquishing the Opposition Leadership.' But with ten of the fourteen members present, caucus elected McQuibban, also a dry; only Sinclair voted for himself. 'I've been thrown out, that's all' an angry and humiliated Sinclair told waiting reporters. 'The trouble was that they wanted something in the nature of a hyphenated name. I have stood by the Liberal party, and in the words of the Scripture, I've fought the battle of Ephesus.' Doctrinal purity had been the foundation of Sinclair's Liberalism, but at the King Eddy meeting Mitch's Nestorian heresies had triumphed. At their first caucus the Liberals accepted Mitch's proposal to form a united opposition group in the legislature. The next session would be 'no political petting party,' McQuibban told reporters, but a 'bare knuckle fight.'[3]

To make certain the gloves were off the Liberals had established a 'brains trust' at Queen's Park to work with the caucus. Directing operations from the OLA office was the board of advisers, or the 'Brigade of Barristers,' including Slaght, Parker, Roebuck, J.C. McRuer, and Jack German, a prominent Catholic lawyer. And despite the anger of Harry Hindmarsh, the *Star*'s editor, Joe Atkinson released investigative reporter Roy Greenaway as a researcher and speech writer. With Roebuck and McRuer well-known drys, it was a little unfair of the Tories to denounce them as the 'besotted board of control of the Liberal Party.' Others referred to it as the Dirty Brigade. 'Militancy is the name with which the programme of the Hepburn party has been dignified,' snorted the *Telegram* with some justification. 'Mudslinging is the name by which it will be more readily recognized.'[4]

Liberal optimism contrasted sharply with the 'depression and apathy' Howard Ferguson had found among the Tories during a visit in the fall. Ferguson urged Henry to follow a short session with an immediate appeal to the people on the sale of beer by the glass. Stay clear of wine, he said, for the Ontario wines were undrinkable, and 'say absolutely nothing until you call an election.' Above all, he told

Conservative election cartoon, 1934,
from *The Straight Furrow*

Henry, provide 'distinctive courageous leadership, and dominate the
Government and the Party' for 'the average fellow likes to be dic-
tatcd to and controlled' and the 'only successful organizations in
the world, whether they be governments, churches or any other
type, are the ones that are controlled and directed in the last analysis by one man.' But George Henry was a conscientious Sunday
school teacher, not a pope, and his excessive caution and perverse
stubbornness dismayed his colleagues.[5]

Henry's promises in the 31 January throne speech were unexcep-
tional: tripling highway construction to relieve unemployment, mortgage relief, more aid to the municipalities, and provincial control of
milk distribution and the grading of agricultural products. Speaking with unusual vigour when he brought down his budget, Henry
spent two hours praising the Tory financial record, forecasting a surplus, and boasting of the government's success in reducing expenditures. Amid desk-thumping applause from his back-benchers, he
thrust one lean shaking finger at Harry Nixon and shouted, 'Go tell

your friend from St. Thomas the truth about this province ... Tell him to sing a song of optimism and not to spend his time going up and down the country sowing the seeds of distrust, dissension and disorder.'[6]

Tory rhetoric did not still opposition criticism. The Liberals mocked the alleged surplus and accused the government of adding millions to the debt by capitalizing relief costs. They charged that the province paid well above the market price for the $40 million bond issue in January and that friendly brokers received huge commissions and were re-selling the bonds on a rising market and making even more handsome profits. While Henry initially stated that the details would not be in the 'public interest,' the Brigade soon provided them: the bankers had set the price, a brokers' committee parcelled out the sale, the government had paid $40,000 for advice, and the bonds had sold in a few hours. Even if it was not unusual, Henry's reticence had again cast a pall of suspicion over the government's integrity.[7]

Like everyone else, Mitch was waiting for Henry to announce his policy on beer and wine. Home Smith had returned to the fold in November on Henry's promise 'to give the public, and especially the working class, or should I say the proletariat, retail sales of light alcoholic beverages' and a June election. Henry had remained silent, however. Home Smith heard that one group within the party had pressed Henry to postpone the election until September and then only to promise an amendment a year later to provide for the retail sale of beer and wine. 'If this is your final decision,' he wrote in an angry ultimatum to Henry, 'then necessarily I must quit in line with our conversation of four months ago, which I only refer to because on this point I have given hostages to fortune over the past two years and I will be no more able to hold as a contribution to party success, the groups which I have built up around me in a two year campaign having largely in view their usefulness to you at election time, and you would be the last person in the world to ask me to stultify myself.'

From Alaska to Florida, he continued, 'the so-called dry vote is dried up' and in Ontario the party's regional organizers knew that without a beer and wine bill re-election was doubtful. With the bill, the party would win fifty seats, and have a good chance of taking half the twenty or thirty doubtful ridings. Home Smith demanded that Henry amend the act and promise to proclaim it after the election. 'In other words, I suggest you deal yourself a good hand, hold it tight against your chest, and play your cards when you choose.'

Until Henry followed through on his promises, Home Smith's organization would simply 'mark time,' but once the decision was reached he would be able to tell his friends, 'Alright, full steam ahead, Go out and slay the Assyrians.'[8]

The Tory caucus met after lunch on 21 March and only a handful of Tories were in their seats when the House opened. For two hours Henry laboriously went through departmental estimates, with Attorney General Price's seat empty beside him. Finally, at 5.30 Price slipped in through a side door, opened his bulging black briefcase, exchanged a few remarks with Henry and McCrea, and at 5.45 when the House moved out of committee, asked leave of the Speaker to give first reading to an Act to Amend the Liquor Control Act. To be proclaimed after the election, the new liquor act would allow the sale of beer and wine in hotel dining-rooms, restaurants, and clubs, all carefully controlled by the Liquor Board. More important, beer could be sold in hotel refreshment rooms and veterans' and labour union clubs. The bar was out but the beer parlour was in. Dry districts would remain dry unless they chose to adopt the beer and wine system. It was a major victory for temperance, Price boasted, because it would cut down the consumption of hard liquor. It was a victory for morality because it would take booze out of hotel bedrooms. It was a major victory for the workingman, who had long begged for beer by the glass. And it would, Price and Henry told caucus, assure a victory for the Conservative party.[9]

Mitch met with the Liberal-Progressive caucus that night. The meeting was tense and stormy as the 'temperance cranks,' as Mitch described them, fought for several hours to oppose the bill. Mitch insisted on party unity and finally caucus unanimously approved a statement that 'Prohibition is not and should not be made a political partisan issue ... We are, therefore, under the circumstances, prepared to acquiesce in the measure without discussion, regarding it as a Government responsibility.' For the moment the disunity in the party had been papered over, but within days dry consciences had been pricked by the persistent lobbying of the prohibitionists and the warnings of their dry constituents. When the decisive vote came on 27 March, principle won over party and nine opposition members voted nay. Among them were six Liberals, including Bill Sinclair, William Newman, and McQuibban.[10]

Mitch was on a northern tour when the bill came to a vote. Some Liberals wanted him to return and read the bolting Liberals out of the party. Outraged at the betrayal, Mitch remained silent, however, and continued his swing through the north before returning early at King's request to assure a Liberal victory in the South Oxford by-election. For two weeks he remained close to South Oxford and refused to comment on Liberal liquor policy or the rumours that McQuibban or Sinclair would lead a dry pro-referendum wing of independent Liberals. In Toronto the bolters were in touch with the prohibitionists and waiting to see if Mitch would drive them out of the party.[11]

After celebrating the South Oxford victory at the farm, Mitch drove to Toronto on 18 April for a meeting of the Board of Strategy, OLA officials, and some of the candidates. There were no leaks and no press statements, but Mitch had clearly demanded a united front. Four days later he issued a press statement in Ottawa describing Henry's policy as 'attempted bribery' and a 'desperate and last minute attempt to becloud the more important problems confronting our people.' His stand was clear: 'I have promised to state the position of the Liberal party without equivocation. I accordingly declare that if we are elected to office in the coming election, now overdue, we shall by order in council, promptly proclaim the legislation and have the same put into effect without amendment.'

Not all Liberals agreed, but most drys agreed with Arthur Roebuck. 'Though I have always leaned against liquor, and opposed those whose talk was freedom and whose motive was money,' he wrote to W.H. Southam of the Ottawa *Citizen*, 'I am a good enough democrat to let the majority rule. There is nothing to be gained in trying to stand between people and what they want. I would rather bend than break, and I am certainly not willing to allow the Conservatives to win the rubber every time they care to pull a beer or whiskey joker off the bottom of the pack.' Poor George Henry was 'not smart enough for his role as election trickster, and apparently has got himself into a pretty mess. He has lost the Drys and not captured the Wets, and has offended all those who resent the use of such a measure for mere election trickery.' Mitch had lost nothing by playing the politics of procrastination.[12]

Despite Ferguson's advice to go to the country immediately after the session, Henry preferred a 'breathing spell.' It was not until the middle of May 1934 that he dissolved the legislature and called an election for 19 June. It was a late spring and farmer George felt that farmers might appreciate a government that gave planting priority over politics. The general economic revival across the province might also improve his chances. Sparked by a surprising consumer demand for new cars, the plants in Oshawa and Windsor were working to capacity and giving a boost to the steel industry. Led by gold, the output of the northern mines was approaching record levels. Recovery in the United States had stimulated the forest industry. By the spring of 1934, industrial employment was reaching levels not seen since 1930 and the numbers on relief were falling by three thousand a week. On the other hand, there was a growing restlessness in the ranks of labour and a wave of strikes around Windsor, in the northern work camps, and in the textile and forest industries.

Time might also give the government additional opportunities to show its concern for the unemployed. Late in the fall of 1933, Henry had grouped a number of projects together in a 'provincial recovery scheme' to employ 61,200 men at a cost of $38 million. The highway budget was tripled. And in April, Henry announced a joint federal-provincial $15 million public works and highway construction program. That same month food allowances in the work camps were increased by 25 per cent and wages from ten dollars a month to 25 cents an hour for an eight-hour day. But while many benefited from the frenzy of road-building that swept the province, those on relief were tired of the continuing indignity of either the cash or voucher system. When the Long Branch Welfare Board bought nine hundred yards of cloth to be made into dresses by good ladies of the local churches, the women for whom they were intended promised to doff their new uniforms and march naked along the lakeshore.[13]

A breathing spell might also give the vaunted Tory organization time to work its wonders. The machine had been thrown into gear in November when Earl Rowe was seconded from his seat in the Commons to organize central Ontario for a $5,000 honorarium and William Ireland and Bill Clysdale, the wily veterans of Ferguson's campaigns, were taken on strength as full-time paid organizers. The results of their labour looked promising. Home Smith reported to Henry that in November 'the general public, and many of our own stalwarts, were dubious as to the Government's chance of success.' But by March the mood was changing because of the more aggressive spirit at Queen's Park and the work of the organizers 'in approaching certain factions and ironing out troubles, and preaching success at the polls.' Home Smith himself had 'even gone the length of visiting that chamber of gloom, the Toronto Club, and other haunts frequented by capitalists of the pre-1929 vintage who are now not quite convinced that the province is going Bolshevik.' But the Tory organizer in western Ontario reported that in the country store, 'recognized as a collecting place of prevailing political sentiment,' six or seven out of ten were predicting a Liberal victory. And in towns like Chatham, where there were 2,900 on relief, the people were talking Hepburn.[14]

Henry's election manifesto was less than inspiring. Warned by one organizer that unless they endorsed unemployment insurance 'we are going to have tough sledding in the large towns and cities,' Henry obliged by promising to cooperate with Ottawa in implementing a scheme. The Tories also ran through a litany of promises to launch a massive program of northern development, reduce interest rates for agricultural loans, increase mother's allowances, reduce municipal responsibility for the King's Highways to 10 per cent, and continue their prudent financial management to 'help prime the pump of progress.' The centre piece of the Tory campaign, however, was Mitch Hepburn.

Mitch was the Liberal party, and in a calculated and sustained attack the Tories were determined to destroy him. The voters were to be persuaded that Mitch was a dangerous radical, a man who flirted with the communists and slept with the CCF. If Mitch Hepburn won, Ephraim Singer told the Todmorden Tories, we would have 'a dictatorship of some socialist administration that is anathema to us British folks.'[15]

Full page ads warned farmers to beware of the Bolshevik from Elgin:

YOU HAVE READ OF RUSSIA

You know what farming in the land of the Soviet has become. S t a t e collectivization, with industrialization the supreme goal, has made the farmer little better than the beasts of the field, the hewer of wood and the drawer of water to the more favored classes, those to whom communism looks for the ultimate success of its state industrialization experiment.

FARMERS MUST BE FREE

Ontario wants no 'swing to the left'. Its farmers must be left free …

Farmer though he is, Ontario's Liberal leader is prepared to sacrifice his own friends, to betray his fellow workers in the fields of a frantic bid for control of Ontario's vast natural wealth.

By his own confession he 'swings well to the left', towards the land where the communists, the socialists and the radicals dwell.

Tory pamphlets carried the same message. In *Communism and the C.C.F.* the Tories asked: 'Are Mr. Hepburn and Mr. Nixon not satisfied with the freedom of speech accorded to the C.C.F.? Would they have the Reds of Russia invited to our parks and regaled with cakes and coffee?' The prize went to an 18 June press release, date-lined New York and issued by the National Press Bureau, a mysterious organization with its offices in the Bank of Commerce building in Toronto: 'Sources close to Amtorg, the billion dollar corporation which represents the Red International refused today to deny or confirm reports that they made a big contribution to the campaign funds of Mitchell F. Hepburn.' Home Smith was satisfied. 'I think we have Mitch firmly nailed to the "left",' he assured Bennett two weeks before the election. 'In other words, I do not subscribe to the theory that the days of miracles are past.'[16]

The attack on Mitch was not only ideological; it was also intensely personal. For three years he had roamed the province mercilessly questioning the personal and collective integrity of his opponents. Even sympathetic journalists were offended by what one described as 'the graceless boisterousness with which he slings mud. In this pastime, his aim is good, but his mud is unnecessarily dirty and indiscriminately applied.' His enemies found stronger words and characterized Mitch and the Liberals as 'Ill-equipped, uncouth, without chivalry, honor or shame, & flagrantly untruthful and unkind & insulting, a party of which all those Liberals, whose Liberalism is not an inherited lesion of the brain are ashamed.'

His critics were just as shameful. General Williams of the Ontario provincial police had hired a Pinkerton agent to watch Mitch's movements around the King Eddy, and zealous researchers in the land registry files found that Mitch had bought more land and paid off over $10,000 in mortgages in 1933. His reply that his mother had loaned him the money from her share of Old Mitch's estate years before did not stop the insinuation that his hands were unclean. There were also rumours that Price and Arthur Ford had resurrected a man who claimed to have initiated Mitch into the Ku Klux Klan and was prepared to go public for a price. Mitch admitted that he had met the man at the Grand Central Hotel in St Thomas in 1927, but claimed that any signature on a Klan document was a forgery. The Tories let the rumours spread, but did not produce the organizer. Perhaps they felt the evidence was too weak or the price too high or, as Ed Carty said, concluded that the voters did not 'care a damn.'[17]

The most likely sources of Mitch's new-found wealth and Liberal campaign funds, the Tories implied, were the private electric utilities in the United States and Quebec. As early as 1932, Hydro chairman J.R. Cooke had asked his engineers to prepare material for a pamphlet attacking the propaganda against Hydro. The commission hired the Chicago firm of Sims & Stransky to investigate 'the connection, financial and otherwise, between the Insull controlled companies and other privately owned companies in the United States with similar units operating in Canada, to discover, if possible, a concerted attempt to secretly undermine the Government controlled Hydro Electric Power Commission of Ontario.'[18]

When Sims & Stransky found nothing, Cooke retained the Commerce Research Bureau, an industrial espionage agency with an office in Toronto. Their operator, a Mr Cathcart who seemed to be familiar with the key people in Montreal, was instructed to identify the private power interests that were undermining Hydro and determine 'whether any political contribution comes from Quebec or the United States in return for attacking Hydro by any politicians or political party.' Cathcart found nothing, and his attempt to persuade Huet Masseau, a Montreal engineer, to sell some of his technical data to the Liberals and thus create the conspiracy he was supposed to unearth, drew from Masseau the curt response that the power question was 'too important to entrust to the mouthings of politicians.'[19]

The unfortunate lack of evidence did not deter Cooke and the cabinet. On 7 June, seven thousand copies of *PAID-FOR PROPAGANDA???: Who Instigates Attacks on Hydro?* rolled off the press. Mitch was not named in the pamphlet, but he was in countless echoes from the platform. Liberal billboards should be labelled 'Beauharnois Billboards,' insisted George Henry, for 'Mr. Hepburn has been playing the game of the private power interests for years ... I'd like to know what assistance he is getting from the power barons in Montreal to carry on his election campaign.' It was a strange and unconvincing scenario from a government that had signed the lucrative contracts with the power barons.[20]

Mitch's Liberals were better prepared to fight an election than the provincial party had been since the turn of the century. His apparent reluctance to agree to a campaign organization was not the result of indecision but of astute planning. As soon as the session was over, he moved quickly and firmly to control the Liberal party. In April the OLA moved its office to the King Edward. He ordered the federal members not to enter the campaign until requested and fired Nelson Parliament. After continuing run-ins with Massey and the NLF fund-raisers, Mitch's bagmen emerged triumphant. So victorious indeed that at a high-level meeting just before the election, Norman Lambert agreed that in raising money for the next federal election the Ontario organization 'would be the same as now if Hepburn returned to power.'[21]

Harry Johnson summoned the members, candidates and key officers of the OLA to a meeting on 24 April. The campaign team that emerged was a completely new creation. Percy Parker was chairman of the overall planning committee, and Mitch's friends were in charge of the regional organizations with Arthur Slaght in command of Toronto. Jack German ran the Speaker's Committee, and with Harry Johnson planned the details of Mitch's campaign. The wealthy president of Famous Players, N.L. Nathanson, chaired the Publicity and Radio Committee and had the assistance of Duncan Marshall and J.F. Mackay, for many years the business manager and treasurer of the *Globe*. Mitch's increasingly close friend, Frank O'Connor, the wealthy owner of Laura Secord and Fanny Farmer, chaired the all-important Finance Committee. The presence of E.G. Long of Canada Trust and Albert Matthews were links with the older Bay Street federal Liberals.[22]

The list of speakers was impressive and revealed the depth and breadth of the new party. In addition to the obvious Liberals, there was old R.H. Halbert of the United Farmers and young aspiring Catholic politicians such as Paul Martin and James Day; Joseph Singer and N.C. Zimmerman (who was also a collector) spoke to their constituency, as did Dr M.V. Cosentino of Toronto and Cesare Saccaro of Windsor. Serving on Hartley McNairn's literature committee were Walter Thompson, Marshall, and Roebuck; the eminent and wealthy Catholic lawyer John Godfrey; Louis Nicolleti, president of the Toronto Italian Liberal Association; and Joseph Clarke, the director of sales at Cockfield Brown Advertising.

Mitch had complained for three years that he had no money for a secretarial staff and little for travel, despite the occasional assistance of Hardy and Parker. By the fall of 1933 collectors were at work, and cheques for a few hundred dollars were dribbling in to the King Street office. But it was not until late in the campaign that there were obvious signs of greater affluence. In September 1933 Johnson reminded Parker that 'Plans should be made to handle the moderation league and the 2,000 hotel keepers of the province. As you know Slaght is a man who seems to have been prepared for the purpose.' Mitch told Ed Carty early in the year that 'the head man of the brewers in Ontario told him that the Tories can "go to hell this time" as the brewers will not put up any money for them' and, despite Home Smith, Mitch may have profited from his peace with the devil.[23]

A number of the prominent Liberals certainly did have close connections with the beer and liquor interests. D.J. McDougald, a prominent Roman Catholic layman and investment dealer, who was making small contributions by the end of 1933, was a vice-president of E.P. Taylor's newly formed Canadian Brewing Corporation. Long and Matthews were directors of Canada Malting and Salter Hayden of Atlantic Sugar. There were other networks as well. Jack Bickell, a broker who made a fortune with the McIntyre Porcupine mine, was vice-president of Nathanson's Famous Players and Alf Rogers of Elias Rogers was a director. Bickell, Rogers, Parker, and Frank O'Connor were also officers and directors of Maple Leaf Gardens. The Liberals also had strong links with the northern gold mining interests. Among his many interests, Percy Parker was an officer of the Mining Corporation of Canada, as was George McCullagh, a young broker. Slaght, Dan Lang, and Jack German also had gold mining interests. R.B. Bennett's 1934 budget certainly encouraged the gold miners to support Mitch when he increased taxes to capture some of the profits as gold soared to $35 an ounce. Although Bennett backed down a little, the miners had good reason to believe that Mitch and the Liberals would treat them more kindly.[24]

Yet the money was slow to come in, and the central office could not meet the incessant demands from ridings across the province. At one point a desperate O'Connor apparently offered to match any contribution. However, by the end of the campaign and with victory in sight, if not certain, O'Connor and his committee seemed to have found 'the necessary.'

The 24 April meeting of the OLA also discussed a party platform. Since 1931 a committee under Roebuck and Colonel A.T. Hunter had been working fitfully on an industrial labour code, and early in March, with the revelations before the Stevens Commission of sweat-shop conditions in Canadian factories, it had seemed timely for the Liberals to steal a march on the Tories. In a statement that was pure Roebuck, Mitch promised to stamp out child labour, improve working conditions for men and women, and police the legislation. 'We are not high-handed and are more inclined to lead than to compel,' he stated, 'but we do not shrink from compulsion when necessary.'[25] Nothing was decided at the 24 April meeting, and Mitch later asked Roebuck to draft a manifesto which, after some reworking, Mitch released to the press on 27 May. As Roebuck had promised, it was a platform which would restore prosperity and make everybody happy, and only Tories or cynics, who looked for means as well as unassailable ends, could take exception to it. It promised cuts in government expenditure without loss of service, a balanced budget and reduction of debt, loyalty to public ownership and lower hydro rates, northern development and marketing assistance for the farmer, increased employment and unemployment insurance, educational reform and improved social services, freedom of speech and the right of assembly, and, above all, honest and progressive government.[76]

Mitch did little to flesh out the platform during the campaign. But there were specific promises that appealed to rural voters. Gasoline taxes would be cut from six to two cents a gallon with the tax and licence fees used to build roads. The 'fossilized' Department of Education would be removed from the grasp of the Toronto bureaucracy and a program of rural education implemented to meet rural needs. Aspiring teachers applauded his promise to abolish the second year of normal school, parents welcomed the end of examination fees, and hard-pressed school boards and municipalities found the prospects of increased grants alluring. Mitch knew his rural audience.

He knew also that rural and city audiences were receptive to his attack on the mismanagement, the inhumanity, the political nepotism, and the corruption of the Tories. Voters without $25 in the bank found it hard to believe that George Henry could forget $25,000 in bonds. Although Harry Price denied he had ever made representations to the Liquor Board, Mitch wondered why his brother had secured the agency for Teachers Highland Cream three days after Harry Price won York West or whether mines minister McCrea was the only cabinet minister to secure a liquor listing for a Tory friend.[27]

But it was less the substance of Mitch's speeches that drew the crowds than the occasion. Every candidate, except the few dry Liberals, demanded that Mitch visit the riding. For three months he obliged, often making four or five speeches a day. He kept his speeches short, never longer than an hour and often a punchy fifteen minutes. Usually travelling by car, with his friend George Ponsford at the wheel and a bar in the back, Mitch hit not only the cities but the small towns and villages and even made whistle stops at country stores. He used the local radio stations whenever possible, dropping in late at night for some local coverage or a province-wide hook-up arranged by the Toronto office. Mitch cultivated the local press as well, never too busy to drop into the office for a chat and say 'Johnny, here are my notes, can you give me a little story on it.' When there was time he drank into the evening with his friends. Not everyone was a friend, however, and so bitter was some of the opposition he encountered that Mitch always carried a revolver in the glove compartment.[28]

Mitch maintained an incredible pace throughout the campaign. In his last northern trip with Peter Heenan late in May, he spoke in Kapuskasing, Smooth Rock Falls, and Cochrane for Joe Habel and was in Cobalt and North Bay the next day. A day later he spoke twice in Sault St Marie and left early in the morning for performances at Thessalon, Blind River, and Espanola in Algoma-Manitoulin. After a day around Sudbury with Eddy LaPierre, he stopped in Sundridge and Huntsville en route to Toronto. In seven days Mitch had travelled over sixteen hundred miles on dirt and gravel roads, made about twenty speeches, and visited ten ridings.

His friends worried about his health. Hardy noted that his 'nerves were not exactly calm' and urged him to let up. Assuring Mitch that 'you are continuously in my thoughts,' King lectured him that if 'you become over-weary and over-strained you do not know into what unforeseen pit you may be brought by some wholly unpremeditated utterance or unintended remark.' King's medicine was an hour or two rest before a meeting, every Sunday free for reflection and rest, and no social obligations. 'Please stick this letter in your pocket and take it out and read it whenever you feel tempted to yield to the demands of others,' he wrote. 'After you have taken the dose six times, it may be repeated at longer intervals.' Mitch would have preferred that King offer some more tangible assistance.[29]

Mitch knew that elections were won neither by prayers nor secular speeches, and that the result on 19 June would very much depend on the effectiveness of ninety local organizations. His punishing forays into every corner of the province over three years and his infectious enthusiasm had done much to bring the moribund party to life. By the spring of 1934 many organizers across the province echoed the assurance from Hastings West that Belleville was no longer a Tory city, for the Liberals had 'the finest machine this city & district has ever had.' The Grits had moved into the parlours and kitchens, the intimate meetings 'reminding one of the old-fashioned Methodist class meetings, where all were asked to bear witness, and an opportunity given to all to take part. Conservatives from all walks of life are flocking to our colours, which could not have been reached otherwise.'[30]

The cities had never been kind to the Liberals. Toronto, with one-sixth of the seats at Queen's Park, had been a solid Tory bastion. Yet even in Toronto there were promising signs that Hepburn's enthusiasm was catching among the young and affluent, and the remarkable spread of the Twentieth Century Clubs throughout the city provided an energetic corps of volunteers. Liberal strategists realized that victory lay in increasing the notoriously low turnout in the cities, and gaining support in the traditionally Tory working-class areas and among the ethnic voters. There were over one hundred thousand members of ethnic communities in Toronto, most of whom lived between the lakeshore and Bloor Street, who could be a decisive factor in the eight ridings from High Park to the Don Valley. Harry Johnson ran large newspaper ads emphasizing the importance of registration and offering assistance. Local organizations canvassed the ethnic voter as never before. The Franceschini brothers of Dufferin Paving entertained thousands of Italians in lineups twenty-five yards long for Tory beer. But the Liberals also had Italian workers in the party. Cesare Saccaro was released by a Windsor contracting firm to get out the Italian vote in Guelph, Windsor, and the Niagara peninsula.[31]

Arthur Roebuck set an example in Bellwoods where there were between five and ten thousand Jews, several thousand Italians, and most of Toronto's thousand strong Black community. Roebuck enlisted ethnic workers, printed posters in Italian and Polish, advertised in the ethnic press, and made a direct appeal for ethnic support in his attacks on section 98 and Bennett's closed-door immigration policy. The sedate and austere fifty-six-year-old in his wing collar even attended the annual Coloured People's Dance and danced with 'the dusky maidens until about 1 o'clock in the morning,' he boasted to a friend 'and take it from me, they can dance.'[32]

Mitch knew that the local organizations were critical because it was on the ground that the party felt the enormous pressure of the Tory machine, the divisive effects of the beer and wine issue, the whispering campaign about Catholic schools, and the thinly veiled innuendoes about life in the fast lane at the King Eddy. A flood of orders-in-council in the months before the election sent hundreds of reinforcements to the local Tory machines across the province disguised as OPP constables, driving examiners, apiary inspectors, dairy instructors, relief officers, game and fisheries overseers, and the additional salesmen the liquor stores needed to handle the increased demand in June and July. But patronage proved to be a two-edged sword. Mitch's promise that all Tory workers and everyone appointed after 1 November would be fired did dampen enthusiasm in the field. Leslie Frost, the Tory hopeful in Victoria, lamented that many of his staunchest supporters were on the government payroll and unable to work in the election. But they had not felt constrained before. Bill Clysdale complained that Mitch was unscrupulous in threatening to dismiss Tory workers and offering appropriate rewards to deserving Grits, or even to converted Tories. Times certainly had changed.[33]

But the thousands of men temporarily put to work on the roads could not be threatened, and the Liberals counted every man with a shovel as a Tory vote. 'Promises are being made all over Northumberland in regards to money and hundreds of men have been put to work this last couple of weeks – in fact they have started two new highways,' Bill Fraser reported to Mitch. 'Number two Provincial Highway is covered with men from Port Hope East and Tory canvassers are going all over the Riding picking up every man they can.' Lucette Valin and Odette Lapointe drove along Number 2 on their way to Toronto to broadcast an appeal to women and francophones. Windows down, they assaulted each contingent of Tory workers with shouts of 'Vote for Mitch' and a blown kiss.[34]

But kisses and threats were no match for money. Bill Fraser estimated that it would take between $8,000 and $9,000 'to offset the Tory crowd' in the swing riding of Northumberland. 'Without a doubt the last three weeks of this campaign, particularly the last one, as far as the Tories are concerned, is going to be hell,' he wrote Mitch asking for $5,000 from the pot. 'These birds are fighting with their back to the wall and money is not going to be an object to them.' Fraser had to pay one local celebrity $500 as an organizer to support the Liberals openly. Four other organizers worked for the customary $5 a day. Hundreds of canvassers, scrutineers, drivers, and countless 'volunteers' asked the market price. In Leeds young George Fulford was spending $18,000 of a family fortune made peddling the famous 'Pink Pills for Pale People' in an attempt to bring the riding into the Liberal camp for the first time since confederation. Like so many other ridings, Leeds had dry polls where the workers had to be paid and others where the wet volunteers had an insatiable and equally expensive thirst. As one Tory organizer admitted, 'You get ten or twelve fellows together to see what can be done and they can't be sitting around and die of South African thirst all the time, they have got to have something.'[35]

Grits and Tories alike faced a new problem in trying to capture the vote of the thirty to forty thousand men in the provincial and National Defence work camps that dotted the roads from the Manitoba border to the Ottawa River. The tactic in the lumber camps was to get a canvasser into the camp a few days before polling with an ample supply of booze, or to provide the camp clerk, who was usually the returning officer, with the proper inducements to tell the boys how to vote. Government-appointed foremen in the road camps may have been less open to Grit inducements, but the game was much the same. The situation in the Hastings and Addington camps was 'nasty,' Bill Fraser told Mitch, but after an evening spent with one of the officials he felt that the votes could be lined up 'providing, of course, we get the necessary.' Tory organizers seemed particularly concerned about the five thousand men in the DND camps, and asked Bennett to move them out of the province. The prime minister replied that, despite his warnings, Price had foolishly provided that thirty days residence entitled the men to vote, and there was little he could do. But Henry persisted, and in the last ten days of the campaign Bennett promised 'to do some shifting that will relieve the situation.'[36]

As Mitch and the local organizations assiduously worked to keep the Liberal-Progressive alliance in place and prevent the dry faction from running independent candidates, the Tories equally zealously encouraged dissident Liberals to run by publicly chiding the drys and secretly offering financial support in a desperate effort to split the anti-government vote. Late in April Clysdale listed fifty ridings outside Toronto where Tory organizers felt that a third candidate was critical. Home Smith advised Henry that 'I am strongly of the opinion that either a dry Liberal or a C.C.F. in any constituency will draw his votes exclusively from those who in a straight fight would vote Liberal.' Three weeks before the election, Clysdale reported that the Liberals were 'moving heaven and earth to get these candidates out of the field' and asked for sufficient financial support to keep them in the race. In the end, however, only a dozen independent Liberals, farmers, and drys ran.[37]

Far more serious was the danger from the CCF. The ardour with which the United Farmers had embraced the CCF had cooled as the party seemed unable to control the communists within the affiliated Labour Conference. Philpott and Macphail had decided that unless they could 'establish an absolute dictatorship within the Ontario CCF and eradicate the communist and anti-Christian element,' they would resign and run as independents. When the inevitable crisis arose in January, with the arrest and indictment of the Reverend A.E. Smith on charges of sedition, the communists were expelled, but not before a special UFO committee severed the connection with the CCF. UFO riding associations were free to nominate their own candidates or to support independents or the CCF, but were advised that since the Progressives had merged 'their identity and independence' with the Liberals they had moved beyond the pale. The CCF contested few rural ridings, but in Peel, Halton, Oxford, and Durham the UFO support for the CCF candidates threatened to affect the outcome.[38]

Mitch was more concerned about the CCF threat in the cities, where the Liberals hoped for the first time to attract working-class support. Any hope of fashioning a working alliance was dashed on 22 May when Graham Spry released the CCF platform and emphatically denied Liberal reports of an electoral bargain. The platform was to the left of the Liberals: minimum wages for all workers and unemployment insurance; public medical and hospital services and improved old age pensions; lower interest rates and sharply progressive taxation; the socialization of hydro services and government control of the distribution of bread, milk, meat, and fuel; and the promise of a referendum on beer and wine. Initially the CCF planned to concentrate on a handful of promising urban seats but in the last three weeks they decided to contest as many as possible. There was no provincial organization, however, and the CCF was very much a platform without a party.[39]

Mitch sympathized with many of the CCF objectives and pleaded in vain for local candidates to withdraw. The Tories meanwhile encouraged the CCF to remain in the race. The CCF executive stated that both parties 'made approaches to the C.C.F. during the election campaign, either offering seats, saw-offs, or contributions to the funds' but all offers were rejected. The 'spark plug of the C.C.F. effort in Ontario,' according to one prominent Tory organizer, was Frank Regan, a good friend of Colonel Price and a 'great admirer' of R.B. Bennett. A Catholic lawyer, Regan ran against Patrick Donnelly in St David's riding and orchestrated much of the campaign in Toronto. The Liberals had good reason to believe that Tory money helped finance the CCF campaign.[40]

The Liberals were not above unethical behaviour in their attempt to counter the CCF appeal. Around the beginning of June, a Liberal organizer asked Hyland, the owner-editor of *The Commonwealth*, described as 'A Weekly Review in the Interests of the Co-operative Commonwealth For Canadian People,' to throw his paper behind the Liberals. He assured Hyland that Mitch's office had agreed that any income lost from losing CCF accounts would be covered. *The Commonwealth* of 11 June argued that 'blind allegiance to our own candidates' would simply serve the purpose of the 'Tory manipulators' and suggested that rather than vote against Mitch the party should conserve its strength 'for the larger accomplishment – the defeat of the arch-enemies of the C.C.F., the capitalistic Ottawa bosses.' Mitch and other Liberals waved *The Commonwealth* from platforms across the province, urging CCF sympathizers to follow the logic of the 'party' organ. An outraged Leo Macaulay, suspecting that a strong CCF vote was his only guarantee of victory, exclaimed that the campaign had reached its lowest point 'when the Liberals forged a document with the CCF signature in a last desperate bid for power.' Rather than listen to *The Commonwealth*, he said, the voters of York South should listen to Dr Teskey, the CCF candidate.[41]

Mitch returned from the north on 2 June for his last swing through eastern Ontario. His good friend Jean-François Pouliot, the MP from Rivière du Loup, was at his side, as he was later in the Essex ridings, to assure the Franco-Ontarians that Mitch had 'l'étoffe d'un homme d'Etat' and was a true friend of the French Canadians. He reached Ottawa on 7 June and took an hour to clean out his desk in the Commons and officially submit his resignation. Senator Spence and other federal Liberals had planned a luncheon at the Chateau for 'Our Leaders,' at which Mackenzie King could be given the opportunity to put the lie publicly to Tory (and some Liberal) charges that he was not supporting Mitch Hepburn. Although King had helped to ease the friction between the federal and provincial Liberals in October, he had consistently refused to offer anything but advice to Mitch in the campaign.

The prospect of the luncheon troubled King because he was still not reconciled to Mitch's success. Following his two appearances on the platform with him in the South Oxford by-election, King had grudgingly admitted that Mitch 'spoke well, telling some amusing stories' but added that 'he is a lightweight for a prime minister of a province like Ontario, – though he cultivates a good many of the young people and has a certain amount of real personality and charm – but lacks experience and knowledge and to some extent character enough. I doubt if he will be elected, though he will make a good run, he has great courage and is not afraid to risk much and to step into the breech.'

When the fateful day arrived, however, King somehow found the guile to say that 'anyone who knows me knows that Mr. Hepburn has not a more enthusiastic supporter than I ... and I want to do all in my power to return to the seat of government my young friend Hepburn because of himself and because of the good government he would give the people ... It is perfectly marvelous the acumen, sagacity and wisdom he has shown.' Mitch did not dally around Ottawa to see what practical support King might offer. After talking to Paul Leduc and seeing Lucette Valin, he campaigned in Renfrew for loyalist Tom Murray. After strategy sessions in Toronto and speeches in Peel and Halton, where he appealed again for the CCF to withdraw from their futile contests, he went home for the weekend.[42]

The rains in southern Ontario that weekend ended one of the longest dry spells on record and Mitch campaigned at home in a constant downpour. He had not spent much time in Elgin, despite the Tory gerrymander. Home Smith had wanted to keep Mitch at home, and reminded Henry that the 'Doctor has the east end in good shape, and we might have our friend Mitch at home during the last week or ten days trying to save his own position and confining his slanders to his own constituency. I think it is of the utmost importance that we crowd him.' The good doctor was Herbert J. Davis. A veterinary surgeon from Aylmer who had won East Elgin in 1929, Davis was assisted by a procession of prominent Tories. According to the Liberals he had been given $40,000 to persuade the hesitant.

Mitch and Davis appeared on the platform of the Masonic Hall for a tumultuous nomination meeting on 12 June. From the outset both candidates were heckled, booed, and cheered. Davis raised the familiar charges of Mitch's new wealth, of Liberal hypocrisy on beer and wine, of false promises during the 1930 federal election. Mitch ran through the litany of Tory sins, including the famous incident a few weeks before in which Liberals hiding in a goat pen swore they heard (and captured) a Tory agent offering Wilbert Fisher, a Lynhurst farmer, a job in the brewers warehouse if he would make charges questioning Hepburn's integrity. The meeting finally disintegrated. Mitch yelled angrily over the din that 'all you people who are booing are paying the shot for all the extravagance at Toronto but you're too ignorant to know it.' Pale with fear and anger, Davis retreated to the rear of the platform as an angry Liberal raced from the crowd shaking his fist and screaming that the Tories were 'a bunch of damned crooks and liars.'[43]

The Catholic School question finally erupted while Mitch was ending his campaign in a strenuous assault on western Ontario. Near the end of the session Henry had announced that the question would again be referred to the courts, but refused to say what the question would be. The Orange Order immediately swung into action and demanded that all candidates oppose any support for the separate schools or 'further concessions' for French-language instruction and insist on 'only one national, public, non-sectarian school system in Ontario.' Henry's statement pushed the Catholics towards intervention in the election. Archbishop O'Brien of Kingston, the most truculent member of the hierarchy and the one closest to Quinn, wrote at once to the ailing Archbishop McNeil of Toronto, that the bishops should meet as soon as possible and decide on their course of action in the closest cooperation with the Catholic Taxpayers' Association. 'While I think there is need of extreme caution and prudence, I feel that we have been given a slap in the face by the Premier,' he wrote. 'If we must take it, well and good; but I don't think we ought to take it lying down.' Most bishops agreed. Others, particularly Bishop J.T. McNally of Hamilton, distrusted Quinn and wanted the hierarchy to remain in control. While the bishops ruminated, even Quinn realized that, although the organization of every parish and every religious institution was being perfected, much was to be gained by patience. He was convinced that if Mitch won there would be 'an immediate ending of "side-stepping and shadow-boxing",' but like many Catholics he was afraid that 'by some untoward action ... we may antagonize the moderate Protestant voter, and give Henry the opportunity to set himself up as the defender of public schools.'

By the end of April, however, the course had been set and the hierarchy had approved a letter throwing the church into the election. On 29 May, with Henry still promising to make the questions public and begging him not to inject a religious issue into the election, Quinn sent the secular and ecclesiastical *mandement* to the parish chairmen. The Henry government had '*treated us with a degree of discourtesy amounting to absolute contempt,*' wrote Quinn, and the time had come to live up to their threat that unless justice were done they would '*elect another government to power* at the first opportunity.'[44]

Although the Conservatives were aware of the increased Catholic activity, they too played a waiting game. Home Smith informed Bennett a week before the election that the 'attitude of the Church is, of course, the stickler! I think they are bluffing and trying to get our fellows into a panic. However, I think I have it fixed up that we will sit absolutely tight until next Wednesday or Thursday [13–14 June]. The Church can either have peace or war and, if the latter, they cannot see the end of it and must swing to the left with Mitch. I do not believe they have the stomach to face such an eventuality. The Grits get 90% of the Catholic vote and we get 90%, or over, of the Orange vote!'

On 13 June the *Evening Telegram* published Quinn's letter under the headline 'Swinging The Big Stick To Destroy Free Elections' and demanded to know what promises Hepburn had made. Believing that they had an issue, as Henry said, that 'will likely consolidate our forces behind us in a more definite way than could otherwise have happened,' the Tories ran large ads over Henry's signature on 15 June.

AT THE LAST MOMENT, a shameless attempt is being made to capitalize to the advantage of the Hepburn opposition the organization of the Catholic Ratepayers Association of Ontario.

I am going to win this election; and win handsomely; and Mr. Hepburn will never have the opportunity of implementing the many secret pledges he has given to bolster up his campaign during which every one of his alleged issues has gone bankrupt.

Whatever secret pledges Mr. Hepburn has given on School taxation are, however, of no importance, as good Canadians will never embitter our situation with a religious controversy and, by their division, enable him and his discredited minority to play with our destinies in business, in religion, and in morals, by allowing him to swing us 'well to the left, where many Grits fear to tread!'

If we swing 'well to the left', we will land in the ditch in which Russia and other European countries now wallow, with state seizure of all Church properties, Catholic and Protestant alike, and the final suppression of all religious training in either school, home, church or elsewhere!

I stand for a policy of 'Straight Ahead!' and of holding tenaciously our standard of morals and our religious beliefs and practices on the solid rock of civilization, order, and fair play, guaranteed under the British Constitution and Parliamentary democracy![45]

Mitch was in Windsor that night, speaking to an exuberant crowd of ten thousand, and drove to Toronto early the next morning. The cheering crowds were three and four deep as his long cavalcade moved along the Danforth from the Bloor viaduct to Pape and south to Withrow Park for a monster picnic. Then it was a procession north through the city to Barker Field on Dufferin for another huge rally. That night Massey Hall and Hygeia Hall were jammed hours before the doors opened for the last Liberal rally of the election, and thousands listened to the broadcast on the streets. The crowd rose to give Mitch a tumultuous ten-minute ovation as he followed a piper down the aisle. Although visibly fatigued, his voice hoarse and raspy, he gave the partisan audience what it wanted.

The crowd roared with approval when Mitch accused the Tories of fanning the embers of religious strife, a plan deliberately 'concocted in the offices of the pink Tely – though I should say the yellow *Telegram*.' He recalled that he had driven a rig for Laurier in 1911, and like Laurier deplored the attempt to make religion a political issue. 'Our Catholic friends have never approached me in regard to the separate school question,' he declared without a twitch, and when they 'do they will receive every consideration a minority should get.' Promising to follow in the footsteps of Blake, Mowat and Hardy, Mitch admitted that 'I have a lot to learn but I am still in the student age and I thank God for it. I always will be. I honestly and sincerely believe I will be able to do something constructive, something worthwhile, with the aid of capable men who will surround me. This is my objective.' The deafening and sustained applause, the spontaneous cheers on the streets outside, the countless hands that stretched out to greet him as he left, convinced Mitch that the Tory bastion was not impregnable.[50]

After spending Sunday with his friends in Toronto, Mitch left for home early Monday morning with Arthur Slaght beside him. At Aylmer a mile-long cavalcade of cars and trucks met him for the ten-mile procession to St Thomas. Crowds lined the length of Talbot Street. There were bands and banners from all over southwestern Ontario. Even a thunderstorm did not dampen the enthusiasm. That night Mitch spoke to the largest crowd ever assembled in St Thomas and over the radio to the province. Not until four young men held him aloft did the massive chorus chanting 'We Want Mitch' quieten so he could speak. It was the time to talk to Elgin, to chastise the *Times-Journal* and London *Free Press* for their Tory politics, to thank all the workers who would keep Elgin Liberal, and above all Eva who has 'stood by me bravely and nobly like a little soldier.' As Mitch was carried from the rink, a burly Italian said to Ed Carty 'I kill myself if Mitch asked me.'[47]

Later that night Prime Minister Bennett, who had sent his ministers into the fray, made a radio appeal to the province to defeat Mitchell Hepburn, a dangerous and reckless radical whose campaign had been nothing more than an attempt 'to raise in the minds of those less fortunate than some of us that feeling of animosity, of envy, of a desire to destroy.' Back at the farm, Mitch switched off the radio and said with a smile that the voters 'will plough a straight furrow to-morrow and it will be long enough and big enough to bury Mr. Bennett and his entire cabinet.'[48]

The heavy rains ended during the night, and across most of the province the polls opened at nine under a brilliant sun. Except for the drizzle in the Ottawa valley there was nothing to keep the voters at home, and with the land too wet to work the farmers could make a day of the election. There were lineups at many polls before they opened, and there was little doubt that 19 June would see a record vote in Ontario. Over 2,100,000 voters had registered, 300,000 more than in 1929.

Although the Conservatives were on the defensive, most organizers agreed with Earl Lawson that 'subject to a landslide (of which I can see no evidence) we are going to win in the province of Ontario. The majority in my opinion will be anywhere from six or seven up, not down.' The danger of a landslide was there, however, after four years of depression, the ineptitude of 'George the maladroit,' and the appeals from so many pulpits the Sunday before the election.[49]

As the day passed the young men and women of the 175 Twentieth Century Clubs worked feverishly to poll the Liberal vote, and the apparent increase in the number of young voters was a good omen. In Toronto, where only about 40 per cent ever bothered to vote, there seemed to be twice as many voters as before. Liberal organizers received similar reports of near record turnouts from Windsor and Hamilton, the Niagara peninsula, Galt and Chatham, and across the north. St Thomas was certainly no exception, and when the polls closed over 98 per cent had cast their ballots. Even the rural ridings, where turnout was traditionally high, reported much more interest than usual. All Mitch could do as he lingered around the farm during the long day was to hope that there were many Tories like George Hardy of Grand Valley who had told him that 'in spite of the "straight furrow" which is crooked, in spite of Hell, I have decided that the time has come for a change and the first time I have done so in my life I shall on June 19 vote for a Liberal candidate.'[50]

At eight o'clock when the polls closed, Mitch and his friends gathered in the small upstairs kitchen in the Masonic Temple, where Mitch had installed a telegraph key and operator. 'I was just thinking,' said George Ponsford as he surveyed the dingy surroundings, 'what a strange place it is to become premier of Ontario – the back kitchen of a Masonic Temple.' Within minutes the advance poll in St Thomas gave Mitch 411 votes to Dr Davis's 221, and at 8:10 Davis conceded. 'Elgin is mine,' exclaimed Mitch. 'Now for the province.'

Before Harry Johnson and others arrived from Toronto shortly after nine it seemed that the province too would be his. The Liberals were leading in thirty-three seats, the Conservatives in thirteen, and the CCF in two. The north was going massively Liberal. As the early returns came in from Sudbury and the surrounding mining towns, there was almost disbelief as even Charles McCrea, who had not faced an opponent since 1923, was suffering a humiliating defeat at the hands of Eddie Lapierre. In Renfrew the returns from some polls suggested that only the road foremen and their close relatives had voted against Tom Murray. Returns from across the province indicated that French-speaking and Roman Catholic Ontario were going solidly Liberal. David Croll and the three other Liberals were piling up impressive majorities in Windsor and Essex. The traditional Grit ridings were holding firm. Along Lake Erie and the Niagara peninsula the early returns left little doubt about the ultimate victors. And with John Glass, Harold Kirby, and Arthur Roebuck running well ahead, Tory Toronto was no more.

At 10:20 the Canadian Press declared a Hepburn victory. Mitch leaped up and hugged Arthur Slaght. There was pandemonium along Talbot Street. When the news flashed on the screen outside the *Star* and *Mail and Empire* buildings in Toronto, there were enormous cheers from the twenty thousand people who had closed King Street. For the next three hours, as the Liberal victories swept on, the downtown crowds grew larger and more exuberant. There had been nothing like it in Toronto since the armistice. Across the province triumphant Liberals lit up the night with long torchlight processions and noisy motor cavalcades. In Ottawa East a crowd of thousands carried Paul Leduc, with Lucette Valin at his side, through Lower Town to the cries of 'Vive Leduc' and the refrain 'Il a gagné ses epaulettes.'

Shortly after victory seemed assured, Mitch and Slaght mounted the platform in the hall to speak to the crowd inside. In Toronto the engineers of the *Star*'s CKCL, CFRB and Bell Telephone had quickly established a line to the Masonic Hall and Mitch's speech went out over the radio and through the loud speakers to the throng on King Street. It was the time for gratitude and modesty, to thank Harry Johnson and the organizations, Eva and his Elgin workers, the Liberals who had faith in him, and the Conservatives and labour supporters who had voted for him. 'I don't believe any political leader in the province has been so subjected to such a campaign of belittlement and vilification,' he observed, 'but to-day my traducers are no more.' Ontario now had a government that would live up to its promises and a premier who would make the province a better place in which to live. Arthur Slaght had less need to be modest. After the great victories in Ontario and Saskatchewan, where Jimmy Gardiner's Liberals had also won that day, he exclaimed, the Liberal battle cry 'is on to Ottawa.'

Mackenzie King was on the line soon after Mitch returned to the kitchen. It was not an easy call for King to make, for he had not expected Mitch to win. The night before the election, Laurier had appeared in a vision to tell King that Mitch would lose, not only Ontario but also Elgin. The prophecy helped to explain the strange telegram Mitch had received from King that morning. 'You have fought a good fight and the real victory is already yours, come what may. In following you, I have been living over again some of my former campaigns. You will discover many parallels along the way and will live to see many more.' Mitch could not have guessed that the parallel was the 1925 election when King had lost his North York seat and the Liberals the election. King had listened to the early returns in his House of Commons office, 'really more anxious (at heart) to have the prophecy fulfilled, that my faith might not suffer a shock, than I was to see a great Liberal victory in both elections.'

More 'upset' than 'elated' King went down to an almost deserted House. Most of the members were listening to the radio in the Liberal caucus room and others were parading up and down the corridors behind Tommy Reid, the piper MP from New Westminster, and frequently bursting noisily through the curtains to pass on the latest upset from Ontario or the west. When Bennett finally gave up and adjourned the House an hour early, King joined the Liberals in a long procession behind Reid which wound up in the Rotunda where he proposed three cheers for Mitch and Jimmy Gardiner. The members added one for King. Back in his office King had phoned Mitch at the Masonic Temple. A simple press release took him over an hour to write, and it was days before he could find a satisfactory reason why Laurier should have misled him.

By the time King called, the last results were in and the awesome dimensions of the Liberal victory were confirmed. George Henry had been re-elected, as had most of the Tories in Toronto and York, largely because the CCF had polled 23 per cent of the vote in the eight Toronto ridings in which they ran and over 19 per cent in the three urbanized York ridings. Parkdale had swung back and forth all night and not until the last few polls were in, with the CCF polling about 4,000 votes, had William Price scraped through with a margin of 212 votes. In Bracondale, High Park, Dovercourt, and York South it was late in the evening before it was clear that the large CCF vote had enabled the Conservatives to eke out slim pluralities. Two of the last to be decided were Hamilton Wentworth and East Hastings, neither of which the Liberals expected to win. In Hamilton it was not until the last rural votes were counted that a Liberal farmer moved 120 votes ahead of his Tory rival. The night of miracles, it seemed, was not over. The Liberals, who had won Leeds for the first time in history and Hastings West for the first time in the century, were even leading in Hastings East until early in the morning when the last northern polls reported.

Mitch had promised he would win sixty-seven seats. Harry Johnson's scoreboard showed that Mitch and his allies had won just over half the popular vote and seventy-one of the ninety seats. And Mitch could expect the sympathy if not always the support of the lone CCF and UFO members whom he had not opposed. George Henry was left with a pitiful rump of seventeen. It was not the biggest landslide in the history of the province, but it was by far the greatest victory Ontario Grits had ever witnessed – or even dreamed of.

With the victory confirmed, it was time to answer the deafening cries of 'We Want Mitch.' Perched on a bench in the back of a large truck, with Eva beside him, Mitch drove behind the Legion Band at the head of a parade two miles long across town and back as twenty to thirty thousand people lined the streets or waved from lighted doorways and second-storey windows. Hands clasped over his head, Mitch acknowledged the cheers and the chant that had changed to 'We've Got Mitch,' waving to friends and leaping from the truck on Talbot Street to embrace Margaret McCallum who said that voting for Mitch was the best work she had done in her 102 years.

It was well after midnight when he returned. A searchlight from the balcony of the Capital Theatre across the street caught him as he emerged to stand precariously on the sill of an open second-floor window. As the crowd repeatedly roared its approbation, Mitch said 'I'm going down to Toronto shortly to form my cabinet ... I want to give you honest and efficient administration ... I want to improve the social happiness of the people.' As for the Tories and their hangers-on, 'They'd better start packing their bags. I'm going to smash that expensive Tory machine when I get down to Toronto so that when the Angel Gabriel blows his horn you'll not be able to find a piece of it.' The farm was ablaze all night, and the sun was up when the last of the well-wishers left and Mitch went upstairs to bed.[51]

'The terrible descent
from Mowat and Blake'

The farm hands had been haying for hours in the big fields south of the house when Mitch came downstairs to hold court in the spacious house on Fruit Ridge Road, soon to be named Bannockburn after the site where Robert the Bruce had defeated the English and seized the Scottish throne. For three days Mitch received supplicants, chatted with well-wishers, and provided good copy for the dozen journalists who hung around the front porch. He then set out on a triumphant tour across the province to Ottawa. Lunching with McQuesten in Hamilton, he invited him to join the cabinet as minister of public works and highways, a position for which he was suited by interest and where his partisan Liberalism would be as essential as his unquestioned integrity.

In Toronto there was little time to chat with the Liberals who jammed the lobby of the King Eddy. After a brief visit to the OLA offices, Mitch joined 'Doc' McCarthy, the genial hotel manager, to look at the large, two-bedroom corner suite with the sitting-room in pale green, which was to be his home for much of the next decade. After a few drinks with the boys, he waved his way through the crowd that milled around the big car George Ponsford had waiting for him. Coly Campbell and Alexandrine Gibb, assistant sports editor and feature writer for the Toronto *Star* who had been with Mitch since election day, waited in the back seat. As they drove along Highway 2, Mitch confessed to Alex that he knew many people wondered whether 'this farmer' could keep his feet on the ground, while the sceptics had written off his campaign as 'just talk, not promises.' But Mitch assured her he was determined not to let success go to his head and would prove that the campaign was not opportunistic rhetoric.

By Sunday noon he was in Brockville, the guest of Senator Hardy and his brother-in-law, George Fulford. Mitch liked the genial Fulford and was deeply indebted to Arthur Hardy, and offered Fulford a seat in the cabinet. At nine he was at the station when the Ottawa-Toronto train arrived, and Peter Heenan and Senator McGuire came to the car for a quick chat. It was long after midnight when Mitch swept through the crowd in the lobby of the Chateau Laurier, as one Tory reported, with 'a great display of hail-fellow-well met ... the darling of the debbies, the apple of the dowager's eyes, the handsome gay young Lothario from Elgin.' The last guest left the suite next to R.B. Bennett's at four in the morning.

Mitch spent the following morning listening to the rival claimants for the promised Franco-Ontarian seat in the cabinet, and fielded questions from two dozen journalists early in the afternoon. Asked why he had come to see Mackenzie King, Mitch admitted that it was his own idea: 'I am perhaps inclined to be somewhat impulsive, but he is a man who can put the brakes on.' Many onlookers shouted greetings and reached out to shake his hand as he walked up Wellington Street. The Commons staff shed their traditional reserve and applauded when he entered the foyer. As he walked along the familiar lobby, Liberals left the Commons to join him while Bennett acknowledged the procession with a scowl. 'Congratulations, my boy,' said King when they reached his office. When Alex gushed that covering Mitch was like travelling with the Prince of Wales, King replied, 'Well, you are travelling with the prince of men.'[1]

Mackenzie King had not looked forward to his meeting with the prince of men. He had delayed meeting caucus for a day, but had then used the occasion to advantage as he pictured Mitch as a true fighting Liberal, 'to point out how much was owing to Hepburn himself in Ontario, for the 4 years he had fought at great odds, without financial assistance or loyalty, or support till the last minute, how he had pulled the party together, got candidates into the field & an effective organization underway, risked his health etc.' But, however unwelcome, the meeting could not be avoided and when the door closed behind Alex the two men talked for an hour and a half.[2]

Although King insisted at once that he wanted nothing to do with Mitch's decisions about the cabinet, he was very generous with his advice. The cabinet was the secret of statesmanship and 'the very essence of our British system of government,' he explained, and Mitch should win the loyalty of his colleagues by taking them into his confidence 'though with respect to many things, there will be much which you will find it inadvisable to share even with them, but best to keep wholly to yourself.' Honesty, character, and temperance were the essential qualities of a good minister, said King with a straight face, as he advised Mitch against 'taking in any man who drinks.' For selfish reasons, however, he was delighted to release Peter Heenan, whose friendship with Mitch, old Senator Charles Murphy snorted, had been consummated when they were 'fellow-devotees at the Shrine of Bacchus.' Given the choice between Paul Leduc and Aurelien Bélanger, King agreed that Leduc was less likely to be drunk for long periods of time. King approved of Roebuck and McQuesten, but was dubious about David Croll in Labour.

King was even less hesitant to offer advice about policy and strategy because his own interests were very much involved. He urged Mitch to establish a royal commission on Tory expenditures on relief and unemployment, which he felt could damage Bennett, and asked him not to meet the legislature until they knew whether Bennett would go to the country. There was merit in reducing the expenses at Chorley Park, he admitted, but danger in having Liberals appear as critics of the crown. Above all, said King, 'the first thing to do is to do nothing & say nothing' until the cabinet was formed and to 'go away & get a complete rest.' King's advice was sound, perhaps a little patronizing. But the meeting left him uneasy. Mitch was too 'full of his victory,' too 'intoxicated in a love of publicity' for King's taste. He remained concerned about Mitch's ability 'to keep away from the gang around him, & exercise the needed judgement in matters of government. He needs prayer to guide him. I told him to pray for strength and guidance.'[3]

Mitch was not given to prayer, and the party at the Chateau that night went on until daybreak. But after meeting some of the gang and discussing the changeover with George Henry in Toronto two days later, Mitch did disappear. He relaxed for ten days at Frank O'Connor's summer home at Roche's Point on Lake Simcoe, where despite the frequent presence of Arthur Slaght and O'Connor's generous hospitality, he put the finishing touches to his cabinet and decided on other key appointments.

There was not too much room to manoeuvre. Nixon as provincial secretary and de facto deputy premier, Marshall in Agriculture, McQuesten in Public Works, and Roebuck as attorney general had already been promised. Mitch had been warned that Roebuck was too radical for the job, but had pushed the objections aside and, at Roebuck's request, also made him minister of labour. Patrick Dewan, the ambitious Catholic alderman from Woodstock, had mounted a campaign to represent the English Catholics. With Senator Murphy's support he hoped that the bishops would let Mitch know that Peter Heenan was not acceptable. But Senator McGuire countered with the appropriate assurances and the 'Clay Pipe Statesman' with the luxurious wig, King noted sarcastically, became 'Minister of Lands, Water, Heaven and Earth etc.'[4]

Dr Leonard Simpson, the Hepburn loyalist from Barrie, in Education and Dr James Faulkner of Belleville in Health were solid appointments. There was little support among the Franco-Ontarians for Paul Leduc in Mines, the Montrealer who had married the daughter of Senator N.A. Belcourt and established his law practice in Ottawa, and l'Association Canadienne-Française d'Education d'Ontario and the clergy were openly opposed. But Leduc had powerful friends at court. Paul Martin claimed that Lucette Valin had nominated him for the cabinet at a late-night party, and to secure his nomination Mitch had overturned a decision of the riding association. David Croll had reasonable expectations, although Mitch had refused to make him a categorical promise. O'Connor and others apparently believed that Ontario was not yet ready for a Jew in the cabinet and there were many who felt that the young man was much too pushy. But Mitch wanted 'minorities' represented and gave Croll Public Welfare and the new ministry of Municipal Affairs.[5]

It was a solid cabinet with a progressive slant, and to some observers was flawed only by Mitch's failure to select a strong spokesman for the business and financial community. Albert Matthews had not run because Mitch refused to promise him a portfolio, and George Fulford had turned him down. But Mitch clearly had his own game plan and there were Liberals who undoubtedly gave offence when they suggested to him, as Thomas Crerar did, that he 'get a man of proven integrity and capacity' as provincial treasurer. In Mitch's mind, the Treasury had been settled long before: he would be in charge of the finances of the province.[6]

Mitch returned to Toronto on 9 July. George Henry resigned the next day, and that afternoon Mitch was summoned to Chorley Park and asked to form a government. The lieutenant-governor, Herbert Bruce, had not taken his advice to resign and, although he had approved a number of post-election appointments, he had, unknown to Mitch, refused to sign an order-in-council paying Dominion Construction $500,000 for their work on the Abitibi Canyon power project. The meeting was brief and cordial. Mitch suggested that since his cabinet was ready, the swearing in could be performed later that evening. Watching the simple ceremony, Mrs Bruce commented that 'Hepburn does not look as bad as his photos make him out to be.'

There were many others, however, who shared some of King's anxieties, even if they did not go as far as Sir Robert Borden who, reflecting on the 'terrible descent from Mowat and Blake to Hepburn,'
concluded that his 'coarseness, his clownishness, his maladroit
approach towards subjects which he obviously does not understand,
stamp him as a man whose future career will be no credit to himself
or to the province.'[7]

Mitch called his first cabinet for eleven the next morning. He
arrived in high spirits at 10:30 and guided a covey of reporters
through his suite of offices and invited them to photograph the first
Hepburn cabinet in the council chamber. The press would always
be welcome, he promised, and when the cabinet met they would be
treated to a daily question and answer period in his office. True to
his word, Mitch emerged from cabinet two hours later to tell
reporters that they had approved the immediate proclamation of
Henry's liquor act and beer would flow on 24 July; cut $2,000 from
ministers' salaries; agreed to investigations of Tory malpractices in
Hydro, the Toronto & Northern Ontario Railway, and the Liquor
Board, with many others to follow; stopped all government construction until the tenders could be examined; and made a number
of key appointments.

The overhaul of the administrative machinery and personnel at
Queen's Park was the immediate priority, and the one closest at
hand. 'That means two things as I see it,' Mitch explained. 'First,
eliminate inefficiency – rip out deadwood, political appointees, hangers-on, those who draw big salaries for doing little. Second, cut out
unnecessary functions of government – those that have outlived
their usefulness or are too paternal.' Asked if his administration
would be governed by the dictates of efficiency or patronage, Mitch
replied that while efficiency was essential, the new government had
to be supported by a sympathetic bureaucracy. 'I am certain,' he
said with a grin, 'that there are enough efficient Liberals around to
do the job.'[8]

Efficient or not, Liberals certainly agreed. Old E.C. Drury, speaking from his bitter experience as premier, warned Mitch not to
'make the mistake I did, being too generous and merciful towards
them. Part of your work during the next two years must be to shoot
them to pieces so they cannot come back ... They deserve no mercy
and none should be shown.' Drury's admonition was most clearly
followed with the dismissal of the most blatant political appointees.
Although some pleaded for their lives, or at least their incomes,
their demise was neither unexpected nor undeserved.

The first to go were the Hydro commissioners, quickly followed by I.B. Lucas and F.A. Gaby, Hydro's highly political solicitor and chief engineer. Five defeated ex-MLAs and a host of party organizers and officers in prominent positions were told to pack their bags. R.A. Stappels had been given the Minimum Wage Board as his reward for deserting the Liberals in 1925 and working as a Tory bagman; his betrayal was not forgotten. Hillyard Birmingham, general manager of the Liquor Board, insisted he had been neutered by his appointment, but within days of his dismissal he was back at his old job as a Tory organizer in Toronto. George Drew not only refused to resign as securities commissioner, but also intrigued with Conservative friends to blackmail Arthur Roebuck. P.D. Ross, the vitriolic publisher of the Ottawa *Journal*, had been a devoted servant of Ottawa Hydro for eighteen years, but his public 'blast' at Mitch during the campaign had earned Borden's praise and Mitch's condemnation as 'the most bitter partisan I know.' Ross was soon free to devote himself to making the *Journal* one of the leading Tory papers in the province, and Drew to covet and finally win the provincial Conservative leadership.[9]

Yet despite the shrill cries for revenge that came from parched Liberal office-seekers, Mitch did not dismember the civil service at Queen's Park. The ministers naturally recruited their own personal staff. Mitch installed Roy Elmhirst, who had worked in the OLA office since 1930, as his private secretary and conduit to the royal ear. Bob Gaskin came from St Thomas as his link with the riding, and Eleanor Parker, his secretary in the Commons, joined him in Toronto. Rather than dismiss Charles J. Foster, George Henry's secretary, Mitch made him civil service commissioner, attached to his office, and never doubted his loyalty. Surprisingly, only six of the twenty senior civil servants lost their positions. McQuesten dismissed the highly political deputy minister of public works, George Hogarth, and replaced him with Chester Walters, a respected Hamilton accountant. Duncan McArthur, who would have been minister of education had he contested Kingston and won, resigned from the Queen's history department to replace Dr A.H.U. Colquhoun as deputy. Roebuck brought in James Marsh, his unsuccessful candidate for the nomination in Riverdale, as deputy minister of labour, and Faulkner placed a medical doctor in charge of hospitals.

Mitch moved quickly to prune archaic growths or excessive foliage in most departments. He began by reducing the staff in the Theatre Inspection Branch and Movie Censor Board and transferring them to his own office. He also took Ontario out of the movie business by closing the provincial studio in Trenton, a studio which employed seventy-five people but with only silent movie equipment had met the onslaught of the talkies by making no movies at all. By closing the Colonization Bureau he took the province out of the northern colonization business. Marshall closed Ontario House in London. Croll informed the 140 unemployment relief inspectors, 'mostly political appointments filling jobs that need never have been created,' that the government would not renew their appointments but would review them individually as it trimmed the bloated department. Nixon transferred the policing of game and fisheries to the Ontario Provincial Police and dismissed 117 game wardens and their five hundred deputies whose local power apparently compensated for the absence of a salary. Faulkner reorganized medical and dental services and inevitably sent many Tories back to full-time practice.[10]

As attorney general, Arthur Roebuck in one bold move reorganized the primary court system. The local magistrates may have been, as he said, 'a vested aristocracy, good men and highly respected personally by the law-abiding citizens.' But their wide-ranging and overlapping responsibilities, their dependence on fees for income, the political and familial incestuousness of that local aristocracy, and their customary non-existent legal training cast a shadow over the administration of justice. Roebuck left the five major urban centres untouched, and organized the province into eighteen districts in each of which two itinerant magistrates would hear cases prepared by local officials. The magistrates were to be lawyers with some experience. Since everyone knew that the justices of the peace held office because of their political faith, Roebuck adopted the English system whereby the JPs were local officials, such as the town clerk, who were paid a small honorarium for their extra duties. Even the Toronto *Telegram* approved.[11]

Watching from a distance, R.B. Bennett commented that the administrative overhaul at Queen's Park seemed long overdue. But Mitch and his colleagues played down the rationality behind the administrative changes and catered to the prejudices of their followers by emphasizing the savings to the province with the exodus of Tory office-holders. Mitch conveniently overlooked that many of the affected civil servants were transferred, paid considerable severance pay, or superannuated early on a reasonably good pension. But as Dr Colquhoun, the 28-year veteran of the Department of Education, told John Dafoe, while his withdrawal was 'hurried, at a day's notice, and with six weeks' pay,' Simpson and McArthur were very courteous. He had assisted them and would continue to do so

both out of personal regard to them and because their policy impresses me as prudent and enlightened ... Of Hepburn I cannot honestly speak well. Much of his policy is fully justified and necessary, but in daily talks with irresponsible reporters he announces the various steps in terms that cannot fail to make the judicious grieve. Regardless of the future, he gives point to the charge that the spoils system is in full swing, whereas if defensible measures were announced differently such a charge, in most cases, could not be sustained. Probably inexperience in social life is accountable and the roughness will wear off.[12]

The roughness was more obvious as Mitch began to fulfil the promise to dismiss all Henry appointees since November 1933. Departmental officials and Charles Foster quickly went through the records, and a monthly count indicated there had been about fifteen hundred temporary and permanent appointments, of whom only one-fifth seemed to be filling a regular departmental position. Some were routine annual appointments: the 185 bee inspectors appointed each season and the 360 driving examiners who received twenty-five cents of the dollar paid for each examination. Some were unquestionably essential. Some, like the appointment the day before the election of Edwin Guillet as historiographer at $3,000 a year, were simply mysterious, since neither a job description nor the historiographer could be found. Made on the eve of the election, many appointments were blatantly political. Although Foster recommended selective dismissals so as not to endanger such essential public services as the inspection of hives, Mitch and the cabinet decided to wipe the slate clean. A steady stream of orders-in-council, which to Angela Bruce's annoyance kept her husband busy at Chorley Park, did just that. A statement of the money saved highlighted each press statement. By the end of July Mitch boasted that he had cut almost a million dollars and the figure moved steadily upward throughout the summer and fall. What he neglected to add was that many of those dismissed were immediately reinstated or were replaced by local Liberals.[13]

Tory cars, like Tory carpet-baggers, were put on the block. Mitch had promised that Liberal ministers would drive their own cars, and the mandarins without a car could walk or take the streetcar. When Senator Hardy complained that Mitch's proposed car auction was undignified, he replied testily that there could be too much dignity in government, and 'this action of ours is going to meet with the wholehearted approval of the rank and file of taxpayers.' Moreover, he added, 'I do not think the selling of these cars is as vindictive as the demand for the scalp of every Tory in eastern Ontario.' When eight thousand people jammed Varsity Stadium on 28 August to watch the hammer rack up $33,385.50 for the eighty-seven cars and trucks, Hardy had to confess that as theatre it had been a smash hit. But the bill for $3,004.45 George Henry received for repairs to his own car looked vindictive. Mitch was vindictive.[14]

The yeomen of Leeds were not alone in their pursuit of Tory scalps. Local riding associations had moved instantly from soliciting votes to demanding jobs, and MLAs and organizers were deluged with IOUs. 'I am having a H—— of a time with this industrial riding of West York,' lamented the victorious Bert Gardhouse. 'All those out of work want jobs and half those with jobs want to better them.' Hardy admitted that the 'rush for office' was not a pleasant sight, but told King that although there had been many dismissals, most were justified and 'the government is now slowing down and I think will be fair if the party allow of it – they are refusing wholesale dismissals on mere request. Even with this, I am one of those who would clean out the whole liquor staff everywhere … as it was a great part of the machine we have to smash up.'[15]

The party, of course, would not allow it. Old friends soon greeted each other from different sides of the liquor store counters. When the men went back to work on the roads in South Renfrew after the freeze, the Tories claimed that fifty of the fifty-five foreman were Liberals and two sons of Tom Murray, the MLA, had jobs as a clerk and a driver. Young Paul Martin was on the lawyers' patronage list and received his first reward as junior counsel on the Hydro inquiry under Arthur Slaght. Roy Elmhirst soon had a list of Grit newspapers, and Jim Franceschini of Dufferin Paving and Crushed Stone quickly became a good Liberal and a Hepburn bon vivant. But it was never enough, and Mitch cynically concluded that every Liberal ballot had been cast in the expectation of a reward on earth not in heaven.[16]

Mitch's selection of his friend Eddie Odette to head the Liquor Board outraged the temperate and astonished many Liberals, who may have lacked Mitch's sense of humour. President of an auto body company, once mayor of Tilbury, and member of the best clubs in eastern Ontario, Odette was a popular local figure. Whatever the truth of the rumours that he had been a rum-runner, no one doubted his fondness for the bottle. The appointment gave

Mackenzie King a bad dream – 'terrible, a handing over to liquor interests in Ontario' – but Mitch assured him that Eddie was 'on the water wagon' and beyond reproach. When the Devil alighted on 24 July, Odette had issued authorities for ninety-nine standard hotels, three clubs, and two steamship companies with a thousand licences to come. There had been long queues in the morning, and with beer at ten cents a glass, business was brisk. By the end of August beer sales were up 120 per cent, and E.P. Taylor's Brewing Corporation had cornered 35 per cent of the market and had secretly formed Mohawk Investments to front Brewery hotels.[17]

Some of the abuses were so obvious that not only the naïve were shocked. Tumble-down shacks suddenly blossomed forth as hotels with only a gesture towards the eating and sleeping facilities required by law. One celebrated case was the Breadalbane at the corner of Yonge and Breadalbane Streets, a broken-down property that Frank O'Connor had picked up hoping to sell on a rising market. But with beer by the glass promising even greater profits, the Breadalbane got a licence, as a thirsty *Telegram* reporter discovered, without providing any rooms. Headlines in the *Telegram* drew the matter to Odette's attention, and the licence was temporarily suspended. The Breadalbane soon had a few rooms and reopened under a new owner, Frank McLaughlin of the Chartered Trust – in trust many believed for Frank O'Connor. There were too many signs of Liberal patronage to be ignored, and, appropriately indignant that Odette had been pressured, Mitch promised a purge of the 'fixers' and declared the Liquor Board out of bounds to members and ministers. Mitch admitted to King that liquor licences were his major headache, but with fifteen hundred licences at stake, his rhetoric did not keep the 'fixers' away from the LCBO and Mitch was not above intervening on occasion himself.[18]

Inevitably there were imperfections in the operation of the new system, and the prohibitionist and temperance forces were roused to a new fury. Beer by the glass, thundered Joe Atkinson, was the Tory Trojan horse that would destroy the Liberals. The Reverend T.T. Shields returned from a European honeymoon to denounce Mitch and his beer parlours for the debauchery, the whoring, and the demoralization of the young that had overtaken the province. Mitch refused to yield to the demands for another referendum, but some response was essential to appease the temperance Liberals. Shocked by reports that women of virtue were being approached by men of evil intent in the beer parlours, Odette promised there would be separate rooms for ladies and escorts. Finally, after long discussions in cabinet, Mitch announced an increase in licence fees and taxes and gave each municipality a 20 per cent share of the beer and wine profits. Of course, that would be of little assistance to the dry municipalities, Mitch dryly commented. An outraged Mayor Stewart exclaimed that Toronto would not accept money so soiled. The cheque was cashed when it arrived.[19]

While some saw the moral fabric of Ontario being destroyed by drink, others feared it was being ravaged by sex. Sex had moved from the bedroom to the movie screen where six million Ontarians a week watched Greta Garbo, Myrna Loy, and Marlene Dietrich portray the sexually independent woman, a portrayal that seemed fully realized off the screen. South of the border the Catholic Legion of Decency had arisen to rid the nation of smut and moved quickly into Ontario. The soon-to-be-dismissed director of the Censor Board told Mitch that the board was the toughest in North America, but the *Star* found that of the fifty-five movies showing in Toronto in July, only twenty-two were clean while the rest were guilty of vulgarity and sexual suggestiveness – bedroom scenes, kisses that were more than a touch on the cheek, and even illicit love-making. With Mitch in charge of the board, it was whispered, movie-goers would soon face the real world unprotected by the censors. Despite the whispers, Mitch was not moved by the tale of Sodom and Gomorrah retold in the *Star* and from countless pulpits. There were, he commented irritably, too many 'pious so-called Christians' with 'souls that would just fit in a peanut shell' and 'moral uplifters' who 'every once in a while have to shout from the house tops to justify their existence.'[20]

But Mitch was on the side of the angels when the government dramatically removed the Dionne quintuplets from the control of their parents. The birth of the Quints on 28 May 1934 was the story of the year, and their survival was widely believed to have been a miracle. Within a few weeks, however, the destitute and semi-literate parents had been persuaded to sign a contract with an American promotional company which in effect would turn the Dionnes into a travelling circus and would almost certainly have killed the babies, who were only kept alive by a constant supply of breast milk provided by the Red Cross. When the details of the contract became known, Mitch and the cabinet authorized Roebuck, as *parens patriae* or 'parent of the country,' to appoint official guardians and break the contract. A few days later the government announced it was building a new hospital for the Quints, named after Dr Allan Roy Dafoe, the reclusive country doctor who had brought them into the world and become an international celebrity. It was to be six months before Mitch saw the Quints. 'Quite the most remarkable sight I ever saw,' Mitch admitted after he, Croll, and Leduc in white smocks were photographed with the babies.[21]

Mitch realized that cutting bureaus and programs and eliminating Tories would do little to balance the budget. Although Tory sleight of hand had made provincial finances an accountant's nightmare, the general picture was bleak. Ontario had a gross debt approaching $650 million, plus contingent liabilities of almost another hundred million (largely Hydro guarantees). The annual interest of $21.5 million on the net debt of almost $350 million consumed 41 per cent of current revenue. The deficit was $30 million a year.

Municipal finances were also a disaster. Thirty-two municipalities had defaulted and Croll said in July that every city except Toronto and Ottawa would be unable to meet its interest payments at the end of the year. Croll's assignment in the Department of Municipal Affairs was to impose fiscal responsibility on the local governments and attempt to negotiate a general refunding of municipal debt at a lower rate of interest. Mitch helped by living up to his election promise of relieving the municipalities of their 20 per cent share of the King's Highways.[22]

Although the ministers slashed their budgets, Mitch believed that there could be no dramatic improvement without coming to grips with the interest on the debt and the crippling burden of unemployment relief. 'Our efforts in cutting down expenditures seem so unimportant when we look at the other side of the ledger and see the increasing demands for relief, caused largely by lack of purchasing power,' Mitch told his 'funny money' friend, Robert Cromie of the Vancouver *Sun*, 'If I were asked to name the greatest contributing factor to our present plight, I would say interest.' Mitch had taken the lead at the July dominion-provincial relief conference when he asked Bennett to call a conference on monetary reform. Ottawa could 'with perfect safety issue millions of currency without affecting the national credit,' he argued. 'There had already been a $40,000,000 or more of inflation and it had not been felt.' Bennett dismissed the proposal as 'ruinous'.[23]

Mitch was determined, however, to lower the interest rate on Ontario's debt. Late in July he boasted that he had secured a rate of 3.5 per cent rather than the customary 4 on some treasury bills. Irked by comments from investment dealers that interest rates were falling dramatically and that he should have been able to secure short-term funds at under 3 per cent, Mitch used a dozen summer picnics to take the offensive. The banks had all tendered for the loan at the same rate, he told his Elgin constituents, and 'we may as well have one bank in Ontario as seven for all the competition they are.' But he warned the banks that he was prepared 'to break their stranglehold.' The bankers accused Mitch of playing to the grandstand because the loan was a joint loan and Mitch had knowingly negotiated with the lead bank and agreed to their terms.[24]

Mitch was playing to the grandstand. He insisted that he would not use a committee of bankers, as Henry had done, to refinance $37.5 million in bonds that matured in September, and another $10 million due in November, and indignantly denied a rumour that he had done so. The denial was true, for Mitch had already made a deal with a syndicate headed by Wood Gundy for $37.5 million of one to five-year bonds at 2.5 per cent. There was outrage on Bay Street when it was learned that the syndicate – Wood Gundy, Ames, Dominion Securities, the Royal Bank and the Commerce – had secured the loan without tenders. To the charge of the disgruntled that he could have got a lower rate by tendering, Mitch replied testily that the banks would simply have engaged in another conspiracy. The rates were the best in Canada, he claimed, and a tribute to Hepburn economies: 'the financial interests of Toronto and Montreal which viewed with alarm ever increasing debts are quite satisfied that loanings in Ontario today are much better risks than in the past. Our economies, I assure you, were a definite factor in establishing an all time low rate for the province and we drove a hard bargain.'[25]

While the Toronto *Star* praised the deal as a warning to the banks that the province expected real competition, the *Financial Post* observed that, with an abundance of short-term money around, a deal 'worth crowing over would have been to sell fifteen or twenty year bonds to the amount of this loan and at a low rate of interest.' Nevertheless, to the public, Mitch appeared to emerge victorious from his first round with the banks. Even Bennett was impressed. 'I confess that some of the statements made by Mr. Hepburn as Treasurer gave me great concern,' he wrote Billy Price with obvious relish, 'but the fact that he was able to get money at 3% is the answer to all his talk against the financial policies of the former administration.'[26]

The half million saved on interest – or even the five million if the entire debt was refunded at 3 per cent – paled beside the staggering burden of supporting the unemployed. By the summer of 1934 the total bill for direct relief and relief projects was almost three million dollars a month and the provincial share had risen from 39 to 47 per cent. There was worse to come. On 12 July Bennett cut Ottawa's contribution to 25 per cent, and summoned the provinces to a relief conference at the end of the month. Surrounded by sixteen ministers, Bennett lectured the premiers on the iniquities of a system which saw local relief rolls packed with unemployables, seasonal and part-time workers, and the downright lazy who were making more than honest taxpayers. Ottawa would no longer encourage sloth by paying one-third of it, but would give each province a lump sum based on a provincial 'means test' of uncertain criteria. Ottawa would continue the DND camps, fulfil its Trans Canada Highway commitments and its own public works projects, but would not fund any provincial projects beyond the grant-in-aid. The amounts might be negotiable, Bennett concluded, but the principle was not.

Since there was no consensus among the provinces, Mitch proposed an adjournment to allow Bennett time to formulate concrete proposals and the provinces to do their homework. The prime minister refused and the next day told Mitch that Ontario's grant would be a paltry $500,000 a month. When Mitch exclaimed that with all costs – including northern highway projects – estimated at five million a month, the minimum required from Ottawa was $1,800,000, Bennett agreed to $700,000 as an advance for two months while the new government at Queen's Park could review the situation. Mitch refused to accept the decision as final, and told reporters that he would be back in two weeks for round two.[27]

Although he had clearly lost the first round, some of the judges were impressed. Robert Manion, the minister of railways, told Mitch that he had 'made a very nice impression on us all down here during the Conference. This was of course due to the fact that you left your wild, turn-to-the-left, demagogic manners at home.' Senator Hardy passed on the word that Harry Stevens 'said you easily stood out as the best of the lot. That's a pretty good recommendation.' Even R.C. Matthews, the revenue minister, confessed that 'Hepburn was not bad when you consider the terrible political bias he has to overcome before approaching any question in a proper frame of mind.'[28]

Mitch returned from Ottawa to face the hunger marchers. Before the election the Ontario Workers' Federation on Unemployment, a Workers' Unity League subsidiary, had announced that several thousand unemployed from all over the province would march on Queen's Park to force their demands on the government. Soon after taking office Mitch had agreed to meet a small delegation, and when

The invitation ... and the welcome!

Mayor Stewart replied that they would be stopped at the city limits, he instructed Roebuck to state that although Stewart had the power 'to employ a body of Cossacks to ride them down ... he cannot prevent the Prime Minister and his Cabinet from giving an audience to these people.' The next day the cabinet approved an order-in-council replacing the two Tory police commissioners with two good Liberals.

There was no police interference as the marchers descended on Queen's Park where a delegation of two hundred met Mitch, Croll, and Roebuck in the government members' smoking room, carefully stripped of its blue leather furniture. For over three hours Mitch and his ministers listened to a procession of speakers, including seven of the ten communist candidates in the 19 June election, demand non-contributory unemployment insurance, generous increases in cash relief allowances, and a $300 million public works program. Occasionally interjecting questions and comments, Mitch and his colleagues expressed sympathy for the plight of the unemployed but emphasized that having returned empty-handed from Ottawa, they could promise nothing except good intentions. There were some cheers, however, particularly for Roebuck's closing comment, 'God bless you in your work. I hope you become strong enough to come to Queen's Park and enforce your demands upon any government in power.'

While good intentions pleased some of the delegation, they inflamed others. Addressing the crowd of five thousand marchers and spectators outside, speaker after speaker denounced the capitalist system and called for the establishment of workers' soviets. Fred Collins, of Stratford fame, accused Mitch of trying to kill communism by kindness, and another warned the crowd not to 'let yourself be blinded by the soft words, the honeyed phrases, the open arms and proffered friendship of a government far more dangerous to our cause than that of Henry which would have crushed us, which turned the police and military on us.' The next day, however, the marchers accepted Mitch's offer of government trucks to take the out-of-towners home and the $50 he pulled from his pocket, supplemented by $40 from his colleagues for food along the way. The meeting had been a public relations triumph for the new government, although Mayor Stewart and other Tories denounced Mitch for throwing in his lot 'with Communists and other subversive elements' and solemnly warned that Ontario was 'sitting on a volcano.'

Ten days later Croll outlined a new approach to relief. Described as 'relief to workers, nothing for shirkers,' the plan permitted municipalities to provide cash relief for work done at the prevailing wage rate on municipal projects approved by the province. A voucher allowance of $40 a month would be earned in cash by eighty hours of work at fifty cents an hour, and relief recipients could earn and keep extra money up to one-third of the allowance as long as it was reported. All those on relief were to be registered within a month. Mitch also repeated his election commitment to a provincial unemployment insurance scheme if Ottawa could not be persuaded to launch a national plan, and hired a consultant to draft a provincial act.[29]

Although Queen's Park demanded most of his attention, summer was the season for political picnics and the summer of 1934 was a time for Grit rejoicing. While Mitch boasted of their accomplishments in Toronto and promised that the inquiries into the Liquor Board and Hydro would reveal Tory corruption in all its nakedness, he also reminded the partisan crowds that much remained to be done, for Lord Gopher of Calgary still reigned in Ottawa.[30] Mitch expected Bennett to go to the country in the fall and the day after his election had ordered the local riding associations to keep their workers in place. Bennett decided against an election, however, but before leaving for Europe late in July issued the writs for five by-elections in Ontario. After the provincial débâcle in June, the Tories were not ready for an election and Home Smith irately reminded Manion of the soldier who refused to join the cavalry: 'When de bugle sounds de retreat I don't want to be bothered with no horse.'[31]

As King began to assign by-election responsibilities, it was clear that he did not realize that Mitch's election had profoundly altered the Liberal party. His comment on election night that in Jimmy Gardiner of Saskatchewan and Mitch he had two young and loyal lieutenants underlined how dangerously he had misread the significance of 19 June, in Ontario at least. Mitch had gone to see King after the election as the victorious leader of the Liberal party in Ontario; the offer he held out was the delivery of the province in the next federal election. If there was to be a Liberal victory in Ontario for the first time since the Pacific scandal election of 1874, it would not be won by the Jim Malcolms, the Jack Elliotts, the Bill Eulers, or even by Mackenzie King – who had failed disastrously in four attempts – but by Mitch Hepburn and the transformed provincial party. King's conceit and suspicion made it impossible for him to see that Mitch Hepburn's offer was that of a comrade-in-arms, not a brazen attempt at self-aggrandizement or a lust for the power and place that was so properly his.[32]

Although Norman Lambert had intimated to King that the tension between the federal Liberals and the OLA persisted and that it was essential that 'the present Ontario office and organization had to be respected on account of Frank O'Connor,' King went ahead as if 19 June had not happened. With no cabinet minister able to manage the by-elections, he decided to parcel responsibility out to a number of MPs, with Mitch assigned Elgin and Johnson and the Toronto office the infertile Toronto East. 'All our forces should be co-ordinated as to work together with the utmost harmony and good-will,' King wrote, with everything linked to Lambert's office 'so that from the centre there would be complete supervision of all political activities.'[33]

While King was drafting what read more like a sermon than battle orders, Bill Fraser was learning the bitter truth in Toronto. 'We had in mind going ahead with actual field work in Ontario,' he reported to King, only to find that 'our plan of field work did not meet with the approval of the Toronto office ... They insist on taking full charge of Federal Organization and I believe it is the intention of Mr. Parker and one or two others to interview you in this connection within the near future.' The federal MPs, he concluded, were opposed to the Toronto takeover 'but my decision was, in order to obtain the maximum unity in the Party, that we should submit to the policy of the Toronto office.'

Vincent Massey also had his ear to the ground and reported to King that the victory had given the provincial Liberals 'great prestige and they are anxious to assume the fullest measure of responsibility for the coming general election. Although I have not discussed the subject with Hepburn ... he will probably reflect this point of view when he sees you in Ottawa.' Massey suggested that Toronto be given the responsibility because the 'more clearly the responsibility for the elections can be placed on the Ontario Liberal Association Office the more likely we are to have the assistance of Frank O'Connor and others who made possible the good work in the provincial fight.'[34]

With Mitch threatening to tell King 'to pull off his brigands & he [would] win four by-elections for him' the two men met late in July. Mitch arrived at Kingsmere with Paul Leduc, 'looking exceedingly well & happy, much more rested, in the best of spirits, quite obviously feeling the power & delight of his office.' The luncheon was a success. King followed Lambert's conciliatory suggestion of proposing a Toronto meeting of federal MPs and provincial Liberals. Although Mitch readily agreed, he insisted that he 'wanted Ontario Ass'n to function properly, & keep federal members from collecting funds.' The cordial discussion continued until mid-afternoon when Lucette Valin and her parents arrived to take Mitch to their cottage on Blue Sea Lake for the night. But as Mitch talked, King had suspected that 'he might be seeking to build up a little machine of his own ... but be this as it may – sufficient unto the day is the evil thereof.'[35]

Lambert, Massey, and Johnson had planned the agenda for the meeting on 3 August in Toronto. O'Connor had agreed to serve on the finance committee, but he happily deferred to E.G. Long as the chairman. Over a long breakfast at the York Club, King, Massey, and the committee straightened out the relations between the Toronto group and Lambert, with King 'a court of last resort to approve or disapprove important steps.' On their way to lunch, King and Massey dropped in to see Mitch as Queen's Park. 'I was quite taken with his manner, and active executive mind,' King admitted. 'The amazing change from what Hepburn has been enduring the past four years is so great that I do not wonder that he continues to feel in seventh heaven.' King also concluded that Mitch's ministers, although 'young, untried, and for the most part immature' and therefore a little risky, were 'honest and sincere in their love for the people, and that they will help along with needed reforms.'[36]

That afternoon King presided over the fateful meeting of the provincial and federal Liberals. Assembled in the King Eddy were the new finance committee, Lambert and Massey of the NLF, a dozen MPs, Johnson, Parker, and Slaght, and Mitch, Roebuck, Marshall, and McQuesten. 'All were in exceedingly good humour,' King recorded, 'and we spent nearly three hours in the utmost harmony the meeting approving the arrangements re raising of finances – the co-ordination of organization effort thro' the Nat'l Lib. Fed. office & plans for the 5 by-elections.' King was content, for the rivalries had been papered over. But he admitted that the federal MPs were upset: 'I can see these men are all jealous, and fearful lest others get the prestige they would like to have and even more a control of patronage. They are even hostile to Mitch – who they think – and perhaps rightly – is already beginning to build up a machine.' Machine or not, the Hepburn Liberals were in charge of all by-elections except Frontenac-Addington. The Toronto finance committee raised $22,000 for the five ridings.[37]

To Mitch the 'little general election' was simply the penultimate step in ridding Canada of the Tories. He was so confident of the result that he bet Manion $25 the Liberals would win all five by-elections. Despite the pressure of work at Queen's Park, he campaigned steadily in the four southern ridings, leaving Kenora in the capable hands of Peter Heenan. Whether talking to the scrub loggers and stump farmers of Frontenac, the Tory working-class in Toronto's east end, the villagers of North York, or his friends in Elgin, the appeal was the same. The real problems facing the country demanded national, not provincial, solutions: free trade with the United States to aid the primary producer, debt conversion at lower interest rates, a government-owned central bank that would encourage inflation, and a national scheme of unemployment insurance. Although it was not clear from King's carefully read speeches in each of the five ridings that he believed in very much except his providential return to power, Mitch left no doubt that all would be possible with Liberal governments in Ottawa and Toronto. And with King beside him on the platform at St Thomas, Mitch denounced Bennett's gold tax as an invasion of provincial rights and promised that after King's election 'one of the first things I am going to do is to bring that matter to his attention.'

With Bennett away in England, the excitement on the Conservative side was provided by Harry Stevens, whose calculated indiscretion in releasing copies of his pamphlet *Price Spreads and Mass Buying* let him pose as the champion of the little man against giants like Eatons, Canada Packers, and Imperial Oil who made enormous profits at the expense of workers, consumers, and small producers. King had trouble knowing just what to straddle on the issue, but Mitch as usual had no hesitation. Recalling his earlier attacks on the monopolies that fattened on tariff protection, he charged that the new-found Tory conscience, the apparent differences between Bennett and Stevens, and the sounds of righteous indignation from monopolists and financiers were a mock battle, a giant cover-up to protect the very interests that were exposed. If Bennett disapproved, why did not Stevens resign? Why was he not dismissed? Was any reform possible with such a Jekyll and Hyde administration?[38]

Mitch's enthusiastic and exhausting campaign and his orders to the party to engage in battle contrasted sharply with King's aloofness before 19 June. Since the federal Liberals had nothing tangible to offer, Mitch responded to requests from the ridings to make some key appointments and have men busily working on the roads. 'We entertained the notion that the leader of the federal Liberal party was *Mr. Mackenzie King*,' observed the Tory Ottawa *Journal*. 'But it is *Mr. Hepburn* who is fighting the Dominion by-election contests now under way.' As the London *Free Press* commented, 'it is something new in politics for the head of the province to close down his office for 10 days and to devote his attention to a federal by-election and Dominion affairs.' Inevitably, the Tories were forced to make Mitch the focus of much of their counter-attack. He was, one Tory MP exclaimed, 'a Dillinger among the Liberal forces,' while another dismissed him as 'a little peanut-eating, wise-cracking boy.' Stevens, Manion, Earl Rowe and other prominent Tories invaded St Thomas and, as Grant Dexter of the *Winnipeg Free Press* wrote, 'the constituency fairly reeks with stories about the alleged wrong-doings of the new Premier.'[39]

Mitch was worn out when the campaign got under way. By the end of August, he was so exhausted that he was unable to sleep at night and dictated to Roy Elmhirst from bed. But he mustered the energy to work the barren terrain in Toronto East; to spend three days drawing thousands to Coly Campbell's meetings at Wolfe Island, Techborne, and Battersea; to help his friend Bill Mulock in

North York; and speak and canvass for Wilson Mills in Elgin. On 18 September he collapsed and his doctor ordered him to bed for a week. But the next day, pallid and drawn, he was up to share the platform with Mackenzie King at St Thomas.[40]

The results were almost all Mitch hoped for, but he paid Bob Manion the $25 – 'not inflated as yet' – because the Tories won East Toronto. The riding had never been Liberal, and Slaght had resisted the pressure from Mitch and King to run against the popular renegade Tory, Tommy Church, who happily denounced his critics in his own party as 'stuffed shirt nobodies' and 'security co-racketeers.' Elsewhere the Liberals won going away, and Colin Campbell had a majority of 2,500 in a riding that had never elected a federal Liberal before. Mitch heard the returns from his bed. A week passed before he was allowed to return to work.[41]

The honeymoon on the hustings over, Mitch faced a myriad of problems at Queen's Park, none more pressing than getting men and women to work. While little could be done in the south where there continued to be signs of recovery, the north presented the greatest challenge and opportunity. An immediate short-term solution lay in putting thousands to work on the Trans Canada Highway and arterial roads under the federal-provincial relief works agreement. But Wesley Gordon, Bennett's minister of labour and member for Temiskaming South, was determined to deny Ontario Liberals any of the political benefits on the eve of a federal election. For months Gordon met every initiative, request, or proposal from Heenan with more questions about alternative routing, traffic volume, engineering data and the weather, finally forcing Harry Nixon to exclaim in exasperation: 'How do I know? Only the Lord knows when the snow will come and block the road!' With eighteen thousand men already at work on northern highways as relief projects, the cabinet gambled and authorized Heenan to spend $7 million on the Trans Canada and other northern roads to employ another eight thousand men working two week shifts.[42]

A promising opportunity to revive the steel industry at the Sault appeared early in November when Dr Roberts, the Liberal MLA, sought Mitch's help in the reorganization of Algoma Steel. Although the name of Sir James Dunn was never mentioned in the official documents, it was generally known that he had been gradually accumulating Algoma bonds. With Algoma showing signs of recovery, Dunn and his Toronto lawyers, Ward Wright, and his uncle, Newton Rowell, had decided the time had come to take over.

Roberts was really only the bearer of a proposition from Wright to the effect that, although the takeover could be done through a simple foreclosure sale in court, the promise of provincial legislation to guarantee the reorganization would speed up the process and, as Dunn desired, 'close the door to nuisance by the minority bondholders' and the stockholders. Given such a guarantee, Dunn had agreed to funnel $5 million into the steel works. After the meeting Nixon assured Roberts that 'we shall give this legislation our support, and facilitate it, in every way possible in its passage through the house.'

Mitch received Wright's official request for such legislation as may be 'necessary' on 15 November and, with the addition of the words 'and equitable,' sent it to Roebuck for his approval. Roebuck replied that he 'did not like it because it is loose and indefinite and we are depending too much on one lawyer, but the guard of the word "equitable" and the importance of the reorganization makes me recommend it.' Dunn moved quickly. The bondholders approved the transaction in December; the sale and reorganization was sanctioned by the court in February; and, although it was unnecessary, the promised legislation was passed in the 1935 session. Algoma and the Sault had a new lease on life. Dunn and Mitch soon became good friends, and Jimmy was later to tell him that 'Algoma Steel is always ready to belch a smokey welcome from many chimneys' whenever he passed that way.[43]

The forests of the Canadian Shield provided the greatest employment opportunity. Recovery in the United States had increased the market for newsprint and lumber, but prices remained disastrously low. Although the production of pulp and paper was the highest since 1930, many mills remained closed and the industry as a whole was working at little more than half its capacity. With grinders and saws often silent, there seemed little chance of an increase in jobs in the bush. Mitch and Heenan moved quickly in September. After meeting delegations of lumbermen, the cabinet approved a 50 per cent reduction in stumpage fees on the condition that the logs be milled in Ontario, and that a large number of men, estimated at ten thousand, were hired at fair wages. Two weeks later they renewed the suspension of the 'manufacturing condition' for pulpwood to allow export from crown lands, and reduced the export fee from 25 to 15 cents a cord on the condition that the wood was not headed for American newsprint mills.[44]

Mitch's determination to get the bushmen to work clashed head-on with the apparent desire of the Lumber Workers' Industrial

Union, a subsidiary of the Workers' Unity League, to shut down the camps. The northern camps had long been extremely volatile, and at the annual conference in Port Arthur in August the union had called for a 'mighty mass struggle this fall.' In September the carefully orchestrated walkouts began in the Abitibi pulpwood camps around Cochrane. The strikers first tried persuasion to send the men down the track, but if that failed the arrival of a gang of men with staves and iron pipes was usually an effective substitute, although some camps met force with force. Late in September Heenan had gone north with an offer to meet every demand except an increase in wages which, he said, the troubled industry could not afford. The offer was rejected and the walkouts continued amid increasing, if often exaggerated, reports of violence. By the time Mitch returned from his sick-bed in October, the industry was paralysed along an eight-hundred-mile front in the north, and the union organizers were turning their attention to the pulp mills, already faced with the prospect of a critical shortage of wood.[45]

The demands for intervention by the northern press became increasingly shrill. Late in October Mitch again sent Heenan north and, although Heenan's attempts to mediate failed, his statement that intimidation and violence would not be tolerated suggested a change of front at Queen's Park. There were also signs of a counter-attack. Reinforced OPP detachments, the RCMP, city and railway police, and newly sworn constables began to clear the stations and escort the cutters safely back to the camps. The strike had lasted two months, and much of the best cutting season was over before life in the camps returned to normal.[46]

Although Roebuck in his capacity as minister of labour was willing to take some of the credit – 'the strong hand is present, but always concealed' – the more general view was that 'the pink-tinged radical,' as he was described by the irate editor of the Rouyn-Noranda *Times*, had been overruled. Indeed, the rumours of strained relations between the premier and the attorney general were so persistent that Mitch was compelled to deny that Roebuck's departure from the labour ministry was imminent. The truth, however, as Harry Johnson told Lambert, was that the 'Hepburn-Roebuck equation [was] none too good.' A growing divergence of views about the benign or malignant influence of the WUL may have strained relations, but the tension was more fundamental.

Whatever his outward appearance, modesty had never been one of Roebuck's vices. He held and expressed strong views, and only rarely could he see the other side of an argument. He had never minimized his own role in the transformation of the party, and was slow to learn that he was playing on a team and Mitch was the captain. He too often used 'I' when he might have used 'we.' And it was not long after the election that one Liberal insider warned Mitch that Roebuck 'has been heard to make remarks to the effect that he is the real premier and you are the window dressing ... Do not underestimate your Attorney Gen'l he is an extraordinarily bright man. DO NOT let him steal your thunder or put himself before THE PREMIER when it comes to being in the limelight before your people. This is unpleasant to say but I have heard it said already that Roebuck is THE MAN and not Hepburn. See that you clip his wings.'[47]

Mitch was less concerned about clipping Roebuck's wings than preventing him from swinging the cabinet too far to the left. There had been some rumblings when Roebuck had told the hunger marchers to return and 'enforce' their demands on the government. The good burghers of Stratford had been incensed when a posse of citizens had forced Izzy Minster, returning for an encore, to kneel before the Union Jack before escorting him from town, only to be told by Roebuck that their action was 'illegal, criminal and unjustified.' Requests for police reinforcements from the Tory mayor of Guelph, when the WUL organized the worst strike in the city's history, elicited Roebuck's reply that 'having failed to change the sympathies of his fellow townsmen by choking them with gasbombs, [he] feels that he has justified himself in the public mind when he screams for bayonets.' But when Toronto's mayor joined the others in accusing Roebuck of being soft on Communism, Mitch not only leaped to his defence but scoffed at the dangers of communism: 'I find no evidence of communism. Such a doctrine cannot make advances, I have found, in a province which is predominantly rural.'

Ontario was not predominantly rural, however, and the York County grand jury took the activities of the WUL more seriously than the attorney general. At the general session in October, the grand jury warned that 'a certain element referred to as "The Workers' Unity League" was exercising an influence which we believe is detrimental to the public welfare' and requested that 'the civil authorities should be given power to deal firmly with such bodies.' Mitch's intervention in the north and a curt warning to the hunger marchers that more demonstrations would not be 'helpful' and would not have 'the slightest effect on the government,' suggested that the cabinet was moving in that direction.[48]

Adding to the Hepburn-Roebuck tension was the conflict in the cabinet over Roebuck's promised industrial codes. The election manifesto had pointed vaguely to cooperative action to establish industrial standards enforced by the government, and Mitch had indulged in equally bland generalities when he mentioned labour reforms. But Roebuck had promised that industrial codes would provide for negotiated 'rates of pay and hours of labour from the lowest to the highest grades of skill. These agreements will be supported by law and the ruthless employer who fails to comply will be put out of business.' In his first day as labour minister Roebuck repeated that with his codes 'the grasping, brutal employer will go out or be thrust out.'

While Roebuck was unclear about the exact form the codes should take, he believed that they must provide a framework for negotiations which would strengthen labour's bargaining power and give the state some power of compulsion, if only as a last resort. But James Marsh, his deputy, was much clearer and surprisingly outspoken. Under the legislation, he stated, labour and management would be encouraged to establish wage and hour codes in all industries, and if the two parties failed to agree the department would impose the standards. The legislation, he added, would also confirm and strengthen labour's right to organize unions for collective bargaining. Company unions would be out, he intimated, but not unions organized under the WUL umbrella.[49]

Arguing that Roosevelt's National Industrial Recovery Act codes, which Roebuck seemed to be copying, had been responsible for much of the 'disturbance and dislocation of industry' in the United States, Charles Burton of Simpson's had asked Mitch to dump the entire idea and later publicly attacked Marsh for his 'wild talk.' Burton was not alone, although few businessmen went as far as W.H. Moore who described the codes as leading to 'state Socialism and fascism.' Moore's outburst led Mitch privately to lecture Marsh on the impropriety of a civil servant discussing public policy and publicly to state that the cabinet had not discussed codes and Roebuck was speaking only for himself. A few hours later, Roebuck told the Board of Trade that the word 'code' was unfortunate, for the intention was simply to provide a forum for the negotiation of voluntary agreements which would then be gently policed by the department. The cabinet did discuss the proposed codes at a lengthy session on 19 November and rejected any form of compulsion. And at a 27–28 November party caucus Roebuck drew a round of applause when he declared that he had never contemplated 'dragooning industry into complying with government ideas of what constituted fair wages and hours.' The grasping, brutal employer could sleep more easily that night.[50]

The caucus had not been Mitch's idea. But as the months passed with no sign of the promised session, there had been quiet rumbling among the back-benchers. By the middle of October Tom Blakelock advised Mitch that 'knowing the talk amongst the members ... I feel you would be wise in taking the members into your confidence.' A week later, Harold Kirby, the outspoken member for Eglinton, publicly demanded an end to the waiting time. The members wanted a categorical admission of their control of riding patronage, he declared, and did not want ministers and deputy ministers publicly announcing policy decisions. As far as Mitch was concerned a caucus was preferable to a session for which he was far from ready.[51]

Arthur Hardy had reassured Mitch that the caucus would go off quietly. 'I am sure you will find all the hot air will have evaporated before the sittings begin,' for 'when they all get together, no one of them will have the courage to do more than voice mild complaints.' The ministers used the first day to good advantage, detailing their actions since the election and explaining how their hands were tied in the unemployment and relief field until Bennett came to some decision about the Trans Canada Highway and other public works projects. The caucus apparently agreed with Mitch that Ontario could not embark upon a long-range recovery program until there were major reforms in economic and monetary policy in Ottawa, and all they could do until Bennett was defeated was to get their own house in order. Skilful footwork kept beer off the floor, and with the backing of a solid block of western Ontario MLAs, the cabinet squelched complaints that the Tories were not being fired fast enough. However, the caucus rejected Mitch's nominee as party whip and elected the outspoken Harold Kirby. Mitch was content. The caucus had served its purpose.[52]

That little could be expected from Ottawa became even clearer a few days later when Mitch, Heenan, and Croll, met Bennett, Gordon, and Rhodes, the minister of finance. The meeting was unpleasant and unprofitable. Bennett not only refused to consider higher relief payments, but cut them back to $600,000 a month with deductions for the overpayments. The Trans Canada consumed most of the morning's discussion. Heenan charged Gordon with stonewalling the project to protect a few ridings (including his own), and Gordon countered with accusations of Liberal boodle and proposals for expenditure controls that would give the Tories half the patronage if they paid half the costs.

The acrimonious meeting was still very much on their minds when they joined King for lunch at Laurier House. King found it 'difficult to get conversation onto any plane' as Heenan 'kept telling how he had told Bennett this & that man was a "damned liar",' and Mitch related how Bennett had threatened to '"get him".' King was depressed: 'I could not help thinking of the contrast of the days of Sir Oliver Mowat, Gibson, Hardy etc. all men of experience, training, background etc. These men all political chances, & professional politicians with little save the party machine & patronage in their minds.' But King was not above asking Mitch again to have only a short session without controversial legislation, particularly separate school legislation, before the federal election.[53]

A session of the legislature was far from Mitch's mind. In October he had returned to his sixteen-hour days at Queen's Park or the King Eddy before he was fully recovered. And as Roebuck told King, Mitch 'gives of himself with unrestrained generosity and he does not himself realize how much he has gone through.' The *Financial Post* offered one solution when it suggested that Mitch move his office to the middle of Lake Ontario for a few days every week. King had also commented that Mitch had become 'very puffy in appearance, eyes leaden, manner that of a man full of antagonism, is losing his natural charm.' Mitch admitted to King that 'fatigue was his great enemy & that when he was tired having only the one kidney, his urine was thick etc. (This means death or worse if kept up).'[54]

Exactly what was worse King did not make clear, but, as he suspected, Mitch's fatigue and puffy appearance owed something to his life outside the office. Although they filled him with 'dismay & humiliation,' King relished the stories of Mitch's alleged debauchery. He faithfully recorded the story of the morning Annie Odette went to Mitch's suite and 'found 3 girls there, who greeted her with the words, "Well dearie, you are too late, we have been here all night".' Senator Hardy's tales of Mitch's 'loose morals – says he spent a night with a woman at a hotel in Kingston and then came on here and spent a night with another woman whom he named at a hotel in Ottawa' were dutifully entered in his diary. Manion told a Bermuda-bound friend that Mitch had left on a cruise that morning 'so if you want any good times you will likely have company. I am almost sorry you are coming back so soon as it would be interesting for you to keep an eye on him down there for a while. They tell me he is running high, wild and handsome.'

A Caribbean vacation with Slaght and O'Connor had been planned for weeks. After a night at the Biltmore in New York, the trio boarded the ss *Monarch of Bermuda* on 6 December. Not long after they cleared the harbour, a young woman approached Mitch at the rail: 'Hi, remember me?' Mitch did remember buying the young Hepburn Liberal a chocolate malt during the election campaign. There was nothing adolescent about the beautiful, full-bodied, twenty-one-year-old who told Mitch that she and some other young people had won the trip in a competition. Until the ship docked in Bermuda two days later and they went their separate ways, she became part of the trio.

From Bermuda they sailed to Nassau, where Angela Bruce heard it on 'good authority that it was arranged to have the Gov. of Nassau lunch with the Captain, Hepburn, O'Connor & Slaght on the boat. Everything went according to plan except that Hepburn & Slaght could not be found. Eventually they were found in a brothel which they had resorted to as soon as the boat put in.' If true, the governor could not have been much offended, for when Mitch and Eva had trouble with their hotel accommodation in Miami over Christmas he invited them to spend a few days with him on the island. Mitch had been away over a month when he returned to Queen's Park from Miami early in January.[55]

'A struggle against feudalism'

The session was to open six weeks after his return and, except for a few long weekends at the farm, Mitch was seldom far from Queen's Park. If the Honourable Herbert Alexander Bruce had his way, Mitch might not have escorted the vice-regal party down the aisle on 20 February. Bruce had not seen Mitch since August and was convinced that his premier was violating not only the courtesies of their official relationship but also the conventions of the constitution. Bruce drafted, but did not send, a letter to Mitch accusing him of improper, disgraceful, and unconstitutional behaviour. Mitch's failure to inform him of the Bermuda trip, advise him who was to be in charge of the government, and consult him about the opening of the legislature, he wrote, were 'subversive of good government.' Angela Bruce predicted 'an open rupture between Hepburn and Herbert' and, on the eve of the session, Chorley Park was convinced that it 'may be before long a Lieut. Governor will be very necessary with this wild man doing what he is.'[1]

The wild man was on his best behaviour when the session opened. His public statement that he and the cabinet would not attend the traditional state dinner led the Reverend Dr Shields to denounce him as 'a boorish, ill-mannered, despotic, vulgarian demigod who cannot be reformed,' but Mitch's friend Mel Rossie of the *London Advertiser* assured him everyone but the 'snobs and socialites' were behind him. Rossie urged him to go further and let the members have their seats on the floor instead of 'being crowded out of them by a lot of Toronto women who are there to get their names and what they wore in the paper.' But Mitch let him down, and with 'all the women on the floor of the House in evening dress despite the Jacksonian democracy of the P.M. & most men in tail coats,' Vincent Massey was reassured of the immutability of the monarchical tradition. In his top hat, cutaway and spats, Mitch looked anything but a Jacksonian Democrat, and Eva, in a long gown of marina blue crepe with a shoulder bouquet of violets and orchids, seemed to the manor born.

Traditions were restored and destroyed. The mace carried by sergeant-at-arms, Walter Bayfield, vc had been taken by the American invaders in 1813 and had just been returned by President Roosevelt. But when the members settled into their seats, the veterans of the House and gallery noticed that much was different. Mitch had adopted the Commons plan where he and Henry glared at each other from the sixth, rather than the first, desk down from the Speaker. And instead of being arranged in straight rows, the three lines of member's benches were arranged in a half-oval so that all the back-benchers could see and hear without straining their neck. Mitch remembered his Commons seat as a freshman MP.[2]

The speech from the throne was more a recital of the government's not inconsiderable accomplishments than a sketch of the brave new world. In both the speech and his own inaugural address a few days later, Mitch emphasized his determination to place provincial finances on a sounder foundation by getting the deficit and the debt under control. Indeed, already he could boast of having done more in seven months than Ferguson and Henry had done in five years. He had slashed administrative costs, though far from the promised 50 per cent. The Treasury had converted maturing debt at a much lower rate of interest, and the $20 million sale of treasury bills in January at 2.25 per cent was the lowest in provincial history. Mitch's appointment of John Cowan as a commissioner to inquire into the Spencer estates in London, with the family's rich Imperial Oil legacy, revealed that he fully intended to tighten up on the collection of succession duties, even if the graves had been closed for years. He was equally determined to straighten out the complicated financial arrangements between the government and the Liquor Board, the Agricultural Development Board, and Hydro. Hydro was critical, as it was responsible for over $200 million of government debt. In the spring Hydro was instructed to do its own financing and convert all government bonds to Hydro bonds as they came due.[3]

The financial community had applauded most of the new initiatives, although there was continued grumbling over Mitch's refusal to tender new issues. But the alarm bells rang on Bay Street when the cabinet announced a dramatic change in the approach to municipal debt. With reductions in federal support and the increasing incapacity or unwillingness of insolvent municipalities to cover their costs, the burden on Queen's Park was increasing dramatically. Moreover, no interest was being paid on over 90 per cent of the municipal debt in default. In January Croll had announced that by the end of the year all forty defaulting municipalities would be forced to so reorganize their finances as to pay interest at 3 per cent and to make a variable lump sum payment towards the cost of their own relief then being borne entirely by the province. This first step towards fiscal responsibility was to be accomplished without borrowing, capitalizing relief expenditures, increasing taxes, or cutting municipal salaries. The message to local councils was clear: tighten controls on relief and other expenditures and be more zealous in the collection of taxes.[4]

To the financial community the message was equally clear, and the dreaded word 'repudiation' was whispered along Bay Street. Bennett anxiously asked Mitch for some clarification so he could respond to inquiries from London. With municipal bonds dropping precipitously and provincial bonds showing signs of weakness, G.R. Cottrell, Toronto manager of the Bank of Commerce and one of Mitch's friends, suggested that he issue a reassuring statement. To save him the trouble, Cottrell enclosed just such a statement. Mitch could not have said it better and that night, in what was described as 'one of his rarely issued formal statements,' he released it without changing a comma.

If certain 'so-called money interests, security dealers and others have seen fit to assume that something would be done by this Government that would ruin the market or value of municipal bonds,' the text read, 'I cannot help it.' What was at issue was debt adjustment, and adjustment 'does not mean repudiation no more than with a private company.' Financial reorganization and debt adjustment were common in the private sector, where it was apparently regarded as good business to get something rather than nothing. Why was it not good business for municipal bondholders as well? In the future, the province would exercise much stricter control over municipal borrowing but for the moment debt adjustment was essential to get the municipalities back on their feet. Sending the statement to Bennett, Mitch explained that his object was to bring the municipality and the bondholder together to reach an agreement based on ability to pay.[5]

A week later W.E. Rundle of the National Trust hosted a dinner for Mitch at the York Club where he could confront his critics. From the reports that reached Angela Bruce, Mitch's speech was 'full of bombast and dirty jokes' and Vincent Massey admitted that he did make 'a breezy speech wh. would have been indiscreet for anyone else but made on the whole a good impression. When Strachan Johnson – a bit tight – interrupted him by shouting out "In hoc signo Vinces" he replied instantly: "I don't know any Latin except 'ne plus ultra' & I saw that on a whiskey bottle." Not bad!' Despite the inspired banter, Cottrell reported that the speech had gone over well.[6]

By the time Mitch began work on the budget, the management of the Treasury was in the hands of Chester S. Walters as controller of finance. With only a high-school education, Walters had trained himself as a public accountant and had opened an office in Hamilton just before the war. After the war he became a federal income tax inspector and ultimately the commissioner of income tax. Like many Canadians, Walters had invested heavily in the market and by 1933 was in financial distress. E.B. Ryckman, the federal minister of national revenue, concluded that Walters' heavy debts compromised his position, and Bennett dismissed him. Walters readily accepted McQuesten's invitation to join the new administration as his deputy minister of public works.

Mitch soon realized that Walters was a man of extraordinary talent and put him on the budget committee. Before long Walters was advising on a wide range of financial and organizational problems, and in January the Treasury was completely reorganized around him. With Mitch's dual mandate to cut costs and increase revenues and with an unlimited laisser-passer, Walters quickly imposed new accounting systems and subjected government programs to a more rigorous financial analysis. Walters had the office directly above Mitch, and the frequent 'see Chester' or 'Chester says' soon led to whispered complaints that Chester was really the master of the administration. Mitch trusted Walters completely. Walters was neither a libertine nor a prude. He loved a good time, and when not reciting endless stanzas of classical poetry or doggerel, entertained with a superb tenor voice. A prodigious worker and a stern disciplinarian, he worked late in the office and even later in his Bloor and St George apartment, and the staff of accountants he recruited for the Treasury could expect to be called at any hour of the night or on weekends. Chester Walters provided the managerial discipline that Mitch lacked.[7]

The Tories were already sniping at Walters when Mitch brought down his first budget on 2 April. For the new April to March fiscal year, adopted by the province to stay in line with Ottawa, Mitch forecast a deficit of $14,600,000, a figure slightly under the expected cost of relief and about half the last Henry deficit. The prospect of reducing relief costs with relief now properly calculated as current expenditure seemed both unpromising and uncertain, for it was 'impossible to either anticipate the constitutionality or effect' of Bennett's New Deal legislation, including unemployment insurance. The province could only 'watch and wait,' but after the federal election he would insist on a federal-provincial conference on unemployment.

Meanwhile, Mitch planned to follow a 'pay-as-you-go' policy. The chore of cutting costs and tightening financial management would continue but, for the moment, he planned no dramatic changes in fiscal policy. While he personally preferred to tax corporate profits, he retained the tax on paid-up capital but extended the definition of taxable capital to increase the return from corporation taxes about 20 per cent. Living up to his promise to soak the rich, he increased the tax on all estates, and gave the government broader investigative powers. Much to the annoyance of Percy Parker and his clients, taxes on the raw materials used by wineries and breweries captured some of their new profits. The largest gain to the Treasury came from a last-minute decision to increase the tax on gasoline. The most unpopular was an increase in the amusement tax, specifically labelled for relief, which the poor claimed hit those who went dancing for a quarter but did not touch the rich with their yachts and tennis clubs.[8]

Everything considered, Mitch was pleased with a budget that projected increased revenues of $10 million without giving too great offence to any single element in the community, except perhaps the very rich. The budget debate was short, and the necessary legislation moved quickly through a House exhausted by the longest and most contentious debate the province had seen.

At 5:30 on Tuesday, 25 February, Arthur Roebuck had begun his maiden speech as the minister responsible for the Hydro-Electric Power Commission. The bulky text of his speech and the pile of documents on his desk left little doubt that his review of the Hydro situation would be exhaustive. Roebuck had waited for that moment since late July when Mitch had first appointed him to the Hydro Commission and had transferred the responsibility for Hydro from his own office to Roebuck's. There had been some raised eyebrows when Mitch picked T. Stewart Lyon as commission chairman. Although Lyon was a passionate advocate of public ownership and the development of provincial hydro resources, the appointment of a sixty-seven-year-old retired *Globe* journalist seemed a strange choice. However, with Roebuck and McQuesten on the commission there could be no pretence of an arm's length relationship between the cabinet and Hydro. 'Keep Hydro out of Politics!' scoffed a Toronto Hydro commissioner. 'Keep the Devil out of Hell!'[9]

In July 1934 the new commission had dutifully endorsed the Liberals' 'Back to Niagara' policy. Roebuck immediately began to investigate the infamous Quebec contracts, and instructed accountants, engineers, and lawyers to examine the contracts, supply and demand, and alternative sources of supply. By early December there was considerable speculation that the government had abandoned any thought of cancelling the contracts, a speculation fuelled by Slaght's public statement that the contracts were valid. However, Roebuck insisted that 'no decision has, as yet, been reached.' He was already beginning to put the pieces together, however, and had selected Richard Jeffery, a senior Hydro engineer, to help assemble the data.[10]

Roebuck insisted on complete secrecy, and for weeks Jeffery often worked at Roebuck's home. One night when they were reviewing some tables, Roebuck exclaimed, 'The Hydro system cannot stand this.' Jeffery agreed: 'No, something will have to be done ... What you will have to do is compromise.' 'Oh, no, we are not going to compromise,' Roebuck shot back. 'These contracts are non-enforceable and invalid. They should be cancelled.' Jeffery had no desire to be a martyr: 'That set me back pretty suddenly and after that, Mr. Roebuck asked me for figures, and whatever figures he asked for, I gave them to him. I did not attempt in any way to influence Mr. Roebuck in what he said, whether it was right or wrong.'[11]

Right or wrong, the speech Roebuck held in his hand was his alone. 'The cabinet knew the line I was going to take,' he claimed later, 'because I told them as fully as I could under the circumstances, but preserved secrecy with regard to any act to the very last moment.' For three hours he discussed Hydro finances, the capacity of the Niagara system and the current and projected costs of Quebec power. The bottom line was clear: by the end of 1934 Hydro had paid over $22 million for Quebec power that it did not need; in 1935 alone the bill for unwanted power would be $6.6 million; and by 1938 without a massive increase in demand the Quebec contracts would absorb half of Hydro's revenues and bankrupt either the system or the consumers. To compound the tragedy, he stated, Hydro's own resources were more than enough to meet current demand with ample reserve capacity. If the House chose not to believe him, he produced a supply-demand graph drawn by Jeffery. When questioned about the graph several years later, Jeffery stated, 'I knew it did not give a true picture.' When asked, 'Did you tell Mr. Roebuck that?', he replied, 'No ... he was drawing the picture not me. I was merely the man that put the lines in under his instructions.'[12]

For three hours the next day Roebuck played the historian. Diligent research through the Hydro files revealed how Hydro money had financed anti-Liberal propaganda during the 1934 election campaign. Roebuck claimed that he had proof that the contracts with Gatineau, MacLaren, and Beauharnois had not been the result of systematic Hydro deliberation and analysis but of collusion between the Ferguson government and the Quebec power barons. In addition to the public contracts, secret agreements protected the companies but not Hydro against every contingency. Moreover, Hydro purchases alone more than covered the cost of the power projects. 'Pizzaro's Spanish freebooters found nothing as fabulous as this in the temples of the Incas. The English buccaneers who singed the beard of the Spanish King never brought home a prize which equalled the splendour of the gift which Ferguson, McGrath and Gaby presented to the financiers of St. James Street.' It was enough drama for one day, and the Speaker called it at 6 o'clock.

The next morning there was chaos in the bond markets, and millions were written off the face value of the bonds and stocks of the power companies. The galleries were full long before the afternoon session began. For two hours Roebuck reviewed the contracts and the political payoffs. His practised oratory reached its peak, his indignation and anger flavouring every phrase, as he waved the contracts before the MLAs and declared them 'illegal, unenforceable, and void ab initio.' Only Mark Anthony's words at Caesar's funeral could express his outrage at the 'burglar's raids' on the people of Ontario with the complicity of their own government: 'O what a fall was there, my countrymen. Then I and you and all of us fell down, whilst bloody treason flourished over us.'[13]

Mitch had not heard Roebuck's oration. He has been speaking in the Nipissing by-election, and returned the next morning with the financial community in an uproar and the party in disarray. Before leaving he had assured reporters that, although the cabinet had not reached any decision, they certainly intended to 'smash the stranglehold' of the power barons. Although he shared Roebuck's view of the infamy of the contracts and did not necessarily disagree about their legality, he had told Roebuck privately that 'it was not the opportune time to say it because we were hoping that we would settle the trouble peaceably.' The attorney general was not a man to take orders. His impassioned brief for the prosecution seemed designed to force the government into the politics of open confrontation and make a peaceful settlement difficult.

Mitch immediately called a cabinet meeting, which Roebuck was too tired to attend. The cabinet was sharply divided on the question of legality, with Nixon, Croll, and Marshall, at least, convinced that Roebuck was wrong. Although Roebuck later insisted that his speech could be searched 'from end to end to find any suggestion of policy included in it,' he certainly had pointed to repudiation and put Mitch in the position where he had to support him or ask for his resignation. The discussion was long and heated. When it was over Mitch stated that while the question of legality had never been discussed in cabinet and Roebuck had spoken only for himself, the opinion of such 'an eminent counsel' as the attorney general would be 'entitled to a great deal of weight in the cabinet.' After another meeting on Monday, 4 March, Mitch told reporters that while there was still no decision on policy, 'you can rest assured that the Cabinet, to a man, is right behind Mr. Roebuck.'[14]

In his determination to salvage Hydro, Arthur Roebuck had endangered the Hepburn government. Few lawyers shared the views of the 'eminent counsel.' On St James Street the power companies huddled with their lawyers over the weekend, and Aimé Geoffrion, an eminent constitutional lawyer, declared that after twenty hours of study he had concluded that not one of Roebuck's legal arguments could be sustained. Company spokesmen left no doubt they were prepared to take Ontario to court. Meanwhile Mitch's financial friends warned him that the prospect of repudiation was leading American investment firms to dump municipal bonds on the market and could jeopardize the successful conversion of the $160 million in provincial bonds about to mature.[15]

More disturbing, as the cabinet debated the options, was the realization that the prosecuting attorney had misled the jury. In the fall Hydro had hired the well-known Boston consulting firm, Stone & Webster, to determine whether the Niagara system could meet the demand without Quebec power. The report from the consulting engineer, William Ryan, was disconcerting. Supply and demand, including the 100,000 horsepower from MacLaren and Ottawa Valley, were already in a precarious equilibrium. The risk of an immediate shortage might be weighed against possible savings, wrote Ryan, but that 'is a question for executive decision on which I cannot presume to advise you.' But with the expected improvement in economic conditions in 1935–6, he warned, there would be shortages and 'prudence would require the provision of at least 150,000 H.P. additional capacity in the shortest possible time.' However, in the House, Roebuck had deliberately overestimated the normal capacity at Niagara and Chat's Falls, and omitted all the engineer's hesitations and qualifications. The simple truth was that Ontario needed some Quebec power. Moreover, eastern Ontario was heavily dependent on 60-cycle power from Gatineau, and if that were cut off, seven hundred thousand people would have to read by lamplight. However, it was also true that unless demand sharply increased it would be some years before Ontario could absorb all the power contracted for and Hydro would have to spend $12 to $16 million on new transmission lines from the Quebec border to feed the additional power into the Niagara system.[16]

For the next few weeks Mitch remained silent. There was little support for outright repudiation. Even the Toronto *Star*, firmly behind the 'Back to Niagara' policy, urged Mitch not to act like 'a bull in a China shop' unless the companies insisted on their 'pound of flesh.' With Ward Wright acting for Beauharnois and Slaght for MacLaren, the power companies received daily reports from Toronto. Wright informed Beauharnois that he was reasonably certain the companies did not face the immediate prospect of repudiation, but rather that 'suggestions will be thrown out as to possible basis of revision.' The companies pointed out that although they might be willing to renegotiate the contracts, the bondholders would have to agree to any revision. However, John MacCormac of the *New York Times* reported from Ottawa that the companies would accept a moderate downward revision not only to survive but also because a settlement would 'drive the last nail into the coffin of any hopes still entertained that Ontario might consent to the initiation of the St. Lawrence waterway scheme' to which Mitch was very much opposed.[17]

Behind the wall of silence the cabinet was devising a strategy that could protect the province and enable the government to negotiate some reduction in its commitments from a position of strength. Roebuck outlined the general strategy to the cabinet early in March:

That we treat with the Gatineau Power Company first because it is in the meanest position & has us in the most delicate position on account of the Eastern power situation. A satisfactory deal with Gatineau will put us in a strong position with the other companies.

We will enter into a new firm contract with the Gatineau Company for 225,000 h.p. at $13 per h.p. and confirm the Eastern District agreement for 60.000 h.p. as of 1937 at the 14/50 rate provided therein ... This must be supplemented by an abrogation of the supplementary agreements and by provisions for renewal.

If Gatineau accepts, we will then offer the Ottawa Valley $11 per horse-power for the power from the Quebec side of the Chats Falls, maximum 96,000 h.p. If they refuses [sic], we will operate our one half, or if that is not practicable we will close down the whole plant, and the 192,000 h.p. can be done without or can be supplied from Gatineau McLaren or Beauharnois.

If they accepts [sic], we will then cancel McLaren & Beauharnois ...

If Gatineau refuses, the attack on Gatineau is delayed until we can protect the Eastern District by 60 cycle power from McLaren, Cedar Rapids, Madawaska [with] frequency changers.

If Gatineau and Ottawa Valley at Chat's Falls accepted the proposal, Roebuck concluded, the annual savings to Hydro would be $6,984,000.

On 12 March, Mitch called Queens 3700 in Ottawa and two days later A.R. Graustein of Gatineau Power slipped almost unnoticed into the Royal York. Although Ward Wright was assured that 'he did not see the Government, or any member of it,' when Graustein left Mitch had a promise that Gatineau would supply 25- and 60-cycle power. Hydro had already approved plans to deal with a power shortage, including rationing, and with Graustein's promise in hand, the cabinet moved a step further towards repudiation. On 25 March Mitch shouted angrily across the floor of the House that he was determined 'to save Hydro from the coupon clippers.' The next day, to counter the massive write-in campaign organized by the bondholders' committee, Roebuck appealed to 'the great court of public opinion' in four radio broadcasts. The die had been cast.[18]

When the House met on 1 April, Mitch introduced Bill 89 for first reading. Article 2 baldly stated that the contracts with all four Quebec companies 'are hereby declared to be and always have been illegal, void and unenforceable' against Hydro. Lawyers had agreed that if the contracts were voided, the companies would have to secure the right to sue Hydro from the government, and while most believed it inconceivable that the right would be denied, others told the Financial Post that so 'many inconceivable things are happening these days that we would not put it past the Government to deny such a right.' Bill 89 abruptly ended that dispute with the blunt provision that no action could be taken in the courts against the Commission.[19]

The banks, insurance companies, and trust companies called emergency meetings to mobilize the opposition. There were questions at Westminster and fear in Ottawa of a massive outflow of foreign investment. Floyd Chalmers of the *Financial Post* was hopeful that the crisis would mark a turning point in the advance of radicalism. 'The banks, insurance companies and others are now definitely aroused and have determined to fight back against the demagogues,' he informed his boss in Florida. 'They are a little late and, of course, there is always the danger that they will use undercover propaganda methods which are never as successful as frank and open publicity.' There were many among the establishment, however, who agreed with Chalmers that the contracts had been conceived in 'political infamy,' but like Clifford Sifton believed that Mitch should use 'every proper legal means' to escape the burden and 'inflict maximum punishment upon every person guilty of deliberate misconduct.' However, the denial of access to the courts seemed to go beyond 'proper legal means.'[20]

With $500,000 in royalties at stake, lobbied by the companies, and afraid that 'Back to Niagara' could mean 'On to the St. Lawrence,' Premier Taschereau was not conciliatory. Delivered to Mitch and Roebuck by Gordon Scott – legislative councillor, one-time provincial treasurer, and St James Street magnate – the warning from Quebec City was clear: unless Hydro took all the power it would get none. Mitch sent Scott back with the message that he would not be clubbed into submission, and if Taschereau wanted war he was ready.[21]

Danger lurked closer to home. At Chorley Park, Lieutenant-Governor Bruce spent Friday evening with Charles McCrea and W.P.M. Kennedy, professor of constitutional law at the University of Toronto. Bruce considered refusing assent, but after a long discussion they decided he should sign the bill and let Bennett decide whether it should be disallowed. However, wrote Angela Bruce, they also agreed, 'that if the stability of the province was affected – i.e. by our bonds being taken off the American and London markets, then it would be H's chance to call upon Hepburn to resign, & either ask call upon [*sic*] the Liberal W.E.N. Sinclair to form a new Gov. or ask for a General Election. But the present issue is not big enough, although it may lead to that.'[22]

Mitch made a short speech when he presented the bill for second reading on 8 April. Although both the Canadian Bankers' Association and the Canadian Chamber of Commerce had warned him that the bill threatened the nation's credit, Mitch declared that the government would never back down, for both its reputation and its credit were at stake. The province could not afford to build a new $20 million transmission and storage system, and Ontario industry would be wiped out if the rates included payments for power it could not use. The bill would not be changed and it would pass if the House had to sit all night.

Sit all night it did. George Henry began a Tory filibuster with a scrappy four-and-a-half hour speech. Liberal whips kept a quorum and members slept at their desks and in the caucus rooms as the filibuster continued throughout the night and all the next day. Only when a sleepy Tory back-bencher missed his cue and the alert Speaker called for the vote did the twenty-six-hour debate end at 5:25 in the afternoon. Mitch was not in the House when the vote was taken, but returned at once to proceed with other matters on the order paper. While most of the members drifted off to listen to the Montreal Maroons defeat the Maple Leafs for the Stanley Cup, the conscripts gave tired attention to other bills and after a short debate approved Mitch's budget resolution. Just after midnight, Mitch forced the House to go into committee on the power bill.

Meanwhile, at the Hydro Commission office, Dr Thomas Hogg, the senior engineer, had decided that the time had come to confront Stewart Lyon. Hogg and the engineers had never been consulted about the cancellation of the Quebec contracts, for the obvious reason that they were opposed. Although he was chairman, Lyon also had been unaware of Roebuck's intention. Hogg came quickly to the point: 'If you persist with the Act as it is constituted now, the minute that goes off we are dependent on our own resources and we cannot carry on.' Lyon was apparently surprised by Hogg's emphatic warning, and immediately called Queen's Park. Early Wednesday morning Mitch introduced an amendment providing that the act would not come into force until proclaimed. Finally, at 4 a.m., after thirty-seven hours of continuous debate, the bill was reported. There was little fight left in the Tories the next day. Roebuck promised that the government would meet with the companies and go 'as far as we can to preserve their interests while protecting our people first ... Those who vote for this bill will, in the years to come, look back with pride on their action.' At 8:40 p.m. the bill passed fifty-seven to seventeen.[23]

The Hydro debate so dominated the session that there seemed little time or energy for the rest of the Liberal's legislative program. Much of the legislation simply implemented changes already announced. Roebuck was unquestionably the busiest minister in the house. He enjoyed the legislature, for it gave him an audience not only on the floor but in the galleries, which he often filled with his enthusiastic admirers. The bundle of bills to implement his radical reconstruction of the primary court system and improve executive control over county and division courts met little opposition. Nor did a bill to bring real estate brokers within sight of the Ontario Securities Commission. With the dismissal of Drew and the appointment of John Godfrey as securities commissioner, the government had already approved regulations which tightened control over the securities industry and prohibited the old 'boiler rooms' where high-powered salesmen used a battery of telephones to entice the gullible speculator.[24]

Mitch had decided to leave Roebuck in the Labour ministry until he had piloted his controversial industrial codes through the legislature. The long meetings he and Marsh had held with trade unions and employers had not reduced the scepticism of the unions or the opposition of business. National and international unions wrestled for position, and agreed only that neither company unions nor the WUL and its offshoots should be recognized as bargaining agents. The business community remained relentlessly opposed. Manufacturers argued that the codes would increase the cost of production, lead to industrial warfare, and result in the flight of industry. Mine owners took their case for exclusion directly to Mitch. 'We have enjoyed peaceful times and pleasant relations with our employees for over 15 years and would deplore the introduction of any legislation which would permit a comparatively small group, actuated by Communistic principles, to disturb these relations,' pleaded the managers of Inco, Hollinger, Lakeshore, Dome, and Wright-Hargreaves. 'As a matter of fact,' they warned, 'such small Communistic groups, thoroughly organized, are now in existence and would be only too happy to avail themselves of this vehicle to create dissatisfaction among the employees.' Moreover, mine workers were men of all trades and all seasons and codes would be unworkable. Lumbermen pressed Mitch with a similar argument, and warned that any increase in costs would damage an industry already pushed to the wall by competition from Quebec and British Columbia.[25]

Roebuck's bill excluded mines, agriculture, and the public sector. It provided that when an agreement was reached on wages and hours by a 'proper and sufficient' group of both parties in an industry in one or more zones across the province, the cabinet could declare the agreement binding on all employers. The unions won a major victory when the act defined an association of employees as one 'free from undue influence, domination, restraint or interference by employers or association of employers,' a clear exclusion of company unions. Fines and imprisonment gave the act some teeth once the codes were put in place.

While Roebuck boasted that the voluntary codes would keep out the wolves and the pirates, who either refused to raise wages or undercut those who did, opposition critics alternately warned of the irresponsible power given to the minister or mocked the bill as 'a simple wooden lathe painted like iron.' Yet however impotent the bill, the pressure on Mitch continued. Percy Parker advised that industry was 'greatly alarmed' and urged him to send the bill to a committee where it might be discreetly killed. Burton wrote, 'For goodness sake before we go further *can* some of this disturbing stuff. Aside from questions of credit this industrial standards bill will undoubtedly move out some of our industries and scare off new enterprise. Why the haste to get into this mess? Delay this and then *can* it. You know I love you. Charlie.' Although Mitch admitted he was not 'enamoured' with the bill and 'tried to keep the brakes on as much as possible,' he refused to back down any further. The bill was pushed through in the last week of the session and became the centre piece of the government's labour policy.[26]

David Croll also maintained a high profile throughout the session, demonstrating considerable poise and praising his leader as often as good taste allowed. He took on new responsibilities when the government, already faced with attempts by Elzire Dionne to break the control of the official guardians, passed a bill making the quints wards of the state until they were eighteen, with Croll the responsible minister. As welfare minister, he strengthened the support provisions for unwed mothers and deserted wives, and included mothers with only one child, instead of two, in the mothers' allowance program. In his maiden speech Croll dealt largely with the new cash relief policy. Later, when he introduced the legislation, he included slum clearance and housing rehabilitation as acceptable projects and boasted that the government had already approved 122 municipal projects, with a labour cost of $5 million.

However, in his maiden speech Croll also lashed out at the relief strikers, hunger marchers, and soft left-wing municipal councils. Earlier that day, with Mitch and Roebuck, he had met another delegation from the two thousand hunger marchers gathered outside the buildings. Mitch and Croll lost their tempers as the words 'starvation' and 'slave camps' and tales of children dying from malnutrition in their mothers' arms flew easily from the lips of the WUL organizers. At night in the House, Croll referred to the wave of relief strikes and occupation of local relief offices. 'I am well aware that these parades and make-believe sieges were cleverly organized by two-cent revolutionaries,' he assured the members, 'revolution- aries who visualize themselves as Lenins, Trotskys or sometimes Kerenskis.' And wherever there was 'agitation and trouble, we invariably find a politically-hostile council falling in with the view and the game of the local Lenins,' a council more often than not in default and paying none of the relief costs. It certainly was true of Windsor, but Croll preferred to speak of Fort Erie where an insolvent council asked the province to take over relief and then passed a resolution demanding a 25 per cent increase. The cabinet handed back the responsibility.[27]

Croll was also minister of the Department of Municipal Affairs. Mitch had long believed that economy and good government demanded the overhaul of the archaic system of local government. But he also knew that the question was politically loaded, and even the rumour of reform had aroused fear of a metropolitan structure in Toronto and a reminder that none of the thirteen local govern- ments in Elgin would willingly disappear. The fierce local opposition to be expected was revealed when the government imposed amalga- mation on the Border Cities, despite the screams of anguish from the wealthy in Walkerville who had no desire to subsidize their Wind- sor cousins. As Mitch confessed to a friend, it was the kind of bit- terly contentious issue that should be delayed until after the federal election. To the Tories, the legislation which created the department and strengthened the Ontario Municipal Board proved once again that the Liberals refused to trust the people, for it gave the province ultimate control over municipal finance and administration. For the moment, tighter control over expenditure, rational approaches to municipal debt restructuring, relief from contributing to the King's Highways, more lenient provisions for the payment of tax arrears, and new income from the sale of beer and wine seemed sufficient for one session. Being burned in effigy in Windsor was enough.[28]

Passing almost unnoticed was Dr Faulkner's legislation to alter radically the definition, admission, and treatment of the mentally ill. Concerned with diagnosis and treatment rather than incarceration, Faulkner scrapped the descriptions 'insane and dangerous to be at large' and 'idiot' in favour of 'mentally ill' and 'mentally defective.' Drug addicts and alcoholics were added to those to be assisted. He also established itinerant mental health clinics to provide local diagnosis and serve as a gathering agency for the mental hospitals.[29]

Legislation trimmed fat and cut costs in almost every ministry and agency, rationalized structures and operations, and tightened accountability. Duncan Marshall confirmed the government's image as the farmers' friend with legislation to give the Milk Control Board greater power and to strengthen the position of the producer, assist cooperatives to build local cold-storage plants, and cut Hydro rates in outlying districts. In Highways, McQuesten tightened safety regulations, improved central planning capacity, and increased departmental control over municipal land acquisition and road construction. There was also increased and often retroactive ministerial or cabinet discretion in expenditures, appointments, and dismissals, sanctioned by law when necessary. Retroactivity did not bother the Liberal conscience very much. The object of 'ride at your own risk' amendments to the highway and negligence acts were rumoured to forestall a lawsuit by a hitch-hiker Mitch had picked up before his car was in some altercation with a fence or a snowdrift. Changes in the Controverted Elections Act conveniently killed a challenge to Charles Cox's election in Fort William (although the Tories did admit the act had encouraged fishing expeditions).[30]

As the days and weeks passed, Martin Quinn and the bishops became increasingly troubled by Mitch's failure to introduce the promised separate school legislation. Mitch had no desire to fire the religious as well as the corporate heather and had only too willingly used King's request to avoid controversial subjects until after the federal election as an excuse to delay the delivery of his promise. In September he asked his friend Monsignor Francis Stanley of St Thomas to explain his problem to Archbishop McNeil of Toronto, but found that neither the hierarchy nor Quinn were sympathetic. Although Heenan was personally disposed to act during the first session, Mitch handed him the task of negotiating with the bishops.[31]

While Mitch was in the Caribbean with O'Connor – with Archbishop O'Brien praying that the Irish Catholic would be persuasive – Heenan and Senator McGuire visited Bishop Couturier of Cornwall, who seemed sympathetic to delay, and Bishop McNally of Hamilton who vociferously was not. O'Brien immediately ordered the other bishops to stand firm. Heenan and McGuire also wasted three hours trying to persuade Quinn to put his party before his church, only to enrage him when Heenan said he was dealing with the question 'as a politician and not as a Catholic.' Compared to Heenan, Quinn later exploded, Judas Iscariot was 'a gentleman. At any rate, he had the decency to be so thoroughly ashamed of himself that he went out and hanged himself with a halter.' Finally, when the 'army of bishops' descended on Toronto on 10 January to welcome James McGuigan, the new archbishop of Toronto, and demonstrate Catholic solidarity, Heenan admitted defeat.[32]

Mitch and his colleagues met Quinn and several leading Catholic lawyers on 22 January 1935. As the Catholics explained that they wanted corporation and utility taxes divided on the basis of school-age population, Mitch interrupted to say, 'As I understand it then, all you are asking for is legislation similar to that in Quebec ... Well, I see nothing wrong with that.' After the meeting, he told reporters that the government had reached no decision on the content or timing of any legislation but assured them that he did not intend to follow the line of least resistance.[33]

Opponents of a new deal for the Catholics had already made it painfully evident that giving in to Catholic demands would not be the line of least resistance. Hundreds of school boards had endorsed a resolution of the Toronto board in September denouncing any diversion of grants or taxes to separate schools. On 14 February Mitch received a delegation of two hundred, representing the Orange Order, school boards, and Protestant churches, who brought the message that funding Catholic schools was 'repugnant to the great ideals of democracy, religious freedom, and absolute separation of the church from the state.' Reminding them that he was a Protestant and a Mason, Mitch gently lectured them on the changes that had occurred in education and the economy since 1863 when separate schools were established, but less gently added that he would not be cowed by their numbers or their propaganda. He was certainly not going to be cowed by scurrilous literature circulated by the Orange Order which, citing higher crime rates among Catholic juveniles, asked, 'What then is the "inevitable fruit" of "sowing the seed" in Roman Catholic religious schools?' Nor would he be cowed by the promise of the head of the Orange Order that no bill would ever get through the Liberal caucus.[34]

Quinn was confident that Mitch would withstand the pressure. After the 22 January meeting, Roebuck asked the Catholic lawyers to submit draft legislation, and Quinn was jubilant when he raised no objections to the draft. 'While there may be further changes, it seems unthinkable that under all the circumstances they will be of a very material character,' he wrote O'Brien, 'and it seems to me the matter is being settled between Mr. Roebuck, and Mr. Hepburn without the intervention of Mr. McArthur, whose influence I feared.' Quinn was in the gallery, where priests jostled Orangemen for a position, when the session opened to hear the brief reference in the throne speech to the 'equitable distribution of the cost of education.' Mitch, it seemed, had not been cowed. His comment later that the reference was to the more general problem of financing education passed almost without notice.[35]

Quinn waited impatiently for the promised legislation, despite the many leaks that it would be delayed until after the federal election. By the end of March the signals could not be ignored, and Quinn was ready to do battle. He wrote to Mitch that the delay was shaking Catholic confidence in the Liberals and giving comfort to 'our traditional enemies.' He absolved him of the sin of opportunism but committed the unpardonable sin himself of reminding Mitch in writing of the March 1933 promise. The next day Mitch informed the House that the illness of the minister of education had prevented a thorough study of the question and there would be no legislation until a fall session. Soon after the end of the session, he appointed a commission under Dr McArthur to study the financing and organization of the public and separate schools.[36]

When the members went home on 18 April, Mitch could look back on a remarkably productive session. But it had not been a model of parliamentary government. Whether by accident or design, almost no legislation was introduced during the first six weeks. And when important bills did reach the floor early in April, Mitch drove them through a small and quarrelsome opposition with scarcely a nod to the courtesies of parliamentary debate. Though usually in a good humour, when tired or impatient he wilfully scorned the conventions and rules of the House, once threatening to answer the 252 questions on the order paper by wiping it clean 'at one stroke.' On another occasion he angrily summoned the back-benchers to defeat the Speaker's ruling that his description of Henry as 'brazen' was out of order.

His own supporters frequently felt the lash of his disapproval, and soon realized that dissent would seldom be tolerated. No one expected Mitch Hepburn to be a sophisticated parliamentarian, but there was a crude arrogance about his behaviour that many found disturbing. Recalling the line 'Upon what meat doth this our Caesar feed, that he has grown so great?' the *Mail and Empire* denounced Mitch as 'a Hitler, a Mussolini, a Napoleon, a Caesar and an Alexander the Great all rolled into one.' Had he read the *Decameron*, the disillusioned veteran Dr McQuibban might also have suggested Giovanni Boccaccio. Over dinner, Angela Bruce was delighted to hear Dr McQuibban give 'a very poor name to all the "front row", saying that every man there now arrived with a good looking "stenographer" and when drunk boasted about them. Hepburn brought his right into the house with him, although she looked "fagged out".'[37]

As the session ran down both the Hydro Commission and the power companies planned their strategy. The key to Hydro's strategy was to protect eastern Ontario against the loss of 60 cycle power from Gatineau. With the debate raging in the House, the commission had sent William Ryan, the consulting engineer, to investigate a story that Westinghouse in Hamilton had stopped work on a frequency exchanger for MacLaren because of the uncertainty. Ryan reported that the work was well along, and with Westinghouse working three shifts, it could be installed at Chat's Falls within six months. Hydro purchased the equipment and ordered the engineers to install it in absolute secrecy. Ryan also outlined emergency measures to safeguard the Niagara system if the contracts were cancelled, including the purchase of 25-cycle power from Niagara Hudson and floating power plants. Mitch refused to meet with the companies, but stated publicly that Hydro would not build a second transmission line and that the maximum purchase under any terms would be 400,000 of the 800,000 horsepower under contract.[38]

Unsure about Graustein and Gatineau but informed at once about the purchase of the frequency exchanger, the other three companies were planning their strategy. They knew that Mitch wanted to use the threat of repudiation to force the companies to the bargaining table, but Loring Christie of Beauharnois argued that 'any compromise or revision of the power contracts at the point of the new legislative pistol is equivalent to repudiation.' As long as Roebuck was in charge, Christie believed nothing could be gained by negotiations, and while the companies might have to compromise in the end, they should stand firm on law and principle. On 1 June Ward Wright reassured Beauharnois that, although there was no news, he felt 'satisfied that if no move is made by the Power Companies this matter will drift along until the fall.'

By then Mitch had reports from Stewart Lyon that the Hydro deficit was increasing at an alarming rate and with 27,000 horsepower from MacLaren to come on stream on 1 July and another 67,000 from Beauharnois on 1 October the burden would be unbearable. Lyon recommended that they negotiate immediately with Ottawa Valley, for with that power 'safely under our control, and the frequency changer that will permit us to use it in Eastern

Ontario – now in process of manufacture night and day – we can procrastinate a bit, without much risk, in coming to a settlement with the other contractors.' Meanwhile, he suggested, Parker should be informed that the commission would not accept or pay for the MacLaren power on 1 July. Parker received the bad news from the commission on 5 June.[39]

This was also the day the province invited tenders for refloating a $15 million maturing bond issue. When Chester Walters had begun to canvass the possibilities late in April, the outlook had seemed less than promising. Ever since the introduction of the cancellation bill there had been thinly veiled warnings that Mitch was endangering provincial credit, and a report from Ottawa cited highly placed sources to the effect that the banks would simply shut off credit and even Mitch would not be able to collect his salary. Jackson Dodds of the Bank of Montreal, and president of the Canadian Bankers' Association, had warned that the banks viewed the situation with genuine alarm and felt 'impelled to urge upon the government with all the force and influence at their command to refrain from deciding upon such a course.' Mitch replied from the floor of the House that 'it will be just too bad for the bankers if they try any collusion to injure Ontario's credit. They can draw their own conclusions from that statement. Bankers in the past have been very fair to us and I don't think they would be so foolish as to try to hurt our credit.'[40]

A long meeting with J. Gordon Weir, of the investment firm of McLeod Young Weir, left Walters pessimistic. After a long explanation of why the time was not ripe because of the continuing downward trend of interest rates and the desirability of floating long-term loans, given the heavy maturities in the next few years, Weir got to the point. The bond houses and seventy-five thousand investors in power company bonds were unhappy, he told Walters bluntly, and until the power contracts were 'settled on a basis satisfactory to the bondholders,' not only would public financing 'be expensive but it might even be impossible to sell any great volume of bonds.'[41]

Mitch then told Walters to ask Graham Towers, governor of the Bank of Canada, if the bank would take any treasury bills. Towers visited Toronto on 18 May. Although he believed he had explained that the bank was not a banker to the provinces unless a province wanted some closer and continuing relationship which the bank might consider, Mitch and Walters believed the question had been left open. The arrival of a bank official to examine the books confirmed that impression and they were surprised a few days later when Towers said the bank would not buy any treasury bills except as an open market transaction, as it might any other security.[42]

Despite Weir's warning and intimations from the financial community that the market for bonds was flooded, with $60 million from a recent dominion issue undigested, and that the proposed rate was too low, Mitch decided to go ahead. On 5 June the province invited tenders for $15 million with maturities from forty to fifty years at rates of from 2.25 to 3 per cent. The tenders were to be opened a week later. That done, Mitch went fishing.[43]

Even before Mitch and his pals unloaded their gear in Algoma, there were rumours on the street that Hydro had refused delivery of MacLaren power. The rumours were confirmed Monday morning, and a bulletin of the Financial News Bureau was in every bank and investment house before noon. By the end of the day MacLaren bonds had fallen from $78 to $67 and Beauharnois issues were much weaker. Breaking the story, the Montreal *Gazette* reported that Hydro's action would 'make bond houses, already doubtful of their ability to sell Ontario's proposed new issue, still more hesitant.'[44]

Mitch returned to Toronto late on 11 June. When the tender box was opened the next day it was empty. After a long cabinet meeting, which considered and rejected a proposal from one syndicate to market the issue on a commission basis, Mitch issued a press statement which made headlines in the morning *Globe*:

NO SURRENDER TO MONEY BARONS IS PLEDGE OF HEPBURN
The financial interests undertook to discipline the Government of Ontario because of its stand on the power purchase question.

Those in control of the centralized money machinery combined in an attempt to coerce the Government into submission by refraining in unison from bidding on the bond offering ...

In their efforts to compel the people of Ontario to continue bearing this impossible burden the financial interests have consolidated and have undertaken to force the Government to surrender.

The challenge is not to the Administration, but to popular government and to the people themselves. Sooner or later the issue had to come.

The would-be invisible government must be taught that the power of money stops somewhere .... The plain issue is whether the country is to be governed by elected representatives or by the dictators in control of the machinery of money.

After another long cabinet meeting the next day Mitch announced that all government accounts were to be transferred to the Ontario

Savings Bank, where the interest rate would be raised from 2 to 2.5 per cent to attract deposits, and that on Monday $20 million in short-term government bonds at from 2 to 3 per cent would be offered directly to the public.[45]

There was something unconvincing in the explanation offered by the president of the Investment Dealers' Association that the absence of tenders was not due to collusion but simply to the unattractiveness of the issue. Even the *Financial Post* admitted that offers could have been submitted even if they were unacceptable to the Treasury. Mitch dismissed the explanation as a tissue of lies. 'They lied deliberately for within an hour after it was shown there were no bids for the bonds they sent an emissary up here to tell me that if we would take a reasonable course with regard to the power contracts they could handle our financing.' Their time would come, Mitch warned, for 'it will be my most pleasant duty to impose a tax on those who make the most money out of the least effort.' Having thrown down the gauntlet, Mitch went home for the weekend.

A *Star* editorial that afternoon anticipated the mail Mitch received from across the country. Whether the banks and brokers had been consulted was irrelevant, for the fundamental issue was the sad truth that Canada was 'ruled by a plutocratic autocracy and is a democracy only in name and that by means of interlocking directorates a dozen men control $9 billion of capital and one-half of Canada's business and commercial life. A move to use the money power to dictate political policy in Ontario will quicken in every province movement for economic freedom and develop political repurcussions of national significance.' The lights burned late in the Treasury as Walters got ready for the bond sale on Monday.[46]

Whether his strategy was entirely conscious, it seemed clear on Monday that Mitch had called the bankers' bluff. No less a commanding financial figure than Sir Thomas White publicly announced that he was personally subscribing 'to the full amount of my cash balance available for investment' and urged his fellow banker investors to 'make this loan a notable success.' White explained to Bennett that he knew his action would be criticized, but believed that failure would be disastrous to the credit of the province 'and seriously affect the market value of its own and all other public securities which are now held by hundreds of millions by the Banks, insurance and other financial institutions of Canada. From such a blow we should not recover for years.' Bennett agreed completely. That day $2.5 million was subscribed and before the sale was over the banks had $5 million of new Ontario bonds in their vaults.[47]

In his battle with the banks Mitch had other powerful, if unexpected and perhaps reluctant, allies. It was unlikely, as one outraged Tory said, that Mitch would extract $20 million from 'the worn out and practically empty pockets of the overalls of the farmers on the Back Concessions and the ragged and empty pockets of the unemployed Under Dog.' But when a subscription for $2 million came from Kirkland Lake Gold, followed by orders for a million from Inco, McIntyre-Porcupine and Imperial Oil, and $500,000 from Hollinger and Eaton's, it was obvious that the financial houses did not have a monopoly on all the gold in Ontario. The banks and investment dealers admitted none of that, of course, but insisted that the shorter maturities at the going rate made the new issue an investment so profitable they could not turn it down. Clifford Sifton may have also studied the bottom line, but the covering letter to Mitch when he ordered $40,000 suggested that he was not playing the bankers' game: 'No Sifton or Sifton concern has held an Ontario security for three years but your administration has restored our confidence as witness my subscription. Your present operation will work wonders in squeezing the racket out of the issue of public security. More power to your elbow.'[48]

Mitch loved the theatre and irony of what Charles Bowman, editor of the Ottawa *Citizen*, called a 'struggle against feudalism.' Three days after the issue went on sale Mitch jubilantly fired off a wire to Eddie Odette, lounging around the Savoy in London. 'Already bond issue over top with subscriptions pouring in. Complete victory for administration and demonstrates confidence of Ontario people.' Recounting the victory of the Back Concessions over Bay Street, Mitch conveniently forgot to mention that about half the issue had moved through the financial institutions whose stranglehold on the Treasury he claimed to have broken. But with the Gundy brothers and other feudal barons at the head table, Mitch told a luncheon meeting at the Centurion Club a few months later that 'he had to play up to the man on the street occasionally, such as taking a crack at the bankers, including his good friend Harry Gundy, but that though the bankers were doing the best they could, you had to give them a ride once in a while or the men of the Aberhart and Stephens [*sic*] type would steal your votes.'[49]

The battle with the coupon clippers over, Mitch could devote more of his attention to the 'unemployed under dog.' Mitch was puzzled by the fact that the economic recovery had little effect on the numbers on relief. Construction contracts and employment in the auto-

mobile and steel industries were increasing dramatically. The pulp
and paper industry was reviving, the mines were booming, and agriculture was enjoying a sharp increase in prices. Yet the numbers of
unplaced applicants for jobs in April was the highest on record and
the number on relief hung stubbornly above four hundred thousand.
Mitch also believed that with the system of cash relief and municipal relief projects and increased allowances, despite the decline in federal grants, his government had been both generous and humane.
His opinion was not shared by those who persuaded the relief workers to strike for increased allowances or, indeed, to refuse to work at
all. By the spring he and Croll had come to the conclusion that many
organizers, usually well-known communists, were more interested in
agitation and confrontation than in the welfare of the workers.[50]

The battle line was first drawn at Crowland Township, across the
tracks from Welland. Organizers of the Unemployed Association
persuaded some of the relief workers to throw down their tools and
demand increased allowances and less work. After three weeks of
intermittent violence, township officials arrived at Queen's Park to
warn Mitch that the situation was out of control. Mitch agreed to
send an OPP detachment to protect those who wished to work and
warned the strikers that if they persisted in 'terrorization, breaking
heads and damaging property, they will go to jail. That's all there
is to it.'

In the next few days, Mitch visited Crowland twice and finally
refused to continue negotiations until the men went back to work.
'I have no desire to be hard-headed on this question,' he told
reporters, 'but it is an impossible situation when about half the people are working to keep the other half in idleness' and 'we will not
tolerate a situation where a municipality provides relief work and
those on relief refuse to work.' The strike leaders wanted to fight
to the bitter end but they could not carry the men. With the collapse of the strike, Mitch returned to Crowland to negotiate a substantial increase in the allowances. 'A good Prime Minister, like a
good General,' applauded the *Globe* reflecting the sentiments of the
daily press, 'never sends his men where he wouldn't go himself.'[51]

Mitch's anger increased throughout the spring. In the north,
where he had again suspended the manufacturing condition, organizers of the Lumber Workers Industrial Union greeted the opening of the cutting season with another attempt to close the camps.
Mitch was outraged that the government's efforts to provide work
were deliberately obstructed by 'a few agitators' and urged the men
to return to the bush before the season ended. But by the time the

men overruled the organizers and trekked back to camp in mid-July, only 60 per cent of the contracts could be filled and thirty-five thousand man-days had been lost. In the south, with farmers complaining of a shortage of labour, Mitch and Croll relaxed the regulations to allow the families to stay on relief while the men worked on the farms. But few found the inducement attractive. And although he did not interfere with the passage of the On to Ottawa trekkers through Ontario, he was blunt in his condemnation of the Ontario contingent, led by his old WUL sparring partner, Ewart Humphries, who were 'willing to walk 300 miles on a futile and useless mission, but will not go out and help the farmers harvest this season's crop at a reasonable rate of pay.'[52]

The relief workers' strike in Windsor in July convinced Mitch that a drastic overhaul of the system was essential. Soon after the June election for the newly amalgamated city, the new council with a strong Communist party membership, abolished the practice of requiring work for relief. To force the issue with Queen's Park, Alderman Tom Raycraft, who had run as a CP candidate against Croll, and his friends organized a strike at the woodyard. Croll was on a working holiday in England and Mitch was acting minister. The government was adamant, Mitch stated at once. 'No work, no relief, that goes for Windsor and every other part of the Province ... It's a man's privilege to refuse work – but it is our duty and policy to refuse assistance if he does so.' After a ten-day stalemate, with the strikers cut off relief and Mitch refusing to bend, the organizers finally conceded defeat.[53]

Convinced that the relief rolls were laden with men who had no intention of working, Mitch called the Queen's Park press corp into his office as the Windsor strike collapsed to announce that the cabinet was going to take a hard look at the whole system of relief. The day of the soap-box agitator was over, and the day of the taxpayer, the 'forgotten man' had dawned. The cabinet met without Croll, still in England, and Roebuck, on holidays in Long Island. Walters presented a sobering report on relief expenditure. Despite the improvements in the economy, the cost of direct relief, work projects, and administration, exclusive of federal contributions, for the past four months was $12.5 million. After the meeting, Mitch announced that a committee under Walters would examine ways of cutting costs, but that as a first step in August all single men or heads of families who refused farm work would be taken off the rolls and where there was a shortage of domestic help municipalities could also strike single women off the lists.[54]

The cabinet studied the report of Walters's committee on 30 July and approved a radical change in relief policy. As of 1 September the province would turn over complete responsibility to the municipalities and pay a sum of $7.50 per capita to the defaulting municipalities and $5.00 to the others. Anticipating the screams from the cities – Toronto would lose $660,000 and Windsor over $1 million – and opposition charges that he was simply dumping a $10 million burden on the municipalities, Mitch argued that with 60 cents of every dollar spent on relief, drastic action was imperative. 'We were almost breaking the back of our own people, and besides there was no uniformity of relief distribution,' Mitch explained. The new policy, he estimated, would save the taxpayers almost a $1 million a month. Local councils, he did not have to explain, could no longer use Queen's Park as a whipping boy. Just how they could assume a larger relief burden he did not try to explain.[55]

To find work for the thirteen to fifteen thousand single men on relief, Mitch ordered Agriculture, Welfare, and Labour to undertake a province-wide campaign to match the unemployed with jobs. The agreement with the federal government on the Trans Canada meant there was work in the north, and the first contingent of 275 single men left Union Station on 7 August. But the supply was soon exhausted, for of the 1,350 men examined in Toronto, only 350 were declared fit for heavy work and an equal number were found physically unemployable. With the heaviest field crop in years, the farmers were desperate for help during the summer. The government offered free transportation and assured married men that their relief allowances would remain untouched. There were 650 placements in the first week and by the end of the harvest over four thousand had been working on the farms.[56]

Mitch's policy shift was widely seen as a repudiation of David Croll, who had been moving towards increasing provincial involvement in relief supervision. Cynics such as the Carty brothers were convinced that Mitch had sent Croll away on a combined conference and holiday trip in order to have a free hand. Mitch admitted that the new policy had never been discussed with Croll, for it was only in July that the Treasury realized some drastic action had to be taken to control the escalating costs. However, he had asked him to return several weeks early. The *Empress of Britain* docked at Quebec on 16 August and Croll was in Mitch's office the next morning. They emerged smiling an hour later to announce that they were 'in complete agreement, there never was any difference of opinion.'

However, it was obvious that the government could not institute such a dramatic change overnight. On 28 August Croll announced that the policy would be implemented in four stages. The delay would cost the Treasury $5.3 million. Meanwhile, the work of purging the rolls of 'cheaters and idlers' would be relentlessly pursued. However, Mitch was soon fully engaged in helping to send a more sympathetic government to Ottawa and delayed implementation until after the federal election.[57]

The battles against the power barons, the coupon clippers and the soap-box agitators had taken their toll. Mitch had returned from his southern vacation in January feeling better than he had in a long time. By spring, however, his doctors warned him that little could be done for his high blood pressure, insomnia, occasional palpitations of the heart, and recurrent attacks of bronchitis unless he got more rest and exercise. But Mitch had never learned how to pace himself, and while the evenings spent with the gang in the King Eddy or the weekend retreats to the estates of his friends outside the city took his mind away from the office, they did little for his health.[58]

As usual, the tales of his extra-curricular activities continued to titillate the curious and shock the puritanical. Charles Murphy passed on the word to his fellow senator, Rodolphe Lemieux, that the 'Big Liberal Medicine Man continues to follow the primrose paths of falliance [sic] formerly trod by Sir Adolphe Caron in the old days and, in later years, by our genial friend from New Brunswick, Harry Emmerson.' A new woman in Mitch's life added spice to the tales. Mitch had not forgotten his shipboard meeting with the young Hepburn Liberal and not long after his return he arrived at her father's farm alone and unannounced. Two weeks later she was working at Queen's Park. The romance blossomed. The beautiful young woman, robust in body and playful in spirit, became his frequent companion. Strongly independent, she resented the term mistress, and would have been outraged if Angela Bruce had included her as one of Mitch's 'tarts.' She was in love with him. Like most of his entourage, she usually called him 'Chief' but there were times when they both preferred 'Uncle Dudley.'[59]

Mitch's family life, which somehow survived the alcohol and the infidelities, also changed dramatically in the spring. On the anniversary of the Quints' birth, the government decided to have an 'Adopt a Child Week' to relieve the congestion in the provincial orphanages. Before any announcement was made, Mitch called Eva, who was delighted at the prospect of adopting a child. For three weeks officials of the Children's Aid branch scoured the province to find an heir for Bannockburn. Finally, one Saturday morning in May, Mitch and Dave Croll went to the children's centre to see a blue-eyed, healthy, two-and-a-half-year-old boy. Mitch wanted to take him right away, but Croll explained there were procedures to be followed. Impatiently, Mitch called Croll several times a day, but it was three days before he could pick up his son and, with Eddie Wooliver at the wheel, drive young Peter Mitchell Hepburn to his new home. Mitch was ecstatic, as they showed Peter his own puppy, the horses and colts in the barn, and the twenty children living in the farm hands' cottages. 'Will he call you "daddy",' Alex Gibb of the *Star* asked? Mitch smiled: 'I presume he'll call me "Mitch" the same as everybody else does. What do you think?' Eva was delighted with her son, and two months later they were looking for a girl 'to match our boy.' But it was not until September 1936 that Patricia Maxine joined the family. Helen followed four years later.[60]

Mitch refused to let reporters talk to Peter or take his picture, for the boy's arrival increased his anxiety for the safety of himself and his family in the spring and summer of 1935. So bitter was the feeling in some parts of the province that during the 1934 campaign Mitch had carried a revolver in the glove compartment. As premier he continued to travel armed. After the election some of the threats to his family's safety seemed to come from Henry Walker, who claimed that the Liberals owed him $1,000 for services rendered during the election. When Mitch refused to pay, Walker promised local organizers that he would get him 'if he didn't come across good and plenty.' And if he could not get Mitch personally, he warned that the 'Premier's wife and mother are still here.' To end the harassment and threats, Mitch finally laid a complaint in July 1935, and at the initial hearing in August, when Mitch presented his case, the magistrate found sufficient evidence to send Walker to jail pending a trial. Yet the threats continued. Mitch installed floodlights around the house and the barn, and while he was away for weeks at a time during the federal election campaign, the OPP maintained a twenty-four-hour surveillance and the St Thomas fire department was prepared for a possible arson attempt.

However, although Mitch was concerned for the safety of his family, nothing was going to keep him off the hustings when Bennett dissolved Parliament in August, with the election called for 14 October.[61]

'A big black X against his name'

The day before Bennett dissolved Parliament, Mitch and King shared the platform in Woodstock. 'I want to take this opportunity of pledging to Mr. King my loyal and undivided support in this campaign,' Mitch said, for 'there is no road too rough, nor night too dark for me to travel in carrying the message of Liberalism.' King's election would begin a new era when the premiers could sit down and discuss 'common policies' for national regeneration. As he followed the accomplishments of Mitch's administration, King replied, he had been a source of great encouragement to him; he 'will play a part second to none for Liberalism in this country.'[1]

Mitch had been waiting restlessly for that day since June 1934 when he had exclaimed that victory would not be complete until Ottawa had also fallen. Before his own session began, Mitch had wanted to discuss the election with the federal Liberal caucus, particularly after Bennett's New Deal broadcasts late in January had indicated the strategy if not the timing of the election. As far as Mitch was concerned there was only one Liberal party. The Ontario branch was located a few floors below him in the King Eddy in the offices of Harry Johnson and Frank O'Connor. The tension between the federal and provincial Liberals during the fall by-elections had continued, but at a critical December meeting it was acknowledged that the provincial organization was very much in command, whatever formal recognition was given to Vincent Massey, Lambert, and the National Liberal Federation. Despite Lambert's concern about the power of Mitch's party, it was the only realistic conclusion. Mitch led a party with an effective organization, access to campaign funds, and the clout provided by a government in power. He was determined to command his army in battle, not turn it over to Mackenzie King and his ineffectual general staff.[2]

Behind Mitch's enthusiasm, King saw only ambition. His suspicions were fed by incessant stories that, even if Mitch did not, others saw him as the Liberal heir-apparent. King even caught Sir Wilfrid 'talking in a friendly way' to Mitch, and only when 'he came out and sat down to talk with me, and let me feel his friendliness towards myself' was King reassured. Mitch laughed off the rumours that he was Ottawa-bound. He decided to take a Caribbean rather than a west coast vacation, he told fellow-inflationist Robert Cromie of the Vancouver *Sun*, because a 'trip across Canada might be misconstrued by those who think I have federal ambitions.' On his return to Queen's Park in January he denied he had any thought of leaving Ontario: 'You can make that as strong as you like.'[3]

As an ally in the battle, Mitch saw nothing improper in his proposal to meet the federal Ontario caucus. Obviously much more sensitive to King's apprehensions, Senator Hardy suggested a smaller meeting on the grounds that anything said in caucus would be in the papers the next day. Mitch then proposed that King 'send someone in whom he had complete confidence to confer with members of this administration in the city of Toronto.' Hardy backed away from warning Mitch that he was treading not only on King's turf but also on his anxieties, and replied that 'the trouble with an intermediary is, to my mind, that Mr. K. is so particular as to every word in such matters.' Hardy volunteered to see King about a meeting, 'now or a little later,' but Bill Fraser pre-empted Hardy's delicate diplomacy at caucus the next day when he said that Mitch wanted to meet with the members. 'King had it checked through Colin Campbell,' Lambert noted in his diary.[4]

Coly Campbell was not the man to send on a sensitive diplomatic mission, and he saw little point in layering the message with King's verbal icing. Mitch claimed that 'he had never felt so hurt in his life' when Campbell told him bluntly that King did not want to see him and immediately suspended diplomatic relations with Ottawa. In Toronto, to beg for money from the Toronto finance committee, Lambert learned from O'Connor that the government had settled a $2.5 million account with Harry McLean of Dominion Construction and had $200,000 left, 'but Hepburn had said it cd not be used for Fed'l purposes.' When Lambert appeared in the role of peacemaker, Mitch angrily told him that 'he had never had a "break" from K. who had no "guts"' and that King was so unpopular he would be beaten if Stevens succeeded Bennett as Tory leader. Mitch threatened to make the rupture public by refusing to attend a testimonial dinner to King ten days later. Always blameless, King concluded that Mitch's 'mind is being poisoned by Campbell or others, or he has a guilty conscience somewhere himself.' But he yielded to Lambert's plea to call him:

He said when I phoned him he had been greatly hurt, by my saying I did not want to see him ... I explained exactly what was meant, & how message had been wrongly conveyed or interpreted. – I told him it was to save both him & me embarrassment by Tories claiming 'a conspiracy' between us. He said something about wishing to be loyal always to the Liberal party. I told him I hoped he would feel the same always towards myself, and know that I was anxious to help him all I could ... It is ridiculous of Hepburn seeking out a grievance, Lambert thinks he is tired & irritable and that it is vanity – I think it is wider ambition, and desire like Bennett to be running everything.

It was a strange conversation, and Mitch must have wondered how a meeting of Canada's two leading Liberals to discuss Liberal election strategy could be seen as a 'conspiracy.'[5]

But an open break was avoided, and Mitch and his colleagues went to Ottawa for the Liberal banquet. The federal members hosted a luncheon for Mitch, and a thousand Liberals gathered at night to pay tribute to King and the party. With Mitch sitting beside him, King found the dinner hour trying, for Mitch was 'wholly wrapped up in himself, and wanted mostly to talk of the majorities that *he* was going to give us in Ontario.' With Ontario safely delivered, Mitch said, 'he didn't care what happened & he would drop out of politics.' King was thrown a little off stride when he was told to make his speech '"short and snappy" that the young people wanted to dance,' but Mitch in his speech was short and snappy and, King grudgingly admitted, 'got a tremendous ovation – they like a fighter.'[6]

King was as unable to realize that the young people preferred dancing to listening to him as he was to accept the fact that his success in Ontario could depend on Mitch Hepburn and the 'machine' he so frequently denounced. As Lambert and Massey knew only too well, the purse strings in Toronto would only be opened by the persuasive intervention of Frank O'Connor and the sense of gratitude felt by the clients of the provincial government. Although King had asked J.C. Elliott to see if Mitch could help finance the campaign in Ontario, when Lambert asked King to intervene personally he received only a long harangue about 'the sordid side of politics,' his lack of trust of 'an Irish Catholic drinking man' such as O'Connor, and that he refused 'to be drawn in any way into any situation which could tie me up to him in matters of this kind.'[7]

By the fall of 1934, however, the situation was desperate. Massey and Lambert were 'in a funk over the absence of funds' and, with Lambert threatening to quit, King accepted the inevitable. After calls to Long and, after some hesitation, to O'Connor, he told Lambert that all would be ready for him when he arrived in Toronto. O'Connor and his assistant Bill Bennett – the man all contractors see Lambert said – got down to work and before it was over the Toronto committee had raised more than $500,000.[8]

Mitch had not been directly involved in the discussions over finance, but with Frank O'Connor based in the King Eddy he was undoubtedly kept fully informed. While Mathews and E.G. Long had their own contacts, and J.S. McLean of Canada Packers, who had joined the Toronto committee in the fall of 1934, was not a Hepburn Liberal, the contributions came largely from friends and clients of Mitch and the provincial government. More than willing to play by the rules of the day, Mitch had told the *Star*'s Roy Greenaway after the 1934 election that he was going to make the liquor interests pay for the next election. With soaring revenues from the new beer and wine policy and Mitch's tolerance for practices which violated both the letter and the spirit of the law, the brewers were easy marks. Distillers, like his good friend Larry McGuinness, were unlikely to slam the door on anyone who had the ear of Eddie Odette. Before the books were closed the brewers had funnelled over $60,000 and malters and distillers another $35,000 into the Liberal war chest.[9]

Mitch had already won the support of the northern gold miners with his attack on Bennett's multi-million dollar raid on the mines. Early in the campaign he asked King to see Jack Bickell, 'a very intimate friend of mine and a good supporter of the party,' who would voice the sentiments of the government of Ontario. 'I believe the time has arrived when there should be some definite pronouncement of policy in order to reassure the prospective investors,' Mitch argued, and if, 'in your wisdom, you consider some joint statement should be made, please believe I shall be only too happy to associate myself with you in this respect.' King promised to keep Mitch's proposal in mind, but refused to see Bickell and J.Y. Murdoch of Noranda. In Toronto the miner's doors remained closed, although there were contributions to local candidates. Finally, in Vancouver on 28 September, King promised a federal-provincial national mining policy, including taxation and administration, that would provide the stability necessary for growth. The miners responded with over $60,000 to the central fund, much of it from Mitch's friends Bickell, Jack Hammell, and Ben Smith, and the $30,000 from LeSueur of Imperial Oil may have reflected the heavy investment he and other directors had in the Kirkland Lake gold fields.[10]

Among the manufacturers, Canadian General Electric stood out with a not inappropriate contribution of $25,000, since the company, partly through Mitch's intervention, had settled for almost 100 per cent of its bills on Henry's Abitibi Canyon project. The gift of $7,500 from Algoma was not excessive, although the larger Stelco felt that $5,000 was adequate. Crawley-McCracken, the giant provisioner on northern construction projects, was an obvious benefactor, as were the three construction companies which had received large Trans Canada contracts in July. But the absence in Lambert's records of gifts from the Franceschinis of Dufferin Paving and all but a few companies with northern timber leases suggested that not all the funds passed through Lambert's hands.

Mitch and O'Connor would have found Lambert's meticulous bookkeeping amusing. The average expenditure from the central fund for the eighty-two Ontario ridings of just over $3,000 was not much more than one-third of what was necessary, and nothing was recorded to cover the costs of travel for Mitch, his ministers, and provincial organizers. Unquestionably, O'Connor and Johnson dug into the provincial account and much of the money raised locally – to supplement the $200 Lambert sent to Kenora or the $100 to Hamilton, for example – came from those more directly interested in being in the good graces of Queen's Park than in saving Canada from chaos. The Irish drinking man rejected the proposal that he buy a seat in the Senate for $100,000 and took his chances with a contribution of $25,000, although with an annual salary from Laura Secord and Fanny Farmer of well over $100,000 and his recent sale of 180,000 shares of Fanny Farmer for $US1,350,000, he could have financed the campaign himself. Mitch claimed that O'Connor and the provincial collectors had financed the Liberal campaign in Ontario and had helped elsewhere – even paying the $6000 to republish King's *Industry and Humanity* – and he could never understand or accept King's insistence that it was all the work of the federal committee.[11]

Mitch had remained silent during the spring and summer but with the federal House prorogued on 5 July and an election certain within two or three months, he simply could not understand why

Mackenzie King would not 'make a key speech which would serve as a chart for the rest of the Liberal party heads to go by.' Although the CCF could not be dismissed in industrial Ontario, Mitch was more concerned about the noisy departure of H.H. Stevens from the Tory party and the appearance of his Reconstruction Party. Stevens and his Price Spreads inquiry had been enormously popular in Ontario, and Mitch was convinced that unless the Liberals had a progressive policy and conducted an aggressive campaign, Stevens would cut deeply into the Liberal vote. Norman Lambert was both sceptical and suspicious when he wrote John Dafoe that 'our friend, Mitch Hepburn, professes to be much concerned about the effect Stevens will have in Ontario. I doubt, however, whether Hepburn is as sincere in this opinion as he might be. He has been very restive of late concerning federal interests and what our policy was going to be, etc., etc., forgetting entirely that he won his election in Ontario without any platform at all.'[12]

King was prepared to follow that example nationally. In the last caucus before prorogation he had delivered something less than a fighting speech when he declared that he did not intend 'to propose any plan or any ism as a cure-all; that these various plans are only possible of execution by means of dictatorship, more in the way of depriving the individual of all his liberties; that I thought we should make our fight for the liberty for which the Liberal party stands and show how strongly the trend had been towards dictatorship in Canada; that all these plans were mere expedients to meet conditions that had their causes elsewhere, namely in the restriction of trade.' Above all, the party should not become 'a target for its enemies to fire at.'[13]

From the beginning of the federal election campaign, with the first of three radio broadcasts on 31 July, to the end King remained an evasive target. He moved leisurely across the country, wisely concluding that too much repetition of his speeches might reveal their lack of substance. It was not 'the fist of a pugilist that Canada needs,' King intoned, 'but the hand of a physician.' There were many, however, who agreed with the always cynical Lambert that a physician relying on sermons about 'Brotherhood and Neighborhood' and 'Dictatorship vs. democracy and freedom' might not attract too many patients. Who cares about Chanak, about which King had spoken for half an hour in Quebec, exclaimed Brooke Claxton, a prominent federal Liberal. 'What the people want to know is what the Liberals will do to raise purchasing power, to reduce the burden of debt, or balance the budget including the railway deficit, to control privilege and provide work.' As the campaign neared its end, Claxton concluded that King 'would have done better never to have opened his mouth,' and described the Liberal propaganda as 'hopelessly antiquated and flabby.'[14]

Echoing the views of his boss, Harry Johnson complained to Chubby Power that the campaign had to be more aggressive, with the 'Provincial Premiers, Mackenzie, Stewart, McPhee, Marshall, Roebuck, Lapointe, Rinfret, yourself, Ralston, and others, speaking almost nightly – sharp, staccato, hard-hitting, stumping.' King's strategy was fine but would never 'stir up the enthusiasm necessary for a sweep,' and the headlines would depend on the 'engine-room crew.' Power agreed. 'I listened carefully over the radio and I even took the trouble to read the speeches,' he replied. 'Like you, I like the line, but I find that the fire is lacking.' The campaign had to be warmed up, 'and I think with Mitch and Ian Mackenzie stumping the country in the English Provinces and raising hell generally; with Cardin and Lapointe in our end; and Rolph in the Maritimes; all of them handling the situation without too much regard for politeness, we may attract some attention in the campaign and get the requisite headlines. As you say, this is the Boiler-maker's job and it has to be done.'[15]

Mitch was more than willing to raise a little hell. During the first two and last three weeks of the campaign he spoke in over fifty Ontario ridings and spent the entire month of September in the west, the Maritimes, and Quebec. Soon after the campaign began he spoke to Liberal organizers and federal candidates in Toronto at a private luncheon at the Centurion Club. Somehow a Tory got in and a report of the meeting was soon on Bennett's desk:

He told the Liberal candidates that as far as the voting public is concerned the Conservative Government is a thing of the past and the people are not interested in the Liberal Party unless constructive policies are enunciated, but they have to remember they are not going to be elected by thinking men and that they have to talk the language of the people they are speaking to; that the farmer is chiefly interested in a better market for his farm products, and to tell him that Mackenzie King is in a position to work out a reciprocal treaty with the U.S.A. that should have been put through in 1911 ... that what we need in the north country is not reforestation as outlined by Stephens [sic], but negotiation of treaties to sell our present matured timber and wider markets for our newsprint; that currency reform is an immediate necessity as Canada as a whole is faced with a service charge on its funded debt of one billion per annum ... and the resources of the country do not permit of meeting this.

The Liberals not only had to advocate constructive policies, Mitch continued, but 'had to promise more than they could give' for they were 'competing for votes with men who would promise anything.' Mitch's performance impressed the Tory interloper: 'I would say that everything said by Mr. Hepburn of a radical nature must be looked at through the eyes of a man who fully expects to be the future Prime Minister of Canada; that is, a man standing for orderly Government but alive to the needs of the hour and trying to gauge public psychology in competition with extreme reformers, or, as he expressed his opinion of Stephens [sic], "an extreme hypocrite".'[16]

Although Mitch varied the emphasis as the audience changed, the seventy-five speeches and radio addresses across the country were much the same. He dismissed the New Deal, ghost-written by Herridge, as the ultimate in death-bed repentance. Stevens was more difficult to dismiss. After his conversion, he sounded like Mitch Hepburn in his attacks on the near monopolies in the tobacco, packing, and canning industries that exploited the farmers; the giant retailers who cut out competition and fattened on enormous price spreads; the captains of finance who curtailed credit, controlled the press, and held the politicians in the palm of their hands. Stevens's solutions also sounded familiar as he ranged far to the left of King's Liberalism without touching the suspect shoals of socialism: the expansion of credit and currency, anti-combines legislation, a massive housing and public works program, progressive income taxes, and heavy taxes on profits.

Since the Stevens platform had to be taken seriously, Stevens himself had to be attacked. While Slaght and Stevens engaged in verbal brawls during the campaign, Mitch denounced Stevens as 'The Great Pretender' who stood with Bennett behind the tariff until the by-elections forecast the demise of the government; who refused to declare himself on the tariff and a government-owned national bank; and whose distracting skirmishing on the sidelines was designed to let the Tories sneak back into office. From one end of the country to the other Mitch told the voters that a vote for Harry Stevens was the greatest threat to the return of a Liberal government.

On the whole, however, Mitch spent less time bashing his opponents than in earlier times and more discussing the issues and policies. The fundamental question was freer trade and reciprocity with the United States. The export market, above all the American one, was the solution to the problems facing the primary producer – the farmers, lumbermen, fishermen, and miners across Canada. He reminded the industrial workers, who were told their jobs would disappear with the tariff, that Canada's per capita industrial exports were the highest in the world in the late 1920s when the Liberals were resolutely lowering the tariff. It was behind the comforting walls of the tariff that monopolies flourished and corporations fixed prices to make unconscionable profits at the expense of the consumers and producers. All that would end, and Stevens be made redundant, with the election of 'the greatest statesman on the North American continent,' who would rectify the tragic mistake of 1911 when 'No truck nor trade with the Yankees' defeated Laurier.[17]

When Mitch turned to monetary reform, he promised much more than Mackenzie King was prepared to give. He argued constantly that the publicly owned Bank of Canada, to which the Liberals were committed, would counter the power of the chartered banks and expand currency and credit. The public debt had to be converted at the current lower rate of interest, for it was high interest on old debt that was crippling not only homeowners and farmers but governments as well. Closely tied to monetary reform was the kind of fiscal responsibility he had shown in managing Ontario's deficit for, while public works served the immediate purpose of relieving unemployment, in principle governments could not spend their way out of the Depression.[18]

Although Mitch was always quick to defend Ontario's interest, he believed that the time had come to take a new look at the old constitution. The Depression underlined the need for action on a national scale to deal with unemployment, minimum wages and maximum hours of work, old age pensions, and other social and industrial questions. Even a province as large as Ontario could not deal with such problems on its own. The answer was not in unilateral federal action which rode roughshod over the provinces, as the dictatorial Bennett had done, but in the calm reconsideration of the old British North America Act. And there would never be a better chance than with a Liberal prime minister ready to sit down with eight Liberal provincial premiers. King agreed. With the Liberals in Ottawa, he promised Mitch, governing Canada would be a united effort, which was 'only possible between governments that enjoy to the full each other's confidence and whose political views are also in accord.' With King as prime minister, Mitch assured the voters, the provincial premiers would be invited to Ottawa before the snow fell to resolve together the problems facing and dividing the country.[19]

King and the Liberals were the only answer. 'Canada needs Mackenzie King at this time; she needs a man of his high statesmanship, his foresight, his ability, his position in international affairs during these troubled times ... We want leaders that know where they are going. We want men at the helm who have vision, statesmanship and all those qualities that we need so badly to-day; I say that because I sat under him for eight years. I know the calibre of man he is.' Although the best the Liberal publicity bureau could invent was the slogan 'It's King or Chaos,' Mitch tried to put a little more content into the King side of the equation and he did not say that King had 'no guts.'[20]

Mitch's trip out west was his first since he had left Winnipeg. The pressure had come from the west, and he readily yielded to the requests of his western friends at the end of August for two weeks of head-to-head battle with the forces of funny money and socialism. As he explained at the Centurion Lunch on the eve of his departure, he was going 'to try and show the Western farmer that the Liberal Party is a party based on reform and that the Ontario Liberal Party is just as alive to the needs of the country as are the Western farmers, and that he is prepared either to make or break the party in the West; but that Western Liberalism needs to have its faith restored, as the election in Alberta vividly showed.'[21]

Mitch's doctors had detected signs of heart strain in August and urged him not to undertake the gruelling trip. But he was not to be dissuaded and boarded a private CPR car on 30 August. Roy Elmhirst and Eddie Wooliver were along to look after the logistics, his good friend Wishart Campbell, the popular singer and radio personality, to warm up the crowds, and Keith Munro of the *Star* to feed the stories of Mitch's conquest of the west back home. The private car, tacked on to a variety of expresses, locals, and even freights, was a blessing for it enabled Mitch to avoid the crowds waiting for him at the hotels and the well-meaning local celebrities who would have been happy to party with him all night. As they passed through northern Ontario, where there had been threats to Mitch's life, the CPR sent an inspection engine over the line ahead of his train and uniformed and plainclothes officers of the OPP mingled with the crowd during his stop-overs at the Sault and Port Arthur.[22]

Mitch was front-page news as he campaigned across the west. Liberal organizers packed the halls and Wishart, the master at pre-game entertainment, usually had the audience singing when Mitch arrived. After speaking in Winnipeg, he filled the Trianon in Regina, where the Conacher brothers and Dick Irvine of the Maple Leafs shared his platform. After driving the forty miles to Moose Jaw for another speech the same night, he went on to Swift Current, with a foray to the small town of Cabri in the heart of CCF country, then on to Lethbridge for a Saturday night speech. They hitched his car to a freight to catch the main line from Calgary to Banff.

Ian Mackenzie joined him for a day of relaxation and then guided him through four days of ultramontane politics with the first stop at Kamloops where the CCF was threatening. Arriving at Vancouver the next morning, they were piped through the station to the CPR wharf where they sailed to Victoria and, after an evening speech, caught the midnight boat back for a day of turbulent campaigning in Vancouver. A day later Mitch was in Edmonton, where his speech from the Empire Theatre was broadcast across the province and, with innumerable whistle stops, he went on to Yorkton where two thousand people waited two hours for the train to arrive. Fourteen days and twenty speeches after he crossed the border, Mitch returned to the welcoming embrace of Peter Heenan in Kenora. But he had never really left the campaign in Ontario, for Keith Munro's reports had been front-page news in the *Star* and all the Ontario dailies had chronicled his war on the western front.[23]

Mitch found western politics 'scrambled' and difficult to analyse, and Roy Elmhirst observed that after leaving Regina the audiences became 'more difficult to understand.' However, Mitch emphasized the same themes as he had in Ontario and preached the gospel of free trade, monetary reform, fiscal responsibility, and constitutional change. Moreover, he argued, because the Liberals would win a majority east of Manitoba, a vote for a third party was a vote wasted and western voters should get on the bandwagon and strengthen their voice within the Liberal caucus. And that caucus would be a 'liberal' caucus, for Ontario Liberals now stood beside the west in the demand for basic reforms in the commercial and monetary policy of the country. Who had bludgeoned the banks into lower interest rates, confronted the St James Street power barons, championed the cause of the primary producer? But you could not spend your way out of the depression, he insisted, for the only money the government has is taken from the people. 'Only over in Alberta, Mr. Aberhart has a different idea,' he told his Regina audience, 'and if it works, no one else will ever have to.'

Forget the illusions of socialism and social credit. The west had, 'as it has not had since 1911, an opportunity to "cash in" on the willingness of the older provinces to put into effect the policies without which there is not the remotest chance of prosperity returning to the prairie country ... the chance of a lifetime for free trade and a sane monetary system ... a national policy built on the lines of western requirements.' His appeal, to some at least, was persuasive:

We, on the prairies, have been accustomed to think and declare that the real vigor of Liberalism was to be found in the West. Mr. Hepburn has, through his visit, dispelled that placidly accepted idea. He has revealed to us an Eastern Liberal moulded along the lines that the most aggressive Westerner desires. By convincing the Western public that this type of Liberalism prevails also in the East, a real service has been rendered. Liberal forces from both sections of the country will unite with greater confidence and closer understanding in a sweeping victory over the most dictatorial forces that have ever threatened this country's freedom since the dawn of responsible government.[24]

Mitch's western audiences found the messenger as intriguing, and as unlikely, as the message. They had read of the new wind that had blown through Tory Ontario, wrote J.B. McGeachy of the _Winnipeg Free Press_, but to hear its premier was 'like hearing a church choir break suddenly into the St. Louis Blues.' Hepburn was a strange combination: a man who had 'a capacity for forming coherent opinions on economic questions, a rare quality' and could present them 'with excellent clarity and force and not too many statistics,' but who remained an 'old-fashioned political buccaneer.' His speech in Winnipeg was the best McGeachy had heard in many years, and his nicely spaced jokes and wisecracks were a welcome verbal lubricant from the tedium of so many political speeches.

Like other columnists, McGeachy found a surprising and appealing informality and naturalness about a man whose self-confidence and ease on the platform enabled him to talk to his audience without affectation. His language, others noted, came off the farm where he was born, a 'down east' touch where the final g's were dropped on the 'comin' and 'goin' and a transition introduced with a confidential 'Lemme tell you.' There was also a disarming openness, an impishness, a combination of satire and levity, that showed that 'he has the courage to reveal to his audience the entire range of his nature and while a few conventional souls may misunderstand the great majority will take him to their hearts. His scorn is wholesome and unreserved.' And there was also the wit, so often turned on himself. Upsetting a glass of water with one dramatic gesture, Mitch joked, 'I am glad I didn't upset an empty glass because an empty glass always annoys me.'[25]

Mitch's least successful meetings were in Victoria and Vancouver. Nowhere had the visit been so carefully publicized. Robert Cromie of the _Sun_ had sent a reporter to Kamloops to catch him as he crossed the mountains, and in a large front-page story had chroni-

cled the meteoric career of Canada's 'Man of Destiny.' Others, like
Mayor Gerry McGeer, had hailed Mitch as an ally in the struggle
for monetary reform and a Bank of Canada, which, as McGeer
wrote Mitch, would 'serve as the nation's most important public utility creating the means of servicing past debts and the progress of the
future.' Although Mitch managed to reach the crowd, the constant
booing of Premier Pattullo and the Liberal candidates in Victoria
suggested they had little to offer. In Vancouver's Denman Auditorium not even his jokes could penetrate the tumult orchestrated by
a few hundred longshoremen who effectively destroyed the meeting.

Mitch may not have been aware that British Columbia's Liberalism was identified with Duff Pattullo's ambitious 'work and wages'
program, with radical social reforms, and varieties of market intervention Pattullo liked to call 'Socialized Capitalism.' 'If anything
was needed to show the total confusion of party politics in this western country,' commented Bruce Hutchison after the Victoria meeting, 'Mr. Hepburn supplied the need with an unstinted generosity.'

One does not recall anything more cruel and ruthless than the spectacle
of Mr. Hepburn standing beside Premier Pattullo on the stage of the Royal
Victoria Theatre here and impaling the Pattullo programme point by point;
and all with quips and minstrel stories to which the ministers of the Pattullo government had to listen and smile, just as if their brain children were
not being butchered at their feet.

Quite evidently Mr. Hepburn didn't know what he was doing ... Quite
evidently he was under the pathetic illusion that he and British Columbia
Liberalism belonged to the same political faith. Quite evidently, despite
all the missionary work of Mr. McGeer, Mr. Hepburn is unconverted and
unredeemed, a Liberal of the old school, a Tory by our western standards.

British Columbia had obviously not sold 'its new deal, its planned
economy, its monetary reform to eastern Canada,' Hutchison concluded sarcastically, and if King formed a government dominated
by Quebec and Ontario 'then British Columbia Liberalism is going
to be a pretty small voice, crying in a pretty large wilderness.'
Ontario's 'luminous comet' had streaked across the Pacific sky, but
instead of 'scattering the political stardust that the Liberal party had
expected, he left only a cinder in the Pattullo government's eye.'[26]

After two days back in western Ontario, where Angus Macdonald of Nova Scotia shared the platform and enjoyed his hospitality
in St Thomas, Mitch was off again on a whirlwind tour of the maritimes, where he drew larger and more enthusiastic crowds than

Mackenzie King. Mitch found that Lunenburg fishermen, Cape Breton miners, and Island farmers knew all about exports and world prices, the tariff and domestic prices, banks and interest rates. And they also enjoyed his rustic humour. Even more impressive was his appearance at a rally at Quebec City on the way home. Chubby Power and Jean-François Pouliot had been pressing him to come and, when it seemed to be impossible, Power demanded that Lambert adjust his schedule. 'You have no idea of the enthusiasm aroused in Quebec City when it became known we were endeavouring to have Mitch Hepburn here,' he wrote. 'Nothing will help more to bring all factions of the Liberal party together than Mitch's visit since the rebels have been telling the people what a great man he is. Besides this I am sure he will draw a larger crowd than Stevens, and between ourselves Stevens, more on account of curiosity than for any other reason will possibly have a bigger gathering than King.' Such a peremptory request from the boss of the Quebec region could not be turned down, and Mitch raced back to Quebec on 30 September.

With Power, Taschereau, Cardin, and a dozen MPs, on the platform, and Wishart at the piano, Mitch received a wild ovation when he appeared. The crowd of eight thousand responded to Lapointe's introduction of him as the 'greatest fighter in Canadian politics' with a boisterous rendition of 'Il a gagné ses epaulettes,' roared its approval as he began 'Monsieur le President,' and cheered lustily as he continued, 'ce n'est pas sans emotion, ce soir, que je vous apporte le salut cordial et l'hommage de la province-sœur d'Ontario. Je tiens particulièrement à saluer les jeunes. Mes amis. Je vous tends la main … Ensemble, nous allions assurer la victoire libérale.' The enemy of the trusts, the fearless opponent of the banks, the critic of the monopolies, the platform artist who could dismiss Stevens with the story of the thief who ran with the crowd shouting 'stop thief,' and the good friend of French Canadians and Roman Catholics lived up to his billing. The crowd spilled out of the hall to march downtown chanting 'Mitch Hepburn, Mitch Hepburn, Mitch Hepburn.' Fighting exhaustion and the dangerous signs of a debilitating cold, Mitch crossed the Ottawa for the last two weeks of the campaign.[27]

Mitch's colleagues in the provincial party were almost as exhausted. The machine that was engineered to win on 19 June had been refuelled to win again on 14 October. The OLA offices had taken complete responsibility for the Ontario campaign and functioned as 'an integral part of the national organization' which Massey had established in the King Eddy. Every provincial cabinet minister was pressed into service. Arthur Roebuck appeared in every riding where there was a strong labour vote, David Croll appealed to the Jewish vote as far away as Winnipeg's North End, Peter Heenan blanketed the north, and Harry Nixon and Duncan Marshall solicited the farm vote across the province. The local members worked their own ridings, with Charlie Cox's intimate knowledge of ethnic and timber politics at the Lakehead ensuring C.D. Howe an easy victory there and the Franco-Ontarian members making certain that not one Tory would grace the Commons from the Ottawa valley and the north. With the purse strings relaxed at Queen's Park, the familiar sounds of pick and shovel rang along the roads and highways. 'If it were not for the mechanics and power of the Provincial Government which has been exercised to the limit,' the beleaguered Tory bagman Don Hogarth lamented, 'King would not be in the picture in this Province at all.'[28]

In the last few days of the campaign, particularly at the Conservative rally in Maple Leaf Gardens, R.B. Bennett trained his guns on Mitch. He accused him of destroying Canadian credit and demanded to know where King stood on the repudiation of contracts and the denial of access to the courts. King was content with a mild restatement of his views on the sanctity of provincial rights, but Roebuck struck back with the suggestion that after 'handing the users of electricity to the power barons, the transportation system to the railway men and control of money and credit to the private banks, he might just as well abolish parliament altogether and hand the country over to a dictatorship with himself as czar.' From Sarnia, Mitch retorted that he would love to have a provincial election on the issue if Bennett yielded to the pressure to disallow the Hydro legislation.

Returning to Ontario, Mitch worked the Ottawa valley and half a dozen ridings along the St Lawrence, filled the Ravina Rink in High Park with ten thousand fighting Liberals from across Toronto, and left for a week of speech-making in western Ontario. He spoke from Midland on a radio hook-up to the Maple Leaf Gardens rally for King on 8 October, appeared for Arthur Slaght in Parry Sound, and was back in Toronto for the last day of the campaign. It was a triumphant tour, the crowds and the enthusiasm recalling the heady days of June. When he left Weston High School late on Saturday night after speaking for Elmer Philpott, who had wandered back into the Liberal party, there was little more Mitch could do for King than return to Elgin and vote.

Mitch waited for the returns in the Liberals' headquarters in the

Masonic Temple. He had boasted that he would win sixty seats in Ontario, but Charles Dunning had believed the Liberals would be lucky to win forty and King, who agreed with Manion that 'the storm centre' was Ontario, hoped against hope for a majority of the eighty-two seats in Ontario. Before the night was over Ontario had sent fifty-six Liberals to grace King's caucus as the Tories suffered their worst defeat in the province since 1874. Only one vote in five had gone to third parties. With the Liberals again in power in Ottawa, Mitch told his Elgin friends, 'I can return to Toronto greatly encouraged and with new inspiration to continue my work as head of the government of Ontario' and to help make Canada 'the great country that grand old Liberal, Sir Wilfrid Laurier, prophesized so many years ago.'[29]

Despite the persistence of the nagging cough and biting chest pains, Mitch was back at Queen's Park three days after the election. The telegrams and letters from across Canada echoed Roebuck's wire, 'This is your victory as well as King's,' and from ridings as different as Cape Breton and Brantford there were personal notes of gratitude for his assistance. The cabinet met for the first time in weeks on the afternoon of his return and ran quickly over the immediate agenda. But the centre of political attention was Ottawa where Liberal hopefuls paraded in and out of Laurier House. Except for a perfunctory telegram, Mitch had not heard a whisper.[30]

There were many Liberals who believed that Mitch should and would be invited to join the cabinet, and two days after the election the *Mail and Empire*'s Ottawa correspondent reported that those closest to King insisted that Hepburn 'to whom full credit is given for the party's spectacular gains in Ontario can have his choice of any of the available portfolios.' Although King recruited the ambitious Jimmy Gardiner and tried to attract Angus Macdonald, the premier of Nova Scotia, nothing was further from his mind than offering Mitch a place in his cabinet. However, Mitch was a disturbing presence throughout his deliberations because Arthur Slaght, victorious in Parry Sound, was the surrogate for his companion of so many nocturnal escapades. Slaght was included in most speculative cabinets, and in his first conversation with Ernest Lapointe, King mentioned him and C.D. Howe as the two new members of obvious cabinet timbre. But King did not want Mitch Hepburn's close friend in his cabinet.[31]

He was not alone. Norman Rogers, once King's secretary and author of his biography who had been elected in Kingston, agreed

with King that Slaght was a man of 'exceptional ability' who would
be extremely useful in the cabinet. But he also believed 'that there
was a danger in taking him in, owing to his being obviously a Hepburn man, and having habits that might get him and others into
serious trouble, though this is more in the way of rumour than of
evidence.' Charles Dunning also opposed Slaght because he 'would
be a Hepburn man, and his moral character was not too good.'
Certainly if morality was in, Slaght was out. Long before he was
known as the Beau Brummell of the Commons, Slaght was re-
nowned as a womanizer, described by one Tory as a 'social and
moral leper of the lowest order ... such a low degenerate that his
wife and family had to break up their home and leave him, on
account of his immorality and drunken blackguardism.' He had left
his wife many years before he met Mitch. At fifty-eight, he was just
beginning a long and loving, if not always faithful, relationship with
a woman less than half his age. She also worked at Queen's Park
and was a close friend of Mitch's companion. But mistresses had
never been a barrier to a seat on the front benches and, as Lapointe
dryly noted, King would have a 'pretty tough time' if he excluded
men who drank.[32]

King soon convinced himself that there was really no need to
include Slaght 'beyond that of recognizing Hepburn's part in the
campaign, which, however, was no more than that of other provincial premiers.' Yet a still higher level of confirmation was necessary.
It came in a vision where he was speaking on the importance of
moral character, which left no doubt that it was character that 'lies
at my determination not to take Slaght into the Cabinet – I know
it will be the wish of Hepburn et al (those who have helped financially etc) but I am quite clear, he is not to come in at this time,
whatever may happen later on. The whole Hepburn forces have to
be faced & opposed in this way.'[33]

The vision had given King courage, but he so dreaded the letter
from Mitch that his secretary, E.A. Pickering, gave him in the
morning that he put it aside until after breakfast. Slaght had been
a great asset in the campaign, Mitch wrote, and whether 'you see
fit to take him into the Cabinet or not, he will be a great asset to
you and the Party.' As you know, he assured King, 'I have no selfish interests myself, except to promote the welfare of the Party. As
a matter of fact I intimated to the Ontario Cabinet Ministers my
intention of retiring from public life in a very short time.' Surprised
and relieved that Mitch's letter was sufficiently general to permit an
evasive reply, King drafted a letter at once and, given its impor-

tance, summoned Lapointe and Dunning to get their approval. The letter arrived at Queen's Park the next day.

I cannot say how much pleasure your letter of yesterday ... has given to me ...

My first thought ... was to communicate at once with yourself, and others who took so all important a part in the campaign, to ask you to come to Ottawa to confer with me in connection with the formation of the new cabinet. However, on giving the matter further consideration, I thought it would be better not to do this for two reasons, one of which you will recall I gave to you at the time you came to confer with me after you had won the provincial elections. My advice to you, as you will remember, was that I thought it would be well for you to seek counsel only of those who were likely to be your colleagues ...

You will also recall that I made no suggestion of any kind as to the personnel of your ministry ...

You will further recall my saying that, as leader of the Liberal party in the federal field, I was most anxious that relations between myself and the Liberal leaders of the several provinces should be such that there would be no understandings, or obligations on the part of either, which were not publicly known. You agreed with me that it was the only way in which each of us could preserve our complete independence in dealing with the questions which might come up for consideration in our respective jurisdictions.

The second reason for maintaining the strict independence of the two leaders and governments, King continued, was that with a dominion-provincial conference on the agenda it was essential that he could 'assure all the governments represented that my action in the formation of the federal government had in no way been influenced by any consideration other than the public interest.' The message conveyed, King wrote that he was 'looking forward with delight to seeing you again in the near future, and to renewing, in ways which have not been possible since you assumed office, the many contacts of our unbroken friendship in the years we have known each other and have been privileged to serve the cause we both have so much at heart.' With the election won, Mitch and the Ontario Liberals were on their own. Gratitude had its limits. It was a letter Mitch neither forgot, nor forgave.[34]

The letter written, King quickly filled the last Ontario seat in the cabinet. He had told Jack Elliott, the 'spent force' from London, that he would not be included, but suddenly reversed field and surprised him with the offer of Public Works. He also decided to have the swearing-in ceremony a day earlier than planned. 'I did not want to run over until Friday,' he told his colleagues, 'with all the contention there would be meanwhile ... I was anxious to avoid all kinds of pressure, lobbying etc.' 'Hepburn's Henchmen omitted from King's New Cabinet' gloated the *Star* when the cabinet was announced. 'Not one Hepburn man got to first base,' reported Grant Dexter. 'Their bodies are strewn all over the province.'[35]

King's declaration of independence did nothing to improve Mitch's spirits as he tackled the other problems on his agenda, the most critical and dangerous of which was a decision on the power contracts. Throughout the summer and fall there had been feverish activity at Hydro as Roebuck, clearly in command, moved relentlessly, almost obsessively, towards cancellation. Niagara Hudson's secret agreement to supply emergency power may have been influenced by the threat that Ontario would take over its plant on the Canadian side. The Special Engineering Committee had canvassed all possible sources of power, including a plan to moor lake steamers at Kingston and connect generators to their boilers, and Hydro had prepared detailed plans for rationing the industrial and domestic use of electricity. On 19 September the commission moved a step closer to repudiation when it advised Beauharnois and Gatineau that it would not accept the additional power scheduled for delivery on 1 October. A day later William Ryan of Stone & Webster informed Mitch that while Hydro was not protected against 'every conceivable contingency,' it could meet 'all of the more probable consequences of an interruption in the supply of Quebec power.'[36]

The commission made the decision despite the caution of its own engineers. Refusing to yield to Roebuck's imperatives, Hydro's chief engineer, Thomas Hogg, argued that Ryan's estimates of Hydro's capacity were too high and of future demand too low, and warned that if its Chat's Falls power was lost 'due to the deliberate waste of water by the Ottawa Valley Power Co or the Government of Quebec then it would be impossible to carry the load in Southern Ontario.' Hogg refused to make any recommendations on the grounds that 'the significance and importance of each angle is a matter on which opinions will differ and that questions of policy must exercise an important influence on the final decision.' Insisting that an early decision was critical, Hogg observed:

One of the strongest features of the Commission's present position, from the point of view of the pending negotiations, is the fact that it is now able to give its customers an interim emergency service in case the Quebec power should be cut off. However, if the Chats Falls plant and the Ottawa and Hull power should not be available, the interim service would be of an emergency character, dependent upon temporary stations and overloaded lines, and, as already pointed out would be hazardous. Moreover, after allowing for Niagara Hudson supply and interrupting the interruptible customers, the estimates show that by 1936 all reserves would be exhausted and there would be an actual shortage of firm power.

Roebuck brought the memo to cabinet on 17 October. Scrawled across the front page with his familiar blue crayon were the words 'Hogg's Memo re Quebec Power saying can give service with all power cut off, see pp. 30.' On page 30 he underlined the supposedly confirming lines above.[37] The cabinet accepted Roebuck's advice and a day later the commission dutifully assured the cabinet that it could provide 'all essential services' and recommended proclamation of the act. Over the weekend Hydro engineers tested all the equipment, pulled the switches on Quebec power other than Gatineau, and issued detailed battle plans for the war that might begin when the act was proclaimed.[38]

The worst-case scenario was unlikely. The companies remained convinced of the validity of the contracts, and for the moment at least Killam would not invite a counter-suit by opening the sluices at Chat's Falls on the Quebec side. Despite his ominous message in the spring, there was no reason to believe that Taschereau would test the law and seal the border. He and Mitch were currently engaged in the more vital task of reviving the newsprint industry, and it was only Taschereau who could prevent Gatineau from continuing to supply the 25- and 60-cycle power Hydro would need.[39]

A.R. Graustein, president of both Gatineau and the International Paper Company, was the key actor in the unfolding drama. Although he was prepared to go to court, he much preferred a different outcome based on the principles of sound ethics, good business, and good will. Moreover, although International Paper had no mills in Ontario, Graustein had no desire to antagonize Mitch at a time when the two provincial governments and the industry were attempting to assist the newsprint industry. Graustein had secretly assured Mitch during the spring session that while insisting on his legal rights he would continue to supply power. Gordon Gale, the Ottawa-based manager of Gatineau, after consulting New York, repeated the assurance late in September that they would continue to supply power 'with the same friendly cooperation.' With these secret assurances and the equipment ready, Mitch could boast that he held the whip hand. It was time to talk.[40]

The council chamber was crowded on 22 October when the cabinet met with the executives from the four Quebec companies and a battery of legal advisers. Earlier that day Mitch and other ministers had met with Honoré Mercier, Taschereau's minister of lands and forests, and Colonel James Ralston, a prominent Liberal attorney, who were in Toronto as part of a delegation to discuss the newsprint industry. Mercier brought Taschereau's appeal to delay proclamation of the power acts until after the November election in Quebec at which time Taschereau promised to meet Mitch 'without delay,' in the expectation that 'we may mutually find a solution for the situation without your being obliged to proclaim your legislation.' When Mitch later met the power barons, although his tone was conciliatory, he told them that Hydro would neither accept nor pay for power under the old contracts and that a solution had to be found quickly that would substantially reduce the impossible burden on Hydro. Graustein insisted that Gatineau was in a different ethical position, and the others suspected he was playing from his own deck. The three companies met the commission the next day and suggested a formula whereby they and Hydro would share the losses 45:55, with an appropriate extension of the contracts so that the total power contracted for would be delivered They left a memorandum detailing the data needed to make the proposal more concrete. A few days later Gale and Graustein slipped almost unnoticed into Queen's Park and Mitch had a promise of under-the-table delivery of 25- and 60-cycle power. By the end of October only Gatineau power was being fed through Hydro lines.[41]

There was another delegation from Montreal camped on Mitch's doorstep when he returned after the election, which had come to appeal for Mitch's assistance in imposing some sanity on the newsprint industry. By 1935 the market for newsprint was recovering. The Canadian industry, as a whole, was working at 72 per cent capacity, although the inefficient Ontario mills, not tied to American publishers, were operating at only 47 per cent capacity. But the price stuck stubbornly at $40 a ton, far from the $68 dollars on the eve of the crash or even the $48 in 1932. Tonnage and price were related, for desperate mills without adequate tonnage were tempted to cut prices, a weakness of which the well-organized American publishers took rapacious advantage. The buyers operated on a system of interlocking contracts where every supplier agreed to meet the price of the competition; if a single firm cut the price either openly or through a variety of discounts or kickbacks the new price became industry-wide. The answer was clearly a producers' cartel to control production and distribute tonnage equitably.

The delegation from Montreal was attempting to create just such a cartel. Taschereau's repeated attempts to force the Quebec companies to cooperate had been dismal failures, so in the fall of 1934 he and Mitch had asked Bennett to threaten to prohibit exports if the suicidal price-cutting did not stop. Finally, the exasperated Quebec premier passed legislation in the spring of 1935 to give the province coercive power over the industry and appealed to Mitch to do the same. 'I may say the newsprint situation is almost desperate,' he wrote. 'We cannot depend on the industry itself to get over its troubles and I never met a group of men so disloyal to each other; the agreements among them are mere scraps of paper and unless Ontario and Quebec will join in common action, I believe matters will become from bad to worse and a more ruinous competition will arise between them. I see it coming.' Mitch was sympathetic, but concluded that the Ontario companies were already at his mercy since they had defaulted on the terms of their timber leases. However, Taschereau's new legislation brought the companies to heel, and they agreed to an independent committee to work out some formula for cooperative tonnage distribution.[42]

Charles Vining, president of the Newsprint Association, spoke for the committee and Graustein, a late but critical convert to the idea of pro-rationing because his International Paper produced 20 per cent of Quebec's newsprint, had also been invited. Vining described the progress made towards rationing production, with the so-called 'long' mills giving tonnage to those who were 'short.' He then explained how the proposed reorganization of Great Lakes Paper at Thunder Bay, part of the Bachus-Brooks empire which had been in receivership since 1931, would mean a return to price anarchy.

The proposed reorganization was the handiwork of John E. Gaefell, a New York newsprint salesman, who had secured long-term contracts which would keep the mill working at capacity. Mitch's Liberal friends at National Trust, the receivers, had appealed to him to approve the Gaefell plan which would bring new life to the Lakehead, return $200,000 a year to Hydro and Lands and Forests, save the bondholders, and make 'only a trifling disturbance in the tonnage position of other Canadian mills.' However, Vining explained, with Gaefell's plan the publishers would pay Great Lakes the market price of $40 a ton but would receive preferred shares and dividends in the company related to the amount purchased. Under the interlocking contract system this thinly disguised price rebate would simply result in another price-cutting war. They assured Mitch that under their proposed rationing plan both Abitibi and Great Lakes would receive tonnage from Quebec mills, largely from International Paper. Graustein also asked Mitch to veto the proposed reorganization.[43]

Mitch and his colleagues reached no decision at the meeting. For the next two weeks he was lobbied by the receivers and bondholders and there was enormous pressure from Thunder Bay. Finally, Mitch summoned the Vining committee to another meeting on 2 November, attended by Clarkson as the Abitibi receivers, Graustein and Sensenbrenner of Spruce Falls for the industry, National Trust, and counsel for the bondholders and Gaefell. The meeting was stormy. Graustein insisted that the scheme would lead to a price war of enormous proportions that could cripple almost everyone but International Paper and the tied mills. Mitch was convinced. The government would not accept the proposed reorganization.

Mitch informed Taschereau of the decision and reminded him of the assurances that Ontario mills would get fair treatment in the distribution of tonnage. A jubilant Taschereau replied at once: 'You will always find our province ready to co-operate with yours to develop the paper industry. I have read with great regret your decision to resign. I sincerely hope that the rest which you are taking will restore your health and enable you to continue. You're a great work in our sister province Ontario. Cannot get along without you.'[44]

When Taschereau's wire arrived, Mitch was on the train to Miami leaving behind an orgy of speculation and a mixture of despair and elation in two bewildered capitals. With the pressure of work and the enthusiasm of play on his return to Queen's Park and the King Eddy, Mitch had not shaken the deep cold. A long weekend at the farm had brought no relief, and he coughed incessantly through the rounds of meetings over Hydro and Great Lakes. The ever-present Eddie Wooliver had publicly imposed a 10 p.m. curfew on all calls to the suite at the hotel, and his doctors warned him that the pace could not be maintained. Most disturbing were the elevation in his blood pressure and the pains that frequently shot down his left arm and left him ashen-faced and short of breath. Adding to his physical distress was his profound sense of betrayal when King announced his cabinet. King had not only summarily dismissed him from the councils of the party, but he had appointed Charles Dunning, a fiscal conservative, to the key finance portfolio although Dunning had not contested a seat in the election. As a back-bencher Mitch had tangled with Dunning, and his open criticism of the contract cancellation had offended the Ontario Liberals. Mitch had let it be known at once that Charles Dunning would not win a seat in Ontario, even if King found one for him to contest.[45]

On the night of 4 November a friend of Mitch's leaked word to the press that he planned to take a vacation and, if his health were not restored, might be forced to retire. The next day Mitch confirmed the rumour. 'My two enemies, fatigue and worry, have pursued me endlessly on this job,' he told reporters, and since it was not fair to the people, the party, or himself that he carry on broken in health, he planned to retire after the 1936 session and go back to the farm. Accosted by reporters on their way to cabinet, his colleagues expressed surprise and disbelief and were convinced that with a rest he would change his mind. Arthur Hardy wrote that it was miraculous that he had managed the 'desperate physical and mental work' of the past five years, and assured Mitch that his friends would see that he went to the Senate.

Mackenzie King was both solicitous and elated. That afternoon, with several colleagues present, King phoned Mitch who 'confirmed the report, saying that the strain upon his kidney had begun to affect his heart and the Doctors had advised him that his condition might become very serious if he tried to keep on.' King expressed his deep sorrow and assured Mitch that 'if, later on, there was anything he might wish to have done, not to hesitate to let me know; that he had a friend in me at all times.' Above all, said King, he should 'run no risks, even in the matter of returning for the Dominion-Provincial Conference, should he find it desirable to prolong his stay.' Mitch's retirement, King gravely told the press, would be a great loss, but a 'sick man is of little value to himself or his country.' Around Toronto, reported the astute bureau chief of the Windsor *Star*, 'the political gossip is that Prime Minister King is not sorry Premier Hepburn intends to retire from active politics.' The gossip was certainly on the mark, as King confided to his diary that he knew 'from the beginning that Hepburn could not last. Indeed, I gave him about a year before he would find it necessary to give up. In many ways it is perhaps fortunate that this change is coming immediately, though the right person for a leader in Ontario is far from being in sight. Men have to be trained for public life, and character must be the basis of all else.'[46]

Mitch spent 6 November at the hotel in last-minute consultations with his colleagues. In a letter to Angus Macdonald, he wrote that he had been 'far from well and propose now to retire from public life as soon as a new sucessor can be selected.' His secretary stopped taking calls at noon, and Eva and young Peter came from St Thomas to say goodbye. The large bevy of reporters and photographers gathered at Union Station that night waited in vain. Mitch's car was picked up at Port Credit near the home of his friend Jack Bickell who, with Frank O'Connor, was going to supervise his recovery in Miami.

Ten days later, Frank wired the office that 'Our friend is fine improving every day spends most of his time on the beach in the beautiful sunshine which we have had every day.' Mitch put the cares of Queen's Park behind him, and Eddie Wooliver kept reporters at bay. Three weeks on the beach was all Mitch could spare. Early in December he left Eva and Peter, who had joined him, to return for the dominion-provincial conference.[47]

Mitch looked tanned and rested when Roy Elmhirst met him at the Buffalo airport on 3 December and drove him to Toronto. He assured the Queen's Park scrum that, although his health had improved, he still intended to resign after the next session. Later he met his colleagues and was quickly briefed on the power situation. During his absence emergency plans had been further refined, as Hydro had warned all industrial users to clean out their boilers and be ready to move back to coal. And at Roebuck's insistence, the commission had refused to supply the capacity and demand data requested by the companies as a basis for their proposal. The next morning Mitch summoned the companies to a meeting with the cabinet.[48]

Beauharnois, Ottawa Valley, and MacLarens tabled an elaboration of their October proposal with a 45:55 sharing of the oversupply (at a saving to Hydro of $2.7 million) but with longer contracts and no reduction in price. After a brief discussion, executives from the three companies were asked to leave the chamber. Graustein, with Slaght as his counsel, remained. Mitch declared that Graustein's refusal to assume the burden of any additional Quebec taxes, as called for in the original contract, made a formal contract impossible. Nevertheless, Graustein promised to supply Hydro with the power needed at the moment, and to increase the supply until the full 260,000 horsepower in the contract was absorbed. After Mitch and his colleagues huddled briefly, the full meeting reconvened and Mitch announced that the 45:55 offer was totally unacceptable and since the companies could not 'surrender the contracts for revision without further authority from the bondholders' the act would be proclaimed. Bruce signed the order-in-council that night.[49]

The final scene remained to be played out. In proclaiming the act, the cabinet invited tenders for both 25- and 60-cycle power. The outraged president of Ottawa Valley exclaimed that his company could not tender because it did not produce 60-cycle power, but offered to wave Quebec taxes or rent their side of the plant. Beauharnois offered to supply the power and absorb any increase in Quebec taxes on the same terms as Gatineau, while reserving their right to sue. But it was the Gatineau tender for the full supply at a price reduced from $15 to $12.50, with power held in reserve until the initial 260,000 horsepower was taken, and with the company agreeing to absorb any increased taxes, that Hydro predictably found most acceptable.

While this met the immediate needs, Hydro also agreed to buy 40,000 horsepower from MacLarens at the Gatineau price. Lyon later explained that old Alexander MacLaren, an honourable man who had always paid his bills, came to Toronto to plead for the solvency of his company: 'That plea proved too much for me, and I succeeded in convincing my fellow commissioners that the quality of mercy should not be strained.' Roebuck admitted that the real reason was a little more calculating. 'You understand that it was our hope to get things settled up with these people, certainly with everybody other than Beauharnois,' he recalled, 'and here was an opportunity to put them out of the picture for the purchase of the comparatively small amount of 40,000 h.p. at a reduced price, and to get rid without a battle, of the balance of 125,000 h.p.' Hydro was also prepared to talk to Ottawa Valley, but the company preferred to go to court.[50]

The settlements saved Hydro $6 million a year, Roebuck boasted, and the ten-year contracts would give Ontario time to develop its own resources. 'I had a great ambition to wrench the system free from what I considered a corrupting and unhealthy alliance as between a public body and private producers,' Roebuck said later. The Toronto *Star* hailed Roebuck and his colleagues as heroes. To Sir Robert Borden, however, cancellation was simply more proof that the Hepburn government was 'guided by the standards and methods of thugs and bandits.' King Edward VIII was not pleased. As Prince of Wales he had bought Beauharnois as a gilt-edged security on the advice of Sir Edward Peacock, the Canadian-born London financial magnate, and as the bonds fell he had sold at a substantial loss. Mitch Hepburn, the King was convinced, was a communist.[51]

Forty-eight hours after the legislation was proclaimed Mitch was on the overnight train to Ottawa for the 9 December dominion-provincial conference in the good company of the three-day-old senator, Frank O'Connor, and Slaght and Elmhirst. The rest of the Ontario delegation – five cabinet ministers, officials, and secretaries – were already there when Mitch moved into the Chateau Laurier. A few hours later they were all in the Railway Committee room to hear Mackenzie King launch what he called 'a new era of harmonious relations between the provinces and the Dominion.' He assured the largely Liberal gathering that while his government did not lack views or principles, he had not called the conference to 'impose a rigid, preconceived program of action.' Indeed, it was not clear exactly why King had called the conference. He emphasized that there was little hope of finding solutions at once, but hoped that the conference could establish the machinery for further study and more conferences.

Mitch quipped that his presence was not 'to be construed as a raid on the federal treasury' and urged the conference to come to grips with the serious problems of relief, debt and overlapping federal and provincial services. 'We are all here representing the Liberal and Reform school of thought,' he said, 'and if we fail in our deliberations we shall have no one to blame but ourselves.' The pleasantries over, the delegates were to spend the rest of the week in committees on finance, relief, constitutional reform, mining taxation and agriculture. Unlike most other provinces and the federal government, Mitch and his colleagues had position papers on each subject as well as on many others King chose not to have on the agenda.[52]

Mitch arrived at the first meeting of the finance committee the next morning 'trailing his coat and daring anyone to tread on it.' Asked by Dunning to lead off, Mitch bluntly stated that the immediate and fundamental issue facing the conference was the need 'to adopt some system of compulsory debt conversion.' Servicing the debt ran to over 40 per cent of revenue in many provinces, and in Ontario reducing interest from 5 to 3 per cent would save the province about $10 million a year and enable him to balance the budget. If refunding were not possible, he warned, Ottawa would have to move out of the direct tax field. Dunning sang a similar tale of woe, pointing to a federal debt of $3 billion and a deficit of $116 million in the past year. 'We must have a solid and unquestionable Dominion credit,' he declared, but on 'that rock it may be possible to work out adjustments of various kinds.'[53]

The tactics became much clearer the next morning when Dunning turned to a discussion of a hypothetical refunding operation with a hypothetical loan council and a hypothetical proposal that cooperating provinces might agree to joint security on a 50-50 basis. Mitch angrily rejected the proposal at once because Ontario would not only have to pay its own share but its taxpayers would also pay over 40 per cent of Ottawa's share. Dunning snapped that the other provinces regarded Ontario as 'the tax-collector rather than the taxpayer of much of the revenue referred to.' When Dunning, under Mitch's questioning, made it clear that under no circumstances would there be any conversion of the federal debt, Mitch exploded: 'I want to make this statement. You declare that the Dominion will not be a party to any policy of debt conversion. I think we might as well end the discussion ... We came down here with the idea of consolidating debts. I don't believe it feasible to do this thing piecemeal. You the Dominion Government are in worse shape than we are.' Dunning persisted. Mitch said Ontario was out, and the discussion turned to taxation.

The rancour continued. Mitch insisted that until Ottawa agreed to a concrete level of relief assistance any discussion of the transfer of tax proceeds was pointless. He warned that Ontario would have to move into the income tax field, and when Dunning refused to make any commitment, he exclaimed: 'If the Dominion is not going to abandon the income tax field we cannot do much ... Mr. Dunning, you have not committed yourself very much.' There was a temporary truce as Dunning speculated on the possibility of turning over the proceeds of a federal sales tax to the provinces to pay for relief, and Mitch replied he would then not levy an income tax. But the truce was shattered when J.L. Ilsley, the minister of national revenue, suggested that if the sales tax proposal were accepted, the provinces might give up succession duties. Absolutely not, shouted Mitch. 'We are going to break up the big estates. Sales tax is on the poor man. I am not sure that the Dominion will get after the big fellow.' And as the discussion wound down, Mitch again said in exasperation, 'How can we get anywhere until someone has authority? We need a declaration of policy on the part of the Dominion.' The committee reached no conclusions, and Dunning was forced to report lamely that the free interchange of diverse views had been extremely valuable and a permanent committee of finance ministers would further explore some of the proposals. Dunning blamed Mitch for the inconclusive results.

In the committee on relief and unemployment, Dunning stressed the need to reduce costs and Labour Minister Rogers argued for increased efficiency and federal control. Both insisted that flat grants were preferable to any form of shared costs. They also proposed a

National Employment Commission to register and classify the unemployed and to set standards and supervise relief spending for federally assisted programs. David Croll tabled Ontario's position paper which suggested that the commission coordinate work and employment programs on a long-term basis; proposed a national youth training program and a lowering of the old age pension eligibility from seventy to sixty-five or even sixty; and recommended that Ottawa and the provinces split relief costs 75-25 with the administration under a federal-provincial board. Ontario's most radical proposal was for a national employment plan 'under which governments may assume the position of being residual employers, as required; such plan being capable of expansion or contraction in accordance with industrial and employment conditions in any given period; so that employment and subsistence income may be available to all who are capable of work.' The committee accepted the enlarged mandate of the commission, the youth training program, and the recommendation that, until the Commission was in place, federal relief grants should be 'substantially increased.' But the idea of the state as residual employer was too radical to receive any serious attention.

In the mining committee, Thomas Crerar, the minister of mines, who was privately sympathetic to a stable and less onerous tax on the gold mines, was bound by the refusal of King and Dunning to consider making any concessions to the provinces or the industry. Mitch arrived late at the first committee meeting after he, Slaght, O'Connor and, Jack Bickell had lunched with King. Mitch spoke to the Ontario brief, which argued that although natural resources belonged to the province and the province had born the full costs of development, Ottawa had over the years 'exacted from the mines of the Province of Ontario vast sums of money which were then used for the general advantage of Canada and not for the Province itself.' Mitch argued that in principle Ottawa should withdraw from taxes on mining operations. The next day Leduc proposed that if Ottawa increased the depletion allowance on gold mines and turned over half the income tax collected on metal mines, Ontario would not increase the tax on mines for five years. Although the proposal meant a significant loss of revenue, Crerar promised that he would bring it to the attention of his colleagues.[54]

The deliberations of the constitutional committee were equally frustrating. In preparation for Bennett's aborted constitutional conference in 1934, Mitch had struck an interdepartmental committee under Roebuck, with Professor W.P.M. Kennedy as the academic expert. Ideologically, Roebuck was a staunch opponent of any form of centralized power, but neither he nor Mitch were rabid provincialists. Although Ontario had opposed the attempt to use the federal criminal law and treaty power to justify some of Bennett's New Deal legislation, Mitch supported a national unemployment insurance program and Roebuck argued before the Supreme Court that unemployment insurance and national labour standards were essential and should be ruled constitutional as matters of national concern under the federal government's residual power. At the conference, Roebuck proposed an amending formula which required unanimity in some areas but provided for changes in the distribution of powers with the approval of two-thirds of the provinces representing 55 per cent of the population. 'Any amendment that runs that gauntlet,' he insisted, 'can be relied upon as expressing the national will.' With an amending formula in the constitution, it could then be patriated. But there was no agreement on procedure or substance, and Lapointe refused to take a position. After three days of talk the committee decided to establish a committee of officials to prepare for another conference.[55]

King had not attended any meetings, but remained close by in the Speaker's chambers for easy consultation. Before the final plenary session he met the cabinet to discuss tactics and found many of his colleagues 'ready to make large grants out of the public treasury in order to meet what they thought was expected by the public and the provinces at this time.' Aghast at such generosity, King argued that 'now was the time to get down to rock bottom.' After considerable discussion, cabinet agreed that 'nothing would be approved or endorsed ... and no commitment of any kind made' except to help the provinces with relief, providing the federal government controlled relief expenditure. 'Those present agreed,' King noted, 'that if I could get away with that, at the afternoon session, it would be a real achievement.' Mitch had concluded that King would have nothing to say, and had taken the afternoon train home.[56]

When Mitch reached Union Station at 9:30, he denied reports that he had left Ottawa in a huff or that the conference was 'a washout,' but he did admit that he was 'disappointed with the Federal Government because at no time was it apparently ready to enunciate matters of policy.' However, at a Sunday night session with reporters at the King Eddy, Mitch shed his reticence and earned the banner headline in the morning *Globe*: CONVERSION OR COLLAPSE – HEPBURN. Asked how long before increased government borrowing would lead to a collapse, Mitch replied, 'I don't know when the bottom of the chest will be reached, but it will be.' Dunning and King refused 'to hold out any hope for the alleviation of conditions for the taxpayer, who is not concerned with schemes to decrease the Provincial tax at the expense of increased Federal taxes, and vice versa.' The rich would leave, increased taxes would crush the middle class, and an inflamed public opinion would ultimately force governments to debt conversion. A day later Mitch confirmed that he was going to follow a 'pay-as-you-go' policy and would introduce a provincial income tax to raise between $12 and $14 million, the approximate cost of relief.

Back in Toronto the day after the conference, Dunning summoned Floyd Chalmers to his Forest Hill residence to plant his side of the story. Dunning admitted that his loan council plan, which would enable the provinces to admit default and then secure a federal guarantee for refunding at 3 per cent, was merely a bargaining position. Taking considerable liberty with the tenor of the discussion, he insisted that all the provinces except Ontario had given 'tacit approval' to the plan. Much more would have been accomplished 'had it not been for the attitude of the Ontario delegation – Hepburn, Roebuck and Croll. They came down to Ottawa with a chip on their shoulder. D. wondered if their strategy was not to force universal government bankruptcy in Canada in order to justify their own policies of repudiation.' As he sat among the accumulated pile of newspapers, Dunning ruminated aloud to Chalmers about the real explanation of Mitch's aberrant views:

D. wonders if some of Hepburn's ideas are not the product of his association with his three-ringed circus of millionaires with whom he travels around. Ordinarily a man who chooses as his travelling and play-time companions men of great wealth becomes conservative and orthodox in his ideas of taxation, public expenditure, living up to obligations, etc. But not so with Hepburn. Dunning wonders if this is not because his friends are all equity speculators ... They have not the mentality of the man whose funds are invested in gilt-edged securities or of the man who is the head of a large corporation occupying a position of trusteeship to the public – such as life insurance. To Hepburn's friends, meeting obligations on the dot is not so important because they are men of the type who benefits from receiverships, bankruptcies etc. They are agile enough to keep their funds moving. When bonds are written down it just removes debts that stand ahead of their securities.

It was an imaginative scenario, but Dunning was convinced that 'checking' Mitch was essential to preserve the financial stability of the country. That Mitch held 'funny money' views long before he joined the three-ringed circus, Dunning conveniently overlooked, and he was perhaps on safer ground in concluding that Mitch was really 'a combination of Robespierre and Robin Hood – ambitious to be the leader of the "have nots" against the "haves" and also convinced that there is no dishonesty in taking from the "haves" to give to the "have nots".'

Floyd Chalmers did not buy the Dunning version and the *Financial Post* provided a different rendering of the inner meaning of the conference. Five days of discussion had left the conference divided between the 'orthodox' and the 'radicals' and from it 'emerged, full-fledged, a left-wing, radical Liberal party with Premier Mitchell Hepburn of Ontario in undisputed leadership.' Mitch drew support, the *Post* continued, from within King's ministry as well as from other provincial delegations and, with his public criticism, he 'is now free to essay the role of a Liberal Harry Stevens against Mr. King's performance as the safe and sound, orthodox statesman ... Mr. Hepburn, as his administration in Ontario proves, is a radical.' There was also an element of pique that gave an edge to Mitch's criticism of King's orthodoxy because King had ignored him in the formation of his cabinet. 'If Mr. Hepburn has come to believe that the King government has put a big black *X* against his name, there is evidence to justify such a belief.'

Before the *Post* appeared, King had reluctantly agreed to a compromise between the liberals in cabinet led by Rogers and the Dunning-King wing and increased relief grants by 75 per cent for three months. Ontario's Christmas present was $1,050,000 rather than the $1,200,000 Croll had requested. Mitch, too, had a Christmas present for the provincial civil servants. His last act in a week of feverish activity before catching a train to rejoin Eva and Peter in Florida was to sign an order-in-council restoring their pay to the pre-Depression level. Six weeks of Florida sunshine might enable him to shake the bronchitis and reflect on his decision to resign.[57]

'Then send us down to defeat'

When Mitch returned from Florida late in January 1936 and dropped by Chorley Park to swear allegiance to King Edward VIII, Angela Bruce felt that despite his bad cough he was looking better. The legislature was to have opened in his absence, but with the death of George V had been postponed until 11 February. Sub-zero temperatures, sleet and snow storms paralysed the city and Mitch developed bronchitis. After a few days at Queen's Park, he went to the farm to rest before his appearance at the trial in London of Henry Walker who, after four days of testimony, was found guilty of extortion and sentenced to eighteen months in jail.[1]

The Legislative Assembly had been sitting for a week when Mitch took his seat. The throne speech had boasted of the economic recovery under a Liberal administration. It promised that the province would honour all its debts and not embark on any scheme of debt conversion unless it was national in scope; confirmed the introduction of a provincial income tax; and forecast legislation 'to provide a more equitable distribution of taxes levied for educational purposes and to improve the organization of the rural schools of the Province.' For two weeks Grits and Tories hurled abuse across the floor, the opposition taking particular aim at Heenan's administration of the north and Roebuck's Hydro policy. As was his custom, Peter the Horsetrader replied in kind. Roebuck adopted the more effective tactic of exhausting the House with another two day, six-hour treatise on the power contracts.[2]

Far less heated, but marginally more substantial, were the debates over Mitch's financial policies, including the first provincial personal income tax. Determined to fund relief costs out of current revenue and move towards a balanced budget, Mitch had been considering an income tax since late 1934. Almost half of the municipalities had an income tax, but collections were low or non-existent and about two-thirds of the total was collected in Toronto. When Mitch instructed a committee under Chester Walters to explore the feasibility of the tax there was an immediate outcry that a tax on incomes would hurt the cities more than rural Ontario. 'What of it?' Mitch retorted. 'Why shouldn't the cities and Toronto in particular pay more? Isn't the wealth of the province constituted there? Do you suggest that big firms do all their business in Toronto? They draw their customers from all over the province ... They can afford to pay.'[3]

When Nixon announced the sharply graduated rates early in 1936, it appeared that, although about one hundred thousand taxpayers would be affected, between 80 and 90 per cent of the tax would be paid by about eight thousand high-income earners. A despondent Sam McLaughlin of General Motors told Angela Bruce that they 'now take 53 percent and soon it will be over 60 percent and next year when tax free bonds are recalled it will be over 100 percent.' Angela agreed the situation was desperate, with all governments 'working overtime to see how they can tax the people. Many are moving out of the country in some cases having to pay 100 percent on their income. Harry Oakes, Sir Herbert Holt amongst them.' R.B. Bennett in despair told a friend that if Ontario added its income tax to the federal tax 'it will greatly retard the development of the Province and in my judgement have most serious effects upon its future.'[4]

In Mitch's absence, Paul Leduc introduced the bill on the first day of the session and Croll followed with bills to provide compensation for the municipalities who would be forced to give up their income taxes. The opposition denounced the tax as unnecessary or too high. Moreover, it would drive business to the United States and would be hard on farmers who had no cash in the spring when the tax was due – an argument Morgan Baker destroyed with the dry observation that not one farmer in ten thousand would pay income tax. Since the tax was only levied on taxable incomes of $1,000 and above, the Liberals could echo Mitch's boast that it would not affect the common man. They also pointed to the provision that if a corporation failed to distribute profits in excess of what it needed to retain for normal operations, the Treasury could decide that the shareholders should be deemed to have received dividends and be taxed accordingly.[5]

Mitch saved his energy for the debate on his 12 March budget. His government's fiscal and administrative policy, he claimed, was a combination of 'social justice with sound economic action.' Buoyant revenues, administrative efficiency and reduced expenditures, debt refunding at a lower rate of interest, and declining unemployment had brought Ontario closer to the cherished goal of a 'pay-as-you-go' budget with the $13 million deficit less than the $20 million relief bill. With the new income tax, optimistically estimated to bring in between $12 and $14 million, and increased returns from succession duties, Mitch forecast a half million dollar surplus in the next fiscal year.

It was not an exciting speech, but it was delivered with a vitality that roused the back-benchers to frequent bursts of applause and suggested that Mitch was on the mend. The budget received widespread approval outside the House, although there were cynics who suggested that Mitch owed more than he admitted to the general recovery. J.H. Gundy felt that it was the finest budget in Canada for many years and told Mitch that 'the people of Ontario – poor and rich – are under a great debt of obligation to you for your splendid service in this regard.'[6]

The debate meandered through the imperatives of constituency politics for two weeks, enlivened one dull afternoon when a shocked premier successfully demanded that Price be censured for stating that for a bit of patronage Dr Roberts of the Sault would have kissed any part of the former health minister's anatomy. Winding up the budget debate, Mitch again swung to the left. Liberals were the foes of privilege, the enemies of the rich who fought death long enough for their heirs to borrow bonds free of succession duties only to return them to the brokers for use again once the estate was settled. Their day was almost over, Mitch promised, for the government was buying all the bonds it could on the open market and was collecting additional millions from families who, with their Tory accomplices, had defrauded the people of the province. Perhaps discretion deterred him from naming names. But he could have mentioned Sir John Eaton's estate from which another half million was collected or that of Wallace Nesbitt, prominent Tory lawyer and briefly Supreme Court judge, which after a more thorough investigation paid an additional $1.5 million to the $448,000 levied by the Tories.[7]

A number of other minor bills and amendments confirmed the modestly progressive tilt of Mitch's government. As minister of labour, David Croll was particularly active in fine-tuning and improving existing labour legislation. He broadened the scope of those protected, strengthened inspection machinery, and provided for fair wages and hours on all work performed under government contract. Croll relaxed the stringency of the penalties under the

Minimum Wage Act which, he explained, was really a positive step since judges had refused to impose the harsh penalties in the act. Most controversial were the amendments which broadened the scope of the Industrial Standards Act and increased the fines for non-compliance. By the spring of 1936 forty agreements covered sixty thousand workers and sixty-three other agreements were under discussion. There seemed little doubt that the act had helped bring labour peace in the northern logging industry, textiles, and the building trades. Despite the criticism of many employers and some trade unions, labour lawyers Jacob Finkelman and Bora Laskin concluded that on the whole the act was beneficial. 'We have for the first time in Ontario, a measure, no matter what its defects, which enables the parties most directly concerned to meet and discuss their common problems and to arrange a solution to their mutual satisfaction. The original act was faulty; the amending legislation leaves much to be desired, but a beginning has been made in a development, the importance of which cannot be overestimated.'[8]

Mitch and Heenan certainly regarded the controversial and coercive legislation to bring the northern forest and pulp and paper industry under government control as progressive legislation. The gradual recovery increased demand for lumber and newsprint. Improved labour relations and increased exports resulting from the suspension of the manufacturing condition for pulpwood had helped the ailing industry. By 1936 there were 410 cutting camps and 17,500 employees, three times the number at work in 1933. Nevertheless, the virtually bankrupt pulp and paper industry teetered on the edge of complete collapse and the government seemed incapable of bringing the fractious companies to heel.

Mitch and Heenan had refused to follow Taschereau's lead in the spring of 1935, but over the next year they were forced to change their minds. Not only did the companies refuse to yield to gentle persuasion, but the determination of the bondholders of Great Lakes to forge ahead with the Aldrich-Gaefell scheme (initially approved by the courts in December) pointed to some form of coercion. As Heenan explained, they had tried 'to coax these fellows to play square with each other, and not to go out and try to take tonnage away from each other, by cutting prices and secret commissions. And they said, Sure, we will promise to be good boys.' But once out the door, the companies concluded that it was 'all poppy cock, and that they would do as they liked; and they continued to do it.'[9]

Heenan announced the day the session opened that the government would seek power to revamp the timber and pulpwood concessions to bring new life to the northern industry. With a draft bill in his briefcase, he went to Montreal ten days later for the first of two meetings with Taschereau and Charles Vining's pro-rationing committee. Assured that Ontario would be fairly treated in any pro-rationing scheme, Heenan then consulted with the industry before a final draft was approved by cabinet and introduced in March. The Forest Resources Regulation Act gave the cabinet the power to reacquire, rationalize, and reallocate cutting rights on crown lands. Heenan admitted that 'my colleagues and myself hated to put that legislation into effect because it was drastic. It seemed to interfere with vested rights and to interfere in business, but we could not see any other way out of it.' The Tories denounced the bill as another draconian measure which gave dictatorial powers to the executive. The industry remained strangely silent and the bill passed in the closing days of the session. Meanwhile, in March the cabinet had approved a modified reorganization of Great Lakes on the understanding that the company would work 'harmoniously' with the industry, accept the pro-rationing scheme, and would not pay dividends until the price of newsprint reached $45.40 a ton.[10]

As the session wore on, the opposition and the province waited impatiently for Mitch to produce the promised legislation to aid Catholic schools. Although Quinn and the bishops had remained quiet during the federal election, they had not been inactive. When the educational commission set up in the spring of 1935 under Duncan McArthur visited Kingston during the summer, Archbishop O'Brien informed McArthur privately that Catholics did not want special grants, however generous, but acceptance of the principle of shared access to taxation. Bishop McNally again made it clear to Heenan that 'the whole Catholic body means business and does not intend to be trifled with.' Quinn was despondent when there was no session after the federal election, but remained confident he could rely on Mitch's promise and O'Connor's gentle persuasion as they lounged on the beach in Miami. O'Connor reassured Archbishop McGuigan on his return that 'we will have the Quebec plan' and was 'so definite about it,' Quinn informed O'Brien, 'that I am sure he will go to the limit in forcing the issue.' After a conversation with Roebuck, Quinn instructed all the parish chairmen to say nothing to stir the somnolent Orange dogs and make things difficult for the Liberals.[11]

But the rising tide of Protestant opposition to any remedial action was distressing. The Toronto Board of Control even refused to comply with provincial regulations allowing the free distribution of text-

THE QUINTS AT QUEEN'S PARK

DR O'CONNOR:
'Not one of them would have survived if it hadn't been for me!'
Conservative political cartoon, c. 1936

books to separate school kids on relief, and Mayor Jimmy Simpson was making a blatant sectarian appeal in his bid for re-election. To demonstrate their political power, Quinn and McGuigan mobilized Toronto Catholics and boasted that the victory of Samuel McBride over Simpson was due to the heavy Catholic vote. Early in the year Nixon told Quinn that a bill would be passed during the session and that Mitch would 'personally make the key speech, and that the single point about which he was concerned at the moment is the basis upon which taxation will be divided.' Pressed to use school population as the measure, Nixon commented, 'Well, we will offend a certain group if we do anything; I suppose that their number will not be materially increased if we do a first-class job.'[12]

While Mitch was wrestling with the problem in cabinet and caucus, Quinn came perilously close to subverting the Catholic cause by dangerously indiscreet threats of political action. If calculated to force Mitch's hand, Quinn revealed that he did not know his man. He wrote to a Catholic friend of Mitch's, that 'the desires of our people will be registered at the ballot box in the way of protest or gratitude, and, as a Liberal, I do hope that it will be in the latter direction.' The letter was on Mitch's desk two days later when Quinn, told that a Knights of Columbus meeting in Oshawa was closed to the press, made the same point. Although the Oshawa correspondent for the *Star* had let the local priest censor his story, Mitch soon had the unexpurgated notes in which Quinn was quoted as having said, 'If that bird doesn't come across now we'll kick him out.' Mitch was outraged and bluntly told Quinn that his denial was a lie and that 'an unnecessary controversy has been created over a matter which has now been projected not only as a political issue but as a challenge to responsible government.' Mitch never spoke to him again.[13]

Mitch was particularly enraged because, although he was personally convinced of 'the justice of the matter,' he knew that Quinn's threats would not make life easier in the cabinet where most of his colleagues, for either religious or political reasons, were reluctant to provide legislative redress. In the end, however, all bowed to Mitch's wishes, and the cabinet spent two long Saturday sessions discussing the most politically astute way to meet Catholic demands and control the predictable political damage.[14]

The caucus was less amenable to direction, but Mitch was determined to take a united caucus into the House. It first met on 25 February amid rumours that the cabinet had approved the Quebec plan. Although everyone was sworn to secrecy, Mitch's warning that they could go only as far as public opinion would tolerate led Catholics to fear that he was backing down. At a second caucus two days later, the party split wide open with members divided between the Quebec plan or some compromise and those who were politically or on principle opposed to any action. The three-hour session adjourned before the rupture became irrevocable, when Mitch struck a committee of ten to work with the cabinet. The *Star* entered the debate to warn Liberal Catholics that it would be unwise to push for anything approaching the Quebec plan because there was 'an overwhelming body of opinion against the existence of separate schools' which, if aroused, could endanger their survival. The 1886 act had permitted but not required corporations to pay separate school taxes in proportion to the number of Catholic shareholders, but the provision had been difficult to implement and was largely ignored. An amendment to change 'may to shall,' trumpeted the *Star*, reflecting a widespread view among the more liberal Protestants and even some Catholics, was all Protestants would accept and all that Catholics deserved. *Le Droit* also entered the debate with a strong editorial to stiffen the French-Canadian members.[15]

On 21 March Mitch and the cabinet met for six hours and three days later met the caucus committee, which had received a petition for delay signed by thirty back-benchers. Following their long luncheon meeting, Mitch told the press he was not backing down. A week later he laid it on the line when he walked into caucus at 2 p.m. before the House met. Despite his doctor's orders the day before that he must quit, he said he was determined to stay on. But there was a price: back-bencher support for the final position the cabinet had reached. Between them, the whip and the doctor worked. Bélanger informed Quinn, who relayed the message to Archbishop McGuigan:

Your Grace

Mr. Quinn phoned to say that the outcome of the Caucus was substantially as he had enunciated Sunday evening.

(1) The 'may' to 'shall'.

(2) where corporations do not or cannot make returns the division will be on relative assessment.

(3) there will be no division of utilities taxes. He further remarked that Mr. Belanger is satisfied this is the best that can be obtained at present. Mr. Quinn seemed elated with the above concessions.

The bill was not ready two days later when Mitch had hoped to introduce it, and late that night the cabinet saw it for the first time. Mitch had transferred the responsibility from Roebuck to Leduc, and he in turn had enlisted Duncan McArthur who, as draftsman, was present to explain the complicated provisions. At two in the morning Quinn and Catholic lawyers had a copy of the bill. When Mitch rose to introduce Bill 38 that afternoon Leduc had already been warned that the legislation had some fatal flaws.[16]

'If I had not implicit faith in the people of Ontario,' Mitch began, 'I would feel like the gladiators going into the arena announcing to the emperor: '"We who are about to die, salute you".' But he was convinced that Ontario Protestants would grant to the Catholics at least some of the benefits enjoyed by Quebec Protestants, and would agree that the modest proposal before the House was a reasonable modernization of the principles of the 1863 act when over half the taxes were now paid by corporations. The bill had two general objectives, he explained, though none too clearly. First, section 33a compelled corporations to direct their taxes according to the percentage of shares owned by Catholics who had declared themselves separate school supporters. Secondly, 33b provided that very widely held corporations, which could not ascertain which of their shareholders were Catholics and separate school supporters, or corporations in which 25 per cent of the stock was owned by another corporation or whose head office was outside Ontario, would have their taxes divided according to the ratio of rateable property owned by separate and public school supporters in the municipality. Mitch stressed that all utility taxes would go to public schools.

It was indeed a modest proposal, Mitch argued, which given the increasing grants to separate schools or the increased taxes that would be necessary to teach the Catholic pupils in public schools would, in fact, leave more money for public schools. But, finances aside, he appealed to the opposition not to provoke 'what we in Ontario want least of all – a religious controversy. I often regret that our ancestors, a thousand or so years ago, decided that there were one hundred or one thousand roads to heaven, and only one road to the other place. It is almost humorous to see us pious Christians fighting like heathens over religious issues.'[17]

If Mitch had quoted Robert Bruce at the 31 March caucus, telling the troops at Bannockburn that the time to desert was before the battle had begun, the Tories soon confirmed Roebuck's charge that they hoped to ride back to power on King William's white horse. The debate raged for three days. The Tories dared Mitch to call off the whips. A few blocks away, the Toronto Board of Education called a special meeting and voted fifteen to zero for a provincial referendum.[18]

Mitch did not force his back-benchers to speak and the Liberals met the Tory filibuster, which repeatedly kept the House in session until the early hours of the morning, with jeers and catcalls. He did try to dilute some of the opposition criticism with minor amendments, however, and also withdrew a bill to create new intermediate schools because the Tories were convinced this would simply allow Catholic secondary schools in through the back door. Finally, just before dawn on 9 April, with the members exhausted and the Speaker barely able to keep order, Mitch rose to close the debate. The bill was a reasonable attempt to provide support for Catholics who have 'just as much a right to an education in this Province as other children.' The time had come for Ontario to shed its past bigotry. But if the Tories chose to make their appeal to 'religious and racial prejudice' he would 'be content to abide by the intelligent decision which the good people of Ontario will give us at the next general election.'[19]

Earlier in the day Percy Parker had begged Mitch to make the act subject to proclamation. There were serious doubts about the constitutionality of at least one section of the bill, he argued, and there were certain to be complex legal proceedings. More important, the issue was tearing the party apart and, after talking to many members, 'I judge that a large number would refrain from voting or even vote against the Bill were it not for a profound sense of loyalty to yourself.' There were, indeed, many Liberals who, like Percy Parker, would back Mitch '100% all the time, right or wrong,' and when the Speaker called for the vote, sixty-five of the seventy-one Liberals rose in their seats. Three Liberals and Sam Lawrence were conveniently absent. Three joined the seventeen Tories and voted nay. The legislature prorogued the next day. When one of the rebels, Joe Crawford from Fort William, came up to say goodbye, Mitch replied: 'Goodbye, and it is goodbye, Joe.'

Mitch was pleased with the session. Despite the fierce attack on the separate school bill, he had been in command throughout and the relative caucus solidarity had been a tribute to his leadership. Mitch dominated the House. The acme of neatness, his double-breasted grey suit immaculately pressed, he often sprawled in his chair, passing comments to his desk mates and asides to the back-benchers, or throwing barbs across the floor. But when he stood erect and fixed the opposition with those piercing blue eyes, contemporaries sensed 'the electricity in the House.' Members and civil servants marvelled at his ability to rescue ministers under attack by the opposition. 'When an emergency arose,' said one Queen's Park veteran, 'he would be called into the House from his office fifty yards away, usually with a sheaf of papers under his arm. In no time he would grasp the situation and come to the rescue. Roy Elmhirst vowed that he didn't know what Mitch had picked up to bring into the House yet he could reach into the bundle and produce the exact document he needed. It was like a magic show.' He was equally in command of the cabinet. The meetings were infrequent and informal. Mitch usually let each minister talk freely and when the time seemed appropriate ended the discussion with the statement 'Alright boys, where do we stand?' But on critical issues there was every indication that, either by command or persuasion, Mitch got his way.[20]

While the numbers on relief had dropped in the summer of 1935, they rose to more than four hundred thousand early in 1936. Over two-thirds of the unemployed on relief were in the nine major urban areas in southern Ontario. Farm relief was negligible. More than 95 per cent of farmers claiming relief were squatters, seasonal workers in the tourist industry in the lake country, settlers in the unorganized northern districts, and urban workers with small holdings in the shack towns outside Toronto, Windsor and Ottawa. Over half those on relief were dependent wives and children, but the vast majority of the rest were employable: seventy-eight thousand out of the ninety thousand heads of urban families and thirty thousand of the forty thousand women. Half of the men were unskilled, but many of the women were classed as domestics at a time when the employment offices reported that the supply of domestic help could not meet the demand.[21]

Before he left for Florida in December 1935 Mitch and the cabinet had agreed on a new relief formula based on their conviction that with improving economic conditions jobs were available and the unemployed were abusing the system. On 3 February 1936 Croll announced a policy designed to force the municipalities to 'house-clean' the relief rolls by the end of March. The government would match Ottawa's grant, but established a maximum grant for each municipality based on what Croll's department decided was the real need. Those to be purged, said Croll, were the 'chisellers – families who have made relief their career,' and those who refused to work or who had hidden income or assets. Moreover, 'no longer would the government subsidize the starvation wages paid by unscrupulous employers,' Croll warned, as he announced that full-time workers whose wages were so low that supplementary relief had to be given to keep the family alive were to be purged as well. 'Need, not greed' was to be the key to government policy.[22]

Despite the housecleaning and a more buoyant economy, there were still 425,000 on relief at the end of March. Mackenzie King's decision to close the Department of National Defence camps did not help. The railways agreed to hire half the twenty thousand men for the summer and Rogers optimistically hoped the other half could find jobs on the farms. Rogers had also introduced a bill to establish the National Employment Commission, which the naive believed was to deal with the problem but whose mandate, in King's mind, was to cut federal relief costs and force the provinces and municipalities to 'find the truth of the saying that every man must learn to earn his bread by the sweat of his brow.' On 1 April, without consultation or even advance warning, Rogers cut Ontario's relief grant another 15 per cent. Mitch was furious. After a cabinet meeting, he wired Rogers that he had no choice but to pass on the cut to the municipalities and the 'defenceless unemployed.' Rogers replied that the original grant had not been carved in stone, and King told the Commons that there could be further cuts in a month. Mitch did not live up to his threat, however, and reduced the grant to the municipalities by only 7.5 per cent.[23]

Mitch led a cabinet delegation to Ottawa for meetings in April and May. Although the sessions were cordial on the surface, Ottawa refused to share relief costs equally and Mitch had to be content with the assurance that the grants would not be cut in May or June. However, a federal public works project provided $3 million in matching grants for highway construction and another $300,000 for building roads into the northern mining camps. As the spring wore on, the numbers on relief dropped sharply and by July had fallen below three hundred thousand for the first time since the fall of 1932. Ottawa's share of the declining burden had in fact been increasing, and Mitch made only a token protest when the grant was cut another 10 per cent in July. Overcoming the objections of rural members of the cabinet, Mitch announced that the province would not pass on the cut to the municipalities, which could not be stretched any further, and he refused to economize on 'empty stomachs.'[24]

In many municipalities the mood of those on relief was uglier in the spring and summer of 1936 than it had been since the Depression began. Most local officials had found it painful, and sometimes impossible, to make the cuts demanded by the new formula and were unwilling or unable to make up the deficit. There were strikes in Penetang, Sarnia, Guelph, and other cities and towns as allowances were reduced anywhere from 15 to 50 per cent. In North Bay, where the closing of the DND camps had thrown another five hundred single men on the rolls, the month's budget was gone by mid-June and the mayor gave permission for married men to beg on the streets. Sudbury simply closed the relief office.

In suburban Toronto, where both unemployment and benefits were higher than elsewhere in Ontario, relief workers began to strike in June and by the end of the month there were more than five thousand heads of families on strike. On 6 July simultaneous protests throughout the suburbs suggested that the violence was well organized.

In Willowdale dozens of women barricaded themselves in the relief offices until extra vouchers were issued. There were angry demonstrations and deputations in Mimico, Long Branch, and

Lakeview. The most serious conflict was in York Township where a crowd of strikers, fronted by women carrying babies, overpowered the police in hand-to-hand fighting, occupied the relief offices at Dufferin and Rogers Road, and imprisoned the staff. A mob of several thousand chanted 'We'll hang old Geggie from a sour apple tree.' A rope thrown into the office convinced a perspiring 'old Geggie,' the relief officer, to take the threat seriously. Leading the occupying forces was Ewart Humphries, of the disbanded WUL, who warned York officials that he could not hold the crowd much longer and held out the prospect of widespread looting. After eight hours of negotiations, the township councillors arrived and in a five-minute meeting agreed to restore the cuts and put the single men back on the rolls.

Two days later an angry mob, five hundred women and children among them, stormed the Sir Adam Beck school in Etobicoke and imprisoned and physically abused the reeve and a relief officer for eighteen hours, until they signed a paper agreeing to their demands. A veteran *Star* police reporter, who had covered the battle of York, told Mitch that well-known communists were behind it, and that many of them had been seen at the other demonstrations.[25]

Mitch had been enjoying a ten-day political holiday in the north and returned to Toronto on 8 July. Croll had already stated that the violence was 'inspired from Communist headquarters in Toronto' and that communist agents were 'covering every relief centre in the province.' Following a cabinet meeting the day after his return, Mitch summoned reporters to his office and announced gravely that 'Mob rule is going to end in Ontario today.' To prove that the strikes had been carefully orchestrated by the Communist party, Croll released what he claimed was an undercover agent's report of a recent meeting of the party's central committee. According to the report, the committee decided to take advantage of the growing unrest among the relief workers and to send experienced organizers into 'every centre in Ontario, to consult with local Communist unit, if any, to find best method of stirring unemployed to action ... and formulate plan of action.' The organizers were instructed to remain 'inconspicuous' and let local Communists 'assume leadership' and utilize them 'to seek the support of local clergy getting them to address their meetings and requesting the use of church basements for such meetings.' Leaders for the Toronto area included Humphries in York Township.[26]

Mitch told reporters that the government would arrest those responsible for the violence. That afternoon warrants were quietly sworn out before the provincial police commissioner. Shortly after midnight on 10 July a squad of twenty-nine OPP and York County police gathered in New Toronto, broke into groups of two or three, and moved quickly to arrest ten strike leaders in their homes. They were charged with forcible confinement under Section 297 of the Criminal Code and released on bail. Early the next morning police arrested another seventeen in York County, among them Ewart Humphries.

The arrests ended the violence. The communists charged that the story of a conspiracy was pure fabrication and retained Jacob Cohen to defend their good name. On 21 September true bills were returned by the grand jury in general session: nine men faced charges of kidnapping and sixteen of being members of an unlawful assembly. Mitch was adamant that the accused would be brought to trial. But in December Roebuck dropped the charges. 'These men are not criminals,' he explained. 'They were just excited and poor people. I thought it wise and in the public interest that the trial should not go on and I told them to go in peace and sin no more.'[27]

The relief strikers were not alone in spoiling what might have been a pleasant summer on the hustings. Mitch also faced a more intense and personal attack by a new Tory leader. George Henry could at times be effective in the House and sneer an audible 'you contemptible cur' across the chamber when Mitch was particularly abusive, but he had neither the stomach nor the talent to battle him on the platform. The 1934 election had sealed Henry's fate, and many wanted his immediate removal. With the federal election over, Henry pre-empted a coup by asking the party caucus on 11 December to call for a leadership convention at the earliest possible date.[28]

Most of the horses were in the starting gate long before the May 1936 convention and the rumours focused on the dark horses that might be drafted. As one of Robert Manion's advocates cynically observed, Charles McCrea 'talks of combing the province for a young man, who must be under 40, who has never been identified with either Bennett or Henry, a young man who will combine the brilliance of Dizraeli [sic] with the bulldoggidness of a Baldwin and, last but not least, one who will ever incline his ear to the counsel of the two kingmakers, Don [Hogarth] and Charlie.' That combination proved to be elusive, and by the middle of May the leading candidate was clearly Earl Rowe. The forty-two-year-old farmer and stockbreeder had sat in the Commons for Dufferin-Simcoe since 1925, after two years in the provincial House, and had become a minister without portfolio six weeks before the federal election. Rowe was young, energetic, a good speaker and a good campaigner, although Hogarth's description of him as 'a combination of Macdonald and Howard Ferguson' seemed excessive even to his friends.[29]

The odds on Rowe dropped dramatically on 19 May with the appearance of half-page advertisements in the press seeking support for George Drew, who planned a number of radio addresses in the week before the convention. The handsome forty-two-year-old bachelor had returned from the war a lieutenant-colonel and, after establishing a successful law career in Guelph, had become securities commissioner in 1931, a post from which Roebuck had summarily dismissed him. There was nothing modest about George Drew, whose advertisements described him as 'a man possessing the highest qualities of leadership' and 'the vision and broad experience so vitally necessary ...' The convention had to decide whether Ontario would 'stagnate in the backwater of petty politics with which both parties have disgusted the people of Ontario during the past few years or is going to return to the vigorous policies of Sir John A. Macdonald and Sir James Whitney.' The Tory party, he stated in his radio addresses, 'must tear itself free from the dead hand of a spineless organization' and must no longer be 'run by that small group in Toronto which boasts that it is the party machine.'[30]

The two thousand delegates who jammed the Royal York for the 27–28 May convention heard Henry's last speech as leader before dutifully approving the resolutions which were, on the whole, a ringing denunciation of Mitch and all his works. The Tory position on separate schools was unequivocal:

Be it resolved that the Liberal-Conservative Party of Ontario in convention assembled hereby put itself on record as unequivocally opposed to the said changes in the Assessment Act without the endorsation of the people at a general election and further this convention pledges itself '*to the repeal*' of the said amendments and furthermore this convention in accordance with traditional Conservative policy reaffirms that the rights of the minorities in the province of Ontario will be respected.

In their short speeches all the candidates echoed Rowe's description of two years of Mitch's rule as 'a carnival of recklessness.' Drew got the biggest laugh when he called him O'Connor's 'little chocolate soldier' and the loudest applause when he declared that he stood four-square for the sacred British principles of democracy and justice. 'We haven't had it in the last few years,' he exclaimed.

'Instead of the Union Jack, the Jolly Roger should have been flying over the Parliament Buildings at Queen's Park.' The first ballot gave Rowe 782 votes to Drew's 480, with five other candidates far behind. Rowe defeated Drew on the second ballot, 1,005 to 660.[31]

Earl Rowe told caucus three weeks later that he planned to secure a full-time organizer and would not resign his Commons seat until the next provincial election. Late in July Rowe announced that Drew had agreed to become chairman of the Tory election campaign. The colonel moved in with a vengeance and it was Drew more than Rowe who took the fight to the man he dismissed contemptuously as 'the little pooh-bah of Queen's Park.'

Rowe and Drew concentrated their assault on booze, power, and Catholic schools. Under Mitch and Eddie Odette, the provincial government had become little more than an irresponsible and corrupt purveyor of drink where 'old cafés, taxi stands, garages – even tabernacles – have been converted into beer halls just to make more money for provincial revenues and secure more friends for the Liberal party.' The separate school legislation was a cynical attempt to get Catholic support at the expense of 'the peace and harmony of the community.' Rowe repeatedly demanded that Mitch prove that the province would not face a power shortage in a few years, and declared that the Tories would support the development of the St Lawrence seaway and power project. Why, he wondered, was Hydro so interested in the Ogoki diversion to run more water over Niagara if supplies were secure?

Higher taxes, contracts without tender, midnight arrests rather than the promised constructive unemployment policy, and a host of other charges were levelled at Mitch in what was generally regarded as 'a first-class show.' Above all, Mitch had no constructive policy, and was afraid to face the electorate. 'Like Old Man River,' Rowe joked at a Port Dalhousie picnic, 'he's "tired of living" and "fraid of dying". Northern Ontario is burning by the thousands of acres while the Minister of Lands and Forests basks in the cool lakes of the West. He refuses to discuss the Hydro policy while the majority of commissioners are on holidays, and agriculture ... he refuses to handle while his minister is in the Old Country buying blue ribbon bulls. Much is being made of the reckless wisecracking of the Premier but the chickens are coming home to roost.'[32]

Mitch was also on the summer picnic circuit. After dividing his time between the office and the farm in the spring, he launched the season with speeches in St Thomas and Woodstock late in June and then headed north for two weeks of fun and politics. On Dominion Day he opened the new highway between Fort Frances and Kenora. Peter Heenan was there for what was both an accolade and an obituary. Mitch had long been unhappy with Peter's administration of the north. In April, balancing loyalty and judgment, he had abolished the Department of Northern Development and moved northern highways to McQuesten's Department of Public Works. Peter was left with only Lands and Forests. But all that was in the past when Mitch cut the ribbon and the cavalcade travelled the 146 miles of the Heenan Highway. He opened another road at Sioux Lookout and spoke glowingly of the mining industry during a flying visit to Patricia Mines. The north was in flames during the visit. Before the rains came late in August fires raged out of control along a hundred-mile front from the borders of Manitoba and Minnesota into Quebec. The Tories charged Mitch and Heenan with 'criminal neglect' because they had fired all the experienced foresters and fire-fighters. Mitch offered a reward for information about northern – presumably Tory – arsonists.[33]

In parched southern Ontario cabbages were selling for a dollar instead of a nickel, but neither the heat nor the late August rains kept the huge crowds away as Mitch stumped southern Ontario making two dozen speeches in six weeks. The refrain was the same – spirited defence of his record, appeal to reason and to justice on the schools question, attack on the Tories and their masters the 'big interests' – all suitably embellished to fit the occasion. He was determined to balance not only the budget but also the distribution of wealth between rich and poor: 'It's the callousness of affluence and wealth that gets me sometimes ... We aren't trying to soak the rich. We are only trying to stop the ever increasing concentration of wealth.'

Among other issues were the national economy and monetary reform, the need for improved hospital and medical services, particularly for the insane, a warning to the Ontario Medical Association that the government was studying health insurance, and government support for an experimental housing scheme in the Toronto suburbs.[34]

As he sipped a Dewar's Special with Mitch at the farm early in May, Ed Carty had asked him if separate schools were worrying him. 'Not a damned bit,' Mitch replied. But separate schools were very much on his mind during the summer and fall.

There were many signs that his appeal to reason and justice would fall on deaf ears. 'Like King William we need two guns,' exclaimed the pastor of Knox Presbyterian in Hamilton as the

Orangemen marched on 12 July, 'one for the enemies of our religion, and one for the enemies of our freedom, education and equal rights.' The president of the Canadian Protestant Alliance described the Roman Catholic Church as 'a blight and cancer to any nation on which it lays its dead and clammy hands.' And Dr Shields paused in his attack on Mitch for turning hotels into whorehouses to assure Protestants that the Roman Catholic Church 'hates the British Empire as I wish it could learn to hate the devil ... All the Communists in Canada put together will never do the harm the Roman Catholic Church is doing every day.'[35]

Mitch knew that the real test on separate schools would come at the polls, and it was a test that he seemed anxious to take. One week after J.F. Hill, the sitting Tory member for East Hastings, died on 15 October, Mitch decided on a 9 December by-election. It was a strange and foolhardy decision. East Hastings was deep in the heart of Tory Ontario. The narrow riding ran one hundred miles north from Lake Ontario between Belleville and Napanee, skirting Bancroft to the west, with its northern edge just south of Barry's Bay. The riding had remained largely untouched by the twentieth century. The population of twenty-four thousand was scattered throughout the small villages, logging camps, passable farms in the south, and scrubland in the north with only Deseronto, Tweed, and Madoc boasting more than a thousand people. Over 75 per cent of the residents were Protestants, and there was only one small separate school in Tweed. Arthur Slaght urged Mitch not to call an election, and his friend George McCullagh, who had bought the *Globe* the day before Hill died, offered the same advice. But, according to McCullagh, Mitch 'seemed to think his own popularity was strong enough for anything' and refused to flinch.[36]

For whatever reason, Mitch made only a minor attempt to sidestep what he knew would be the central issue when he spoke to the East Hastings nominating convention on 6 November. Handicapped by a severe bronchial cold, he spent the first ninety minutes with a familiar review of the accomplishments of his government and a ringing indictment of his Tory opponents. Finally, he made, what he called a 'fair offer.' Unless he could demonstrate that rural Ontario would benefit from the separate school legislation, he would expect the riding to vote against the Liberal candidate and his government at the next election. The new tax law was a long overdue measure of justice to the Catholic minority, he argued, and was also a measure of justice to Ontario farmers. The Henry government had increased the grants to separate schools but at the same time had reduced support for public schools. In East Hastings, he pointed out, public school grants had shrunk by 40 per cent since 1930, while grants to urban Catholic schools across the province had increased. His legislation was simply putting the burden where it belonged – on the cities and the corporations. 'If defeat is the penalty for doing what is right and just,' he ended amid thundering applause, 'then send us down to defeat.'[37]

For the next month the rustics of East Hastings were treated to an endless procession of the great and not-so-great. Reporters for the big dailies who filed from Tweed and Madoc, Maynooth and Plainfield fought for headlines with the reports from London that Edward VIII preferred an American divorcée to the Crown. Harry Johnson set up his headquarters in Madoc and Mitch almost lived in the riding. All the cabinet – with the discreet exception of Heenan and Leduc – and many of the rural Protestant back-benchers swept through the riding. Road engineers worked overtime to comply with orders from Queen's Park to get men to work. The number of day labourers jumped from 385 in August to 922 in December. Leslie Frost, the prominent Lindsay Tory, reported that truckloads of flour were being distributed in the north of the riding, while cash seemed to be a more satisfactory inducement in the south. The brawls that erupted at many meetings suggested that both sides offered liquid refreshments. Les Frost urged the Tories to see that 'our strong Orange supporters are in the hall[s] to see that fair play is given.' Fair play there was not. At Madoc on 2 December Earl Rowe survived the bedlam and finished his speech but Mitch gave up trying to shout over a screaming, shoving, and fighting crowd of two thousand.[38]

It was a nasty, dirty campaign. Earl Rowe, the gentlemanly victor in many a harness race, attempted to take the high road, challenging Mitch's facts and figures without calling him a liar, and accusing the Liberals of stirring up racial and religious passions. Mitch's record was a 'boulevard of broken promises,' and the party stained by the Beauharnois scandal was now unblushingly bribing the East Hastings voters with their own money. With a venom fed by his dismissal as securities commissioner in 1934 and the accusations of almost criminal incompetence that were used to justify it, George Drew knew no restraint. When Mitch denounced the 19 November decision of the Ontario Court of Appeal declaring the act cancelling the power contracts *ultra vires* as a 'hollow verdict...a hog's head of law and a thimbleful of justice,' Drew insisted he should resign for contempt of court. 'Who is this Mussolini, this puppet of Frank O'Connor? This is Fascism. Mussolini has suspended the courts recently in his totalitarian State. Now this man says he will suspend Ontario's courts. He should haul down the Union Jack and hoist the Jolly Roger. He is a pirate.' A vote for the Liberal candidate, screamed the Tory handouts, was a vote for the Hepburn-O'Connor government. 'I have every respect for a man's religion,' Drew assured audiences throughout the riding, 'but I say that it is up to Ontario to decide whether any fraternal or religious group can organize itself into a temporal political power with the end of dictating to the Government.'[39]

But the statement that aroused the most intense controversy concerned the French Canadians. As interpreted by a young *Star* reporter, Drew stated at Plainfield on 26 November that 'It is not unfair to remind the French that they are a defeated race and that their rights are rights only because of the tolerance of the English element, who, with all respect to the minority, must be regarded as the dominant race.' Drew immediately denied that he had made the statement, and explained that his remarks 'were a mere reference to historical background in which I referred to the conquest of Quebec and noted that the laws and religion had been retained under British rule. If we have reached the state where the conquest of Canada can no longer be referred to we will have to tear up all the history books.' Privately, Drew insisted that it was a deliberate frame-up, written by a reporter in Hepburn's pay, less to win East Hastings, where there were few French Canadians, than to enable Mitch to pose as the champion of French Canada as part of the O'Connor-Hepburn on-to-Ottawa strategy. The *Star* reporter undoubtedly took considerable liberty with Drew's remarks, but Plainfield was to haunt George Drew for the rest of his life.[40]

A confident Frank O'Connor had offered Don Hogarth, his counterpart as the Tory financier, $5,000 or $25,000 on the outcome, but Hogarth had not taken the wager. It was bitterly cold on December 9 and deep snow made the roads impassable in many parts of the riding. But whether it was the issue or the 33,000 Liberal dollars, probably matched by the Tories, there was a record turnout of 85 per cent. The Tories gained 861 votes to the Liberals 143 and won with a majority of 1,136.[41]

The election was widely seen as a plebiscite on separate schools. 'The government's separate school legislation accounts for its overwhelming defeat in this strongly Protestant constituency – that, and nothing else,' the *Star* declared. 'The electors discarded all but the one issue, they listened to only one appeal – the sectarian appeal.'

Mitch initially agreed that his defeat was due in part to religious bigotry, and to the turnout of traditional Tories who were too 'disgruntled' to vote in 1934. Later, with a poll-by-poll analysis showing that the Tories had gained more in areas with the largest Catholic population and the Liberals in some polls with almost 100 per cent Protestant voters, he concluded that the Catholics must have been intimidated and stayed home. As he explained to King, the Irish Catholics had 'double-crossed him. They had been bought out by the power interest. That part of the constituency had lost votes; in the Protestant sections, he had gained, though the Protestants were supposed to be Tories.' Mitch concluded hopefully that the 'School bill had not helped him with the Catholics, and had not injured him with the Protestants.'

The result in East Hastings did indeed defy analysis, and Les Frost was perhaps closest to the mark when he dismissed the explanations of a friend with the comment, 'I think to sum up that we are simply chasing each other around a tree. There are too many cross currents to arrive at any real conclusion.' But no such rational reflections tempered the Tory jubilation. After such a 'crushing defeat,' Rowe insisted, Mitch's clinging to office could only be termed 'an act of deliberate usurpation' and his only 'honourable course' was to face the people. Back at the farm Mitch replied that he saw no reason for an election until 1938 after two more sessions and a much-needed redistribution.[42]

On the day of the East Hastings election, Charles Dunning was opening a three-day session of his newly established National Finance Committee. A day later Norman Lambert chaired the meeting of the National Liberal Federation Advisory Council. Dunning had refused to delay his meeting because of East Hastings, and Mitch sent Paul Leduc and Chester Walters to represent the province. But there were no representatives of the provincial Liberals at Lambert's gathering because Mitch had seceded from King's federation.

The December 1935 conference had confirmed Mitch's fears that with Dunning in Finance little could be expected from Ottawa. Chester Walters's report of the discussions at the January 1936 meetings of the finance committee, when Mitch was recuperating in the Florida sun, was even more ominous. Dunning was not only after provincial succession duties, it seemed, but corporation taxes as well. Describing the corporate tax structure as a disgrace, Dunning had expected Ontario, with 42 per cent of the collections, and

Quebec, with 25 per cent, to object. 'They are at the centre,' he observed, 'and the further you get towards the circumference the more difficult it is to collect from Dominion corporations because their head offices are in Ontario and Quebec.' Under any revised scheme, he confessed, Ontario and Quebec would inevitably get less, and he warned Walters that 'you would not enjoy the advantage which you now enjoy of taxing other parts of Canada, because that is what it really amounts to.'

Walters in turn carried Mitch's message that the province had no objection to Dunning's cherished loan council but would not participate, had cash in hands to meet its maturing obligations, and, as far as the western provinces were concerned, believed the 'damage to the credit of Canada is greater, would be greater if you continued to temporize, to use your word, than if you let them go into default.' There seemed to be little doubt that Dunning and J.L. Ilsley, the tax collector, were interested in more than eliminating waste, duplication, and inefficiency.[43]

There were also disturbing rumours that King and Lapointe were seriously considering a petition from Beauharnois to disallow the Power Commission Act. Although King believed it should be disallowed, he realized that 'a larger political issue of a party character would have been raised' and wanted it rejected before the session opened. But Lapointe found it impossible to easily dismiss an appeal from the apex of Montreal's financial power and wanted a defensible report. As the rumours persisted, Mitch had declared that his answer to disallowance would be 'to dissolve the Legislature and make an immediate appeal to the people. This course, while forced on us, would do irreparable damage to the Liberal Party.' Although the cabinet approved Lapointe's carefully worded recommendation against disallowance on 31 March, the observation that the legislation was discriminatory and of doubtful constitutionality did not sit well at Queen's Park. A day later came Rogers's cut in the relief grants. By the spring it was also clear that Ottawa was dragging its feet, if not being wilfully obstructive, on Mitch's request to secure permission from Washington to run the water from the Ogoki River diversion through the generators at Niagara.[44]

Although Percy Parker had warned King of an impending battle with Ontario early in the new year, the first hint of a break had come in March 1936 when Lambert, in Toronto on a begging expedition, learned from O'Connor that there was 'nothing doing' and from Harry Johnson that Mitch did not want any federal Liberals on a platform with his ministers. Matters were worse a month later when Lambert saw O'Connor and Bill Bennett who told him 'that "Mitch" very sore at Ottawa over relief adjustments & alleged failure of Ottawa to notify him or Peter H. – M. had asked Frank O'C not to send any money from Ontario to Ottawa – O'C said he would talk to Mitch later about it. He wanted K. to make overtures toward reconciliation re & he (F) intended to approach K. about it.' But King was not in a conciliatory mood. Dropping into Rideau Hall when the Bruces were visiting, he 'disassociated himself from Hepburn immediately' and told Angela that 'the less he saw of Hepburn the better he got on with him.'[45]

However, on the surface relations between the two men were cordial when Mitch, with Walters, Croll, and Heenan, had been in Ottawa for two days of meetings at the end of April:

At the office, I had a quarter of an hour with Hepburn alone, before having a conference with his colleagues, and Rogers, Elliott and Mackenzie. Hepburn brought with him two signed photographs of himself, one of the two of us together, which he had framed and addressed to me as 'my chief'. It was apparent that he was anxious to hold friendly relations with myself, and is discovering that some of the advice I gave him, it would have been well for him to have followed.(...) He told me of the feeling of hatred which was growing up between the Ontario ministers and our own, and spoke with peculiar bitterness of Ilsley refusing to co-operate with his Dept in tracking out frauds under the succession duties.

King had them all to Laurier House for dinner, and spent an hour with Mitch after the others left. At cabinet that afternoon, wrote King, 'I pointed out the necessity of viewing the relations with the provinces in a friendly way, and doing our utmost to restore good feeling between the two governments. Hepburn is in a decidedly different frame of mind than he has been on any previous occasion.'[46]

Mitch was in the Commons gallery when Dunning delivered his 1 May budget. He had been too close to the ground not to be aware of the tension within cabinet and even more in caucus over the direction of Liberal policy. Not all Liberals were as obsessed as King and Dunning with protecting the public treasury from marauding provinces or shiftless unemployed. The warmed-over Bennett policies in the 1936 Unemployment Relief and Assistance Act and the efficiency-oriented National Employment Commission were singularly unimpressive assaults on unemployment. Not only advocates of 'funny money,' such as Gerry McGeer, criticized King's refusal to nationalize the Bank of Canada completely and direct it to pursue an expansionary monetary policy. King lectured a truculent caucus about the causes of revolution and finally warned his more outspoken critics that 'if they were not prepared to work within the party in a co-operative spirit, there was lots of room for them outside.' On every count Mitch's views coincided with those of the caucus radicals.

Mitch also agreed with Thomas Crerar, the minister of mines, who had fought a long and losing battle to stimulate the mining industry through tax concessions for depletion and exploration. The best he could extract from King and the cabinet was provision that new mines would be exempt from taxes for three years, a provision Crerar insisted was a far cry from King's vague campaign promise to give the industry security and stability. In the end, Dunning was able to cap the projected deficit at $100 million but only by increasing sales and corporation taxes by almost $30 million. Publicly, Mitch said that the budget was the best that could be brought down under the circumstances and applauded the concession on new mines. But there was little in the budget or other decisions in the first nine months of the new government to convince him that King intended to do much about unemployment despite his campaign statements that it was a national problem.[47]

Mitch attempted to still the rumours of tension between Laurier House and the King Eddy. 'When I speak of Mr. King, I speak of a man for whom I have the greatest regard,' he told the annual convention of the Ontario Women's Liberal Association in May soon after his return from Ottawa, 'a man who will go down in history as one of Canada's greatest statesman. I am one of his most loyal followers.' But Ottawa remained under the fund-raising ban. An unhappy Lambert learned late in May that although O'Connor had been slipping him a few thousand now and again, he was through collecting for Ottawa 'because he didn't want Hepburn to hear that he was doing anything. He referred particularly to Jack Bickell who, he assumed, had said to Mitch that O'C had solicited 10m from him for federal purposes.' Although Lambert insisted that the situation could not continue, it did. At a June meeting of the National Liberal Federation brass, O'Connor caustically stated that 'we wanted to work with the [federal] Ministers but it was up to them. We were as good as they were; & we did not propose to be pointed at as undesirable because we were connected with the [Ontario] organization.' The two bagmen were driven to desperation. In September O'Connor told Lambert that he was going to ignore Mitch's injunction and if Lambert 'quit he would do so too.'[48]

At the end of the year Lambert asked Mitch, 'as a personal favour, if nothing else,' to attend the federation's annual meeting on 10 December and the big dinner being tendered to the King government that night. Mitch replied a week later:

During the past few months I have given a great deal of thought to the question of the relationship which should exist between the Ontario Association and your Federation, and after many conferences with my colleagues it has been decided that we will not be represented at your annual meeting. I am also asking Mr. Johnson to keep his organization separate and distinct from yours. I believe this to be in the interests of both Governments. I am constantly being pressed from all sides to make representations to the Federal Ministers and in accordance with the intimation given to me by Mr. King shortly after the Federal election I have carefully refrained from doing anything of a nature which I know would ultimately be embarrassing not only to Mr. King, but to myself as well.

In future it will be our intention, and may I make this very clear, to keep our organization separate and apart from yours.

Told of the secession, King concluded that Mitch's antagonism must have been caused by someone else. But Lambert wisely decided to substitute a quiet reception for the testimonial dinner. Mitch consolidated the secession by asking O'Connor not to collect for Ottawa and not to attend the NLF meeting. O'Connor agreed to stay away, but he also decided that he had had enough. In January 1937, he announced that he was through collecting for anyone and closed his office in the King Eddy. For the moment at least, O'Connor went back to making chocolates and the invaluable sherpa, Bill Bennett, went into insurance. The Tories gloated that both the Liberal party and the Hepburn machine were beginning to crack.[49]

'A much divided crowd'

Mitch was irritable, exhausted, and sick. Confident that his personal popularity and the government's record would win converts even in the Orange lodges, he had gambled on East Hastings and lost. Mitch was not a good loser. He had also been subjected to an unprecedented torrent of personal abuse that he found difficult to take and ironically, while Protestant Ontario was rendering its verdict on Catholic schools, the legislation itself was proving to be unworkable. Worse still, while the Tories were denouncing the contract repudiation and warning of a power shortage, the courts were shredding his Hydro policy.

With Roebuck's assurance, Mitch had repeatedly boasted that the 1935 legislation was 'bombproof.' Chief Justice Rose had agreed in June when he dismissed the appeal from Ottawa Valley on the grounds that no action could be brought against Hydro without the consent of the attorney general. But on 19 November, in a three to two decision, the Appeal Court held that the 1935 act repudiating the contracts was unconstitutional. Equally disturbing was the knowledge that the publisher of the newly merged *Globe and Mail* was going to appeal to a different tribunal to force Mitch to renegotiate the contracts. It was a bleak December.[1]

George McCullagh was a dazzling example of the self-made man. Born in London, Ontario, in 1905, the son of a cabinet-maker of Ulster descent, he had endured high school for less than six months and clerking in a bank for less. His success in peddling *Globe* subscriptions along the concession roads of western Ontario brought him to the London office, where he doubled circulation and soon replaced the manager. Toronto beckoned and within a few years he had graduated from chasing fire engines to the financial pages, where he became the assistant editor with a special interest in mining. His energy and apparent brilliance caught the eye of the brokers, and at twenty-three he left the *Globe* to manage the business of Milner, Ross & Company on the Toronto Stock Exchange. The market collapsed, but George prospered. By 1933 he was a partner in Barrett, McCullagh and Company with a seat on the Toronto Stock Exchange. He became a director of the Mining Corporation of Canada whose president was his good friend Percy Parker. Like Parker, McCullagh was a good Liberal and had been one of the founding members of the Centurions. McCullagh was also fond of the bottle, a fondness that threatened his marriage and, it was said, led him to the hospital periodically to dry out.²

Mitch and McCullagh were good friends, and Mitch may have taken a perverse delight in asking the young, intemperate, high-school dropout to take Parker's seat on the University of Toronto board of governors when Percy died in April 1936. McCullagh at first refused, on the unusual grounds that while alcoholics might be acceptable on Bay Street, they would be out of place in Simcoe Hall. But Mitch persisted and after six weeks on the wagon and resolving never to drink again, McCullagh became the youngest member of that august body in September.³

A few days later he dropped by the *Globe* to thank the editor for the eulogy on his appointment. The paper, visibly run down, was losing a $1,000 a week. The decline owed something to the fundamentalist views of Colonel W.G. Jaffray, who had inherited the paper from his father. Jaffray had been determined to remain the conscience of Ontario as long as he lived but, by the summer of 1936, two operations and the financial haemorrhaging had weakened his resolve. A few days after his visit, McCullagh knocked on Jaffray's door and bought the paper. His friend William Wright, the Croesus of Barrie whose northern gold mines had made him one of the richest men in Canada, had put up the money.⁴

One of the rejected suitors for the *Globe* was Isaac Killam, the Montreal magnate who owned the morning *Mail and Empire*. Editorially, its support of the Tories was 'inscribed not by a pen but by a grease gun,' noted a critic, but its political reporting was the best in the city and the miracles wrought by the Tories on the editorial page were often refuted in the news columns. By 1936 Killam was also overextended and the word was out that the *Mail* was also for sale. The Tories were frantically trying to raise money to buy the *Mail* when on 19 November the headlines in the *Globe* told them it was too late. Four days later the first edition of George McCullagh's *Globe and Mail* hit the streets.⁵

Much more than the smell of printer's ink had drawn McCullagh back to journalism. The young man was extraordinarily handsome, gifted with a forceful and magnetic personality, and capable of infinite charm. He was also enormously ambitious, far too ambitious to be content with mere wealth, exotic holidays, and his large stable of prize-winning horses. George McCullagh wanted power, and he believed that now he had it. His voice would be 'a power in Canada,' he promised, which would 'set a pace for the future.' Although King told McCullagh that he was delighted to see the paper in the hands of a man who assured him that it would be 'a courageous and fearless exponent of Liberalism,' he was disturbed by the morning monopoly. 'I fear,' he confessed to his diary, that 'it may become in time a big interest, Fascist organ, at a time when the real Liberal publication would be of great service from national point of view.'[6]

McCullagh believed the world belonged to men of action, like himself, who knew how to run industries and brokerage firms. He was, reported Sir Anthony Jenkinson, a visiting British journalist, 'intolerant of those who did not possess a similar knowledge – especially college professors and theorists.' After a chat with him in Mitch's suite, above the chatter of some young ladies and the tinkle of ice in the glass, Jenkinson concluded that he had 'no particular ideas about Dominion politics, except that radicalism should be fought on as wide a front as possible.' Despite his Liberal connections, McCullagh put capitalism before party and believed that unless the two older parties 'put an early end to their practice of mutual recrimination and mud-slinging, it may place in power the advocates of some dreaded ism.'[7]

In his first *Globe and Mail* editorial McCullagh had declared that despite some 'glaring weaknesses,' the Hepburn government deserved support in East Hastings. He wrote King that although he was 'a great believer of Mr. Hepburn's sincerity, honesty and courage ... some of the acts of the other members of his cabinet at times make me shudder.' After the by-election McCullagh intended to 'review some of the acts of his government' and hoped that Mitch would accept the criticism 'as helpful and friendly, and realize that it does give him an opportunity to effect a much needed house cleaning.' In private, McCullagh made no secret of his determination to have Mitch reverse his Hydro policy and renegotiate the contracts, back away on the separate school question, remove Roebuck, Croll, and Heenan, and stop drinking. George McCullagh had set his course.[8]

He wasted no time. During a weekend visit to his parents in December he slipped over to Bannockburn for a chat. But Mitch refused to back down on the contracts, and McCullagh concluded that he had been assured by the commission that there was no danger of a power shortage. Mitch also listened to McCullagh attack Roebuck as a fanatic who, in his more extreme 'we-they' speeches, sounded more like an advocate of class warfare than an attorney general. Mitch admitted that Roebuck was an extremely difficult colleague, but he refused to dismiss him and, in fact, immediately warned Roebuck to expect an attack in the *Globe and Mail*.[9]

It came two days later. 'THE PRICE OF REPUDIATION,' as McCullagh titled his editorial, was a slur on Ontario's good name which threatened to undermine the 'moral structure' of its citizenship, destroy its credit, and hurt thousands of innocent holders of insurance policies from companies that had invested heavily in power company bonds. Roebuck's inflammatory attack on the 'power pigs' was driving 'a wedge into public sentiment by setting up one class against another.' The only honourable solution was renegotiation without 'coercion or recrimination on either side' in a spirit of 'give-and-take.'

Mitch spent the morning with Roebuck and Nixon drafting a reply. Held back to run in the morning *Globe and Mail*, the statement was issued by Mitch but bore the unmistakeable Roebuck imprint:

The cat is out of the bag.

When one hears that a multi-millionaire has opened his money-bags to the extent of three and a half to four million dollars for fun, one is surprised and pleased. It is a pretty picture. Then when you learn that all this money is being used to purchase a great newspaper with a national circulation and historic prestige in order that the philanthropy of the multi-millionaire may be used for the influencing of public opinion in the interest of humanity, rectitude, good government and everything else that is high-minded and noble, you pause, and you instinctively say, 'What is the game?'

Now we know ...

The editorial was 'the opening gun in a carefully prepared and considered campaign of propaganda,' but the government was no more prepared to back down than it had been when Taschereau threatened 'to club us into submission.' Handing the statement to the press, Mitch added that he would be happy to meet company representatives if they came 'as businessmen and not brandishing a club' and if they were prepared 'to take the jokers out of the contracts, and to write equitable agreements in the interests of the users of Hydro in Ontario.'[10]

Roebuck was dismayed at Mitch's conciliatory comment, and the *Telegram* was even more convinced that the Hepburn-McCullagh 'combination play' was a sham battle to enable Mitch to save face. Bay Street also seemed to feel that some settlement was possible and Beauharnois bonds ran up to $63.50 before closing at $61, and the common stock jumped 1⅜ to 7⅛. McCullagh responded with soothing editorials. The threat from Taschereau was certainly 'enough to arouse the anger of a quick-acting and hard-hitting Premier,' and now with both Mitch and the companies prepared to negotiate there was 'a way out without hurting anyone and it should be sought instead of permitting the Attorney-General to run around playing checkers with the legal system.' From the farm after Christmas, Mitch insisted that 'this thing will be fought to the finish' and legislation would pre-empt any adverse decision by the courts. Although Ottawa Valley advised Hydro that it was prepared to negotiate, the offer drew a curt reply from Roebuck that in going to court they were attacking 'the long-established constitutional authority of Parliament.' Ottawa Valley countered with a suit for $1.5 million. Surveying the scene of battle, the *Financial Post* said there was increasing evidence of an approaching power shortage and that with McCullagh's attack the handwriting was on the wall for Arthur Roebuck.[11]

Mitch returned to Toronto early in the new year. After a long cabinet meeting on 4 January, he announced that a short session of the legislature would open on 19 January to pass legislation protecting the province against any adverse decision on appeal to the Judicial Committee. Roebuck and Ian Humphries, his deputy, had the three draft bills ready by 13 January when the Ontario Supreme Court awarded Beauharnois $573,750 and the company immediately filed a second suit for $2.98 million. Minutes before the court decision was announced Mitch commented that 'They think they are not going to get money from us and we know they are not. They haven't got a chance of collecting anything.' The three bills certainly seemed to provide complete immunity of Hydro and the province from any suit or seizure. But on this occasion Hydro's council, R.S. Robertson, advised caution. Was it wise, he asked Roebuck, to pass such inflammatory legislation when the case was on its way to the Judicial Committee? The court might resent legislation 'designed to defeat any judgement they might give unless it is favourable to our appeal,' he observed, and in Ontario there were many who regarded 'interference with the Courts as somewhat of a revolutionary measure and likely to lead to the unsettling of the foundations of our social order.' Roebuck was not to be deflected or deterred.[12]

Nor, Mitch learned to his dismay, was Franklin Roosevelt to be deflected from his determination that the St Lawrence seaway would be built 'as sure as God made little apples,' a determination which stood in the way of the 'Back to Niagara' policy. At its first meeting after the June 1934 victory, the new Hydro Commission had confirmed that the water flowing over Niagara was 'the most convenient and economical' source of power for Ontario. With Niagara producing 100,000 less horsepower in 1935 than in 1928, the first step was remedial work at the Falls which would increase efficiency by 15,000 h.p. Another 120,000 h.p. could be generated at Niagara by damming the Ogoki River and sending some of the water from the Albany watershed, which ran unmolested into James Bay, south to Lake Superior and on to the Falls. However, under the terms of the Boundary Waters Treaty of 1909, any change at Niagara needed the consent of the United States. The commission asked Mitch to request Bennett to begin the negotiations with Roosevelt to enable Ontario to divert the water and enjoy the exclusive use of the additional power generated. It also instructed Hogg to report on the fullest possible utilization of Niagara.[13]

Neither response was promising. Hogg's report that it would take five years to secure the necessary agreements and complete the engineering works before the water reached Niagara was contemptuously rejected by Roebuck as pessimistic and narrowly technical. Fully aware that Roosevelt wanted to move ahead on the St Lawrence, Bennett replied that it would 'seem desirable – if an orderly and progressive supply of power for provincial use is to be worked out – to consider all the possibilities of the St. Lawrence and other projects' where federal-provincial cooperation and an international agreement were essential.[14]

King's victory in October 1935 offered more promise and soon afterwards Stewart Lyon asked O.D. Skelton, undersecretary of state for external affairs, to begin negotiations with Washington. Skelton's long-delayed reply was unsatisfactory. He had not referred the request to the State Department, but lectured Lyon on the history and diplomacy of the issue, telling him in so many words that, without agreement on the St Lawrence, 'seeking action on the Ogoki question alone would not seem to have any prospect of success.'

Although the letter was discussed at the next commission meeting, Lyon did not send it to Mitch until April, when a press report suggested that he might be wavering on Ogoki. 'The necessity for additional water both for the Nipissing [sic Nipigon] plants and the Niagara generators becomes more urgent daily,' Lyon wrote. 'The Commission cannot wait indefinitely for the problematical action of the Government of the United States.' Skelton's evasive letter was a clear indication that unless Ontario 'yielded to coercion,' it would not be permitted to use its own water at its own power sites. 'This whole issue of who owns the water that originates in Ontario,' Lyon argued, 'must be settled as speedily as possible, and I have been trusting that you would take as firm a decisive action in regard to this question as Sir Oliver Mowat took a generation ago, when he fought Sir John Macdonald on the question of who owned the bed of streams.' When Mitch met the commission on 20 May and agreed to go ahead with the surveys, Lyon was elated: 'It is a good rule to settle upon one's destination before taking the road, and your action yesterday settled the destination of the Niagara district in the matter of power supplies.'[15]

There was only one problem. The White House was determined the St Lawrence would go ahead despite King's explanation to the Americans in May 1936 that with Ontario and Quebec opposed, the west indifferent, and the railways antagonistic there was little support for it. Roosevelt and his advisers, particularly Frank P. Walsh, chairman of the Power Authority of New York State, saw the public development of the St Lawrence as the way to free the state from the grasp of Niagara Hudson and the private power monopoly controlled by the Aluminum Company and the Mellon interests. They were not going to allow Mitch Hepburn to stand in the way, and with the cancellation of the Quebec contracts and the decision to go back to Niagara, Walsh told the president that they had Mitch in a corner. Unless he agreed to the St Lawrence, they should not consider any additional diversion at Niagara.

However, Walsh continued, the president had to understand the political realities in Ontario. If the courts upheld the power companies, Hydro would not face a power shortage but would have a very expensive surplus. It was therefore impossible for Mitch to accept any plan for the development of the St Lawrence 'which involves large obligations prior to the actual marketing of the power.' The solution was one in which Ottawa would agree that Ontario 'need assume obligations only as and when the Ontario market absorbs the power. Fortunately, such a solution is entirely practicable.'[16]

Roosevelt did not press matters in the fall of 1936, but within weeks of his November re-election he sent a high-powered delegation, led by Walsh and John Hickerson of the State Department, to Ottawa with the proposal for a new treaty. Over dinner at Laurier House, King and members of his cabinet explained at some length the opposition in Canada, particularly in Ontario. However, in discussions with Skelton, Walsh made it clear that they would not agree to any diversion at Niagara unless Canada agreed to the St Lawrence. At the end of the two days of discussion, 'during which it was developed that Ontario actually needs additional power at this time, and may in the next couple of years face a serious power shortage,' Hickerson wrote, 'the Canadian officials informed us that Prime Minister King would in the next few weeks take up the whole question with Premier Hepburn in an endeavour to persuade him to cooperate in going forward with this project.'[17]

Although King was anxious to please Roosevelt, he had no desire to proceed with the St Lawrence or to contact Mitch. A month later the American minister asked Skelton what progress had been made. Skelton replied 'that in all frankness the present moment was not a very propitious one to press matters, so far as Ontario was concerned ... However, the matter had to be tackled soon or later, and the sooner it was done, Dr. Skelton felt, the better.'

The pressure was sufficient. Three days later King informed Mitch that Roosevelt was anxious to move ahead quickly on the 'co-ordinated and orderly development' of the entire St Lawrence–Great Lakes basin for both power and transportation. The Americans were opposed to strengthening 'the position of the private companies which now own or operate all the plants on the United States side of the Niagara River,' King wrote, and even if that obstacle could be overcome, it was clear that Roosevelt would never let more water run over Niagara without an agreement on the St Lawrence. However, all was not lost, for the Americans had suggested that an agreement might be reached on the St Lawrence with the proviso that construction of the powerhouses on the Canadian side could be delayed for six or seven years after ratification. 'Whether or not in that case it would be possible to provide for an early utilization of additional power by Ontario at Niagara ... is a further question that would require consideration.'[18]

Mitch responded by sending Roebuck and Hogg to Ottawa. Roebuck made the startling proposal that Ontario should proceed with the Ogoki diversion with or without a treaty. If Roebuck had not understood the linkage, Skelton undoubtedly made it clear, as he did the legal impossibility if not the audacity of Roebuck's proposal. The discussion then turned to the advantages to Ontario – as seen by Ottawa at least – of the development of the entire basin 'based upon a new agreement between Ontario and the Dominion for the absorption by Ontario of St. Lawrence power, upon some mutually satisfactory arrangement. Niagara Convention power and Ogoki diversion power available as soon as the Convention and Treaty ratified by both parties.' The prospect of using the northern water as soon as it reached Niagara would be enticing, Skelton suspected, for he also believed that Ontario would soon face a power shortage.[19]

Mitch was in no condition, physically or mentally, to deal with the unravelling Hydro policy. Soon after his return to Toronto in January 1937 he was confined to bed with bronchitis at the King Eddy. He was also drinking heavily, so heavily that the born-again George McCullagh decided to have it out with him. McCullagh told Mitch that drink was destroying his character and making him 'prey to influences' that he was not conscious of himself. His excesses were partly due to 'the group of men who were wealthy but who liked drinking and that fast sort of life,' he continued, but who would not go 'near him if he were back on the farm.' Unless he gave up his 'mistaken life,' warned McCullagh, he could no longer count on his support. Mitch took it 'very well,' McCullagh claimed, and 'admitted the truth of it in large part.' Arthur Slaght also warned King that 'there may be a very bad smash-up as far as Hepburn is concerned; that alcoholism and excesses in other ways are at the bottom of it, and it is very doubtful whether he will be able to continue the leadership.'

On the afternoon of 15 January Dr R.N. Irwin, accompanied by Dr Faulkner, the minister of health, told reporters that Mitch was suffering from an acute flare-up of bronchitis complicated by dangerously high blood pressure caused by his kidney affliction, and they had ordered him to get away to a warm climate for several weeks of complete rest. Before leaving the next day, Mitch dictated a brief letter to King reiterating his view that the St Lawrence could not be 'justified on economic grounds as we are neither in need of a new avenue of transportation nor additional electrical power.' Moreover, he reminded King, if their 'efforts to protect the hydro consumers of Ontario against the power interests of Quebec prove futile, it would mean we would have to immediately pay for Eight and a Half Million Dollars worth of unsaleable power which, in my opinion and in the opinion of our technical experts, would take care of our ordinary consumption over a period of many years.' In his parting exchange with the press, Mitch again denied that the province was facing a power shortage, but promised on his return to go into the matter thoroughly with the commission, its engineers and independent consultants, if necessary, 'to acquaint myself first hand with the situation.' Four days later, with Eva, Peter, and Patsy, he was breathing the dry Arizona air.[20]

Harry Nixon was a very unhappy man when Mitch left him with the unpleasant task of seeing the power legislation through the House. 'He seemed most worried and said he was not looking forward to what was ahead of him at all,' commented Angela Bruce after Nixon had briefed the lieutenant-governor, 'as he did not favor the Hydro legislation at all and yet he had to force it through. He hopes to leave the Bill to be proclaimed and still get the Power Companies to come to terms.' Nixon was not alone. Slaght was strongly opposed to legislation 'in advance of a decision by the British Courts' and laid the blame squarely on Roebuck for a decision which 'savoured of communistic action.' He told King that the cabinet was sharply divided, with 'some of them almost broken-hearted over the power legislation.'[21]

Nixon faced strong opposition in caucus on 18 January, but McQuesten whipped the members into line and Roebuck insisted all be in their seats for what turned out to be a six-hour speech over two days. Roebuck dismissed the charge of a power shortage as 'errant nonsense' for there were ample reserves and work was underway on the Ogoki diversion. But the back-benchers seemed more convinced by the opposition attack than Roebuck's assurances, and found McCullagh's editorial that 'the integrity of the judiciary must not be destroyed to gratify political ambitions' compelling.[22]

Roebuck was less than convincing, perhaps, because he was not telling the truth. In November and December Hydro had to take up the remaining 40,000 horsepower from Gatineau; in January the engineers had to make some heavy cuts in interruptible contracts, and the capacity of the system was moving perilously close to the demand. At their 7 January meeting Hogg informed the commissioners that any emergency could lead to an interruption in service and they authorized him to buy another 20,000 horsepower from Gatineau if necessary. Moreover, while it was true that the cabinet had authorized the northern diversion, Roebuck knew that if the water ever reached Niagara it would run unmolested on to the sea unless Ontario agreed to the St Lawrence.[23]

Liberal back-benchers were not fully aware of the situation inside Hydro or the White House, but they were sufficiently disturbed after

Roebuck's speech to urge the chief whip, Harold Kirby, to write to Mitch in Arizona:

At our first caucus there was only one member who absolutely refused to support the legislation and in my opinion, though many did not like it, but through loyalty to you and the Cabinet, they were prepared to give the bill their full support. Since the bill has been introduced the A.G. has held forth for two whole afternoons but as he progresses a number of our strongest members are becoming disturbed. The press and Opposition attacks during the last two days have no doubt contributed a lot toward breaking down the general morale of the members.

Rumours have been freely circulated that the Ottawa Valley Co. made reasonable overtures which were turned down by the Commission and that you were not in possession of the true facts and that there is a general feeling that we have failed to take every step to work out an amicable settlement to the benefit of the Province. The authentic source from which the reports are coming, as to the shortage of power is most alarming and many of the members are far from satisfied that the legislation proposed is not a serious blow at our courts and constitutional government.

Kirby appealed to Mitch to 'make every effort to arbitrate and to end the feeling of dismay which undoubtedly exists, not only among the members but among many of our supporters in the province generally.' Kirby's letter was not the only one on its way to Arizona. On 22 January, David Croll left for El Paso bearing letters from Nixon and Hogg.[24]

Nixon had met Hogg in the Royal York cigar store on 19 January. When to his casual 'How are things going?,' Hogg had replied gloomily 'Not very well,' Nixon asked to see him the next day. Hogg's report astounded him. Demand was increasing rapidly and, if there was only the 120,000 horsepower in the Gatineau contract to call on, the province did face a power shortage. And if Ottawa Valley turned nasty and opened the sluices to force Hydro to pay or negotiate, the province would be 'tremendously embarrassed.' Hogg reported that this had been made very clear to the commissioners, but they had refused to accept his figures because they did not like the obvious conclusions. Nixon sent Hogg's technical report with a long covering letter to the 'Chief':

I am very sorry indeed to have to trouble you with the Government affairs at this time, but frankly things are not going so well. The Province is tremendously inflamed over the legislation now before the House, and the

Members are disturbed to such an extent that I doubt very much if they can be held in line. – the whole trouble being that they have no confidence in the A.G., and are not prepared to sacrifice themselves under the circumstances ...

As you know, Roebuck has always held that an Agreement could not be negotiated with the Ottawa Valley, that they walked out of the Conference and entered a law-suit, that they have refused to enter into anything that looked like a sincere attempt at a settlement. Recently the Ottawa Valley people gave a statement in all the papers which very strongly indicates the opposite to be the case, and I personally sent for Mr. Symington, and asked him what the actual facts were. He said that they would be more than delighted to agree to any settlement that would be at all reasonable and fair, that they would abandon all litigation, forget everything that is past in the way of bills for unused power, cost of litigation, etc. ...

Nixon recommended negotiating with Ottawa Valley, leaving Beauharnois, which had less leverage, to be dealt with 'at our leisure.'[25]

Croll arrived at Teddy Hayes's ranch near El Paso, where Mitch had gone after seeing a chest specialist in Tucson, on 24 January. Mitch was aware of the crisis at Queen's Park because George McCullagh had phoned 'all excited' soon after his arrival, and Mitch had wired Roy Elmhirst to tell Nixon if there was further trouble in caucus to adjourn the session for a month. After reading the letters and listening to Croll, Mitch agreed the situation was critical. He authorized Nixon to negotiate with Ottawa Valley and to assure caucus that the two most controversial acts would not be proclaimed until the cabinet had accurate engineering reports on the power supply. With these assurances party lines held and after eight days of debate, which raged along the Tory benches, the bills passed. Nixon at once wired Symington of Ottawa Valley that if they desired to 'negotiate sincerely' the government was ready.[26]

The commissioners were less willing to negotiate. Lyon refused until ordered to do so in writing, and Nixon had to put pressure on both Roebuck and McQuesten. The mood was bad, the negotiations tense, for Symington found it difficult to have all the 'jokers' removed from the old contract because some were part of the company's lease. The deadline for agreement was 10 February, the date for the appeal to the Judicial Committee.

Mitch had not planned to return until the House resumed on 16 February. Despite claiming to be 'high and dry on the well known wagon,' he was enjoying life at the ranch. Hayes was a congenial host, and Jimmy Dunn and Ben Smith, a New York broker, joined the party. He shook his bronchitis and shed sixteen pounds. But the Ottawa Valley negotiations demanded his intervention and he returned to Queen's Park on 8 February. Three days later he reached an agreement with Symington that met most of his conditions. Symington reflected on his experience in a letter to John Dafoe:

... I made a fairly satisfactory adjustment with Hepburn after ten days intensive negotiations, during which I came to the conclusion that they were definitely on the way out and that probably nothing could save them. Hepburn has a peculiar and incalculable character, doing some good things immediately followed by inexcusably stupid ones. They are a much divided crowd, fighting viciously among themselves and it won't be long before they have to pay toll for their misdeeds.[26]

Mitch was in his seat when the session continued on 16 February. For the first time he brought Eva and the kids to Toronto. They rented a house on Riverside Drive, on the east bank of the Humber near Grenadier Pond, and Peter and Patsy went to Dr Blatz's school then achieving a reputation for innovative pre-school education. With many of his buddies wintering in Florida and Nassau, the suite in the King Eddy was unusually quiet and Mitch spent much of his time being a good father, a role that led to a sprained ankle during a bedtime tussle with Peter. However, with the power crisis, problems in the cabinet, and the feeling that if the economy kept recovering the fall might be an auspicious time for an election, Mitch did not join Mackenzie King at the coronation of George VI.[28]

The mood was bad and the fuses short as the members roamed through the political underbrush during the throne speech debate. Coming off their victory in East Hastings, the leaderless but feisty Tories found Liberal patronage, contempt for the courts, the alleged power shortage, and rampant drunkenness congenial subjects. But the motion of non-confidence was predictably a demand for the repeal of the separate school legislation, which the Grits turned back fifty-six to sixteen. Mitch carried much of the defence and parried Tory thrusts with ill-humoured attacks on his critics.

The government did not have an ambitious legislative program, and much of it was approved with little opposition. Croll promised that a new five-member Industry and Labour Board, with one labour and one employer representative, would help ensure industrial peace and provide greater security for Ontario workers. The board would administer the Industrial Standards Act and under a new Minimum Wages Act could set minimum wage rates and maximum hours of work, which could vary for communities of different sizes. The legislation, said Croll, would provide protection and security for the 430,000 men and women not protected by trade unions or the Industrial Standards Act. There was some apprehension that the unspecified rates could give Quebec industry a competitive advantage until Mitch told the house that his good friend Maurice Duplessis, who had become premier of the province in August 1936, would pass similar legislation. Croll also faced little criticism of legislation to relieve the municipalities of all responsibility for mother's allowances and old age pensions. Duncan Marshall had an easy time with the passage of bills to establish a Farm Products Control Board, with powers to regulate grading and marketing of farm products, and a board to bring some order to the production and marketing of milk. And the House happily endorsed the *trillium grandiflorum* as the floral emblem of Ontario.[29]

No Tory denounced Mitch for selling out to his friend Jimmy Dunn when Leduc introduced a bill to increase the bounty on iron ore mined in Ontario. Dunn was not alone in dreaming of reviving the Helen mine north of the Sault, which had been abandoned in 1918, to reduce Ontario's complete dependence on American ore and create an integrated steel industry in Algoma. But the bounty of fifty cents a ton offered by the Ferguson government in 1930 was not enough to compensate for the quality of the low-sulphur ore which would have to be mixed with high phosphorous American ore to feed the blast furnaces. But if it could be profitably mined, there was also a market in the States where part of the production could be effectively traded for high phosphorous ore.

Although Mitch had shouted at Ward Wright in January that Sir James had never 'done a damn thing' to live up to his earlier promises, he was sympathetic when Dunn had raised the bounty question because the prospect of a thriving industry at the Sault in the Depression was compelling. He raised the question when he and Mitch were at Teddy Hayes's ranch. Two days after his return, Mitch summoned the MLA and the MP from the Sault, as well as James Curran, the editor of the Sault *Star*, to a meeting in Toronto. As he admitted to Curran, 'I am frank to confess that I am quite ignorant about the iron industry and will have to be guided by the views of those who have given the matter a great deal of thought.' Mitch also gave the appropriate data to a mining consultant, D.H. McDougall of McDougall Engineering, who advised him at once that on the basis of the estimated cost of production, which seemed reasonable, a bounty of one dollar a ton was appropriate. After talking to the Algoma manager, Curran suggested the same figure. At a banquet in the Sault on 15 February Sir James heralded the dawn of a new era for the Sault. Backed by Mitch's promised dollar a ton bounty, he planned to invest a million and a half on the development program.[30]

Seated at the head table, Dr Roberts, the MLA for the Sault, was outraged: 'Was astounded to hear private financier announce Government policy,' he wired Mitch, 'while the people's representative who for two years loyally supported a supposedly democratic Government whose policies will not be announced and I trust not dictated by financial interests. I am discouraged but not defeated by such discourtesy and cheap autocracy.' Two weeks later Roberts read his telegram to a hushed House, and attacked the 'blind, unreasoning loyalty' of the party system, the dominance of the cabinet, and the total lack of consultation with back-benchers except on minor matters of patronage. The next day on the floor of the House Mitch, in a cool rage, read Roberts out of the party and suggested that his anger was fuelled by his failure to secure a lucrative medical contract with Algoma. He later agreed with the riding association that 'it would not be in the party's interest to endeavour to carry Dr. Roberts in another election.' The good doctor could devote himself to his practice.[31]

The Tories were mysteriously reticent when Croll unexpectedly announced that with his heavy ministerial responsibilities he found it impossible to continue as the guardian of the Dionne Quintuplets. Croll had taken an unusual interest in the business affairs of the Quints since they had become wards of the crown under his department in 1935. The Quints were the hottest commercial property in the world, and within a year Croll and Joseph Sedgwick, who had been partially seconded from Roebuck's department for the purpose, had negotiated thirty-six contracts, from baby syrup endorsements to a variety of media rights. By the spring of 1937 the Quints had earned $535,000, with another $300,000 owing on current contracts.[32]

Croll drove a hard bargain in their interests. He also took a personal interest in the details of the agreements. When Jack German, a prominent Catholic Liberal lawyer, suggested he consider a contract with Paramount for a comedy starring Harold Lloyd, Croll refused and pointedly added that any contract was impossible without his personal approval of the story line, dialogue, and actors. He had signed a contract with 20th Century Fox for the film Reunion, and in November 1936 had made a much-publicized trip to Hollywood to view the opening. Croll enjoyed being cast as a celebrity.

'My flying visit to Hollywood has had a bad effect on me,' he wrote to a friend, 'in that I continually want to get back there for another week.' However, the film was banned by the Chicago Board of Censors and, after seeing it in Toronto, German could not resist a jocular note to Croll about watching the Quints in a picture 'with characters portraying an ex-convict and pick-pocket, a suggested adulteress, a weakling Doctor who was courting a married woman, and a broken-down actress who attempts suicide – not that I personally object to any of the failings of human nature, but I can understand the reason for the Chicago Board's censorship.' Croll was not amused and his testy demand for a written apology suggested that German had touched a raw nerve.

Waiting on his desk when Mitch returned from Arizona was a note from Dr Allan Roy Dafoe, doctor to the Quints, urging him to prevent Croll from signing any new contracts until they could meet, and a pencilled note stating that Nixon had done as Dafoe requested. Mitch moved quickly, so quickly indeed that Bill 50, which transferred the authority to the official guardian, was not printed when Croll suddenly announced his resignation on 24 February. The Tories refused to begin second reading until they had seen the bill, and later demanded to see the contracts. Mitch finally agreed to make the gross figures public, but not the details of the individual contracts. There was widespread suspicion that more than overwork lay behind Croll's resignation, and his Tory opponent in the October election asked bluntly if his management of the Quints had anything to do with his dismissal from the cabinet in April.[33]

The high point of the session for Mitch was the budget he brought down on 9 March. He had not given the back-benchers any details, but told them to be in their seats to hear the good news. And good news it was as Mitch announced that Ontario was the first government in Canada to balance its budget during the Depression and pass on some of the benefits to the deserving taxpayers. The Grits repeatedly punctuated his address with such wild ovations that as Mitch soared through his final oration the demonstration in the House spread to the galleries. 'I hope that we can reculcate in our minds and hearts the hope, faith, courage and vision of our noble forefathers, and accordingly, Mr. Speaker, may I urge that we turn our faces, not toward the shadows, but toward the sun and view in that direction a brighter and happier day for this great land.' Amid the bedlam even his sparring partners crossed the floor to congratulate him, and visitors lined the corridor to get his autograph. 'FROM THE SHADOWS INTO THE SUN' was McCullagh's high praise. The *Star* was rapturous, the *Telegram* apoplectic, and the *Financial Post* convinced that Mitch had set a standard for all governments in Canada.

There was no fire in Tory bellies to keep the debate going. They could gain little by arguing that Mitch owed much to the rapid recovery which began in the spring of 1936 and showed no signs of faltering a year later. Nor could they win many votes by suggesting that only his draconian pursuit of the dead had brought an extra windfall of $4 million, and certainly none by opposing amendments to the Income Tax Act which prevented residents from evading income taxes by creating personal corporations in Bermuda or the Bahamas. Indeed, so enticing and widespread were the benefits that Mitch had to deny that it was a pre-election budget. Not only did the province assume the municipal share of old age pensions and mothers' allowances, but it also gave them one mill on the dollar of their assessments on condition they pass it on to the taxpayers. He abolished the amusement tax, 80 per cent of which was collected on tickets under twenty-five cents; cut commercial vehicle licences 25 per cent; increased subsidies for township roads to 50 per cent; promised to spend $15 million on new highway construction; and committed $2.5 million for new hospitals.[34] The Tories chose not to oppose the details of the budget, but spent the six day debate in a wide-ranging and ineffectual critique of Liberal policies.

There was some nastiness during the debate on the amendments to the securities law. With the appointment of John Godfrey, after Drew's dismissal, the government had made important changes in the monitoring of the securities industry in an attempt to prevent fraudulent sales of unlisted securities, misleading promotional advertising, boiler-room activities, and false or misleading drilling results. During his first speech in the 1937 session, Mitch announced that he planned to arm the government with even greater powers which would be used to investigate the 'nefarious Abitibi deal,' which he claimed was a 'cold and calculated scheme to defraud the people for Meighen's benefit.'

Meighen was outraged and demanded that King establish 'a truly Judicial enquiry, under the Enquiries Act of Canada, into the charges so made by Mr. Hepburn, and everything related thereto.' Meighen's friends were also outraged. 'I see by the papers that the mad dog of politics has had another fit,' wrote Mr Justice P.H. Gordon of the Saskatchewan Court of Appeal. Well, he asked, 'what are you going to do about it? Do you want me to come down and shoot the son of a bitch? I suppose there is another opportunity of paying Slaght 200 bucks a day. I used to think that you would require a million at your elbow now I know you need a gangster. There is no use fighting a devil with holy water.'[35]

Roebuck's bill gave the government unprecedented investigative powers which were not limited to the securities industry and went well beyond the traditional definitions of offences. It gave the attorney general power to investigate and prevent 'any act which may be unfair, oppressive, injurious, inequitable or improper' or which discriminated against any party or gave an unfair advantage to any party in a transaction. The bill, which also removed the Ontario Securities Commission from the attorney general's department, was retroactive. Roebuck hailed his bill as giving the government a 'much needed searchlight;' Leo Macaulay denounced it as a Star Chamber. The *Financial Post* was hysterical, and blamed legislation which was paving the way 'for revolution and the destruction of our democracy' on 'Canada's No. 1 legislative Red – the Attorney-General of Ontario.' Such a bill, the *Post* added a week later, 'should have shaken the legislative buildings to its foundation.'

The buildings were shaken to their foundations on the last days of the session. East Hastings had convinced the Tories that Mitch could be beaten on the religious issue, with Protestant Ontario convinced that the Pope was about to move the Vatican to Casa Loma. There were more than rumours of dissent in Liberal ranks, and the Protestant Liberal League was determined to run a candidate in the Wellington North by-election to end 'the rule of rum and Rome.' More moderate opponents, both Catholic and Protestant, feared the longer-term results of a religious war, and some feared that such a divisive issue was tailor-made for communist agitation. Yet it all seemed irrelevant, for although the constitutionality of the act had not been challenged, defects in either intent or drafting had turned school financing into a shambles.[36]

Within hours of seeing the school bill in 1936, Senator Louis Coté, a prominent Ottawa lawyer long involved in the separate school question, had concluded that without drastic amendments it would prove to be '*much ado about nothing.*' Although Mitch had boasted that Ontario Catholics would enjoy the same benefits as their brethren in Saskatchewan and Alberta, Coté pointed out that the act did not achieve its purpose. In the west all Roman Catholics were assumed to be separate school supporters, while the Ontario act limited the direction of corporate taxes to Roman Catholics *and* separate school supporters who themselves filed notice with the company. The provision therefore excluded all non-property holders such as wives, sisters, children, roomers, estate executors, corporate shareholders, and all non-residents of Ontario.

The provision (33b) that widely held corporations unable to ascertain the number of separate school supporters would have their taxes divided on the basis of relative assessment was flawed by the absence of any sanctions to force them to make an attempt. Unless compelled, the corporation could simply declare the percentage of those shareholders who had given notice under the other section. As company returns began to come in during the summer, with what were often minuscule proportions of Catholic shareholders, it was clear that many widely held companies had simply ignored the provision. The Toronto Separate School Board decided to appeal about 75 per cent (2,475) of the corporate assessments. By September 1936 the sixteen largest boards had agreed to seek legal advice on the likely interpretation of the act. Mr Justice Macdonnell in county court found for the separate schools on several critical issues, but his decision was appealed.[37]

The Court of Appeal decision on 11 January 1937 confirmed Coté's predictions. Only Roman Catholics named on the rolls as separate school supporters could direct their corporate taxes, thus even preventing J.E. Clements Inc. of Quebec City from directing its taxes to the separate schools as it had for years. Since corporations were deemed to have no religion, the taxes of all subsidiaries whose head offices were in Ontario would go to the public schools. Companies which had made a mockery of section 33b were upheld. An officer of the Bank of Commerce was not alone in admitting that he could ascertain how many of the 11,764 shareholders were Catholics and separate school supporters but 'since there was no obligation on the part of the corporation to make the attempt, there was no reason why they should incur the expense necessary.' The Commerce thus filed under section 33a which gave the separate schools .5963 percent rather than 7.4 per cent if the distribution was based on relative assessment in Toronto. As a result of the decisions it appeared not only that many boards would actually lose income, but there was also the likelihood that those banks and other widely held companies that had filed under 33b would follow the Commerce precedent.[38]

Quinn was determined to take up arms again. Enclosing a letter to Mitch demanding either amendments or repeal, he urged Archbishop McGuigan to mobilize the faithful. Already under attack in the House, the press, and the courts, Mitch warned O'Connor, who had earlier asked McGuigan to put a muzzle on Quinn, that the letter would 'cause considerable trouble if given publicity. As you know, I have absolutely no use for him. I believe he is so hot-headed and irresponsible that he makes little headway in any undertaking.' Although the hierarchy continued to support Quinn, Mitch's view was increasingly widely shared among leading Catholic laymen, and at a stormy meeting of the executive committee of the Catholic Taxpayers' Association on 6 March they pushed Quinn aside and appointed a committee of three to see Mitch. Lawyers Albert Murphy of London and James McNevin of Chatham, both of whom had always believed that any act which gave Protestant taxes to separate schools would be unacceptable, told Mitch that in the Catholic interest, repeal was a more judicious course than amendments that were bound to be bitterly divisive within caucus, cabinet, and the country.[39]

George Henry had placed a bill to repeal the 1936 legislation on the order paper and, to end a Tory filibuster of the estimates, Mitch agreed to bring it forward late in the afternoon of 23 March. He sat in stony silence as Henry detailed the financial chaos in the system and argued that any further support for Catholic schools would destroy Ontario's magnificent public school system. When Henry sat down, Mitch did not respond but adjourned the debate. There was a two-hour cabinet meeting that evening, with rumours that only Croll and Leduc opposed repeal with Heenan, as usual, fence-sitting. In the House, the Tories continued their filibuster until three in the morning.

By then the early edition of the *Globe and Mail* was on the streets with McCullagh's powerful editorial 'Mr. Hepburn's Duty Is Clear.' His duty was to repeal the act and prevent a religious war, with Catholics and Protestants 'fanning the flames of hatred, something which has no place in a God-fearing country such as ours,' and from which Ontario would not recover in decades. Mitch would not find it easy to confess error, wrote McCullagh, but would be universally admired for his courage. There had been nothing in the history of Ontario to equal 'the abject panic and terror that seized Mr. Hepburn's followers,' wrote Quinn. 'They were running around the Parliament Buildings like mice in a deep tin dishpan with an angry cat's eye glaring over the rim, and that most of them would have refused to support the Liberal leader had he decided to oppose the Globe's dictation none of those close to the centre of things had the slightest doubt.'[40]

That evening Mitch held the House and the galleries in suspense for an hour as he spoke to Henry's motion. Stating at the outset that he had not caucused his party, he reviewed again the history of separate schools in Ontario and his attempt to be just in the 1936 legislation. 'I must confess that I did not anticipate the violent opposition we got from the Conservative Party and the Conservative Press,' and in East Hastings the Tories 'opened up religious sores which will not heal in the lifetime of this country.' Nevertheless, Mitch continued, it was clear that the legislation was unworkable. For that reason, 'I am going to accept the motion of my honorable friend the Leader of the Opposition.'

When the desk-thumping from the opposition benches had subsided, Mitch solemnly continued. 'An even greater responsibility than bringing justice to a religious minority rests on the Government. It is the responsibility of maintaining peace and harmony' and 'I am not going to allow the opposition ... to inject a religious issue to satisfy their own lust for office and their own political ambitions.' When Laurier was advised he could win an election with an appeal to race and religion, he replied, 'and I commend his words to the Opposition – "I do not want to open the door of power with a bloody key".' Liberal applause continued unbroken as Mitch said he would have no part in a religious war. 'I am man enough to stand up and take it on the chin for what for me is a bitter pill ... No doubt my friends on the opposition side will have ample opportunity to gloat over the situation,' but just as he sought economic justice for all so did he promise the Catholics of Ontario that the Liberals 'will give justice and equity to all people, regardless of race or religion.'

The session had been long and bitter, Mitch concluded, and no doubt there would be 'more harsh words said before it is over.' Pausing as Henry threw 'No worse than your words' across the aisle, Mitch continued. 'I am going to forestall it. I am going to move, seconded by Mr. Nixon of Brant, that the question now be put.'

The members were stunned by a motion that prevented further debate. As the Speaker was about to call the vote, an enraged Leo Macaulay leaped to his feet. Ignoring the Speaker's call for order as the House and the galleries erupted, Macaulay screamed: 'You can put me in the tower or take me to Whitby, but I am going to have my say.' Looking up to the press gallery, he shouted: 'Take this down, you fellows. It is the dirtiest, rottenest trick ever perpetrated in this or any other Legislature.' With no other recourse, as Macaulay repeatedly ignored his orders to sit down, the Speaker summoned the sergeant-at-arms to usher the still shrieking Macaulay from the chamber. The Speaker then ruled the motion non-debatable and was upheld, sixty-three to fifteen. As the division bells rang, George Challies rushed from the House and returned moments later to drape a Union Jack over Macaulay's chair. The motion passed eighty to zero. The session ended the next day and the weary members went home.

Mitch's action, wrote McCullagh in another front-page editorial, was an exhibition of 'the triumph of statesmanship – which is all too rare in this day and generation.' While Catholics were disappointed and determined to fight another day, most agreed that Mitch had acted wisely and laid the blame for his failure on defective drafting and Tory bigotry. Perhaps the highest praise of all came from Arthur Ellis, the talented Tory member from Ottawa South with whom Mitch had crossed many swords: 'Dear Mitch – You have my most profound respect – that took courage all kinds of courage.'[41]

Many Liberals agreed with George McCullagh that if Mitch had real courage he would do some housecleaning in his cabinet. Divided by personal and ideological feuds, united only by the accident of power and a sometimes trying loyalty to Mitch, and unable to reach any decisions in his absence, they were indeed, as H.J. Symington had observed after ten days around Queen's Park, a fractious crew. Harry Nixon was solid, reliable, and loyal. Simpson was a good man who let Duncan McArthur run the Education Department, but he had little influence in cabinet. Although Leduc was competent and loyal, the Ottawa lawyer had never been accepted as leader of the Franco-Ontarians. Dr Faulkner was well-meaning, but with the need for more hospitals, particularly for the mentally ill, sterilization, and state health insurance on the agenda, Mitch needed someone with more imagination and drive. There was little criticism of the ebullient Duncan Marshall in Agriculture, despite his vulgarity, but as the butt of many a Tory joke when the prize bulls he had bought with much fanfare in Britain for the Agricultural College at Guelph did badly at the Winter Fair, Mitch had to remove him from the breeding business. His major concerns, however, were with Cox, Heenan, Croll, and Roebuck.

Why Mitch brought Charles Cox into the cabinet in December 1936 was a mystery to everyone. He was as powerful in the north as he was controversial, but the suggestion that Cox should have anything to do with timber policy or northern administration was hardly believable. Cox had been a notorious timber pirate when the Tories were in office and profited mightily from the continuation of pulpwood exports under the Liberals, a policy for which he had taken credit. Ruggedly handsome with jet-black hair, Cox was further compromised, and his appearance marred, early in 1937 when the 'Flanagan girl,' said by some to 'be in the family way,' threw acid in his face. There was no love lost between Heenan and Cox, and later during the October 1937 election campaign, Heenan shouted to Cox's Tory opponent: 'Say, George, if you don't lick that black s.o.b. I'll come back after the election and give you the worst licking you ever had.'⁴²

Only Mitch's fierce sense of loyalty and, perhaps, the absence of a strong northern member on the back-benches had kept Peter Heenan in the cabinet. Heenan was so inept in the House that Mitch often had to come to his rescue. Catholics believed that he wore his religion lightly, and he was never able to shake the widespread conviction that he found donations, political and personal, as persuasive as reason. The enormous power given to the government to reallocate timber limits tested both his ability and his ethics, and there were many who believed the 'Horsetrader' was not up to the challenge. Don Hogarth, lord of much he surveyed in the north, had seen the writing on the wall, and no one suggested that his new friendship with Heenan was based on the sudden discovery that they liked the same brand of whiskey. Peter did enjoy his whiskey, but Mitch indignantly denied a story that Peter had thrown a colleague cross the table during a heated discussion in cabinet. And the galleries at Queen's Park knew that after the dinner recess Heenan was often verbally rambunctious, and that on one occasion Mitch had had to adjourn the debate when neither he nor the Speaker could restrain Heenan when he tried to cross the floor and fight George Henry. By the spring of 1937 Mitch was trying to get him a job on the federal Transport Commission.⁴³

As early as the fall of 1935 Mitch had admitted to Ed Carty that he had made a mistake when he appointed David Croll and Arthur Roebuck to the cabinet. Croll was a congenial colleague, so eager to please and willing to compromise that many distrusted him. On the surface at least he seemed a good minister. Less fond of left-wing rhetoric than Roebuck, despite his Lib-Lab past, he had accepted responsibility for bringing relief costs under control, imposing some discipline on the municipalities, and taking the labour portfolio when Roebuck became an embarrassment. Obviously Nixon had trusted him enough to select him for the mission to El Paso. Yet Mitch repeatedly confided that he was having trouble with Croll in the cabinet. And Chester Walters told Angela Bruce that he 'hates Croll who, he says, is not even honest and is a great trouble to the Cabinet.' The Dionne affair had not enhanced his reputation.[44]

Arthur Roebuck was humourless, self-righteous, and dogmatic. In his lexicon, compromise was a synonym for unprincipled. From the beginning there had been tension between Mitch and Roebuck, and by March 1935 Roebuck was so 'unhappy' in the cabinet that he was thinking of resigning to run in the federal election. Mitch admitted that he 'could do nothing with him, and found him extremely difficult,' McCullagh reported to King. Roebuck had few friends in the cabinet or the caucus, and his most recent performances as Hydro commissioner and attorney general destroyed much of his credibility.[45]

It had not been an easy session. Six weeks after returning from Arizona Mitch had begun to 'flag' again. His face seemed a little flabby, and the double-breasted suits strained uncomfortably across a less than trim belly. With the session over, Mitch put politics behind him and flew south to Miami in Jack Bickell's private plane, where Eva and the children planned to join him for a month in the sun. Arthur Roebuck, too, fled Queen's Park for a working holiday in South Carolina. David Croll was also anxious to get away, but before he did there was a minor dispute between General Motors and its workers that needed to be tidied up.

'If necessary we'll raise an army to do it'

After years of short rations the Ontario workers wanted their share of the benefits as the country seemed to be moving out of the Depression. Trade union membership increased significantly in 1936 and leaped 40 per cent in 1937, when the number of days lost through strikes more than tripled. There were the expected strikes for higher wages, but the new militancy was most obvious in the demand for union recognition. That demand was due less to the return of better times than to critical decisions made in Washington and Moscow.

When the American Federation of Labor refused to embrace industrial unions at Washington in October 1935, John L. Lewis created the Committee for Industrial Organization (CIO) as a separate organization whose immediate goal was to organize industrial unions in the mining, textile, rubber, automobile, and steel industries. In Moscow in the summer of 1935 the Seventh Comintern had ordered the international communist movement to disband communist unions and, as in other fields, to work with socialists – or even liberals – in a popular front against fascism and capitalism. Though long regarded as an opponent of the communists, Lewis welcomed the marriage of convenience, for the CIO needed their experience and unbridled militancy. Attacked for courting the communists, Lewis replied, 'Who gets the bird, the hunter or the dog?'[1]

Mitch was well aware of the new strategy as it unfolded in Ontario. The press devoted considerable unsympathetic attention to communist activities. Ontario Provincial Police reports, some from undercover agents and informers, underlined the close links between the CIO and the Communist party. The communists had found the older unions difficult to penetrate and concentrated on organizing new industrial unions that were, or could be brought, under the CIO umbrella. Operating from their Toronto headquarters, where Joe Salsberg was director of trade union tactics, CP organizers, including Americans, were soon in control of the drive to organize the textile, packinghouse, rubber, electrical, steel, and automobile workers across southern Ontario and the miners and bush workers in the north. In October 1936 a dozen Canadians, almost all of them members of the CP, attended the first organizational meeting of the CIO in Pittsburgh. The CIO selected the automobile and steel industries as priority targets and the sit-down strike as one of the preferred weapons in the battle for union recognition. Their strategy was to organize unions on both sides of the border, 'so that if necessary a General Strike could be called affecting both countries,' and Canadian locals were bound by decisions at headquarters. Mitch soon had an informer's report on his desk.[2]

The United Automobile Workers (UAW) selected Wyndham Mortimer, its communist vice-president and leading advocate of the class struggle, to direct the first attack against General Motors. Canadians, like Americans, watched and heard the bloody drama as sit-down strikers occupied GM plants in Cleveland, Flint, and Anderson in January and February 1937. There was no doubt that the communists were supplying the strategists, tacticians, and shock troops for the assault. Nor was there any doubt that strikers, company guards, and squads of local vigilantes were prepared to take the law into their own hands as local and state police and the National Guard stood by, unwilling, unable, or instructed not to intervene. Before the first phase of the battle ended on 11 February, GM was paralysed, 136,000 workers were idle, and a score of American border cities had lived through what was described as armed insurrection or civil war.[3]

The sit-down strike and the inevitable violence that accompanied it was unanimously condemned by the Canadian press, the *Daily Clarion* excepted. The *Financial Post* was not alone in asking if Flint could happen here, 'where Canadian temperament is traditionally more stable than across the border and where respect for law is generally regarded as further advanced.' In December sit-downs at Hamilton Cotton and Kelsey-Hayes in Windsor, both called by CP organizers for the CIO, had been short-lived failures. But the *Post* warned that Flint could happen in Canada unless 'there is swift and decisive action to prevent it at the moment of its first outbreak. It may prove to be a test of Canadian law enforcement in the interests of peace, order and good government, and it may cost the lives of those who are charged with the task of keeping the peace. But in the long run it would be worth it.' A week after the *Post*'s 13 February editorial a UAW organizer was in Oshawa to direct the battle against GM in Canada.[4]

By 1937 General Motors in Oshawa seemed on the road to recovery, with production reaching levels not seen since before the crash. With many of the thirty-six hundred employees working twelve hours a day at straight time and management reluctant to concede major improvements in hours and wages, the time seemed promising for a more effective organization than the company union formed in 1935. There were a number of underground cells in the plant whose members were in touch with Joe Salsberg in Toronto. In February 1937 Tim Buck, Salsberg, and their friends inside GM weighed the possible danger of giving control to the UAW against the benefits of a strong union organization. They decided to take the risk and Salsberg called Homer Martin, the UAW president in Detroit, for help. Coincidentally, a day later the men in the body shop walked out to protest a new production-wage rate GM had proposed to reduce the 30 per cent efficiency gap with its American plants. After meeting with management and Louis Fine of the Labour Department, a delegation of workers recommended to a general meeting that they try the system for two weeks. The meeting was then told that a UAW representative from Detroit was present and wished to speak. Despite Fine's objection that 'outsiders would only complicate matters,' the visitor was given the floor.[5]

Slight, carefully groomed, and well-spoken, Hugh Thompson looked more like a clerk or a cleric than an experienced union organizer. An Irish immigrant to Canada, the thirty-three-year old Thompson had worked in Windsor before moving to Detroit. After GM fired him for union activity, he had become a full-time organizer and soon established a reputation that belied his gentle appearance. Thompson had organized the Anderson, Indiana, sit-down, and had only escaped a severe beating, or worse, at the hands of a mob besieging the union headquarters, when at his request, local police escorted him to the safety of the local jail. Soon after he returned to Detroit, Martin sent him to Oshawa, where he had arrived on the day of the meeting. Thompson's message that night was that a UAW union could also bring General Motors in Canada to its knees. Over the next few days a thousand workers joined what became Local 222 UAW.[6]

While Thompson organized Oshawa and other GM plants and afffiliates, the workers at Holmes Foundry at Point Edward, a few miles from Sarnia, gave a definitive answer to the *Financial Post's* question. For several months organizers for the Steel Workers Organizing Committee (SWOC/CIO) had been working the plant, whose Port Huron parent across the river had been organized and struck. Although they had succeeded in signing up fewer than half the workers, most of them Polish and Ukrainian immigrants, a group of militants sat down at their machines and closed the foundry. Destroying a summons for trespassing and anticipating an attack by police, vigilantes, or non-strikers, the men barricaded themselves in the foundry while friends and relatives formed a protective picket outside. Repeated calls to Roebuck in Toronto went unanswered and the OPP said they were powerless to intervene. On the night of 3 March a mob of several hundred men armed with crowbars, chains, pipes, and axe handles marched on the foundry. Brushing aside the pickets, they broke through the barricades and engaged in hand-to-hand combat with the strikers, most of whom were attempting to escape. Twenty of the 'Reds' and 'Hunkies' were injured and the victors handed over the 'haggard, blood-spattered and disillusioned' men to the police and ran up the Union Jack. A detachment of OPP arrived soon afterwards and arrested the organizer and other strikers.[7]

The next day in the legislature Sam Lawrence demanded to know why the strikers rather than the strike-breakers had been arrested. Mitch sprang to his feet before Roebuck could answer. 'My sympathies are with those who fought the strikers,' he exclaimed. 'Those who participate in sit-down strikes are trespassers, and trespassing is illegal in this province ... there will be no sit-down strikes in Ontario! this government is going to maintain law and order at all costs.' The UAW's reply came from Martin Bishop, a veteran of Flint, who had crossed the river to organize in Windsor. 'When you are going to pull a sit-down you are not going to ask the Premier,' he scoffed at a union meeting. 'Do just like we did. We sat down and asked the Governor what he was going to do about it. Don't let the Premier scare you into submission ... You haven't got enough Police or Militia or Vigilantes here to keep you out.' Mitch had a full transcript forty-eight hours later.[8]

Mitch found Bishop's open defiance intolerable. Soon after Thompson's arrival he had asked Ottawa either to close the border to CIO organizers or deport them. After a full RCMP investigation Crerar, the minister of immigration, replied that Thompson had entered the country legally and there were no grounds for deportation. When Bishop 'openly advocated violence in defiance of law and order,' as Mitch put it, and another CIO organizer denounced the spineless GM workers in St Catharines for refusing to disobey a by-law prohibiting the distribution of handbills, he called Crerar again and offered 'to accept full responsibility for stopping them at the border.' The offer was not accepted. All Mitch could do was instruct the OPP to cover CIO meetings and, hopefully, secure evidence that could be used in court.[9]

The response from Ottawa changed perceptibly ten days later when Richard Steele, the CP organizer for SWOC, and Thompson struck the Coulter plant in Oshawa which produced parts for GM. Faced with violence on the picket line, the company closed the plant and the police released an arrested striker to placate the mob. Mayor Hall warned the strikers that while industrial conditions in Canada 'may be similar to those in the United States, *methods approved there will not be tolerated here*. We are today instructing the police to apprehend all cases of law breaking, and we promise that they will be prosecuted and punished, *promptly, severely and inexorably*.' Advised that the eighteen-member Oshawa police force could not maintain order if there was CIO-inspired violence, Hall asked Roebuck to send OPP reinforcements, only to be told that it was settled policy not to interefere in industrial disputes.

In the Commons Ernest Lapointe declared that the sit-down strike was illegal and that the government was 'prepared to utilize all the resources and agencies at its command and to the extent of its legal powers to the end of restraining and eliminating this illegal mode of procedure in Canada.' A week later he told the Commons that he was considering a league of Canadian citizens to fight both communism and fascism, and counteract those who advocated force and violence, to ensure that 'peace, order and good government may be maintained in our dominion.' His speech was 'at once a warning and an invitation,' wrote the *Globe*, convinced that the CIO came within Lapointe's definition of public enemies. 'Some one has to start this movement and some authority has to finance it.' Back in Ottawa after a Florida vacation, King noted that an 'emissary of Lewis is at Oshawa to foment trouble there. Canada's only salvation is to compel respect for law & do it promptly.'[10]

The strike at Coulter's was not an auspicious beginning for the negotiations between GM and the newly elected officers of Local 222 that had begun the day before. Thompson had waited to begin negotiations until the terms of the agreement with GM in Detroit had been finally settled on 12 March. Although the agreement had not given the UAW the exclusive representation they demanded, it did recognize the union as the collective bargaining agency for its members. And while there were compromises on the role of union shop stewards in the grievance procedure, seniority, and production standards, victory had clearly been on the side of the UAW. General Motors' executives in Oshawa were well aware of the UAW's strategy and tactics. Before the negotiations began they insisted that while they 'were prepared to discuss Company business with any group of employees at any time, whether they belonged to an outside labour organization or not,' they would not permit 'the presence at such a meeting of any labour organizer not an employee of the Company.' Charles Millard, the president of the local, agreed. On that basis negotiations began on the afternoon of 18 March.

It became obvious at once that the real issues were not work and wages, but the role of Thompson and recognition of the UAW. Millard insisted that GM Oshawa was bound by the agreement signed in the United States; J.B. Highfield, the factory manager, and Colonel Frank Chappell, the director of industrial relations, insisted that they were 'completely self-supporting, having perfect freedom of action ...' Millard repeatedly asked whether GM would negotiate with the UAW local and Hugh Thompson; Highfield replied that they would negotiate with their employees, whether or not they belonged to a union. The meeting was cordial, but the battle lines were drawn. It took less than fifteen minutes in a second meeting on 23 March to reveal that they remained drawn.[11]

With GM immovable, the UAW sent Edward Hall, a vice-president, to Oshawa to strengthen Thompson's hands. Hall was not a man to be trifled with. He had helped engineer the alliance with Mortimer and the communists, played a leading role in the sit-downs, and had once summoned his president, Homer Martin, back to the battlefield with the words, 'You dumb son-of-a-bitch, you get your ass back here or that'll be the last trip you ever make.' The OPP was on hand and a crown attorney was ready to arrest Hall if he advocated a sit-down, but he merely instructed the men only to picket 'so damnably tight' that no one got in or out. Although Hall promised the 'full support' of the UAW, he told Thompson privately that the cupboard was bare and, whatever they might be told, the Canadians could receive nothing more tangible than rhetoric and moral support. The next day Highfield warned Millard that unless the disruptive activities and intimidation of non-members stopped, 'steps that suggested themselves' might be taken. The shop stewards responded with a vote to strike unless GM agreed to negotiate directly with Thompson, although Hall had announced Millard's appointment as a full-time UAW/CIO organizer.[12]

The threatened strike was postponed when David Croll intervened and invited Chappell and Thompson to a meeting at Queen's Park on 31 March. Chappell again stated that the company was willing to negotiate with its employees, 'but would not consider the presence at any such meeting of any foreign organizer not an employee of the company.' Croll then turned to Thompson: 'Well, this narrows the issue down to one thing. It looks as if these people could get along alright if it were not for one person. I would suggest that you withdraw out of the picture.' When Thompson refused, Croll suggested that he select a representative and 'not lose face.' For an hour the three men debated the wording of a press statement Croll wished to make. Thompson insisted that Millard, his surrogate, be named as a CIO organizer; Chappell equally strenuously insisted that Charlie was a GM employee on leave of absence. Exasperated, Croll said that he would use his own judgment and adjourned the meeting.[13]

Highfield made GM's position perfectly clear at a meeting with several hundred shop stewards that evening. With the Department of Labour mediating, the company was prepared to negotiate all the concrete issues on the table, some of which were virtually settled. But it would not negotiate with the CIO, whose agents were deliberately moving towards a strike. With almost four thousand jobs and $50,000 a day in wages at stake, the city of Oshawa should not be the victim of a movement that was not 'a spontaneous drawing together of workers for mutual protection and betterment, but the result of a careful strategy, skilled solicitation and coercion by a highly organized wing of labor in a foreign country.' If the objective was 'to obtain exclusive bargaining rights with General Motors in Canada then the union's cause is lost right now. It was not conceded to the U.A.W. as a result of their sit-down in the United States, and it will not be conceded here, strike or no strike.'

Despite the firmness and clarity of GM's position, Croll attempted a clumsy sleight of hand that he hoped would satisfy Thompson and pass unnoticed by GM. He issued a press statement that negotiations would begin in his office on 2 April with Millard, 'the recently elected President of local Union 222 who now becomes the international representative of the negotiating committee of the United Automobile Workers of America.' Thompson would act in an 'advisory capacity to the negotiating committee of the United Automobile Workers of America but will not be present at the meeting.' At noon on 1 April Millard quit his job at GM and boasted that he was no longer the chairman of the elected bargaining committee but a paid employee of the international UAW working under Hugh Thompson.[14]

Highfield and Chappell arrived in Croll's office on 2 April with fire in their eyes. If the press statement was correct, all Croll had done was substitute Millard for Thompson and, if Millard was the representative of the UAW rather than an employee on leave of absence, there would be no negotiations. Croll invited them into an ante-room for a discussion that was long and acrimonious. He professed to be puzzled by their concern over Millard's status. Why not let him call himself anything he likes, Croll suggested, while you can continue to regard him as an employee on leave of absence. Moreover, 'you don't have to sign anything you don't want to, so why worry about that until you come to it?' Because, Highfield replied, 'I would rather tell them straight out now the position in which we stand ... I tell you flatly that I won't sign my Company away to the C.I.O. and I don't want these boys to be kidded into the idea that I will.' Unable to move GM, Croll ended the discussion with 'Well, we are going in now, leave it in my hands.' As they moved to the door, Highfield warned 'but remember, Mr. Minister, I won't sign an agreement with the C.I.O.'

Back in the office, where Millard and the negotiating committee had been waiting, Croll said simply, 'Well, Gentlemen, you will now adjourn with Mr. Fine in his Board Room to commence your negotiations.' Croll abruptly cut off Millard's 'Well, Sir, is it understood...?' with the curt statement, 'Everything is understood.' With that Croll fled Queen's Park on a Friday afternoon to enjoy a Carolina spring. It was very clear when the two sides met Fine on Monday, 5 April, that if everything was understood, nothing was agreed. Millard woodenly demanded that the company negotiate with the union and accept the American agreement; Highfield insisted that 'any agreement would be an agreement arrived here' and would not be with the UAW. Croll had accomplished nothing.[15]

After Louis Fine left for Oshawa on the morning of 6 April, Roger Irwin, Croll's secretary in the Labour Department, sent a note across to Harry Nixon. 'We are convinced that negotiations have taken a turn for the worse and that a strike may be anticipated,' he wrote, and there was also the danger of a general walkout in the carpet-manufacturing plants in the province and the Kitchener rubber factories. In Oshawa the meeting dragged on for three hours, until the talks broke down over the demand for union recognition. When Fine adjourned the discussion until the next day, Millard shrugged: 'Tomorrow is too late.'[16]

Mitch was on his way to Toronto as the crisis approached in Oshawa. He had planned to stay in Florida longer and had rented a car to drive over to the Lake Wales district when he was summoned home on 6 April. He caught a plane from Miami to Buffalo in the afternoon and drove to St Thomas for the night. When he arrived at Queen's Park the next afternoon reporters asked whether his sudden return pointed to an early election. Denying any such intention, Mitch added with his customary grin, 'We live in unusual times and anything is likely to happen.'[17]

That same afternoon in Oshawa there had been some movement on minor issues, but none on the question of union recognition or the American agreement. As the meeting adjourned until the next day, one of the committee intimated that if they could not take a satisfactory report to the men 'there might be a disruption at the plant the following day.' The stewards met that night and, after Thompson had received the go-ahead from Detroit, agreed to strike. The next morning, five minutes after entering the plant as usual at seven o'clock, thirty-seven hundred workers walked out. Within minutes four hundred pickets had sealed the plant.[18]

With the battle under way, on 8 April Mitch's office became the headquarters for the defence of Ontario against the CIO. Although the first report from Oshawa indicated only that pickets had prevented anyone from entering the grounds, Mitch ordered General Williams to cancel all OPP leaves and mobilize one hundred officers for possible use in Oshawa. He then called Ernest Lapointe and later confirmed his request for a RCMP detachment in a wire: 'Report just submitted to me indicates situation becoming very acute and violence anticipated any minute also impairment heating plants and fire protection service.' Lapointe reported to King that Mitch had told him there was a 'sit-down strike' and King replied 'if that were the case, he would be justified in sending police.' One hundred Mounties were on the train to Toronto that afternoon. When Mitch warned him later that trouble could be expected in a few days, Commissioner J.H. MacBrien ordered RCMP detachments in Regina and New Brunswick 'to hold their quota in readiness' and asked Lapointe to authorize the deployment of another hundred men if Mitch asked for more help. But when Norman Rogers told King it was not a sit-down, he ordered Lapointe to keep the RCMP very much in the background.[19]

After spending much of the day with GM, Louis Fine and members of the cabinet, Mitch issued a long statement to the press late in the afternoon. 'This is the first open attempt on the part of Lewis and his C.I.O. to assume the position of dominating and dictating to Canadian industry,' he declared. The government supported GM in its determination 'to remain clear of the domination of professional labour agitators of the C.I.O.' and believed that 'the time for a show-down is at the start.' Mitch promised he would not interfere in a peaceful strike, but there 'will be no illegal sit-down strike or illegal picketing', such as barring company executives from the plant that morning, and 'the entire resources of the province will be utilized, if occasion warrant, to prevent anything in this country resembling that which is taking place across the line due to the failure of constituted authority to take adequate action. We know what these agitators are up to,' Mitch told the reporters. 'We are advised that they are working their way into the lumber camps, the pulp mills and our mines. Well, this has got to stop – and we are going to stop it. If necessary we'll raise an army to do it.'[20]

Mitch's declaration of war made the front pages across the continent, and the *New York Times* kept him there for two weeks. Floyd Chalmers reported from Washington that Roosevelt told him 'he admired the stand' Mitch had taken. Sir Herbert Marler, the Canadian minister, told Chalmers that the challenge to Lewis had aroused 'tremendous interest' on Wall Street and that 'one of the big financial men with large interests in Canada (Henry Fuller)' had said that Mitch's statement 'had put Canada on the map and it would mean millions of dollars of US investment in that country.' In Toronto McCullagh's front page editorial, 'A Menace to be Stopped,' warned that 'the motor industry, steel plants, pulp and paper mills and the mines are in the line of march. If the Lewis agitators get a foothold, the country will pay dearly.'[21]

Hugh Thompson replied to Mitch at a strikers' rally that night. If the reports of Hepburn's statements were true, 'then God bless him, we are glad and happy to know it, because he has done you more good in Canada, and he has done more harm to General Motors than anything General Motors could have done to us.' If GM attempted to import cars into Canada, he promised, they would never make another car in the United States. 'That doesn't come from Hugh Thompson, that comes from 171,000 General Motors workers to-day through the person of Homer Martin, telling me we will support the Canadian workers to the limit.' As the crowd cheered, Thompson shouted, 'I say to the Premier of the Province of Ontario, you can send 50,000 of your militia in, but you still can't build automobiles because we are the ones that build them, and General Motors can't make ten cents until they sign with this

Sweeping back the sea
Toronto *Star*, 16 April 1937

International Union, and they will do it before they make another car in Canada.'[22]

Arthur Roebuck returned from vacation the next morning, 9 April, and learned that Mitch had been trying to reach him. He arrived in Mitch's office after lunch to find him in a heated discussion with Joe Atkinson, who was supporting the strike. Roebuck said nothing, as he recalled, 'because I did not wish to appear, when an argument of that kind was going on, on one side or the other.' But when Atkinson left, Roebuck said that he agreed with him and their policy should be one of 'impartiality and conciliation; and if that was done the strike would peter out in a very short time and be settled and be forgotten about.' At one point, Mitch later claimed, Roebuck had shrugged, 'Let them smash a few heads and destroy a little property' – (or words to that effect) – 'and then this thing will blow over.' Clearly, Roebuck was not on side.[23]

Later in the afternoon Mitch spent two hours with Charlie Millard, an old school mate from St Thomas, listening to his side of the story. The meeting left him optimistic about an early settlement, he said, and Millard's promise that the staff of the parts department would not be molested when it opened the next morning had averted a possible crisis. At a closed-door meeting of the shop stewards in the evening, Thompson denounced Millard and issued a statement that 'anyone going to work at the request of General Motors are strike breakers, regardless of what they may think. Representatives of the union promise that these people will not be molested going into or out of the plant, if they wish to go to work, but after they leave and return to their homes we will not take any responsibility for anything that might happen to them.' Asked what that meant, the veteran of Anderson snapped, 'Accidents may happen.' Mayor Hall believed Thompson's 'veiled threat of terrorism and gangsterism' provided grounds for his arrest on a charge of intimidation, but the crown attorney, Gordon Conant, awakened at 2 a.m., felt that the charge would not stick and that his arrest would lead to the violence they hoped to avoid. There were threats of violence, but no more, when GM began moving parts out by truck in the morning under the watchful eye of Mayor Hall and the Oshawa police.[24]

Mitch was to have met with Millard's committee and with GM on Saturday afternoon, 10 April, but when Millard arrived with Thompson in tow, Mitch refused to meet them. 'Thompson is the issue right now,' he told reporters, and 'I will have nothing to do with him.' The delegation left to consult Jacob Cohen, retained that morning by the CP as the union solicitor, and returned to Oshawa to hear Homer Martin assure the strikers that he had told William Knudsen, the president of GM, that if the company would not make cars in Canada under union conditions they would not make cars in the United States. He had no desire to meet 'Herr Hepburn' because the strike would be settled in Detroit not Toronto. That outcome seemed more likely on Monday, 12 April, when the American Supreme Court upheld the 1935 Wagner Act which, in effect, meant that the UAW was the sole bargaining agent in a plant where it had signed up 51 per cent of the workers. Mitch insisted that the American decision was irrelevant and repeated that the CIO was the issue and on that 'I won't budge.'[25]

Late on Monday afternoon Mitch appealed to the Oshawa workers through the press. He pointed out that GM had accepted most of the demands, including the compromise steward system in the American agreement, and despite recent pay increases had agreed to another five to seven cents an hour. The automobile industry was poised for an even greater future, particularly to serve export markets, and there was 'no doubt that many manufacturers, fearing a continuance of the chaos which exists across the line, will be willing and anxious to either extend existing plants in Canada, or establish new industries and take advantage of an enviable situation which can be established by the citizens of Oshawa on this occasion.' Mitch appealed for a made-in-Canada settlement and offered to meet GM and any group of employees' at any time, at any place, or at any hour, if I can contribute in any way to a settlement.' A mass meeting in Oshawa shouted down his appeal and accepted Norman Rogers's offer of federal mediation.[26]

Mitch's conciliatory tone had vanished on Tuesday morning, 13 April, when he brusquely refused to talk to reporters and remained closeted with General Williams, Chester Walters, and some members of his cabinet. Mitch instructed Ian Humphries, the deputy attorney general, to draft an order-in-council, approved later in the day, authorizing the OPP to appoint a force of special constables with province-wide jurisdiction. Before ten o'clock, he told Lapointe that the situation was becoming increasingly tense and asked for another hundred police. There appeared to be nothing on the picket lines to justify the request, but Mitch told Horace Hunter of the *Financial Post* that he had 'definite proof' that the CIO in Oshawa was 'linked up' with the CP in Toronto, where plans had been made 'in the event of trouble starting in Oshawa, to go down there in large numbers.' Stewart Smith, provincial secretary of the CP, indignantly denied any connection at all with the strike and described as 'pure fiction' the suggestion that communists 'are going to Oshawa or have ever contemplated going to Oshawa'.[27]

Smith's denial was itself pure fiction. Both in Oshawa and Toronto the CP had been at the centre of the strike strategy and tactics. Although Thompson did not want the participation of the CP to appear obvious, he welcomed the support of the truckload of Toronto workers that arrived each morning to work the streets, the picket lines, and deliver the *Daily Clarion*. Reporters and police noticed the presence of Joe Salsberg, Sam Scarlett, Felix Lazarus, and members of the Ukrainian Labour and Farmers' Temple on Bathurst Street. The Toronto and District Trades and Labour Council, allegedly under communist control, had sent a message of support, and Fred Collins, properly described by the RCMP as a 'Communist' if not 'notorious,' arrived at the Sunday rally to state that the TDTLC was 'one hundred percent' behind the strikers and to challenge Mitch and GM 'to drench the Oshawa workers in blood.' Behind the scenes Jacob Cohen and others were attempting to mobilize the local trades and labour councils to prepare for vigorous province-wide demonstrations. On 14 April the *Oshawa Times*, friendly to the strikers, warned its readers that 'one grave danger threatens this community in connection with the deplorable deadlock which now exists – THIS MENACE IS COMMUNISM.'[28]

Mackenzie King refused to support Mitch in his crusade against the twin forces of evil. Lapointe wanted to reinforce the Mounties, but King believed it would be a 'great mistake to do so' and Lapointe reluctantly told Mitch the matter would be considered in cabinet but assured him that 'in case of trouble breaking out all possible aid will be sent.' Soon afterwards Mitch learned that the union had accepted Rogers's offer to mediate and angrily wired King: 'While I have not consulted with General Motors executives I am satisfied they will not be party to such treachery or make my present unhappy lot more embarrassing. This action is quite in common with the treatment that this government has received from most of your Ministers and in my opinion constitutes an overt act.' Although King believed that Mitch 'had become pretty well beside himself' over Oshawa, he also realized that Rogers had given him 'just the kind of material he wants for a real grievance, his mind being full of suspicion and his nature full of jealousy so far as Rogers was concerned.' With Rogers and Dunning at his side, King told reporters that they were ready to assist if asked but Mitch had 'made it perfectly clear' that he wanted no help from Ottawa. McCullagh agreed. In a front-page editorial, 'Canada's Man of the

Hour,' he wrote that Mitch had 'taken up the battle without Ottawa's aid ... and he is the man to see it through.'[29]

Roebuck and Croll, who had returned on 10 April, had been conspicuously absent from the conferences at Queen's Park. The *Telegram* labelled them 'sit-downers' and the *Globe* declared that all ministers would 'be advised to swing into line with their Leader or swing out of the Ministry.' Mitch agreed that 'in the course of time' he would want to know 'if every member of the government is solidly behind me in our fight against the forces of John L. Lewis and communism which are now marching hand in hand.' The course of time came at 10 a.m. on 14 April when Mitch arrived at the office and, with reporters standing by, summoned Roy Elmhirst to take a letter:

My dear Colleague:

It is with deep regret that I find myself in a position where it is necessary to ask for your resignation as a member of the present administration.

It is quite clear to me and all concerned that you are not in accord with the policy of the Government in fighting the inroads of the Lewis organization and Communism in general. To my way of thinking, Ontario is facing one of its greatest economic crises. For that reason there must be solidarity and unanimity within our ranks.

Needless to say, the decision I have arrived at is one that is causing me both grief and unhappiness, but I am determined to carry out the policy which I believe to be in the best interests of the people I was elected to serve.

I deeply appreciate your loyalty, up to this point, and shall always remember our close and intimate association, both in a political and social way, and I am unhappy indeed that we have arrived at the parting of the ways on a matter of policy.

Please believe there is nothing personal in this and I hope I shall always enjoy your friendship in the future, as I have in the past.

The letter finished, Mitch assured reporters that 'This is a fight to the finish ... we know that the Communists are standing by, by the thousands, ready to jump in at the first sign of disorder. If the C.I.O. wins in Oshawa, it has other plants it will step into. It will be in the mines, demoralize that industry and send stocks tumbling.' When Roebuck, who had been trying to see Mitch for several days, arrived at his office half an hour later reporters told him he and Croll had been fired. The news did not come as a surprise, for the headline in the morning *Globe and Mail* stated emphatically that their resignations were expected sometime that day.

Mitch had their replies later in the day. Both men reaffirmed their belief in the right of workers to organize, to affiliate with any union of their choice, to engage in collective bargaining, and to use, what Croll called 'their final effective weapon – the strike.' Both reaffirmed their commitment to the maintenance of law and order, but opposed, as Roebuck put it, 'massing force prior to the absolute necessity arising.' Both declared their opposition to communism. After a long statement of his 'ideals as a Reform Liberal,' David Croll continued:

So much for my general principles. You will see that they were offended in your policy toward the strike at the General Motors plant in Oshawa. You quarrelled with the right of these workers to join the union of their choice. That it was a union sponsored by the Committee for Industrial Organization was incidental to the fact that these thirty-seven hundred men and women decided that they wished to exercise their liberty to affiliate with that organization. You based your attack upon a conviction that the C.I.O. should not be permitted to invade Canada, when you must have known that agreements had already been signed by the C.I.O. with the Coulter Manufacturing Company of Oshawa and the Goodrich Tire Company of Kitchener. Indeed, there are today and have been for many months, some ten thousand workers in the Province of Ontario who are members of unions affiliated with the C.I.O. – and most of these ten thousand enjoy the protection afforded by our own Industrial Standards Act. Certainly I had never heard of it until you made it, any suggestion of an alliance between the Lewis Unions and Communists ...

I regret that I have been led to the necessity of passing an opinion upon your policy ... I had intended merely to say that I had disagreed with it. You know my origins: I have always been with, and one of, the workers, and I have neither the desire nor the ability to swing at this late date to the other side. In my official capacity I have travelled the middle of the road, but now that you have put the extreme alternative to me, my place is marching with the workers rather than riding with General Motors.

Unlike Roebuck's cold assurance to the 'Prime Minister' that 'this relief from responsibility is received with equanimity,' Croll heaped praise on Mitch, even admiring 'the courage and honesty with which you are following the path which you believe right. It is the same fearlessness and determination which have given to the Province so many wise and generally helpful decisions since you first became

Prime Minister.' The end of their official relations, Croll hoped, 'will in no way mar the personal friendship which began between us long before the present Government took office, which has continued uninterruptedly during the years of our administration, and which I firmly hope will survive for all time to come.'[30]

There was little sympathy or support for Croll and Roebuck. With the exception of the Ottawa *Citizen* and Atkinson's *Star*, the provincial press regarded the dismissals as necessary and justified. Mitch's mail, too, was overwhelmingly favourable. Senator Hardy, who had the habit of speaking for everyone, assured Mitch that 'Everyone seems glad that someone had buckled up against this new attempt to dictatorship.' And it was not surprising that Angela Bruce noted that 'Croll and Roebuck resigned today much to most people's joy.' There was also support within King's cabinet. Lapointe was outspoken in his belief that the CIO should be crushed. Other ministers were opposed to 'the idea of organization of an entire industry' and some, like Thomas Crerar, supported Mitch's policy if not his methods. Crerar was convinced that Lewis was 'attracting all the subversive elements' and his 'representatives thought they could apply the same methods in Canada that succeeded in the United States, and it will probably prove in the end that Hepburn's standing up to them in the way he did, will teach them a lesson: in fact they appear now to have learned it.' Croll and Roebuck, he added, were already 'under suspicion; the first because he was not trusted, and the second because he has more than one foot in the C.C.F. camp.'[31]

The news had reached Ottawa when the cabinet was discussing Mitch's request for more police. King was opposed. He was not alone in surmising that Mitch was

in the hands of McCullagh of the Globe, and the Globe and McCullagh, in the hands of financial mining interests that want to crush the C.I.O. and their organization in Canada. The situation as he has brought it into being has all the elements in it that are to be found in the present appalling situation in Spain. Hepburn has become a Fascist leader and has sought to have labour in its struggle against organized capital, put into the position of being under Communist direction and control. Action of the kind is little short of criminal.

Lapointe argued that the Lewis organization had to be stopped, 'kept repeating that they had organized sit-down strikes in the States etc.' But King, as usual, carried the cabinet and Lapointe grudgingly sent Mitch the reply 'that under the existing circumstances having regard to our responsibilities in all parts of the Dominion it would not be advisable to withdraw a larger number of the members of the force from their present location.'[32]

Ian Mackenzie had been enjoying a three-hour lunch with Mitch and McCullagh in Toronto when King's cabinet met. The *Globe*, which was on the street that night at 9:30 p.m., contained a statement by Mitch that his friend from Ottawa had promised all the aid that was necessary, 'all we have to do is ask.' In another front page editorial, 'Outcome Not in Doubt Now,' McCullagh wrote:

If anything were needed to ensure the success of Premier Hepburn's campaign against the throttling of Canadian industry by the invasion of Lewisism and its handmaiden, communism, there can be misgivings no longer.

The Federal Government is behind him 100 per cent.

The message was brought from Ottawa by Hon. Ian Mackenzie, Minister of Defence. But, more significant, it was brought by a member of the Ottawa Cabinet who has a reputation as a radical, and is perhaps the most uncompromising friend of organized labor in the Federal Ministry.

This is the fortunate outcome of what appeared for a few days to be a conflict between the two Governments.

From Peterborough that night a troubled Mackenzie wired King: 'Saw no reporters and regret alleged declaration of attitude. Had private luncheon with the Premier and McCullagh but would not dream of even suggesting government policy. Personal friendship construed deliberately into government attitude ... Obviously no minister could pledge defence forces assistance ... Am exceedingly embarrassed by publicity but probably best I could ignore it.' But Mackenzie was not allowed to ignore it. The *Globe* story convinced King that there was a sinister conspiracy under way:

The Globe's article is simply terrifying indicating a combination of Dominion and Provincial Governments to destroy labour organization by force. I cannot imagine anything worse ... The way matters are developing, there is coming to be enough in the whole situation as to undermine the strength of the Liberal Government at Ottawa as well as effectively to destroy, as already is the case, the Government in Ontario ... What I now fear is that Hepburn, at any moment, may dissolve Parliament and make the fight against the C.I.O. an issue in the campaign. That would be inviting a revolution in Canada.

Mackenzie told cabinet that 'he had made no mention of any-thing of the kind.' and King forced him to issue a statement deny-ing the whole story. Mitch was not prepared to back away, however, even for his friend. 'He said it all right,' Mitch told reporters. 'I didn't ask for any assistance and his offer was entirely voluntary.' Bethune Smith, who had also been at the lunch, added 'As I recall it, Mr Mackenzie said that all the resources of $40,000,000 of estimates will be behind you.' Mackenzie had not realized that it was war and the ground was mined. Too much of Mitch's whiskey had probably loosened his tongue, and McCullagh had taken more than full advantage of his indiscretion. King accept-ed his denial, but when Lambert saw Mackenzie a few days later he 'was still smarting under the Globe's indiscreet publicity of his conversation with Mitch in Toronto.'[33]

Mitch met with General Williams early on the morning of 15 April. The OPP had learned of the plans to mobilize labour organi-zations to create disturbances around the province, and Mitch authorized Williams to recruit another two hundred constables, described by critics as 'Hepburn's Hussars' or, in Oshawa, 'Sons of Mitch's.' He then wired Lapointe that because of the 'vacillating attitude' of the King government he no longer wanted federal aid and demanded that the RCMP be withdrawn. The absence of the RCMP would not be a great loss, he angrily explained to the press, since he had learned from Williams that they were secretly under instructions not to get involved unless the inability of the provin-cial police to handle the situation made it absolutely necessary. King's secret orders were a 'double-cross' Mitch never forgot. How-ever, events in Oshawa and Detroit during the day made it unlike-ly that the Hussars would ever see action.[34]

In Oshawa, by 15 April, there was a growing disenchantment with Hugh Thompson. While the shop stewards insisted they would not negotiate through Mitch, a delegation of strikers, including Millard, met secretly with W.H. Moore, the local MP. Moore then drove to Toronto to tell Mitch that the men wanted to negotiate and sug-gested that he call Millard. Mitch agreed. As he said later, 'After all, Charlie Millard came from my bailiwick and if he wants to save face with the men I am willing to be the goat. My one concern is to get the men back on the payroll.' After a quick check with GM, Mitch invited Millard to bring Cohen for a meeting with GM in his office the next morning. A few hours later in Detroit, Martin and

GM issued a statement that after 'due consideration' it was agreed that the issue would be settled between GM Canada and 'the committee representing the various local unions involved.'[35]

Martin arrived in Oshawa on 16 April, as the workers began to drift back to work and the picket lines thinned. Late that night, after meeting the stewards and the strikers, Cohen was authorized to confirm a meeting with Mitch the next afternoon. Just before the meeting, Martin stated at a press conference that he had just completed a conference call with forty-five UAW locals in the United States, representing 110,000 men, who were determined to see their Oshawa brothers triumph. When Lorne McIntyre of the *Globe* suggested to Cohen that it was simply a ploy to make GM officials 'feel they had a general strike threat hanging over the head,' Cohen replied grimly, 'It is not a threat.'[36]

When the bargaining committee reached Queen's Park, the men were left in an ante-room and Thompson stayed discreetly in the background while Millard and Cohen met Mitch in Elmhirst's office. Mitch asked them to sign a statement that they were representing 'the Canadian workmen of the Oshawa GM plant and the Local Union and we are not acting as representatives of the International c.i.o. and that is the basis of the conference to which Premier Hepburn is giving us audience.' Mitch and Cohen fenced for an hour, with Cohen determined to secure some recognition of the UAW and Mitch, frequently consulting Highfield and Chappell in his office, equally determined to avoid it. Finally all agreed that the committee represented the 'organized workers of General Motors of Canada' and, with Mitch's consent, Cohen called Martin in Oshawa to secure his approval.

The discussion then turned to the concrete issue of work and wages. Cohen and Millard soon withdrew to review the proposals with Thompson and again decided to call Martin. Directed by reporters to a phone in a small room housing the office vault, Cohen was dialing Oshawa when Mitch came down the hall and asked, 'Is this another long distance call?' When Cohen admitted he was calling Martin, Mitch exploded. 'Then that ends it. Good afternoon. I'll have no more of this remote control.' Mitch explained to reporters later that he had allowed Cohen to show the various texts to Thompson and to call Martin, but when it became clear that the negotiations themselves would really be handled by Martin and Thompson, not Millard and the workers, he realized it 'was obviously just another Martin and Thompson set-up.' Stopping to talk to the bargaining committee, who had never got into the meeting, Mitch said 'I am very sorry this had to happen, but there was no other alternative.' Send a delegation of Oshawa workers, and you 'will find me a friend in court.'[37]

Homer Martin was a busy man on the weekend. He flew to Flint and Detroit, and led the *New York Times* to believe that he had threatened GM with a strike or at least a slow-down if it did not order its Canadian subsidiary to recognize the UAW. He then flew to Washington for a Monday meeting with John L. Lewis and the general executive board of the UAW. In his report to the board, Martin stated that the UAW hoped to secure recognition of the union at Oshawa, but he candidly opposed the sympathetic strike he had threatened because it would be 'jeopardizing our entire union.' There was no dissent, and when the question of financial support arose no one answered George Addes's question, 'What do you mean financial support?' Martin wired Thompson the next day that the UAW board had 'unanimously voted financial aid.'[38]

The deception was timely for there were too many signs that the men wanted to return to work. While Martin was engaged in his duplicity in Washington, Mayor Hall was determined to live up to his earlier ultimatum that unless Martin pulled out the American workers by Monday, 19 April, he would advise the Oshawa workers to forget the UAW and negotiate a settlement. The mayor spent Monday flitting between GM and Thompson and Millard and believed he had a settlement which Thompson allowed him to present to a general meeting that evening. Hall urged the men to accept what he felt was an acceptable work and wages offer. However, the strikers had to return to work before a contract was signed and the question of an appropriate formula for union recognition was to be left open for further negotiations.

Before the discussion began, Thompson ordered the press from the collegiate auditorium. For the next two hours, as the argument raged behind closed doors, twenty-five reporters were kept prisoner in a basement classroom. Unknown to Hall, Thompson had persuaded the bargaining committee and stewards to hold out for union recognition and, still believing in Martin's promises of a sympathetic strike and financial support, the men and women with a roar of 'ayes' voted to have a settlement before they returned to work. Flushed with anger, the mayor shouted over the din of mixed boos and cheers, 'You are being fooled. You are being duped. You are being hoodwinked. Take this damn seriously. You boo me now but you'll be coming to me later and admitting I'm right and I'll do my best to help you.'[39]

The unity was more apparent than real. At noon the next day, 20 April, a delegation claiming to speak for a thousand workers, many of them admittedly not union members, saw Mitch and told him they wanted to go back to work on the terms outlined by Hall. With additional information that the strike was almost broken, Mitch wired Colonel Sam McLaughlin, president of GM, Canada,then approaching New York on the *Queen of Bermuda*: 'Would urgently request that you advise Carmichael to suspend any negotiations with strikers until your return Thursday morning. Would also ask you to give no statements regarding situation until I have had a chance to confer with you. Confidential reports indicate total collapse of the strike imminent.'

In Oshawa a troubled Jacob Cohen, whose efforts to organize widespread demonstrations had failed, called Martin in the morning and wired in the afternoon: 'Since talking to you on phone situation acutely aggravated by 8-column newspaper announcement your executive board turned down suggestion for sympathy strike further aggravated by report of delegation of 12 visited Hepburn stating they speak on behalf of hundreds of men anxious to return to work imperative clear and specific word be received by you no later than 4 cannot overemphasize urgency of this.' But Martin had no specific word to give. That night Mitch declared that if the union dared a secret ballot, 90 per cent would vote to return to work and if the company decided to open the plant he would guarantee 'absolute peace and order.' General Motors had insisted that he participate in the negotiations, he added, and would not recognize either the UAW or the CIO.[40]

All that remained was to find an acceptable form of words. After three hours of discussion in Mitch's office on 21 April, Cohen and Millard finally agreed to a statement that they 'represented the employees of General Motors at Oshawa,' and neither 'were instructed by, or represented the Committee known as the C.I.O.' They also promised that neither Thompson nor Martin would return to Oshawa or Toronto. With those assurances the stage was set for negotiations the next day. When Mitch arrived at his office at 12:45 he refused to say anything to the dozen reporters from across North America outside his office. Cohen, Millard, and the bargaining committee were also silent when they arrived fifteen minutes later. But they all knew that many of the strikers had picked up their last pay cheque that morning and were ready to go back to work.

The possibility still remained that the UAW in Detroit would try to prevent a settlement that did not recognize the union. While the meeting was in progress, Lorne McIntyre of the *Globe* wired Queen's Park that he had been informed that the CIO was still in the picture and that even if the committee agreed to 'a local settlement barring C.I.O. they at mass meeting will take matters out of hands of negotiating committee and hold out for union recognition.' Their suspicion seemed confirmed with the sudden arrival in Oshawa of a Claude Kramer who was in immediate touch with Mrs Thompson and the shop stewards. When the news reached Queen's Park there was a flurry of excitement in the corridors. Mitch immediately forced a now-docile Jacob Cohen to sign a statement that he did not know Kramer and 'had no intention of discussing with him any features of the agreement which we are now in the course of working out.'

After two hours of discussion the bargaining committee streamed out and headed for the cafeteria, while Mitch and GM enjoyed a brief catered lunch in his office. Finally at 5:57 on 22 April Mitch opened his door and, with a wide grin, called 'C'mon in, boys' to the reporters who had camped outside his office for two weeks. That night Mitch celebrated at the King Eddy with his good friend Ned Sparks, the Hollywood comedian, and other congenial companions.[41]

The terms of the agreement were roughly what GM had offered two weeks before: a forty-four hour and five-and-a-half-day week with time-and-a-half for overtime; the seniority system requested by the union; a combination of the traditional unit foremen and elected shop committee as agreed to earlier; the pay increase offered earlier; a reduction in the production rate in 1938; and an agreement that 'no discrimination of any sort will be practised either by the Company or the employees, by reason of any activity, past or future, of any employee with, or in respect to, trade union activity or trade union membership.' The agreement was to be concurrent with the agreement in Detroit. 'This agreement covering the Oshawa Factory of the company,' read the last clause, 'is signed by the union employees hereunder who signed on behalf of themselves and their successors in office representing the employees of the company who are members of the local union.' That night the stewards enthusiastically endorsed the agreement, and when the doors of the Armoury opened at ten the next morning, two thousand strikers were lined up to vote. At 1:45 Cohen announced the results: 2,205 for and 36 against. The agreement was signed in Mitch's office at 3:10 that afternoon.[42]

The 'incendiary lunatic,' as Eugene Forsey described Mitch, was content even if the battle, at best, had been a draw. With most of the provincial, national, and American press, Canadian and American business and labour leaders such as A.R. Mosher of the All-Canadian Congress of Labour, his critics in the pulpits, and what seemed to be public opinion generally, singing his praises for defending the province against the lawlessness of the CIO and Lewis's communist allies, Mitch could afford to be magnanimous. It was difficult 'to find words to express to the employees of General Motors and the citizens of Oshawa my appreciation for the splendid cooperation extended to me which culminated in the bringing to a successful conclusion the most important strike with which we have been confronted. The true Canadian spirit asserted itself, in the final analysis, and all Ontario today, I am sure, joins me in extending to you an expression of thankfulness.' With the return of prosperity, he added, 'all people must realize that labour shall request and be entitled to a greater share of the increasing profits of industry. To this end I shall lend the support of the present administration and hope to attain such objectives in an orderly and constructive way.' With that Mitch left the battlefield to spend the weekend at Bannockburn.[43]

In Oshawa the next afternoon it was the union and the CIO which claimed the victory. 'I know, and they know, and the world knows that the union has been recognized,' boasted Charlie Millard. 'All the business of trying to avoid saying so, in so many words, is just child's play.' In fact, added Cohen, 'the agreement was so worded and the interpretation was so planned that there can be no doubt about the union's recognition.' Despite Mitch's strong protest to Crerar, Martin and Thompson crossed the border to attend the Oshawa rally. The strike was not settled in Canada or at Queen's Park, said Thompson, it was settled at Grant Boulevard and Woodward Avenue, Detroit, between 'a foreign corporation and foreign agitators.' Even while the final negotiations were under way in Mitch's office, he boasted, the union was in touch with Martin in Washington and Martin had been conferring with GM in Detroit. Martin promised that the UAW would soon organize the entire Canadian industry, and advised Mitch to stay on the onion farm. But to George McCullagh, Oshawa was 'a permanent defeat for Lewis and Communism in Canada ... No matter what false and flimsy claims may be put forward by Lewis agents and their comrades, the Reds, the C.I.O. is repudiated.'[44]

Before the strike was over Mitch faced the charge that the Oshawa strikers were only pawns in a larger game, that his hardline against recognizing the CIO was due less to his concern for GM than for his mining friends. With the strike over, the story that he had proposed an anti-CIO coalition to the Tories reinforced the suspicion that the same interests were deploying the political chessmen at Queen's Park. Listening to Mitch and reading the *Globe and Mail* did indeed recall the confusion of the dying Isaac that 'The voice is Jacob's voice, but the hands are the hands of Esau.' It was no secret that Mitch and McCullagh were in constant communication, sometimes closeted together for hours at a time. And the similarity in content and timing between Mitch's statements and the editorial and news columns of the *Globe* were suspiciously coincidental. Mitch agreed that McCullagh was 'co-operating in the fight,' as were all but two of the province's newspapers, but he insisted that McCullagh was not determining policy. Privately McCullagh boasted that it was 'the *Globe* that had made the C.I.O. issue and had really used Hepburn to further it.'[45]

It was not until Mitch emerged from seclusion on Sunday night, 18 April, to tell Lewis that 'he and his gang will never get their greedy paws on the mines of Northern Ontario as long as I'm Prime Minister' that the conspiracy theory blossomed. Mitch claimed to have 'definite knowledge' that CIO organizers were working feverishly to be in a position to pull out men across the north, and promised that if Lewis's 'invasion of the north' became more menacing he could find it necessary to take more drastic steps than at Oshawa. While the owners did not seem to share his concern about the immediate danger of strikes, they did share his resolve that the CIO should be stopped. Jack Bickell promised that if the CIO struck he would simply shut down McIntyre-Porcupine and 'when I say "shut down" I mean shut down ... until the men are ready to go back to work.' J.R. Timmins of Hollinger said he would never recognize the CIO and welcomed the government's assurance that should the CIO strike, 'ample protection' will be provided for the men who want to work. And Julius S. Bache of Dome, lamenting that there was no one as reliable as Mitch in the United States, suggested that because of their 'loyalty and cohesion' the mine owners would act in concert. From his perch on Parliament Hill, Norman McLeod reported that Ottawa believed that Mitch's uncompromising stand was due to the powerful influence of the 'gold mining millionaires' who were determined to crush the CIO.[46]

Although not alarming, the reports from the RCMP and the OPP since early 1936 had chronicled the increased activity of CIO and local communist organizers in the mines and the bush. The appearance of George Anderson, who had spent a year in jail for seditious statements at Lethbridge in 1931, as the Mine Mill organizer was not reassuring. Paid-up membership in the three CIO locals chartered by the summer of 1936 was low but the enthusiasm and rhetoric of the organizers was high, and by the spring of 1937 there was talk of a strike in the mines. Oshawa gave a great stimulus to organization and the union had invited Thompson to come north as soon as he had won the battle with GM. Police reports confirmed the opinion of Hollinger's manager who warned Mitch on 16 April that the CIO was 'only waiting for the Oshawa results before mobilizing the mines.' George Anderson assured a large meeting at Timmins on 18 April that the miners were behind their Oshawa brothers 'to the last cent, to the last breath,' although he denied a widespread report that he had threatened a general strike.[47]

In a long interview with John Marshall of the Windsor *Star* on 20 April, Mitch agreed that the mines certainly were at risk. Showing Marshall an OPP report just received from Timmins that 'about 1200 have joined up and they are just holding off awaiting the result of the strike at Oshawa,' Mitch said a strike would leave five thousand people with no means of support. With the afternoon paper reporting that gold stocks were tumbling, he urged Marshall to think of 'the women and others who have invested their savings in stocks. Think of these savings being wiped out.' Marshall commented that there were others who would lose even more in a stock market crash and bluntly asked if McCullagh and his friends were determining policy. McCullagh was providing 'welcome support,' Mitch replied. So were the mine owners, although he had talked to his friend Jack Bickell only 'once, for a few minutes, on this matter.' Whatever the opinion in Ottawa or the Toronto *Star*, he was not against unions or even international unions such as the A.F. of L. 'whose attitude to the Lewis crowd is the same as my own.' But, like all the law-abiding citizens of Ontario, he was against the CIO with its contempt for law and order and its close ties with the communists.[48]

The leaked report, a week after the Oshawa strike was over, that Mitch had proposed an anti-CIO coalition to Rowe again suggested that powerful influences were at work to shape the pattern of Ontario politics and policy. The finger of suspicion pointed at McCullagh and his friends. Nominally a Liberal, McCullagh viewed the party system as a cynical competition for the spoils of office and had long championed a non-partisan approach to the problems of the deficit, the railways, and more recently the CIO. The coalition idea was his, he later told King, for 'he could get millions from Americans, and other capital invested in Canada, if he could make it clear that both political parties were united in suppressing the c.i.o. and movements of that kind. He had gone to Hepburn, and suggested Hepburn talking it over with Rowe, which Hepburn said he would be glad to do, and which he did.'[49]

Mitch had spoken to Rowe on 12 April and asked his support in the battle with the CIO. Despite pressure from many of his followers, Rowe had remained silent until 16 April when he issued a statement so ambiguous that, as the *Star* said, it left the province 'where Moses was when the light went out – in the dark.' But there were many Tories, including Drew, who were appalled that Rowe refused to take a strong stand against the CIO and the communists. With Roebuck and Croll on the side of the CIO and Mackenzie King neutral at best, Mitch was not prepared to reject the coalition proposal, particularly given its genesis. That it also seemed so unpromising was even more reason to float the proposition.[50]

On Friday, 23 April Mitch informed the lieutenant-governor that in view of the seriousness of labour troubles 'he might be calling for a dissolution at any time and asking for a union government.' At home for the weekend, Mitch spent an hour flying a coalition kite with his friends Pete Birdsall and Tom Keith of the *St Thomas Times-Journal*. Both men supported the idea, but Keith urged him to 'move warily for a few days until you feel out the "other side"' and have some understanding on Hydro and separate school policy. While Mitch was at Bannockburn, the veteran Tory MLA Wilf Heighington arrived at Chorley Park on Sunday afternoon to tell Bruce that he had been approached about entering the cabinet – 'that the P.M. would make 4 vacancies' – and would like to be attorney general if he joined. George Drew arrived a little later 'with the same story only a little more definite. As he has been offered the Attorney-Generalship, H.[erbert] advised him to do nothing without taking Rowe with him, which he had not planned on doing.'[51]

When they met at Queen's Park on Monday morning, 26 April Mitch asked Bruce 'to interview Drew & Rowe separately and find out their views with regard to joining him.' He was prepared to take in Heighington, Drew, Rowe, and Bob Manion, and Bruce suggested that he add Leo Macaulay to the list. Drew saw Bruce later that afternoon and 'seemed very hopeful of everything going well, but H. warned him that he should do nothing without the consent of Rowe.' Bruce also saw Donald Hogarth who, as party financier and wire-puller, Angela Bruce noted, was the 'key man, and is difficult to argue with.' Since Hogarth was against the proposal, Bruce made the case for coalition 'impartially, and left it at that.'[52]

Neglecting to mention the overtures made to him, Drew made his position clear in a letter delivered to Rowe the same day. While he disagreed with Mitch 'in regard to many of his utterances,' Drew wrote, 'I am in entire agreement with him in principle in the present issue, and cannot publicly take any other position.' It was not a question of the right of labour to organize, he continued, but whether 'we are going to stand by and permit an organization to become established in Ontario which has shown that it is prepared to use force, and to disregard law, whenever it feels that it is stronger than those whose duty it is to enforce the law.' Rowe had not explained in detail what Mitch had proposed on 12 April, 'but if it was that a coalition should be formed which would give the Conservatives and the Liberals equal expression in meeting this issue, I am convinced that party politics, for the moment, should be forgotten and the offer should be accepted.' Drew asked for a decision the next day.[53]

There was no decision when Mitch met Rowe secretly in the Royal York at 10 a.m. on Tuesday, 27 April. He explained that McCullagh and other 'interested parties' had urged him to form a coalition with the Tories to combat the CIO and communism. Rowe claimed that Mitch offered him half the seats in the cabinet, even offering to resign if necessary, and assured him that the parties behind the proposal would cover all his debts and pay him several hundred thousand dollars. Rowe concluded from the discussion that Mitch wanted to be free to sell the idea of a union government nationally and 'get rid' of Mackenzie King. Whatever their private thoughts, Mitch was sufficiently content to tell Bruce there was no need for him to see Rowe as 'things were going alright.' Rowe spent the afternoon in a long session at the Albany Club working over a statement of labour policy, drafted by Cecil and Leslie Frost, which Drew felt was not sufficiently forthright on the CIO issue and, at his request, was not issued to the press. After dinner Rowe went to Chorley Park where, for an hour and a half, Bruce begged him 'to accept the offer for the good of the province.' Rowe agreed to consult 'a few of the men who were working with him' and left the next day for Ottawa.[54]

As point man in the coalition manoeuvres, Herbert Bruce was a busy man on Wednesday. Hogarth phoned at noon and asked him to tell Mitch that 'the door was still open.' Mitch called after lunch to report that he was seeing Rowe again on Friday. Drew told him in the afternoon that 'he had more or less decided to join the Govt even if Rowe did not and was preparing a statement.' Hogarth arrived at nine and left the impression that 'he would be willing to come to an arrangement, at any rate he was so interested in it that he took the midnight train to Ottawa to see Rowe (who had gone there) Meighen & Bennett.' When Hogarth left, Bruce immediately phoned Drew and 'told him on no account must he do anything that would hurt negotiations.'

The gathering of the tribal elders in Ottawa passed unnoticed by the press but there were no secrets among the backroom boys. Rod Finlayson, Bennett's private secretary, told Lambert that Hogarth, Meighen, and Rowe had met with Bennett to discuss Mitch's offer of half the cabinet and the 'P'Mship' if Rowe wanted it. According to Finlayson, Bennett 'was inclined to union' but 'Hogarth & Meighen were so much opposed that Rowe went back with his mind made up to refuse.' Rowe was to have seen Mitch with his answer on 30 April, but 'Rowe et al were inclined to stall for a few days because they distrusted George McC in a plan to spring a demonstration vs. labor on May Day.' A few days delay would also give Bennett time to get away to the coronation before the news broke.[55]

Rowe met Drew twice on Friday, 30 April, after his return from Ottawa. In spite of the decision reached in Ottawa, Rowe intimated the door was not closed and that he was going to see Mitch 'sometime during the next week.' However, Drew concluded that Rowe was not convinced of the seriousness of the CIO menace and made one final effort to change his mind. In a long letter he asked Rowe to meet him over the weekend and examine evidence he had just seen that afternoon which would 'remove any remaining doubts in your mind that this is one of the most serious issues that this country has ever faced' and which, he later claimed, was 'positive proof that every member of the Ontario executive of the C.I.O. but one was a member of the Communist Party.' That menace alone was sufficient justification for coalition, but even if it were exaggerated, coalition would provide 'an opportunity to do things for the future welfare of the Province that it seems to me unlikely could ever be done by one party alone,' such as scrapping the detestable legislation denying access to the courts and reforming the Hydro Commission and the civil service.

The fundamental issue, however, was the CIO. While Mitch's words may have been 'somewhat provocative to labour, I cannot agree, after careful reading of the statements that he has made, that he has shown any antagonism to properly constituted labour organizations, whether national or international.' The issue was not the right of labour to organize, but whether the CIO, controlled from

Washington and with its contemptuous disregard for law and order, should be allowed into Ontario. It was an issue which could 'no longer be faced on the basis of party expediency.' If the party was true to its principles, Drew insisted, 'it has no choice but to take an uncompromising stand against the inroads of an organization which is an exact counterpart of the Soviet in Russia and is directed by men who have actually gone to Russia to study their organization methods.' But if the party chose not to be true to its principles, the colonel would be true to his. As party organizer, 'I have, of necessity, been forced to remain silent. I can no longer, however, refrain from expressing the opinion I now hold ... For that reason, I have no choice but to ask you to accept my resignation as your organizer until such time as we are in agreement on this issue.' At Rowe's request Drew did not announce his resignation.[56]

A discreet call from Lambert to Harry Hindmarsh at the Toronto *Star* blew the coalition story open. The late edition on 1 May carried a report from Queen's Park that Rowe had been invited to join a coalition government and, although he had not formally replied on 30 April as scheduled, he had declined the offer. Rowe admitted that he had had a couple of short interviews with Mitch 'at his request on matters he thought of public interest. Nothing was settled at all, so far as that is concerned.' Asked explicitly about union government, Rowe replied: 'No, no. There is nothing in that at the present time. There's nothing so far as any agreement is concerned and there is not likely to be.' Mitch admitted the two had met as 'old friends' and he had given Rowe some information which he thought the opposition leader should have. 'There was no mention during our meeting,' Mitch insisted with a flagrant disregard for the truth, 'of any proposal for a coalition.' With the rumours persisting, Rowe issued a press statement on 3 May: 'If the two brief and informal interviews I have recently had with the Hon. Mr. Hepburn have given rise to a rumour that a coalition government was being formed, I may say most emphatically that no such plan is even contemplated.'

For the moment at least what *Saturday Night* described as a 'Business Men's Putsch' had failed. That Mitch 'gave unofficial assurances of his willingness to take a few Conservatives into his cabinet is quite believable,' concluded its editor. 'That he ever authorized anybody to offer Mr. Rowe the premiership is believable only on one condition, namely that he was perfectly sure Mr. Rowe would not take it.' Over a year later when Rowe and Drew had revealed more of the details, Mitch claimed that he had never personally offered Rowe a coalition. 'In fact I was opposed to it ... But third parties – plenty of them – came to me proposing it but Mr. Rowe was also opposed to it.' The April putsch had failed, but the idea lingered in the office of the publisher of the *Globe and Mail*, where it began.[57]

'It is the "Fellows" that count'

Mitch had decided on a fall election long before Oshawa. The normal political cycle had been three years and he had every reason to follow tradition. With the sharp upswing in the provincial economy almost every sector and every region were enjoying what, after seven years of depression, seemed like a boom. Farm income was double the 1932 low and the prospects were excellent for 1937 prices. The stock market had reached its highest level since 1930. In manufacturing employment was up more than 11 per cent, the construction industry was busier than it had been since 1931, and more men were at work in the bush and the mines than ever before. Mitch's March budget reflected the return of better times and so wide was the diaspora of its benefits that an election seemed almost inevitable.

By March it also seemed politically astute, perhaps imperative, to secure a new lease on life before the government faced a humiliating retreat in its Hydro policy. Strangely, Mitch had paid so little attention to the details of the Hydro Commission's policy that he did not sense the inconsistency between its advice that Ontario did not face a power shortage but desperately needed more power at Niagara. Nor did he seem to appreciate that if everyone else was right on supply and demand, the commission was misleading if not deceptive. By January 1937 McCullagh had become convinced that the commission was 'concealing' the power shortage from Mitch, and the mail that Croll had brought to Arizona revealed the incompetence of the commission. Although settlement with Ottawa Valley provided a short-term solution, it left Mitch with the inevitable longterm problem of trying to square the circle with Beauharnois and the courts on one hand and with Roosevelt and the St Lawrence seaway on the other.[1]

A few days after his return from Arizona, Mitch had reviewed the power situation with the commission. Hogg's engineering reports indicated that all the reserve power in the Gatineau and MacLaren contracts would be absorbed by 1939. Even with the additional horsepower from the Ogoki diversion and a smaller diversion planned at Long Lac, where the cabinet had approved a canal for running pulpwood south to Lake Superior, the province would need more power between 1943 and 1945. However, there did seem to be a reasonable prospect of securing American approval for the diversions. When Croll had returned from Arizona the commission, with Hogg added to the team, met the New York Power Authority. Frank Walsh, the Authority's chairman, explained that the president was determined to go ahead with the St Lawrence but might be sympathetic to the diversions if Ontario agreed to the St Lawrence. After his meeting with the commission, Mitch informed King that he had changed course.[2]

Late in February Lyon and McQuesten proposed to King and Skelton that in return for the immediate utilization of the greater flow over Niagara from the Ogoki and Long Lac diversions, Ontario 'would be willing to negotiate an agreement with the Dominion for the utilization of St. Lawrence power, providing that a 10-year period, from the date of signing the Treaty (or preferably from the date of commencing construction work) was allowed for taking the first block of power and making the first payment.' After the meeting King told the cabinet of the proposal and also of the invitation he had received that morning to visit the White House. The change in Mitch's strategy was not entirely welcome for, although it might please Roosevelt, King's colleagues felt as he did 'about not getting into the St. Lawrence Waterway Project at this time, if we can keep out of it.'[3]

King dropped in to see Mitch on his way to Washington. The federal government was not interested in the St Lawrence, he admitted, but wanted to accommodate Roosevelt – and now Ontario. Mitch explained that he did not want to make any commitment until the court case was settled, for if they lost, Ontario would 'have more power than they could deal with for years to come,' but if they won, he 'could make some suitable arrangement with the Dominion.' However, he wanted to do nothing until after a fall election. King outlined Mitch's position to Roosevelt the next day and was relieved when the president said that with the heavy backlog in Congress the treaty could stand over until 1938.[4]

Roosevelt's decision did nothing to meet Ontario's need for more power. Although engineering reports inside Hydro continued to underline the impending power shortage, the position taken by the commission was becoming increasingly remote from reality. Lyon assured Mitch in March that 'it is still true, as it has been every day since your Government came to power, that there is an ample supply of reserve power available in the system for the use of any customer, present or prospective.' However, he told William Ryan of Stone & Webster that more was needed 'and if the diplomats have not succeeded by the time Ogoki water flows down the Niagara, in giving us legal right to the sole use of the water in our generating plants there, I would then favour making the necessary arrangements without international sanction.' The commission 'as at present constituted,' he assured Ryan, had no intention of ever taking Beauharnois power.[5]

The composition of the commission changed a few days later when the dismissed Roebuck rejected Mitch's ambiguous invitation to remain a commissioner. 'The impulse to accept your suggestion has been strong,' he wrote in a draft letter of resignation, but 'I am of the opinion that for the protection of the System from the milking that is planned I would be less effective on the Board than I will be off it.' In the end, however, he wrote only that staying on the commission while disagreeing with Mitch's labour policy would lead to a 'serious misunderstanding.' Nevertheless, he diligently encouraged the rumours that his resignation would pave the way for a deal with Beauharnois, and told King that the 'true explanation' of his dismissal from the cabinet 'lies in the Hydro, and in the fact that I have apparently stood in the way of future private profits from that public enterprise.'[6]

When the increase in demand passed 10 per cent in the spring and showed no signs of levelling off, Hydro engineers estimated the shortfall would be an alarming 360,000 horsepower by 1940. With Lyon adamantly rejecting the data and their implications, Richard Jeffery, the senior municipal engineer, drove to St Thomas on 8 June to see Mitch. Not only had the commission persistently ignored its engineers, he explained, but 'most of the leading legal men of the Province' were convinced that Beauharnois would win in court and he 'could see financial disaster facing the Commission unless immediate steps were taken ... to negotiate compromise settlements with the Power Companies.' Even worse, Lyon was determined to prevent any settlement with the Quebec companies. Lyon had stated in his presence – 'and made no secret of the same' – that he was going to cut rates in the Niagara system 'so low that the resulting financial condition of that System would ... make it financially impossible for the incoming Commission and/or Government to negotiate any compromise settlements with the Eastern Power Companies.' Mitch listened for half an hour, asked only a few questions, and promised Jeffery that he would arrange for Nixon and Leduc to meet with him and Hogg.[7]

Mitch had already realized that Ontario might have to fall back on Beauharnois power, if he could reach a settlement that would not bankrupt Hydro. Negotiations would not be easy. With the courts deciding in the company's favour, the bondholders, led by Holt of Montreal, Light, Heat and Power who effectively controlled Beauharnois, held a reasonably good hand. Moreover, Gatineau had the contractual right to supply the first 120,000 additional horsepower. Finally, the transmission lines from the border to the Leaside transformer station were almost at capacity, and new lines would cost $16 to $20 million. Public negotiations were out of the question, for Mitch was determined to secure a new mandate before voters became aware that the commission had put the province in an embarrassing, even critical, situation. As George McCullagh later told Angela Bruce, 'Hepburn knew that he was running short of power & said to him Roebuck & McQuesten have fooled me on this. And instead of admitting it he was going to call a quick election on "Back to Niagara" policy all the time making plans with the so called "Barons".'[8]

Although Lyon had insisted in April that the commission would never take Beauharnois power, Hogg had intimated during his conversations with the New York Power Authority in March that Hydro might buy 50,000 from Beauharnois, an amount obviously dictated by the capacity of the transmission lines. The prospect of lowering the 'black flag' of repudiation was mentioned during the coalition manoeuvres in April, and Earl Rowe stated early in May that it was 'generally understood' new contracts were being discussed. There were few secrets on Bay and St James Streets and by June brokers were advising their clients that there were 'excellent grounds for believing that the company within a reasonable time, will dispose of 250,000 h.p. to the Ontario Hydro-Electric Commission.' There were also few secrets among the power barons and on 19 June Gordon Gale of Gatineau wrote as a matter of fact that Hydro would have 'a surplus of 25 cycle power if they complete their new agreement with Beauharnois.'[9]

Three days later the Ontario Court of Appeal made a settlement imperative when it gave Beauharnois what was in effect a $7 million judgment and, in scathing language, struck down the 1937 statute preventing a suit against Hydro without the consent of the attorney general. 'We have been expecting it, and we are ready for it,' Mitch stated defiantly. The province would appeal to the Judicial Committee and would also proclaim the acts that declared it would not be bound by the decision and gave the commission immunity against any judgment. And Mitch assured Lyon that before the sheriff arrived at Hydro to serve a judgment, 'he would no longer be an employee of the Province of Ontario.'[10]

But Mitch's bravado did not stop the rumours on the street. By early June there were reports that Lyon's days were numbered. Financial circles were also aware that late in June Mitch had asked Hogg if he would accept the Hydro chairmanship. It was no secret that Hogg detested repudiation and believed that both the need for power and sound business ethics demanded a revised contract with Beauharnois. The market responded with Beauharnois bonds moving from $55 to $65 between the end of May and the end of July. A day after the cabinet had secretly decided on a fall election, the *Globe and Mail* stated categorically that 'a contract on a favourable basis was prepared' but was not signed for political reasons.[11]

Mitch had decided to face the people before dealing directly with Beauharnois. But to cover all eventualities he had instructed Nixon to formally ask Ottawa to secure American approval of the northern diversions and Ontario's right to use all the additional flow. However, with Hogg likely to be in charge and Bethune Smith, solicitor for MacLaren and Liberal treasurer, deeply involved, it was really only a matter of settling the details of revised contracts after the election. Even Gatineau was alerted in September when Jeffery told them that they could expect to hear from Hydro after the 6 October election 'about the weather and other matters.' Asked if they wanted to discuss 60-cycle power, Jeffery replied: 'I don't think so; 25 cycle power is what we have in mind.' Since negotiations on Beauharnois's 25-cycle contract would trigger renegotiations with Gatineau, the meaning was clear. By September Mitch was well into the campaign, patiently reassuring the voters that with the reserves in hand and the developments planned there was no danger of a power shortage. It was also a campaign in which Mitch neither wanted nor received the support of Mackenzie King.[12]

Mitch's decision to break openly with King and the federal Liberal party on the eve of an election inspired an orgy of speculation. The occasion was an after-dinner speech on 3 June, when Mitch was in his usual after-dinner form. Near the end of a meandering forty-five-minute talk, during which he praised his new friend Maurice Duplessis as 'a great national character,' and claimed that Ontario and Quebec should have a voice in national public policy, he turned to the tumultuous labour situation south of the border. 'There will be no lawlessness in Ontario,' he assured his audience, but 'I cannot speak for Canada because we have a vacillating Canadian government in Ottawa.'

Mitch paused, glanced briefly at George McCullagh, and leaned into the microphone. 'And now I am going to make a statement that will probably make headlines. I am a Reformer – but I am not a Mackenzie King Liberal any more. I will tell the world that and I hope he hears me. As far as I am concerned I am ready to forget partisanship in the interests of my country.' The time had come to stand up for 'what we think is right just as my good friend George McCullagh is doing.' The optimistic Liberal view that whiskey had again loosened his tongue was shattered the next day when he told reporters that he had in fact severed relations with the federal party in November 1936.[13]

Duncan Marshall swore that as Mitch got up to speak, McCullagh had whispered 'now go after the Ottawa crowd if you want the headlines for tomorrow' and, although McCullagh denied it, he enthusiastically endorsed the break. The news columns of his paper explained it as the result of Mitch's growing disaffection since the October 1935 election; his editorial, 'MORE URGENT THAN PARTYISM,' hailed the statement as proof that Mitch was determined to put principle over party in his war against the CIO and its communist allies. With or without Ottawa, 'there is a job to be done in behalf of the people of this Province ... The C.I.O. is not in Canada a party issue. Mr. Hepburn has the backing of both Conservatives and Liberals in his efforts to keep its illegal operations out of Ontario.'[14]

Publicly Mitch did not detail his criticism of King; privately he was bitterly outspoken. That 'son of a bitch' was happy to have him stump the country in 1935, he told the Carty brothers, and then became a 'welcher' on all his promises. He even tried to renege on Frank O'Connor's appointment to the Senate and refused to find Wishart Campbell a job with the CBC. The last straw was King's failure to do anything for the widow of Archie McCoig whose tubercular son was dying in a London sanatorium, although Archie had gladly given up his West Kent seat in 1921 so that King could parachute James Murdock into the cabinet. Mitch detested King's lack of compassion and gratitude and gave her a job as a mother's allowance inspector in London.[15]

Mitch emphasized policy and politics in a long letter to Duff Pattullo, another Liberal premier disillusioned by two years of Mackenzie King. Despite King's public and private assurances, he wrote, he
had failed to lower the tariff to pre-Bennett levels, nationalize the
Bank of Canada 'in the true sense of the word,' consult with the
provinces on relief, and accept responsibility for the unemployed.
For two years King's policy had been 'one of studied insults, one
heaped upon another' and, although it was 'friends of our Government who financed the Federal candidates from Quebec to British
Columbia,' those friends 'have been treated even more shamefully
than the members of the Government.' Moreover, 'due to its callousness towards its own supporters,' the federal party was so unpopular that 'I arrived at the point where I decided to break with
them. I am quite prepared to answer for the sins of my own Government, but not to carry King's as well ... in brief I am sick and
disgusted with King and his whole outfit and want nothing more to
do with them, politically or otherwise.' After lecturing Ian Mackenzie on King's sins for three hours, Mitch sent the message to Ottawa
that the rupture was complete: he did not want federal support in his
election and would not support King when he went to the country.[16]

Most pundits refused to believe that Mitch's statement was either
another of his impetuous after-dinner outbursts or a straightforward
reflection of his disillusionment and disaffection, but preferred to see
it as a calculated move inspired by some deeper and more sinister
motive. Already there were what one informed journalist described
as 'dangerous' rumblings in the Liberal caucus because of the conservatism of King and Dunning. And there were frequent discussions of a new realignment of forces within the party in the
aftermath of the King era. Some predicted a Hepburn–Jimmy Gardiner alliance, backed by Chubby Power and Ian Mackenzie, with
Gardiner – or even Mitch – seeking the leadership to prevent the
accession of Charles Dunning. There was no doubt about Gardiner's
ambition and few took seriously Mitch's declaration that he would
not take the federal leadership if 'it was handed to me on a platter.'
But if Mitch's break with King had been designed to pave the way
for that realignment, many analysts concluded his judgment was ter-
ribly flawed for, as the *Financial Post* put it, Gardiner was too much
of a 'machine politician to be party to a complete insurgency.'[17]

Others speculated that Mitch was planning a new coalition of
interests outside the Liberal party. When King received the news in
London he immediately concluded that Mitch's break was the opening move in a plot engineered by McCullagh and his friends. His

assumption was reinforced when he received a summary of Lambert's analysis from his secretary, W.J. Turnbull:

He says he has been told that Hepburn has been seeing Duplessis, and he believes it is a combination of McCullagh of the Globe pushing Hepburn in this direction, while Bassett of The Gazette is working with Duplessis. Mr. Lambert understands that McCullagh and Bassett are sailing together, early next week, for England. The alliance seems pretty definite, and it is surely significant. My own opinion is probably valueless, but the inspiration for the move probably comes from McCullagh and Bassett who are more concerned with the interests they represent than anything else, and are hoping to make a real stand against Labour, counting on the backing of the Catholic Church, particularly in Quebec, and of the Ontario farmers. The mining interests in both Provinces have an identity of interests and feel that a Fascist programme under the spellbinders, Hepburn and Duplessis, may permit of a successful last ditch stand.[18]

With Duplessis carrying on his own war with the CIO and publicly promising to collaborate with Mitch to resist the 'penetration of subversive ideas,' the journalists found the trail easy to follow. Confirmation came from Montreal where both the *Gazette* and the *Star* enthusiastically hailed the prospect of an alliance against 'mischievous foreign intervention.' With Mitch and Duplessis extending the hand of friendship across the Ottawa, argued the *Star*, it 'would seem only sensible that the two peoples of these two central provinces should get together on so vital a subject and form a solid bloc in the Federal Parliament – under whatever party name or none – to defend our fundamental national interests, our cherished freedom from outside intervention and the established principles of finance, economics and outstanding self-respect.' *Le Devoir* also speculated on the possibility of 'un bloc ontarien-quebec' and *L'Unité* predicted a Duplessis-Hepburn coalition. Even the governor general believed there was some sort of alliance between 'Hepler' and 'Duplessini,' as *Saturday Night* dubbed them, but described it as 'a pinch of temperament rather than of policy.'[19] Mitch repeatedly dismissed the stories as idle speculation, but he warned Ian Mackenzie that he 'might link up with Duplessis to defeat the Ottawa Liberalism unless there was more co-operation.' With a touch of shared policy interests, a mutual hostility to Ottawa, and a bonding lifestyle, the rumours persisted that there was more to their close association than a pinch of temperament.[20]

Saturday Night's astute observer, 'Rideau Banks,' reported that the more common view among federal Liberals was that Mitch's remarks were designed to pave the way for a 'union ministry' in Ontario, with at least Drew representing the Conservative element, and an early election on the CIO issue. Reports from usually reliable sources had been circulating in the spring that such a move was planned, he continued, but Drew's departure for England late in May scotched the rumours and Ottawa Liberals 'breathed freely once more.' However, Mitch's speech had reawakened the suspicion; otherwise his secession remained 'an act without a definite motive.'[21]

In Conservative circles it was much more than a suspicion. When she returned from the coronation, Angela Bruce heard that Drew had broken with Rowe and that he and Stewart, the former mayor of Toronto, would enter Mitch's cabinet. Don Hogarth warned Rowe on 5 July that Mitch planned 'to re-organize his Government in the comparatively near future and in the re-organization to include three prominent Conservatives, and when I say prominent I mean just that.' The Frosts did not have hard evidence, but Les sent his brother a Hepburn-Drew dossier in case 'there should be a Hepburn-Drew coalition. I have not included references about the French being a "defeated race" but you will have it.' One of Drew's political confidants from Guelph was mildly amused. Informing the Colonel in London that 'the cat is out of the bag ... getting out by way of rumours,' he wrote that the local politicians were tremendously mystified and were 'flapping about like a tent without any guy ropes.'[22]

The accusing finger again pointed to 'the Rasputin behind Mr. Hepburn' who was alleged to run Queen's Park from his office at Yonge and Melinda. McCullagh's contempt for political parties was well known and his 10 June editorial praising Mitch for being 'one jump ahead of the procession' as usual in acting for the best interests of the province regardless of 'party strings' was clearly a call for non-partisan support. The *Globe* was even more extravagant in its praise of Drew who, after his resignation, had bought time for two radio addresses in which he endorsed Mitch's stand against the CIO and warned of the real and present danger of communism. McCullagh told King that he had discussed the possibility of an alliance – 'a sort of National Government again using the C.I.O. as the excuse therefore,' as King described it – with both Drew and Mitch. He claimed that Mitch had agreed, and that he had left for England in June 'with the understanding that when he returned arrangements would be made and an election brought on.' But when he returned from England in mid-July, Mitch told him the deal was off: 'That he had settled matters with Beauharnois ... that McQuesten had said the arrangement would ruin his political future, and that he was opposed to it.' According to McCullagh, Mitch 'threw up his arms and went on like a mad man, said he did not care what the agreement had been that he had with McCullagh, he would have to go ahead and would go as the Liberal Party.'[23]

Most Liberals, like McQuesten, opposed any idea of a non-partisan government and assured Mitch he would win thousands of Tory votes without it. There was also a good deal of opposition to Drew personally, most bluntly expressed by the Bothwell Liberals who told Mitch that 'We have on file every speech of that bloated and bastard son of class-hatred and privileged plutocratic exploitation ... Let him go back where he belongs, at the breast of Tory Financialism and Tory Plutocracy, where he was suckled and bred to hate and despise the poor and defenceless.'[24]

McCullagh's grand design had never moved far from his drafting table, despite his claim that Mitch had agreed. Drew admitted that he had been approached, but insisted that he had refused 'to even discuss it unless it was accepted by the party as a whole.' Nevertheless, the rumours persisted that Mitch would fill the vacancies in his cabinet before the election with Drew as attorney general. And when the reorganization failed to materialize, Drew's decision to run as an Independent Conservative, after failing to secure a Tory nomination, was widely believed to be the first step towards joining Mitch after the election. Drew later dismissed that suggestion as 'utterly false,' but R.B. Bennett, who distrusted Drew, was not convinced. 'The evidence before me is that the Premier of Ontario requested one candidate at the general election to contest his constituency as an Independent Conservative,' he later wrote Drew. 'He even went so far as to suggest to reputable persons that you were contesting South Wellington on that basis and after the election would, if elected, be Attorney General in his government.' McCullagh's enthusiastic backing of Drew during the campaign convinced many that a Hepburn-Drew alliance had been delayed not aborted.[25]

Although Mitch had decided on a fall election long before Oshawa, he assured one of his backbenchers in May that there would not be an election in 1937 'unless some great crisis should develop, which I hope will not be the case.' The only crisis seemed to be Mitch's health. He spent a week in bed at the hotel in June with what was first reported to be an asthmatic condition, but was later said to be bleeding in his stomach probably from over-indulging. As McCullagh informed the 'Bruiser,' who had left Mitch's entourage to move north and dry out, 'Habits and forms of entertainment have not changed much since you left here and as I have told you so often, there is nothing that you or I can do to change a person who will not help himself.' Colin Campbell told King late in July that Mitch's kidneys and liver were 'out of order' and he needed injections. The news was of some comfort to King, who 'saw only tragedy ahead so far as Hepburn is concerned, and possible defeat of his government ... He is an alcoholic – in bad shape – dissolute I fear and will come to his grave in dishonour I greatly fear.' Mitch eventually escaped the perils of the King Eddy to spend many restful days at Bannockburn. Since Roy Elmhirst was often there, the work of government did not come to a complete stop.[26]

By the middle of July, Mitch's denials of an approaching election had become less convincing. Following a long cabinet meeting on 22 July, Nixon told Bruce unofficially that 'it was best to go while the going was good' and Mitch chose his forty-first birthday, 12 August, to announce the date of the provincial election and establish his agenda. Circumstances had changed in the past few months, he told the expectant crowd at Pinafore Park, and an election could not be delayed until after the promised redistribution. Earl Rowe was challenging his position on the CIO, and only the people could decide 'whether they want Lewis and lawlessness in this fair Province of ours or whether they want it to remain a decent, law-abiding place in which to live.' With the courts deciding against Hydro, he needed the support of the people to protect Hydro against a final adverse decision. Mr Justice McTague had struck down a provision in the Succession Duties Act which effectively killed further investigations, and he needed a mandate to pass a new act and recover the $50,000,000 still owed to the taxpayers. Finally, he wanted the voters to pass judgment on three years of the Hepburn government – years that had fulfilled his promises of a balanced budget, progressive social legislation, and efficient and honest administration.[27]

Mitch undoubtedly believed that his crusade against the CIO and its allies was popular among the voters, for whoever had won the battle of Oshawa, he had won the support of the provincial press. And in the months after Oshawa the CIO organizers in Ontario and the United States made certain that he kept it. Between April and the October election there were almost one hundred strikes in the province – an epidemic not seen since 1919 – affecting a dozen centres across the north and three dozen cities in the south. Most of the long strikes, often marred by violence on the picket lines, police intervention and arrests, were called by organizers associated with the CIO, many of whom were well-known members of the Communist party. By the summer of 1937, as Mitch and Drew charged, communists dominated the CIO leadership in Ontario. Drew, in fact, claimed to have 'positive proof that every member of the Ontario executive of the C.I.O. but one' was a member of the party.[28]

The Ontario sub-regional Council of the CIO, operating within the Buffalo Region, had delegates from each of the dozen CIO-affiliated unions. Stewart Smith, the most prominent communist after Tim Buck, was chairman of the council, which took over the offices of the Workers Unity League on John Street. In May Joe Salsberg was promoted from director of CIO activities in Toronto to 'chief field organizer' for the province. The leaders of the drives to organize textiles, steel, rubber, shoes and leather, miners, seamen and longshoremen were members of the party, and a member of the Young Communist League organized caddies that struck Woodbine Golf Club in June. The communist Ukrainian Labor and Farmer Temple Association and the Polish People's Association sent organizers into plants with large ethnic work forces, such as the rubber factories in Toronto and Kitchener. The trade union section of the Communist party determined much of the organizational strategy, and the party bought sound trucks to use during strikes. 'I come bang up against the Communists in every walk of life,' Graham Spry warned David Lewis. 'The situation now is that the Communists are powerful in the unions, just as powerful almost as they are in some of the foreign language associations. Even when they are not powerful in numbers, their representatives constitute a voting block that trade union officers have to consider if they want to hold either jobs or offices.'[29] The slaughter south of the border as Tom Girdler and 'Little Steel' fought off the CIO invasion with the aid of local and company police, vigilantes and the National Guard seemed to confirm Mitch's charge that the CIO and lawlessness invariably went hand in hand.

Despite his tough stance, Mitch, as his own minister of labour, and Louis Fine, whom he had promoted to chief conciliation officer, worked continuously to secure negotiated settlements which would give the strikers some of the benefits of better times, but stopped short of recognizing CIO-affiliated unions. But if local authorities asked, he was always ready to send the OPP. He sent detachments to Windsor in May, when the city police needed help to protect the workers at the Walker and Young plants who refused to join the UAW strike and to the tobacco country around Delhi in July, when farmers with shotguns stood off Toronto communists attempting to organize the tobacco pickers. The OPP in Peterborough used tear-gas to end weeks of intermittent violence in August after Alex Welch had pulled out the textile workers.

With the violence in the United States and the strikes in Canada a timely counterpoint, Mitch seldom let an opportunity pass without some outrageous reference to Lewis and his allies. Despite his vicious attacks on the CIO, however, Mitch insisted throughout the campaign that he was not against trade unions – or even the strike weapon – but against lawlessness whether it came 'under the guise of the CIO or Al Capone,' but not it seemed if it came in the guise of Tom Girdler or Henry Ford. Although even the *Star* commended him for his softer tone and his more deliberate distinction between the right to organize and the methods used, the ambiguity remained.[30]

Like many of his contemporaries, Mitch did not believe in the closed shop; workers had the right to strike and those who refused had the right to work, under police protection if necessary. He also believed that his labour legislation had been beneficial and that the new Industry and Labour Board, with representatives of management and labour, would acquire the experience to enable it to recommend new legislation which would protect 'the rights labour possesses' and help to 'eliminate strife in industry in this province.' Moreover, he warned, hundreds of millions of new capital investment would be lost if industrial peace were not assured. 'If next Wednesday you go out and return your present Government to power,' he told his own constituents, 'you will see the greatest era of industrial expansion Ontario has ever known; but if, on the other hand, we lose, no one knows what the outcome may be, because the Lewis forces are hovering around, ready to come in given the opportunity.'[31]

Mitch could afford to take the high road because the low road was crowded. In Oshawa, Gordon Conant waved American propaganda pamphlets, such as *Join the C.I.O. and Build a Soviet America*. Even Mitch's enemies in the Protestant churches took up arms. 'It is not by evolution, but by revolution, that the C.I.O. and communism hope to conquer,' intoned the Reverend Dr John Inkster of Knox Presbyterian in Hamilton. 'They are the greatest menace to our three great pillars of civilization – the home, the school and the church ... I am opposed to the C.I.O. and communism because I am a Canadian and a Briton. I am more than that, I am a minister of God, and I say that they are anti-God, anti-Christ and anti-Bible.' Mitch could hardly have asked for more.[32]

However, the central issue in the election, Mitch insisted, was the record of his administration. He boasted of a balanced budget, relief to the municipalities, improved social legislation and allowances that benefited the working class. Harry Johnson's office had prepared a statement for each riding of just how much the Hepburn government had saved the local taxpayers in highways, township roads, old age pensions, mothers allowances, municipal subsidies, the liquor refund, and reductions in Hydro rates. There were, of course, promises of even more to come: major reforestation programs and extensions to the Trans Canada for the north; a new chain of provincial parks across the province with land already acquired near Sarnia; a new liquor commission, composed of a Supreme Court judge and two MLAs, one Grit and one Tory, with even a hint that women might be kept out of beer parlours; and provincial unemployment insurance if King failed to introduce a national program. And a week before the election Mitch implemented the promise of a $5 reduction in car licences.

The Conservatives were convinced that Mitch was most vulnerable over Hydro. Rowe seemed sufficiently confident of his facts to challenge Mitch to have Hogg and two engineers sign a statement denying there was a shortage: 'I know he can't secure those engineers to sign such a statement, and he knows it ... I challenge him to say he is not negotiating with Beauharnois.' Mitch denied the charge and ignored the challenge. But as the American minister, unlike his Tory opponents, astutely observed, Mitch's language was evasive. The denial of a power shortage was always carefully cast in the context of the availability of additional power at Niagara from the northern diversions, and although Mitch admitted the necessity of an agreement with the United States, he neglected to point out that an agreement was equally unlikely. Even more slyly he said that more Quebec power was available from Gatineau and MacLaren if needed, and that even Beauharnois was standing by eager to sell Hydro 250,000 horsepower. If Rowe could tell him where power was needed, he promised to buy 400,000 horsepower from Quebec and build a $30 million transmission line to get it there.[33] After all, Mitch explained, he had not repudiated the contracts but simply cancelled them to force the companies to renegotiate: 'I did what I did to give you people cheaper power, and I would do it again if ever faced with the same situation.' However, he often added almost as an aside, the government 'is going very slowly with regard to contracts for power from Quebec.' But the one source he would not touch was the St Lawrence. 'Mr. King is in favor of it. Mr. Roosevelt is in favor of it. The State of New York is in favor of it. Earl Rowe is in favor of it.' Mitch Hepburn was the 'last stumbling block' in its way. If the taxpayers wanted to saddle the province with another hundred million dollars of debt, elect Earl Rowe, the friend of the power barons, who would buy the original 440,000 horsepower from Quebec and develop another million on the St Lawrence. If the railwaymen in Belleville and St Thomas wanted to lose their jobs, then vote for 'this unnecessary new avenue of transportation.' The choice was theirs.[34]

Time put the crusader against Lewis and the CIO on its cover. The story pictured the election 'not so much as a contest between parties as the sort of plebiscite staged by a Dictator when he wants the blanket approval of the people for all his measures.' It was very much Mitch's campaign. Despite his summer illness he managed to regain his strength and maintained a feverish pace for seven weeks on the hustings. He had put on weight since 1934, but he was still the magnet that drew large and enthusiastic crowds to the fifty meetings he held in as many days, many of them broadcast over local radio or province-wide hookups. He endured the record-breaking heat wave without visible strain as he criss-crossed southern Ontario by car and enjoyed his forays into the north in Harry Maclean's Dominion Construction seaplane.

Although Mitch had spearheaded the campaign, there was a powerful organization behind him. From the central bureau in the King Eddy, Harry Johnson had been in touch with the ridings since the spring, giving local organizations a timetable for checking the voting lists and selecting poll captains. Throughout the campaign, a deluge of handbills outlined the Liberal largesse in each riding, while from hundreds of posters a smiling Mitch promised more of the same. In the last weeks, the Liberals saturated almost every newspaper in the province with its advertisements and a cartoon of Rowe and the Old Gang in The Rowe Boat over the caption 'You Just *Think* You're Steering Earl.'

The only distance between Queen's Park and the King Eddy was the mile from College to King. By August, local members and candidates were being allocated temporary jobs. Candidates had lists of people receiving old age pensions, mothers allowances, and other benefits but were told to use them discreetly. After three years in office the Liberals had built up their own network, and for every riding there was a patronage list for insurance, printing and advertising, and a wide variety of supplies and services from butchers and bakers to men's clothing. In April, McQuesten had unveiled a $10 million highway program, and there were few ridings where men were not busy on the roads during the summer and fall. From St Thomas, Pete Birdsall reminded Mitch that the Aylmer voters would be happier if he paved 'about a mile south of Aylmer on the Port Bruce road as well as three miles north this summer and fall.' Elgin had already been given new bridges at Port Stanley, Vienna and New Sarum, as well as a mental hospital, a home training school for girls, and a high school at Aylmer. But early in September the men were at work on the Port Bruce road.[36]

As early as the spring of 1935, Frank O'Connor had been at work to have 'a good fund of a million in hand' for the next provincial election, and on the eve of the election, Paul Nathanson had told King that the methods Mitch used 'to obtain money for his party would shame Tammany itself.' Bethune Smith, the party treasurer, and Bill Bennett, recruited again as collector and distributor, could count on the customary percentages from contractors and timber wolves and tangible expressions of gratitude from businessmen and financiers for Mitch's stand against the CIO. The president of Chrysler was not the only executive to tell Mitch that he hoped the people would appreciate 'the magnificent things you have done.' Clifford Sifton was 'strong' for Mitch. Dunn said he was prepared to go into the Algoma mill and tell every man that he owed his job to Mitch Hepburn. Lord Rothmere, trying to unravel the Abitibi mess, wanted Mitch to know how much he admired him 'as the only man in Canada with enough guts to stand up to the C.I.O.' And the word from François, the maitre'd at the Waldorf Astoria, was that 'everyone with whom he has talked says that you will sweep in again.' There were, of course, the usual charges of a toll-gate, and Rowe said, but did not prove, he had evidence. The *Globe* reported that the Hotelmen's Association was collecting funds 'to protect the continuity of their business' and the manager of the Royal Connaught in Hamilton admitted that while they had been collecting on a gallonage basis, 'there have been as yet no political contributions.'[37]

The most persistent rumour was that Beauharnois and other Quebec and American power companies were financing Mitch's campaign. Despite all the rumours and the whispered insider knowledge, neither the Tories nor the CCF could unearth a scrap of evidence to document the charge that Mitch received money from the power companies or anti-CIO interests in the United States. Indeed, they were unable to trace a penny of Bethune Smith's ample supplies.[38]

Whatever the source, there was no doubt about the munificence. Although local candidates raised some of the money, most of it, said to be $5,000 for each riding, came from the central fund. There were no complaints, as there had been in 1934, that the ridings were starved for funds. In fact, claimed Don Hogarth, the Liberals 'could not spend all the money that was handed to their organization.'[39]

Mitch also enjoyed a relatively good press. The only major paper to support the Tories aggressively was P.D. Ross's Ottawa *Journal*. The Toronto *Telegram* found it impossible to support Rowe's labour policy, and traditional Tory papers such as the Hamilton *Spectator* and the London *Free Press* remained more or less neutral. Despite Atkinson's contempt for Hepburn, the *Star* reluctantly endorsed the Liberals. Although relations between Mitch and McCullagh were never the same after he returned from England to find that his pet non-partisan scheme had been aborted, McCullagh had also decided by the end of August to support Mitch. 'The political campaign is starting to warm up here and neither candidate is fit to be the premier of a pub,' he wrote Eddie Wooliver contemptuously. 'However, of the two evils we have to choose the lesser, and time will tell the wisdom of our course.'[40]

The support that Mitch did not need, or even want, was that of King and the federal Liberals. King had returned from England early in July to find his party deeply divided after Mitch's declaration of independence and anxiously waiting for him to provide some guidance. The cabinet agreed on a 'local option' policy, with support for Mitch not to be taken as disloyalty to King. Ian Mackenzie went to see Mitch. He reported that Mitch did not want the support of the federal cabinet ministers and advised King that they should maintain 'an attitude of complete aloofness at the present time. I would even go further than we decided the other day and recommend that no Federal Minister take part in the coming campaign.'

When Mitch dissolved, King immediately cancelled all his political picnics in Ontario and said he would follow his usual practice and take no part in the provincial campaign. But federal Liberals in Ontario did not have that luxury, for with their own re-election a year or two away, they realized only too well that although Mitch may not have been the spiritual leader of Ontario Liberalism, he was undoubtedly the political boss. Most of the MPs worked for the provincial candidates and before the campaign was over every Ontario minister had spoken, however faintly, in his own riding.[41]

There was nothing faint about the support of Gardiner and Ian Mackenzie. Speaking for Colin Campbell, Gardiner was fullsome in his praise of Mitch. 'You know and I know that Hepburn did not join General Motors against labour during that strike – he joined General Motors against Lewis and lawlessness. The lawlessness of Michigan and Illinois never got beyond Sarnia.' The brief reports in the *Star* and *Telegram* ended there, but a fuller report by Gordon W. Fowley in the *Globe* quoted Gardiner as stating: 'Your Government in the first few days of trouble at Oshawa thought Ottawa should become more active. Ottawa disagreed. Mr. Hepburn did not wait to fight out the fine point with Ottawa, but took charge of the situation in his own energetic manner, using all the powers our federated form of government gave him. Criticize his methods if you like, but results speak louder than criticism.' The next day Ian Mackenzie stood shoulder to shoulder with Mitch in St Thomas to praise him as the 'fearless champion' of law and order and to tell a province-wide radio audience that the Liberal party was one hundred per cent behind him.[42]

It was too much for Norman Rogers, who stormed out to Kingsmere and threatened to resign unless King repudiated Gardiner. King admitted that he was surprised at Gardiner's statement, but argued that to make an issue of it would 'only play into the hands of Hepburn, etc ... & I wd. be given the credit of being the one really responsible.' Gardiner claimed to have been misquoted and the cabinet agreed to let the matter rest. However, the incident increased the pressure on King to make his position clear to counter Tory claims that the federal Liberals wanted Mitch defeated. King believed he had gone a 'good way' by telling the press he intended to vote for Paul Leduc and letting his sister Jennie have Mitch and Dr Simpson to dinner in Barrie, but he confided his true feelings to his diary:

He will pay for the attack he made before this campaign is over. He has never retracted what he said about being against myself, not being a 'Mackenzie King Liberal, which he hoped I wd. hear' & which I have heard, & been perfectly silent about. It is for him to say he is what he wants to be, but not to expect me to ask the people of Ontario to return him as head of a Liberal Govt. meanwhile. Rogers thinks Gardiner is ruthless, very ambitious & wd. be disloyal to win his own ends. – I doubt that. I believe however that Mackenzie & Power are Hepburn men & Gardiner is listening in, to be as far as he can "on all sides" – but I believe he is loyal to me. If there is treachery, I shall certainly go out to meet it, but will be cautious & take the right moment. Meanwhile I have no reason to think that any of my colleagues are in a conspiracy.

King did want to see Mitch defeated. But when he reluctantly concluded Mitch would win, self-interest dictated that he be on the winning side. Mitch's comment at Collingwood on 4 October that despite their difference over the CIO, King had done 'a tremendous amount of good for the country' eased his conscience. After the cabinet meeting on 5 October, King told reporters that he did not want to see a Tory government in Queen's Park.

I felt it was unwise to leave this till after tomorrow's results & permit it to be said that I had allowed the Tories to capitalize [on] my feelings against Hepburn, – should he lose I would be blamed for it, should he win I would get no thanks for any part taken in the campaign & emphasis wd. be placed for all time on not having helped – tho the battle was a Liberal one. My duty as Leader of the Party for all Canada is to heal its divisions, keep it united & as a Christian to forgive, to heap coals of fire if need be on my enemies head ... I feel it is right to have shown my colours, unmistakably, – the party will appreciate it, & as the Fed. leader I owe it to the party to do this.

His dream that night confirmed that 'I was right, had been magnanimous, done the right thing, – that I had helped to heal a breach, & helped politically at a moment when help might be necessary.' Only King believed that his election-eve repentance or his sister Jennie's hospitality would win many votes for Mitch.[43]

The Conservative platform was an enlightened pot-pourri of promises to aid almost every occupation and region, but there were too many of the old guard around for it to sound convincing. Mitch and the press generally ignored it, and even the Tories found attacking Mitch and his millionaire friends more congenial. Before it was over the Tory campaign had degenerated into an almost hysterical attack on what the Frost brothers labelled 'HEPBURNISM.' In three years at Queen's Park, Cecil Frost told a province-wide radio audience, Hepburn had hoisted the black flag of repudiation, preached class hatred, destroyed the morale of the civil service with his vicious patronage system, and encouraged disrespect for the courts and the law.

He fanned into flames the smoldering fires of religious animosity, by interjecting the school question into party politics, causing boys and girls who had grown up together to walk on opposite sides of the street. Under Mr. Hepburn's leadership the Legislature has fallen into the lowest state of dignity ever known. The amenities of public life have been degraded. We have had government by whim, by moods, by tantrums, and often violence.[44]

Rowe had believed that his labour policy would swing the labour vote to the Tories. After weeks of equivocation, during which Drew had resigned, he had outlined the policy in a speech at Arthur on 5 May. A Conservative government would insist on 'the maintenance of law and order in all industrial disputes,' Rowe promised, but would also guarantee 'the right of employees to bargain collectively through their own representatives chosen by workers through the medium of a secret ballot free from improper influence, coercion or intimidation.' The role of government was not to take sides, but 'to maintain law and order without the display of unnecessary force.' The statement was far milder than many Tories would have liked, while others were dismayed by his refusal to exclude CIO unions from his collective bargaining process.[45]

On the eve of the election, Don Hogarth warned Rowe that he was courting disaster. The province of Ontario was overwhelmingly British, he observed, and 'definitely against anything which savors of disrespect for the law.' And the CIO, 'rightly or wrongly, is classified in the minds of the people as a lawless, outlaw organization.' However enlightened, Rowe's policy marked him as a CIO sympathizer, while Mitch Hepburn was 'earmarked as the "Defender of the Faith"'. Mitch's courageous stance, he continued, 'has obliterated all other factors and considerations. *So much so, in fact, that I say without hesitation that he will sweep the Province if this is to be the issue on which the Election will be fought.*' Hogarth begged him to 'clarify' his position and condemn the CIO, and remember 'that wherever I use the phrase "c.i.o." I mean Communism. The general public have got it in their minds that the two are associated and the fact that there is no substance to this impression cannot be got over to the public.' But throughout the campaign Rowe insisted on 'the right of the toiler to join the union of his choice and not the union Mr. Hepburn and Mr. McCullagh may say he should join.' There were many Tories in cities hit by the epidemic of strikes, like those in Peterborough, who were 'frothing at the mouth over Earl's stand on the c.i.o.' and Mitch remained the undisputed Defender of the Faith.[46]

Mitch was the issue in the Tory campaign, but they needed someone with more power and imagination than Rowe to find the jugular. 'Poor Rowe stumbled along, doing his utmost, but effecting nothing,' one Tory lamented. 'And all the time, day and night, the air was filled with the same stuff, droned out in the same unimpressive way.' While Mitch sounded strong and convincing on radio, Rowe was 'halting, sounding anything but logical. For tens of thousands of electors, whose only acquaintance with Mr. Rowe was a radio acquaintance, these faults were fatal.' And there was not enough Tory money to compensate for the fatal flaws. The traditional sources had dried up and the party found it difficult, Don Hogarth claimed, 'to find sufficient funds to carry on a skeleton campaign. In fact, if it had not been for a couple of Conservative Dervishes, the campaign would have fallen flat from the lack of financial support.'[47]

If the Tories failed to dent Mitch's armour, the CCF only skirmished on a distant front. If 'we miss this election seriously,' Graham Spry wrote to Frank Underhill on the eve of the election, 'I see nothing but years of a CCF that like a wounded snake drags its slow length along.' If not an accurate prediction of the future, it was an apt description of the party's impotence in the campaign. The CCF lacked a solid base in the older trade unions, and had stood helplessly by as the communists ran many of the new unions and skilfully penetrated the local trades and labour councils. As David Lewis, the national secretary, wrote, the 'crux of the matter is that the people in Toronto simply don't seem to get the significance of the present development in the working-class movement.' With the 'political consciousness' of the trade unionists 'being fostered, inspired, developed, led and naturally used by the Communists,' he lamented, 'you have another reason why the hidebound partisan C.C.F.'er will be cautious and ineffective.'

A federation of meetings, rather than an organization, the party had not devised a strategy to combat the communist-directed United Front movement, and while the 1936 national convention had decisively rejected any form of political collaboration there were many in Ontario who believed that to stand aloof would hand the leadership of the working class to the communists. When Mitch called the election, theoretical questions suddenly became matters of immediate and practical tactics, which left the CCF spending more time fighting the communists than helping Rowe nail Mitch's hide to the wall.[48]

Cautious and ineffective they were. Although their platform roundly denounced Mitch for his 'parade of storm troopers' and boldly promised compulsory negotiations with representatives of unions freely chosen by the workers, 'including international organizers,' once the campaign began, CCF speakers were told not to be drawn out on the CIO issue. Moreover, the initiative was seized and retained by the communists who proposed a united Farmer-Labour Party and easily gained control of the labour representation committees formed by local trades and labour councils to select labour candidates. The CCF constitution prohibited the official endorsation of communist candidates, but many agreed with David Lewis that the CCF should cooperate to gain a foothold in the trade unions. Others, including J.S. Woodsworth, agreed with the Ontario organizer, E.B. Jolliffe, that the communists could not be trusted and that cooperation would be 'politically suicidal.'

Internally divided and without an overall strategy, CCF tactics ranged from open war to covert cooperation. By 5 October the CCF had only thirty-nine candidates in the field, while the communists ran six as Farmer-Labour and about a dozen, including Joe Salsberg and George Anderson, the CIO organizer in Sudbury, under Labour banners. Only Salsberg caused the Liberals much anxiety, and the controversial decision of the CCF to run a candidate against him in St Andrew delighted Toronto Liberals.[49]

The loose canon who ran the Catholic Taxpayers' Association was more menacing than the communists or the CCF, and unless he was tied down Mitch faced the prospect of more East Hastings across Protestant Ontario. Quinn warned Nixon in June that if they expected that 'the Heenans, McGuires, O'Connors and others among our people who have attained some political prominence will be able to whip the Catholic vote into line' without a firm commitment on taxation, they were in for a 'rather rude awakening.' Frank O'Connor called Quinn at once to say that Mitch, although 'unwilling to make any definite commitment, had assured him that if we would say nothing and would take no action, he would treat us generously after the election.' Outraged, Quinn was prepared to sound the call to arms when he was told that the hierarchy would call him off.[50]

The hierarchy clearly did not want more East Hastings. As Quinn fumed restlessly, Archbishop O'Brien warned him that 'prudence and caution' were essential and no action should be taken until 'after very careful consideration on the part of all concerned.' On 2 September, the bishops met in Ottawa and decided that 'Catholic papers and organizations should not discuss the school question during the election as no good can come of it and our enemies might gladly seize upon anything said to make this an election issue.' However, if the schools question became an issue Catholics would defend their position, but the archbishops, not Quinn, would be in charge.[51]

The schools question was an issue. 'Today and together we must think of and act for a united, British, English-speaking Canada,' trumpeted the manifesto of the Orange Order. 'To-morrow may be too late; the enemy is at the gate.' Tory candidates pounded the Protestant drum. The issue in the East Hastings by-election, Rowe said at Madoc, was 'the same issue Ontario is considering this fall' and Hepburn owed the voters 'if not a full explanation of his trickery in the past, at least some indication of his policy on this issue in the future.'[52]

Mitch's continued silence convinced Quinn that the Catholics had to force him 'out into the open.' Although McGuigan and Kidd agreed, O'Brien cautioned the archbishop that 'the Conservatives have not resorted to their tactics used in East Hastings, but let Mr. Quinn say a word and I have no doubt that the woods would be fired and with as much success as in East Hastings.' Quinn was finally persuaded to remain silent, only to sneer later that the bishops were men 'whose valor is nine parts discretion.' Albert Murphy passed on the good news to Mitch. The Catholics 'are prepared to sacrifice what present advantage or benefit might come form a public appeal,' he wrote, 'and are prepared to risk the suspicion that they are failing, at this time, to push their claims as vigorously as may be, rather than precipitate a religious issue.' But that decision, he assured Mitch, was 'dictated by the continued trust in yourself and your Government, inspired by your efforts in 1936 and your words on the occasion of the repeal of Bill 138.'[53]

In the last days of the campaign the religious issue was stripped of its modest veil. The Ontario Public School Defence League, secretly organized by the Tories, began an advertising campaign to convince public school supporters that the only issue was 'Hepburn's Attempt to Disrupt Our Public School System. DO NOT BE MISLED, HE TRICKED YOU IN 1934 DO NOT GIVE HIM A CHANCE TO DO IT AGAIN! Vote Conservative.' By the end of September a chain letter was spreading like 'wildfire' across the province.

The challenge is now before you – Hepburn has made another agreement with the Roman Catholic School Taxpayers Association – Re-elect Hepburn candidates and he will amend the Assessment Act to satisfy Roman Catholic Separate School Supporters demands.

Irrespective of your past political affiliation, the fight today is, – 'Will Rome be permitted to control Ontario as it does Quebec? 'There is no middle course. YOU are with Hepburn and the Roman Catholics of Ontario or you are against them and their Sectarian Schools.

Mitch and Duplessis, 12 August 1938: two 'incipient dictators' in the onion patch

'On to Ottawa': with King and Woodstock,
12 August 1935

OPPOSITE

'There is no road too rough, nor night too dark for me to travel
carrying the message of Liberalism.'

'There you have the promise of one,' said King, 'who will be second to
none in furthering the policies of Liberalism throughout the country.'

A cast of two, a crowd of thousands

The 1937 election: the challenge

'One issue emerges of transcendent importance – HEPBURNISM …
We have had government by whim, by moods, by tantrums, and
often violence.'

OPPOSITE

The result, 6 October 1937

Election night on Talbot Street – and King Street, Toronto, outside
the *Globe and Mail*

Queen's Park, 17 April 1937: 'I'll have no more remote control' of the
Oshawa strike, Mitch tells reporters with Harry Nixon beside him.

Birthdays, the beauty of nature, and 'pressure from millionaires,'
12 August 1938
Front row (left to right): Bickell's pilot, Judge D.C. Ross of St Thomas,
Larry McGuinness, Maurice Duplessis, McLean's pilot.
Second row: Isaac Ilslev (contractor for the St Thomas mental hospital),
Maggie, Eva, Peter, Mitch, Patsy, Harry McLean, Bill Tapsell.
Back row: D.A. McIntyre (manager of the St Thomas employment
office), Harry Johnson, Colin Campbell, L.H. Dingman, and L.B.
Birdsall of the *Times-Journal*. Dunn and Bickell were busy when the
photo was taken.

Three reasons for returning to farm and family

Beyond politics: 'listening to the grass grow'

Are the traditions of your forefathers and heritage which we should hand down in our Public School worth 30 c/ to you?

If they are, copy this letter at least 10 times* and 3 c/-sealed mail them, within the next 24 hours, to Public School supporters in Ontario and remember your duty Oct 6.

If you delay or fail us in this invisible chain of united Protestant effort and the Roman Catholic minority again got support from enough indifferent Protestants to elect sufficient Hepburn candidates, you can be prepared for further concessions and greater diversion of taxes to the Roman Catholic Separate Schools at the expense of the Public School supporters of this province.

Your Protestant Friend

*Oftener if you
can afford it

No one claimed authorship, although the finger of suspicion inevitably pointed to the Orange Order or the Public School Defence League. However, the Liberals put it to good use. One French-language newspaper included the letter in a special edition which it sent to Franco-Ontarians across the province. 'Whoever got that letter out was responsible for the loss of 4 northern seats,' exclaimed the defeated Tory in Manitoulin, where the Liberals had placed a copy in every Catholic home, 'and I would personally like to have the pleasure of shooting him at dawn.' The letter was so effective in marshalling support for Mitch that the Frost brothers concluded it probably had a Liberal origin. As unlikely as that was, the chain letter was certainly a useful reminder to the Catholics that the Tories were not their friends.[54]

Mitch had left the assault on Tory Toronto until the last weekend. With all the local Liberal candidates except Roebuck on the platform behind him and thousands listening to loudspeakers outside, Mitch contrasted the glories of his administration with the pitiful ineptitude of the Tories under Henry and Rowe. Again he linked communism and the CIO, boasting that had it not been for his show of force, fifteen thousand Reds from Toronto and Hamilton could have intervened in Oshawa and started trouble in other cities as well. Although Earl Rowe denounced him, Mitch was convinced that if 'a bunch of lawless thugs went down to take control of Mr. Rowe's farm, including his horse Spark Plug, he would be the first to call for help.' Mackenzie King turned off the radio and commented wearily: 'It is a pity that the affairs of a great province should be administered with so little dignity and real ability. – He will win, probably handsomely.'[55]

Mitch did not have to go to Oshawa, but after considerable discussion among the party strategists he willingly agreed to enter the 'den of lions.' Gordon Conant's campaign manager recruited 'a bunch of strong men from Toronto' to handle the hecklers and, after his speech, an escort 'comprising Conachers, Admiral Sharpe and all the big men we can find' was to get him safely to his car. The precautions were wise. Tumultuous boos and cheers greeted him when he entered the Armouries. As he walked down the aisle behind a piper, one of the overloaded platforms collapsed sending three hundred people crashing to the floor or precariously clinging to the grill work along the wall. When order was restored, Mitch fought an hour-long battle with a crowd divided between very vocal supporters and equally determined hecklers. 'I'm game,' he shouted over the bedlam. 'I can stay here all afternoon. I say this exhibition of rowdyism is not only a terrific indictment against Oshawa, but will do more to elect Gordon Conant tomorrow than anything else.' Mitch did not make much ground, but he lost none. From Oshawa, he drove to Galt and Kitchener for his last speeches of the campaign. It was long after midnight when he arrived at Bannockburn.[56]

Mitch slept late on 6 October and it was early afternoon before he and Eva drove to Union to vote. He had not spent much time campaigning in Elgin. But with over ten years as a member, the hard work of Eva and his organization, and the visible signs of his largesse, he expected to be more than a match for Norman Martin, the wealthy Tory dairy farmer, or John Tough who, with the aid of J.S. Woodsworth and M.J. Coldwell, solicited the support of the railway workers. He showed no signs of anxiety as he spent the afternoon showing his prize Percherons to the assembly of journalists and, despite Liberal sceptics, still felt that his boast of winning seventy-four seats would not be wide of the mark. After an early supper, he and Eva again went to the kitchen at the back of the Masonic Auditorium. Outside on Talbot Street the crowd gathered early to celebrate another Hepburn triumph.

Mitch danced excitedly around the room as the first returns from St Thomas showed that he was increasing his majority among the railwaymen, a happy omen for other heavily unionized centres. A few minutes later the early returns from Brantford assured MacBride's re-election. With Simpson retaining a slender lead over Rowe in Simcoe Centre, he was ecstatic – 'Tell the boys outside.

Tell them the old rowboat is going down.' There were some disappointments. Leeds was rediscovering its Tory allegiance, and Mitch's good friend George Fulford was biting the dust. Duncan Marshall was not holding off the popular Tom Kennedy in Peel and Leslie Frost was running well ahead in Victoria. And even with all the resources of the government and the party, Colin Campbell was not shaking the fifty-year Tory hold on Addington. But the early returns from the north showed that francophones had remained solid and Catholics had not wavered in their allegiance. Industrial Ontario was going heavily Liberal, as Peterborough deserted the Tories and Hamilton East the CCF. Rowe conceded defeat before nine.

The cliff-hangers were in Toronto. Many ridings see-sawed back and forth all night. Not until after the recounts would it be clear that Lionel Conacher could hold his lead of a dozen votes or that John Glass would survive Joe Salsberg's effective campaign among the workers and ethnic minorities in the south end of St Andrew. But by morning Toronto was no longer Tory. The Liberals had won seven of the thirteen seats and split with the Conservatives in the four Yorks.

When it was all over, the Liberals had captured sixty-four seats, including those of Croll and Roebuck, and had not contested three won by Liberal Progressives and the United Farmers. Mitch had lost six seats; the Tories were returned with twenty-three. The Liberal popular vote had increased slightly to 51 per cent; the Tories held at 41 per cent as their increased support in rural ridings balanced their losses in the cities. The CCF had not won a seat and lost almost a third of its support, some of which undoubtedly went to candidates running under the Farmer-Labour or other extreme left-wing banners.[57]

King's dream that night was 'a vision of the forces that had helped Hepburn to victory – good fellows, mining interests, drinking & its associations – underground methods in politics – play *against* the U.S., – Gladstonian tradition thrown to the winds etc., – a real merry-go-round, – perhaps it is.' But the victory deserved and received a more secular analysis. Although such issues as the CIO, the battle against the big interests, and the balanced budget played an important part, King also conceded that much was due to Mitch himself. 'People believe he is honest; know he is fearless; and regard him as efficient in Administration. His manners, evidently, as well, catches the man on the street. – It is the "fellows" that count & he is one of them in language and spirit.' With Mitch's continued access to campaign funds, King was afraid that he would 'seek to control the province federally as well as provincially from that source – mining interests, etc., etc.' The victory also forced King to speculate about the future:

Whether it will strengthen Hepburn at expense of myself, in federal field, remains to be seen. It is natural younger men may wish to take hold of federal arena, but I imagine the party as whole will not want a change in Leadership at Ottawa, tho' formation of Cabinet for next campaign, may involve some change & bringing in new blood from the provinces. I will be responsible to the will & wish of the party, – but will tolerate no treachery or treason, should I ever have evidence of such. Meanwhile I do not propose to undermine my peace by suspicion –

But the pathological suspicion would not go away, and that afternoon, as the cabinet discussed the Ontario election, King confessed that he was 'struck by the lack of frankness of Mackenzie & Power. I am inclined to feel they have an understanding with Hepburn, & that we shall see an effort to get younger men in control, a sort of Toronto group – however it will not be easy to break up the party that is behind me, & much water will have to run under the bridge first.' The crown rested more uneasily after 6 October.[58]

'We are ready for the fight'

There was general approval of the cabinet Mitch took to Chorley Park to be sworn in on the evening of 12 October. Gordon Conant, the new attorney general, had a reputation of judicious, if stodgy, reliability. Harold Kirby, a Toronto lawyer and a power in caucus, succeeded Faulkner in Health. Catholics and farmers applauded the appointment of Patrick Dewan of Woodstock in Agriculture. Morrison MacBride, the Brantford veteran, was a popular choice for Labour. Eric Cross, the bright but abrasive thirty-three year-old Osgoode graduate, brought several years' experience as chairman of the Ontario Municipal Board to the Department of Municipal Affairs and Public Welfare. William Houck of Niagara Falls and Arthur St Clair Gordon from Kent West became Hydro commissioners and sat in the cabinet as ministers without portfolio. Those who knew Mitch were not surprised that he appointed his good friend Colin Campbell to Public Works, despite his defeat, and those who knew Campbell had little doubt that he would not overlook the interests of the party in his administration of the department.

Mitch's most difficult task was to find some suitable reward for Duncan Marshall. With the vacant Ontario senatorship apparently committed, Marshall envied the lieutenant-governor's box at the Royal Winter Fair, a position for which his lack of refinement and sorry personal finances ill equipped him. However, although King was aware of Mitch's commitment to close Chorley Park when Bruce's term expired at the end of October, he had informed Bruce a week before the election that he intended to extend his term by at least a year unless Hepburn disagreed, in which case he could 'further consider the matter.' A letter from King making his proposal was on Mitch's desk when he returned after the election. Angered by such an obvious and unnecessary pre-emptive move,

Mitch replied that he would not endorse Bruce's extension and intended to close the residence. If King wanted a nominee, Mitch recommended Duncan Marshall.[1]

Suitably aghast at the thought of Marshall representing the crown, King brought the proposal to cabinet. To his dismay, his colleagues on the whole 'thought it should be done as a first request from Hepburn Govt. with their new authority, *& fearing* the consequences if it weren't. I decided the first thing would be to make Hepburn declare that Govt. House would be closed – then to make Ont. Ministers take the responsibility of writing on the apptmt.' However, Mitch was not really pressing Marshall's appointment, for he knew he would 'be like a bull in a china shop,' and sent word privately to King that if he would appoint the deserving Marshall to the Senate he would agree to an extension for Bruce, after which Chorley Park would be sold.[2]

King immediately concluded Mitch's offer put him 'in this matter, just where I am glad to have him' and embarked on a course that only he seemed to understand. Privately, he was prepared to send Marshall to the Senate 'as I think he might really be of help & service to us there & wd. know he owed his appointment to me.' But he neglected to inform Mitch or his cabinet. A week later he continued his devious course when he saw Mitch in Toronto. It was, he confessed, 'a day of agony in the garden. The call on Hepburn in the morning – the entirely different attitude towards myself by Hepburn – My photograph removed from his desk, from the side of Sir Wilfrid no doubt, this done with some oath that I was no longer his Leader and intent to "betray" me at some time – .'

In what King described as a 'stormy' meeting, the two men ranged over Mitch's grievances against King's ministers for an hour before turning to the matter at hand. King was bewilderingly evasive. Instead of telling Mitch he would appoint Marshall in the Senate, he said only that while his colleagues did not believe Chorley Park should be closed or that Marshall was a suitable vice-regal appointment, he was prepared to make him lieutenant-governor if Mitch wished. Seated beside Angela Bruce that night at dinner, King spent most of the time 'running down Hepburn,' sneering that a 'black dog' could have beaten Henry in 1934, and urging them 'to stick it out.'[3]

A few days later George McCullagh appealed to Mitch on behalf of the Bruces. He reported that Mitch 'let off very badly on King's treatment of him, and said he was through with him. He had never done a thing to help him, and he would never ask him to do any thing again.' However, they persuaded Mitch to agree that if King sent Marshall to the Senate and Bruce remained, he would keep Chorley Park open. Informed of Mitch's position, the governor general, Lord Tweedsmuir, passed on the message to King. Although King told Tweedsmuir that Mitch had never asked him to send Marshall to the Senate, he finally agreed, in view of his 'qualifications for the position,' to send Marshall to the Red Chamber at some later date and reappoint Bruce. If Mitch closed Chorley Park, however, he would appoint Marshall as lieutenant-governor. Tweedsmuir advised Bruce of King's response on 30 October, but Mitch had left that weekend on an extended hunting trip. McCullagh planned to inform Mitch of King's agreement when he returned to Toronto on 15 November. Mitch did not return as expected, however, and that morning the staff told Bruce that because the appropriations had run out on 31 October there was no money for light bulbs or chimney cleaning. Bruce resigned.[4]

Whatever his object, King's strange diplomacy had failed, and he immediately sought to escape the public disapproval of Marshall's appointment. Without communicating with Mitch, he offered the position to Leighton McCarthy, Senator Hardy, and finally to Albert Mathews. When Mathews accepted, King sent a very reluctant Jack Elliott to Queen's Park. Elliott phoned King the next day and told him that 'Hepburn would not yield on apptmt. of Marshall, intended to close Govt. House, had had a row with McCullagh of the *Globe*, said *Globe* was not going to run the Govt. & insisted on Marshall being made Lieut. Govr.' Although Elliott urged him to back down, King refused, 'regardless of the consequences,' and later in the day, when Elliott reported no progress, told him that 'if Marshall did not fall in line & help us, he wd. get neither the Lieut. Govr. ship nor the Senate.' The ultimatum worked and Mitch called to say that Marshall would accept a seat in the Senate. A few weeks later the furniture in Chorley Park was moved to the Speaker's chambers and cabinet ministers' offices. Mackenzie King admitted that he 'should not be sorry to see the social set that think Govt. House their preserve, given a blow or a shock,' and he was mainly responsible for closing Chorley Park. As King said, it was an opéra bouffe, and he had written the score.[5]

More serious than the comic opera was the final act of the Beauharnois drama. Fresh from his success in preserving untarnished the image of the crown, Mackenzie King took up the defence of parliamentary government against the fascistic tyranny of an accomplice in an international power conspiracy. Mitch was not aware that his request for a federal licence to export power could become a drama of such profound ideological significance.

Nor was he aware that his relations with Mackenzie King would dominate the rest of his political career. Mitch's overwhelming victory had done nothing to diminish the arrogance and impetuosity that even his friends were finding increasingly distasteful. With his position as leader of the country's premier province so solidly confirmed, Mitch was even less willing than before to accept King's preeminence in either the country or the party. The election also seemed to have deepened King's implacable hostility, even hatred, and he seemed determined to cut Mitch off at every pass.

Mitch had waited two weeks after the election before requesting Lyon's resignation, for 'we must now shape our course for the future,' and another ten days before appointing Dr Thomas Hogg as chairman of the Hydro Commission. But even before Hogg's appointment the broad parameters of a settlement were being discussed in Montreal. George Montgomery of Beauharnois recalled having heard on 16 October that Bethune Smith was in Montreal trying to 'work out some scheme by which Beauharnois power could be exported to Niagara Hudson through the medium of the Ontario contract.' On 26 October the directors of Gatineau, told to expect such a request from Hydro, removed one obstacle to a settlement when they agreed in principle to postpone delivery of some of their power in return for a longer term contract 'if it does not cost too much to get it.'[6]

There were no surprises when Hogg met R.A.C. Henry of Beauharnois on 4 November. Hogg did not have to tell Henry that the transmission lines from Chat's Fall and the physical facilities at Leaside could only handle an additional 70,000 horsepower from all Quebec sources. Henry also knew that the line from Beauharnois to Chat's Falls, where the power was fed into the 25-cycle grid, could only carry an additional 125,000 horsepower unless Beauharnois built another transmission line. It was also true that in the short term Hydro did not need additional power. The problems seemed insurmountable. Yet when Henry reported to the bondholders committee the next day they quickly authorized him to pursue negotiations with Hydro. The journey to the Judicial Committee was postponed.[7]

The export of surplus power through the Hydro contract was a key factor in Hogg's negotiations with Beauharnois. The solution, for problems on both sides, was for Hydro to become a de facto part of the interlocking private power community in Quebec and the United States. The three large Quebec companies – Montreal Light, Heat and Power (which owned Beauharnois), J.E. Aldred's Shawinigan, and Saguenay, owned by the Canadian subsidiary of the Aluminum Company of America – were closely bound together by transmission lines and the interlocking directorates that reflected investment and control. Largely through the Aluminum Company (ALCOA) they were also linked to Niagara Hudson, which controlled 90 per cent of the power in New York.[8]

By 1937 both ALCOA at Massena and Niagara Hudson needed power and the Quebec companies had a surplus. In April Duplessis had reversed Quebec policy and approved an application from Montreal Power to export 40,000 horsepower. The company then requested an export licence from Ottawa. King persuaded the cabinet to reject the application 'notwithstanding Duplessis govt. had given consent, until Parliament had a chance to consider the whole question & reviewed it anew. This means I put all the big interests – the Beauharnois crowd of Montreal at bay, – and in their place. They will find they cannot force my hand.' What King had in mind was a strategy to avoid direct responsibility for a decision on power exports. The 1907 legislation had given cabinet the power to license exports. A private member's bill to make Parliament the regulatory body had passed the Commons in the 1927–8 session, but had been defeated in the Senate. Claiming that Parliament really had spoken, King planned to place the responsibility in Parliament through the medium of a private member's bill, thus avoiding overt responsibility but retaining political control whenever he chose to exercise it.[9]

When Mitch returned from the north on 18 November, Hogg had outlined the terms of a settlement with Beauharnois and asked Mitch to secure King's permission to export 120,000 horsepower to Niagara Hudson and Alcoa. Mitch had discussed the matter with Jack Elliott during the Marshall negotiations and Elliott returned to Ottawa with Mitch's request for an early meeting with the cabinet. King realized that it would be 'a most contentious matter' and, with his nerves 'all on edge,' decided not to attend cabinet when Mitch's request was discussed. Since cabinet was well aware of his position, King was relieved but not surprised to learn that, without turning Mitch down, Lapointe had persuaded his colleagues that the wisest tactic would be to ask Mitch to communicate his reasons 'in detail' instead of coming to Ottawa. When Euler informed him of the decision, Mitch immediately called King and demanded a meeting before King left for Florida two days later. King reluctantly put off his vacation for a day so that Mitch could not say 'that we had refused even to hear him.'[10]

Mitch arrived on the morning train on 29 November, took a room at the Chateau, and faced King and ten of his cabinet at noon. He explained that permission to export would enable him to settle with Beauharnois and end the possibility of losing before the Judicial Committee, recover the cost of the surplus power, and even provide Dunning with some additional revenue. King followed with a long history of the export question designed to show that it was really a question for Parliament to decide. Despite McCullagh's advice to remain cool, Mitch became impatient and angry and 're-quired a little cooling down from one or two of the Ministers.' His request was 'a matter of business' crucial for his government, while King's long lecture was 'a matter of mere words.' After forty-five minutes of heated discussion, Mitch concluded that he was wasting his time. Demanding a formal decision before he caught the three o'clock train, he returned to his room at the Chateau. As he left the room, Mitch snapped that Duplessis was far more accommodating than King and warned that if it came to an open fight, the people and the MPs from Ontario would back him, not King.

The cabinet was sharply divided. Fortunately for King, three ministers – Elliott, Mackenzie, and Gardiner – who might have supported Mitch were not in town. But Crerar, Power, Cardin, Euler, and Michaud believed it was politically astute to meet Mitch's request. Even Dunning, to King's dismay, sat on the fence. Only Lapointe, Ilsley, Rogers, and Rinfret were firmly on his side. After his mini-lecture on the cabinet being the servant of Parliament, King somehow concluded that since support for Mitch had been 'to say the least equivocal,' he 'proposed to say to Hepburn that Council had considered the matter very carefully, but that we could not agree to grant the application he had made. I asked if there was any exception on the part of anyone to my saying this. All were silent.'

King carried the bad news to Mitch at the Chateau. As Mitch saw him to the door, he warned that 'this means an open break with your Government.' King left the encounter saddened by the prospect of a deeper rupture in the party. 'He is of the nature or character that in order to destroy me, he would be quite prepared to destroy the Party, and, no doubt, we shall find intrigue continuously from now on,' he confided to his diary. However, when the time came to take the platform against him, Mitch would find 'that the people are on the side of those who stand for maintaining liberty

through Parliament as against introducing Fascism into Canada.'
With that reassuring thought King left Ottawa to bask in the sun
at George Fulford's winter estate at Lake Wales, Florida.[11]

Mitch was silent on his return to Toronto, but exploded privately
to McCullagh that King's refusal was not going to stand in his way.
Hogg patiently continued the negotiations and on 10 December,
after cabinet approval, he issued a formal statement on the terms
of new agreements with Beauharnois, Gatineau, and MacLaren. The
total amount of power purchased remained the same but the contracts were lengthened to compensate for the interruptions since
1935. The cost was reduced from $15.00 to $12.50, as in the Ottawa
Valley agreement. Beauharnois and Gatineau agreed to stagger their
increased deliveries to allow Hydro to absorb the power more easily. Hogg stated that the agreement ended all fears of a power shortage, eliminated costly and dangerous litigation, saved the province
$70,923,000 and enabled Hydro to maintain its current rates. Under
the old contracts the cost of surplus power would have been over
$25 million between 1938 and 1945; under the new contracts the cost
of surplus power would be less than $7 million and would be 'large-
ly eliminated' if Ottawa granted permission to export surplus
power.[12]

Power exports, as well as King's Royal Commission on Dominion Provincial relations and the ailing newsprint industry, were on
the agenda when Mitch and four of his ministers met Duplessis in
Montreal on 13 December. After the meeting Mitch publicly questioned the constitutionality of federal control over exports, and
Duplessis branded Ottawa's interference with provincial control of
natural resources as 'intolerable.' If Ottawa 'wants a fight on its
hands, we are ready for the fight,' Mitch promised, and he challenged any Quebec or Ontario MP to vote against his request to
export power if a resolution came before Parliament. When King
met the cabinet on 16 December, a day after his return from Florida, he found his colleagues 'pretty indignant' over the dictators' tactics, and Lapointe, who had been wavering on exports, now agreed
that retreat was impossible. The government would not be moved
by this 'ganging up,' King told reporters, and no exports would be
permitted until Parliament had spoken.[13]

Mitch stormed out of a cabinet meeting the next day to deliver
an angry and bitter denunciation of King. Ottawa's policy was
made in Washington, and until 'such time as we weaken under the
pressure of Ottawa and Washington for the St. Lawrence, we'll
secure no rights for further development at Niagara.' Despite

Nixon's formal request in July, King had never asked Washington to approve the northern diversions but, as his letter of 7 September proved, had simply assumed and readily accepted the answer. As a result, work on the Long Lac and Ogoki diversions had stopped except for the pulpwood canal, over two hundred men had lost their jobs, and plans for a pulp mill and a much-needed hydro plant were cancelled. (Although Mitch did not mention it publicly, King had again yielded to pressure from the White House and had asked him to reconsider his position on the St Lawrence, a request Mitch had rejected since the Beauharnois settlement provided Ontario with enough power for 'many, many years to come.') King's obstruction was also dictated by personal spite, he added with unseemly malice, for he 'is still licking his wounds from personal defeats suffered in this province and he hasn't recovered even though for the first time in his political career this province sent him a majority in the last federal election.'[14]

In a long press release, King replied to what he privately described as 'a vicious & lying attack.' He denied categorically that the refusal to grant an export licence was the result of an agreement with the United States and insisted that 'at no time has pressure been brought to bear' on Ontario with respect to the St Lawrence. Mitch's 'allegation that an agreement exists between Ottawa and Washington that Ontario should not be allowed to develop more power at Niagara until the province becomes party to the St Lawrence development,' he concluded, 'is also wholly without foundation.'[15]

Mitch repeated his accusations and publicly demanded that King publish all the official correspondence, including the letters which 'with his usual cunning' he had marked confidential. King wired Mitch that the documents would be tabled when Parliament met and again denied the charge of an Ottawa-Washington conspiracy. Mitch responded by releasing all the power correspondence with Ottawa since July 1937. The fundamental question, he declared, was 'whether Ontario is to be dominated by Washington and Ottawa ... I tried to get the federal government to separate the two problems – that of diverging the waters above Niagara from the problem having to do with the St Lawrence but he insists in tying the two together.'

King spent the day drafting another statement which he issued that night. As the correspondence revealed, he argued, all he had done was to communicate Washington's position to Queen's Park. There was no agreement with the Americans or anything to substantiate Mitch's assertion that there had been 'any attempt at domination or coercion ... What Mr. Hepburn stated, and what I denied a day or two ago, was not the existence of correspondence or conferences between Washington and Canada or between himself and myself, but the existence of an "agreement" between the authorities at Washington and at Ottawa with respect to either the export of power, or to the St Lawrence waterways project, or related matters.' King's carefuly worded statements were literally true, but he and Skelton had become the apologists for the American position rather than Ontario's advocate. And King had found it expedient to use Mitch's opposition as, what Skelton later called, his 'alibi' for not proceeding with the St Lawrence.

At cabinet the next afternoon King found his colleagues solidly behind him, but he did berate Dunning for lacking 'backbone' and complained that several others 'could not see where we were drifting by seeking to meet Hepburn in the loose manner that some of them thought we should.' King met the press afterward. 'It was like being in a calm after a storm,' he wrote. 'Hepburn had not been able to come back with any word in reply to what appeared this morning, and I had no news to give out.' Mitch, in fact, was deeply engaged in two days of discussions with Duplessis in Toronto which ended with a long liquid buffet dinner at Frank O'Connor's. 'You and your friends, especially Jack [Bickell] and Frank, will always be welcome in the province of Quebec,' Duplessis wired soon after his return.[16]

On 21 January Mitch formally requested permission to export 90,000 horsepower for which Hydro had no immediate need. To strengthen his defences, King finally instructed the minister in Washington to inform the State Department that Ottawa supported Ontario's request to divert the northern waters and that the water be 'regarded for power purposes as national waters exclusively,' as recognized in the aborted 1932 treaty. Citing the 27 January note from the legation to the State Department a few weeks later, King was shocked that Mitch could ever have thought that he did not support Ontario's request.[17]

King was concerned that his bill to allow the export of power only with the consent of Parliament would run into trouble in caucus or, when it passed, the Liberal members could be trusted to vote against Mitch's request. Before Christmas Mulock had warned him of the serious political consequences and suggested to King to leave it an open question, 'especially if there be a division of opinion amongst your own supporters in the House.' With the bill on the order paper, King gave caucus his version of his relations with Mitch and another long lecture about the cabinet as the servant of Parliament. However, although party solidarity was important, he said, 'I wished the party to understand that the party was perfectly free to exercise, as individuals, their own judgement in the matter of the export of power.' However, when he introduced the bill a week later, King believed that his bill would pass but trusted that the Senate would not pass a private bill for the export of power from Ontario. 'Should it, in this way not reach the Commons,' he gloated, 'Hepburn will find all his threats of what he was going to do to Liberal Members who voted against the export of power, pretty much set at naught.'[18]

There was no doubt the bill would pass, but there was some question whether King back-benchers would vote against a private bill embodying Mitch's application. Ralph Maybank, the Winnipeg MP, advised King that unless he provided firm guidance, 'most of the Ontario members would, to some extent through fear of Mr. Hepburn, support the application for export of power,' as would most Manitoba MPs for different reasons. There was also the danger that some Quebec members would kick over the traces in view of the well-known wishes of the power companies and Duplessis's vigorous support of Mitch. King did not issue firm instructions when he moved second reading on 10 March, but it was clear that he opposed the export of power. However, Arthur Slaght, whose task it would be to sponsor the private bill, was optimistic if Mitch were to be less belligerent. 'I trust that from now until the Private Bill is disposed of,' he wrote, 'you will not find it necessary to make any public utterances reflecting on the Federal Government in connection with this matter because there is a genuine desire here to help put this Bill through for you and it would be most unfair to me and your other good friends here for you to pursue such a course while we are so doing.' While the export bill was still in committee, King entered the House at 10:30 p.m. on 21 March and gleefully announced that communications from Washington made the question academic.[19]

Mitch's determination to export Quebec power was of more real concern in New York and Washington than in Ottawa. The New York State Power Authority and the State Department had been tracking the export question for years, particularly since 1935–6 when Beauharnois was looking for markets and Niagara Hudson for power, because the availability of large amounts of Quebec power threatened the public development of the St Lawrence. The Power Authority was convinced there was an international private power conspiracy to kill the St Lawrence as a public utility, and it now seemed that Mitch was an innocent or willing accomplice in the conspiracy. With the export bill in the Commons, Frank Walsh reviewed the situation for President Roosevelt.

Circumstantially, he argued, it appeared that Hepburn was reflecting 'private power interests in Ontario politics': Bethune Smith as party treasurer; the renegotiated contracts; the fight with King and the alliance with Duplessis; and the public accusation of a King-Roosevelt alliance to force him to accept the St Lawrence. Moreover, Ottawa had finally endorsed the request for the diversions and, when the export bill passed, Ontario would likely get an export licence. Ottawa would then request Washington to agree that a later withdrawal of the power would 'not be deemed an unfriendly act toward this country.'

The issue was of fundamental and critical importance, Walsh continued. If Mitch secured his export permit, Ontario Hydro would become part of 'a power pool of international proportions,' with ALCOA at the centre. Although there were many scenarios, Hydro would probably retain the 110,000 horsepower exported to Niagara Hudson at the Falls, closer to its load centre, and in addition to the new request, export the equivalent at Cornwall. In effect, over 300,000 horsepower from Beauharnois and other Quebec sources would flow into the Niagara Hudson system. What was at stake was nothing less than harnessing the St Lawrence as a public utility.

Walsh's recommendations were blunt. The State Department should reject the request for the northern diversions and inform Ottawa that it would consider only a comprehensive Great Lakes–St Lawrence plan. The president, with plenary power to prohibit imports, should inform the Canadian government before the bill passed in the Commons that the proposed export request and the international power pooling under private auspices was unacceptable, and that withdrawable exports were unacceptable unless coupled with the development of the St Lawrence. With the dangers so starkly outlined and the circumstantial evidence that the international power trust had somehow caught Mitch and Hydro in its web, Roosevelt needed no urging. Cordell Hull sent official notes based on Walsh's recommendations to the Canadian minister on 17 March.[20]

'Nothing could have happened more opportunely,' wrote King when he received the notes on 21 March, 'not an hour sooner nor an hour later. A complete vindication of my whole course ... Without doubt, the confidence established between my Administration and Roosevelt's has operated to effect this result without a request or even a suggestion of [sic] my part.' The next day, when Slaght berated the opponents of exports but admitted there was no point in introducing Hydro's bill, King concluded that 'Hepburn has only to thank himself for this. His antagonistic attitude toward the St. Lawrence Waterways and the President has brought him this rebuff, and shut the door of the United States in his face ... Our record is clean as a white sheet, and Hepburn is left now with his whole problem to work out as best he can.' Contacted by reporters that night, Mitch exploded that while 'the whole thing is off,' the pressure from Washington would not change his mind on the St Lawrence. However, Slaght again urged him to be both realistic and diplomatic. Since Washington adopted the 'horse-trading' tactic, Mitch should do the same and sit down with Hull and Roosevelt and try to find a solution which 'would be short of impelling you to agree to the St Lawrence Waterway project at this time.' Moreover, he should say nothing to antagonize Roosevelt, for with war on the horizon the goodwill of the White House was of critical importance. Mitch accepted Slaght's advice and, until provoked, curbed his temper in public.[21]

Mitch was halfway through the first regular session of the new legislature when Roosevelt ended the controversy over power exports. The session had opened on 23 February 1938 with a throne speech that was fulsome in its praise of the administration but promised little to bring the members back after dinner. In the short December session, when Mitch had plugged the holes in the death tax legislation, Leo Macaulay, the new house leader, quickly revealed that he would be far more effective than George Henry. Cut of much of the same cloth as Mitch, he was a more congenial adversary and the debate, though sometimes acrimonious, was usually good-humoured, and Mitch and Leo often retired to the premier's office for a drink.

The most controversial issue was the new Hydro contracts. Macaulay insisted that Mitch had deceived the voters during the election and demanded an investigation by a committee of the House. Mitch's reply was less than convincing. 'It is true I said there was no power shortage,' he admitted. 'It is true that I said we would have no dealings with Beauharnois.' There had been no negotiations 'carried on by the Government and the power companies'; Hogg had assured him in writing that 'no negotiations were taken by him prior to his appointment'; and he had not 'directly or indirectly' been party to a deal with the Quebec companies before the election. It had been King's refusal to support Ontario's request for the northern diversions – a refusal Mitch claimed to have learned only after the election – which had killed the prospect of more power at Niagara. Moreover, as Conant earnestly confirmed, as the new attorney general he was so convinced they could not win in court that he and Hogg, 'ganged up' on Mitch and begged him to negotiate.

Mitch finally agreed to a select committee, as Macaulay's persistent accusations clearly laid the burden of proof on the government. In their testimony, Mitch and Hogg, and Henry and Montgomery of Beauharnois, all stuck to their story. Although the suspicion lingered, the Tories could unearth no hard evidence of a deal before the election – perhaps because Bethune Smith, Sweezey, and McCullagh had not been called.[22]

The ubiquitous R.O. Sweezey featured prominently in the opposition's attacks on the administration of the 1936 Forest Resources Reallocation Act. Under the act, Heenan had reacquired thousands of square miles of undeveloped crown timber lands, usually held by dormant or bankrupt companies. With the dramatic increase in demand and price for exported pulpwood, there was no shortage of ardent suitors, and Heenan had quickly negotiated agreements with new companies usually created for the purpose. Most of the agreements provided only for the export of pulpwood, but in return for two thousand square miles of reacquired timber limits, Lake Sulphite, another R.O. Sweezey venture, agreed to build a pulp mill immediately at Red Rock. There had been the usual criticism that the government had simply handed out the new contracts to its friends, many of them large American concerns with an assured market. The Tories had been particularly critical of the contract with F.J. Sensenbrenner of Kimberley Clark at Kapuskasing, a friend of every government since the United Farmers, to take out one hundred thousand cords a year through the Long Lac diversion canal. However, with more men at work than ever before and local jobbers happy to cut for any employer whose wages were regular, the criticism did not affect Liberal popularity in the north during the election.

The price of pulp peaked in August 1937, however, and then declined as dramatically as it had risen. Over production, high inventories held in anticipation of price increases, and slumping markets as the business cycle turned sharply downwards in the fall crippled the industry. By winter many of the camps were closing, and thousands of men were thrown out of work. Lake Sulphite, after spending $4 million on a mill at Red Rock, declared bankruptcy.

Was it possible, Macaulay asked on the second day of the session, that the Ontario Securities Commission was less thorough in examining Sulphite's stock prospectus because Sweezey was the underwriter and Bethune Smith the solicitor? Mitch denied that the government was responsible for Sulphite's financing, and refused to accept Macaulay's demand for an investigation unless he made a definite charge of impropriety. Macaulay kept Heenan and Sulphite on the agenda throughout the session, but it was not until 1939 that Mitch agreed to a Select Committee to investigate the Department of Lands and Forests.[23]

Apart from the power agreements, the law to require the comulsory pasteurization of milk attracted the most attention and aroused some of the most stubborn public opinion. The matter had been on the public agenda for twenty years. The Ontario Milk Distributors and the medical profession had persistently pressed for legislation, and by 1937 between 85 and 90 per cent of all milk sold in the province was pasteurized and fewer than 100,000 people lived in areas where pasteurization was not compulsory. But successive administrations had refused to grasp the nettle of total pasteurization because of the noisy opposition of small dairy farmers who sold their milk locally.

Early in December 1937, when the distributors made another pilgrimage to Queen's Park, Mitch and Nixon agreed that the time had come to act. The medical evidence was conclusive. Dr Allan Brown, the chief physician at the Sick Children's Hospital, sent Mitch a National Research Council report which proved that more than 10 per cent of the 490 tubercular children at the hospital suffered from bovine TB. In every instance the child had been fed raw milk. Not one was from Toronto where milk had been pasteurized since 1915. Tens, if not hundreds, of thousands of other milk-borne diseases, from typhoid to septic sore throats, could have been prevented with pasteurized milk. Just before the session opened, Mitch walked through the TB ward with Dr Brown. These children would not be here, the doctor said, if you people at Queen's Park had the courage to make pasteurization compulsory. Done, said Mitch, and done it was. If his action saved only one young life, Mitch lectured many angry supporters, he was prepared to lose the support of every dairy farmer in Ontario.[24]

There was not a hint in Mitch's second sunshine budget speech on 18 March that the business cycle had swung sharply downwards and Ontario was entering a recession. Provincial income from all sources was up dramatically, the receipts from liquor, gasoline, and automobile licences and the increased deposits in the savings banks all reflecting higher personal incomes. There would be no increase in taxes, Mitch promised, despite rising relief costs and the refusal of the federal government to increase its support. The increased expenditures for education, health, and agriculture would probably equal the projected surplus for 1938-9. Although Mitch boasted that the funded debt had been reduced, the opposition had little difficulty demonstrating that the total debt had increased dramatically in the past four years. The *Globe and Mail* was also critical of the increased debt, but felt that the $35 million in highway expenditures, particularly for the divided highway between Toronto and Hamilton, which the Tories scoffed was only to enable Mitch and McQuesten to get home faster on weekends, was a good investment for the future. The *Globe* also echoed Mitch's praise for Chester Walters, whose 'efficient and business-like management of affairs' had kept ministerial spending propensities in line. Graham Towers, the conservative bankers' banker at the Bank of Canada, also told Walters that 'in the circumstances he was no doubt accomplishing a great deal,' but observed that 'the continuing substantial increases in debt – in spite of unprecedently high revenues and general prosperity in the Province – were somewhat disappointing, since it meant that none of the ground lost during the depression was being regained, and no margin provided for the debt increases which would inevitably take place if and when there was a period of depression.' Walters replied that he was doing 'the best he could' to keep expenditures down, and that if revenues dropped they would have to cut expenditures.[25]

Mitch was content when the session ended on 8 April. The work had been constructive and generally free of contentious issues and the bitter wrangling that had marred earlier sessions. The opposition had not damaged the government's reputation, and two by-elections indicated the party was still strong in the province. The leaderless and squabbling Tories decided not to contest Hamilton Centre, and the CCF left the field to the communists. Although Lambton East was not in danger, Mitch spent two days in the riding. With King's Royal Commission on Dominion-Provincial Relations soon to arrive in Ontario, the subject was very much on his mind. 'It is all very well to talk of a national viewpoint,' he said in Petrolia. 'But as head of the Government of Ontario, it is my duty to protect Provincial interests as well as co-operate with the Dominion authorities for the welfare of Canada as a whole.'[26]

Mitch had insisted that Mackenzie King's royal commission delay its arrival in Toronto until late April when, with the session over, the provincial brief could be completed. In February 1937, after months of opposition, equivocation, and procrastination, King had finally yielded to pressure from his own officials and the Bank of Canada and agreed to a commission. But despite frantic warnings by O.D. Skelton and others that delay could spell disaster, he refused to decide on the terms of reference or appoint the members before leaving on an extended trip to the coronation and the imperial conference in April. It was August before King selected Newton Rowell, chief justice of Ontario, to head the commission, with Thibodeau Rinfret of the Supreme Court of Canada and John Dafoe as commissioners. R.A. MacKay and Henry Angus, political scientists from Dalhousie and British Columbia, were added to provide a more balanced regional representation. The technocrats trusted that the commission would pave the way for fundamental changes in the collapsing federal system; King hoped it would recommend a return to classical federalism and relieve his government of responsibility for coping with the enormous social costs and economic dislocations of the Depression.[27]

Mitch had approved of the commission and hoped that it would recommend a 'thorough revision' of the federal system 'with full regard to the taxpaying capacity of the people in regard to the taxes properly collected by the Dominion, by the provinces, and by the municipality.' Although Mitch promised to 'co-operate in every possible way,' his friend Norman McLarty, the freshman MP from Windsor, warned him that cooperation might be difficult. The maritime and western provinces were almost certain to demand some form of fiscal compensation for the alleged injustices of the tariff, he predicted, and were likely to find a sympathetic audience in Dafoe, MacKay, and Angus. Since the interests of Ontario and Quebec were 'practically identical,' McLarty suggested a defensive alliance with Duplessis.[28]

McLarty's predictions were confirmed when the Commission began its hearings in Winnipeg on 29 November 1937. Premier Bracken and his colleagues proposed that to compensate for the cost of the tariff and as part of a major reallocation of revenues and responsibilities, Ottawa should assume responsibility for provincial debts and relief, while the provinces would surrender their succession duties. 'It is perfectly plain that the case for the western provinces and the Maritimes will be along the same lines,' wrote Dan Lang, a member of Mitch's planning team who was at the hearing, and Ontario should not only prepare its defences but 'develop an attack of our own on this basis.'[29]

On the eve of a meeting with Duplessis in December 1937 to discuss the newsprint industry and power exports, Mitch suggested that the commission might also be on the agenda. Ontario and Quebec might have to form an 'economic alliance' to withstand demands from the western provinces which, if accepted, would mean additional taxation in Ontario which already contributed 47.5 per cent of Ottawa's revenues. The news report was wired to King in Florida. It was 'just as well to have these two incipient dictators out in the open linked together,' he reflected. 'The public will soon discover who is protecting their interests and freedom ... It is an important departure in Canadian politics, – an outrage that this young upstart should seek to array central provinces against West & East, as he is in attacking representations before Rowell-Commission. – We will win on a "United Canada" cry.'[30]

Although neither he nor Mitch divulged the nature of their discussions, Duplessis's intemperate boast at Shawinigan two days later that Ontario, Quebec, and the maritimes would not be driven by Ottawa or the western provinces provoked a flood of protest. In an outraged editorial, 'MR. DUPLESSIS RUNS WILD,' McCullagh denounced Duplessis for thinking only of Quebec and appealed to Mitch to think of Canada. If there was a narrowness of vision in the west, he asked, must the east prove that it could be worse? 'As to Premier Hepburn, we wonder what he thinks now of the bedfellow of his political and economic alliance ... One half of the alliance has shocked the country with an open challenge to national integrity. Can the other half be better?'[31]

There were more meetings in Toronto and Montreal in December and January and, although newsprint and power exports were the most pressing issues, the commission was also discussed. 'I am proud to say that Quebec and Ontario have got together to get justice for themselves in the belief that charity begins at home,' Duplessis said at a Montreal banquet. 'It's not a matter of ganging up but to stop a raid against Confederation. We believe in unity through diversity and our policy in Quebec is to live and let live.' Mitch could not be – and was not – as categorical. However, as he wrote Duplessis in February, he believed a common front was essential.

The more I read of the representations made by the other provinces the more convinced I am of the necessity of Ontario and Quebec resisting together, and in no uncertain way, the ever increasing, unreasonable and impossible demand ... I can readily understand the advantage it would be to the other provinces for them to raid the Federal Treasury, particularly when Ontario and Quebec contribute 80% of the revenue.

I have further information to the effect that the King Government is determined to take over the collection of succession duties. This would deprive us of our greatest source of revenue.

Duplessis was also pleased to learn that Mitch had withdrawn his earlier support of a constitutional amendment enabling Ottawa to introduce unemployment insurance.[32]

Mitch had long advocated national unemployment insurance and in November 1937 had told King that he would 'waive any constitutional objection' to the necessary constitutional amendment. But when he received a very vague draft amendment in January, Mitch immediately told Duplessis that he suspected that King 'is simply asking for a blank cheque insofar as amending the British North America Act is concerned and is using unemployment insurance as the thin edge of the wedge.' Ontario remained 'solidly behind the principle of a national unemployment scheme,' he added 'but not at the expense of Confederation.' Mitch refused to agree until he had seen the details of the proposed measure; King refused to discuss the details until the necessary amendment was passed.

Dissatisfied with King's position, Mitch told Duplessis that 'I rather regret that I was in a position of having to first endorse the proposed national scheme of insurance ... However, if this means we have to sacrifice Confederation I am quite prepared to withdraw any support whatsoever. It is clear to me that with the Western provinces hopelessly bankrupt, any national scheme of unemployment insurance will have to be borne by the two central provinces, and if unemployment insurance is necessary it probably will be better to run our own show.' Even with Duplessis, Aberhart, and Dysart of New Brunswick opposed, Dafoe felt that King would call their bluff unless Mitch joined 'the gang.' Mitch did not join the gang, but after his criticism King was only too happy to shelve the proposal in April. By June Mitch had a task force studying a provincial program and in November hired Jacob Cohen to draft legislation.[33]

Mitch was also at war with Ottawa again over relief. The numbers on direct relief had climbed from a summer low of 163,000 to over 200,000 in December and reached 272,000 in March 1938 as the recession deepened. But Ottawa refused to increase its payment of $465,000 set in October and the provincial burden rose from 38 to 46 per cent of the cost. When Cross led a delegation of mayors to Ottawa in February to request a 50-50, or at least a 40-40-20, split, Rogers not only categorically refused, but demanded that the province cleanse the rolls of the 'large numbers of unemployables and charity cases' who were their responsibility. Mitch was furious. 'We are getting back to the "not a five-cent piece for Ontario" policy of Mr. King,' he exclaimed. The time had come to call a halt to 'this milking of Ontario' and he would challenge Ottawa's right to harvest the major share of personal income and mining taxes. Mitch carried his war with King into the Assembly where the members unanimously and enthusiastically passed a resolution asserting Ontario's prior right in the income tax field.[34]

The commissioners could not expect a warm welcome at Queen's Park in April 1938. Cooling his heels in Toronto waiting for Mitch to appear, R.A. MacKay told his wife that Duplessis had spent his forty-eighth birthday in the city with Mitch a few days before and the meeting, 'with everyone smiling and saying nothing for publication, seems to have greased the "axis".' Duplessis would probably boycott the commission, he accurately predicted, and Mitch would do the same if he thought it would hurt King more than himself. 'The real bond between Maurice & Mitch,' he added, 'is a common hatred of WLMK and Lapointe.'[35]

Mitch did not boycott the Commission, but he had deliberately remained at Bannockburn and asked Conant to welcome it, which he did, wrote J.B. McGeachy of the *Winnipeg Free Press*, much 'as a man welcomes poor relations with cautious warmth and few words.' The commissioners heard private briefs for a week while they waited for Mitch to appear. '"Mitch" comes on Monday afternoon, and he is out apparently to damn the Dominion Government and the West,' wrote MacKay to his wife. 'We haven't seen the brief yet. It has been held back to the last minute, but we've got an inkling of the tenor, or at least the tenor of the introductory stat. from the Canadian Press man who has a copy.' They had a copy when Mitch and his entourage arrived on 2 May, but rather than speak to it Mitch read it verbatim. For ninety minutes, head down and rejecting questions, Mitch raced through a speech. It was certainly not his speech. Indeed, it sounded as if he had not read it before as he stumbled over words like formidable, awry, and seriatim.[36]

Students of the punditry of W.H. Moore had little difficulty identifying him as the writer of the first part of Mitch's statement, with its lavish praise of individualism as the foundation of freedom and its warning that 'the accumulation of power leads to autocracy; its distribution is the safety-zone of democracy.' Recent history revealed that Canadians must 'strengthen the hands of government closest to the people – or get ready to look back on the past seventy-five years as merely an interlude in freedom.' The accumulation of more power in the hands of an already overburdened central government was a threat to democracy and if national programs were essential, perhaps they would be 'better arranged by compact' between the provinces than by federal legislation. While Ontario was ready 'to co-operate with all the provinces, whenever it is found desirable to equalize social condition,' it was also determined to ensure that 'the provinces charged with social services should make the initial levy on incomes arising within the province. The federal income-taxing officer should only step in when the provincial needs have been satisfied.' It was 'poor politics, and worse economy, that one government should tax for another to spend.'

With the language still reeking of Moore, but with more of the substance provided by Professor Kenneth Taylor, the McMaster economist on the planning team, and Chester Walters, Mitch turned to the more congenial task of countering the western demands for a massive diversion of funds 'from the sorely pressed provinces of Ontario and Quebec.' With the aid of their American professors, the western provinces had performed a valuable service in presenting their 'Account Rendered' in terms of real money based on the alleged costs to the west of national tariff and monetary policies. But the account neglected to point out that the collapse of the wheat economy was due, in part at least, to the world overproduction of wheat, with the Economic Committee of the League of Nations pointing out that the increase in Canada was of 'the greatest absolute and relative importance.' The west was, therefore, at least a co-author of its own misfortunes. 'I have every sympathy for those 99 thousand farmers whose main source of revenue has declined; but really I do not see that it is necessary to upset Confederation on their behalf; nor do I believe that we should re-make a fiscal policy that was established long before most of them ever turned a furrow, with a tractor, on Canadian soil.'

With the prairie provinces claiming \$58 million a year compensation for the cost of the tariff, Mitch set out to 'clean up the charge of "eastern industrial exploitation"; for a sense of sectional injustice has too long retarded the national aspirations of the Canadian people.' His own economists and statisticians had worked through the statement of claim against the tariff and found it a combination of hopeless economics, flawed methodology, and even bad arithmetic. In short, said Mitch, the 'long-drawn cry of "Eastern Dominion" lost its savour the moment it was converted' into money. 'Personally, I confess I thought the West had some grievance, but began to suspect there was deep-water in sight when the economists introduced their items for the Account Rendered with the statement: "No claim is made for its accuracy than what ordinary common sense and objectivity can provide."'

If the west really wanted to balance accounts, Mitch insisted, Ontario wanted to include the debt and expenditures on western railways; low freight rates for western wheat; the tariff disability on Ontario's use of imported coal; and the cost of special grants to the west for export subsidies, the wheat pools, and state aid in the marketing of wheat. With a few more of Moore's platitudes behind him, Mitch concluded with the argument that, despite the revolutionary changes in the world economy, within the Canadian federal system, 'with its balance of powers,' the provinces, with 'the exercise of prudent economy,' could prosper and 'still preserve their political heritage.' The commissioners had agreed beforehand 'on the policy of a soft answer that turneth away wrath.' After a few polite words from Rowell and his assurance that the commission was a fact-finding body with the power to recommend changes only within 'the strict limits of a Federal constitution,' the session was over.[37]

'The great Hepburn, defender of hard-pressed Ontario, against the idle-rich of Saskatchewan and Manitoba took the stand today,' McGeachy informed his *Free Press* readers. 'Mr. Hepburn looked as sleek and round as usual but less vivacious. Accustomed to an audience which responds with loud cheers to wise-cracks and declamatory periods, he was subdued and out of character in this judicial atmosphere.' Mitch was expected to battle for provincial rights, McGeachy continued, 'but nobody supposed his statement would be quite as full of half-baked economics, appeals to prejudice, jumbled logic and parish politics as it was.' The *Star* found it 'ill-tempered,' and the *Globe and Mail* described it as 'an instrument of destruction from the standpoint of national unity.' Even those who sympathized with his position found the tone distressing – and attributed it not to the fulminations of W.H. Moore but to Mitch's animosity towards Mackenzie King.[38]

For the next four days Walters, Taylor, and members of the cabinet worked through the long statement with the commission. Although Walters was occasionally heavy-handed, his natural scowl 'frequently dissolved into a smile,' observed McGeachy, and he was 'fluent, facetious, merry and even literary at moments, quoting Dickens, Aesop, the Winnipeg Free Press, and a close friend of Adam Smith.' Taylor's presentation and interventions were so intelligent and clear-headed that he was later invited to join the commission staff. The central thrust of Ontario's argument was that regional and social diversity precluded the centralization of powers and revenues advocated by the western provinces which, if adopted, 'would convert the provinces to mere names upon a map, and their legislatures into little more than county councils.' Over 45 per cent of federal taxes were collected in Ontario, far more per capita than from any other province, but Taylor's cautious estimates suggested that the province received the benefits of only 28 per cent of federal expenditure. 'We do, sir,' Taylor replied to a question from Dafoe, 'say we feel in Ontario we have borne a reasonable share, a full share, perhaps some of us think a little more than our full share, of the burden of taxation.'

Ontario had balanced its budget by the application of 'the sound business principle of levying taxation to cover all ordinary expenditures' but faced a continuing demand for increased expenditure on education, housing, and social services. Nevertheless, Ontario did not wish to transfer social services, however costly, to Ottawa, for it believed they could better be handled at the provincial level. Nor could it give up 'any present source of substantial revenue, and must in fact, insist on a more strict recognition of its clearly established legal and moral rights in the field of direct taxation and natural resources.' Walters refused to agree that because fortunes were made across Canada succession duties should be in the hands of the federal government. Taylor dismissed the argument that the tariff had concentrated industrial development in Ontario and Quebec as 'an entirely unwarranted assumption.' A different commercial policy might have led to more or less industrial development, 'but such industrial development as would have occurred would still have been concentrated in the Lower Lakes-St. Lawrence area.'

Conant concluded the presentation. Ontario viewed with 'very great alarm' any attempt by Ottawa to 'take over the griefs, worries and responsibilities that are confronting some of the provinces' for the already heavily burdened taxpayers of Ontario would have to pick up much of the cheque. 'We are not Midas ... the villain in the piece, sitting back without obligations but unbounded wealth ... And we must say to this Commission that if the field of taxation which is, for lack of a better name, now called "direct tax" is invaded by the Federal Government, our financial structure, our whole fabric of Government is, and must be very seriously jeopardized.'[39]

Before the commissioners left, Mitch had repaired relations on a personal level at least. Two days after his presentation he invited all the commission and the staff, visiting dignitaries, the lieutenant-governor and the cabinet to dinner at the King Eddy. The evening began quietly but after the departure of Rowell, a staunch teetotaller, the party began. R.A. MacKay naïvely sent a full report to his wife:

Under the lead of Chester Walters and Conant there was soon a bunch around the piano   Seeing what was coming I had a good drink of Scotch to remove my inhibitions – I can't quite play the fool when completely sober. A little later there were demands for something from 'Mitch', he proceeded to oblige by leading a chorus with his arm around Cronkite, Dean of Sask. Law School who has been representing Sask. He and 'Cronk' then sang a duet. I've forgotten the song, but as I recall it wasn't quite printable. At the close of which he or Cronk announced 'Ontario-Saskatchewan axis'. After which choruses again, then a demand for the recitation of a famous ballad – again unprintable – from Mitch, which he did superbly, again more choruses and stories. In some of the choruses Mitch insisted on my joining in – which I did to the best of my ability, one arm around Mitch or Cronk. And there were French songs, and of course, Allouette (how do you spell it) from Leduc, Savard, and Chester Walters who sings a superb tenor. And a couple of Irish songs from Peter Heenan. The party broke up about 11.30 with a rousing chorus of 'O Canada' after which 'Mitch' presented me with his rose, and I with mine, and Mitch and 'Cronk' finished each others glass. All of this sounds as if it was a drunken ordeal. It really wasn't … And it wasn't all merely fun … on one occasion, just when a song was at its height, Mitch quit singing and remarked in my ear to the effect that after all Ontario wasn't so damned provincially minded and that we were all Canadians anyway. Again two different Cabinet ministers and Chester Walters as well as Lang more or less apologized to me during the evening for the PM's speech the opening day, and remarked that circumstances were such that he more or less had to do it (no doubt his bargain with Duplessis) though he thoroughly disliked it. The upshot of the party was twofold – a much better tone to the proceedings, and a special telephone call from 'Mitch' to Duplessis urging him to appear before the Commission – whether it will have any effect or not remains to be seen.

I think we all – that is those of the Commission who stayed and the staff – came home more or less under the undeniable spell of Hepburn's personality. One can't help liking him, even though he might thoroughly disagree with him.

Mrs MacKay was not amused, and he wisely neglected to tell her of their encounter with Duplessis. Mitch's call did not persuade

Duplessis to appear before the commission, but he followed Mitch's example and threw a party at the Chateau Frontenac that one journalist described as 'something not much better than a drunken brawl, with dishes smashed and a big chandelier damaged.'[40]

'Something in the wind'

If not the spell of Mitch's personality, the menacing shadow of his ambition had confused and immobilized the federal Liberals. There were many who shared Thomas Crerar's suspicion that the alliance with Duplessis went much deeper than the scanty news reports indicated. 'It is not difficult to see Duplessis and Hepburn leading the way to a business government,' he had suggested to Dafoe in December, 'part of whose job will be to solve the railway problem ... When one looks at this it seems incomprehensible that such a thing could ever be thought of, but Hepburn and Duplessis are both drunk with power; they are both impulsive and little given to reflection.' George McCullagh, too, was convinced there was more to the entente than met the eye, and according to King warned him that Mitch was 'aiming at the leadership of the Party at Ottawa, and that he was going to make this the issue, and with the help of Duplessis, supplant myself. I said this did not cause me any concern. Rather smiled at it.'[1]

There was little to smile at in the rumours that reached King early in 1938. He had always suspected that Bill Fraser of Trenton, Ross Gray of Sarnia, and several other Ontario MPs were in Mitch's camp, and he did not need Elmore Philpott's warning that several of his ministers were 'playing ball' with Mitch to reawaken his suspicions. Lambert heard in the middle of March that Mitch was boasting that he would take '20 seats from Ontario out of the Federal House,' and Dunning relayed the report that while Mitch was prepared to see King remain as leader, Howe, Rogers and, presumably, himself had to go. At the first cabinet meeting after the Easter recess the cabinet discussed relations with Queen's Park, and King optimistically 'stressed the need of avoiding the cleavage

between the two becoming wider, and some positive efforts of bringing the two together.'²

King learned just how wide the cleavage had become the next day
when three Toronto MPs told him of their discussions with Mitch.
His complaints were familiar, but the threats were menacing. Mitch
stated that he would not support King in the next election, expected early in 1939, and might actively oppose him. He had already
closed the financial pipeline, and he would also raise Hydro rates
to remind the voters of King's duplicity, stop all public works, and
prevent his ministers from participating, although he 'might' allow
provincial members to work in their own ridings. Asked what could
be done to resolve the differences, Mitch snapped that 'Rogers,
King, Lapointe & Rinfret had to go.' Mitch also warned the MPs
that although Duplessis had quietly supported the Liberals in a January by-election, he had become so 'sore' at Lapointe and Rinfret
that he had 'elected' the Tory in Argenteuil in February. 'The infer-
ence appeared to be,' they told King, 'that if Lapointe and Rinfret
got out, Duplessis might agree to quietly support the federal Liberal party or at least mind his own business.' Further confirmation
of a Hepburn-Duplessis alliance came from Harry Johnson who had
told them that Mitch was 'the only man who could influence Duplessis and that he could get Duplessis to do anything he (Hepburn)
wanted.'³

When Paul Martin returned to Ottawa with the same report, the
conversation turned to the root causes of Mitch's antagonism. Martin believed that it was based less on Mitch's criticism of policy than
his discomfort in 'encountering trained minds, like Rogers' and Ils-
leys',' and 'that their way of speaking antagonized him.' King
agreed that Mitch was 'an upstart and knows it' and that it was
really a question of character. 'Men of the Hepburn and Campbell
stamp are unprincipled men, fond of drinking, good fellowship, and
are really uncomfortable in the presence of men of perspective, culture and integrity.' The lines in *Isaiah* sprung to mind:

> His watchmen are blind: they are all ignorant,
> They are all dumb dogs, they cannot bark;
> Sleeping, lying down,˙ loving to slumber.

Mitch's bark at the royal commission hearings had raised the
question of whether Ottawa could afford to slumber any longer.
Afraid to take on Duplessis in Quebec, Lapointe favoured an immediate assault in Ontario. Rogers agreed. But Mackenzie, Dunning

and, King suspected, most of the other ministers 'felt it wiser to wait and not create an open cleavage of the Party immediately, the hope being that, in the interval, some means of bringing Hepburn to his senses might be found.' King maintained that he was ready to launch the attack, but only on the understanding that 'the entire Cabinet and Federal Party kept it up'. On balance, however, he preferred to let the dog slumber until the eve of a general election 'and then go at it without reserve.' The realization that a convention of the Ontario Liberal Association, if one could be called, would force a showdown or bring Mitch into line, was tempered by the unwillingness of the Ontario ministers to take the initiative. The best that Bill Mulock, the MP for York North, could suggest was that Harry Johnson might be bribed with a seat in the Senate.[4]

Although King had pressed Lambert to have a good representation from Ontario at the 18 May 1938 meeting of the National Liberal Federation, no member of the provincial party attended. But Mitch's shadow hung over the proceedings. The resolution on national unity underlined the need for harmonious relations between Ottawa and the provinces. Another strongly opposed 'the promotion in Canada of Communism, Fascism, Nazism, Separatism, Sectionalism and Provincialism, and all other "isms" inconsistent with Liberal principles,' several of which might have been meant to include Hepburn-ism. King's in-camera speech was a charge to the party to take up the cause of national and party unity in the face of the 'trying circumstances' under which he had tried 'to apply the principles of Liberalism' to Canadian problems. King worried that he had spoken more pointedly and forcefully than he had intended and, as he looked at the looks of consternation on the faces of the MPs was afraid that he 'said things which, divorced from context, would add fuel to the fire.'

When I sat down, I did not know whether I had made things better or worse ... It is pretty clear that our members are loyally behind me. Also that they are all very fearful of what the effect of Hepburn's behaviour is likely to be. My own feeling is that he, himself, will be out of the way before any general election comes. Though, if he is not, we may expect to see battles in Ontario similar to what they have been in Alberta, and in Quebec where we will have a crop of dictators of a bad breed.[5]

If Mitch heard of King's speech, he made no comment, but in the next few months he vocally escalated the war with Ottawa. Privately, he told Crerar that he looked forward to the day when the voters would send a government with 'some practical horse sense' to Ottawa, and he made it clear publicly that he found little 'horse sense' in King's belated and parsimonious attempts to stimulate recovery. Moreover, among the measures passed in 1938 to stimulate construction were two that invaded provincial jurisdiction: the Municipal Improvements Act offered loans to municipalities, and the National Housing Act made $30 million available to local governments for low-cost housing. Dunning admitted the federal government was moving into fields it had 'no constitutional right to occupy' but, without any consultation, attempted to circumvent the constitutional issue by providing that in both cases the provinces had to approve the loans and guarantee repayment. With the muncipalities emerging from insolvency, Mitch was not prepared to let them start borrowing again. Ontario would not approve the improvement loans, he told Dunning, or provide the necessary guarantees for a 'foolish housing scheme which exists only on borrowed money.'[6]

With the royal commission examining the entire tax structure, Mitch also found unilateral federal changes to the income tax particularly infuriating. Dunning's action, he wired, was 'little short of effrontery [*sic*] to the provinces' and a snub to the commission. Two weeks later Mitch informed King that because of these unilateral changes his government was 'no longer interested in further deliberations or the findings of the Royal Commission on Dominion-Provincial Relations.' With Quebec and Alberta refusing to participate, Mitch's secession killed the plans for a round-table conference in the fall. 'I am afraid it would be quite an anti-climax and would add considerably to the acrimony of the situation,' Alex Skelton, secretary to the commission, concluded. 'It would certainly strengthen the impression that the Commission is primarily designed to bail the "have nots" out of their difficulties at the expense of the "haves", rather than attack certain national problems of fundamental importance.'[7]

The suspicion grew over the summer and fall that the 'national problem' uppermost in Mitch's mind was Mackenzie King. No one saw anything sinister in his trip with Jack Bickell to see the second Louis-Schmelling fight, but when they dropped down to see Duplessis and announced they were going to fly across the country to the Arctic and the Pacific Coast, with stops in Regina, to see Gardiner and Premier Patterson, and in Edmonton, the strategy seemed clear. The *Star* suspected that it was 'not a view of the earth from the clouds' which explained Mitch's 'wave of air-mindedness' but, as Ottawa concluded, the creation of 'a new political party in the

Federal arena.' Whether Mitch and Maurice, who believed they could deliver forty seats each to a new party, could swing Gardiner and, perhaps, Aberhart and Pattullo behind them was the question. Gardiner would lead the party, the *Star* suggested, and Mitch and Duplessis would provide the financial muscle. Lambert also reminded King that Mitch had already assisted Gardiner and Patterson with financial support in the June election in Saskatchewan. Mitch's insistence that it was a holiday was not believed.[8]

With Ben Smith on board, they left Toronto in Bickell's twin-engine Grumman amphibian on 17 July. Gardiner, Patterson, and the cabinet were at the Regina airport and took them to lunch. In Edmonton the next day Mitch denied that he was linking up with his good friend from Quebec, admitted that Gardiner was very popular in Ontario, and defended his position before the commission as a necessary defensive posture. Mitch told reporters that he had no intention of leading or assisting a new federal party. He was still a Liberal, but he was not a supporter of Mackenzie King. The thrust of his comments seemed too pointed for his denial to be believed.

Politics were left behind when they flew north to Yellowknife, Port Radium, the mouth of the Coppermine, Fort Norman, over to Aklavik, and south to Dawson and Carcross. Mitch was overwhelmed by the north, particularly Yellowknife where the gold rush was in its fourth year. The Bank of Commerce's newest branch was an eight-by-ten-foot log cabin and Bickell, a bank director, manned the counter while Mitch and Ben Smith opened accounts. Despite the warnings of the Carcross telegraph operator, they set out for Juneau in a blinding snow storm, but a zero-zero ceiling forced the pilot to turn back. After a hazardous flight through a narrow gulch, where Mitch felt he could hear the wing tips scrape the side of the mountain, the pilot brought the plane down.

When they failed to reach Juneau, the press reported they were lost. Harry Nixon asked Duff Pattullo to launch an all-out search and a young teenage clerk in Mitch's office led a prayer meeting in the vault, before the morning papers headlined the news that they were safe. While Bickell waited for the weather to clear, Mitch and Smith took a train to Skagway and a boat to Vancouver. After a few days at Smith's lodge near Lillooet they flew east across the northern states and on 7 August buzzed Bannockburn on their way from Detroit to Toronto.[9]

That evening Mitch talked to reporters on the veranda of Bickell's estate in Mississauga. He was soon back to politics. Asked about King's decision early in August to peg the price of wheat at

80 cents a bushel, Mitch replied: 'I never heard of anything so assi-
nine … It's like trying to defy natural laws. It's a colossal blunder.'
Asked if Ontario farmers should get the same support, Mitch
laughed 'Sure. If he's going to be crazy he might just as well be
crazy all over the country.' Back in St Thomas a few days later, he
made public his refusal to cooperate with the royal commission.[10]

Mitch had gone to St Thomas to celebrate his forty-second birthday. Among the thousands of the local faithful who trooped out to
Bannockburn were his friends Ed and Art Carty of London.
'Mitch's first words were in regard to his fight with Premier Mackenzie King,' said Ed. '"Am I right or wrong?" he asked. "Right",
I said, and he seemed pleased.' The Cartys were at the London airport when Mitch greeted Duplessis, who had flown in with Bickell,
and Harry McLean and Ben Smith who flew in a few minutes later
from New York. When Mitch introduced Ed to Duplessis as a
friend close enough to be a brother, Ed joked 'I'm going to make
Mitch Premier of Canada for that.' 'That will not be hard,' Duplessis replied. Later in the day, Mitch told the Cartys, 'It is not I
who am leaving the Liberal party. It is King who is driving me out.'
King, he added bitterly, was a 'sweet-scented hypocrite.' Mitch
showed off his latest onion-grading machine, paraded his prize horses, and with Duplessis provided an abundance of photo opportunities as they drove around in a painted wagon and pitched sheaves
into the barn. For the first time he allowed photographs of Peter
and Patsy. Despite the best efforts of the press to draw them out
on politics, Mitch and Maurice countered the questions with comments about birthdays and the beauty of nature. The only exception was a brief comment by Duplessis that the provinces 'must
have more autonomy or there can not be unity in Canada. The individual members of a nation must be given their rights or there can
be no nation.' Mitch nodded in agreement.[11]

There was a good deal of talk about King and national politics
as Mitch and his friends drank into the night. Duplessis was 'hell-
bent' for an immediate entry into federal politics with Mitch leading a new party while he delivered Quebec and French-Canadian
votes across the country. Jimmy Dunn believed that only a national government could save the nation from financial disaster. He
wondered, however, whether the time was right, and if Mitch had
the national reputation to lead the movement, a question he had
put to Floyd Chalmers of the *Financial Post* in May. Mitch was
noncommittal, but certainly did not reject the proposal outright.
Harry Johnson felt trapped as he contemplated a movement that

would shatter the provincial party, and later admitted to Lambert that he was '"on the spot" as a result of developments over the weekend. He said Mitch had Duplessis in his hip-pocket & spoke of "pressure from millionaires".'

Larry McGuinness had also been uncomfortable when Duplessis pressed Mitch to go out 'like David alone to meet both Manion and King' and warned him a few days later that he would 'bear the burden of things outside Quebec' and 'wind up broken down in health.' Although King should retire, McGuiness did not believe he would, and 'things are not sufficiently crystallized for a third party.' His advice was to stay on the sidelines and let King and Manion fight it out. Manion would propose policies 'much more foolish than King and if you let the boys beat themselves to death,' McGuinness assured him, 'you will ride to Ottawa more triumphantly than was ever done before and will stay there as long as you desire.'[12]

Ever since his victory in 1934, Mitch had denied any interest in returning to Ottawa. By the summer of 1938, however, his apparently irreconcilable and bitter conflict with King, the widespread and deep-seated dissatisfaction with King's leadership in the country, the party, and even the caucus, and the flattering pressure from friends and colleagues drove him towards national politics. Although seemingly inevitable, his course was equally unclear, for only a coup could remove King and there did not appear to be the ingredients for a national government party.

After the last birthday guest had departed, Mitch spent the next few days around the farm monitoring the harvesting of his record crop of onions. He was still there when Roosevelt came to Kingston on 18 August to accept an honourary degree from Queen's University and to share the honour of opening the Ivy Lea Bridge across the St Lawrence with Mackenzie King. Mitch had not been invited. At Queen's in the morning, Roosevelt delivered the dramatic promise that 'the people of the United States will not stand idly by if the domination of Canadian soil is threatened by any other Empire.' Opening the bridge in the afternoon, he made a passionate appeal for construction of the St Lawrence seaway and dropped what he promised King would be a bomb. And it was the bomb, not the president's interest in the defence of Canada, that won headlines in the Toronto press.[13]

The Americans had moved ahead with a new draft of the St Lawrence treaty within weeks of their despatch giving the coup de grâce to Mitch's request to export power. In a long memorandum for Roosevelt, Leland Olds, chairman of the Federal Power Commission, outlined the features of a new treaty which would be so attractive that neither Canada nor Ontario could turn it down. Roosevelt accepted the proposal at once and, on 28 May, the secretary of state, Cordell Hull, forwarded a draft treaty to the Canadian legation in Washington. King sent it to Mitch on 31 May with the comment that it had not been reviewed in Ottawa.

The very attractive proposal reflected Roosevelt's determination to develop the river as a public utility before some political misadventure, such as a Republican victory, might give the advantage once again to the private power interests. The Americans proposed that they move ahead with the International Rapids section, but that Canada be permitted to delay its share of the project until Ontario could absorb the power. Meanwhile Ontario would be permitted to divert the northern rivers and have the right to all the additional power generated at Niagara. Mitch had not replied to the proposal when Roosevelt dropped his bomb.[14]

After extolling the magnificence of the river beneath them, with its power running largely unused to the sea, Roosevelt said that it was true, 'as has been true of all natural resources, that a good many people would like to have the job – and the profits – of developing it for themselves. In this case, however, the river happens to be placed in the hands of our two Governments and the responsibility for getting the results lies plainly at our doors.' After a brief pause, he continued:

Let me make, now, an unusual statement, I am sure you will not misunderstand. I consider that I have, myself, a particular duty in connection with St. Lawrence power. The almost unparalleled opportunity which the river offers has not gone unnoticed by some of my friends on our side of the boundary. A conception has been emerging in the United States which is not without a certain magnificence. That is no less than the conviction that if a private group could control the outlet of the Great Lakes basin, that group would have a monopoly in the development of a territory larger than many of the great empires of history.

If you were to search the records with which my Government is familiar, you would discover that literally every development of electric power, save only the Ontario Hydro, is allied to, if not controlled by, a single American group, with, of course, the usual surrounding penumbra of allies, affiliates, subsidiaries and satellites.

The astute Skelton was aghast. 'The moment I saw a press report,' he warned King at once, 'I felt certain that he had pressed a button that would automatically result in Mr. Hepburn coming out with a blast against it within 24 hours.'[15]

The blast, in the form of a letter to King, was released to the press in less than twenty-four hours. King's letter of 31 May had not been answered, Mitch wrote, because Washington had made its proposal to Ottawa and 'I would like to know what your policy is, if any, and should you have a policy, what proposal you have to submit to this Government for consideration.' Not only did Ontario have adequate power, indeed a 'huge surplus – for which it must pay and receive no benefit,' but 'as the keystone province of the Dominion, we are also interested in the railway situation which has not been improved since you have been head of the administration at Ottawa. Until such time as you solve what is considered to be one of the major problems of Canada – that of national railway deficits – I cannot conceive how you could seriously consider spending public funds for the purpose of creating another public, competitive avenue of transportation' which would increase the CNR deficits, throw railway men on the relief rolls, and threaten the credit of the country. 'Irrespective of any propaganda or squeeze play that might be concocted by you, you may rest assured that this Government will resist any effort to force us to expend public funds in such an unwarranted manner or to foist upon the people of Ontario an additional burden of debt and taxation.' When reporters asked if the Ivy Lea speech was part of a squeeze play, Mitch replied: 'You can draw your own conclusions.'[16]

Floyd Chalmers interviewed Mitch later on 19 August. Mitch rejected the suggestion that he would reconsider the St Lawrence if he got a better financial deal from Ottawa, 'because Ontario was half of Canada and he intended to do what he could to keep the Canadian government too from going bankrupt because Ontario would have to pay the bills anyway.' As far as he could determine, Mitch continued, the 'campaign for the Waterway was merely political propaganda inspired by Roosevelt. Roosevelt wanted it because he wanted to ruin the United States private power companies. He, Hepburn, had no intention of being a party to a dirty game like that.' Chalmers was intrigued, and speculated that

it is just possible that back of Hepburn's opposition to the Waterway there may be some influence that was not revealed in my conversation with him. For instance, it is possible that Hepburn is fighting the Waterway because he does not want it developed while Roosevelt is in power, because the

Mellon-Morgan interests (Aluminum Corp. – Niagara-Hudson) have sold him on the idea of blocking the waterway until Roosevelt is out of office and it will be possible to develop the St. Lawrence and divert the U.S. share of the power to private interests? Where does 'Ben' Smith sit on this? Where does Sir. James Dunn fit in? Dunn, I happen to know, consistently urged Hepburn not to go ahead with the Waterway on the ground that it would bankrupt Ontario and both of the major railway systems.

Convinced by his earlier conversations with Hogg that Ontario would need St Lawrence power as soon as it could be generated, Chalmers asked Mitch what he would do if Hydro needed more power. Duplessis was going to create a Quebec version of Ontario Hydro, he replied, and the two public power systems 'would get together on joint developments on the Ottawa River, when they were needed, or might adopt the alternative of "swapping" power sites – Quebec developing say, the Carillon Rapids and Ontario developing Ste. Joachim.' Agreeing that he and Hydro engineers seemed to be 'poles apart' on future demand, Mitch observed that Hydro had been wrong before and could be wrong again.[17]

King spoke at Bill Mulock's picnic in North York the day after Mitch's blast. The tone of his response was clearly dictated by the widespread criticism of the coarseness of Mitch's outburst, even by those who agreed with him on the St Lawrence. McCullagh, whose relations with Mitch had improved, agreed that the St Lawrence was uneconomic, but warned him editorially that he was 'alienating public sympathy by his crude performances and his obvious attempt to crash into the limelight on his own terms. This kind of vituperation cannot be laid to anything but petty jealousy ... It is getting tiresome and nauseating.' King's response was the language of reason and moderation. The treaty proposed by the United States provided a solid basis for study and negotiation which, he added to applause, would be carried out 'in a manner befitting the importance of the issue at stake, and according to the wishes of the Canadian people as to how public business should be conducted.'[18]

In his official response, King proposed that Mitch agree to detailed technical studies. Mitch replied that, as King had pointed out, 'most of the matters arising within the proposed Treaty can be determined and settled only by the Government of Canada. For me to participate in any negotiations or discussions looking to the formation of Dominion Government policy could only lead to confusion. It is your responsibility, not mine, and it would be equally embarrassing to both of us if I took any part in it.' If King persisted in moving ahead, Mitch warned, 'I wish to be entirely untrammelled in my discussion of any proposal which may come from your Government when and if you decide to announce a policy on the St. Lawrence development.' Ontario remained convinced of the enormous benefits of the developments above Niagara, he concluded, and if King was 'interested in supporting a constructive development policy for Ontario, I shall be pleased to renew representations already made to you on this subject.'[19]

As far as Mitch was concerned the door was closed. And King was happy to leave it closed, for he had never been enthusiastic over the project and did not want to engage in a battle with Mitch, Duplessis, and the powerful anti-St Lawrence interests centred in Montreal. But the Americans had an ally in Dr Hogg, who also believed that 'the door could not be closed.' In a long talk late in August with Leland Olds, Hogg 'reflected Hepburn's indignation at being put on the spot in his own backyard and suggested that, as a result, he was more obstinate than ever on the St. Lawrence project.' But Hogg told Olds that King could break 'the jam blocking the treaty if he would accept the responsibility for agreeing with the United States without waiting for Hepburn's consent.' King would not be taking a risk because Ontario would need the power before 1949.

With this information, Frank Walsh pressed Roosevelt to tell King that he was 'unwilling to stand by and let the personal pique of one man threaten the ability of the great Ontario Hydro Electric Commission to meet its requirements seven years hence,' a requirement acknowledged by Hydro itself. The treaty offered the promise of employment, the upstream and downstream benefits of the northern diversions, and removed the long-term prospect of a power shortage and 'hand-to-mouth dependence on more costly power from some other source.' Finally, King should be told that 'negotiation of the treaty enabling the United States to obtain power which it needs for the production of supplies in case of war is no more than a gesture of reciprocity for the good neighbour attitude expressed by its President. A dog-in-the-manger policy would hardly be compatible with that country's many friendly acts.' Such gentle American pressure, Walsh suggested, might 'show the Prime Minister the safe grounds on which he could take action without Hepburn's consent. It would certainly have the effect, by giving him a glimpse of our view of the situation, of making it more difficult for him to evade the responsibility by shifting it to Mr. Hepburn's shoulders.' Fortunately for King, neither the White House nor the State Department chose to follow Walsh's Machiavellian strategy and, for the moment at least, the door Mitch had slammed remained closed.[20]

By the fall of 1938 the relations between King and Mitch were moving inevitably to some kind of open political confrontation. Mitch had broadened his attacks on the King government, moving beyond concrete bilateral issues to more general questions of national policy, including rearmament. As the recession deepened, he spoke more frequently of the need for credit expansion and monetary reform to avoid national bankruptcy. Mitch was vague, but in general he seemed indistinguishable from Liberal inflationists, such as Gerry McGeer of Vancouver, or W.D. Herridge, who was about to launch the New Democracy Movement with Aberhart's support, or even Aberhart himself. Moreover, he had become the mouthpiece for Colin Campbell's argument that if gold were held at home instead of exported, it could be used to expand currency at a ratio of four to one. But Mitch admitted privately he knew little about the details of monetary reform, and when asked what he meant, replied, 'Oh, a little more inflation. Make money cheaper.' That, he felt, could be achieved by lowering interest rates and expanding the currency to raise commodity prices and create a pool of capital to finance public works projects.[21]

Mitch's political machinations were much more menacing than his excursions into economics. Rumours reached Ottawa in August that he would help Manion in the next election by running his own Liberals in every riding. At Sarnia in October, he said that he would never 'live down' his participation in the 1935 election and remarked that he was looking forward to the day when his host, Ross Gray, and other Liberal MPs would bring about a change in party leadership. In November, he put South Waterloo under quarantine during the federal by-election and, despite the intervention of the Ontario federal ministers, the Liberal candidate lost his deposit. Since his embargo on contributions to Lambert's bagmen by anyone seeking favours from Queen's Park was already having the desired effect, Waterloo South seemed an ominous forecast of defeat in the election expected in 1939.[22]

More menacing was the prospect of a Hepburn-Duplessis alliance in the federal field. Allied in their opposition to communism, the CIO, the St Lawrence, and the expected thrust of the royal commission, they seemed to be bound by more than a pinch of temperament. The possibilities of some alliance, on policy at least, were certainly being promoted by Sir James Dunn when he returned to

Canada in the fall. He had several long talks with Mitch, and dropped him a note on the morning of his return to London:

Maurice breakfasted with me and I told him of our last interview on policy with which I understand he is in agreement. I gather he has some idea of an independent report before putting the railways together but I do not think he holds any strong view on the subject that would be out of line with your policy. On defence I found him in entire agreement, stressing Canadian independent preparation ready to act with both Britain and the United States in defending this Continent but strongly preferring the British political association to the American. I understand him to see with you the necessity of putting our financial house in order to Canada before calamity overtakes us ... Maurice is 100 per cent for your leadership and I understand is going to see you on the 15th.

Also mailed from Rimouski was a letter thanking Duplessis for the roses in his stateroom: 'After our talk this morning I wrote Mitch that I thought your views and his harmonized and that together you could do as fine a service to Canada as MacDonald [*sic*] and Cartier did seventy odd years ago. The ship they launched on the seas of fortune is having very rough weather now but I believe my two friends are the navigators who can bring her safe to port.' Senator Dandurand was also on the *Empress* and Dunn indiscreetly boasted that he had carried 'messages from Hepburn to Duplessis concerning the two combining together for the next general elections.'[23]

In the middle of November, after Duplessis had been Mitch's guest at the Royal Winter Fair, John Dafoe instructed George Ferguson at the *Free Press* to 'keep a complete file of those Dromios: Hepburn and Duplessis ... A certain pattern is beginning to appear in their speeches: Lack of action by the King govt is deplored; the great possibilities in the way of recovery given a govt of action; and so forth.' Dafoe suspected that 'the pair are grooming themselves – or being groomed' for the federal election expected in 1939 and were deliberately

pre-empting wide areas of discussion. Mr. Hepburn's colleague Campbell wants a new-fangled currency system based upon our gold production; both Hepburn & Duplessis employ vague language capable of being interpreted as a sort of overtone for a campaign of soft money, social credit, currency depreciation or some such panacea ... There is something in the wind. One wd say that this hinting at monetary 'reform' wd at once build a barrier between them and big business, C.P.R. etc; but I don't know that this is necessarily so. I would not be surprised if Beatty and his pals wd support any movement calculated to break up the two old parties, neither of wh will take orders from him. The whole thing wd be a grand adventure and a great game of grab; each of the players wd hv his own hopes of the fish he wd get in the troubled waters. I don't think there is a definite organization yet but the possibilities are being explored. I am rather happy at the prospect of A.G. D.[exter] being available for the purpose of getting the low-down on these gentry.[24]

There was something in the wind, but Dunn's sailors had neither set their sails nor selected their port.

Whatever other objectives he may have had, Mitch seemed obsessed with removing Mackenzie King from the leadership of the country and the party. Jimmy Gardiner was also at the Winter Fair and Mitch hoped to see him, perhaps to show-off his prize-winning Percherons, perhaps to talk politics. With King's approval, Gardiner saw Mitch on 17 November and warned that he would report the substance of their conversation to Laurier House. Gardiner informed King that Mitch had told him that the prime minister was so unpopular in Ontario and 'he was so strongly opposed to the attitude toward Ontario of the Federal Government, as led by Mr. King' that there would be South Waterloos across Ontario unless the federal leadership changed before the next federal election. Mitch had already warned friends of the Ontario government not to assist the federal party and was determined to defeat King 'whether it destroyed the Liberal Party or not.'

What Gardiner did not tell King initially was that in his attempt to be conciliatory, he suggested that Mitch, like any other Liberal leader, should not hesitate to make recommendations about key cabinet or senatorial appointments and discuss important policy matters with the provincial ministers and the prime minister. Gardiner's suggestion must have led Mitch to wonder whether he was the only Liberal told to stay in his own backyard after the 1935 election, but he replied bluntly that he would have nothing to do with Liberal patronage so long as King remained in office. From the discussion, Gardiner stated, 'grew the suggestion that he was prepared to support the nominee of the Liberal Party when he came before the people with a progressive policy and intimated that he would be prepared to support me under those circumstances.' Gardiner replied that 'while he appreciated the compliment,' he would remain loyal to King as long as he was leader of the Liberal party.[25]

A few days later, Mitch called Gardiner to say that after talking to some of his friends he had reconsidered his position and asked him to return for another talk on 25 November. King summarized the substance of Gardiner's second report in his diary:

Hepburn had said that he had gone much too far in what he said about me; that he had come to the conclusion that, for the sake of the Liberal Party, he might, when the time came, tell his own followers that he would give up the leadership in Ontario, so as to avoid embarrassment. Neither Gardiner nor I were sure whether this was genuine or another device to make the breach deeper indefinitely – a fight between the two of us, Hepburn believing his own popularity is so great. I told Gardiner it was for Hepburn to do as he pleased. He said he had given my message that I still did not know what the difference was and had no feeling in the matter, but would like to see the gulf breached; Hepburn had again said it was not anything I had done but things I had not done, and spoke of the power business, export of power, and the diversion of water from the North at Long Lac and Ogoki, which, by the way, he has given orders to discontinue. He knows this to be quite untrue.

Initially, King felt that Gardiner had been frank in his explanation, but later, when he gave a slightly different version to cabinet, King suspected that 'there had been much more in the way of seeing and staying with each other than seemed to be necessary in a man who was as treacherous throughout as Hepburn has shown himself to be.'[26]

Mitch continued to press Gardiner's leadership as the price of Liberal unity. When Gardiner's friend T.C. Davis, the attorney general of Saskatchewan, dropped by Queen's Park early in December, Mitch said that the entire weight of his government and organization would be in the field with Gardiner. Harry Nixon and Bethune Smith agreed. With King as leader and without his support, Mitch warned that the Liberals would win no more than a dozen seats in Ontario and twenty-five at the outside in Quebec. 'He seemed to be particularly pleased with this prospect,' Davis informed Gardiner, 'and I was satisfied that this matter had been the subject of discussion by him and Duplessis.'[27]

Mitch's scheming seemed more menacing when King learned on 2 December that Harry Johnson had attempted to convert two leading Liberal fund-raisers in Montreal, Gordon Scott and Senator Donat Raymond. In his conversation with Scott, Johnson was vague about the purpose of his visit, and only after 'milling around for a time,' said that the breach between Hepburn and King would destroy the party at the next election unless it could be overcome.

However, he could 'guarantee Hepburn's support a hundred per cent' if Scott and others would support Gardiner for the leadership and, in apparent contradiction to what Mitch had told Gardiner, 50 per cent if Mitch had the right to nominate two cabinet ministers. Pressed by Scott to say who sent him, Johnson hesitated before replying that he had come with 'Hepburn's knowledge and consent' to ask Scott to see Mitch in Toronto. As Johnson must have anticipated, Scott immediately informed his close friend Norman Lambert and the prime minister. King thought it might be a good idea for Scott to go to Toronto and draw Mitch out further, but Lapointe said it would be a mistake for Mitch was 'such a liar; would misconstrue the situation.' If Mitch wanted to talk, he could go to Montreal.[28]

On 8 December King and Gardiner reported to cabinet on their respective meetings with Scott and Mitch. It was obvious, said King, 'that Hepburn was a traitor, false to myself, false to the Government, and that the time had come when I should openly denounce him.' He had expected that some of his colleagues 'would have been the first to denounce Hepburn's treachery when directed against myself,' but since they had not, when he spoke out he would 'spare no one that I had reason to believe was in any way false.' When Rogers innocently asked if he objected to ministers speaking out, King replied he was surprised they had not done so. The discussion then turned to tactics, and King felt that 'I should not appear to be defending myself, but that it would be preferable I thought for the Ministers themselves to say something which would bring forth a protest from Hepburn at which time I could then follow the matter up.' It was a virtuoso performance before a largely unsuspecting audience.[29]

Tired of King's caution, and suspecting that Mitch and Charles Cox, the MLA, were intriguing to prevent his nomination at Port Arthur, Howe had already decided to attack Mitch at the convention. King was delighted when Rogers agreed to deliver the major address and 'did not give a damn about the consequences.' The nominating meeting itself, on the afternoon of 10 December, was uneventful when, with Cox on the platform with King's ministers, the convention dutifully nominated Howe and passed resolutions of confidence in both King and Hepburn. But Cox had learned of the impending attack and was not there in the evening when Rogers was to be guest speaker.[30]

The time had come, said Rogers, when the 'conspiracy and intrigue' in the land had to be subjected to the purifying sunlight of publicity, when those responsible for the 'instability and menacing growth of sectionalism' had to be named, and when the Hepburn-Duplessis alliance, with its 'basis in personal and political animosities' had to be exposed and denounced. 'But that is only part of the story,' he continued:

I want you to listen carefully to what I am about to say – within the past few weeks it has become increasingly apparent that Mr. Hepburn has determined to use all the powers at his disposal to bring about the retirement of the Prime Minister of Canada, with the evident purpose of setting up a Government at Ottawa which would be largely dependent on and largely controlled by the provincial Governments at Toronto and Quebec.

However fantastic this may sound, I am convinced that it is the sober truth. Whatever dispute there may be as to details, I believe that this objective has become the underlying purpose of this unnatural alliance between Mr. Hepburn and Mr. Duplessis. That attempt has failed. It will continue to fail ...

If this deliberate attempt to supplant Mr. King had succeeded, it would have had far-reaching and disastrous results. A national government, controlled in the interests of two of the nine provinces of this Dominion, in their own interest, would be an outright contradiction of Federal self-government. It would be a political monstrosity, It could not survive. The people of Canada could not and would not long submit to it. But before it was destroyed, it could do untold damage to this country.

Although the attempt had failed, Hepburn and Duplessis had been ready – 'and perhaps are still ready – to make overtures to Dr. Manion, the Conservative leader, with the same object.' 'We have been exceedingly patient,' Howe added in his acceptance speech, but 'there is a time when patience ceases to be a virtue. There is a time when plain speaking and blunt words must be resorted to. There comes a time when a spade must be called a spade. That time, ladies and gentlemen, is now.'[31]

The front pages of the Monday morning papers carried the story from Port Arthur and a long reply from Mitch at the farm. Mitch denied categorically that there was an alliance with Duplessis and insisted again that he had no desire to go to Ottawa. But he did not deny that he wanted to get rid of King.

Let me ask this simple question: What has the King government, in its three and a half years, done to deserve the support of those who elected it in 1935? ... I don't think there ever was a government which was elected with greater promise, and which has failed more dismally. Its attitude on all important policies has been one of laissez-faire. Its performance has been one of drifting. Its ministers appear to be living in another generation altogether ... Why shouldn't I – or anyone else with the welfare of the country in mind, for that matter – take exception to the half-baked, impracticable, unworkable theories which emanate from Ottawa? Most of their policies are predicated on the assumption that Ontario will cooperate with them and embark on a spending spree. Do they face their share of responsibility? Oh, no! They pass legislation that does not implement the purpose they have in mind. They won't stand on their own feet, but they pass the buck to Ontario. Let Ontario shoulder the burden of their unworkable schemes. That, in a nutshell, is their tactics.

If Rogers and Howe wanted to make an issue of which government was shirking its responsibilities, he was 'prepared to go out on the hustings and fight them to the limit. If that's the sort of thing Rogers and Howe are looking for, let them say so. All they have to do is toss the gauntlet down to me, and they'll get all they're looking for. More too.'[32]

After reading the morning paper over breakfast, King wrote a statement for the press. He had already decided 'to see that my own Party show their colours at once, and that no one is left until the end of the Session to show where he stands. Those that are not openly and above board with us from now on will be put in this category, and given a place outside the party.' In his statement, King unequivocally declared that he believed the charge of the unnatural alliance was true. For a year and a half he had done nothing to widen the breach, in the hope that 'legitimate differences, whatever they might be, would disappear or be removed.' The issue, as it had developed,

transcends the narrower considerations of personalities and parties. It has become one involving the standards which are to prevail in the public life of Canada, in the relations between the provinces and the Dominion, and the whole question of national unity. This issue must be and will be squarely faced. To that end, as a first step, I intend, as soon as Parliament reassembles to discuss the situation in all its implications with members of the party in the House of Commons and the Senate. That is all I have to say for the present.

With speculation on the Hill that Ian Mackenzie and Gardiner had been involved in the conspiracy, the *Star* ran its story under the headline KING MAY PURGE CABINET OF HEPBURNITES.[33]

Arthur Carty was interviewing Mitch that afternoon when his editor phoned with the news from Ottawa that Mitch had approached Gardiner to lead an insurrection. Privately, Mitch told Carty his reply to them was 'Damned be he who first cries, "hold! enough",' but for publication said only: 'This is a time for taking stock and inventory. It has been put up to me as a challenge. I could go out and take the platform against King, but I am not in a position to make any declaration. This situation has flared up too suddenly.' But a few more attacks would bring the fight into the open and King could 'find out how the wind blows by opening up a few more Ontario seats.'

Mitch denied ever having approached Mackenzie or Power. 'As I said of Mr. Gardiner, they would not discuss the possibility of accepting the party leadership while members of the King cabinet.' Mitch described the charge of conspiracy as a 'contemptible lie,' and was blunt about his own position. 'Rather than submit to another five years of such apathetic rule, and callous indifference to the needs of the people of Ontario, I would support another party, but I would not lead a third party.' Asked if he would vote for Manion or King, Mitch replied: 'Vote for Bob Manion – at least he's human. I can forgive a man for making mistakes, as most Tories do, rather than have a man who does nothing and never tries.'[34]

Mitch returned to Toronto for a major luncheon address to the Empire Club on 15 December. Given the circumstances, it was one of the largest meetings in the club's history. Speaking largely from a prepared text, Mitch vehemently denied that in putting Ontario's case squarely before the Rowell-Sirois commission he was out to destroy Confederation. Ontario taxpayers were already subsidizing the economies of the prairies and the maritimes, while the federal treasury sucked in three-quarters of the revenue from resource development in the north, and the other provinces looked rapaciously at the estates of the millionaires in the audience. Ontario had put its financial house in order, but Ottawa was running up enormous deficits and the growing debt charges could only be met by borrowing and increasing taxes. Admitting that his views on monetary reform were not popular, Mitch again called for a national refunding scheme before the country went bankrupt. However, he had no confidence in King's leadership, and reminded the applauding audience that the man who now preached national unity had in 1930 said 'Not a 5 cent piece for any province with a Tory government!' King was 'getting so near to the 5 cent piece, so far as relief is concerned,' he added, that 'I'm questioning my own political affiliations at this moment.' The audience of conservative businessmen had been 'distinctly chilly' as Mitch outlined his heretical monetary views, but 'he was so good humored, made so many quite witty remarks and told jokes including some against himself,' noted Main Johnson of the *Star,* that before it was over 'he won the increasing sympathy and applause of the audience.'

Soon after he returned to Queen's Park, Mitch felt dizzy and nauseous. He returned to the hotel and before the day was over had been examined by five doctors. The diagnosis: extreme hypertension, with blood pressure between 230 and 240, and the very real danger of a heart attack or stroke. Mitch stayed in bed, amid reports that he planned to resign, until he was well enough to travel to St Thomas on 19 December.[35]

Meanwhile in Ottawa, King had finally decided that the time had come, as he said, to separate 'the wheat from the chaff', although he refused to tell cabinet on 13 December what should be done. In answer to a question from Euler, he replied coldly 'that if he discovered a viper gnawing at his breast he would know, I think, what to do.' He pointedly stated that dissolution was his prerogative and that he planned to leave any cabinet appointments until he 'had found out where the different men stood, each man to be given a chance to show his colours.' Nothing could be clearer, and within twenty-four hours the Ontario ministers had called a caucus of members and defeated candidates for Monday, 19 December.[36]

On Saturday Arthur Slaght phoned King to say that Mitch was 'very, very ill' and he hoped that neither Rogers nor Howe would make matters worse by issuing a statement 'such as, that gentleman is to be read out of the party, etc.,' for Mitch would resign in a few days and retire from public life. King had no intention of letting sympathy influence caucus and said nothing of the conversation. He concluded at once that when Mitch 'found he was squarely faced with a fight, he has taken to drink and is probably in a bad way.' But the fact that Slaght had discussed the caucus with Ian Mackenzie, who opposed an open break with Mitch, rekindled the embers of suspicion that all was not well in the kingdom:

Personally, I have, for a long time past, watched with interest the eagerness of some of my colleagues to associate with Hepburn in a provincial campaign, and to identify themselves with him since. Power, Mackenzie, and Gardiner have been conspicuous in this way. I have not doubted their loyalty to myself so long as I was Leader, but I felt that they realized that sooner or later, I would be dropping out and that another group would come probably into control; that Hepburn, having the machine in his hands, would probably be the successor or dictator. Mackenzie and Power, through their habits, are dangerous men for an association of this kind. Gardiner has his ambitions but is quite different in character. I think all of them now realize the precarious position in which they have placed themselves.

However, though his hatred was undiminished, King's political instincts led him to call Rogers on Sunday 'cautioning him against having anything done tomorrow which might serve to alienate Ontario Ministers, to confine what was being made of record to the Resolution regarding confidence and organization; to be firm in exposing treachery and the causes for action at the time it was taken in case it had to be continued, but to keep in mind the possibility of Hepburn dropping out and the need then to get the Party united.'[37]

The strategy had been carefully prepared in an all-day meeting at Lambert's on Sunday. When the caucus met on Monday at eleven, the members had before them a carefully drafted document which, after noting that King had been 'the subject of criticism' in Ontario, resolved that in view of his 'courageous public services ... wisdom and statesmanship ... we declare our unbounded confidence in his leadership, and unreservedly pledge our loyalty, devotion and support for the future.' Despite its lack of punch, caucus did not adopt the resolution immediately and enthusiastically. In the discussion the members supported King, but there were some, like Bill Fraser and Ross Gray, who argued that it was important not to break irrevocably with Mitch and divide their own supporters. It was after two before the handful of dissidents gave way. Only H.A. McKenzie, the MP for Lambton-Kent, slipped out while the resolution was being passed around for all to sign. That afternoon W.A. Taylor, the caucus chairman, took the resolution to Laurier House. Moments after Taylor left, King wrote him to thank caucus for the 'unqualified expression' of confidence.[38]

Mitch laughed at the report that he was to be excommunicated, for he had taken the provincial party out of the national party two years ago. Indeed, there had been no excommunication because, as one journalist put it, the rank and file 'didn't like the idea of a feud between two Liberal leaders threatening to make a Tory Roman holiday of them in the constituencies.' The caucus had appointed a sub-committee of seventeen under Euler to consider party organization, but stopped short of opening up shop in Toronto. Moreover, Gray and Fraser had insisted on going to see Mitch and, as

Howe explained to King, 'caucus had acquiesced but had issued no instructions.' Informed of the mission, Mitch said there would be 'no compromise' and the OLA would have nothing to do with Euler's committee of reconciliation. If some of the Ontario MPs had sufficient 'backbone,' they would come out in the open and fight the battle in the constituencies because ultimately the voters would decide whether they wanted another five years of 'drifting' or a government with a 'national spirit.'[39]

Gray and Fraser returned from their 'peace mission' to Mitch's sick bed at Bannockburn, and reported that he was 'prepared to keep quiet' and that 'a united front from now on was to be the word.' Listening to the discussion at cabinet that afternoon, King 'felt they had a knowledge that Hepburn intended to drop out and they were seeking to have themselves appear as the great conciliators in the management of Ontario affairs.' He concluded, however, that 'some progress had been made in the way of "appeasement". It is clear that Fraser and Gray and those who have been associated with Hepburn are anxious to get things cleared up as rapidly as they can.' Fraser and Gray boasted publicly that the 'Ontario Liberal Party, provincial and federal, will be out to fight Tories, both Manion and Drew, in the next election.'

Mitch said nothing. He told the Cartys that Gray and Fraser had agreed that there would be no more attacks on him and 'I agreed to lay off King for a while, and that's how matters stand. But I did not agree to support King in the next election. Fraser had no reason to make that statement.'[40]

Rumours that over-indulgence and ill-health would force Mitch to retire had circulated among the *cognoscenti* since the spring. Late in May Mitch's doctors confined him to quarters for two weeks. By the summer it was common gossip that his doctors had told him he had either to leave politics or risk his life. He was sick on and off during the fall and his friends and colleagues found him increasingly irritable and unpredictable. From what he heard in Toronto late in November G.W. Gordon reported to King that he 'would blow up and Nixon would succeed.' His collapse on 15 December was not unexpected.[41]

Mitch had recovered sufficiently the next day to receive a number of his colleagues at the hotel, whose reticence on leaving persuaded the press that Mitch was through. According to Slaght, Mitch had decided to resign at once and had selected Conant as his successor, but Nixon and others refused to attend the coronation.

Reluctantly or not, Mitch yielded to their pressure and agreed to hang on through one more session. At the farm a few days later he told reporters that although he felt miserable there were 'a few kicks in the old horse yet.'[42]

If stress contributed to Mitch's hypertension, it could hardly be attributed to his arduous tasks at Queen's Park. Apart from his running battle with King, it had not been a trying year. The session had gone well. His ministers were solid and reliable and Chester Walters kept his hand firmly on the rudder. By-elections had confirmed his government's popularity, and he had generously withdrawn the Liberal in Parkdale in October in favour of ex-mayor and Tory strongman, W.J. Stewart, 'in recognition of his outstanding public service.' Although he was concerned about the growing number of jobless, widespread layoffs had destroyed the CIO momentum, union membership was dropping dramatically, and the labour scene was remarkably peaceful.[43]

There seemed to be so little to do that Mitch was seldom to be found at Queen's Park. The *Star* estimated that after the session he had averaged about a day a week at the buildings, and then for only a few hours. The 'absentee' premier obviously preferred to run Ontario from his suite in the King Eddy, the onion fields and stables at Bannockburn, or, the *Star* unkindly put it, 'remoter points which usually only a few of the premier's intimate friends know.' Mitch did find his $100-a-month suite more congenial than his office, and his friends more fun than his colleagues. Harry Johnson was downstairs; Frank O'Connor kept a room in the hotel; Jack Bickell's office was just a few blocks away; and McCullagh and Slaght were just around the corner. Selected friends among the gentlemen of the press – Bill Shields, even though he worked for the *Star*, Vernon Knowles of the *Telegram*, and Ken McTaggart of the *Globe* – had ready access to the suite and occasionally accompanied him on his political or extra-curricular jaunts. Mitch enjoyed the relaxed and carefree environment, with good company and good drink. Harry Johnson feared that Mitch's indiscretions were politically dangerous and others, such as Paul Martin, found the excesses distasteful, but Mitch seemed unconcerned about the possibility of scandal.[44]

Mitch did live on the edge of scandal. The allegations of a Dr Shields could be dismissed as the ranting of a lunatic fringe of 'sanctimonious, psalm singing preachers.' And the repeated digs about his private life by the Tories – Mitch Hepburn should be interested in the tariff on eggs, quipped the Tory MP for London, 'as he takes such a keen interest in the chickens' – might be laughed off. But the report of Sir Anthony Jenkinson, a visiting British journalist who clearly did not know the rules of the King Eddy game, was a little more damaging. After Mitch greeted him at the door, Jenkinson wrote, he introduced his friends. 'They were his doctor and a member of his government and two attractive girls who sprawled on a sofa and called the Prime Minister "Chief" and who generally lent an unparliamentary air to the place. A big broad-shouldered fellow with the supple movements of a trained athlete mixed drinks ... It was evident that he acted as a sort of bodyguard-cum-gentleman's servant to the Prime Minister. The latter called him "Eddie", but the girls called him "Bruiser".' When B.K. Sandwell printed excerpts in *Saturday Night*, Mitch expressed his displeasure and Sandwell assured him there was no 'personal animus' in his decision. Mitch contemplated suing Jenkinson and Sandwell and turning the $250,000 over to charity, with Heenan and McCullagh as his star witnesses. 'It sounds very good except for one thing,' said McCullagh. 'And what's that?' asked Mitch. 'That you won't be able to get me to commit perjury,' George replied.[45]

That Mitch drank to excess was hardly a point worth making. Howard Ferguson was a notorious drunk and many on the Tory front bench, including Leo Macaulay, found coherence difficult in the few after-dinner sessions. But booze was damaging Mitch's career and his body, and even hard-drinking friends such as Slaght and O'Connor urged him to take it easy. McCullagh, the self-proclaimed reformed alcoholic, threatened to destroy him unless he took the pledge, but Mitch remained immune to both his blandishments and threats.

But while whiskey went to some men's heads, one journalist joked, it went to Mitch's penis. Mitch did not disguise his fondness for women; indeed, he rather revelled in it. Knowing he would not be displeased, his friends relayed to him the stories and jokes that circulated about his escapades. And the born-again Bruiser reminded him that it was always a good idea to keep a couple of pairs of pajamas under the pillow – 'in case of fire.' Although some Liberals feared that Mitch's indiscretions could destroy his career, others believed they were part of his appeal. During the York South by-election in 1942, when an anonymous letter accused the sixty-seven-year-old Arthur Meighen of having a mistress, George Drew observed that 'It is a strange thing that when a boisterous, full-blooded fellow like Hepburn is charged with fairly extensive amorous adventures, people seem to look upon it as a not unattractive weakness and perhaps many of them get some vicarious pleasure in recounting some of the fabulous tales which have made his performance in this field of activity something of a legend. But there is always something coldly repellent to the general public about the thought of a bishop, or a frigid senior statesman, dallying with the pleasures of Venus.'[46]

Mitch was not a handsome man, like George Drew or George McCullagh. But he had a charm, an electric vitality that drew women to him. Mitch loved Eva. She was a warm and compassionate woman, loved and respected by everyone who knew her. But Mitch needed women with more zip, more fire, women who played, women who put him at risk. He had loved Lucette. He still loved the young girl on the ss *Bermuda* and she was deeply in love with him. Their affair was no secret, even among the journalists who frequented the King Eddy. Occasionally Mitch took her away and she often accompanied him on excursions to Frank O'Connor's lavish farm in Scarborough, Bickell's mansion in Port Credit, James Franceschini's house in Mimico, or his famed stock farm at Dufferin and Sheppard. Mitch was faithful to her after his fashion. Eva was aware of his adultery, but seemed unable or unwilling to impose any marital discipline. She was inclined, at times, to believe it was men such as Slaght who had led him astray, but, said Slaght, 'had come to see that it was part of his own nature.'

Mitch's closest friends were unlikely to keep him on the straight and narrow. By 1938 he was seeing less of Arthur Slaght, who was busy with his flourishing law practice and seat in the Commons, but they remained very close. Slaght turned down King's invitation to join the cabinet because even at sixty-one he was unwilling to give up his 'Bohemian life.' Slaght's mistress was still the beautiful woman who had left a bank to join the civil service early in 1935. She and Mitch's companion had remained intimate friends and, with her younger sister and several other favourites of ministers and courtiers, were referred to as 'the stable' by some of the more proper secretaries in the Whitney Block.[47]

Jack Bickell, the multi-millionaire bachelor who loved fast cars, fast planes, and the fast life, was more than a decade older than Mitch. Bickell was not known for turning down a drink, and at least one of his mistresses stirred the most jaded of men. Bickell brought Ben Smith, the errand boy who had become notorious as 'one of the shrewdest, coolest and most to be feared market operators' in North America, into the circle. The 'Bluff Bear' was as earthy in life as he was fearless on the street and was usually included in the northern hunting and fishing expeditions that looked like small encampments, with a dozen tents and nurses to attend the wounded. Frank O'Connor, widowed in 1931 at the age of forty-six, was less addicted to excess, but he enjoyed life as part of the gang and was never accused of being an overly conscientious chaperon.

Mitch's association with the Bickells and O'Connors, the McCullaghs and Smiths, inevitably fathered rumours that through their hot tips on the market he had become a rich man. Mitch had never been poor. Before the crash of 1929 he had been in the market in a modest way and by 1934 was looking for blue-chip investments. For a time at least, McCullagh volunteered his help and, on at least one occasion, took him in as a silent partner in the purchase of some speculative gold stock on which, with luck, he told Mitch, 'we might make a killing.' That venture might have made Mitch suspicious of McCullagh's advice for the stock, bought at 11 cents had fallen to 2½ cents nine months later. Nevertheless, Mitch had great faith in Ontario's gold mines and, despite the volatility of the stocks, in 1938 told his friend Ned Sparks to hold on to his stock and even bought three hundred shares of Dome himself. However, although Mitch may have profited from 'Sell 'Em' Ben's 'good things' and McCullagh's hot tips, the reports of his killings seem grossly exaggerated.[48]

Yet there were too many signs of wealth to still the rumours or silence Tory whispers that he had made $100,000 on the 1935 bond sale. By 1938 he had forsaken the Buicks that he had driven for fifteen years for a five-passenger Cadillac and a deluxe LaSalle convertible, leaving Eva to drive a Buick. More telling, the Tories believed, was his investment of over $20,000 between 1934 and 1938 to round out his property at Bannockburn.

With over one thousand acres he was one of the largest landowners in the county. He had also invested heavily since the early 1930s in clearing and installing miles of drains in the 100-acre quagmire of the swale grass, weeds, and stunted cedars across the road from the house. From the rich black muck he share-cropped between thirty and fifty thousand bushels of onions, which he graded and processed on the farm, and a rich harvest of potatoes. A new barn he built in 1936 was one of the showpieces of Elgin. His Percherons, including a perfectly matched set of six, were probably the most photographed horses in Ontario and his fine stable of Clydesdales included Torr's Transformer, the grand champion of Canada and the International Stock Show in Chicago in 1939. At times there were as many as 175 horses at Bannockburn. Mitch also had a splendid herd of beef steers and Holsteins. There was also a small army of brood sows and hogs and a thousand or more laying hens. Seven silos stored the corn, wheat, hay and oats that he harvested each year.

Mitch was hardly a farmer's farmer. After 1934 Bill Tapsell, who had started work at Bannockburn in 1928, was the farm manager. As the farm expanded after 1934, with the improvement in agricultural and land prices, Mitch built more houses for the farm hands. By 1936 there were fourteen families, mostly Russian or Ukrainian, with thirty-one children living on the farm. There were twenty regular farm hands, and in the planting and harvesting months as many as fifty worked for Tapsell. Bannockburn was big business. The value of what was described as his 'model farm' was estimated to be over $200,000. Tapsell was never sure it made any money, but Mitch told the Cartys that it had paid its own way and 'had yielded his living at $7,000.00 a year net on the average.'

Mitch especially loved the pond he had converted into the nine-acre Lake Laurier, which he stocked with trout and bass and made into a bird sanctuary. He built a small cottage beside the lake to which he and his friends often retired and enjoyed cruising in a small rowboat with an 'egg-beater' on the stern. Mitch was prouder of Bannockburn than he was of the large mahogany desk and the other trappings of his position at Queen's Park. He opened the farm to friends and neighbours and to delegations of visiting journalists, Rotarians, or agriculturalists. If Mitch could not be there, Eva was a charming hostess. And when he was there, he mastered the ceremonies from atop the Bannockburn Farm wagon drawn by his Percherons. To some the farm resembled a cross between Coney Island and Grand Central Station, but Ed Carty hailed it as a 'glorious place,' where Mitch lived 'in feudal splendour.' As he walked through the fields on his birthday, Mitch turned to a reporter and asked: 'Why am I in politics, when I have all this?' It was a question he must have asked himself again as he recovered at Bannockburn waiting to board the train on new year's eve on his way to Australia.[49]

'A famous man of the Empire'

Long before his collapse in December Mitch had planned to take a long vacation. When Colin Campbell said he was going to Australia to visit a cousin, who had been involved in the various Australian schemes to combat the depression, Mitch decided to join him. Chester Walters had also been interested in Australia's debt conversion and devaluation policies and Mitch invited him and Roy Elmhirst to join the party. 'Australia has applied the necessary remedial measures for her troubles,' Mitch had told reporters on 15 December, just before his collapse. 'She may or may not have a real cure – reports are conflicting – but we are going over there to find out.' Professor Wynne Plumptre hurrumphed that Mitch could find anything he needed to know in the University of Toronto library.[1]

Mitch's friends were concerned that that trip from San Francisco to Sydney would be a nineteen-day happy hour. But he looked tanned and rested when the premier of New South Wales and a minister from the Commonwealth government went out to meet him as the ss *Mariposa* steamed into Sydney harbour. It was just as well that only Chester's expenses were charged to the Ontario taxpayers for there was little time to study. For the next ten days there were receptions, state dinners, concerts, and even parties like those in the King Eddy. 'We would welcome more guests from Ontario,' wrote a friend in the prime minister's office, 'but of course cannot expect the high standard set by your party to be consistently maintained. They still remember you at the Hotel Australia in Sydney and other places and especially "the one with the beautiful voice".' But there were meetings with financial experts, cabinet ministers, and chambers of commerce in Sydney, Melbourne, and Canberra. After ten hectic days they sailed on 3 February and reached Los Angeles on 20 February. 'NO HITS NO RUNS NO ERRORS UNCLE' read the telegram that sped from California to the Toronto friend who playfully called him Uncle Dudley.[2]

Mitch returned home more convinced than ever that what Canada needed was courageous leadership in Ottawa to solve the country's economic problems. While Australia was not a utopia, he concluded, the debt conversion had worked, the central bank had pursued a beneficial monetary policy – 'ours is a donkey engine' – taxation was low, foreign investment healthy, and social legislation advanced. Compared to Australia, Ottawa had been 'asleep at the switch' and unless King abandoned such 'false economic policies' as a guaranteed price for wheat, realistically faced the railway problem, and refunded government debts at current interest rates, Mitch saw only bankruptcy ahead. Canadian problems could be solved, but not by 'burying our heads in the sand like so many ostriches.' Unlike Australia, Canada was also living in an atmosphere of 'false security' while events in Europe and Asia proved that international relations were governed by 'the law of the jungle.'[3]

Mitch's trip to Australia was the last stage in his conversion from the young man who denounced Meighen's 'ready, aye ready' during the 1925 election to an outspoken disciple of the doctrine. As a newly elected MP he had been reluctant to see King attend the 1926 imperial conference, for he was deeply suspicious of British motives and believed Downing Street hoped to get Canada 'to subscribe to some scheme of Imperial Defence.' As the war clouds darkened in the mid-1930s, Mitch had not changed his mind. He approved King's repudiation of Dr Riddell over oil sanctions against Mussolini in 1935, and when King assisted in the castration of the League of Nations at the 1936 Assembly, with his lecture on the role of the good Samaritan, Mitch said that he expressed the view 'of 90 percent of the people of the Dominion. If the 'War Lords of Europe' were determined to have war, he told his friend Ed Carty, he hoped that Canada would 'not be dragged into it.'[4]

By 1938 his position was changing, although it was difficult for contemporaries to know exactly where he stood. Early in the year he argued that Canada should strengthen its own defences and cooperate with the United States in continental defence 'so other countries will consider it advisable to leave us alone.' With Chamberlain on his way to Munich in September 1938, Mitch praised him as a man who 'makes us all proud that we are British, all part of the British Commonwealth of Nations and pledged in loyalty to one King and one cause.' But Canada could no longer 'hide under the paw of the British lion or the wings of the American eagle' and had to rearm. 'When I was a member of the House of Commons I was one of those who strenuously opposed any major armament policy in Canada,' he admitted. 'Today, through force of circumstances I have changed my mind.'[5]

S.M. Bruce, the Australian high commissioner in London who had been called home for foreign policy discussions, was on board the ss *Mariposa*, and he had given Mitch a bleak picture of the prospect for peace in Europe and the Pacific. During his two-week visit Mitch found that, although the Australians still hoped for peace in the days after Munich, they were feverishly preparing for a war that could involve a Japanese attack on the island. He also found them puzzled about Canada's position because the impression left by the Canadian delegation to the Commonwealth Relations Conference in Sydney in September 1938 was that isolationism was strong and the Commonwealth connection weak. Mitch replied that the academics, led by Frank Scott, spoke for no one but themselves, and that Canada was deeply attached to Britain and would not rely for its security on the United States. While the country lacked national leadership, he admitted that even King was spending more on defence than at any time since the war. As he left Australia, Mitch said that he was determined 'to force the issue of proper defence in Canada' when he got home.[6]

Arthur Ford, the Tory editor of the London *Free Press*, and Ralph Hyman of the *Globe* were waiting for Mitch when he reached Chicago on 23 February. Far more concerned about Mitch's political future than his study tour, they reported that although he had shed fifteen pounds, his blood pressure remained high and he had not completely recovered. While Mitch toyed with Hyman about his future, Ford was sufficiently convinced that he would retire after the session to headline his story 'HEPBURN TO QUIT POLITICS.' Privately, Ford claimed that Mitch had told him that 'by getting out of office he could take the platform and go after King, and this is just what he would do.' Publicly Mitch stated that Canada's problem remained the lack of leadership in Ottawa. 'I see no hope in Government which has been tried and found wanting,' he told Ford. 'There are others I believe who will provide the necessary leadership, crystallizing public thought and sentiment in solving our problems.'[7]

George McCullagh had already decided that *he* was just the man to provide the leadership Canada needed. In January he had taken to the air with a series of broadcasts appealing for an end to politics and the formation of a national government. In his final broadcast on 12 February, McCullagh had announced the creation of the Leadership League as a pressure group. Mitch approved of McCullagh's initiative but, despite King's suspicion and Don Hogarth's conviction, he was not part of the conspiracy to use the National Government drive to get rid of King. Indeed, although McCullagh was more friendly to Mitch on his return, the logic of his policy pointed to George Drew, the new Tory leader, as the obvious champion of the cause. By the end of April, however, the League had collapsed for lack of financial nourishment. McCullagh had also collapsed and gone to Santa Barbara suffering from 'complete mental and nervous exhaustion.'[8]

Mitch faced a new and far more talented leader of the opposition when the session opened on 8 March 1939, with a throne speech that indicated the government was marking time. George Drew had easily won the leadership at the December convention despite the concerted, almost obsessive, opposition of Hogarth and the old guard, Rowe and the Frost brothers, and Bennett and the federal party. Over the years Drew had attracted a large following across the province. He seemed to be the only match for Mitch in the House or on the hustings, and he had the powerful support of George McCullagh and Colonel J.B. Maclean and his publishing empire. As Drew took his seat, the press gallery agreed that the tall, well-built man with the slightly greying hair, the faultlessly tailored suit, the poised and dignified bearing, was easily the most handsome man in the House. Although Drew had been bitter in his attacks on Mitch during and after his leadership campaign, Mitch greeted him with a warm smile. He had faced three opposition leaders in five years, he said, and he expected to face three more in the next five.

Mitch had promised to 'go to the mat' with Drew on leaders' day. Drew's maiden speech was not the traditional recitation of false and failed promises, and tales of patronage and corruption. Instead, he launched a vigorous attack on Mitch for his running feud with Mackenzie King and his misguided defence of provincial rights. Indeed, Drew's entire speech sounded vaguely like McCullagh's call for an end to political games and regional squabbling. Drew declared that he believed in 'one strong government dealing with national affairs,' while Mitch's statement before the Rowell-Sirois commission that the provinces must remain 'sovereign and autonomous' was a short step from separation. If the exchange between Mitch and King had taken place on the international scene it would have led to the suspension of diplomatic relations, Drew continued, adding with a smile that he had expected King to follow Chamberlain's example and charter a plane to St Thomas.

His motion of non-confidence regretted that the throne speech 'contains no statement covering the past failure and future intention of the Premier of Ontario to confer with the Prime Minister of Canada for the purpose of considering joint action to increase employment and reduce the cost of Government.' Addressing the Liberal back-benchers, Drew appealed to them to declare

no matter what party is in power in this House, that the head of this government shall co-operate with Ottawa for the welfare of Canada as a whole … Nothing would stimulate Canada more than if this House exerted its free right to vote and put the usurper out of office. Nothing would so restore public confidence in democracy by proving here, when the vote on the amendment is taken, that the members have the courage to forget politics and vote for a united Canada.

Since there was nothing in the throne speech to discuss, said Drew as he sat down, caucus had agreed that his speech would be their first and last.

Mitch clearly had the mat taken from under him. Surprised that Drew had leapt into bed with Mackenzie King, he challenged him to get out on the hustings and explain to the farmers why the price of western wheat but not theirs should be pegged; to the taxpayers why they should pay for even larger federal deficits incurred in bailing out the improvident western provinces; or why King should be praised for trying to saddle Ontario with the St Lawrence while denying it the right to export power or use the northern waters. He was prepared to cooperate, to support unemployment insurance, to avoid duplication; he was not prepared to place the province in bondage. Mitch refused to follow Drew's advice to have the vote and get down to work, and the Liberals droned on for days. Drew's amendment was lost sixty to twenty-two, with only Arthur Roebuck accepting the invitation to vote the usurper out.

Despite a bit of nastiness when Joe Habel dragged up Drew's statement about the 'defeated race,' the mood during the session was good. The Tories were better organized than before, and relaxed House rules allowed for more motions and questions. Drew used the opportunities well and spent much of his time in hot pursuit of Peter Heenan until Mitch agreed to the appointment of a select committee to examine the administration of the Department of Lands and Forests.

There was little controversy over most of the legislative program. The Tories did not object to a wide-ranging bill incorporating the recommendations of a labour-management commission on the Mining Act, chaired by Robert E. Dye of Dome Mines, to improve health and safety in the mines, provide greater protection for prospectors, and license refineries to prevent high grading, but leaving the mines out of the scope of the industrial standards codes. Hippel secured legislation that tightened the minimum wage provisions in the Industrial Standards Act and added more protection for workers under the Workmen's Compensation Board. Speaking on a bill enabling the government to enter into an unemployment insurance agreement with Ottawa, Mitch promised that Ontario would act if Ottawa did not, but warned that King should act before he 'dares to face the people' in another election.

Once again Mitch faced the prospect of a disruptive debate on separate schools. Early in the 1938 session a delegation had met Mitch and the Catholic members of the cabinet requesting legislation to provide Catholic schools with an equitable share of corporation taxes. Mitch sympathized with the objective and, when told that the Conservatives might cooperate if the legislation 'would not take from the Public Schools money rightfully belonging to them,' assured them that 'if the matter could be removed from the sphere of party politics, and if religious conflict could be avoided, he would support legislation fair to both branches of the school system.' Leading Catholic Conservatives agreed at once that the issue should be removed from politics. But Mitch received no guarantee that Macaulay could, or would, discipline the Tory caucus, and at a second meeting he promised only that a more equitable system of financial support would be based on the report of McArthur's commission into the cost of education.[9]

Before mounting their lobby at the 1939 session, the hierarchy and leading lay Catholics forced Quinn's resignation and placed the movement in the hands of a general committee. Each bishop was to write Mitch, Drew, and all the members from his diocese. Early in March a committee of the reorganized association met Drew, who assured them 'of his desire to see justice done' and 'of his willingness to co-operate in every way consistent with his position, in securing a satisfactory solution of the school tax problem.' Although sceptical of Drew's promises, Mitch told the committee he was prepared to appoint a joint committee of the legislature, with five members from both parties, to make recommendations, and stated that he would 'abide by such recommendations and immediately enact legislation to give effect thereto.' When the committee saw Drew again on 23 March, he had changed his mind. Habel's insertion of the 'defeated race' issue, he explained, 'was a violation of an understanding between the Premier and himself that personal matters were to be omitted from debate during the session.' And on 4 April, Drew formally rejected the joint committee proposal on the grounds that 'it was preferable that the ordinary parliamentary procedure be followed by which the Government would take the entire responsibility of introducing the legislation.'

When the committee met Mitch two days later, it found that the stand taken by Drew had confirmed Mitch's earlier view that the 'introduction of school tax legislation would cause religious conflict and would produce fatal consequences for the Party which would risk legislation without a previous understanding and agreement with the Opposition.' Naively believing that as a result of their lobbying they had the support of a majority of the cabinet and caucus, the committee urged Mitch to place the matter before caucus. He did so the last day of the session. Before leaving for a vacation the next day, Mitch phoned James McNevin with the predictable report that 'the unanimous decision of the Members in caucus was in favour of assistance to schools by grants ... and against the amendments to existing legislation.' That spelled the end. As a circular letter to the CTPA in the spring of 1940 stated, it was clear that Mitch intended to do nothing: 'You will, therefore, not expect that your requests for school tax legislation will be presented again during the lifetime of Premier Hepburn's Administration.'[10]

Mitch faced surprisingly little substantial criticism of the budget he brought down on 30 March. He had been able to balance the budget, although the estimated surplus was only $236,000 and increased expenditures on health, education, and municipal assistance were only possible by increasing taxation. Since the succession duty bonanza was over Mitch had to look elsewhere. The Chevrier Commission on Transportation had recommended an increase in the gasoline tax from six to nine cents a gallon. Despite screams from the oil companies and opposition in caucus, Mitch settled on eight which would raise the take from $18 to $25 million and provide over a quarter of the treasury's revenue. Although Mitch also increased the tax on corporation profits from 1 to 3 per cent, and he referred to the increase as a 'readjustment' because it was accompanied by a cut in the tax on paid-up capital, business was not deceived. Mitch admitted that he had failed to live up to his promise not to increase taxes and acknowledged that he had increased the provincial debt by borrowing millions for highway expansion and new hospital construction.[11]

One issue united the House even more than Catholic schools could divide it: the conviction that Ontario, at least, stood 'Ready, Aye Ready' to answer the call of empire. With the visit of King George VI and Queen Elizabeth scheduled for May, Mitch introduced a resolution on the second day of the session praising the imperial connection as the backbone of civilization. Liberals and Tories followed Drew in endorsing the resolution. W.J. Stewart drew applause from both sides of the House when he declared that Professor Frank Underhill should be fired for his subversive remarks about the shrinking Union Jack. Colonel Hunter denounced those who had passed the Statute of Westminster in 1931 for destroying the unity of the empire. J.J. Glass said that as a Jew he applauded the spirit of fair play which was part of the British heritage. Only J.A. Habel cautioned that such hyperbolic flag-waving was not the essence of patriotism.[12]

In the spring of 1939 more than resolutions of loyalty were needed to make Ontario's position clear. Mitch had returned from Australia convinced that a war, probably on two fronts, was imminent and that Canada, unlike Australia, was prepared neither materially nor psychologically for the catastrophe. Hitler's occupation of Prague on 14 March ended the illusion of appeasement. In the legislature on 20 March, Colonel Hunter and Ian Strachan moved that the government of Ontario

should take cognizance of the fact that the present international crisis in Europe calls for immediate action on the part of the component parts of the British Empire in support of any action which it may be necessary for the Imperial Government to take.

And this House hereby requests the Government to introduce a Bill at the earliest possible moment for the purpose of conscripting the property and civil rights of every individual in Ontario to the defence of our free institutions.

Drew and Mitch concurred at once with the sentiment, but Mitch argued that it was not advisable at 'this inopportune time' to embarrass Ottawa in any way. But if Ottawa refused to take a stand, he promised, Ontario would. If war came, he added, 'I believe we should have equality of sacrifice in this country.'

After days of agonizing over a statement of Canadian policy, King had chosen that same afternoon to declare his position. The latest 'disturbance,' he confessed, had come as a surprise. Whatever the circumstances, Parliament would decide on Canada's participation. However, while he did not believe that Canada should be involved in some conflict over trade or prestige 'in some far corner of the world,' if 'there were a prospect of an aggressor launching an attack on Britain, with bombers raining death on London, I have no doubt what the decision of the Canadian people and parliament would be. We would regard it as an act of aggression, menacing freedom in all parts of the British Commonwealth.'

Like much of English Canada, Mitch did not find King's statement sufficiently forthright. Nor did it deter Hitler, who sent his troops into Memel and made aggressive demands for Danzig a day later. On 23 March Mitch continued the debate on foreign policy. With Germany determined to master Europe, Italy to dominate the Mediterranean, and Japan certain to conquer southeast Asia once it had swallowed China, Canada itself was endangered.

I believe that a national emergency exists. I have said we would await a definite pronouncement from the Federal Government, and I don't want to be particularly critical of the Federal Government at this particularly critical time, because I realize that this Dominion is a most difficult country to govern, with its various factions and different schools of thought. But I speak here as the head of the government of Ontario, and I believe that if the government of Canada does not consider itself in a position to make a declaration, as far as open sentiment is concerned, we in Ontario can at least do that.

And in a tight, clipped voice he moved an amendment to the last paragraph in the Hunter motion, declaring that the House 'hereby petitions the Federal Parliament of Canada now in session to immediately pass Legislation providing that in event of a War emergency the wealth and manpower of Canada shall be mobilized by proclamation of the Governor-in-Council for the duration of the war, in defence of our free institutions.'

Drew endorsed it all and more; Liberals and Tories leapt to their feet to applaud; the galleries cheered; and the loudest cheers were for Aurelien Bélanger, who found the resolution too sweeping but promised that the descendants of those who fought in 1775 and at Châteauguay to keep Canada free and British would be loyal to the last man. 'Ontario struck for the Empire yesterday, and for all the Empire stands for in this hour of crisis,' began McCullagh's headline story. 'In dignified but determined terms – with a forcefulness of action that brooked no interference – with a unity of purpose before which racial passion and political prejudice and parochial pride crumbled like moths in a candleflame,' Ontario without a dissenting voice had taken its stand.[13]

On the eve of Queen Victoria's birthday Sir James Dunn decided 'to strike an Imperial note' and urged his good friend Lord Beaverbrook 'to have the glare of your incomparable limelight turned on Mitchell Hepburn who will dominate our country because of rare political flair and first-rate courage to fight a cause through or turn quickly if he gets on the wrong road ... He carried every vote in the Ontario House on his motion to stand with Britain while the straddlers at Ottawa dithered and jellied.' The next day's *Daily Express* carried a column 'On Empire Day let us praise a famous man of the Empire, Mitchell Hepburn, Premier of Ontario.'[14]

When the session ended there was general agreement that it had been the least acrimonious since Mitch had taken office. Although ill with the flu when the session began, Mitch soon recovered and looked better than he had for a long time. Eva and the children were in town for the session, and the hours he spent in the rented house on Riverside Drive were undoubtedly easier on his system than the nocturnal pleasures at the King Eddy. He was almost always in his seat, and was almost always in good humour. He and Drew had agreed to keep personal matters out of the debate and, with a few exceptions, lived with their agreement. Mitch found that Drew improved with age, and told Frank O'Connor that after a few weeks he was 'not the pompous individual who came in when the session opened.'

Mitch remained the master of the front benches, coming to the aid of colleagues when they were in trouble, and encouraging the back-benchers. He was 'still the king pin of the ready wisecrack and the devastating defence by attack,' a journalist noted, but 'he seems to have less interest in the fight for the fight's sake.' There were some who suspected that his less belligerent, almost benevolent, manner suggested that he was bored and would soon find new excitement in national politics or retire and enjoy life. King heard from Slaght that Mitch would resign after the session and advise the lieutenant-governor to call on Conant. Late in April the Tories picked up the rumour that King would not go the country in the fall because Mitch's resignation would enable the Liberals to select a more cooperative successor. Mitch as usual kept his own confidence. He reminds me of the great Honus Wagner, said Tom Murray, the Renfrew MLA who had caught for the Barry's Bay baseball team until he was forty-four. 'He used to steal second and third quite often. An old catcher once was asked why he let him do it. He said that the trouble was you never knew what he was going to do. He always keeps you guessing. Just like my leader, who I admire very much.'[15]

There was no hint of resignation when Mitch climbed abroad Jack Bickell's plane hours after the session adjourned. He planned to spend some time at Bickell's estate on Sea Island in Georgia and enjoy a leisurely Caribbean cruise on his yacht. Mitch was not certain when he would be back at Queen's Park, but certainly in time to receive the royal visitors on 22 May.

Mackenzie King was apprehensive when the royal train pulled into the North Toronto station at 10:30 a.m. on 22 May. His decision to accompany the royal couple across Canada had drawn the nasty comment from Mitch that trailing after them 'like a poodle dog was an effort to gain cheap publicity for his own political aggrandizement.' Asked if he planned to join them for the tour of Ontario, Mitch replied, 'No, I don't think it would be safe for King and myself to be so close together.' Yet together they were from the moment King introduced Mitch and Eva at the station until the train left that night.

Given the occasion, the two men were on their best behaviour. At Queen's Park Mitch introduced the Quints and explained that *this* Mr King was the prime minister of Canada. Sitting beside Eva at the Hart House lunch, King asked if she would like Peter and Patsy presented and a note sent down the table to Mitch brought an affirmative nod. At Woodbine racetrack King invited Mitch to join the king and queen in the royal box to watch McCullagh's horse, Archworth, win the King's Plate. Mitch was overwhelmed by the royal presence, unable to describe his emotions, and treasured the autographed picture of King George and Queen Elizabeth.

Perhaps it was the Scotch he took before dinner that led King to believe that his day with Mitch would 'help to end the feud that he has been seeking to provoke. I think his own Ministers were tremendously relieved and pleased when they saw what I was doing. I think they will persuade him to ease up on his attacks.' However, if he had not 'paved the way for the end of discord,' King concluded that he had positioned himself for 'the inside running of a contest if he begins to participate in a bitter way.' Asked a week later if the day had changed his mind about King, Mitch replied, 'My position is unchanged.'[16]

Mitch's position had dominated much of the political planning by Lambert and the Ottawa Liberals. King intended to have an election some time after the session but, despite the loyalty oath, the party in Ontario was a mess. As an exasperated Lambert exploded at a meeting of the Ontario ministers in January, who is the leader in Ontario, 'Hepburn or whom?' Was Ontario going to return to the National Liberal Federation? There were no answers. When Euler asked him what he proposed, Lambert replied there was only 'one obvious course, a convention in Ont, to set up our association, elect officers & prepare for election.' They drafted a resolution to be presented to the Ontario caucus the next day, but caucus turned it down and cautiously 'supported general instructions to see McQuesten' and find out whether the Ontario Liberal Association, which had not met since 1932, could be revived.[17]

Forewarned by Rogers and Howe not to take too strong a line, King met the full caucus the next day. The feud with Hepburn, he began, was an issue affecting the whole party and the country. It was not a 'personal quarrel' and until Mitch demanded the right to export power, 'I had had no words which could be regarded in the nature of a difference' and even then he had only attempted to explain that Liberals were 'the servants, not the masters of Parliament.' King then spoke of the messages brought by Gray, Fraser, and Gardiner; of the threats of more South Waterloos; of the Hepburn-Duplessis alliance and Johnson's trip to Montreal, all of which 'disclosed the kind of treachery' exposed at Port Arthur. It was not the Liberal party that was at stake, but 'the cause of Liberalism and the furtherance of its principles. That where the party was being made to serve ends of individuals and corrupt ends, I thought it was time that as guardian of the party, I spoke out clearly.' After a long review of his leadership of the party, he returned to Mitch insisting that he was 'far from ever having said a word against him to anyone ... That even today, if there was anything I could do to save him, my arms would be stretched out to him.' However, King concluded, the life of a party was built on loyalty, and 'if there were some who did not feel they could be loyal, the sooner they got out of the party the better ... That no man could ride two horses without falling between them sooner or later.' It had been an impressive performance; the message was unmistakable.[18]

Loyalty was also uppermost in King's mind as he considered Elliott's replacement in the cabinet. Ross Gray and William Fraser, two obvious candidates, were, if not disloyal, 'sort of facing both ways.' By January 1939 King and Rogers agreed that Slaght would bring the most strength to the cabinet if they could be certain about his loyalty, and might also 'be useful in healing the breaches.' Slaght assured King that while he would try to keep Mitch in line, he much preferred the good life to a portfolio. When King finally informed cabinet he had decided on Norman McLarty of Windsor, despite Chubby Power's support for Mitch's friend Ross Gray, he caught 'a look of surprise and dismay' on the faces of Mackenzie and Power which persuaded him that his decision 'helps to break up still further the little combination I have said little about but have watched carefully.' Conveniently forgetting the offer to Slaght, King also concluded that his rejection of Gray would 'let the country see that so far as I am concerned, I am not in any way seeking to placate Mr. Hepburn, but rather, if need be, to fight him and his sympathizers in the open.'[19]

It appeared that King would have to fight Mitch in the open. Much to Lambert's disgust the strategy team had done nothing. When Euler saw McQuesten early in April, he learned that King had established the tone and nature of the relations between Ottawa and Queen's Park in a letter to Mitch soon after the 1935 election. The information came as a surprise, and it was weeks before Jack Pickersgill could pry the letter out of King's files. But McQuesten refused to call a meeting of the OLA. Finally, at a tense meeting on 26 April, the Ontario caucus decided that a rally in Toronto on 8 August, the twentieth anniversary of King's accession to the leadership, would do more for the party than fighting Mitch in the open. The only encouraging news was that Mitch had told his caucus at the end of the session that the members were 'free agents in a federal election.'[20]

There was more encouraging news late in May when King instructed Lambert to ask Frank O'Connor to intervene. Lambert reported after his visit to Toronto that 'altho he looked very badly,' O'Connor promised to see Mitch and 'was emphatic about his stated efforts to restrain Mitch.' O'Connor was dying and spent most of his time in an oxygen tent, and it was Mitch who dropped in to see him on Sunday, 4 June. Deeply moved by the conversation with his good friend, Mitch went at once to see Arthur Slaght and told him that if he was going to run in the next election, he would do nothing to embarrass him or the federal Liberals – providing they left him alone. Slaght felt the conversation was so important that he boarded the royal train at South Parry the next night and, although it was after midnight, got King out of bed for a two-hour chat. He advised King to say nothing, for if the press got hold of it 'it could turn Hepburn the other way in a minute.' The next day, as the train headed into southwestern Ontario, King wired Mitch to join the tour and use his car. But although Mitch had thought of meeting the king and queen again in London, he was not to be seen.[21]

In fact Mitch was not to be seen for most of June and July. Soon after the royal visit he was confined to bed with what was described as a severe bronchial attack. His physical deterioration again led him to consider resigning, and Queen's Park was alive with rumours about his successor. Early in July Ian Mackenzie visited Bannockburn as a 'dove of peace' and told Lambert that Mitch's 'last & only grudge was Howe & Rogers.' Publicly, Mitch stated that although his 'attitude towards Premier King and disappointment in the record of his government is well known' he had not come to any decision about his personal role in a federal election. Ultimately, it would 'be on the basis of country before party.' While individual members were free to do as they wished, the organization would take 'no active part, either way.'[22]

What role Mitch and his machine might play was the unknown factor as the Tories calculated their chances and King considered the wisdom of going to the country. Although Manion had never believed that Mitch would throw his support to the Conservatives, he asked Drew to continue the political truce in Ontario, so that Mitch would not be distracted from his battles with King. Drew agreed that nothing would please the federal Liberals more 'than to have me engage Hepburn in a rough and tumble on provincial issues at the present time.' The truce attracted a good deal of attention in Ottawa and, after spending an afternoon in the Rideau Club, John Dafoe wrote that there was considerable discussion about the implications of the 'semi-cordial relations' between Mitch and Drew. 'One view (held in high places) is that they are both working to bring about a national government in which case one will have Ontario and the other will come to Ottawa,' he wrote George Ferguson in Winnipeg. 'By no means improbable I would say.'[23]

The prospect of some united action by Mitch and Duplessis was also factored into the equation, but with war looming, and the demands for a national government already in the Toronto air, that prospect was even more remote. Determined to 'wreck King,' McCullagh assiduously cited the obligatory reliable sources in Ottawa that despite his reticence, Mitch would be 'very much a factor in the anti-King forces' and that he and Duplessis would actively support Bob Manion. Believing that the report was of 'more than ordinary interest and significance,' Don Hogarth excitedly wrote

Manion that with Mitch's support he would win sixty seats in
Ontario, with Mitch neutral about fifty, and if he supported King
about forty. 'H & D are like two peas in a pod,' he continued.
'They will operate as a unit. If H supports you so will Dup & Quebec should do almost as well for you relatively as Ontario – Moreover such a development will have a 'settling' effect on the money
bags.' Mitch said nothing to scotch the rumours and told the *Star*
only that he did not believe that Duplessis would support King. As
for himself, he said on 20 July, 'I won't take the platform one way
or the other. Everyone knows where I stand and what I think, but
I am not going to make any election speeches at all.'[24]

While the speculation swirled around Ottawa, King had been
pondering the advisability of a fall election. He had hoped to get
the 'goods' on Mitch from the White House and in January
instructed Sir George Marler, the minister, to see the president: 'To
let him know I was expecting him to see that what he had told me
he knew of, when we were at Kingston, should be made public ...
That I wanted to have material where there could be no question
about it, and that as he wanted the St. Lawrence issue cleared up
properly, that was the way to do it.' King learned to his dismay,
however, that 'the matter was not being proceeded with' and that
Roosevelt knew little about it. Late in June he asked Daniel Roper,
the new American minister and a friend of the president, to secure
all the information the State Department had on the 'close tie-up
or any informal working agreement between the large private power
interests in the northeastern United States with any Canadian power
interests, or, in particular, with Mr. Hepburn.'

The plea was in vain. As Cordell Hull wrote to Roosevelt,
although there were rumours of concerted action by the private
power companies on both sides of the border to obstruct the St
Lawrence, 'there is no definite information on this subject in the
possession of the Department of State. Even if we had such information, I should hesitate to communicate it to the Prime Minister
because of the likelihood that his relations with Mr. Hepburn will
play a considerable part in the Canadian election campaign.' Roosevelt agreed, and wrote Roper that the St Lawrence 'should not
be pushed before the Canadian election, but I really count on action
as soon as the election is over.' Roosevelt would not be King's ally
if Mitch joined the battle.[25]

In July King asked all his ministers for a written report on the
chances of success. On 20 July, with many replies on hand, he discussed it with Crerar, Rogers, Power, and Euler. Ontario was the

question mark. Although they believed they could not hold their fifty-six seats, the consensus, King noted, was that they 'should go ahead, regardless of the attitude of the Ontario government; that the people were really with us and would show that, and Hepburn would learn his lesson as to where he stood when his own campaign comes.' King finally picked 23 October, the anniversary of the day he entered Parliament as leader of the opposition, with a dissolution early in September: 'by 11th of Sept. we should know if war probable in Europe – & wd. be justified in going to people if not probable – if war comes before, would be wise in not having made this move earlier.'[26]

The national rally on 8 August was to kick-off the campaign. Mitch said he would not be there and, 'in his usual hateful manner,' King noted, encouraged his colleagues to follow his example. King's speech was a disaster – a testimonial to his own leadership, his parents, and the octogenarians who remembered the great days of Laurier. And it was Laurier on whom he pegged his implicit references to Mitch. For it was Sir Wilfrid who said, 'It does not do to cherish resentment in public life.' Long before it was finished King desperately wanted a drink, and when the ordeal was over he 'walked about for a time, being in almost a desperate frame of mind, and humiliated in my eyes beyond expression.' He recovered quickly, however, and by morning had found many excuses, said Lambert, 'including Heeney, Mitch Hepburn, Pickering and the weather.' But he was spared the immediate ordeal of an election when, three weeks later, despite King's personal appeal to him, Hitler marched into Poland.[27]

'The cloven hoof of the gang'

Just hours before the Germans struck across the Polish border, Mackenzie King 'feared that knowing Britain and France were at their side the Poles might, with their war-like natures, prefer to fight' than to accept Hitler's ultimatum. Mitch was at Magnetawan that day speaking at Arthur Slaght's nominating convention. 'Two million men were on the march' and a war that could destroy western civilization seemed inevitable, he solemnly told the Parry Sound Liberals. Canada must support Britain, he said to resounding cheers, and 'when Parliament meets, as apparently it must in a few days, I hope Canada's voice will be heard in no uncertain way.' Parliament did meet on 7 September and three days later Canada was at war. The most moving speech of the debate was made by Ernest Lapointe, who denounced the thought of neutrality and prayed that 'God give Canadians the light which will indicate to them where their duty lies in this hour of trial.' From Toronto Mitch wired: 'You were absolutely magnificent and are still my Sir Ernest.' To a friend in the Ottawa press gallery he wrote, 'Make no mistake about it, Tommy, this is going to be a long war, and a bad one, and I agree with you that conscription should be in force at once.'¹

Mitch and Conant had already placed Ontario on a war footing. At a meeting in April with senior officers of the Department of National Defence and the RCMP, Mitch had agreed that Hydro would hire its own guards at once, and if the situation grew worse the OPP would recruit a force of special constables. Mitch insisted, however, that in the event of war the military should take over the defence of key Hydro installations. With war imminent Mitch met Defence Minister Ian Mackenzie and federal officials on 29 August and asked for military protection of Hydro installations, which he believed would be prime targets for saboteurs. Hogg pointed out that the Niagara plants could be easily bombed from small American airports and wanted anti-aircraft guns at Queenston. J.F. Mac-Neill of the Department of Justice was unyielding. Protection against sabotage, Ottawa had decided, was a matter for the local police not the army. Mackenzie raised the matter in cabinet, but could only promise further meetings in case of a real emergency.[2]

Mitch had not waited for the real emergency. A war council on 1 September called up one hundred additional OPP constables and mobilized the 'Hussars'; gave Hogg complete authority to protect Hydro plants with armed guards, barbed wire, and river nets to intercept floating bombs or torpedos; established a committee within Conant's ministry to deal with fascist organizations, already under surveillance by the Criminal Investigation Bureau; and created the special branch to specialize in anti-sabotage and counter-espionage operations. On 5 September Mitch wired King that the government of Ontario was at his disposal, an offer King noted that was 'done in the right spirit.' Later in the day, behaving as if an invasion were imminent, Mitch flew to the Niagara war zone to inspect the defence force of police and 380 veterans armed with shot-guns. He stated that the provincial air force had been moved from the north to Toronto Island, and that a flying squad of the OPP were bedded down at Queen's Park ready to move anywhere along the border. When war was declared, Conant asked Lapointe to re-enact section 98 of the Criminal Code and give the province authority to deal with unlawful or disloyal associations, individuals, and publications.[3]

Mitch had planned a short fall session for 19 September to amend the succession duty legislation which had again been successfully challenged in the courts. With Poland under attack, Drew had written Mitch that 'I believe that evidence of unity in the House will be of great public service in these critical days. I therefore hope that no matter what may have been contemplated before the present emergency developed, no legislation will be introduced other than that which is necessary to hasten our preparation for war.' Unity there was as Mitch, Drew, and Conant outdid each other in their pledges of loyalty. Mitch admitted that he had intended to comment on the critical situation in which Canada found itself, but 'I decided to refrain, as my remarks might have been construed as criticism of the administration charged with the pursuit of the war.'

But his restraint was short-lived, as he added that Canada was 'entering the war less prepared than any other country in the world. There is no use in disguising the obvious fact. There is the one need of unity. Canada can only be successful if every man does his duty to the State, from the top to the bottom, the Federal Cabinet as well as the man on the street.' Conant had put together a package of emergency legislation, most of which passed without objection, including bills which gave the attorney general command of a centralized police force and power to arrest and seize without warrant; changed personal and corporate income taxes to allow 10 per cent deductibility of donations to the war effort; extended the franchise to everyone who joined up, including Indians; and gave Hydro the authority to ration power. Only the draconian Act respecting Public Meetings and Public Processions, which gave enormous arbitrary power to local authorities, aroused much criticism. However, Drew attacked the succession duty legislation, which made recourse to the courts more difficult, as 'one of the most vicious and badly drawn acts that has ever been introduced in any British Parliament.' Tabling a list of thirty fraudulent cases that had yielded the treasury $26 million, Mitch insisted that he was not going to allow legal technicalities to protect the rich, particularly in wartime.

There were rumours that Mitch and Drew would use the session to call for a national government. A few weeks before the session opened, he and Drew had appeared together at Niagara Falls. After praising the colonel's war record and his criticism of King's defence policy, Mitch said 'when and if the time comes for me to throw the torch I don't know anyone I would rather have carry on than Colonel Drew.' Mitch denied that a union government was in the wind, and Drew added that 'any argument which might apply for national government in the Dominion field does not seem to have any application in the Provincial field at the present time.' However, in Toronto on 19 September, Manion heard that 'there was to be a blast put forward by a certain group (the names I did not give them but they were given to me as Mitch, George Drew, Nixon, Macaulay and Conant) in favour of National Government.' But the predicted blast did not materialize, perhaps because Mitch could not carry his caucus. The rumours persisted, however, for many agreed with Les Frost that 'a political upheaval in both the old Parties for a union in federal politics of people of like mind is the only way. At the moment Hepburn and Drew appear to be the only ones who would have the slightest chance of effecting such a Dominion movement and the difficulties in the way are very great.'

The establishment of the Organization of Resources Committee under the lieutenant-governor, Drew, and Mitch underlined the non-partisan nature of the session. Before it ended Mitch announced that the committee would meet King and offer Ontario's support for a total war effort. 'We will go down there and find out everything that is required,' he stated. 'We will base everything on that information.' The committee, enlarged to include representatives of labour, industry, and agriculture, would coordinate the mobilization of all the human and physical resources of the province, including assisting in the work of recruiting for the armed forces with 'the least possible disturbance to agriculture and industry.' Queen's Park wanted to be a participant not a bystander in the war. The session over, Mitch and some of the 'old gang' got together. 'Notwithstanding the increase in the excise tax on scotch whiskey,' he wrote a friend, 'we did our duty nobly – damn it.'[4]

King was dismayed when Mitch asked for the meeting, suspecting that it was 'part of the foundations of a scheme to further Union Government later on from Ontario.' The possibility of Mitch joining or even leading the drive for a national government was the subject of endless speculation, and King had no doubt about Mitch's ambition. Any doubts were removed when King received a letter from Slaght on 9 September urging him to invite Manion and other Conservatives, even members of the CCF and Social Credit parties, to join the administration. 'My conviction is profound, wrote Slaght, 'that no single political party can successfully run a war and that now is the time to avoid the mistake of Sir Robert Borden.' To King it was all very clear:

I am as certain as I am living that it has been the McCullagh-Hepburn combination which probably includes Drew as evidenced by Hepburn's friendly relations with him from time to time. Certainly Conant whom Lapointe mentioned as embarrassing him all he can in Justice matters; very likely Bassett, and in particular the mining crowd and also power interests that have been helping Hepburn. McLaughlin, of General Motors, and others who have been using the Canadian Army Corps – a body of gangsters – seeking to get possession of the Government of Canada at this period of war. How far railway interests may be with them, I cannot say.... Theirs will be an effort to establish Fascist Government in Canada.

King neutralized Slaght by persuading him to speak to a caucus called for the purpose, rather than in the Commons. As King expected, Slaght received no support. When Lambert told King after caucus that Slaght had been heard to say that the drive for a national government would force King out in six months – 'that there were a group combining to see that this was effected' – his suspicion seemed confirmed. He was 'convinced that the whole business is part of a conspiracy in which the cloven hoof of the gang is only too apparent.'

The real purpose behind Mitch's request for the meeting, King reasoned, was to demonstrate that 'we are not imperialistic enough, and a lukewarm Liberal party not throwing enough energy into the war effort.' Arthur Hardy tried to persuade him that it was a tribute to King's leadership and a sure sign that Mitch was 'running for cover.' King was not persuaded. 'Between ourselves,' he replied, 'I am not at all sure that it is not one more attempt, on the part of those who are anxious to have a national government at Ottawa, to prepare the way for a demand of that kind to be made later on, probably at a moment when conscription may become the issue. We shall wait and see.'[5]

When the 3 October meeting began Mitch admitted at once that he had been openly critical of King's tardy and indecisive preparation for war (although he did not suggest as he had to Tom Wayling of the Press Gallery that King should be impeached). But Canada was now at war, and he had come to pledge his total support to the war effort. Mitch reiterated many of the proposals and offers that his government had made concerning buildings, the use of interned aliens on Trans Canada road work, freeing up prisons by allowing short-term prisoners to enlist, and the services of Dr William Avery, the 'clap doctor' as he was called, whose successful research into 'social diseases' would be of value to the armed forces. He criticized the delay in securing adequate uniforms and supplies for the recruits and, although King had announced the formation of a division for possible despatch overseas two weeks earlier, Mitch bluntly stated that the feeling in Ontario was that 'the government was not taking' quick enough steps for getting expeditionary force under way, etc.' As the industrial heartland of Canada, the protection and expansion of power resources were essential. He could not adequately guard Niagara with civilians, but if King would supply the militia, Ontario would pay the cost. And finally, if King and Roosevelt would agree to the northern diversions at once, he would withdraw his opposition to the St Lawrence project. For the moment he wanted his agreement kept secret, but needed a quick decision, for without the northern diversion or other additional sources Ontario would face a power shortage.

King explained that the issue was not simply an expeditionary force, but a navy, air force, defences on two coasts, and cooperation in the defence of Newfoundland and the West Indies. Moreover, he argued, accomplishing the almost miraculous feat of bringing a united Canada into the war had necessarily involved 'restraint in some directions' He then asked Colonel Ralston, who had joined the cabinet as minister of finance on 6 September, to run over the dimensions of financing the war. Ralston discussed the estimated billion required to support the first two years of the Commonwealth air training program, the enormous credits requested by Britain, and the necessity of ensuring that Canada would have the financial strength to fight a long war. However, said Ralston, he was doing everything he could to cut through the red tape and secure the funds to get the essential requirements under way.

King had been generally non-committal during the meeting, but that afternoon in cabinet said that the meeting 'had really been helpful' and he was 'prepared to start anew all relations with the Ontario government and to make no reference to the past.' He asked Lapointe to consider the question of work camps for aliens and the enlistment of prisoners, and secured the general agreement of cabinet that a good case could be made for military protection of 'bridges and power plants along the U.S. border, including, possibly, interprovincial bridges as well.' The cabinet agreed to go ahead with the St Lawrence to keep 'the good will of the United States.'

After the meeting Drew and Mitch compared notes. Neither was impressed. Drew's 'most vivid impression was of a group of extremely tired and befuddled old men, with the exception of Ralston and Rogers. Ralston appeared anything but befuddled, although he did look extremely tired. Rogers looked young, befuddled, tired and insignificant.' Drew welcomed Ralston's firm statement, but remained unconvinced that 'there was any real driving power behind the war effort' or any purpose 'in the mind of the man who is driving the machine.' Mitch generally agreed, but because of Ralston he had 'reason for confidence,' a conclusion, Drew reasoned, that revealed 'that what was really on his mind was that on looking over the situation Ralston's statement had given some reason to believe that he could still safely be a Liberal.'[6]

Mitch unburdened himself in a long off-the-record talk with Jack Hambleton of the *Toronto Star*. Only with great difficulty had they been able to hold their tempers for they could get no definite answers to anything. 'The only man in the cabinet who seems to know anything is Ralston,' said Mitch, and 'he is about to quit in disgust.' Mitch assured Hambleton that he went to Ottawa with the best intentions and the determination to submerge any personal feelings:

But honestly, it would make you sick to see how confused and distraught everything and everyone is in Ottawa. I wanted to break the story and tell the country just what is going on, but I realize my personal feelings towards King would neutralize any effort I made. Surely, some newspaper will sooner or later open up. It would be a great national service because we are unprepared for this war and we aren't getting anywhere towards getting prepared.

A report of the interview was in Lambert's hands within two days and on King's desk a day later. King read the 'thoroughly deceitful and lying report' to cabinet on 10 October and the next day declared that Mitch's statement 'ended everything.'[7]

Mitch remained silent for weeks. But he was deeply pessimistic. He believed it would be a long and costly war, with Britain laid waste by German bombers and Japan certain to take advantage of British weakness in the Pacific. The best we could do, he told Floyd Chalmers, was 'just win.' He also told Chalmers that he had no confidence in the King government:

He thinks it is a very weak Government with only one good man in it – Ralston, who is not well. Ralston, he says, has his eye on the Supreme Court bench and wants to succeed Duff as Chief Justice.

He thinks Canada cannot make an effective contribution to the war under Mr. King whose traditional policies of inertia, and of side-stepping every serious problem while he waits for the breaks, will not work in wartime. But he suggested that until the casualty lists become very large and the war really got going in earnest there might not be any public demand for the strengthening of the Cabinet. In the meantime, he intends to give no support to this Government and if there is an election next year he couldn't 'as a Liberal' honestly support a Government that is letting down the Empire this way.

Mitch broke his long silence late in November. His informal talk to a group of local farmers and businessmen in St Thomas was an earnest appeal to everyone to pitch in, but the press was quick to emphasize his critical comments. 'I don't think that the war is being prosecuted the way that Canadians want it to be prosecuted,' he said. 'A modernly mechanized force of 2,000 men could lick the whole Canadian Army, today, gentlemen, and I don't mean anything disparaging to the Canadian forces when I say that ... But they are not getting a break and are not getting the training and equipment they must have.' The next night at Aylmer, unaware that the pace of Canada's industrial mobilization reflected in part Britain's refusal to provide designs or place firm orders, Mitch accused Ottawa of fiddling while 'Rome burns. Therefore, I say that if those in Ottawa are not ready to prosecute this war they had better get out and get out in a hurry.' Ralston replied on the CBC with a long review of the government's war program and financial commitments: 'In certain quarters, the government has been charged with inactivity ... I had an idea that we here in Ottawa were trying to do a fair bit of work, but if our efforts of the last ten weeks can be classed as inactivity then heaven help us if we ever have to get down to work.'[8]

Other than the two criticisms of King's war effort, Mitch lived up to his promise of total support. Although the federal surtax in the 13 September budget trimmed $350,000 to $400,000 from the provincial income tax and the increased tax on liquor cut sales $244,000 in October, Mitch told King he was quite prepared to forgo a balanced budget and would not raise taxes or liquor prices to recover the lost income. But he wanted some assurance there would be no further liquor taxes. The best that Ralston and Ilsley could do was to assure Mitch that while they could make no firm promises, 'we are not disposed to further increase in the tax in respect of this particular commodity unless the exigencies of the general situation make it imperative.' Mitch was delighted when Ralston asked him to sit on the National War Loan Committee for the first war loan campaign scheduled for the spring. He was particularly anxious to see the St Lawrence agreement confirmed, and Hogg urged Skelton to hasten the negotiations because of 'the precariousness of the present truce between Ottawa and Toronto.' But it was not until 21 December that King officially informed Cordell Hull that Canada was ready to reopen negotiations. King now saw the St Lawrence as 'another great progressive stroke' of his administration, and one which, as a bonus, might avoid a troublesome dispute with Mitch in the next election.[9]

The Ontario legislative session opened on 10 January 1940, with a long throne speech that praised the government's war effort and its cooperation with Ottawa. Mitch paid tribute to the patriotism of Private David Croll, who took his seat in the kilt of the Essex Scottish, and Lieutenant Colin Campbell, who was ill. The occasion prompted Mitch to observe that Canadians did not seem to be taking the war very seriously. The war was not of Britain's making for it had a peace-loving prime minister. In Canada, he added with a smile, the prime minister was so peace-loving that even 'I have not yet been able to provoke him into an open quarrel, although I have tried to do so with great dexterity on frequent occasions.' Drew agreed with Mitch that it would be a long war and insisted that the true path of patriotism was not 'to remain silent in the face of incompetence.'

Drew had warned an astonished and mistrustful Manion that, despite his earlier agreement to remain more or less within provincial politics, he planned to attack King from his seat in the House. In a powerful speech critical of King on leaders' day, he insisted that the war was not the 'exclusive prerogative' of the federal parliament. 'This is the first of the Canadian parliaments to meet in 1940. We have an important role to play. We represent one-third of the population and one-half of the industrial production of Canada. We have the right to speak ... we can sound a clear trumpet call to action, or we can utter pious and ineffective platitudes about our faith in democracy.' There was no doubt that Drew's criticism of King was to be the trumpet call to action.

Mitch had not anticipated Drew's speech. After assuring the House that he and Drew agreed on 'matters that were basic,' he embarked on a long rambling account of men without uniforms contracting TB; of Coly Campbell falling sick because he had no greatcoat; of the hasty evacuation of the fourteen hundred inmates of the St Thomas asylum because Rogers needed it urgently for the RCAF only to see it sit empty for months; of the prospect of half-trained men with antiquated equipment being sent into battle. 'And the men responsible for sending those men over are the men who are going to some day answer to the Canadian people for the lack of preparation, regardless of the radio speeches,' Mitch promised. He agreed with Drew that the time had arrived 'to speak our minds, because national security, to me, is much greater than any political affiliation.' After the cheers subsided, Mitch promised to study Drew's address in detail, 'after which time, I can tell him, the Government will be in a position to make its own position clear.'[10]

Before the orders of the day were called on 18 January, William Duckworth criticized Ottawa's sale of a million bushels of wheat to the Soviet Union and Mitch supported him. When Morgan Baker approvingly referred to a King speech, Mitch snapped, 'Why should we be subject to that kind of twaddle?' When Baker went on to say that Drew's 'vitriolic attacks' do 'more harm and cause more confusion than all the German bombs and tanks and poison gas,' Mitch whirled to face Baker. 'I ask to be associated with Colonel Drew in his attack on the King government to which you refer.' And when Baker joked that Mitch's statement was not quite as vitriolic, Mitch shouted, 'Well, if it wasn't, it was not because I didn't mean it to be.'

The donnybrook continued despite many appeals from the Liberal side of the House, until the Speaker finally called the orders of the day. But Mitch challenged the decision and not one member voted to suspend the debate on the war. As the mêlée continued, Mitch moved restlessly around in his seat. Suddenly he was on his feet, waved down a Liberal back-bencher, and said that he was going to test the opinion of the House. After a bitter review of his relations with King, Mitch declared that it was not a 'personal matter, so far as Mackenzie King is concerned, his insignificance protects him,' but 'the calloused attitude of the King government. I haven't sounded out the members of the government. But I believe Mackenzie King harbours a hatred of this province, probably because he could never be elected in Ontario.' The real issue, however, was not political, it was national security. Then came an astonishing ultimatum.

I don't care if I am defeated – and you must construe the resolution I am about to read out as a Government measure – I shall have done what I consider to be the right thing. Of course, if I am defeated, there is only one course open to me – to resign. If I am wrong, if in the opinion of this House we are not reflecting the overwhelming opinion of the people of Canada at this moment, then I shall bow to the decision. I am ready to take my political future in my hands. I am not going to take it on the chin as Federal Cabinet Ministers have and go down without fighting.

Let me say again that I stand firm in my statements that Mackenzie King has not done his duty to his country – never has and never will.

As the members sat in stunned silence, Mitch then read a resolution he had scrawled on a yellow piece of paper:

That this House has heard with interest the reports made by the Prime Minister and the Leader of the Opposition of the result of their visit to Ottawa to discuss war measures with the National Government and this House hereby endorses the statements made by the two members in question and joins with them in regretting that the Federal Government at Ottawa has made so little effort to prosecute Canada's duty in the war in the vigorous manner the people of Canada desire to see.

A few moments earlier Mitch had handed the resolution to Nixon and asked him to second it. Nixon whispered: 'Oh Mitch, it is very foolish, I do not think it is at all wise to do it. However, I have stuck with you this long and if you insist I will, but it is a — — mistake.' Mitch grabbed it back and turned to McQuesten: 'Here, you are the President of the Liberal Association, second this.'

There was pandemonium on the floor and in the galleries. Some back-benchers appealed to the Speaker to rule the motion out of order or delay the vote, while others scurried for cover. But the Speaker put the motion and after a voice vote declared that victory lay with the yeas. Determined to force the issue even more, Mitch demanded that the nayes be recorded. As the division bells rang, other Liberal back-benchers fled. Two dozen gathered in the Liberal room and asked the whip for a caucus, but the word came back that 'the premier wants this finished now.' More than twenty Liberals, including the assistant whip, refused the call. Ten dared Mitch's wrath and voted nay. But with the support of a dozen back-benchers, all the cabinet in the House, and the opposition, the resolution passed fourty-four to ten. As Thomas Blakelock, who voted aye, explained to his constituents, each member was left on his own and 'we had only two or three minutes to decide how to vote. At least I didn't get down on my knees and sneak out. I have voted for the Hepburn government when I knew it was right and I've voted for the Hepburn government when I knew it was DAMN well wrong.'[11]

When King heard the news, he concluded at once that it was 'the most important night since the war began. It is of such importance, that on tonight's decision depends pretty much the future of the government.' Mitch's vote of censure gave him the excuse for a snap dissolution which would silence the opposition in Parliament, preempt the possibility of Drew and Hepburn agreeing on an election with a union government the issue, and assure his re-election before the war turned nasty in the spring. 'If ever a prayer to confound one's enemy was answered,' King wrote, 'it seems to be at this moment. I have felt all along that given enough rope, Hepburn will hang himself. This he has certainly done at this time. If the truth of the old saying: "Whom the Gods wish to destroy, they first make mad" had ever needed verification it will be found in the case of Hepburn and his intemperate act.'[12]

King's strategy was so secretive that only the privileged few in the war cabinet knew his real intentions, and even there Ralston believed that the proper course was to allow a debate before dissolution.

King included a paragraph in the throne speech declaring that the government had decided on 'an immediate appeal to the country,' but how immediate not even his colleagues knew. When Parliament met on 25 January he decided that he would dissolve that night, pre-empting all but the briefest discussion. Just two hours before Lord Tweedsmuir read the speech from the throne, Lapointe informed a shocked cabinet of King's intention. After a tumultous afternoon session, the Commons recessed at six, the members expecting to return after dinner. But King was on his way to Rideau Hall and at 7:07 Parliament was dissolved.

King began his campaign in caucus the next morning. Mitch Hepburn was responsible for the election and to back away from the vote of censure would have deserved the charge of cowardice. And if Mitch was the cause, he was also in part the issue. King demanded one hundred per cent loyalty to himself and the government. 'There could be no other than Mackenzie King Liberals as candidates,' and anyone who had any doubt about his loyalty should leave at once. Nor could any King Liberal countenance the thought of a national government, the first step toward dictatorship.

Mitch had refused to comment until after the weekend, and the galleries in the Assembly were crowded on Monday. Drew immediately denied that he had seconded the resolution or knew it was to be introduced. Nor had he called for an immediate election as King had charged. Both Drew and Mitch mocked King's argument that the resolution necessitated an election. In an act of cowardice comparable only to the commander of the *Graf Spee* who had scuttled his battleship rather than face three British cruisers, Mitch exclaimed, King had 'scuttled the ship of state rather than face the criticism of Manion and his thirty-nine followers.'[13]

While the federal election campaign got under way, Mitch finished the session. He had been sick when it began and there were the usual reports that heavy drinking explained his displays of bad temper and unusually bad taste. Fortunately there was little on the government's agenda and the House often sat for less than two hours as ministers were content with routine housekeeping. Mitch and Walters had planned to wait for the federal budget before bringing theirs down, but there was to be no federal budget. As expected, Mitch's 15 February budget was a wartime budget. 'In Ontario, no sacrifice will be considered too great ... The people of Ontario are determined to see this war through to a victorious conclusion, and with this in view, are prepared to stake their last dollar and furnish the last man, if need be, that the world may be rid of this constant threat of war.' The war had already cut deeply into provincial revenues from the gasoline and liquor taxes and the province had absorbed the loss when Ottawa imposed a 20 per cent surtax on 1939 incomes. With the loss of an estimated $3.6 million in succession duties as a result of another court injunction, the projected surplus of $150,000 had become a $4.4 million deficit.

Although declining revenues pointed to a bleak future, Mitch promised to show leadership and balance his wartime budget. In addition to freezing expenditures, the government would increase the corporation income tax from 2 to 5 per cent, with equivalent increases in the taxes on utilities and financial institutions, to raise an additional $6 million which would offset the decline in succession duties. If his forecasts were correct, Mitch anticipated a surplus of $356,000. The Tory offensive was spirited but not damaging, and came to an end after four days of meandering discussion. After the usual last-minute flurry over the estimates, the members went home on 24 February.[14]

When the session at Queen's Park ended, the federal election was only a month away. After his initial denunciation of King for the snap dissolution, Mitch had remained silent. The new federal organizer, Bart Sullivan, advised Lambert that 'having shown a commendable and for him an unusual restraint,' Mitch 'should not be goaded into another outburst by repeated attacks from our speakers.' Support for King could not be expected, but hopefully Mitch and his machine would remain on the sidelines.

The Conservatives hoped that Mitch would be an ally. On several occasions he had spoken warmly of his friend Bob Manion, and when the federal House met on 25 January, Billy Price had written Manion that Mitch was 'anxious to cooperate and is waiting for your speech.' The sudden dissolution pre-empted Manion's speech, but the Tory caucus endorsed a policy of no conscription for overseas service and, somewhat paradoxically, the formation of a national government composed of 'the very best brains available' whose objective it was usually assumed would be conscription. Prominent members of the Tory hierarchy pressed Manion to promise that after the election he would step aside and leave the national government supporters free to choose the new prime minister. He refused.

Mitch featured prominently in the backroom discussions of Tory strategy. According to Grattan O'Leary, Manion explained to Drew that the national government proposal was 'to facilitate Mitch Hepburn's bolt from the Liberal party, to invite him in.' Drew apparently thought the invitation was 'clean crazy,' O'Leary informed

Grant Dexter. 'He doesn't want Mitch in the field in a big way and he does not think Mitch will bring any strength to the Tory party.' Manion was also told that Mitch was among a group in Toronto, which included McCullagh, Drew, Meighen, and Price, who wanted to agree to leave the leadership an open question. Manion was sufficiently confident of Mitch's support that he told him of the report and said he doubted its authenticity.

Although Mitch had promised Manion his support and had urged Herbert Bruce to run as a national government candidate in Toronto Parkdale, he said nothing for public consumption. When the Ottawa *Citizen* called him on 1 March to query a report that he planned to resign and take the stump for a national government, Mitch replied, 'I haven't anything to say about the report. I am not ready yet to enter a political controversy.' The election had not yet crystallized, Mitch continued, and everything would depend on events in Europe. 'If there is a great German offensive, and I believe there will be by an attempted push through Belgium within three weeks or so, I think the Canadian people will be awakened from their state of apathy and the King Government will be thrown out.' There was no doubt where Mitch stood.[15]

There was even less doubt on 4 March when, as head of the Motion Picture Board of Censors, Mitch banned the release in Ontario of the film 'Canada at War' until after the election. The film was John Grierson's first wartime propaganda film, as national film commissioner, and was a joint production of the National Film Board and the March of Time, an enormously popular American film series. The film had been rushed through production a month ahead of schedule to be released during the election. A eulogy of Canada's war effort, the film told of the departure of the first division with its regiments 'made famous by Canadian valor,' of the forts defending the coasts, of torpedo boats that 'will be the fastest craft afloat,' and of a voluntary enlistment system that attracted more recruits than were needed.

A few days after the film was released one of Drew's speeches on the shortcomings of King's war effort was censored. Mitch responded quickly. 'Canada at War,' he said, was 'pure political propaganda' and would not be shown until after the election. Had it been 'Canada's Lack of War Effort,' the decision would be the same. 'In banning this picture we are only following out the policy laid down in the 1937 election here in Ontario,' he claimed. 'It was suggested then that we show scenes of c.i.o. riots in plants in the United States, and if we had it would be to the advantage of the Liberal

Party. But I said no then and we are still adhering to that policy.' Mitch was unmoved by the torrent of criticism from friend and foe alike, even by the argument that the film, designed for international consumption, was good propaganda for Canada and might even 'warm up' the United States. Mitch was 'attaching undue importance to himself if he thinks the March of Time spent three months filming "Canada at War" to refute his charges that Canadians are lagging in their war effort,' observed the New York producer, Louis de Rochemont. Indeed, he was following in the footsteps of Huey Long, 'who banned the March of Time from all Louisiana theatres whenever its contents displeased the Kingfish.'[16]

Mitch responded to the criticism by lashing out at his critics. In particular, he asked Norman Rogers to deny that on 10 February several hundred men at the air force base at St Thomas had left the base without leave and it had taken the military police three days to round them up. 'They were disgusted and fed-up because they got no training and were doing nothing but shining door knobs and polishing floors,' Mitch claimed. Moreover, he continued, Rogers 'gave them leave of absence so that he could say that no one was away without leave of absence' and the press was warned 'not to publish it. I challenge Rogers to deny it. I make the statement as Premier of Ontario and let the censors say they can't publish that.' The *New York Post* headlined its story 'Mutiny in Royal Canadian Air Force – Men Rebel at Polishing Door Knobs – Quit Ontario Camp.' German radio beamed the story to Britain and Russian radio praised the 'Brave Britisher' for daring to criticize his country's war effort. Describing the charge as 'absolutely untrue,' Rogers stated that 'each time Premier Hepburn indulges his flair for abuse and for groundless statements, for loose and violent speech, he is a party to the betrayal of Canada.'

Mitch persisted in the attack, Rogers in his denial. Finally Mitch instructed the attorney general's department to conduct an inquiry. After examining witnesses and participants, OPP Commissioner W.H. Stringer concluded that between two and three hundred men had walked into St Thomas and that it had taken the military police three days to round them up. Mitch claimed the victory, although Stringer had found no evidence of the 'violent disturbance' he had mentioned. That the walkout was apparently the result of administrative incompetence and not the near-mutiny he had described, Mitch said, was irrelevant. Both the Board of Censors and the *Times-Journal* denied that the story had been censored, but Mitch took some comfort from the editor's qualified statement that 'we endeavored, while giving the public the facts, not to say anything that would conflict with the regulations.'[17]

The condemnation of Mitch's exaggerated accusations and intemperate language was widespread. King concluded that Mitch was 'now completely done for. It is apparent that his judgement is just appalling.' The Toronto *Star*, whose editorials on Hepburn's 'ravings' had become almost hysterical, asked 'Is there no way in which his associates in the government of this great province can bring him to his senses?'[18]

That weekend Harry Nixon brooded about the situation at his farm near Paris. He returned to his Royal York suite early on Monday morning, 11 March, called a public stenographer, and dictated a letter of resignation and a long press statement. He wrote Mitch that 'I find myself so completely at variance with your recent policy statements and acts that I am convinced it would not be fair or honest to you as head of the Government, to the people of Ontario, who have honored me so greatly with their confidence during my twenty-one years in the Legislature, or to myself, to continue longer in my position in your Government.' He hoped that his resignation would not end their 'warm friendship,' however, and assured Mitch that he would give him 'all possible support' in the legislature. The press statement catalogued his growing disaffection. 'Particularly repugnant' was the alliance with Drew, 'so obvious for many months' and which 'seems to exist for the sole purpose of concentrating every possible attack and embarrassment upon the federal government.' The vote of censure made him realize that 'the time had come for the parting of the ways,' but out of personal loyalty and the desire to avoid an election and defeat of the government, he and others had reluctantly acquiesced. Since then matters had 'rapidly gone from bad to worse,' and he was convinced that 'the break must come now, and I must dissociate myself from his actions.'

Mitch first heard the news from a Windsor *Star* reporter who raced to St Thomas. Asked if Nixon's resignation would propel him openly into the campaign, Mitch replied that would be a 'natural reaction.' Later, in a long interview with the *Globe and Mail*, Mitch expressed surprise that Nixon had suddenly become a King supporter and, given their earlier decision that cabinet solidarity and party discipline applied only to the provincial field, felt that he had to resign. There was no alliance with Drew, and there would not be a coalition or an election. Mitch scoffed at the idea that other ministers would follow Nixon because he had received assurances of support from all of them during the day.[19]

Mitch called a meeting of the cabinet for 3 p.m. the next day. That morning the lieutenant-governor called the secretary of state in Ottawa to seek advice, but with Lapointe, then acting minister, out of town, the undersecretary insisted on seeing King:

He began by saying that the Lt. Gov. expected a call from Premier Hepburn at 3 this afternoon. Before he went any further I said: 'Tell him to act upon the advice of his Prime Minister.' Then Coleman went on to say that the first question he wished to ask was whether he would be justified in asking the Premier, before acting on his advice, whether the views he was presenting to him were those of the entire Cabinet or whether there were differences in the Cabinet concerning the advice he was tendering. I said to tell him that his duty was to accept the advice of the Premier, ... If he was not willing to accept his advice without question he should dismiss him as being unworthy of enjoying his (the Lt. Gov.'s) confidence ... Coleman said he felt sure that that was the view I would take, but wished to make doubly certain of it. He said the next point raised by the Lt. Gov. was that he thought he might be called upon to form a coalition, the government to be composed of Hepburn and Drew. That he wondered whether, as the Legislature had prorogued, after supply voted to the present government, he would be justified in allowing another government to carry on ...

I said that the relations between the governor and his Prime Minister remained the same. That either he would have to accept his advice all along or not at all. If a mistake was being made, the remedy lay with the members of the Legislature or the people. It could not be the governor's mistake.

King believed that Mitch had been planning a coalition with Drew ever since he was not defeated on the 18 January motion of censure. 'Their game from the start has been to get underway with it' before the federal election, and 'Hepburn will now make an effort to get underway with it before the present elections are over. I am pretty sure that the day will witness an effort to effect this end. Whether he will be successful or not will depend upon how far seeing or short-sighted his colleagues are.' If Liberalism was not dead in Ontario, other ministers would follow Nixon's lead and force Mitch to resign; but most of them, he concluded sadly, 'will not act on principle at all, that is to say Liberal principles but will do the thing that they think will enable them to retain office.'[20]

There were some provincial Liberals who did believe that others would follow Nixon's lead. Although all ministers refused to comment, the *Star* reported that off the record two of them had revealed that at least four ministers condemned Mitch's actions and there would be 'some plain talking' at the afternoon cabinet meeting. But after an hour and a half, McQuesten emerged from the meeting to tell the press that there was 'absolute solidarity behind the premier' and no further resignations. 'Was there any demand that the premier stop his criticism of the King administration while his cabinet ministers were all supporting the Dominion Premier?' 'No demand,' replied McQuesten, 'it had always been agreed that each member was "at liberty" to do as he likes.'

When the meeting was over, Mitch called reporters to his office. 'It was the most harmonious meeting,' he insisted. Every minister 'expressed his loyalty – and it was all voluntary. And we expressed our regret at Mr. Nixon's resignation.' Mitch repeated that every minister was 'free in his own riding. I have not told them what to do or say and they have made no requests of me.' Asked if he would replace Nixon with Drew in a coalition government, Mitch replied tartly: 'Absolutely not. Dissipate that silly rumor of a coalition government. Mr. Drew and I share ideas about certain measures on the conduct of this war. On all fiscal policies we are wide apart as the poles. I don't think he would come in if he were asked. He has no desire to come in under me, aspiring as he is to be prime minister himself.'[21]

But according to two ministers, who indiscreetly spoke to Jack Hambleton of the *Star*, although all denied it, there had been 'plain talking.' With several other ministers apparently threatening to resign and precipitate a general election, and with all emphasizing the disastrous effect of Nixon's resignation on the party, Mitch had been either persuaded or forced to try 'to patch up the quarrel.' At nine o'clock that night he arrived at Nixon's suite in the Royal York and after an hour's chat invited reporters in to watch him rip up Nixon's letter of resignation. Throwing his arm over Nixon's shoulder, Mitch explained that the prospect of not having his old friend by his side was too much to bear. 'After Cabinet Council today I felt very much worried and concerned over his resignation. I decided that before attending next day's council I would see him myself and talk over the whole situation. I repeated what I said in caucus a year ago: that members of the Cabinet and my supporters in the House were privileged to vote and speak as Canadians on national issues.' Slightly ill at ease, Nixon agreed. 'The unfortunate misunderstanding which arose regarding the principle of Cabinet solidarity has been cleared away and I am happy now to rejoin my colleagues.'

But the *Star* insisted there was more to the new understanding than freedom of speech and association. To persuade Nixon to return, it claimed that Mitch had agreed not to attack King during the campaign and to end his dalliance with George Drew. Although Mitch angrily denied the *Star* story, he was somewhat ambiguous during his 13 March press conference. 'I am just as free to criticize the King Government as my Ministers are to praise it' and 'I want the people of Canada to judge the Mackenzie King Government's war record when the full fury of this conflict strikes us within the next few months.' He did not expect 'to take any part in platform activity,' however, and while reserving his right 'to criticize where I feel criticism is due, I don't intend to take either side.'[22]

Mitch remained at home during the rest of the campaign and refused any comment. Many provincial members appeared at meetings with their federal counterparts and the ministers gave at best lukewarm support to the federal candidates in their ridings. None openly endorsed the King government. The provincial organization took no part and, with no federal organization, Power and Lambert were afraid of major losses in Ontario. Some of Mitch's more generous supporters – among them the Franceschinis, Algoma Steel, and his gold-mining friends – threw their support to Manion, and Bethune Smith's contribution of $10,000 could have come from the provincial war chest.

Lambert and Power had little reason to fear the results in Ontario. With the party divided and Manion's leadership both suspect and inept, the grab-bag of national government candidates offered little alternative to the Liberals. Even so, the Liberals gained only one seat in the province and both Grits and Tories increased their popular vote by 7 per cent, as the CCF virtually disappeared. With the exception of the Atlantic provinces, however, the Liberal gains in Ontario were the lowest in the country. Mitch may not have helped the Tories, but he did not hurt them. Manion thanked him for all he 'tried to do on our behalf – or at least against the fat little jellyfish from Kingsmere, but somehow he seems to come out on top.'[23]

Many Liberals regarded King's victory as Mitch's defeat, among them King himself who, with the Tories beaten, immediately turned his troops against the enemy within. The day after the election he ordered Lambert to get rid of Mitch and added a few days later that the 'move to get rid of Hepburn should come from within Ontario.' The tactics were discussed at cabinet on 2 April when Euler reported that the Ontario ministers had decided to have Lambert call a meeting of the federal and provincial members in Ontario and 'get Hepburn out of office.' King agreed it was 'the only way Ontario Liberalism could be saved – name a new leader at once, and make an immediate appeal to the people, and have one hundred per cent support of the administration.' King was pleased that even Ian Mackenzie had finally agreed that Mitch had to go. Lambert, Euler, and McLarty met the next day and decided to call a meeting on 8 April in Toronto of a special Ontario committee of the federal caucus to plan the coup d'état.

The prospects seemed promising, for there were signs that Mitch had lost the support of the provincial party. The Toronto *Star*, which insisted that the election had been a vote of non-confidence in Mitch, diligently encouraged and published demands from local riding associations for a leadership convention. Morgan Baker, the MPP from York North, and other dissident members quietly solicited support in the caucus for a move to replace Mitch with Nixon. By 3 April Bill Mulock informed King that fifty-four members were prepared to support Nixon. 'I spent an hour and a half with Nixon last night and he quite naturally will not commit himself,' he wrote, 'but I am satisfied that he realizes the feeling of hatred against Hepburn in the Party, and that he will accept the leadership in his place, but Mr. Nixon wants the appointment from the Provincial Members of the Party throughout Ontario as a whole, and does not want it through Hepburn handing it over to him and so have his hands tied to deal in any way with matters that might arise.' A day later, Mulock wrote that the dissident members numbered sixty-two, which if true left no Hepburn loyalists. 'Hepburn saw Nixon today,' he added, 'and said "Harry I have got to get out" Nixon did not commit himself.'

Mitch confined his public comments to the simple statement that he was not a 'quitter' and had no intention of resigning. McQuesten, the president of the OLA, met the demand for a convention with the blunt statement that 'nothing could be gained by such a convention.' The pressure continued for a few weeks, and finally sputtered and died. Despite their decisive victory on 26 March, the King Liberals became faint-hearted when they had to face the prospect of a frontal assault on Queen's Park. As *Saturday Night*'s Politicus observed, the feeling seemed to be, 'Take it easy and watch you don't get your fingers burned.' The coup failed.[24]

'With blood in my eye'

Mitch's contempt for Mackenzie King blinded him to the fact that in the days of the phoney war Canadians seemed content with King's limited commitments and found the rhetoric of all-out war, with the menacing prospect of conscription, unnecessary and unseemly partisan. Mitch remained convinced, however, as he told a disconsolate Manion, that 'when the real fury of this thing strikes us the people of Canada will realize they have made a tremendous mistake in endorsing King and his half-hearted war effort.' The real fury struck on 9 April when Hitler's forces swept through Denmark and into Norway. Mitch was seldom far from his radio, morbidly listening to every foreign report. He told his friends that the Germans would smash through the Low Countries, the French army would collapse, and Hitler's troops would be in Paris by 15 May, London by 15 June, and on the shores of Canada by 15 September. In May the blitzkreig he had predicted shattered the pitiful defences in the Low Countries and swung into France. At Westminster the 'appeaser' resigned and Churchill formed an all-party government. In Canada Mitch was not alone in praying that an inflamed public would force the resignation of the appeaser in Laurier House. Nor was he alone in attempting to make his prayers come true.[1]

On 21 May, with German panzers at the Channel, Mitch broke his long post-election silence when King released the report of the Rowell Sirois Commission which he had conveniently delayed until after the election. King had released the report, Mitch charged with his customary hyperbole, 'with the design of shielding the heads of a Government leading a defenceless people.' Ontario would not attend a conference to discuss fundamental changes in the federal system; instead Mitch asked King to enlist the support of the provincial governments 'in saving ourselves from what seems to be obvious destruction.' Acknowledging the plot to remove him, Mitch exclaimed that 'they can call a Provincial convention if they wish – they can call two Provincial conventions – they can call a Dominion convention if they want to – I don't care. The issues are beyond that now.'

King was already concerned about the widespread criticism of his government and the open scepticism – even in his party, caucus, and cabinet – of his capacity as a wartime leader. Mitch's attack, he assured caucus and cabinet, was part of a Toronto-based conspiracy to force his resignation and pave the way for a national government. The iron hand was seldom more faintly disguised in the velvet glove as he warned caucus that his resignation would bring down the government. The message was clear, and King was 'amused later to see how some members, especially Moore came nearby to shake hands in the House. Fraser came to my office to assure me he was 100% behind me, that he despised Hepburn. Ross Gray made a remark or two on the floor which helped to excuse him a little.'[2]

But as the tragic miracle of Dunkirk unfolded, criticism of King mounted. With many Liberals openly discussing the prospect of Ralston taking command, King intimated to his colleagues that he was prepared to resign in favour of Ralston. But as long as he was in office there had to be an end to the treachery and the conspiracy to replace him with a national government. Confirmation of the conspiracy came from his friend Charlie Bishop of the Ottawa *Citizen*. The barons of the press – including Grattan O'Leary of the *Journal*, Grant Dexter, Dafoe and the Siftons, the Vancouver *Sun*, and, of course, McCullagh and his friends – said Bishop, were engaged in a plot to replace him with 'some more warlike person.' True or not, the sudden appearance of bitterly anti-King display advertisements, 'Calling Canada,' in newspapers across the country made the story credible.[3]

'Calling Canada' was largely the work of Judith Robinson, the fiercely anti-King columnist for the *Globe and Mail*, and Oakley Dalgleish, who had resigned from the paper a few months earlier. The European war was a tank war, Robinson wrote on 21 May, but thanks to Mr King the first Canadian division would soon face the enemy without tanks. 'Tank Soldier's Wife Presses Plea for Tanks' followed a day later. Robinson's articles drew a quick and angry response and inspired the 'Buy a Tank' campaign in Kitchener and other cities.

Mitch was among those who encouraged Robinson and Dalgleish to broaden the attack. He promised them $10,000 from one of his stockbroker friends and assured them of more to come from others, Robinson later reminded Mitch, 'if we gave proof of our ability to do a job.' Late in May they created 'Calling Canada.' The first full-page ad on 27 May – 'Canada Sold Out' – documented Canada's lack of tanks and lack of preparation for tank warfare. A day later came 'Will Sixteen Scout Tanks Stop Hitler – Canada Makes No Tanks – Have any been ordered – Ask Mr. King.' 'McNaughton Bring Him Home – Canada Needs "Andy" McNaughton' followed on 31 May. As effective as the ads, which ran until the end of June in Tory papers across the country, were thousands of posters and bumper stickers with anti-King slogans.

Picked up by Tories in the Commons, the venomous campaign was a success. King summoned a delegation from the Canadian Manufacturers' Association to Ottawa to explain that Canada was not yet producing tanks because the British had not settled on a design. And Howe followed with the promise that contracts would soon be let for the production of tanks. Despite its success, however, 'Calling Canada' soon disappeared. Although McCullagh knew that Robinson was going out on a limb, he 'cut off the limb' and fired her. Mitch's stockbroker reneged on his promise and the financial support never materialized. Robinson and Dalgleish appealed to Mitch to save 'Calling Canada,' but their letter lay unanswered as he was engaged in what was widely believed to be a battle to save his life.[4]

Mitch and Conant had also been pressing Ottawa to wage a more vigorous war against the fifth columnists in Canada, whose European cousins had allegedly facilitated the easy German advance in western Europe. Since the outbreak of war, Conant had demanded that Ottawa take action against what he described as 'these slimy subversive elements' that opposed the war in Canada. In December 1939, he had arrested Charles Millard under the Defence of Canada Regulations for such statements as 'there was not a great deal of sense going to Europe to fight Hitlerism, while there was Hitlerism right here in Canada.' On 15 May Conant succeeded in having Mr Justice Chevrier of the Ontario Supreme Court rule that the Communist party was an illegal organization, a step Lapointe had refused to take. Conant immediately demanded that Lapointe act on the decision and intern all members of the party without the right of appeal. Although Lapointe's initial reaction was cautious, in response to public opinion he banned the party on 4 June. Many Communists were arrested, and interned, and Tim Buck and others fled to the United States or went underground. Conant remained frustrated in his semi-hysterical war against subversion, however, for Lapointe refused to prohibit the right to appeal.[5]

The alleged danger of subversion also demanded a more vigorous defence of Ontario. After meeting his war cabinet on 21 May, Mitch wired King that he could no longer be responsible for the defence of the Niagara frontier. King replied at once that an infantry regiment would be moved to Niagara as soon as possible. With many municipalities already organizing Home Guard units, Conant urged Rogers to create a civil defence force within the Defence Department. To avoid criticism, King forced Rogers to announce a plan to enlist twelve Veterans' Home Guard companies. However, three thousand Home Guards across Canada did not allay Ontario's anxiety and on 4 June, with Mitch's approval, Conant stated that the government would help local municipalities establish their own units.[6]

The anxiety increased on 10 June when Italy entered the war. The RCMP and OPP quickly arrested and later interned hundreds of suspected Fascist sympathizers. The next day Mitch emerged from his sick-bed at Bannockburn to make his wildest statement ever. Special Branch agents had warned the government that there was a Nazi fifth column in the United States 'only waiting for orders from across the Atlantic' to move into Ontario. Mitch warned that Ontario lay along 'the most thickly populated sections of the United States, where undoubtedly there are hundreds of thousands of Nazi and Fascist sympathizers.' He promised total support to local governments in organizing the 'able-bodied' men of Ontario to defend 'their homes and factories, their wives and children' because by the time the King government was ready to act 'the damage would be done.'

In the Commons, Lapointe stated that Mitch was 'merely spreading rumours in a way that is not conducive to the public good or the proper prosecution of the war.' But J.G. Ross, the Liberal from Moose Jaw, seriously suggested that Mitch himself deserved to be treated as a saboteur. There had been no subversion and no sabotage, Ross exclaimed, but there had been 'repeated sabotage in high places, for instance, Premier Hepburn of Ontario.' No one had done more damage to national unity and the war effort than Hepburn, who 'could not be a better servant of Hitler and Mussolini – if he were a paid agent' and if an 'ordinary citizen had said one-tenth of what Hepburn has said he would long since have been charged under the regulations.'

'My own opinion,' Chubby Power told reporters, 'is that Mitch Hepburn is crazy and I don't think I am alone in that opinion.' In

Washington, General George Marshall did not say Mitch was crazy but suggested that he was 'fishing in thin air ... We know there are many Nazi sympathizers in the u.s. and a big proportion of foreign-born population in Michigan, near the Canadian border. But does the premier think anybody of this ilk could organize a strong force in the u.s. without the government knowing about it – strong enough to do any damage?' If Mitch would give him the facts, Marshall promised, the American army would prevent the invasion. Nevertheless, Conant was about to make a public appeal for ten thousand rifles and shotguns when, on 18 June, King, who a month before has said he would resign before he would 'accept any move in the direction of conscription,' announced the conscription of men for service in Canada. With sixty-five thousand men already under arms as well as the Home Guard, Power suggested to Conant that the country was well defended. And although most of 57 municipalities which had organized Voluntary Civil Guards still wanted weapons, Conant reluctantly suspended his appeal. There were many who agreed with Les Frost that the pressure from Queen's Park and Mitch's outburst played an important part in 'arousing our people to an overwhelming demand for the mobilization of man-power, industry and wealth' which led to King's 18 June decision.[7]

Mitch was a very sick man in the spring of 1940. Obsessed by the war, he became increasingly depressed as he contemplated the ultimate tragedy of the invasion of Britain by Hitler's apparently invincible troops. Frank O'Connor's death was a blow in no way softened by the $2,000 a year that Frank had left him. The acute bronchial attacks he had endured during the session recurred in May. Dr Avery confined him to bed at the hotel and on 7 June sent him to Bannockburn and prohibited visitors. A week later, heavily bundled up, he drove around the farm and walked in the sunshine. But that night he suffered a relapse and Bob Gaskin issued a bulletin that he had severe bronchial pneumonia in the right lung. At Queen's Park his colleagues hoped for the best; in Ottawa Mackenzie King prayed for the worst. 'I don't often wish that a man should pass away' he confided to his diary, 'but I believe that it would be the most fortunate thing that could happen at this time.'[8]

On 26 June Mitch was carried on a stretcher to Jack Bickell's plane bound for the Kellog Sanatorium in Battle Creek, Michigan. Although Dr Avery insisted he was going only for a complete check-up and total rest, Eva's tearful farewell suggested that Mitch was much sicker than his doctor admitted. At Battle Creek the doctors began a round of tests and placed him on a controlled diet. Although Mitch had expected to be away from four to six weeks, he was soon up and around and returned to the farm in two weeks, eighteen pounds lighter and looking better than he had in months. He was supposed to rest for several weeks, but he returned to Queen's Park a week later and met the cabinet on 18 July for the first time in two months. Mitch seemed a different man after his recovery. 'The change in him is deeper, subtler, than could rightly be attributed to a stomach ache or its cure,' a journalist noted. 'In a serious conversation the new Hepburn shies away from controversial subjects. Throughout an interview lasting more than an hour he did not once mention the name of Mackenzie King.'[9]

His health restored, Mitch tried to enlist or get war work in London. He had appealed to Ian Mackenzie in the fall of 1939 and soon after his return from Battle Creek raised the question of enlisting with Ralston. He was more hopeful of securing a position in London through his friend Jack Bickell, who had been recruited by Lord Beaverbrook's Ministry of Aircraft Production to organize the North Atlantic Ferry Command. After lunching with Bickell in London, Colin Campbell wired: 'You were discussed. Offer may be made soon. Advise acceptance. Miss you.' Bickell also missed Mitch, but told Campbell privately that 'I'm not going to get in wrong with Bill King by doing anything.' The best he could do was send best wishes from 'one dead drunk to another.'[10]

As the Luftwaffe began its July raids over the Channel to soften up Britain for the invasion, Mitch admitted that he was 'more apprehensive than ever regarding the outcome of this war and greatly fear that Britain will not be able to withstand the German onslaught when it comes.' He was heartened when King reorganized the cabinet after Rogers died in an airplane crash in June and put Ralston in National Defence, Power in Air, and his friend Premier Angus Macdonald of Nova Scotia in Naval Services. He met the three war ministers soon after his return from Battle Creek, and found them much more supportive of his plans for the defence of Ontario than in the spring. They not only approved of Ontario's Home Guards but also agreed to provide the force with arms 'if and when Ontario decided to place the units under what would virtually be war footing.' Although Ottawa did not officially delegate responsibility for civil defence to the provinces until June 1941, the government created a Civilian Defence Committee in the fall of 1940. By the end of the year forty thousand men, many of them trained and armed, enrolled in the Volunteer Civilian Guards. On 1

October Mitch announced the formation of the Ontario Voluntary Constabulary as an auxiliary force to aid the municipal and provincial police. Veterans' guard units continued to protect essential industries and installations not guarded by the military.[11]

Although Mitch continued to lament Canada's lack of preparation, he directed his speeches in the fall at the apathy of the Canadian people rather than the shortcomings of the King administration. But as time passed he became convinced that Ottawa's 'propaganda mill,' grinding out exaggerated stories about squadrons of all-Canadian Spitfires flown by Canadian pilots and Canadian shipyards building all-Canadian corvettes for the battle of the Atlantic, was creating a false sense of the Canadian commitment. 'They know they are misleading the Canadian people,' Mitch exclaimed. 'If the people knew the truth they would not tolerate this inaction. We need planes and we need tanks; and we need artillery and we have wagon wheels with fence posts between them.' Before Chubby Power took over the Air Ministry, 'it was nearly as pitiful as when Churchill took it over.' King claimed to have known war was inevitable three years before it broke out: 'Did we do anything? No, we did not do a blasted thing!' Apologizing to Lapointe for his impatience, Mitch wrote that 'this situation is infinitely more serious than most of us realize and unless the United States comes forward almost immediately with merchant ships and protective escorts it is very doubtful as to how much longer Britain can stand up under concentrated U boat and air attacks.' Mitch was somewhat relieved a month later when Roosevelt asked Congress to approve a massive lend-lease program to aid the allies, and in April extended the U.S. navy's 'sea frontier' beyond the mid-Atlantic.[12]

Mitch was so obsessed with the war that he could not think about local politics or carry on the work of government. Increasingly reclusive, he seldom called cabinet meetings and often missed those that were scheduled. His colleagues found him distant, almost unapproachable, particularly if they differed with him, and the tension was often acute at Queen's Park. Despite pressure from within his own party, he refused to consider an election in 1941 and even refused to fill the five vacancies in the legislature. However, by-elections became legally necessary when he appointed two new ministers from outside the legislature. Simpson had died in August and Duncan McArthur, his deputy, was sworn in a week later. When Paul Leduc resigned in September to become the registrar of the Supreme Court in Ottawa, Mitch's choice of Robert Laurier could only be explained because he bore his uncle's name and had served as Ernest Lapointe's secretary. Laurier had hesitated because of Mitch's feud with King, but Lapointe suggested he 'could be a sort of liaison' and Mitch agreed that he 'could keep him in line if he went too far.' Neither the Tories nor the CCF contested the by-elections, but Laurier faced a disgruntled Liberal and a Social Crediter in Ottawa. Mitch and Lapointe appeared on the same platform, where Mitch delivered his ten lines of practised French, and their warm handshake suggested that all was quiet on the domestic front.[13]

Federal Liberals conceded that Mitch was firmly in control of the party in Ontario. Even many of those who had criticized his anti-King behaviour had swung around after the full fury struck. Although King had assured a reluctant Angus Macdonald that it was safe to run in Rogers's Kingston seat because 'Hepburn was as dead as Julius Caesar as far as his influence was concerned' this opinion was not shared by King's Ontario ministers. Throughout the province, wrote Lambert late in the year, the federal and provincial Liberals 'are moving together again to support Hepburn in his by-elections and coming general election. This movement meets with the approval of local federal Members and Ministers. Harry Johnston's [sic] office in Toronto becomes once more the centre of Liberalism in Ontario, and no one can seemingly prevent his revival of strength in that quarter. There is no one to say that Johnston's office is not a truly representative Liberal office, or that Hepburn last January forfeited the right to be regarded as a Liberal.' No one, that is, but Mackenzie King.[14]

'"Mitch is friendly," one hears on all sides. "He wants to heal the breach," they say,' Lambert informed King late in 1940, 'but it should not lull the federal Government into a sense of security in connection with the approaching conference on the Sirois Report.' Until his outbursts early in December, Mitch had been friendly. But, as King knew only too well, he had not changed his mind on the appropriateness of discussing the report during the war and was highly critical of the recommendations themselves.[15]

King had also wanted to postpone any discussion of the report until a distant future. He did not like proposals which added new federal responsibilities and were certain to arouse the opposition of some of the larger provinces. And on reflection he concluded that the recommendations had been too influenced by Queen's University economists and their 'orthodox money theories' and, with Rowell's death, had become largely a Dafoe report' which was 'too highly coloured by the needs of the Prairies,' sentiments which Mitch endorsed completely. But under pressure from Graham Towers of the Bank of Canada and the Department of Finance, King reluctantly established a special cabinet committee which quickly concluded that the time was now. Finance Minister Ilsley was instructed to consult with the premiers and warn the recalcitrant that provincial revenues would be drastically affected by higher federal taxes and the likelihood of liquor and gasoline rationing.[16]

Ottawa was 'eagerly awaiting Mitch's reaction' to Ilsley's proposals, Dexter wrote to Dafoe. 'It is almost certain to be against and the feeling is that Mitch will leap into print with the charge that Ottawa is using the war as a screen or a blind, behind which to rape the provinces.' There was good reason for Ottawa to be apprehensive. On the basis of the 1937 figures used by the commission's research staff, the benefits to Ontario were meagre at best. And the report had admitted that if the burden of unemployment relief fell, the benefit to Ontario 'might be reduced, might disappear entirely, or might even in prosperous years be converted into a loss.' By 1940, with relief costs down and revenues up, there was no question that the province would lose an estimated $17 million and the municipalities another $5 million. However, 'this "compulsory insurance", if we may so designate it,' paid by Ontario, the report argued, 'is a low price to pay to safeguard the financial stability for all the Canadian provinces and the autonomy which is closely linked with that stability.' The commission also realized that the compulsory insurance, which would enable Ottawa to take over the almost worthless paper in several provinces, would lead to 'unearned profits for a favoured few,' but saw no way around such 'fortuitous' results.[17]

When Ilsley came to Toronto on 21 October, Mitch was 'very friendly and a little wistful in his desire to improve relations with Ottawa,' but said he was unalterably opposed to the recommendations of the commission. He believed that the Commission had been 'biased, unfair and out to get Ontario,' and was particularly indignant that the formula for the federal assumption of provincial debts heavily favoured Quebec. When Ilsley reported to cabinet, Grant Dexter learned that the '"hotheads" ... were for carrying the issue to Hepburn, for fighting it out.' With Ilsley apparently on the fence, the opposition to 'any militant action' was led by King and Lapointe who 'were unwilling to risk an open break with Mitch on this issue. Their reason is that they would not divide Canada on a domestic question while the war is in so precarious a position. It is the old national-unity-first line.' The cabinet agreed with King that since

Mitch was opposed, it would be unwise to have a conference on the report. The report would never be accepted, said King, 'till Hepburn and in all probability his government along with him would be removed.' The special cabinet committee was asked to recommend the action government should take in view of Ilsley's gloomy report. Dexter was convinced that King's view would prevail.[18]

However, he underestimated the powerful influence of Graham Towers, Dr Clifford Clark in Finance, and hotheads such as Ralston, Howe, and Crerar who believed that financial imperatives overrode any political consequences. On 25 October the committee recommended a conference, despite Mitch's opposition and the likelihood of criticism from Pattullo, Aberhart and even Adelard Godbout, who had defeated Duplessis in October 1939 with the powerful backing of the federal Liberals. By placing before the public the 'powerful reasons from the national point of view' for implementing the report, Ilsley's committee argued, even in Ontario the 'favourable conditions presently existing would bring wide support for a strong Government lead.'

Perhaps because King was sick, cabinet agreed. Even a failed conference would set the stage for the necessary invasion of provincial tax fields. 'The report commends itself strongly to our judgement,' King wrote on 2 November, summoning the provinces to a conference, and its adoption is 'necessary to put our country in a position to pursue a policy which will achieve the maximum war effort and, at the same time, lay a sound foundation for postwar reconstruction.' Mitch replied that he had hoped that discussion could be delayed until after the war but, however reluctantly, Ontario would be at the table.[19]

Mitch was trapped in a no-win situation. As King believed, the conference would fail and Mitch, more than anyone else, would be blamed. Moreover, if Lambert's judgment could be trusted, the conference could be extremely important in undermining Mitch's political power. In a long memorandum for King, Lambert argued that if 'the federal government's course is determined definitely to go ahead, then it can do much to consolidate the Liberal federal position in Ontario, as well as to help Canada as a whole, by refusing to let Hepburn and his associates stall off any definite conclusions by this Conference. Hepburn cannot face Ontario as the outstanding opponent of a stronger federal structure for Canada's war burdens.' If the other provinces supported the recommendations, he concluded, all the federal Liberals with whom he had spoken agreed that Mitch 'could not maintain an isolationist position in his own province.' And obviously if it failed because of Mitch's obstinacy, his advocacy of an all-out war effort would lose credibility and his position would be seriously weakened.

To make certain public opinion would crystallize against opponents of the report, the Ottawa propaganda machine moved into high gear, and Walters complained to federal officials about the 'extensive propaganda.' The *Globe and Mail* and the financial press insisted that national salvation depended upon the adoption of the report to such an extent that, given the self-interest of financial institutions in recouping their losses on provincial bonds, King was afraid they were 'mitigating against acceptance of the Report.' As Mitch maintained a public silence, the *Star* tried to bait the trap with a provocative headline story: 'Great Sirois reform may founder on rock of Hepburn's politics; Even Aberhart suggesting only revisions but Ontario Premier wants whole far-reaching plan scrapped.' But Mitch refused to be drawn out. Unaware of the political strategy or naively believing that Mitch might accept the report, Towers begged King to tell Atkinson not to provoke Mitch into taking a categorical position against the recommendations.[20]

With everyone in the cabinet except Crerar agreeing that the conference would amount to nothing, King was convinced that it would be foolhardy to take a strong line and defeat the grand strategy that it was Mitch and other premiers who stood in the way of success. Moreover, he was afraid that if he took an 'arbitrary and dictatorial position' Mitch would dissolve the legislature on the issue and 'run his provincial campaign on the effort of Ottawa to take from Ontario all its powers, privileges, rights, to sacrifice them to Quebec or to the Prairies.' He told cabinet that in his opening speech he would 'have to construct a mattress that would make it easy for the trapeze performers as they dropped to the ground one by one.' Although his colleagues may have wondered if they were numbered among the performers, they agreed that the soft line was the best. The bureaucrats did not. Sandy Skelton, who felt pride of authorship, had reached the point, reported Dexter, 'where he no longer believes the pen is mightier than the sword and would like nothing better than an assignment to scrag Mitch with his bare hands.'[21]

To the dismay of his officials, the opening statement was King at his equivocal best: 'We do not say "all or nothing"; or "everything at once".' The aim was not 'to re-write the constitution, or to rebuild the structure of confederation' but simply to distribute the burden a little 'more evenly.' Although some would suffer in the short run all would benefit in the end because of increased stability and prosperity. Mitch seemed not to listen as King spoke, and did not join in the polite applause.[22]

As Mitch had warned Chubby Power, he was coming 'with blood in my eye and dandruff in my moustache.' Whatever the merits of the Report, he argued, the timing was not only inopportune, but almost treacherous. Surely this was not the time 'to send a courier to bomb-torn London' and ask the British Parliament to debate a new constitution for Canada. 'And while you have obligated yourselves to fight this war with the last drop of printer's ink and to the last page of *Hansard*, confusion, utter confusion, would prevail in all governments as existing tax machinery bogged down.' Ontario had cooperated fully in every request made by Ottawa; but if the 'propagandists' believed that because of its opposition to the report 'we will remain silent while insinuations are broadcast deliberately for the purpose of branding us as unpatriotic, unneighbourly with our sister provinces, or guilty of doing anything to block Canada in achieving our maximum war effort, then I say to them, "We shall defend ourselves from that kind of attack here, on the floor of the legislature, and on the public platform".'

Ontario had asked for nothing and there was certainly nothing for it in the report, 'the product of the minds of three professors and a Winnipeg newspaper man' who, he added the next morning, 'had always had his knife in Ontario.' There would be no fiscal stability when all that was left was the revenue from the Liquor Board, car licences, and the gasoline tax, with the federal government likely to ration gasoline and curtail the sale of liquor. And although there were 'extenuating circumstances' it was widely believed that Quebec's $8 million a year adjustment grant smacked of 'preferred treatment' and was a threat to national unity. Citing the statement of a broker who estimated that its adoption would add $120 million to the value of the bonds of the three prairie provinces, Mitch said that there was 'a fast developing body of opinion, not without cause, now promoting the idea that behind this untimely move, ostensibly as a war measure, is a well-cooked, nefarious deal to make good the losses in depreciation of certain bonds held largely by financial houses, to collect unpaid interest on Alberta's bonds and to cause a sharp appreciation in bonds of certain provinces' with the capital appreciation exempt from federal income tax.

Under the War Measures Act Ottawa possessed 'extreme, even dictatorial power' to prosecute the war. If King wanted support from the provinces, 'say so, and I am sure every province will assist by immediately passing the enabling legislation.' Ontario had cooperated fully and would continue to do so. 'But this is a peace-time document, and we believe honestly and sincerely that the time to discuss it is not now, but only when the menace to our democracy, christianity and freedom is removed by the complete defeat and even annihilation of the ruthless axis powers.'

Aberhart and Pattullo attacked the centralizing substance of the report, as well as the argument that its implementation was necessary to prosecute the war. Godbout was non-committal, but felt it was inappropriate to make fundamental changes in the federal system during the war. The three Atlantic provinces were less than enthusiastic converts to the proposition that it should be studied. Only Saskatchewan and, particularly, Bracken of Manitoba were wholehearted in their support.[23]

King had proposed that they discuss the recommendations in four committees – finance, constitution, labour and unemployment, and special problems – and he instructed Lapointe and Crerar to meet the premiers the next morning to discuss procedure. The meeting was 'the god damndest exhibition circus you can imagine,' said Sandy Skelton, as it became apparent within five minutes that Mitch, Pattullo, and Aberhart would not agree to the procedure. 'They all stated they were quite willing to sit down in committee with the Federal Government to discuss how the provinces could further aid the war effort,' Crerar relayed to Dafoe, but they would not go into committee to discuss the recommendations.

When the conference resumed at 2:30 p.m., Lapointe reported the failure of the morning session and the three 'sinners' explained that they would be willing to continue to discuss ways in which the provinces could cooperate in the war effort. But King refused and suggested that Finance Minister Ilsley provide an overview of wartime finance. Ilsley painted a gloomy picture of billion-dollar budgets that would consume almost half of national income, and suggested how implementation of the report would simplify the tax system, save provinces from bankruptcy, establish important national minimum standards, and lay the basis for post-war reconstruction, a task which Churchill had already set in motion while London was burning. He warned the provinces that he would have to increase succession duties and income taxes and take other steps that would cut into provincial revenues. Rather than use power under the War Measures Act, he explained, he preferred the democratic method to the 'big stick'; but 'we shall do it reluctantly, but do it we will, if necessary to win this war.'

Mitch intervened twice before the conference ended. He warned that he would withdraw from the conference if King insisted it was the report or nothing. But he insisted that he was not objecting to Ottawa moving into provincial sources of revenue. 'I say to the dominion: "We are not behind you; we are ahead of you, and if you want to do something as a war measure, go ahead and do it. But don't smash this confederation and stir up [a] possible racial feud in your efforts".' And as the conference moved towards adjournment, Mitch once again tried to make his position clear.

I just want to summarize the whole situation in a few words, by saying that the Sirois report was conceived as a peace-time measure. What has happened to it in the interval? You have dressed it up with the garments of patriotism and cloaked it with the exigencies of war as well, and have said to those of us who represent the provinces, 'We want you to accept the findings of this report as a war measure in perpetuity'. Now this is where we disagree. We say that we will help you in every conceivable manner so far as prosecuting this war is concerned, but we are not going to sell out our respective provinces, and generations yet to come, under the exigencies of war.

That, in short, is our position, and that is the position to which we are going to adhere. If you can meet us on that basis of discussing our problems, without any degree of finality in so far as our constitution is concerned, we are prepared to sit here to-morrow and next day, and next week.

Angus Macdonald sent a scrawled note over to King: 'Mr. Aberhart is willing to consider the Sirois Report, along with other matters. Hepburn is willing to talk about the war. If we accepted the idea of discussing *something*, could we by degrees get to a consideration of the Report?' But King was not prepared to snatch defeat from the jaws of victory and death came at 6:35 p.m. Mitch passed up King's dinner at the country club.[24]

Mitch was remarkably restrained on his return from Ottawa, but three days later he issued a statement, approved by cabinet, on financing the war. The war should not be financed by raising taxes and borrowing at 3 per cent, but the Bank of Canada should imitate Roosevelt's policy and expand the currency supply and pay only a reasonable service charge for borrowed money. The crux of his argument was that 'sound' money occupied the driver's seat in Ottawa. King immediately anticipated a violent agitation between the advocates of hard and soft money. While the dangers of inflation were very real, he reflected, it was important that 'the extremists of sound money bend a little before the breeze rather to see themselves broken in front of the storm. There will have to be some yielding.'

Ilsley refused to yield. He delivered a long public lecture on the misconceptions and flawed economics in Mitch's 'rubber money' panacea, which was not dangerous when confined to western lunatics but was more menacing when it came from Toronto. The Bank of Canada had expanded the currency substantially, he explained, and would ensure there was ample credit to meet wartime requirements. But with the county approaching full employment, further expansion would simply lead to inflation. Moreover, he lectured, taxing and borrowing out of current savings were necessary not only to raise money but also to divert labour and resources into war production. Above all, he concluded pointedly, what the war effort needed was not talk of an impending financial crisis, but a solution to 'our present system of overlapping jurisdiction in the field of taxation to spread the burden fairly and equitably over the people of Canada as a whole.'[25]

Despite the deserved public spanking, Mitch was not contrite. He was so incensed by the criticism of his stand at the Conference that the government placed large ads in provincial newspapers. Contrary to press reports the delegation had not withdrawn, and he had agreed to discuss all avenues of cooperation to maximize the war effort. The recommendations not only cut into provincial revenues, but added hundreds of millions to the federal debt much of which was borne by Ontario taxpayers – an illustration of the sailors' description of marriage as 'giving one half your grab to get the other half cooked.' Not only would adoption of the report threaten the high level of education and social services, but would also lead to the centralization of power and the growth of a bureaucracy which would undermine federalism and threaten democracy.[26]

Both the Tories and the federal Liberals were afraid Mitch would take his case to the people. A Tory strategist reported that Mitch was 'generally popular, except with a limited class of investors, a limited group of King Liberals, and possibly the Roman Catholics. He is more popular than he was a year ago.' Among the Tories, Cecil Frost confessed to Drew, there was a 'feeling of helplessness and defeat ... of dullness and lethargy.' All we can do, Drew mournfully admitted, was to 'keep plugging.' In Ottawa the Liberals continued to waffle. The *Star* reported that all fifty-seven Ontario members would stand behind King if Mitch called an election, but Billy Taylor, the whip, told Lambert 'he did not think Federal members would be a unit vs. Hepburn.' Certainly, no Liberal left cabinet or caucus with his sword unsheathed.[27]

Mitch's wooing of Ontario farmers strengthened the prospect of an election as no rural member was likely to oppose him. Ontario farmers were much less interested in the Rowell-Sirois Report than the price of butter and bacon. Farm prices had not kept up with the increased cost of living or of inputs and, with labour drained off to the armed forces and industry, farmers could not get help at affordable wages. Yet they were being asked to increase the production of dairy products for the British market at prices they claimed were below the cost of production. Mitch's repeated lament about primary producers being ground down by high taxation and lower prices found a receptive audience.

Murmurs of a farm revolt across Ontario became rumbles in December when, after putting price controls on bacon, which gave western farmers an advantage because of their cheaper feed costs, Ottawa capped butter prices. Mitch sympathized with the protests and encouraged the farmers to create a non-partisan farmers' union. Stung by Mitch's move, the federal minister of agriculture, Jimmy Gardiner, immediately met a delegation of farmers at London and argued that the cap on butter was designed to prevent windfall profits by companies which had large amounts in storage. But the farmers were not convinced. Early in February Mitch and his farmer ministers held a two-day conference with farm leaders. After the meeting, Mitch announced that the government would spend $3.5 million on subsidies for cheese and bacon. 'The farmer is willing to bare his back, but he wants the other fellow to bare his back also,' he said repeatedly. 'We want equality of sacrifice. The government of Ontario stands firm as the friend of the farmer.' There was no doubt about the outcome if the friend of the farmer went to the people in the spring or summer of 1941. However, Mitch insisted there was no need to put the province to the expense of an election – estimated at six or seven squadrons of Spitfires – and went ahead with the session as planned.[28]

Mitch had been sick with the usual colds and bronchitis during the fall and winter and was not well when the session opened on 19 February 1941. The throne speech catalogued the government's contribution to the war effort and defended Mitch's position at the Ottawa conference. Drew was not to be envied when he and Mitch went head-to-head during the leaders' day debate on 25 February. For months, while Drew had remained silent, the Tories had test-

ed party and public opinion on the report. The overwhelming conclusion was that Ontario would get a bad deal and even Les Frost,
who hoped that the 'national interest would prevail,' believed there
had to be substantial changes in the financial arrangements. Moreover, with the pegging of butter prices Ontario farmers were unsympathetic to any aid to the western provinces. And among the Tory
militants there was the conviction that Quebec municipalities were
'graft ridden and that the Catholic church which runs the whole
province has a property worth $600 million with an annual income
of $50 million free from income tax and that they did not see why
the province of Ontario should be made a party to perpetuate a
condition of this kind.'[29]

Drew chose to ignore the substance of the report while blaming
Mitch for scuttling the conference. And now the advocate of 'rubber money' was walking 'hand in hand through the same bewildered
maze with Alberta's silver-tongued apostle of economic lunacy.' His
amendment urged the government to propose another conference to
'adopt such measures as may be necessary to assure our greatest
possible war-effort by inter-Governmental co-operation,' assist agriculture and protect labour, and lay the basis for post-war reconstruction.

In his short speech, Mitch replied that he had begged King to discuss broader issues only to be told that it was the Report or nothing. Moreover, King himself had questioned the wisdom of holding
the conference in war time and, when he proposed adjournment,
had asked '"What do you think Mitch?" He still calls me Mitch to
my face. I don't know what he calls me behind my back,' he
quipped, 'but I don't think it is Mitch.' He repeated his criticism
of the report, described the takeover of provincial debt with no
restrictions on future borrowing as 'the biggest bond deal in Canadian history,' and for good measure said that Drew could not reach
Aberhart's boot tops in understanding monetary questions. While
some Tories echoed Drew's call for a conference, most ignored it,
and Holland Acres, the MPP for Carleton, confessed that he would
not have spent as long in Ottawa as had Mitch.[30]

The session was uneventful. Other than earning their indemnity
there was little to keep the members at work for six weeks.
Although the Tories argued that the farm subsidies were inadequate,
they could not oppose them. And when the federal government
stunned the municipalities by ending all grants for relief, Mitch
stunned them again by picking up 75 per cent of the costs. There
was little criticism of bills tidying up the public health system, great-

ly expanding the venereal disease prevention program which had become even more essential in wartime, and embracing real estate brokers and collection agencies within regulations policing the white-collar world. At long last Conant was able to enact his grand design to rationalize the judicial system, but both caucuses rejected the proposal that women could sit on juries. Drew had hoped that the Select Committee on Lands and Forests, established at the previous session, would reveal the depths of Liberal corruption and Heenan's mismanagement. There was little in the report to suggest that Heenan was an able administrator, but nothing to prove he was a scoundrel. Drew's motion to establish a commission, like Hydro, to administer the department was defeated, as was his proposal for a Town and Country Planning Commission.

Mitch boasted that his 14 March budget was proof of his commitment to an all-out war effort. Ontario had absorbed the massive increase in federal taxes and had helped hard-pressed farmers increase production. He had lived up to his promise to Ottawa not to borrow and to control expenditure. With a $12.6 million dollar surplus and a forecast of a $9.4 million surplus for the next fiscal year, there would be no additional taxes and a modest reduction in the provincial debt. The best the opposition could do was to charge that having a surplus was unpatriotic and it should be given to Britain for food aid. When the session limped to its end, Mitch was very much in command of his caucus and the House.[31]

The suspicion that Mitch would hold a provincial election was heightened by his reaction to Ilsley's 29 April budget. Faced with the necessity to raise more than $2 billion, the federal government had little alternative but to increase personal and corporate income taxes. After long debates, the cabinet decided to couple the heavy tax increases with an offer to the provinces that guaranteed them their current revenues if they would withdraw completely from the personal and corporate income tax field. If they refused, they would have to answer to their voters for a system of double taxation. Cabinet agreed there would be no consultation with the provinces before Ilsley announced the decision in his budget.[32]

From Bannockburn, Mitch's initial response was that he had instructed Walters to examine the impact of the budget on provincial revenues. A week later, after two long cabinet meetings, he wired Ilsley that while he was 'reluctant to voice the slightest opposition' to the budget proposals, he did object to a 15 per cent tax on interest paid to non-resident holders of provincial bonds, a provision which, since it did not apply to federal bonds, was 'discriminatory and destructive of provincial credit.' With Ilsley unbending, Mitch appealed directly to King. His dark intimation that King was threatening the success of the June victory bond campaign, was followed later by the statement that in view of 'your latest provocative act' the province would not vacate the direct tax field. Moreover, Mitch questioned the legality of the act and had instructed bankers not to deduct the tax.[33]

Only with great difficulty did King persuade Ilsley that 'it was never too late to retreat.' King agreed the tax was discriminatory and could jeopardize both the war loan and the budget proposal. He also warned cabinet that Mitch might dissolve and 'bring on a political fight just at the time when the war was at its worst. I felt we had to reckon with that possibility and should take care not to be responsible for it.' King sounded the retreat in a wire to Mitch stating that Ottawa would withdraw the tax if he would agree to vacate the direct tax fields. Mitch's reaction was as predictable as it was outrageous. In a 'move worthy of Hitler,' King stood 'unstripped and unmasked,' he exclaimed to the press, for it was now clear that the non-resident tax was conceived as a device to strengthen Ottawa's hands in forcing Ontario to vacate the direct tax fields.[34]

Officially, however, Mitch did not reply to King's proposal and the rancorous debate began again in the cabinet. King was even more convinced than before that the tax should be abolished to prevent Mitch from calling an election on a provincial rights cry.

That what I emphasized most was that I doubted if a member of the Federal Party would get out and fight Hepburn defending the Dominion position. The Ontario Ministers present: McLarty, Mulock, Howe and Gibson instantly agreed that our men would not oppose Hepburn; that would mean siding with the Tories. I then said that the Federal Government and our own party would be in a fine position before the eyes of the public. We would stand condemned by the action or rather the inaction of our own men, and this I thought was an impossible situation.

After another long debate the next day, during which King ridiculed Ilsley's comment that Mitch would give in, King finally got his way, and Ilsley agreed to remove that obstacle to the tax agreement.[35]

The belief was widespread that Mitch might seek a new mandate with King's leadership inevitably an underlying issue. Although McCullagh had urged King to encourage a revolt in Mitch's cabinet, even the *Globe* commented in June that but 'for the fact that it would be sabotage to call an election in wartime, Premier Hepburn could easily demonstrate that there is no one, either in Toronto or Ottawa, who could defeat him in an appeal to the people. Loose talk about his political security is nonsense.' When a cabinet shuffle late in May moved Heenan out of the sensitive Lands and Forests ministry, suspicions were reinforced and the Tories reactivated the party machinery.[36]

Mitch was also under strong pressure from his cabinet to go to the people in the summer of 1941. Before Drew left for England, Nixon and Oliver pressed Mitch to tell him to stay at home because the cabinet wanted an election. 'I'll never forget Hepburn,' Oliver recalled. 'He was very sentimental about the course of the war ... He felt he wasn't doing right by us and he thought we were losing the war and all this sort of thing.' The Tories picked up the rumours that an election was imminent and Cecil Frost cabled Drew on 5 September asking him to make it known that 'while Hepburn government open to serious criticisms ... war effort demands Ontario be spared an election' and to agree to extend the life of the Assembly. Frost then asked Tom Kennedy to appeal to Mitch. 'He discussed the matter very fully and in strict confidence, as his Cabinet wants an immediate election,' Kennedy wrote Drew after the meeting. 'He promised me that there would be no election this year if you will not oppose the Bill that he intends to introduce to extend the length of Parliament one year, if the war is still on. He wants to know immediately.' Kennedy was 'much impressed with his earnestness about the war and how he would hate to have to call an election this year,' and assured Drew that Mitch would live up to his promise. Drew was more than willing to agree. Nothing could have pleased Mackenzie King and the federal Liberals more.[37]

Mitch's likely electoral success had he chosen to go to the people was in no way diminished by his renewed war against the CIO. The war had dramatically altered the balance of power in industrial relations as the unemployment rate approached zero and wages fell behind the increased cost of living. But the federal government usurped labour's ability to use its advantage by placing industrial relations in all essential industries under its control. During the spring of 1941 Mitch watched as CIO unions struck vital war industries in the United States, which led to demands in Congress that strikes be outlawed. He applauded Roosevelt's decision to send the troops in with fixed bayonets when the communist-led UAW defied a government order and struck North American Aviation in June. During that spring and summer in Canada, there were also pro-

longed slowdowns in the coal mines, work holidays at Canadian
General Electric, and strikes in Montreal and Hamilton steel plants.
Generally sympathetic to the demands of labour, King resisted pressure from industry to outlaw strikes. Only when C.D. Howe submitted his resignation because of his impotence during the crippling
strike in the Arvida aluminum plant did King approve the use of
troops and an order-in-council giving the minister of national defence authority to call out the militia.[38]

Mitch agreed with Howe that King and Norman McLarty, the
minister of labour, were guilty of too much 'pussyfooting' in dealing with strikes in war industries. There was no pussyfooting at
Queen's Park when CIO organizers called a strike at the Campbell
Soup factory at the height of the canning season. When the organizers rejected an improved wage offer Heenan had negotiated and
demanded union recognition, Mitch invited the tomato growers to
come to Toronto and operate the plant. The government would pay
their way, the company provide accommodation, and the OPP guarantee safe passage. Within twenty-four hours one hundred men and
women from Kent County were in Toronto and the strike was broken. Senator Hardy echoed a widespread opinion that if 'we could
only get McLarty to handle some of his strikes the same way I
think we could get on a bit better.'[39]

There were inevitable comparisons when the UAW struck McKinnon Industries in St Catharines for wages higher than those recommended by the conciliation board. McKinnon made anti-aircraft
guns and munitions, and although McLarty denounced it as 'a
deliberate attempt to undermine the wage policy of the Dominion
Government,' Ottawa did nothing to get the thirty-seven hundred
workers back to work. A day after the strike began, Mitch discussed
the situation with Howe by telephone on three occasions. Believing
that Howe had accepted his offer to intervene, Mitch wired that he
would step in if Ottawa gave the province complete power over all
labour difficulties, delegated its authority under the War Measures
Act, agreed that troops could be used at Ottawa's expense, and
empowered Conant to intern anyone deliberately blocking the production of war materials. Howe replied that he had been misunderstood, and that 'the best results will be obtained if the provincial
and federal governments each exercise their own respective powers
and authority and each accept their own respective responsibilities.'
When the RCMP requested a detachment of the OPP to maintain
order, Mitch refused. 'In view of the fact that you have decided to
exercise federal powers in connection with a strike in a war industry,' he wired Howe, 'I wish you every success and hope that this

serious impairment of Canada's vital war effort can be ended without delay.' Before the strike ended on 29 September, fifty thousand working days had been lost – more than in all the strikes in the province in 1940.

Mitch did not openly criticize the King government during the strike, but he did suggest that the strikes were 'clear evidence that there is something lacking in the driving force needed to keep our war effort going at full speed.' Children would ask, 'What did you do in the war, daddy?' And the answer for too many would have to be, 'I went on strike, son, and helped to slow up the production of vital war materials while ill-equipped soldiers overseas were being killed by an enemy which had all the modern equipment it needed.' It may not have been nice, but it was effective.[40]

Two months later, during the strike in the Kirkland Lake gold mines, the reeve requested a squad of thirty OPP officers. But Conant sent a force of 180, and Mitch promised to 'recruit an army' if necessary to maintain law and order, prevent intimidation, and protect those who wanted to work. While Conant's police were certainly no friends of the strikers, it was King's refusal to intervene that ultimately ended the strike, a refusal many believed was the result of his fear that Mitch was 'just waiting to denounce the government for selling out to the CIO if he can find an excuse.'[41]

Long before Kirkland Lake, Mitch had taken his plea for an all-out war effort and American aid to Britain to the United States. Sponsored by his friend Gene Tunney, the boxer, and Lowell Thomas, the well-known broadcaster, Mitch was initiated into the infamous Saints and Sinners of the Shriners' Circus. 'Don't pull any punches on my account,' he had told his hosts and they obliged. As a 'fall guy' Mitch delighted the Shriners, but there was more to his visit than the raucous and bizarre roast of the onion farmer from the boonies. CBS and Mutual, with a potential audience of eighty million, broadcast his two speeches.

The occasion demanded a restraint and discretion that Mitch seldom exercised at home. He asked Americans to contemplate for a moment the awful prospect of the defeat of Britain and Japanese domination of the Pacific. Would the lust of the dictators not turn to the rich resources of North America? Yet it was those resources, if marshalled, that could be turned into the instruments of victory. Churchill had asked for the tools to do the job, and to 'my American friends, I say this. Give them the tools with which to defend Britain, because Britain is the outpost of America and if Britain falls the United States and Canada ... will face the fury of Hitler isolated and alone.' Much depended on Churchill and Roosevelt, but

LOOK! AN INTERNATIONAL VICTIM —
AT OUR OPENING LUNCHEON

WED.
SEPT. 24

TEX O'ROURKE & CO.,
ANARCHISTS OF GOOD
WILL, WILL PRESENT THAT
THRILLING DRAMA

"GETTING HEP
TO HEPBURN"

HONORABLE
MITCHELL HEPBURN,
THE COLORFUL, DYNAMIC,
"I'LL-MAKE-CANADA-HAPPY"
PREMIER OF ONTARIO
WILL STAR
IN THIS PRODUCTION
——
12 NOON

HOTEL ASTOR

WRITE, 'PHONE, WIRE THE RIGHT HONORABLE LESLIE NAPOLEON KRAMER,
292 MADISON AVE. (MURRAY HILL 5-1838) FOR RESERVATIONS – AND DO
IT DAMNED QUICK UNLESS YOU JUST WANT TO READ ABOUT THIS LUNCHEON.

in the end it was a 'People's War.' And yet among the people there were those who were 'creating unrest and disturbance at the most critical time in our history, playing unwittingly, if not deliberately, into the hands of Hitler … In Canada, there should be no room for such trouble-makers. They should be listed, classified, condemned and divorced from society.' Canadians were 'outraged,' he added at his press conference, because an 'apathetic' federal government refused to intervene in strikes and slowdowns that were seriously hampering the war effort. 'I would prohibit picketing and intern those holding up vital war supplies,' he declared, but at Ottawa 'they don't consider anything but their political hides.'

The Liberal MP for Halifax immediately phoned King's secretary to pass on the word that although he disapproved of Mitch 'and all his works,' he was 'voicing the feelings of many people in Canada, including, by far, the great majority of Maritimers.' Commenting on Mitch's New York speech, the usually critical Ottawa *Citizen* reflected that he 'is nearer to expressing the spirit of the Canadian people to win the war' than the inhabitant of Laurier House. That assertion would soon be tested.[42]

'Somebody else's war'

In the winter of 1942 conscription did not appear to be a military necessity – even the tragedy of Dieppe lay ahead. But Mitch and many others believed it was not only inevitable and just, but also used it as the metaphor for unlimited national commitment. Senator Arthur Meighen's selection as Conservative leader in November 1941 brought the simmering movement for conscription and a national government to a boil. The Conservative member for York South, on active service in the army, resigned his seat to enable Meighen to run for the Commons. King also needed seats for two new ministers, Louis St Laurent and Humphrey Mitchell, his minister of labour, who was nominated in Welland. The by-elections were to be held on 9 February 1942.

Before issuing the writs, King had hit upon his subterfuge. Although he had told caucus on 14 November that he was firmly against conscription for overseas service, because it would be 'playing Hitler's game by creating disunion and would be destroying our total war effort,' he realized that with public opinion and key members of the cabinet, led by Ralston, strongly pro-conscription, some evasive action had to be taken. On 17 December he more or less decided on a plebiscite and for a month drew on all the political acumen, semantic ambiguities, and spiritual guidance at his command to find the words that could mean all things to all people. The well had never been deeper, and on the eve of the session he persuaded his colleagues to agree to a statement in the January throne speech that the government would seek 'release from any obligations arising out of any past commitments restricting methods of raising men for overseas service.' King's ploy had the intended effect of dramatically undermining the opposition in York South and Welland because conscriptionists, including those in the cabinet, believed that with a strong yes vote conscription for overseas service would follow. As Dafoe commented to Dexter, 'in the next world he [King] may have the occasional reminiscent conversations with old Nick (of course I mean Machiavelli).'[1]

Mitch had positioned himself for the battle when it was rumoured that King planned a plebiscite. 'It is the responsibility and duty of the Dominion Government to make a decision, and if they are not prepared to make a decision they should get out of office,' Mitch stated, echoing the views of the Ralston wing of the cabinet. However, he dismissed reports that he was planning a pro-conscription coalition at Queen's Park and, more evasively, that he would introduce a pro-conscription resolution when the House met in February. 'It may be,' King noted hopefully, 'that Hepburn's opposition to it will help to bring Quebec friends to see that it might be the means of preventing conscription in the end.'

When King revealed the question, Mitch denounced the plebiscite as 'one of the most dastardly, contemptible, and cowardly things ever perpetrated on a respected and dignified country by any government, 'with its sole object' to perpetuate in office a government which obviously is not in sympathy with an all-out war effort, but which has been forced into a declaration of a total war effort – a policy which will be deliberately evaded when this government is supposedly entrenched by the smokescreen of a referendum.' That was also a suspicion of some of King's less trusting colleagues. 'I appeal to Grits and Tories alike to show their indignation quickly and forcefully against this cowardly suggestion from Ottawa today,' Mitch told a wildly cheering audience, 'which will make Canada and Canadians the laughing stock of the Allied nations fighting our battles for freedom.'[2]

The federal Liberals had decided not to oppose Meighen in York South and there was an understanding that the Tories would not oppose Mitchell in Welland. However, the president of the Welland Liberal Association wired Mitch that King's plebiscite had 'changed everything. Must have an independent candidate. Will you back such an effort?' Mitch was more than willing. He spent several days in the riding, often on the platform with Drew. In South York a Citizen Committee, which included Bethune Smith and Colonel Fraser Hunter, the Liberal MLA for Toronto St Patrick, soon emerged to support Meighen. With Meighen's approval, Mitch announced that he would participate in the York South campaign as well, but delivered only one radio address.[3]

Mitch denied during the campaign that he was motivated by his dislike of King or even by his conviction that he lacked the qualities of a wartime leader. His sole object was to prevent the 'gross deception' of the plebiscite. The election of Meighen would bring his powerful advocacy of an all-out war effort into the Commons and, combined with Mitchell's defeat, would force either King's resignation or an election on conscription. As it was, King's 'Frankenstein' was threatening to tear the country apart. Refusing to state his position if released from his commitment, King was willing to let people believe that a yes vote was really a vote for conscription, while in Quebec the Liberals echoed Adelard Godbout's assurance that King could be trusted for he was opposed to conscription and had always been the 'defenseur acharné ... du pont de vue canadien-française.' 'Imagine such duplicity in a time of national crisis!' Nor could anyone demanding a total war effort support the CCF, for it was their ally, the CIO, which was responsible for crippling strikes in American war industries and 87 per cent of the days lost, many of them in essential industries, in Canada. In his last speech Mitch said that he had already lost colleagues, friends, and supporters, and if King's candidates won with 'overwhelming majorities,' he could even lose his job. But country came before party, and that was a risk he was more than prepared to take.[4]

King certainly hoped that Mitch would lose his job. 'If there is any true Liberalism in the party at Toronto,' he noted, 'his ministers and followers would tell him to get out.' But with Toronto silent, some response was demanded from Ottawa. As usual, King placed the burden on caucus when he warned the Ontario members that if they lost the by-elections he would consider resigning. As usual, the threat worked. 'Many Ontario men volunteered to go up to Toronto at once,' King reported. 'Roebuck said he intended to work against Meighen. Altogether, they became quite roused and, I think, wakened up to the real situation.'

A few days later the Ontario caucus discussed a resolution stating that Mitch was 'endeavouring to discredit and undermine the present government of Canada by indiscriminate and ill-considered criticism of the measures taken for the effective prosecution of the war.' The resolution asked the members to reaffirm their loyalty to King and to 'record their disapproval of the actions of Mitchell F. Hepburn and express the belief that he no longer represents Liberalism in the province of Ontario.' Caucus unanimously voted confidence in King, but more than a handful of the forty present refused to vote on the last sentence.[5]

In both York South and Welland the federal Liberals declared that the election was really between King and Hepburn. In radio speeches and on the platform, Roebuck launched a savage personal attack on Hepburn. Mitch was not acting on principle but out of 'a settled hate and loathing' for King 'which colors all his thoughts and makes of him the easy cat's paw of those who sick him on.' Such a man was 'a false prophet,' a political renegade who had 'joined the clique of the wealthy men who foisted Arthur Meighen on the Conservative party, and would seize power for their own ends.' While Ottawa was fighting fascism abroad, the fascist at Queen's Park, whose outspoken defeatism and denigration of Canada's war effort was being hailed in Axis countries, would 'draft you each as guerilla privates under the command of himself and his millionaire chiefs of staff.' And the man who had betrayed the Oshawa workers and sent his police to Kirkland Lake, he assured the largely working-class voters of York South and Welland, had nothing but 'hatred and contempt of working people.' Roebuck's evangelical earnestness was effective, as was the small army of supporters he sent into the battle, and the CCF admitted that he had been a useful ally. Useful, too, were the several thousand dollars the federal Liberals sent in to aid the CCF cause.[6]

In both Welland and York South the CCF also trained their guns on Mitch. Basing their campaign on the argument that conscription was a red herring and that the real issue was social and economic reform after the war, they found it convenient to portray Mitch's intervention as part of a capitalist plot to seize power and prevent 'a people's victory and a people's peace.' Why did Hepburn wreck the Rowell-Sirois conference, asked M.J. Coldwell. 'Because he was afraid if certain powers were placed in Dominion hands, some of his powerful mining and liquor friends would have to pay the shot.' Why did Hepburn and his rich friends want to overthrow the government? So they could be in a position after the war to prevent the new war industries 'into which we have poured millions of dollars' from interfering with those 'established by private capital.' Coldwell read even more sinister motives into Mitch's denunciation of King:

Mr. Hepburn has interesting associations in Canada, but how many of you know of his associations and achievements beyond our borders? Have you heard of Ben Smith – who reportedly returned from Vichy in 1940 with a Nazi peace offer; that Mitch spent a week on a yacht owned by the owner of the most anti-British newspaper in the States; that he was predicting defeat of the Russians and thus providing U.S. isolationists and Lord Haw

Haw with arguments to show the hopelessness of Britain's position and the futility of wasting further aid upon her? In short it would appear that every time Mitchell Hepburn meets his U.S. isolationist friends, he emerged with a program designed to divide the Canadian people and to undermine confidence in the struggle of the united nations.

It was a little difficult for Mitch to assure Coldwell that some of his millionaire friends wanted him to stay out of Welland. The mine owners liked King's new minister of labour. 'He is certainly a fine fellow,' observed Dr W.P. St Charles of Lakeshore, 'he played the game very squarely with the mining interests [at Kirkland Lake] and has as much contempt for the c.i.o. as the rest of us.' The boys selected Jack Bickell, then in the country, to see Mitch; but Mitch would not back off. That pleased Bill Wright, at least, who congratulated Mitch on his stand. 'In my book you are Canada's Churchill,' he wrote during the by-elections. 'He used to be a little erratic too. That your big time will come is the hope of yours sincerely.'[7]

Mitch did not carry a united cabinet or party into the by-elections. Conant, McQuesten, and Houck openly supported him. But other members of the cabinet and most members stayed out of the line of fire. Peter Heenan let King know he was prepared to 'pitch into Hepburn,' but King sniffed pressure for a seat in the Senate and gave him no encouragement. Robert Laurier intimated to Mitch that as the bearer of his uncle's name he might have to resign and, with King's comforting assurance that 'his friends would wish to remember his action,' he did so on 5 February. The next day Harry Nixon issued a statement in which, while remaining free to criticize King as he had in the past, he appealed for an end to 'this strife which is distracting everyone's attention from the main purpose ... This I must say, however, that I believe it would be a national calamity if Arthur Meighen were returned to public life by South York on Monday.' He could never 'be party to an alliance with Drew and Meighen,' he wrote Mitch, and asked him to accept his resignation if his statement 'embarrasses you or interferes with your plans or policies for the future.' Nixon remained in the cabinet and Laurier returned after the spring session.[8]

Although King was convinced that 'Hepburn's machine will be combined with the Tory machine and will spare neither liquor nor money for bribes of any kind to insure Meighen's return,' the smart money had Meighen the underdog from the beginning. No one could have saved the scion of Bay Street parachuted into a riding where almost 90 per cent of the voters were working class. The CCF had successfully defined the issue as post-war reconstruction and an army of as many as a thousand workers worked for Joe Noseworthy, a popular high-school teacher who had run a respectable third in 1940, in the first door-to-door, poll-by-poll, saturation campaign in Canada. Noseworthy defeated Meighen by 4,500 votes, as many Liberals and Conservatives stayed home or voted CCF. In Welland a strong Liberal campaign, aided by a $20,000 war chest and a large CCF vote, enabled Mitchell to defeat the independent by the narrow margin of 1,800 votes.[9]

King was more than jubilant; he was, said Brooke Claxton, 'psychopathic.' Those who 'for personal or partisan ends have been guilty of provoking unnecessary and bitter political controversy at this very critical time have been roundly and soundly rebuked,' he stated, and their duty now was to support the government in its prosecution of the war. Mitch admitted that he had been badly 'spanked,' but again blamed the apathy of the electorate. With the next morning's headlines heralding the fall of Singapore, Mitch claimed that if the news had arrived the day before rather than the day after the election the outcome might have been different.[10]

There were more spankings to come, this time from Washington. On 10 February the American press reported his earlier comments in Chatham that the Japanese had naval supremacy and the American navy was 'in hiding.' Canadian journalists recalled that during the Welland campaign Mitch had said that when he returned from Australia with his dire prophecies of a Pacific war his critics had boasted that the American navy would wipe the 'tissue paper navy' off the seas. 'Well, you've seen what that tissue paper navy has done.' Angus Macdonald quickly declared that Mitch did not speak for the Canadian government and King sent the same message to Roosevelt. 'Please do not worry about what our friend said about the navy,' the president replied, 'I, too, have a lot of backseat drivers.' While Frank Knox, the secretary of the navy, claimed that the navy was trying to make contact, Mitch retorted, 'I'll tell you where they are. They're right at Manila, surrounding a gallant force of American troops. They're at Singapore and Shanghai where the once-proud U.S. Marines are now being humiliated by being forced to drive rick-shaws through the streets.'

Although there had been widespread criticism of the navy for handing out sugar-coated press releases or no stories at all, Mitch's widely reported slurs, wrote the director of British United Press, 'aroused *white hot bitterness* against Canada generally.' Coincidentally, perhaps, the navy chose to release a grossly exaggerated report that the enemy had been engaged on 31 January in the Gilbert and Marshall Islands and had sunk sixteen ships, damaged eight, and destroyed forty-two aircraft. 'I can tell you where the Japanese fleet is' shouted Mitch in a *New York Post* cartoon. 'So Can We,' replied a US sailor with a wink as he totalled the score. For the moment Mitch was silenced. But he remained deeply, almost pathologically, disturbed about the likely course of the war. He agreed with John Dafoe's 'Grim and Desperate Danger' editorial that with unity, courage, and self-sacrifice the war could be won but before it was over it was not unlikely that 'our coasts will suffer their own share of the perils and destruction of war.' Mackenzie King also feared a Pacific invasion, but that prospect left him with the comforting reassurance that the conscripts would never have to be sent overseas.[11]

The 1942 session opened two days after the by-elections amid rumours of a back-bencher revolt. Many members had agreed with Nixon and Laurier. And Roebuck, ambitious to become elected provincial leader, was actively stirring up the dissidents to demand a leadership convention. On the eve of the session, the press reported that from twenty-five to forty members would condemn Mitch's participation in the by-election, insist that he cool his war with Ottawa, and oppose any attempt to pass a resolution of censure on King for having the plebiscite. Asked if he planned to introduce a motion calling for conscription for overseas service, Mitch replied that 'We will have to wait and see until after the caucus. Of course I can't say what the Conservatives will do.'

The rumoured revolt failed to materialize in the four-hour caucus held a few days after the session opened. There were prolonged cheers when Mitch entered the room, and he quickly seized the initiative. With seventy thousand British troops surrendering at Singapore the day before, Mitch insisted that the demand for an all-out war effort overcame any domestic political considerations. However, although there were few leaks to the press, Mitch apparently intimated that he would 'cool' his war with King and not introduce a resolution condemning the plebiscite. He also told caucus that the rumours of a coalition with Drew existed only in the minds of the reporters. With these assurances the caucus, including Nixon and Laurier, gave Mitch a vote of confidence. 'Everything's fine,' said Mitch, as he greeted reporters outside the room. Robert Laurier reported to King that 'the whole thing had turned into a chorus of glorification of Hepburn as he had come into the Caucus with his resignation written out to hand to the Lt. Governor. There was at once a demand that the resignation should be destroyed.' 'It was a bit of a stage play on Hepburn's part,' observed King, who knew the tactic well, 'but succeeded in producing the result desired.'[12]

Mitch had already decided to adjourn the session when he met the caucus. The long throne speech had boasted of Ontario's contribution to the war, but promised nothing in the way of legislation except a bill to provide for the takeover of the direct tax field by the federal government. The truth was that even the minor pieces of legislation were not ready. Moreover, until the details of the tax agreement were settled, Mitch said he could not bring down a budget. After six days of almost pointless afternoon sessions, he adjourned the legislature for three weeks.[13]

The negotiations on the tax agreement had begun on 30 September 1941, when Mitch led a large delegation to Ottawa and saw the detailed federal proposals for the first time. With his victory on the non-resident tax, Mitch was quite willing to vacate the personal and corporate income tax field. But the province also faced rising expenditures, and was left with only three flexible sources of revenue: gasoline taxes, vehicle licences, and Liquor Board profits. Would Ilsley guarantee that those revenues not be impaired by gasoline rationing or increased federal taxes on alcohol? Ilsley replied that there was no present plan to ration gasoline and that he would guarantee gasoline revenues at their current level. Both he and Clifford Clark indicated that increased taxes on liquor were unlikely for they would 'pass beyond the point of diminishing returns and lower receipts for both.' However, Ilsley refused to exclude municipal corporation taxes from the package, although he agreed with Mitch that swelling urban populations would lead to what Mitch warned would be a 'terrible row' with the municipalities.

The clause providing that when the agreement lapsed after the war Ottawa would reduce its rate of tax to enable the province to re-enter the direct tax field was, as Conant said, the question of 'fundamental importance.' The federal proposal mentioned only a 10 per cent reduction in corporate taxes, and Clark admitted that no suitable formula had been found for the personal income tax. Ilsley asked them to accept 'an honourable obligation on the part of the Dominion not to act sharply' and, although Conant and Walters demurred, Mitch felt the honourable obligation was sufficient and quickly turned the discussion to a broader question. 'Frankly,' he said, 'I would like to see the Dominion stay in the field of income tax, stay there alone. I think the worst farce in the world is the double personal income tax. It is a nuisance, confusing, and everything else.' An agreement should be reached in which Ottawa occupied the field and returned an agreed amount to the province. When Ilsley suggested that other provinces would not agree, Mitch replied, 'Let us not close the book at the moment anyway.' Although important matters of principle and detail remained to be settled, Mitch was pleased with the day's work. 'We have got along splendidly,' he told Ilsley, and 'I am very satisfied with everything.'

Mitch had planned to attend a second meeting on 18 December, but was bedridden with pleurisy and in his absence the discussions were less amicable. With Ilsley adamantly refusing to exclude the municipalities, Walters warned that it would be difficult to get the agreement through the legislature because the province would not agree to assume the responsibility for their foregone revenues. In the end, after months of negotiation, Ottawa finally agreed to allow the municipalities to collect their corporation taxes until the end of 1943. The agreement was signed in March.[14]

When the session resumed on 24 March – with the tax agreement freezing the budget – the legislature was, as Mitch said, 'a glorified county council.' He was sick much of the time and attended infrequently. Drew was preoccupied as opposition counsel on the inquiry into the government's agreement to send ill-equipped troops to Hong Kong just before the Japanese invasion, and was seldom in the House. But he returned from Ottawa for Mitch's 2 April budget. Mitch reported a surplus of $1.4 million and forecast a modest surplus for the following year. He also promised to continue the agricultural subsidies and grants to municipalities and extend free medical services to pensioners, the blind, and women receiving mother's allowances. Drew left comments on the budget to Les Frost, and used the opportunity to urge Mitch to draft a comprehensive program to ensure large-scale British immigration after the war to keep Ontario British. Like the throne speech the budget passed without division.[15]

There were no divisions during the session. Drew agreed with Mitch's legislation to protect the Abitibi Power and Paper stockholders against the bondholders, although the act in effect set aside a court decision. Drew also supported a bill to assist Cyrus Eaton in the development of iron ore beneath Steep Rock Lake. However, opposition from both the Liberal caucus and the Tories forced Conant to withdraw his bill to tighten provincial control over the municipalities. Both sides of the House supported a total overhaul of measures to control venereal disease that gave health officials 'no-knock' rights to seek out VD carriers and the government power to send those infected to detention centres for treatment. With the Liberal caucus and Drew in agreement, there was no opposition to the extension of the life of the legislature for one year.[16]

There was an air of expectancy around Queen's Park as the session drew to a close. Apart from a few opening salvos at Ottawa during the leaders' day debate, Mitch had been unusually quiet. However, just before the dinner recess on the last night there were rumours of a resolution concerning the plebiscite. Although Robert Laurier and the Franco-Ontarians asked Mitch to prevent it, Tom Kennedy, seconded by Ian Strachan, introduced a resolution after dinner calling for a yes vote on 27 April. There was no debate and the resolution passed unanimously without a recorded vote. But with Tories demanding a formal division, the six Franco-Ontarian Liberals were scrambling for the exits when Mitch escorted Lieutenant-Governor Matthews into the chamber to end the session.[17]

George McCullagh had urged Mitch not to recall the legislature until after the plebiscite so that the members could campaign. In Ontario that was hardly necessary. 'The anti-conscription viewpoint in Canada,' Mitch informed the editor of the *Detroit Free Press*, 'is confined very largely to those who are not of Anglo-Saxon descent and who are prepared to defend Canada's own shores, but, at the same time, religiously refrain from anything which might be connected with what they call "British Imperialism." The vote to be recorded here on the 27th will illustrate that in no uncertain way.'

However, on the night before the vote Mitch issued a long statement from Bannockburn referring to the shelling of a California refinery by a Japanese submarine, the sighting of subs off Vancouver Island, black-outs on the west coast, and Roosevelt's concern about the security of Alaska. There was the possibility of a 'two ocean attack on this continent,' he warned. 'The Japanese may or may not continue to hold naval supremacy in the Pacific. No one knows. The surrender of the French fleet to the Axis may or may not give naval supremacy in the Atlantic to the enemy. No one knows.' Canada was an inviting piece of real estate and, like Australia, had the enemy at its doorstep. 'Tragically, we in Canada continue to believe that it is somebody else's war.' Only an overwhelming yes vote would convince the government that Canadians demanded mobilization for total war. In Ontario 83 per cent agreed while in Toronto and Elgin more than nine out of ten voted yes. Mitch was content with a result which partially compensated for the crushing defeat in the February by-elections. Like most Canadians, including the Ontario members of King's cabinet, he believed that conscription for overseas service would soon follow.[18]

Mitch had been a sick man during the fall and winter. In addition to his usual bouts of pleurisy he had suffered for over a year from debilitating headaches which his doctors could not diagnose. They were not apparently due to over-indulgence, for Mitch claimed to have gone on the wagon in the fall of 1941 and there had been none of the outbursts when liquor seemed to have loosened his tongue. The doctors concluded that the headaches were caused by badly infected remnants of tonsils and early in May he spent a week in Wellesley Hospital to have them removed.

But his health and his spirits remained precarious. Eva had scarlet fever in June and, although Mitch escaped, he was quarantined at the farm for a week. The children also escaped – the third, Helen, had been adopted in the fall of 1940 – but there were anxious weeks. The make matters worse, his mother, to whom Mitch was devoted, had survived one operation for cancer, but tests in July found another malignancy. 'At the moment it is a question of whether she should undergo a second and more serious operation, or let the growth develop again,' he sadly wrote Arthur Slaght. 'It is very doubtful if she could survive the shock.' His private life, too, was less stable. His long affair with the girl on the ss *Bermuda* had ended in 1941. Among his new companions was one who his friends feared was far too calculating, demanding, and perverse for his own good. There was also Bannockburn where Bill Tapsell, like other Ontario farmers, was attempting to increase production in the face of an critical shortage of farm labour.[19]

There had been an acute labour shortage on Ontario farms in 1941 and, despite the increase in wages to an astronomical $50 a month, farmers could not compete with war industries. So critical was the expected shortage in 1942 that the Cabinet War Committee considered 'freezing' farm labour, even at the expense of recruiting. In 1941 the Department of Education had encouraged local boards to alter the school term to release students for work on the farms and there was even talk of lowering the school-leaving age to fifteen for the duration. Dewan and the cabinet organized the 'Farm Service Force – We Lend a Hand' which by the end of the summer hand enrolled ten thousand high-school boys in a Farm Cadet Brigade, brigades of men and women, six thousand Farmerettes, and almost ten thousand older public school boys who stayed in camps organized by the YMCA. Perhaps it was the shortage of farm labour that led Mitch to agree to accept Japanese evacuees in Ontario and muted, but did not silence, criticism of his decision.[20]

When the federal cabinet in mid-January had decided to evacuate Japanese males from the west coast, but with little idea what to do with them, James Marsh, Ontario's deputy minister of labour, suggested that two thousand could be put to work on Ontario's sugar-beet farms. However, two weeks later when Ottawa made a formal request to use a construction camp at Schreiber as a staging depot for evacuees en route to logging camps, where an equally acute labour shortage existed, the cabinet decided that 'under no conditions or circumstances is this government willing that Japanese be brought in for any kind of work.' While Hugh Keenleyside of External Affairs was prepared to go ahead, regardless of the 'fulminations' from Toronto, Norman Robertson, the more politically astute undersecretary, wisely advised King that it was best to wait until 'the smoke from the by-elections' had disappeared.[21]

Three weeks after the by-elections, Humphrey Mitchell asked Heenan if Ottawa could use camps along the Trans Canada as work camps on the highway and hostels for men going to the logging camps. In response to Heenan's questions, he stated that they would not be internees, would remain in the camps unless authorized to leave by the RCMP, and could not acquire property. Ottawa would pay all the costs, but Mitchell could not promise that the government would remove them after the war. 'Obviously it is too early to say what the general policy will be in regard to the Japanese after the war,' he wrote Heenan, 'nevertheless any representations by the provinces in this regard would have to be given serious consideration.' Mitch and the cabinet agreed to the general terms, and announced on 18 March that Ontario would accept three thousand British subjects of Japanese origin. The first contingent left Vancouver a week later.[22]

Even before this agreement, Mitch had said he would accept some Japanese at Bannockburn. 'I don't believe in any mass movement of Japanese so they would be concentrated in any one Province,' he observed, 'but I do believe the other Provinces should do something to help British Columbia, which has an acute problem. I wouldn't have anything to do with Japanese nationals, but I do believe Canadian-born and educated Japanese should be given special consideration.' Austin Taylor, chairman of the B.C. Securities Commission, wired at once: 'Very much impressed by your patriotism and co-operation ... It would be a great help in this period of emergency if you would take the lead in endeavoring to impress upon the other provinces of Canada their responsibility to assume [*sic*].' Mitch and Bill Tapsell quickly arranged accommodation for eight, and six young men left Vancouver on 12 April.

The men were forced initially to come without their families, but Mitch soon decided that Ontario farmers should accept families. 'Family tickled with the good news,' wired Eji Yatabe, secretary of the Citizens' Council at Hastings Park, when told that he and his wife could join their three sons at Bannockburn. A second family arrived in July and another in August when Mitch had over twenty Japanese Canadians working on the farm. By the summer he was praising their work and encouraging his neighbours to follow his example.[23]

There was no criticism in the legislature of the arrival of the Japanese, but resolutions of the Orange Lodges, in line with their policy to 'oppose the admission of any person or persons that cannot become British Subjects in mind and deed,' demanded that they be kept out. Trades and labour councils, insisting there was no labour shortage, opposed their admission on the grounds that they would lower the standard of living. Local councils also protested. In Aylmer public opposition and threatened violence prevented the arrival of a group of tobacco pickers; the Toronto Board of Control passed a resolution prohibiting the entry of any Japanese; and the Chatham city council demanded that no Japanese be allowed to settle permanently or remain in Kent County after the war. Irate local citizens continually pressed Mitch for assurance that they would be evacuated after the war. Initially Heenan had said that Ottawa had agreed to remove them after the war, but by fall Mitch was much more evasive. Before the war was over there were 3,742 evacuees in Ontario, and most of them remained.[24]

More disturbing than the shortage of farm labour was the shortage of power. Demand had escalated in southwestern Ontario and, despite the addition of 170,000 horsepower since 1938, by the spring of 1942 the province faced a shortfall of 350,000 horsepower Since March 1941, when the three governments signed an agreement to go ahead with the St Lawrence, other major Hydro developments had been on hold. However, although Roosevelt did not officially end the prospect of the wartime development of the St Lawrence until September 1942, H.J. Symington, Ottawa's power controller, confirmed rumours in March that Ontario 'might as well forget it,' and urged the government to develop other sources.

The most obvious was the Ottawa River where water power could be concentrated at seven sites, from Carillon near Montreal to Rapides des Joachimes above Deep River, to produce over one million horsepower divided more or less equally between Ontario and

Quebec. In April 1942 Mitch authorized Hogg to begin exploratory discussions with Quebec and on 20 April Hogg met Premier Godbout. The premier was more than willing to accommodate Hydro, but rejected joint development in favour of dividing the sites, with each province harnessing the full flow of the river on both sides of the interprovincial boundary. Godbout proposed that Quebec develop the lower river and Ontario take equivalent power on the upper Ottawa. Since that made engineering and logistical sense, Hogg agreed in principle, but realized that Godbout's proposal to alter the interprovincial boundary to encompass the sites would be difficult, if not unacceptable.

Mitch also agreed in principle, and on 2 May the cabinet authorized Hogg to proceed with detailed negotiations but, given their political delicacy in both provinces, ordered him to maintain the utmost secrecy. Hogg had no doubt that Quebec was, as he said, 'in the driver's seat' because Quebec did not want the power for fifteen years and, given the boundary line at Carillon, Rocher Fendu, and Bryson, could claim more than half the power. However, by the end of May the government had reached an agreement on the division of sites, Quebec passed the necessary enabling legislation, and Ottawa indicated its consent. All that remained were the details of land ownership, offsetting claims for construction, land acquisition, and compensation for land damages as a result of flooding. Mitch had considered a special fall session to approve the agreements, but the ominous evidence of opposition from eastern Ontario and the Conservatives, as well as uncertainty about an election and his own political future, convinced him it was best to wait on events.[25]

Despite York South and Welland, Mitch was still the uncontested head of the provincial Liberal party. 'My Ontario friends tell me he is still strong with the voters,' lamented Dafoe, 'which makes me blush for my native province.' No one disagreed with Fred Gardiner when he assured the Conservative executive committee that 'there was no issue to ensure a victory over the Hepburn administration.' Federal Liberals agreed, and, at a 30 April meeting, the Ontario ministers decided that discretion, as well as valour, dictated that Mitch be left alone. Howe sent a memorandum of their discussion to Mackenzie King:

The provincial political situation in Ontario was discussed. Roebuck is insisting that a Convention of the party must be called immediately to set up a Provincial Liberal organization. Roebuck makes it clear that he intends to compete for the leadership of the provincial party. Failing the calling of a Convention, Roebuck states that he intends to leave the Liberal Party and organize a C.C.F. Provincial Party. He is obsessed with the idea of becoming provincial leader of a party, and there is little doubt that he will carry out his threat if no action is taken by the Liberal Party.

While our Provincial Caucus seemed to be strongly in favour of a Provincial Convention at the time of the recent by elections, it was agreed that this feeling had died down and that very few of the private Members now favour any political move in the Province at this time. It was the feeling of the Ministers that the calling of a Convention in the present time of crisis would not be in keeping with the Government's war policy.

It was decided that Mr. Howe would discuss the matter with the Prime Minister and indicate the wish of the Ontario Ministers that Roebuck be offered a judgeship. It is believed he would accept such an appointment. The Ministers believe that his removal from political activities would be a great help to the party in Ontario.

A few days later, however, the ministers met with the whip of the Ontario caucus, fund-raiser Peter Campbell, and Lambert. 'After showing situation in Ont. now in hands of C.C.F. and a prospective Union of Hepburn & Drew followers,' reported Lambert, 'it was decided to have an Ont. caucus to decide upon a convention for Ont. by July 1st.'[26]

Any attempt to seize the initiative in Ontario would depend on King's response to the overwhelming yes vote in Ontario. Although King had told his colleagues 'not to interpret the vote as a vote for conscription,' he was about the only person in Canada who did not. Mitch certainly did. So too did the Ontario ministers, who warned King that 'unless prompt action is taken, the Opposition' – and Mitch they might have added – 'is in a position to place Ontario Ministers and Ontario Members in an impossible situation. All present,' Howe reported after the 30 April meeting, 'believe that the initiative must be ours.' But after six weeks of skilful and tortured diplomacy, King was able to bring the hard-line members of the cabinet to accept the removal of the clause in the National Resources Mobilization Act limiting the 'zombies' to service in Canada as the only way to keep the party united and his government in office. It was the most he would concede; it was the least they could accept.[27]

Meanwhile, Mitch was not restrained by King's threats. Like many Canadians, he saw unqualified conscription as a proof of an unqualified physical and emotional commitment which, despite the enormous financial, military, and industrial accomplishments of the government, he did not feel would be achieved under King's leadership. Like Humphrey Mitchell, Mitch believed that 'majorities had rights as well as minorities' and like Angus Macdonald, believed that King was 'a twister and wobbler.' During the summer he left his bundle of jokes at home when he embarked on the traditional tour of fairs and picnics and spoke almost exclusively about the war. Did King's refusal to act after the plebiscite, he asked, mean that our policy has changed 'from can't to won't?' Shall a bitter posterity say of Canada that 'in the great struggle for human freedom, Canada did not do her part very well? ... Think of the burlesque in the House of Commons at Ottawa. Ask your Federal members how much longer they are going to put politics above country.'[28]

As usual, King was convinced that Mitch was in league with a Tory cabal, whose demand for a national government had not been silenced by York South, 'the combination being Meighen, Drew, Hepburn, McCullagh, John Bassett and some others associated with them. Really a gangster gang with white collars ... These men are merely a Nazi Fascist output with characteristics and methods comparable to those of Hitler and Goering and others.' What King denounced as 'the imperialist point of view' was strongly represented by the conscriptionists in his own cabinet. And he was assured by Louis St Laurent, during the crisis with Ralston over conscription early in July, that 'at the bottom of everything else lay the desire to get me out of office; that those who felt like Ralston and Macdonald did, regarded me as an impediment to their having their own way and would, therefore wish to have me out; that, of course, was the Tory attitude in Toronto, Montreal and elsewhere.' It was certainly the attitude at Bannockburn.[29]

Mitch had now found new allies in his crusade against Mackenzie King. After Hitler's invasion of Russia in June 1941 Canadian communists had moved abruptly from their condemnation of the imperialist war to ardent advocacy of total commitment to 'a just war, a people's war of national freedom and liberation.' Tim Buck secretly returned from New York in July 1941 and, from his hideout on the outskirts of Toronto, called for a 'National Front' in the war against fascism. By the spring of 1942 the heroic defence of the Russian homeland had evoked a strong response in Canada, and in June Mitch sent a message of support to the founding rally of the Canadian Aid to Russia Fund. 'There have been no half-way measures in Russia's fight for freedom, but heroic sacrifice of land and home life. Only by such all embracing effort can victory be won. As we in Canada pay tribute to the courage and devotion of the Russian people,' he concluded pointedly, 'let us also pay heed to the example they have set.'[30]

There was soon a demand that King release the interned communists and lift the ban on the party. Considering his past, Mitch embraced the movement with an enthusiasm that some found puzzling. Before publicly supporting the cause, however, he had secretly sought out Tim Buck to determine exactly what strengths the communists could bring among the working class to a more vigorous war effort. Through Ian Strachan and Alex MacLeod, editor of the *Canadian Tribune*, Mitch met Buck at Strachan's house in Rosedale. 'What would you do if your Party was restored to legality?' asked Mitch after MacLeod and Strachan left the room. 'I would go on a tour across the country making statements – somewhat like you are making,' Buck replied, 'but with less emphasis on the criticism of the King government.' Buck admitted he was critical of King, but argued that Mitch's attacks on King were divisive at a time when national unity was essential. Eventually they agreed to disagree on the conditions necessary to achieve national unity. Buck maintained that he and his friends could bring the labour movement behind a unified war effort. 'I think you're right,' concluded Mitch. 'I'm going to see if I can help.'[31]

Not long afterwards Mitch issued a long press statement. Conveniently forgetting that he had supported Conant in his determination to get every communist behind bars, Mitch stated that the internment 'of prominent political and labour leaders has astounded those of us who believe in British freedom and justice ... A total war effort is not possible so long as an autocratic political party in office abuses its extreme power and persecutes those who criticize its policies and record, and differ in economic theory.' Mitch also wired St Laurent requesting that the communists incarcerated in the Don Jail since the outbreak of the war either be released or brought to trial. And he was not above taking the credit when they were released at the end of July.[32]

Meanwhile, pressed by the opposition, King had been forced to accept a special Commons Committee on the Defence of Canada Regulations which, on 23 July, recommended the release of other interned communists and the removal of the ban on the party. Fearful of repercussions in Quebec, King refused to consider lifting the ban. Pressure mounted when Tim Buck and sixteen others 'surrendered' to the RCMP on 25 September and were at once lodged in the Don Jail. The Department of Justice intended to release them after an investigation if they, like the others, agreed not to engage in anti-war activity. But while the wheels in Ottawa ground slowly, Mitch ostentatiously sent the prisoners cigarettes and candy and publicly demanded their freedom. King was furious. 'Hepburn and Conant had known of the intention in this regard,' he wrote, 'and Hepburn came out with the request he did for their release making the situation more embarrassing both pollitically [*sic*] and judicially.'

While St Laurent waited for the report of his advisory committee, Mitch wired King that, given his failure to act, 'we are bound to conclude that minority influences in the government have been successful in thwarting the will of parliament and the people of Canada.' Buck and the others were 'conditionally released' on 5 October. But St Laurent refused to lift the ban and suggested to Mitch that 'a majority of the people, even in Ontario, still felt that there would be danger in giving any encouragement to the Communist Party.' The resistance of the Russian people, he continued, was due to their 'vigorous Russian nationalism rather than to any virtue of international communism; and even if one were to admit that their Russian nationalism has been stimulated by their adherence to Communism, I am not at all convinced that we require the prodding of Communism in our constitutional set-up.'[33]

Mitch had also promised Buck that he would help him organize meetings and even speak from the same platform. Just a few days before Buck surrendered, Mitch had spoken at a 'Total War Rally' in Maple Leaf Gardens where eighteen thousand people hailed three heroes of the Soviet Union, particularly Lieutenant Lyudmila Pavlichenko, the young female sniper who had shot three hundred German soldiers. The rally was organized by three CIO unions, two of them communist-run, and two of the three keynote labour speakers were just out of jail. The star performers were the Russian soldiers, but Mitch also got an enthusiastic reception, even though he reminded the audience that Britain and the United States were also in the war. Admitting that he had not been a friend of the CIO, Mitch insisted that there were now only two camps in Canada, those willing to accept Ottawa's '50 percent effort' and those who were not. Three weeks later he was on the platform for Buck's first speech. The purpose of the rally was to demand removal of the ban on the Communist party, but Buck used the occasion to pledge his full support for the war and insist that conscription, ultimately inevitable, be introduced at once. All appeals to King to legalize the party could not overcome the opposition from Quebec, however, and Canada remained the only allied country where the party remained under a ban throughout the war, although it surfaced in 1943 as the Labour Progressive party.[34]

Standing shoulder to shoulder with the Communists, while both Drew and Edward Jolliffe, the newly elected leader of the CCF, cautiously stood aside, was only one of the strange twists and turns that Mitch took in the summer of 1942. He was deeply pessimistic about the outcome of the war. Victory seemed far off as the Russians fell back on Stalingrad, Rommel massed for his all-out attack on Egypt, and the Japanese secured the Aleutians. And the heavy cost of victory, if there was to be one, was tragically revealed to Canadians on the beach at Dieppe in August. 'I think we must admit that we face the possibility of absolute defeat in this war,' Les Frost wrote to Drew. 'This possibility overshadows everything else.' That possibility drove Mitch to the verge of melancholia, as he cast about with an obsessive, almost irrational, determination for ways to accelerate King's downfall or at least to drive him to a total commitment to the war.[35]

King's stock had never been lower. Support for the Liberals had dropped dramatically from 55 per cent in January 1942 to 44 per cent in February. By September it had fallen to 39 per cent. Although his colleagues reluctantly accepted what Dafoe described as his 'unheroic expedient' on the plebiscite and its aftermath as a politically necessary and probably short-lived gamble in the interest of national unity, there were many Liberals who did not. Liberals as well as Tories spoke sullenly of appeasement. By the summer of 1942 anxiety about the war and its aftermath was shaking Canadians loose from their old political allegiances and pointing to a realignment of political parties. The October 1941 election in British Columbia and by-elections in Edmonton and Ontario seemed to confirm the polls which revealed a dramatic increase in CCF support from 10 per cent in January to 21 per cent in September and showed the CCF running neck and neck with the Liberals from the Ottawa River to the Pacific. The politicians had to think seriously about the future.[36]

In mid-July Aberhart met secretly with Mitch and Drew in Toronto. Aberhart was convinced that the effective prosecution of the war demanded a new political alignment that could also adopt a progressive post-war program that would prevent the CCF from capitalizing on the leftward swing in public opinion. After he returned to Edmonton he wrote to both Mitch and Drew that 'something along the line of our discussion should be started without delay.'

The political situation is unique in Canadian history. The old party alignments have ceased to have any real meaning for the majority of people ...

The only course of action likely to succeed must be such that it cuts across all party alignments and unites the people in an enthusiastic determination to 'see the job through' at all costs. And the key to that 'will-to-victory' lies in the vision they must have of the social order which will be created out of the havoc and suffering of the war and an unquenchable determination to attain it ...

I would suggest that as a preliminary, you and Drew (if you both concur in the views I have expressed) should get together and draft a popular platform, brief and progressive, to give the people a chance to choose their proper course. You people must give leadership to Canada! You will pardon that statement – I say it as a challenge ... We must not fail the people at this time.

A month later, when he read that Mitch was planning a provincial election, Aberhart begged him not to go to the people 'before tackling the larger issue ... for I am convinced that you will not only strengthen your position in the Province by coming out on the national issue *first*, but I think you run a grave risk of weakening your position in the national field, should the Socialists make a good showing in the provincial election ... Every moment counts if we are to be organized for an All Canada organization ... Have you talked with Col. Drew and what was the result?'[37]

But Drew was marching to his own drummer, and Mitch realized that if any movement was to originate in Ontario, it could not be led by either of them. Early in August he met Herbert Bruce secretly at the King Eddy and asked him to lead a coalition government. Mitch claimed that all his colleagues agreed except Nixon, and Nixon could be left out. He would also stand aside if Bruce wished. Astonished by Mitch's preposterous proposal, Bruce gave him little hope that he would agree. 'When you approached me with the suggestion that I head a coalition government in Ontario,' he wrote a few days later, 'I felt coming from you it merited serious consideration. After giving it some thought I am not able to see how such a proposal would contribute to the important object we are both most concerned about, namely, the more vigorous prosecution of the war and, therefore, I would not be willing to act in the role you suggest.' The coalition door was closed.[38]

Aberhart continued to plead with Mitch and Drew to take the initiative. To launch the movement, Aberhart invited them to speak at a conference in Edmonton. The speech could provide 'an excellent springboard for the whole country,' and the people will respond enthusiastically to the definite policy of post-war reconstruction and a courageous lead on the war effort.' 'Please let me have another week to take stock and inventory of my own problems here before making a definite reply,' Mitch replied. 'Needless to say, I am whole-heartedly in support of the general idea.'[39]

Despite the pressure for an election within his own cabinet and caucus, Mitch had no intention of going to the people. The Toronto *Star* and the CCF, however, were determined to force him to have by-elections for six seats, five of which had been vacant for over two years. Confident their star was rising, the CCF sought a court order forcing the clerk of the crown in chancery to issue a writ for the riding of High Park. Mr Justice Greene rejected the appeal on 3 June on legal grounds, and threw in an *obiter dicta* that there was no evidence of any demand inside or outside the legislature for a by-election. While the appeal was being considered there were reports that if forced to call the by-elections, Mitch would hold a general election instead. On 16 October the appeal was denied. The decision, said Mitch, was 'exactly what I had expected' and simply legal confirmation of his conclusion that only the CCF wanted an election, a view confirmed by a Gallup poll which found that 71 per cent were opposed to an election.

That evening Mitch spoke to the Queen's Park War Services Guild. He appealed again for a new and vigorous national spirit that would end the vacillation in Ottawa, for 'We will pay in human lives – as we have already paid – and will continue to pay to a greater degree for the ineptitude at Ottawa.' But there was more than a hint of melancholy at the end. 'I do not know what the events in the future will bring forth, whether I will be Premier or whether George Drew will be Premier and I the leader of the opposition, but whatever happens I hope you will carry on your work and I can assure you that you will always have my very best wishes.' That said he went home for the weekend.[40]

Mitch returned to Toronto on Tuesday, 20 October, to resign as premier. The decision had been made long before. Although some doubted his sincerity, he had told the cabinet in the fall of 1941 that he wished to resign – and had even proposed that Nixon succeed him – but was persuaded to lead the government through another session. When the CCF had gone to court, he believed he should not leave to others the possibility of having to fight a 'miniature general election.' However, when Mr Justice Greene delivered his decision in June, the way was clear and he asked Nixon to accept the premiership. But Nixon refused again and apparently told Mitch that after twenty-three years at Queen's Park he was also ready to go back to his farm. Mitch then decided to wait for the decision on appeal which was delivered on 16 October.

Mitch did not regard himself as simply *primus inter pares*. To the dismay of many Liberals he increasingly saw the government and the party as very much his own. Some of his colleagues, he knew, would accept his planned course of action. There seemed little need to consult them. Others would be adamantly opposed and, although he could go through the motions of consultation, persuasion would be impossible. A meeting of the cabinet would simply reveal the deep-seated divisions within it and a meeting of caucus would be equally divisive. Whether his earlier proposals to Nixon were sincere, Mitch had no desire to turn Queen's Park over to the leader of the pro-King cabal in the party. Farquhar Oliver, whom Nixon had once recommended for the succession, was unsatisfactory for the same reason and ever since York South had been a dissident in cabinet. Mitch did speak to Oliver on his return, however, and when Oliver said he would only be interested in the leadership if he had the approval of caucus, Mitch replied, 'To hell with the caucus. I can get someone to take it without going to caucus.'

Mitch had decided on his successor before his return to Toronto – perhaps even months before. When he reached his office on 20 October he summoned Gordon Conant to the office and offered him the job. Dumbfounded, Conant begged Mitch to stay on, but when he refused, said the only course was to let the cabinet decide on the succession. 'No, this is it,' Mitch insisted. 'You are going to take over for me.' Conant called his wife. The answer was yes. They agreed that the deed would be done at six the next night. Robert Laurier was one of the few ministers to be informed. When Laurier suggested that Nixon was the heir apparent and the cabinet and caucus should be consulted, Mitch said simply that 'he had made up his mind what he was going to do. Had intended to take this step at different times. It was settled now once and for all.'

When Nixon heard of Mitch's intention, he went home to ask his wife if he still had a job on the farm, and returned to Toronto late Tuesday night. But Mitch was not to be found on Wednesday – there were reports he had spent the morning with Bickell, Sam McLaughlin, and others at the hotel – and Nixon did not see him until after four. He emerged, tight-lipped, fifteen minutes later. At six Mitch and Conant drove to the lieutenant-governor's home in Rosedale. Conant's first act as Ontario's twelfth premier was to receive Mitch's letter of resignation as provincial treasurer and to reply that following their discussions he was holding it 'in abeyance.'

Back in his office, Mitch told reporters that his resignation should not have come as a surprise for he had said repeatedly that he intended to leave after the session. As a Laurier Grit, he laughed off the suggestion that he planned to enter federal politics as a Tory, but admitted that he was not a supporter of Sir Wilfrid's successor. There were three good reasons for returning to the farm and family, Mitch grinned, holding up a picture of Peter, Patsy, and Helen. In St Thomas Eva told reporters the family had been praying for the homecoming for a long time. In Ottawa King prayed that he had seen the last of Mitch Hepburn. 'Ambition, combined with venom, has helped to bring about his destruction,' King wrote. 'I feel this morning as if the atmosphere has been cleansed, as if the province and the Dominion had been freed of a corrupt and corroding influence, something really loathsome.' But few believed that love of the land and the bosom of his family had drawn Mitch back to Bannockburn – or at least would hold him there very long.[41]

'The Hepburn jitters'

Mitch's resignation inspired endless speculation about his future. Of all the roads he might follow, almost everyone agreed with Agnes MacPhail that none 'leads back to the onion patch.' Some believed that it was a typical impetuous act, due either to despair and frustration or alcohol, that Mitch would soon regret, while others saw a deeper and darker meaning. There were a few, however, who did believe that after sixteen years in politics, with his health increasingly problematic, Mitch did feel that family and farm demanded his attention. Robert Laurier relayed to King that Mitch had said that 'his wife had not been well lately, was having a change of life, and was much upset. That he also had heavy investment in his farm, and felt it needed his attention.' Patrick Duff of the British High Commission reported that he had been told 'by one good authority, with a good deal of circumstantiality, that his resignation was forced upon him not only by his own state of health but by his wife's and that the lives of both of them depended on his withdrawal into private life.'[1]

His other private life was the stuff of stories in the newsroom of the Toronto *Star* where it was said that Joe Atkinson had finally driven Mitch out of politics by threatening to release compromising pictures of him with a girl friend. But Mitch had lived too close to the edge of scandal to be easily intimidated. He had been under surveillance by private investigators, however, and Roebuck, presumably among others, had received reports that the manager of at least one hotel, where passage was easy from the beer parlour to rooms upstairs, said he was not afraid of the police because it was 'one of Hepburn's hotels. I only manage it.' The female investigator claimed that the hotel was a 'chain-store proposition for the gentleman we are watching ... I know you realize that success of our investigations depends entirely upon keeping results absolutely private until we are ready to pull the plug.' There was not a whisper of evidence in October 1942 that anyone had pulled the plug.[2]

Some suspected, however, that Mitch's millionaire friends had pulled the plug. Roebuck concluded that Mitch's 'kissing of the C.I.O. and leading the cheers for Tim Buck' made him look ridiculous in the eyes of J.P. Bickell and other members of 'the brains trust, representatives of power, gold and liquor interests. It was these men,' he told George Gordon, 'who became convinced that Hepburn was through and decided they must have another front man.' Eric Cross agreed that although the root cause was Mitch's frustration in not being able to fell King, the immediate cause was his support of Buck and the communists which had put him 'in wrong with his own gang.'[3]

King had concluded initially that 'something pertaining to his health or conduct' had led Mitch to resign, but that was far too simple to satisfy his egocentrism and conspiratorial anxieties. Mitch's decision, he speculated, may have been caused by his own announcement on 15 October that there would be a gradual curtailment in gold production. But in his scenario the 'millionaires who control gold mines' did not want to dump Mitch but 'having been exasperated at the government's action, have promised to spend any sum in an effort to defeat me, and they may feel that they can find means of securing him the leadership or at all events a lieutenancy in the national government that is to be.' The next move, King thought, would come at the Conservative leadership convention in Winnipeg in December with Mitch lining up with Drew and Meighen. Some of his colleagues on the War Committee agreed that Mitch would be at the convention.[4]

John Dafoe also wondered whether Mitch's resignation was not 'designed as a bridge over which he can more easily pass from the Ontario premiership to a prominent place in the ranks of a national government dominated by the Meighen-Drew-Globe and Mail wing of the Conservative party?' For it was certain, Dafoe wrote, that Mitch 'will not be satisfied with the humdrum routine of his onion farm until he has made at least one more attempt to unhorse Mr. Mackenzie King.' Grant Dexter reported that unofficial but reliable reports reaching Ottawa from Toronto revealed that Mitch's resignation was the first step in moving into federal politics. If the Tory convention could be persuaded to draft him, wrote Dexter imaginatively, Mitch was prepared to fly out and take the job; but if this admittedly 'fantastic scenario' failed, Mitch planned to run for the Commons as 'an advocate of total war.' 'If people want to believe that, it is their privilege,' Mitch replied tartly, but 'I am still a critic of the King government, and I am going to remain one.'[5]

Whatever his political future might hold, Mitch's immediate task was to keep Conant's precarious crown on his head. As expected, Nixon had resigned at once. Professing friendship for Mitch, he admitted that the feud with Ottawa and the refusal to have an election had made life difficult in the cabinet. The succession could not be passed around 'like a dirty shirt,' he commented bitterly, and Conant had no mandate to remain in office. Farquhar Oliver resigned a few days later. Both demanded a leadership convention. King and the federal Liberals also wanted a convention, as they had for many months. King instructed Norman McLarty, the political minister for Ontario, to cultivate the cry for a convention, already so vocal in the *Star*, but to remain discreetly in the background.[6]

The concerted drive for a convention, described by the *Globe and Mail* as an attempt by Ottawa to take control of Queen's Park, forced Mitch to support Conant and give another explanation of why he had felt compelled to resign. The resignations from the cabinet and the 'loud voices being heard from party politicians who are already organizing for a convention, an election, or both' should make it obvious why he resigned. His long advocacy of monetary reform and his unrestrained criticism of King's war effort, in short, 'my adamant and consistent stand, my lack of blind adhesion to Party welfare against national interests ... annoyed the purely partisan section of the Liberal Party, and as a consequence my position as leader became untenable.' He had refused to bow 'to the Ottawa political machine' or to accept the argument that getting re-elected was more important than winning the war, particularly when the polls indicated that almost 80 per cent of the electorate felt an election was unnecessary. Country had to be weighed against party.

The statement was, as Ralston told his son, the 'muddiest possible' and did more to encourage the belief that he was either part of some deep conspiracy or that reason had deserted him. 'Hepburn is the Laval of Canada,' exclaimed King. His 'diabolical statement' was a deliberate attempt to focus agitation and hatred upon myself for not having National Government and conscription' and part of a deep plot that was somehow linked to the Tory convention at Winnipeg. Mitch's statement was even more preposterous, because he 'knows that so far as the Federal machine, as he calls it is concerned, we have not even a Federal organization, and it is impossible to get Federal Ministers from Ontario to even direct the course

of action and Federal Liberal members to meet and declare themselves.'[7]

The most immediate danger did not come from Ottawa but from
the provincial party, and Mitch decided on a test of strength in the
caucus. A week before the critical 25 November meeting, he had
written to each member describing the conspiracy that led to his resignation with details even more incredible and for which he provided no evidence:

Three months before I resigned I was warned by Mr. McCullagh of the
Globe and Mail that the board of strategy at Ottawa had decided to force
a General Election in Ontario believing that out of it all would be raised
a racial issue comparable with the 1917 bitterness engendered by the slogan TAKE THEM OUT OF QUEBEC AT THE POINT OF THE BAYONET. This and
this alone in the opinion of the Ottawa Board of Strategy would hold the
wavering Quebec support against a common enemy to be created in
Ontario ...

With Judgeships and Senate positions as bait, the Ottawa crowd was
able to create considerable dissatisfaction in this government and Provincial Liberal Party as only master strategists like themselves could do, but
always working under cover.

I do not need to discuss this further nor to say how unhappy and untenable my position as leader of a political party became as a result of outside
interference.

So serious were the rifts in the party, Mitch continued, that if a caucus had been held to select a successor 'we would have been torn
to shreds.' His selection of Conant made eminent sense for he was
'the real truck-horse for the Party on the front benches' when Mitch
was so frequently sick. Mitch asked the members to support Conant
through the session, after which a convention could deal with the
leadership. He had no desire to see his letter floating around the
press rooms: 'As a favour to me, I would be pleased if you would
destroy this letter after you read it.'[8]

'Up to the moment that members went into caucus, there was a
persistent lobby by pro-King, pro-election and pro-convention federal Liberal interests to upset Premier Conant and force a general
election,' said Mitch after the caucus, but the result was 'a complete
rout of the King forces.' Mitch was asked to speak first. Nixon and
Oliver followed, and before the session was over every member had
spoken. At one point Mitch reminded them that he was still leader of the party and if caucus insisted on an immediate convention,

he would 'dissolve the house to-morrow,' a warning which apparently was taken seriously despite the fact that a request for a dissolution was the premier's prerogative. Nixon and his allies had hoped for the support of about twenty-five of the members, which they felt would be sufficient to force a convention. But after four hours of straight talk, with surprisingly little acrimony, and with the promise of a convention within two months of the session, the demand for an immediate convention was defeated forty-seven to five. Eight members chose not to vote.[9]

The promise of a convention slowed the rebellion for a while; it did nothing to stop the rumours. Eric Cross told King that Mitch planned to restrict the convention to provincial Liberals. Kenneth Cragg of the *Globe* reported that rumours from usually reliable sources suggested that Mitch would return as premier before the session and call an election during the planned recess or immediately after prorogation. From other indirect sources, Cragg added, he learned that at a King Eddy party for Tim Buck and others, Mitch left the definite impression he was going to return to office. 'Some of this stuff came from men who were pretty high directly after the party,' however, 'which means that they either did not know what they were talking about or had their tongues loosened.'[10]

Mitch's unpredictable and often irrational actions and statements once again forced the federal Liberals to consider a Queen's Park coup. Peter Campbell, the unofficial treasurer, after discussions with Lambert and the Ontario ministers, briefed King on party organization in Ontario. If the national party were to be 'revived and resurrected,' Campbell began, Ontario was the place to begin. Given an alternative, many provincial members and ministers would leave Hepburn and Conant, but without leadership 'few of these members are willing to make a break with the present leaders in Ontario as they are thinking of their own future with the Provincial party and their indemnities.' Hepburn's resignation had opened the door for more cooperation, he continued, but should Mitch 'decide to continue in public life and again lead the Ontario Provincial party, I believe he would get a good deal of support from members of the Provincial Legislature.' His solution was a meeting of the federal Ontario caucus to demand a convention. Leadership and direction had to come from the Ontario ministers, he warned King's secretary, W.J. Turnbull, and unless 'something were done immediately there was little hope for the party in the next election.' Passing the memorandum to King, Turnbull commented: 'In spite of the good intentions of the Ontario Ministers in their conversations with Mr.

Campbell, I doubt if they will make a concerted effort without a further word.'[11]

Realizing that the Ontario ministers would not move and determined to topple Conant and seize the crown himself, Arthur Roebuck called a meeting of the Management Committee of the OLA for 15 February. 'That will put the train on the tracks and I hope some steam in the boiler,' he wrote McLarty. 'Hope you'll be able to attend for we must make sure we have a quorum.' Meanwhile, McQuesten, as OLA president, had promised Lambert an open convention and, to prevent Roebuck from controlling the process, Harry Johnson persuaded the Liberal caucus to appoint a committee to meet with a similar committee from Ottawa. Roebuck was cut off at the pass; the 'olive branch (or white flag),' as he described it, could not be rejected. The meeting was scheduled for 22 February.[12]

Meanwhile, in increasingly inflammatory language, Mitch had escalated his attack on a government he described as the 'only lunatic asylum operated by the inmates themselves.' King's lack of 'guts' had made conscription impossible, for the 'situation has gone too far' and 'through it all the French Canadians have been used as a political football.' The CBC, the funnel of government propaganda and censor of opposition criticism, was little better than the Gestapo. To prove that he could play the same game, Mitch held up the release of John Grierson's National Film Board production 'Inside Fighting Canada' which boasted that behind the leadership of Mackenzie King 'stands a people disciplined for war ... a people who make a national policy of voluntary service.' He finally relented, but not until Chubby Power admitted that the claim that the success of the war in the air owed much to the 'hundreds of thousands' of fliers who had graduated from the Commonwealth Air Training Program was a gross exaggeration. Chubby did add, however, that if the war lasted long enough that number could be reached.[13]

There was good reason to believe that Mitch had not only left the federal Liberal party but had joined the Tories. Although he was not at the Winnipeg convention in December, he approved of the election of John Bracken, the Progressive premier of Manitoba who in 1932 had coalesced with the Liberals and in 1940 had formed a non-partisan government. As an advocate of conscription and supporter of a national government Bracken was the choice of Meighen and McCullagh. He also appealed to the party's progressive wing which had moved the Tories to the left at the Port Hope conference in September. His 'People's Charter,' confined largely to national issues, appealed to Mitch, and especially a speech strongly critical of King which suggested there would be no waffling on conscription. 'Please believe me when I say you are voicing the sentiments of the overwhelming majority of citizens,' Mitch wrote before the convention. 'Keep up the good work.'

In February Mitch was on the platform with Drew when Bracken made his first speech in Toronto as leader of the 'Progressive' Conservatives. Both men rose to lead the applause after Bracken outlined his charter on post-war security and the need to bring farm income into line with other industries. Already openly critical of the impact of King's policies on Ontario farmers, who were liquidating their farms while western grain elevators were overflowing, Mitch asked the farmers in the audience to 'throw politics in the ashcan' in the next election and vote as a bloc. A month later he stated unequivocally that he was 'going to vote for John Bracken, a decent, progressive, kindly man, who is out to give the people of Canada a decent government.' When Grattan O'Leary read the press report, he commented sarcastically, 'This is the first time John Bracken's luck has failed him.'[14]

Mitch was also incensed by the broken pledge on liquor rationing. Despite Ilsley's commitment when the tax agreement was negotiated, King was determined to seize the wartime opportunity to impose temperance on the country. He had argued in August that consumption had to be controlled and that 'it was a crime to let revenues be the first consideration or any fear of Hepburn and others, when great national interests were at stake.' Although his colleagues did not see any national interests at stake, King's determination was strengthened by a promise he had made in September to a temperance delegation. Despite the opposition of most of the cabinet, including Ilsley, who warned that the provinces would have to be consulted and compensated, King wore them down. None of his ministers chose to make the announcement and, after labouring over his speech for hours, King went on radio on 16 December to inform the nation of cuts in the supply of alcohol, wine, and beer. Temperance at home was essential to keep faith with those making the supreme sacrifice, said King solemnly, and 'To be equal to the ordeal to come we must put on the armour of God.'

With the pubs running out of beer in mid-afternoon and near riots in the long queues outside the Brewers' Retail stores, it was little wonder that Mitch received a rousing reception from an audience of hotelkeepers in January 1943 when he mocked the 'moral depredations of the Federal leader in Ottawa' who had 'put on his red underwear and flannel socks and decided he would track demon rum to its lair.' Like King's ministers, Conant argued that there was no industrial justification for restricting the sale of beer and demanded that King meet the provincial premiers. For two hours King listened to their lamentations about the loss of revenue but, despite Conant's warning that beer would cost the Liberals the next election, the premiers went home empty-handed. Queen's Park was fed up being the suicide squad for Ottawa's regulations, Conant exclaimed. 'We are not going to act as shock troops for the Dominion any longer.' On 8 February Ontario filed a statement of claim for lost revenues of $7.1 million and Mitch stated that it was impossible for him to bring down a budget until the issue was resolved.[15]

When the session opened on 9 February, the Queen City was alive with the 'Hepburn jitters.' Torontonians, reported a St Thomas *Times-Journal* editor who spent a few days in the city, were 'roused to such a pitch of uncertainty about how, when and where Mitch is to make his next leap, that it ranks in the epidemic line with the 'flu. There is this difference, however: the 'flu can be cured – the Hepburn jitters can't – at least not in Toronto.' Mitch's appearance with Bracken and Drew had fed the rumour that he planned to run federally in Elgin either as a Tory or an anti-King Liberal. A more immediate prospect was that he would soon be premier again and form a coalition with Drew or go to the people during the recess or after a short session. One thing seemed certain: whatever his intentions when he resigned in October, Mitch still ruled the roost at Queen's Park.

If proof were needed it came at the first caucus when Conant tried to persuade the members to accept the principles of the collective bargaining bill, not an easy task with the OPP at Wallaceburg to contain a tense strike for recognition of the CIO union. 'Look what happened at the party caucus when the proposed labour legislation was discussed,' a prominent Liberal told the *Times-Journal*. 'Conant tried to explain the proposed measure. Heenan tried. Finally things got into an unholy mess. Then Mitch jumped in and had things all smoothed out in no time. The old Hepburn fire, a bit of whiskey and a dose of whatever it is that party politicians take to tame them down, and they were a happy family again – or are they?'[16]

Not even the most imaginative script writer could have written the next act. Drew came out fighting on the first day of the session and forced a division on Conant's motion to defer debate on the throne speech and give immediate approval to the Quebec power agreements. The colonel and other Tory speakers insisted that there was a 'hidden agenda,' that Hydro policy was 'dictated by the Premier of Quebec,' and the good residents of Ontario, working on the Quebec side, would be forced to become Quebeckers. Visibly upset, Mitch claimed that the Tory criticism confirmed his view that an election in 1942 would have been fought on a racial issue and justified his resignation in October:

I was more anxious to have this bill brought before the house than I was to remain as premier. While we were negotiating the agreement the pressure was on me to call an election. The federal authorities wanted an election. It would have injected a racial issue into the campaign ...

I warn that anything we may say in this house will be magnified by the isolationists in the Quebec house and I want to avoid that.

I am a Britisher, an imperialist, but if the Plains of Abraham had gone the other way I couldn't feel the same way toward France as I do toward Britain, and that's the same with the French. You can't push them around.

When Drew angrily interjected that Mitch was deliberately attempting to create 'an impression utterly remote from the debate,' he insisted that if an election had been held 'the federal machine would have made it a racial issue by claiming that Quebec was refusing to negotiate with Ontario and was thereby holding up hydro development indefinitely in Ontario.' There was little doubt that, given the mood of Ontario after the plebiscite, the Tories would have injected a racial issue into the campaign, but Mitch did not explain how the federal Liberals could profit.

At cabinet on 12 February, Mitch proposed an extraordinary and desperate course. Unable to present a budget because of the broken promise on liquor sales and aware that the federal Liberals could influence, and possibly control, the April leadership convention, he said that he was going to resign and asked every member, including Conant, to resign with him and bring on a general election. There was a long sixty-second silence. Some stroked their chins and mumbled about the wisdom of such a move; Conant said he would be embarrassed; others said frankly it was not a good idea. When all had spoken, Mitch insisted they meet again the next day when he would see 'who has the guts to follow me.' One minister, formerly close to Mitch, said a meeting was unnecessary: 'I know where I stand; I won't.' That night he met with all the ministers except Mitch, and they sent word to the hotel that the answer was no.

The press learned nothing of Mitch's bizarre proposal, but Harry Nixon heard that Mitch was trying to force an immediate election and phoned King to see if it could be prevented. King replied that since Nixon and others had been demanding dissolution, 'I did not well see how they could afford to ask that it not be granted. I said I doubted, however, if Conant would yield to Hepburn's demands.' King advised Nixon not to take the many rumours about Mitch too seriously, concluding that nothing would come of it. Meanwhile, Mitch had met with the cabinet and, given their decision, said he would go alone. But his colleagues eventually persuaded him to stick by Conant through the session as he had promised, although Mitch warned them that he would be supporting Bracken in the next federal election.[17]

Mitch had lost the skirmish and the battle. For weeks some of Conant's colleagues and members of the caucus had been pleading with him to get rid of Mitch, whose malevolence and uncontrollable eruptions suggested to G.N. Gordon of Peterborough and others that he was 'either drunk or crazy.' There were many prominent Liberals who were 'just itching to take a kick at Hepburn,' Gordon told Roebuck, and 'Now I think is the time to put on the squeeze.' Although Conant was too loyal to the 'Chief' to be easily persuaded, Mitch's wild proposal to the cabinet followed by his outburst on 19 February left him no choice.

A budget was impossible until the liquor taxing question was settled, Mitch said irritably on 19 February, and unless those 'despoilers, violators of a sacred trust' made up the losses he would have to increase taxes or cut social welfare spending. Members sat stunned as Mitch shouted angrily: 'They acted the way Hitler acts. These are Nazi tactics.' Liberal backbenchers applauded when Eric Cross criticized Mitch by recalling the words of Shylock, 'I'll feed fat the ancient grudge I bear you.' In Ottawa Ilsley did not deny that a promise had been made, but stated acidly that he dismissed Mitch's accusations and language 'without comment and with contempt. From any other public man in Canada, these words would be an insult. From Mr. Hepburn, all they mean is that he was in a fit of temper when he uttered them.' An apoplectic Gordon immediately wrote Conant that everyone to whom he had spoken agreed that Mitch's attack 'was a disgraceful and disreputable back alley politician's performance of such a digusting and contemptible character that you, by his remaining in your cabinet, are suffering from the ignominy and discredit of his being a member of your political household.' Gordon's sentiments were shared by many Liberals; his argument was persuasive. If Conant hoped to retain the leadership, Mitch had to go. When the 22 February joint federal-provincial meeting decided that the convention would be open to all Liberals it ensured that federal members would be a critical factor. Mitch's fate was sealed.[18]

Mitch had gone to the farm when the House recessed. Conant phoned on 28 February. He told Mitch that although he was also concerned about the financial position and autonomy of the province, the situation was not likely to be improved by Mitch's 'attitude and statements concerning the Dominion Government,' and he had decided to accept his 21 October resignation as provincial treasurer. Mitch's distemperate reply to Conant's confirming letter contained no expression of friendship or regret: 'The Ottawa political machine has long endeavoured to put up a Quisling Government in Ontario and has now succeeded temporarily by employing the Hitler policy of breaking an agreement and by autocratic use of power.' King was ecstatic when he heard the news. 'Liquor has been the occasion of his downfall,' he wrote triumphantly, 'and in all that has taken place toward that end I have not so much as moved a hand. The whole story is like the old Greek tragedies, based on nemesis.'

Mitch was seldom in the House after the session resumed on 9 March. Conant survived without him, and St Clair Gordon dutifully read Chester Walter's budget speech. The Quebec power agreement had been approved before the adjournment, and the most contentious issue was Mitch's collective bargaining bill. Originally drafted by J.L. Cohen, the bill established a labour court to certify bargaining agents determined by majority vote, encourage bargaining in good faith, and police unfair practices and discrimination. The bill also exempted unions from civil conspiracy in restraint of trade actions and gave them legal status for the first time. While the act was by no means what labour wanted, the Trades and Labour Congress admitted it was 'a step in the right direction,' and it was far more than management wanted to concede. Uneasiness in the Liberal caucus over the labour legislation was much less than over Conant's decision to seek another extension of the life of the legislature. Although the caucus had voted almost unanimously against an election, eight Liberals, led by Nixon and Oliver, joined the Tories in opposition.[19]

Long before the session ended on 14 April, the convention dominated the political agenda. Conant was naive if he believed he could win the convention by dumping Mitch and cuddling up to King and Ilsley. He was fatally tarred by the Hepburn brush, and had few friends in the caucus and little support in the ridings. And if Roebuck believed that his opposition to Mitch and his labours in securing an open convention would endear him to either the federal or provincial Liberals, he too was naive. Although few doubted his abilities, many questioned his judgment, and his colleagues had too long endured his self-righteous conceit and undisguised ambition to place him in charge at Queen's Park.

If he were a gambler, Mitch said at Brantford with Nixon beside him, he would bet on Harry to carry the Liberal convention. Mackenzie King felt the same way, and he was in a position to influence the odds. Delighted that Nixon had told him that 'on no account would he let Hepburn participate in his campaign or give him any support,' King believed that Nixon was 'the man who deserves to be chosen. Has more judgement than Roebuck. More real principle. Roebuck too extreme. My own feeling is that the Ottawa delegation will swing to Nixon.' Most Liberals agreed that Nixon deserved the job, and some urged Roebuck to stand aside and be satisfied with a position in Nixon's cabinet. Roebuck refused. 'I have had enough of doing the fighting and supplying the industry while somebody else took the glory and wielded the whip hand,' he replied. 'I have no ambition for the experience I went through from 1934 to 1937.' Nixon could not be relied upon 'to push a battle through to the bitter end. He would be much more likely to make a comfortable arrangement during the course of the battle. Moreover, do not forget that Nixon has been quite ready to stand for all Hepburn's antics till he was himself overlooked, with the one exception when he marched up the hill and down again in the last Dominion election.'[20]

A poll of MPs a few days before the convention indicated that three-quarters of the federal Liberals were solidly behind Nixon, as were all twenty-seven federal ridings in western Ontario. Billy Fraser, the Ontario whip, opened a committee room for Nixon and many of the MPs were actively lobbying. Conant knew the game was up when he saw eight cabinet ministers and six senators at the opening session. Early the next morning he checked into the Toronto General Hospital, suffering from nervous and physical exhaustion, and withdrew from the race.[21]

Mitch was not at the convention, and was reported to have left for New York on the advice of his doctors. Rumours of a last-minute appearance gained some credibility on the morning of the voting when thousands of white cards, courtesy of his colourful hôtelier friend Mickey Wilson, were scattered throughout the hotel bearing the message 'We Want Mitch.' Mitch issued no formal statement, and it was uncertain whether the rumours that he supported Nixon were spread by Nixon's supporters or opponents. From Mitch there was only a note delivered by Harry Johnson to the chairman: 'I wish to tender my resignation as leader of the Ontario Liberal Party.' Despite Roebuck's last-minute warning that although Nixon could deliver the rural vote to him, he could not deliver the urban vote to the Brant farmer, the die had been cast. Nixon won easily on the first ballot with 418 votes to 85 for Roebuck and 40 for McQuesten.

'It was a King-Hepburn battle,' wrote a triumphant King, 'with a complete routing of all the Hepburn forces, and he and his right & left bowers left wounded and bleeding on the field.' The final victory over 'Hepburn and his gang,' had been long in coming, but in the end was proof of loyalty to him and 'a remarkable evidence of the moral forces that work in the unseen realm, and of the vindication of right in the end.' Spring in 1943 had been long in coming, but King believed that winter was finally over: 'it has lasted till the last possible moment – the end of April with its wind on into May – Hepburn & his gang & their control – now behind – their evil influence being gradually swept away by the new beginning made at the Convention – the warmer weather, sunshine, green grass blossom & flowers coming at last.'[22]

For a few days, however, it seemed that summer might be far off. Conant was bitter in defeat and toyed with the idea of staying on, as both the *Globe* and the *Telegram* suggested he could and perhaps should. He finally swallowed the bitter pill after meeting the cabinet on 13 May when many, if not all, of his colleagues warned him that they would resign if he clung to office. Harry Nixon was sworn in on 18 May. Ten days later, when Conant was appointed master of the Supreme Court at Osgoode Hall, George Drew commented scornfully that the 'new era of public purity, proclaimed in advance by Mr. Nixon, died before it was born.'[23]

Mitch watched the summer election from the onion patch. Nixon felt he was morally bound to dissolve and King advised him that 'the sooner he brought on the election, the better.' If the polls were accurate, it would be a close election with the Liberal and Conservatives running neck and neck at 35 and 36 per cent and the CCF a step behind with 27.

Nixon did not use the two months between his election and the 4 August election to good advantage. Time was too short – perhaps any amount of time would have been too short – for the amiable, ambling Brant farmer to establish an image of being anything other than just one of the folks. There was no one in the unreconstructed cabinet who could match Drew on the platform or feel the pulse of the urban Ontario that was emerging from depression and war. Other than a few vague platitudes about post-war reconstruction, the Liberals had no program to offer as an alternative to the progressive stance of the Tories or the radical manifesto of the CCF. The Liberals were forced to run on their record. But it was Mitch's record and, as the American embassy reported, although he ran as an independent Liberal, he remained 'ominously' silent. The Tories were happy to have him remain at Bannockburn and deliberately avoided any provocation that would draw him into the wider battle.

Large ads showed Nixon on the bridge of the 'Ship of Liberalism' promising to 'Keep the Light of Democracy Burning' while Drew and Jolliffe, the CCF leader, were fighting to keep the leaking SS *Socialism* afloat. Given the mood of the province they were counter-productive if not pathetic. Moreover, Mitch's break with King and his convolutions since October had left the party organization in a shambles, and those interests that had looked with favour on a government in office were either hedging their bets or, like George McCullagh, had switched to the Tories. Above all, Harry Nixon had the impossible task of carrying the heavy burden of Mackenzie King on his sloping shoulders.[24]

The Conservatives were more than ready for the election. By the summer of 1941 the rejuvenation and reorganization of the party had begun in earnest under Drew and Cecil Frost. On the eve of the election the redoubtable Alex McKenzie, perhaps the pre-eminent backroom organizer in Ontario history, became chief of staff. Under E.W. Bickle a formidable group of bagmen made certain that McKenzie's well did not run dry. Drew not only had a machine, he also had a platform well suited to the times. Revealed to a large organizational meeting on 3 July and released as the '22 Points' in his first radio address of the campaign, the enlightened and progressive program for post-war reconstruction even won the grudging approval of the Toronto *Star*. More immediate and effective was the promise to revise the property tax system and pay half of local educational costs at once. A Drew government would cooperate with Ottawa to establish a social security system after the war, but would preserve 'the constitutional rights of the people of Ontario.'

Cooperation was one thing, lectured George McCullagh in one of his two inflammatory radio addresses, 'fawning subservience' to a 'one-party Government at Ottawa' that was steadily encroaching on provincial rights was another.[25] And fawning subservience was all that could be expected of Ottawa's 'toady' who had been elected at a convention rigged by the Ottawa Liberals.

Following Nixon's victory, Tory strategists had decided immediately to identify Nixon with King and fight a provincial election on national issues. This great province 'no longer has a government of its own,' said Drew, setting the tone of the anti-King campaign. 'The voice may be the voice of Nixon but the words will be the words of Mackenzie King.' There was no doubt about King's unpopularity as the country found the wartime restraints and regulations more painful now that victory, however far off, seemed certain. In addition, a strong current of anti-Quebec feeling ran through the election. Ontario was fed up with the 'timidity, log-rolling and compromise of a government dominated by Quebec,' wrote Les Frost. 'I have come to the conclusion that there has been enough appeasement in that direction and that it has reached the stage where so-called national unity will be harmed if there are further concessions.' And although it was a provincial election, it was Nixon, the man who said he was loyal to King 'come what may,' who had to bear the responsibility for King's coddling of Quebec, with the cowardly plebiscite, the refusal to abide by its results, and St Laurent's untimely invention of false figures on French-Canadian enlistment and his bitter attack on critics of Quebec and the influence of Catholic hierarchy. 'If Mr. St. Laurent had wanted to lose the election for his party in Ontario,' wrote the *Round Table*'s analyst, 'he could not have made a more effective speech.'[26]

The CCF also hoped to capitalize on the unpopularity of the King government among labour and farmers, and party strategists knew that this feeling was largely responsible for their surprising increase in popular support. With the election of Ted Jolliffe – journalist, Rhodes scholar, lawyer, and architect of the York South triumph – the provincial party had an aggressive and articulate leader for the first time. The platform dealt almost exclusively with post-war planning, and the advice to candidates was to avoid any contentious provincial issues. For the first time the party had the open support of labour, big and small, in the Canadian Congress of Labour and the local trades and labour councils. It was not difficult to persuade workers that they had suffered most from wage and price controls, and reports from the factories and CNR shops in London, Ed Carty noted, 'show workers down on the Liberals because of heavy war taxes and taking them out of the envelopes of workers without the workers' consent.' Ralph Maybank, the perceptive Liberal MP from Winnipeg who worked in the campaign, reported to King that among the working class there was a 'positive dislike, almost amounting to hatred, of federal labour policies.' With Ottawa incapable of resolving the crippling strikes in Hamilton and Galt in the summer of 1943, there was even the danger of a general strike.[27]

There was also a hatred of King for depriving workers of their beer, a hatred not tempered by soaring temperatures in July and August. As far as workers or farmers were concerned, King's restrictions were identical to prohibition for there was seldom any beer left when they finished work. Ever since King had cut the supply of beer, he had been warned that his action could defeat the Liberals in Ontario and Quebec. With the police forced to keep order along the queues outside the beer stores and pubs before they opened, with citizens sporting 'NO BEER NO BONDS' buttons as the war loan drive approached, King's colleagues begged him to relent. His answer was a threat to nationalize the industry and prosecute the buttoned for interfering with the war effort. The bitterness was so 'astonishing,' reported one Liberal organizer, that it alone could have cost Nixon the election. When Howe and Mulock offered the same observation after the election, King dismissed it as 'ridiculous.' The Liberals were defeated because of Hepburn's attack on him, King stated categorically, and if beer was an issue, it was simply because his colleagues had 'done nothing to explain the policy or defend it. It was like everything else.'[28]

Mitch Hepburn reminded the St. Thomas railwayworkers that he had not deprived them of their beer. Running in Elgin as an Independent Liberal, Mitch denounced King for putting party before country and did not retract his declared support for Bracken in the next federal election. Appealing for non-partisan support, Mitch said he would support Nixon if he did not sell Ontario 'down the St. Lawrence' as well as anything in Drew's 22 Points that would benefit the province. Although he worked hard in the last two weeks of the campaign, Mitch counted on his record to offset the anti-Liberal swing. 'KEEP ELGIN ON THE MAP by re-electing Mitch Hepburn. Mitch Hepburn Isn't Through. You Can't Re-elect Mitch By Staying Away From the Polls,' read one ad. Another asked, 'Can Elgin County Afford to Lose Mitch Hepburn? Ask Yourself That Question Before You Go Out and Vote.' Just over half of the Elgin voters decided they could not. Mitch's election was the first to be conceded in the province and, after the traditional cavalcade up and down Talbot Street, Mitch said he would return to represent all of Elgin at Queen's Park 'as your white-haired, bald-headed Mitch.'[29]

Few Liberals were as fortunate. Despite the polls which showed that 56 per cent were satisfied with the government, Nixon's optimism, Slaght's prediction that the Liberals would be returned with sixty seats, or even King's more pessimistic conclusion that Nixon would be lucky to win a majority, the party was crushed. One million registered voters failed to go to the polls. Of those who did 36 per cent cast their ballots for George Drew, 32 per cent for the CCF, and 31 per cent for the Liberals. Urban and industrial Ontario totally deserted the Liberals. And in rural Ontario both the Tories and the CCF cut deeply into their traditional farm vote. Nixon's Liberals were reduced to a pitiful rump of fifteen members. The CCF won thirty-four seats, sweeping the north, Hamilton, and the Niagara peninsula and winning the four Yorks and four Toronto ridings. Toronto also sent Alex MacLeod and Joe Salsberg, two communists running under the Labour Progressive banner, to Queen's Park. Drew won thirty-eight seats as the Tories regained their traditional strongholds in eastern Ontario, won seven ridings in Toronto, and took seats from the Liberals in western Ontario.[30]

'In my inner nature,' confessed King, 'I feel a sense of relief that a cabinet that has been so unprincipled and devoid of character has been swept out of Queen's Park ... Instead of injuring the Federal party excepting temporarily it may help to save us in the end.' That he may have been partly the cause of Nixon's defeat did not occur to him. He was not prepared to accept the conclusion of Ralph Maybank, that 'Nobody ever heard anything of Ontario politics. The Federal Government was the target and the cause of defeats.' Indeed, on the contrary, the re-election of Nixon, Oliver, and Laurier – the ministers who had stood by him – convinced him it had been another battle between the forces of good and evil, and that anyone associated with Mitch was 'doomed.' Mitch, on the other hand, regarded the election as a defeat of Mackenzie King: 'Ontario has said to Ottawa today in no uncertain terms, "Hands off".'

There was a flurry of rumours of possible alliances and coalitions. Admitting he knew little of constitutional practice, Roebuck wanted Nixon to remain in office and have another election later in the year, and warned King that if Drew became premier, Mitch would enter the cabinet as minister of agriculture and 'do us great harm.' But Harry Nixon was not prepared to play games with the constitution, and when he resigned on 17 August, Lieutenant-Governor

Matthews asked George Drew to become the fourteenth premier of Ontario. There were informed reports that Drew asked Mitch and three other Liberals to join him, but the cabinet sworn in on 17 August was pure Tory.[31]

'More joy in Heaven'

No one knew what the future held for Mitch Hepburn, but of all the roads he might follow none pointed back to the Liberal Party. In his infrequent public appearances he seemed to be only a step short of joining the Tories. On the same platform with Drew in November, he said he was going to support him in the House. 'I won't say I'll do it blindly, but so far as my conscience will permit – it's almost unbelievable how far you can stretch your conscience,' he threw in to cheers and laughter. And in his first speech of the session, members on both sides pounded their desks when he exclaimed that 'You can't cooperate with the bureaucracy we have in Ottawa. They are the most incompetent, vacillating, hypocritical government we ever had.' There was Mackenzie King, who had donned the armour of God to deprive the working man of his beer while the breweries exported millions of gallons to the United States.[1]

Mitch was not invited nor did he ask to join the Liberal caucus, and sat with the other loose fish, MacLeod and Salsberg of the LPP. The session was uneventful. Neither the CCF nor the Liberals wanted an election and Drew briskly began to implement many of his 22 Points, including the popular increases in the school grants. Mitch was seldom to be seen in the House and rarely intervened in the debate. The session over, he returned to the farm.[2]

In mid-August Mitch was packing halls in northern Ontario during the Victory Loan campaign. He was in Port Arthur on 14 August when Angus Macdonald and Senator Joseph Bench arrived for C.D. Howe's nominating convention. A thirty-nine year-old St Catharines lawyer and businessman, Bench had been appointed to the Senate in 1942 and had been involved in the futile attempts to reorganize the party in Ontario. Bench had known Mitch for years and was also close to Archie Haines who, after losing Lincoln in the 1943 election, had become president of the Ontario Liberal Association. Bench sought out Mitch and suggested that it was time 'he ought to be in the fight with the Liberals.' Mitch was non-committal, but after meeting Bench again in Hamilton late in September he invited him to the farm for the 30 September weekend.[3]

Bench's proposition, unquestionably sanctioned in Ottawa and perhaps Toronto, was that Mitch not only return to the fold but that he also return as leader of the party. As King later realized, his colleagues had concluded that Liberal fortunes would not be restored with Nixon as leader. Their immediate, if not their only, salvation lay in getting Mitch back in harness. Mitch was willing, once he had got his complaints against King off his chest, and the question was how to explain the return of the prodigal and how quickly it could be accomplished. Bench believed that the process had to be gradual. Over the weekend they drafted a statement that Mitch would release a few days later when he turned down an invitation to contest Elgin as a Liberal in the next federal election.

The explanation for his conversion as a born-again Liberal was to be the record of the Drew administration and particularly the colonel's brutal speech on 9 August attacking King's family allowances. 'If the Ontario Government submitted to the arrogant usurpation of power in passing the baby bonus bill,' Drew had warned, 'then we would be handing over the rights of the Province to a Government which has shown only too clearly that it submits to the will of Quebec.' Even for one as politically supple and agile as Mitch, however, it was a difficult task. Late in July he had also expressed grave apprehensions about the baby bonus and other federal giveaways and, with his customary hyperbole, had suggested that King stop bribing the people with their own money.[4]

But Mitch seldom let consistency stand in his way. And in the statement drafted over the weekend, Mitch said that after 'due consideration' he had concluded that his 'main responsibility as a Liberal is to do battle against reactionary Toryism in Ontario.' Drew's speech on 9 August was 'the most irresponsible utterance ever made by a Canadian public man within my memory. It was, in the first place, a clear incitement to hatred against a neighboring Province, but, worse than that, it was an incitement to hatred against one-third of our own Ontario population ... While I no longer wear the mantle of leadership,' Mitch concluded, 'I am satisfied to take my place in the ranks of reform Liberalism to rally the forward-looking people of Ontario against the new Tory menace, whether it be in the Provincial or Federal field.'

Interviewed at the farm a few days later, Mitch indicated that his conversion was almost unqualified by any lingering political heterodoxy. He admitted that he had been critical of King's war effort and had hesitated to re-enter the political arena until he had become convinced that Drew was attempting to 'breed racial disunity' in Canada. The Liberal Government at Ottawa has not come to me about this matter,' he added, semantically shading the truth, 'and I have not gone to Ottawa.' Privately, Mitch told Wilson Mills, the retiring MP for Elgin, that 'you know I do not like King very well but still I believe he can do the best job for Canada of any of the leaders.'⁵

King saw Joe Atkinson in Toronto the day Mitch's initial statement appeared in the press. 'We were laughing about Hepburn's attitude,' King wrote. 'He thinks Hepburn will be effective against the Tories. That the Party may gain by his action. He would not be surprised to see him become leader of the Liberals in Ontario at Tuesday's caucus.' When Bench gave King the background to the return of the errant son – hinting that Nixon might exit gracefully through the Red Chamber – he brooded over the deeper meaning of the secret negotiations.

The conclusion I have come to is that Howe and others of the Ontario Liberals have felt the Liberals would get nowhere with Nixon at the head. That they could see no other person in sight who had dynamic powers or powers of leadership than Hepburn and that it might be well to try and get him back into line ... It is clear now that there is an effort on foot to have Hepburn again brought into the leadership of the Ontario Liberals. Whether they are seeking to convince him that if he plays the game with the Liberals for the balance of the term of this Parliament, and that I should [sic] be defeated at Prince Albert, or not wish to continue the leadership, then Hepburn might be brought forward as leader in the federal arena, I do not know. I am quite convinced in my own mind that whatever may be thought of in that way today will not be countenanced by the party as a whole. On the other hand, I am quite prepared silently to acquiesce in having Hepburn used in any way possible by my colleagues in help winning the election and I have no fears whatever to the consequences. He will never have the confidence of the people of Canada as a whole and only the confidence of the worst elements in the province. Unfortunately, all men have votes and for that reason all means that are honourable can be used.⁶

Bench and Mitch met again before the provincial Liberal caucus on Tuesday, 10 October. They agreed that Mitch would arrange that the leadership question would not be discussed. Bench also put a little gloss on his earlier discussion with King when he told Mitch that King would be 'pleased and anxious to co-operate with him in every way' in the interests of the country and the party. 'I think I can say that this news pleased Mr. Hepburn,' Bench reported to King, 'although he fully recognizes the danger which presently is inherent in any untoward public display of any mutual sentiment in this connection.' The return of the sinner had already had 'an excellent tonic effect' on the party, wrote Bench, and was 'an earthly application of the Gospel assurance that there is more joy in Heaven over one sinner doing penance than ninety-nine just who need not penance.'[7]

After the caucus Nixon informed a radio audience that his 'good friend and former Chief' attended the caucus 'fully restored in health and old time fighting vigour. I know of no one better able to speak for himself than Mr. Hepburn, but I am satisfied and you can accept my assurance that his outstanding abilities will be directed to the advancement of sound Liberal policies and the defeat of reactionary Toryism in this Province and Dominion.' Mitch's vigour and abilities would soon be tested, for caucus had decided that, in view of Drew's shocking speech on 9 August, the political truce was over. The CCF willing, the minority government seemed doomed.[8]

Although Mitch was back in the fold, there were many who agreed with Bench and Sir James Dunn that he had some 'coming back' to do. After spending a few hours with Mitch the day after the caucus, Sir James wrote a perceptive letter to McQuesten, the substance of which he trusted would be passed on to Mitch:

He seemed in good form and ready to bury all the hatchets with the Government at Ottawa. If Mitch will keep emotionally stable and not allow himself to be rushed into decisions, some of which he would regret tomorrow, I think he can come back in the estimation of his friends and of the country. I think his friends will do him service by making it clear to him that he has some 'coming back' to do for he certainly let all his friends down very badly when, without consulting them he threw over his responsibility onto very poor shoulders and walked out of the picture leaving the rest of us who had always stood by him in the air. Another thing I hope you will realize is that he cannot maintain the dignity of a great political position by harbouring drunks who drop in at all hours of the day and night to hinder his repose and interfere with his serious engagements. A man with two kidneys and two hearts could not again go through what Mitch went through for many years before his collapse – so Mitch with

only one kidney and one heart although very big and generous cannot successfully come back to be a great leader in his country with the dragging
attachments of a few years ago – he has got to have the dignity of the
position.[9]

His penance served, Mitch was unanimously elected House leader of the Liberals at a caucus on 6 December 1944. In his letter of
resignation, Nixon stated that ever since Mitch's return in the fall
he and all the members wanted him back, and a survey of party
supporters indicated that he enjoyed 'tremendous support throughout the province.' Nixon would remain as leader of the party until
a convention could elect his successor. Roebuck was dismayed and
assured King that Mitch was 'thoroughly unworthy and corrupt'
and 'we would now have all the liquor interests and corruptionists
and others coming into the fold of the party under Hepburn.' The
appointment of Harry Johnson as Roebuck's assistant in the federal organization, however, suggested that Roebuck, too, was prepared to get help wherever he could find it.[10]

There was endless speculation before the session opened on 15 February 1945 on the likelihood of Drew's survival, or, if defeated, on
whether the CCF and the Liberals must form a government. Following Drew's speech on 9 August Jolliffe had been convinced that
he would call a fall session during which he expected to be defeated and fight the election on 'the anti-King, anti-Quebec and anti-
zombie feeling prevalent in Ontario.' At an emergency meeting of
the caucus in September the CCF decided to take the initiative and
be responsible for Drew's defeat. Caucus also agreed that if the lieutenant-governor refused Drew's request for a dissolution, Jolliffe
would agree to form a government. However, Drew did not call a
fall session, and when the House met in February the continuing
CCF drop in the polls made Jolliffe far less enthusiastic about defeating Drew.[11]

Unless Mitch agreed to support a Jolliffe government, however,
there was little chance that a dissolution would be refused. Soon
after the session opened, Agnes MacPhail apparently approached
Mitch with the strange proposition, endorsed by MacLeod, that the
Liberal, CCF, and LPP members send a petition to the lieutenant-governor asking him to call on Mitch if Drew was defeated. A more
rational scenario, apparently proposed by Mitch, was that if Jolliffe joined him in defeating Drew, he would support Jolliffe's claim

The Prodigal

to the premiership and join a coalition cabinet. Whichever alternative was the more plausible, Jolliffe apparently rejected both.[12]

Although Mitch had decided to defeat the government in the first two weeks of the 1945 session, the federal Liberals were unhappy with the prospect of a spring election in Ontario when they were also planning to go to the country. On 19 February Howe, Peter Campbell, and Lambert met Mitch in Toronto. Lambert believed that 'it was finally agreed (or agreement was implied) that no election or change of Govt. should be forced in Ont. just now. Give more time for Drew to kill himself, and the C.C.F. to split.'[13]

Mitch's behaviour in the House did not seem to reflect such an agreement. From the opening day he constantly engaged in testy, sometimes nasty, exchanges with Drew, who did nothing in reply to curb Mitch's desire to defeat the government. During one stormy session, Drew said he was not going to let 'the honourable and irritable member for Elgin ... reduce the level of debate in the House to what it was when he was prime minister,' and referred sarcastically to Mitch's 'ill health,' a frequent euphemism for his drinking. On several occasions Drew backed away from decisions on a Speaker's ruling and avoided a motion on family allowances. Jolliffe, on the other hand, seemed ambivalent. He promised Drew that he would support all progressive legislation and supported the Tories on two of Mitch's motions. However, his amendment to the throne speech criticizing the government for failing to live up to its promises and threatening national unity seemed sufficiently free of socialist rhetoric to enable Mitch to support it. Mitch's sub-amendment a few days later condemned the government for introducing religious instruction in the schools and planning large-scale British immigration after the war without a legislative mandate, and 'before providing adequate safeguards to ensure full employment for our war veterans and present war workers.'

Incensed that Drew suspended debate on the throne speech to enable Frost to bring in his sunshine budget, Mitch made a valiant effort to have the procedure ruled out of order and seemed to have the House rules on his side. But Jolliffe refused to support him and Frost brought down his election budget on 9 March. Again, on 14 March, Mitch insisted that according to parliamentary procedure the throne speech debate had to be concluded before the House was asked to vote supply. He stated categorically that he intended to vote against the government and accused Jolliffe of attempting to escape. When Jolliffe interjected, 'There is no question of any escape,' Mitch continued: 'All right. Then the Government is doom-

ed and it simply awaits its death sentence.' But Jolliffe replied that
he wanted a vote on principle, not procedure. 'I can set my Hon.
friend from Elgin's mind at rest, that we are going to vote against
the government – I think he has known that since the first of
August – but we are not going to be diverted to vote against the
passing of sufficient funds to assist the school boards of Ontario.'

The resumed debate on the address reached its end on 22 March.
The members and the packed audience in the galleries waited impa-
tiently as the government introduced a host of bills for first reading;
Tom Murray meandered through the Renfrew underbrush; Mrs Luc-
knock made her maiden speech; Bélanger unfavourably compared
Drew with Laurier on national unity; and, after the dinner recess,
Carlin of Sudbury expounded on the dangers of sulphur fumes. After
Harry Nixon spoke, the floor belonged to Jolliffe. The CCF refused
to lend itself 'to partisan warfare upon any religious issue,' he declared, and members of his caucus would vote on the Liberal amendment as their consciences dictated. 'The lines are clearly drawn,'
Drew warned, the time has finally come. The fate of the government
was in the hands of the 'leader of the Liberal remainder.'

It was midnight when the vote was called. The CCF split neatly
down the middle on Mitch's motion and Drew survived, fifty-two
to thirty-five. When Mitch stood in his seat as the ayes were called
on the CCF motion, there were wild outbursts of approval and dismay on the floor and in the galleries. When the Speaker declared
the non-confidence motion had passed fifty-one to thirty-six, Jolliffe
was immediately on his feet. 'In view of what has taken place in this
House, I think the House, and the people of the province, require
some time to consider what has taken place here to-night.' Drew
accepted his motion to adjourn the House until Tuesday, 27 March.
On 24 March, despite Jolliffe's willingness to form a government if
called and Mitch's desire to continue the session and vote supply,
Lieutenant-Governor Matthews granted Drew a dissolution.[14]

A week later, on 2 April, more than 250 leading federal and
provincial Liberals met in Toronto to go through the motions of
unanimously electing Mitchell Hepburn as leader of the party.
Arthur Slaght, among others, had told Mitch he was not prepared
to support him unless he unequivocally endorsed King and 'have
an end to the continual harping and criticism which he had indulged
in for many years.' In an address to the Canadian Club on 1 March
Mitch had refused to back away from his earlier criticisms of King's
policies, but he did admit that he 'probably erred in attacking
Mackenzie King in a personal way.' The major issue before the

country was now national unity and only the Liberal party could maintain it. He repeated his statement in the House a few days later, but quickly added that 'there have been no overtures made by him to me or me to him, and so I am perfectly free to criticize his government.' Despite the face-saving qualification, King believed his victory was complete: 'I had waited long for his confession but he had found that he had had to make it in the hope of getting back into a strong position in the party. I have never asked for anything from him.' And when Mulock informed King that in persuading Mitch to recant he had suggested the reward might be the federal leadership, King noted in his diary that 'I can see, however, stronger men of the party will not quickly pass by Ilsley, Gardiner and possibly others for Hepburn.'[15]

Although King welcomed the prospect of a united party in Ontario contesting the federal election, the cabinet had to weigh the negative effect of a possible Liberal defeat in the provincial election. King had been toying with the idea of going to the country on 25 June. But Jack Pickersgill came to him, 'disconsolate and discouraged' with the news that Drew planned an election for 11 June. Pickersgill warned King that 'this would in all probability give Drew a chance to get the Ontario elections over before ours, in which event should the Liberals run second or last in Ontario – last seems in every way the most probable – the effect on the Federal campaign which would come later would be disastrous indeed not only in Ontario, but a defeat which might hurt us in all the provinces.' In cabinet on 12 April Howe suggested that they should also appeal to the people on 11 June and, although most ministers were opposed, King found the proposal attractive. That afternoon he talked to Roebuck, the Ontario organizer, who agreed with Howe, and told him to be prepared for the 11th. When King announced on 13 April that the federal election would also be held on 11 June, Mitch wired that 'Liberals everywhere can now join forces for the defeat of Toryism and get the whole job done at once.' However, the enemy was not to be out-manoeuvred. On 15 April Drew pushed his election ahead to 4 June. King was outraged. 'It is a form of highway robbery to seek to get into power by destroying right constitutional procedure.' As usual, he found grounds for optimism: 'I can see that our forces will be working hard with the Ontario Liberals. All will be welded into one and even if our men get the worst of it provincially they will be perhaps keen to get even federally.' But King had his doubts about what 'Hepburn can do and whether he will last through the campaign. I am quite certain that he has not the balance of a leader for any length of time but it would certainly be helpful to have his forces and my own working together against a common enemy.' [16]

If Mitch and Jolliffe believed they could defeat Drew, they had lost touch with reality. Although some of Drew's legislation was cosmetic, it was a creditable beginning for a minority government. Drew's position on family allowances, once 'clarified' as a question of Ontario's rights, not social policy or the fecundity of the French Canadian, was in the best tradition of Mowat, Ferguson, and even Mitch Hepburn. The Tory organization was in excellent shape. Harry Gundy and his colleagues had made certain that Drew had more money than he could spend; Major Baxter, the director of publicity, devised the most massive advertising campaign in the province's history, and long before the campaign began had purchased the best time on radio stations across the province; and Alex McKenzie had ensured before dissolution that riding associations were in fighting trim and candidates in the field.[17]

Above all, CCF rhetoric enabled Drew to polarize the issue as a straight fight between free enterprise and socialism. By the summer of 1945 Drew was harvesting the crop that he and others had so assiduously sown. Since the election of 1943 the interests opposed to 'State Socialism' had been fully mobilized by the zealous and well-financed efforts of W. Gladstone Murray, Burdick A. Trestrail, and Montague A. 'Bugsy' Sanderson, whose Reliable Exterminators included socialists and communists among the pests to be destroyed. Corporations and business organizations inundated the province with anti-socialist literature and advertisements which held out the spectre of the nationalization of industry and occasionally sank to the level of equating democratic socialism with National Socialism and Fascism. The colonel set the tone of the campaign when he solemnly stated that 'the issue to be decided is well defined. The decision between Freedom and Fascism right now at home.' In this battle for freedom Mitch Hepburn was an irrelevant irritant; but those who were tempted to vote Liberal should remember that it was Mitch Hepburn and his communist friends who had joined the socialists to bring down the government.

Jolliffe and the CCF were not optimistic. Neither he nor the party had established a clear and positive image during the two sessions. Financial resources were meagre. Although membership was up, morale had slipped since the euphoric aftermath of the near victory in 1943. The party could not find an antidote for the malignant communist cells within the big CIO unions that had delivered the vote in 1943 but had repudiated their association in 1945, or the smooth-running communist machine that had captured local trades and labour councils in many industrial ridings across the province. Most important, Jolliffe had no answer to the anti-socialist campaign of the Tories other than his faith in the intelligence and common sense of the voter.[18]

Ten days before the election those qualities failed him when he accused Drew of 'maintaining in Ontario, at this very minute, a secret political police, a paid government spy organization, a Gestapo to try and keep himself in power.' Drew admitted the existence of a special branch within the OPP, which had been created as an anti-sabotage detachment in September 1939, but he categorically denied the accusations, called Jolliffe a 'liar,' and immediately appointed Mr Justice Lebel as a royal commission. He refused Mitch's demand to delay the election until Lebel reported, but promised to resign if the charges were proven.

There was little doubt that Jolliffe's desperate gamble failed. Even if the alleged evidence contained some truth, the bizarre cloak and dagger work of D208, Captain William Osborne Dempster, hardly justified the term Gestapo. In spite of George McCullagh's passionate partisanship and anti-socialist convictions, many agreed with him when he insisted that the Honourable George Drew could not be guilty of the crime as charged and that the accusations simply demonstrated the lengths to which the socialists would go to seize power. 'Even as I speak,' he told a province-wide radio audience, 'a fresh crop of lies is being manufactured for the morning. Surely it is time for people to stop muttering in their parlors and kitchens about the dangers of the C.C.F. That won't stop them. Get out and join arms with your neighbors regardless of past affiliations.'[19]

Mitch fought on the sidelines of the battle between the forces of light and darkness, and he fought very much alone. Only his supreme self-confidence and his egotistical belief that he could work the same magic on the hustings as he had in 1934 and 1937 could explain his determination to force an election. Mitch needed time after the twists and turns since 1940 to restore confidence in his leadership and to rebuild a party shattered by those same contortions. The Liberals had no organization and in many ridings it was difficult to find candidates. There was no money as his one-time provisioners found the anti-socialist embrace of the Tories more comforting. And Mitch had no place to stand – or hide – as the Tories and the CCF polarized the electorate.

Mitch opened his campaign on 23 April in Windsor when he

released a long party platform. The Liberals promised assistance to the returning veterans; a minimum wage of $25 a week and equal pay for equal work by women; a new labour code guaranteeing workers the rights of free association and collective bargaining; improved old age pensions and the fullest cooperation with Ottawa in social security, including universal health insurance; aid to agriculture, tourism, forestry, and mining, the assumption of 90 per cent of the cost of education, scholarships for university students, and a new university in the north; and a return to a pay-as-you-go fiscal policy and ultimately a reduction in taxation. A week later he released a special manifesto promising a vigorous development policy for northern Ontario.

Although Mitch did pull out the appropriate platform planks as he toured the province, he much preferred to attack Jolliffe's 'State Socialism,' with its threats to free enterprise, and Drew's attempt to ride to power with an anti-Quebec crusade. He also denounced Drew's pledge to keep Ontario British by flooding the province with British immigrants when a major task facing the province would be to absorb into peacetime jobs the 400,000 men and women in uniform and the 375,000 in war plants. Unlike Drew, he promised the fullest cooperation with Ottawa. 'Such cooperation is not always easy,' he admitted in a 12 May broadcast, 'as I have learned from personal experience. There were times when, as Premier of this province, I didn't give it. That was one of my mistakes. I admit that I have made mistakes, but when I make them, I make big ones – good ones – that teach me not to do the same thing again.'[20]

Among the big ones he had made was his war with Mackenzie King and, although he did not explicitly refer to it, his support for conscription. 'Whether ardent imperialists like it or not we have to live in harmony with 4,500,000 French Canadians in this country,' he said in Owen Sound. A Tory vote is 'a vote for national discord,' he insisted in Barrie. What Canada and Ontario needed were governments committed to national unity, he added in Kenora, and only Mackenzie King could maintain national unity in Canada.[21]

Mitch received little assistance from Ottawa in return. Although King was willing to accept whatever assistance the provincial Liberals could provide, he suggested to cabinet that 'each of us had better arrange our own meetings, make pleasant references on the platform but not work out joint meetings, etc. though each one to do what was best.' With the deep-seated split in many ridings between the Hepburn and King factions, it was the only course to follow. Soon after the campaign started, Roebuck informed King that the two parties were cooperating at the headquarters level and in many ridings: 'We are advising that they work together but without merging or losing identity, or accepting the Hepburn licking where it can be seen that such is coming.'

In the middle of May Roebuck reported that the provincial campaign was 'going badly. They have no money. There is every evidence of a flop. Hepburn himself is getting good meetings and is struggling manfully and alone, but he is pretty much the whole campaign. His candidates are being carried by ours, and are using our committee rooms. We are making splendid progress and Hepburn evidently would like us to carry him too.' There were, he continued, many voters who would support Drew but switch to King a week later. 'Our problem, as I see it,' Roebuck concluded, 'is to keep our case as distinct as possible in the public mind from that of Hepburn and his following. We must be ready to step out of the wreck on the 4th and drive on with all vigour to the 11th.' King was more than willing to keep his distance. Although he placed a reluctant blessing on the provincial Liberals, he never mentioned Mitch by name.[22]

Except over the radio, Mitch made little attempt to woo the voters of eastern Ontario or in the industrial ridings around Toronto, Hamilton, and the Niagara peninsula, but divided his time between the north and southwestern Ontario. He boasted before dissolution that he would win every riding from North Bay to the Manitoba border, which the CCF had swept in 1943, and trusted that the Ottawa Valley voters would return to their Liberal allegiance. In the north and in southern urban ridings Mitch apparently hoped that the presence of communist candidates, running under the LPP or Labour banner, would cut into the CCF vote.

Mitch and Alex MacLeod had become good friends and when the national CCF rejected the application of the LPP for affiliation in September 1943, the communists had turned to the Liberals as allies in the war against the forces of reaction – and CCF opportunism. 'What is wrong with the C.C.F. position?' asked Leslie Morris in the *Canadian Tribune* during the 1945 session.

Nothing but the continuing habit of parallelling Drew with Hepburn ... If Jolliffe were realistic he would know that the only practical way of replacing what he is now commencing to call 'the forces of reaction represented by the Conservative Party' is to forge an alliance of the forces of Labor and the Liberals ... All the sneering in the world, all the gibing at Hepburn, all the reminiscing about Kirkland Lake and Oshawa, all the wisecracks at the L.P.P., will not gainsay the political truth that in a Labor-Liberal alliance lies the only hope of defeating the Ontario Tories and giving Ontario a majority reform administration.

The Liberal party, he wrote later, 'despite its actions against the people's interests, is responding to the pressure of progressive thought   Far from sneering, we welcome the accession of Mitchell Hepburn back to the leadership of that party as a hopeful sign pointing towards a new orientation of politics.'

Only in Windsor, however, was there a formal working agreement between what Morris described as 'the proud, pulsating, virile labour movement' and the Liberals. The UAW, which had left the Political Action Committee of the CLC, asked the three opposition party leaders to support UAW-sponsored candidates. Mitch and Morris of the LPP agreed but Jolliffe contemptuously replied that he did not want a 'mulligan stew' in the legislature. Three UAW officials, one a communist and one a fellow-traveller, were nominated and all ran as Lib-Lab candidates with Mitch's blessing. In two other ridings, however, the LPP ran against Lib-Lab candidates, and the Liberals did not withdraw in favour of any of the thirty LPP candidates, including MacLeod and Salsberg. The *Tribune* criticized the Liberals for not accepting a 'clear-cut coalition' but condemned the CCF for its 'virulent' opposition. During the campaign the communists were equally virulent in their criticism of the CCF, but did not openly endorse the Liberals.[23]

Voters did not find Mitch the lamentable and sorry figure described by George McCullagh in his radio address. Whether they turned out because of the medium or the message, Mitch played to full and overflowing houses throughout the campaign. He was subjected to some tough heckling in Windsor, North Bay, Sudbury, and Kirkland Lake. But he held his ground and insisted that he would run 'bogus' labour leaders, such as John L. Lewis and Two-Gun Martin, out of Ontario again. In Windsor he invited a CIO organizer to do his questioning from the platform. In Kirkland Lake, the hecklers even agreed to be quiet during Mitch's broadcast when he promised to debate with them on the platform when it was over.[24]

It had been a strenuous campaign, with more than fifty meetings in thirty days. Mitch returned exhausted to St Thomas on 1 June for the traditional Talbot Street parade and a rally in the Granite Arena. He had spent only two days in the riding since the campaign began and large newspaper ads were a poor substitute for his presence. If Mitch had run as an independent, the *Times-Journal* speculated, he might have had an acclamation, but his abrupt recantation and conversion gave the Tories new life.

The Tory candidate in Elgin, Fletcher Stewart 'Tommy' Thomas, ran as an independent in fact if not name. Born on a farm in Peel, a veteran and graduate of the Ontario Agricultural College, Tommy had been the county agricultural representative since 1927 – the best Elgin had ever seen Mitch once said – and knew every farmer in the county by his first name. 'I don't know much about politics,' he observed quietly, but matters had reached a sad state when the people were being told what 'somebody thinks they should have and what they will get when somebody was elected. My idea is that such things still start back home where the people themselves think out what they want and instruct their representatives accordingly. That may be an old-fashioned idea but I'll stick to it.' The politicians could make all the extravagant promises they wished; but the less government interfered the better, for in the end the taxpayers paid. Thomas never attacked Mitch personally and expressed only mild support for Drew. It was a homey, old-fashioned message and it recalled the days when Mitch talked beans and tobacco with his farmer friends along the concession roads.[25]

Mitch had boasted that he would win fifty-six seats. But as the results were fed into the Masonic Temple on election night it was immediately clear that Mitch would not return to Queen's Park. He was the first to concede defeat when the early returns showed Tommy Thomas winning every municipality in the county except the small Liberal village of Vienna. When the last votes were counted, the Liberals and their Lib-Lab allies had won only fourteen seats in the north, the Ottawa Valley, and southwestern Ontario. The only consolation was that Mitch had retained the support of 30 per cent of the electorate. The CCF fared even worse, with seven seats in the north and one in southern Ontario, and fell from 32 to 22 per cent of the popular vote. George Drew won sixty-six seats. The Tories swept southern urban Ontario, losing only two Toronto seats to the communists, kept eastern Ontario, and cut deeply into Liberal strongholds in central and southwestern Ontario. The result, King reflected, was a natural 'working out of God's law of justice and retribution on Hepburn and the Liberals for their behaviour.' But as usual God worked in secular ways for Mackenzie King. 'The Tories winning Ontario,' he predicted, should 'give us a near solid Quebec.'[26]

Mitch took his defeat gracefully. 'For the first time in my political life I have tasted defeat, but I can take it on the chin and come up smiling ... The people have spoken and I accept their verdict. I said during the election that I would not be elated by victory nor downcast by defeat. I am happy at the thought of coming back home and living with my wife and children and listening to the grass grow.' Disturbed by a few boos from the crowd, Mitch said sadly that he felt he deserved better from people he had served so long and so well. So did Tom Keith of the *Times-Journal* who called for three cheers for Mitch. With the cheers ringing in his ears, Mitch waved good night and, with a few friends, drove home to Bannockburn.

His friends on the *Times-Journal*, which had opposed him, were less gracious in their 5 June editorial. Although the riding and the paper had traditionally been Tory, the paper had supported him 'until, as time went on, his political methods and speeches began, we frankly assert, to alienate even some of his best friends. He was reckless and erratic, crude and rude in statement and we and others felt he was not the sort of political representative, especially in the high position of premier, the Elgin electors could be proud of. Slowly but surely he lost favour with his own people as well as with the Liberals of the province, and on Monday he reaped what he had sowed.' Others said more simply that over the years Mitch had become too high and mighty and had forgotten his friends in overalls.[27]

When Mitch drove home to the farm that night it was to leave politics behind. While Drew moved his machine into the federal campaign, Mitch remained mute at Bannockburn. Politics was a dirty game, he had told Coly Campbell twenty years earlier, and he was glad it was over. Mitch was not bitter in defeat and made no excuses for his failure to restore the fortunes of the party he had brought to power and done much to destroy. But he was disillusioned and saddened when his friends and neighbours in Elgin, even in Yarmouth, deserted him. There were so many tangible testimonials to his concern for the riding and so many beneficiaries of his private generosity that he felt betrayed. Even if he did not completely understand, Mitch sensed that his encore had been out of tune with the times.

Mitch was honorary president of the East Elgin Liberal Association, but he played no part in local politics. There were groundless rumours that he intended to seek the provincial and federal nominations in 1948, and even that he might be a candidate for the federal leadership when King retired in 1948. He received top billing and drew large crowds when, against the advice of his doctors, he was persuaded to speak for his friend, Henry Parker, in the 1951 provincial election. Although the fire was gone, the wit and the warm human touch remained. 'They say there will always be an

England,' the Liberal leader, Walter Thompson, told a cheering Elgin audience. 'I say there will never be another Mitch.' Mitch drew the crowds, but Tommy Thomas, a new member of Frost's cabinet, headed the poll. Apart from that brief excursion, the 1945 campaign was Mitch's last performance.

Whether he felt humiliated or betrayed or had simply lost touch with his Elgin friends, Mitch became a recluse. Unlike the old days, he was never at the ball park and, although he sent a cheque for $1,000, he was not on the platform when Syl Apps, the great Maple Leaf centre, dropped the puck in the campaign for a community centre. And when they met him in St Thomas or along the back roads at the wheel of his truck, Mitch seemed too busy or preoccupied to stop for a chat. Old friends and colleagues occasionally dropped in, and Coly Campbell, who returned from the war a brigadier and became a party organizer, was a frequent guest. Paul Martin visited with his wife and, despite Mitch's reputation, she was totally captivated. There was a great change in Mitch a few years after his retirement, Martin recalled, 'but his charm, his personality, his conviviality were still there.'[28]

For the first time in twenty years Mitch could be a full-time farmer. During the war when the farm hands who looked after the herd of Holsteins had struck for high wages, although they were paid more than the going rate, Mitch had ordered Tapsell to fire the men and sell the entire herd. After the war he restocked the farm with beef cattle bred from foundation stock from the McIntyre Ranch in Alberta. Gambling on improved pork prices, he also went heavily into swine. He replaced the famed Percherons and Clydesdales with lighter riding horses for the family and the fourteen teams of field horses with tractors. But there was no room at Bannockburn for two farm managers. Bill Tapsell soon tired of Mitch's impulsive and erratic decisions and his imperious 'I'm tellun yu' and left in 1947.

In fact, as Tapsell lamented, the farm soon 'went to hell,' particularly when Mitch decided to harvest the large sand and gravel deposits near Old Mitch's farm on Highway 4, three miles south of St Thomas, and the rich deposit of masonry sand above the onion field. He invested in a washing and grading plant and was more often at the wheel of his gravel truck or at the pit than working on the farm. While the gravel business was sometimes brisk, the profits were as meagre as they were from the farm. Over the years he sold much of his farm stock and even rented out some of his land. There was little time to listen to the grass grow.[29]

Mitch's retirement from politics did little to improve his health. The colds and bronchitis returned each winter, and he was frequently in the hospital. In the spring of 1949 he had a serious abdominal operation from which he did not recover for over a year. But in the winter of 1952 he seemed to be in excellent health as he wheeled his gravel truck to the site of the new hospital and stopped to say hello to his old friend Archie Coulter, one of the delegation that had persuaded him to run in 1926. He was struck by a heavy cold on 3 January 1953 but was up and around the next day and looking forward to a Texas holiday with Eva. That night he retired early and at 1:30 a.m. on Monday, 5 January he died in his sleep in the room in which he had been born. He was fifty-six.

The man who had made such a fortune on hot tips from his mining and broker friends, who the Tories had said pocketed $100,000 from the 1935 bond deal, had bequeathed more in his last will six months before his death than his liquid assets could provide. The most rigorous examination by National Revenue and the Comptroller of Revenue at Queen's Park could not uncover the wealth he was supposed to have acquired. His estate was valued at $297,534.46, with only $8,000 in cash and less than $5,000 in stocks. Some of the land had to be sold to pay the succession duties and provide for gifts to the veteran farm hands and legacies to Eva, the children, and his sister Irene. Eva got the one-hundred-acre Bannockburn home farm and any other three hundred acres she chose, as well as the income from the farm and the gravel business. In the end, it was to be Peter's. Whatever was left by 1976 was to go to the Elgin and St Thomas Memorial Hospital.

Colin Campbell and George Ponsford were in charge of the funeral arrangements on 7 January. After the last quiet respects were paid to Mitch at the cemetery, the men returned for a Board of Trade reception. When many of the guests departed, the wake began. Among those with his oldest and closest friends, Coly and George, were Ross Gray and Arthur Slaght, Roy Elmhirst and Bethune Smith, Bob Gaskin and Charlie Foster, Croll, Dewan, Hippel, and Cross, and Earl Rowe and George Drew. Each had his recollections: of life in dynamite alley and the nocturnal visits to Hull; of the campaign trail in '34 and '37; of the nine years at Queen's Park and the King Eddy. It was a party where Mitch would have been at the centre. 'You know,' one said as others nodded in quiet agreement, 'Mitch could still be premier of Ontario or even prime minister of Canada – if only — '

'If only ...'

If only Mitch had combined 'knowledge, serenity, a capacity to sit back and contemplate' with his 'very great determination,' Paul Martin reflected years later, 'he could have been Prime Minister of Canada, and he would have been a good one.' So impressive was Mitch the politician and so magnetic his personality, even to those who found his excesses distasteful, that many contemporaries agreed with Martin. Mitch had admirable qualities in addition to determination, but serenity and contemplation were not among them. His unquestioned natural abilities could not compensate for his deficiencies.[1]

There were so many, too many, if only's. If only Mitch had followed King's advice and found a few hours each day for rest and reflection. If only he had spent more time at Queen's Park and less with his fast and famous friends. If only he had been less sensitive to criticism and less abusive and vindictive when crossed. If only he had been less impulsive and impetuous, and had cultivated a capacity for patience and moderation. If only he had traded the street fighter's broadsword for the physician's scalpel and more often treated raw wounds with salve, not acid. If only the devil had been born in a manger.

Mitch Hepburn was an enigma: at once dogmatic and iconoclastic, impressionable and independent, vain and self-effacing. He was mean and vindictive, compassionate and generous. He was neither well educated nor well read, his knowledge of economics, history, and politics came from cursory reading, conversation, and observation. Without firm principles or guidelines, he too often permitted personal relations to govern his actions. His behaviour, like his policies, was inconsistent, an often erratic response to events. But similar comments could be said of many politicians, for as Walter Lippmann observed, 'the character in which men deal with their affairs is not fixed ... Nobody confronts every situation with the same character. His character varies in some degree through the sheer influence of time and accumulating memory, since he is not an automaton. His character varies, not only in time, but in circumstance.' As Paul Roazen said, 'everyone plays roles that events assign.'[2]

Mitch satisfied most of the definitions of an extrovert: sociability, a craving for excitement and action, impulsiveness, and an inability to control emotions. At times his hostile and aggressive behaviour, outrageous abusiveness, and self-destructive excesses, which suggested the absence of a strong sense of personal responsibility, seemed to mark a man who was mildly sociopathic or 'either drunk or crazy.'

Many of his contemporaries believed that Mitch became intoxicated with fame and power. As a young man he was something of a local celebrity, who bore a well-known name and cast the spell of his personality along the Port Stanley boardwalk. His early political success and dramatic rise to power may have nourished an incipient megalomania which, in the absence of self-discipline, became more evident as time passed. Particularly after his re-election in 1937, an authoritarian streak became more evident and more distasteful. He dominated cabinet and caucus as much by intimidation as persuasion, and he often paid too little attention to the courtesies and conventions of parliamentary and political discourse. His familiar car licence, I H I, a journalist unkindly quipped in 1942, stood for 'I Hepburn the First.'[3]

In his public life Mitch defies any conventional analysis, as do other populist rhetoricians spawned by the Depression: Aberhart, Gerry McGeer, and Duff Pattullo, H.H. Stevens and, perhaps, Duplessis, or Huey Long and Father Coughlin and, perhaps, Roosevelt in the United States. Writing of Long and Coughlin, who for a brief period rivalled Roosevelt in popularity, Allan Brinkley observed that they 'occupied a murky realm that belonged clearly to no conventional category. At times they sounded like spokesmen for the left, with their denunciations of entrenched wealth and power, their defense of the common man against the "special interests," and their insistence upon the duty of society to provide for the minimal needs of its citizens. At other times, they seemed to resonate with the themes of the right, with their opposition to socialism, communism, and statism, their emphasis upon a few hidden enemies rather than an unjust economic system, their concern with the control of money rather than ownership of the means of production.'[4]

A hatred of one evil seemed to link them together: the accumulation and entrenchment of wealth in a few hands, the power of financial institutions, the unequal distribution of purchasing power, and the crippling burden of individual and public debt. Expressed in various forms, the common solution was state control of financial institutions, breaking up the large accumulations of wealth, and a variety of 'soft money' expedients to increase purchasing power and reduce debt charges. Indeed, it is impossible to believe that Mitch was not influenced by Father Coughlin's enormously popular Sunday sermons, beamed across the river from Detroit, which by 1932 were a powerful secular appeal to pump more and cheaper money into the economy through a government-owned central bank and the nationalization of credit.

Although Mitch was not free of cynicism or demagoguery, he was not the cynical demagogue so often portrayed. His pursuit of the dead, increased taxes on corporations, the modestly progressive tilt of his personal income tax, and closing the hatch on the rich who hoped to flee the province were moderately and consistently progressive. Although his economics now seem flawed, he championed a central bank that would follow what would later be called a counter-cyclical monetary policy. He supported much of Bennett's New Deal legislation, though not the legal arguments for its constitutionality, and endorsed national unemployment insurance, minimum wages, and old age pensions. His government even put forward the controversial and radical proposal in 1935 that the state should act as residual employer. That he was also a fiscal conservative, committed to a balanced budget and an escape from crippling interest charges, was not surprising with debt charges absorbing 25 per cent of provincial revenues. Nor was it surprising in a provincial treasurer who had an accountant as his chief adviser, not the Keynesian economists who finally penetrated Ottawa very late in the decade.

Mitch's legislative accomplishments in the five sessions before the war were substantial. He reduced the cost and numbers of boards and commissions, streamlined the civil service, restructured the judiciary, and rationalized departmental organizations. He increased the scope and benefits of most provincial social services and assumed some of the municipal burden. He built hospitals, improved care for the insane, and flirted with medical insurance. Between 1935 and 1941 the percentage contribution to education doubled. Increased grants to rural and Catholic schools, and the much-needed reorganization of the thousand rural school districts helped equalize educational opportunities. In the best populist, if not pedagogical, tradition he decentralized management of curriculum, exams, and promotion, and to the dismay of the universities, allowed entrance for the best students on principals' recommendations.

Mitch's hostility to the CIO and the charge that he was in the camp of the capitalists tended to overshadow his attempts to stimulate economic development and employment in the forest industry, the mines, the highways, and the farm. Mitch was not an enemy of labour, organized or unorganized. He might have said that some of his strongest supporters in 1937 worked in the St Thomas railway yards and the Hamilton steel mills. In the 1930s, like most of his contemporaries, Mitch did not believe in the closed shop or the automatic check-off; workers had the right to organize and to strike, but unions did not have the right to demand membership or pickets the right to stop others from working. As the long-awaited recovery brought jobs and larger pay cheques, he was outraged when union organizers seized the opportunity to strike. As premier he was ready to protect both property and the right to work. As an employer he responded to a strike of his dairymen by firing them and going out of the dairy business. However, while the codes of the 1935 Industrial Standards Act and the 1937 Industry and Labour Board were not landmarks of progressive legislation, they were positive steps which were not forced on a reluctant government by popular demand. By 1942 he had turned another corner sharply. Despite long and determined lobbying by the business community, in 1943 the Conant govenrment passed the collective bargaining legislation which Mitch had initiated. If only he had realized in 1937 that it was organization and protected collective bargaining that could equalize the power structure in industrial relations.

And if only Mitch had learned how to deal with Mackenzie King his political career would have been vastly different, though he may not have come closer to those heights so many predicted. If Mitch had realized the extent of King's paranoia and, in the words of Hugh Keenleyside, that King's approach to people was controlled by his 'suspicious mind' in which lay 'the unvarying question, "What can this man do for me, or against me?"' If Mitch had realized that King opposed his election as leader in 1930 not only because of his lifestyle or age but also because he was a threat and if he had known that King's letter of October 1935 was not a declaration of independence but of war, he might have been able to devise a personal and political strategy to counter King's implacable hostility and Machiavellian tactics.

But the result would have been much the same. The personal qualities Mitch needed to deal with King – patience, self-discipline, forward planning, a talent for semantic ambiguity – were precisely those he lacked. King had declared war, but he refused to fight in the street. Mitch's broadsword could not dint the defences of a man who donned the armour of God, but whose commitment to a higher calling always seemed to serve some more secular end. Mitch's relations with Mackenzie King drove him to despair and did much to destroy his precarious equilibrium.

If only Mackenzie King had been willing to share power, to accept Mitch's companionship in the battle for the Liberal party, to use his undeniable talents for persuasion and accommodation on the boy from Yarmouth, Mitch Hepburn's career might have been profoundly altered. On the other hand, if only Mitch had gone to the people in the gloomy fall of 1941 and received the sweeping mandate everyone predicted, both his and King's career might have had a much different ending.

But there are no ifs in history or in life, and Mitch was not one to look back and wonder if only ...

Notes

This volume is much shorter than earlier drafts. The notes have been substantially reduced. The citations have been shortened as much as possible, and since many collections have been reorganized I have not given full volume, file citations. Anyone wishing to examine the longer version of the text, and particularly the notes, for a fuller elaboration or documentation may consult an earlier draft deposited in the York University Archives.

ABBREVIATIONS

AO	Archives of Ontario
ACFEO	Association Canadienne-Française d'Education d'Ontario
BCA	Bank of Canada Archives
CTPA	Catholic Taxpayers' Association
D. Hist.	Directorate of History, National Defence Headquarters, Department of National Defence
FP	*Financial Post*
GM	*Globe and Mail*
HCD	House of Commons, *Debates*
HP	Hepburn Papers
HQA	Hydro Quebec Archives
JLAO	*Journals of the Legislative Assembly of Ontario*
KD	King Diary
KP	King Papers
LD	Lambert Diary
ME	*Mail and Empire*
NAC	National Archives of Canada
OH	Ontario Hydro
OHA	Ontario Hydro Archives
PC	Private Collection
PCO	Privy Council Office

STTJ   St Thomas *Times-Journal*
TDS   Toronto *Daily Star*
TET   Toronto *Evening Telegram*
USNA   United States National Archives
WSU   Wayne State University, Archives of Labor and Urban History

PREFACE

1 Peter Gay, *Freud: A Life for Our Time* (New York 1988), xv

CHAPTER 1: 'INTO THE PROMISED LAND'

1 Parochial Register, Newborough, Fifeshire (courtesy of Mrs Jean Griffin,
   London, Ontario). In his will Andrew refers to 'a boy who has resided with
   me and known by the name of Michael Hepburn but whose proper name is
   Michael Broom' (AO, Surrogate Court Registers, Middlesex County, Will
   dated 18 Sept. 1850). The early land transactions are also in the name of
   Michael and Mitchell Broom (Yarmouth Township Land Records, Registry
   Office, St Thomas).
2 Yarmouth Township Land Records; NAC, Manuscript Census on Microfilm,
   1861, 1871; *Elgin County Atlas* (Toronto 1877)
3 Records of the St Thomas Cemetery; HP, Will Mustard to W.F. Hepburn, 1
   Oct. 1894, 4 May 1899. A Fulton family genealogy prepared by Kenneth A.
   Fulton states that William was born on 23 Dec. in 1870 or 1871 (*The James
   Fulton Family 1867–1964*, privately printed). Interviews, Don Cosens, Jean
   Griffin
4 AO, Surrogate Court Records, Will No. 2235 (Eliza Hepburn); HP, Thirza R.
   Moulton to W.F. Hepburn, 21 Aug. 1894; W.F. Hepburn to Margaret
   Fulton, 14 Sept. 1893
5 *St. Thomas City Directory*, various years; Records of the Wellington Street
   Public School, Elgin County District School Board, St Thomas
6 On the Orwell affair see Ontario Legislative Assembly, *Report of the
   Commissioner ... into the conduct of W. Andrews* (Toronto 1909), which
   contains Hepburn's statement of 22 September 1906 (obviously written for
   him); St Thomas and London papers Sept.–Oct. 1906; St Thomas *Evening
   Journal*, 8 Nov. 1906. Butler was obviously persuaded to incriminate himself
   in the interests of the Tory party.
7 HP, W.F. Hepburn to Margaret Hepburn, Feb. 1907; Alex Darrach to W.F.
   Hepburn, 4 May 1908; Fulton Papers, Margaret Hepburn to Sam Fulton, 9
   Mar. 1909
8 General Register, St Thomas Collegiate Institute; CBC interview, George
   Gray; *The Collegian*, St Thomas Collegiate Institute Library. All dates for

his employment with the Bank of Commerce were provided by the Canadian Imperial Bank of Commerce, Department of Personnel Records. The culprit in the apple-throwing episode was Claude Dunn, who was not a student. Mitch joked when he became premier that he imagined Greer, then chief inspector of schools, would be interested in seeing him again (*Border Cities Star*, 25 June 1934).

9 AO, Drew Papers, D.G. Macpherson to Drew, 16 Aug. 1936. Macpherson was the officer commanding C squadron.

10 Fulton Papers, Sam Fulton to Clara Wismer, 24 Aug. 1915, 6 May 1917; HP, Frank Palmer to Hepburn, 17 Oct. 1936; NAC, Dept. of Militia and Defence, II B4, vol. 8, Register of Officers, 25th Regiment.

11 The reconstruction of Hepburn's military service has benefited from the invaluable assistance of Barbara Wilson of the National Archives and the sleuthing of George Drew who used his friends in the service to find the records, including those of his enlistment and discharge from the RAF (AO, Drew Papers, Misc. Documents, Hepburn File). Drew's interest was provoked by Mitch's stretching of the truth. His entry in the *Parliamentary Guide* read: 'Lieut. Can. Infantry and served Royal Air Force, 1918.' More misleading was his statement that 'I qualified as a Lieutenant and served in the Royal Air Force, but, unfortunately was injured and did not get overseas' (HP, Hepburn to O.L. Dubeau, 16 Feb. 1932). Mitch stated that when he joined the Royal Air Force 'after some delay was accepted as a cadet pilot and started training at Long Branch.' Drew's information, secured privately from the RAF, was that 'cadet pilots were never officially recorded as Air Mechanics 3rd Class,' the rank Mitch held. Drew's suggestion that, in fact, Hepburn had failed to go with the Fort Garry and was later drafted was as misleading as Mitch's gloss of the truth. Corrected by Colonel D.G. Macpherson, Drew replied: 'This correction does not, of course, change the general effect of his mis-statement in regard to service, as there is no question about his conscription and the fact that he was drafted into the Western Ontario training regiment at London in May of 1918. I do not intend to labour the point at all, but I must admit that it did get under my skin when he appealed to the veteran vote on the ground of his supposed effort to get overseas and his service as a cadet pilot, which he never had' (AO, Drew Papers, Drew to Macpherson, 20 Aug. 1936).

12 HP, Dr. G.C. Brink, report on medical examination, Nov. 28, 1932

13 Fulton Papers, Sam Fulton to Clara Wismer, 9 Sept. 1918; *TDS*, 22 June 1934

14 Yarmouth Township Land Records; drafts of the will in HP, Personal; HP, W.F. Hepburn to Hepburn, 20 Apr. 1921, 23 Sept. 1924; *STTJ*, 15 Oct. 1922; HP, Hepburn to Col. J.A. Currie, 1 Mar. 1927. Mitch may have received between $15,000 and $20,000 in bonds (interview, Colin Campbell). Mitch remained in touch with, and occasionally visited, his father, who

settled in Minnesota, married and had children, but does not seem to have been divorced. Mitch never mentioned his father and let pass uncorrected statements that he had died when he was a youth. In an interview with John Marshall after his election as leader of the party, Mitch said that Marshall could ask him about his mother, but not his father (John Marshall, *Shelburne Free Press and Economist*, 2 Apr. 1977).

15 *STTJ*, 29 June 1927, 6 Sept. 1930; HP, Hepburn to Inspector of Income Tax, London, 28 Jan. 1930
16 Interview, Pete Lang; KP, Darrach to King, 4 Feb. 1927
17 *STTJ*, 19 Oct. 1925
18 KP, Darrach to King, 4 Feb. 1927; *STTJ*, 15–28 Oct. 1925
19 KP, Darrach to King, 4 Feb. 1927; *STTJ*, 28 July–18 Sept 1926; HP, Hepburn to Peter Heenan, 9 Oct. 1926; KP, Darrach to King, 16 Sept. 1926; *TET*, 23 Sept. 1926; KP, McNish to King, 20 Sept. 1926

CHAPTER 2: 'LET THE RAFTERS RING'

1 Interview, W.H. Taylor; HP, Arthur Conley to Hepburn, 8 Dec. 1926; Hepburn to Conley, 10 Dec. 1926; KD, 9 Dec. 1926
2 KP, Darrach to King, 6 Jan. 1927; King to Darrach, 21 Jan. 1927; J.G. McLean to King, 13, 29 Jan. 1927; King to McLean, 18 Jan. 1927
3 The divisions were on 14 Feb., 15 Mar., 23 Mar., 11, 13 Apr. 1927. HP, Hepburn to A. McIntyre Bruce, 25 Mar. 1927; KD, 13 Apr. 1927
4 *FP*, 18 Mar., 15 Apr. 1927; *HCD*, 5 Apr. 1927: 1924–5; HP, Hepburn to Darrach, 9 Apr. 1927
5 HP, Hepburn to Blake Miller, 23, 29 Mar. 1928; Hepburn to W.H. Hammond, 14 Apr. 1928; *HCD*, 17 Apr. 1928: 2112–15. Blake Miller, the MLA for Elgin East, had informed Mitch that 239 shares had sold on the New York exchange at $1,970 (HP, Miller to Hepburn, 20 Mar. 1928).
6 KP, T.B. Macaulay to King, 30 May 1928; King to Macaulay, 5 June 1928; *HCD*, 5 Mar. 1929: 1001. Mitch and the Progressives fought a similar battle with Bell Telephone from 1927 to 1929 and ultimately forced Bell to accept an amendment giving the Board of Railway Commissioners power to approve any new issues. The *Canadian Annual Review* (1927–8: 94) described it as 'one of the most determined battles of the Session.' Mitch had promised the Toronto City Council he would do all in his power to defeat the bill, and he did (HP, Hepburn to Toronto City Council, n.d.).
7 United Farmers of Ontario (UFO), Minutes of the Annual Meeting, 12 Dec. 1923; 9, 10 Dec. 1925; Minutes of the Executive Committee, 10 Feb. 1926
8 *Farmers' Sun*, 1, 8 15 Sept. 1927; *TDS*, 8 Sept. 1927
9 *Farmers' Sun*, 27 Oct. 1927; HP, Hepburn to Jones, 8 Nov. 1927; *TDS*, *Globe*, *STTJ*, 30 Nov. 1927; *TDS*, 12 Dec. 1927

10 UFO, Minutes of the Annual Meeting, 6–8 Dec. 1927; *Farmers' Sun*, 8 Dec. 1927; *Globe*, 9 Dec. 1927

11 *TDS*, 15 Dec. 1927

12 *STTJ*, 21 Feb. 1927; NAC, Dept. of Agriculture, Report ... by G.E. MacIntosh, 8 Mar. 1927. Data on agriculture may be found in Ontario, Dept. of Agriculture, *Annual Report of the Statistics Branch*. An excellent annual review of farming conditions is provided by the reports of the county agricultural representatives (AO, Dept. of Agriculture, Agricultural Representatives Annual Reports).

13 HP, Hepburn to Rodgers, 1 Mar. 1927

14 Dominion Bureau of Statistics, *Historical Series of Tobacco Statistics* (Ottawa 1950); *Globe*, 9 Dec. 1927; NAC, Dept. of Agriculture, Archibald to Motherwell, 29 Nov. 1927; Report of the Tobacco Inquiry, Mar. 1928; *STTJ*, 17 Dec. 1927, 16 Jan. 1928; *TDS*, 21 Dec. 1927; *Farmers' Sun*, 12 Jan. 1928; HP, Hancock to Hepburn, 9 Dec. 1927

15 *HCD*, 2 Mar. 1928: 960; *Winnipeg Free Press*, 24 Dec. 1930

16 HP, Hepburn to W. Parson, 26 Mar. 1927; Hepburn to John Thornicroft, 1 Mar. 1927; J.H. Becker to Hepburn, 22 Apr. 1928; Hepburn to Gray, 24 Mar. 1928; *HCD*, 25 Mar. 1930: 133

17 HP, Hepburn to George H. Jackson, 4, 12 Mar. 1929; Hepburn to G. Kolb, 23 May 1929; Hepburn to P.J. O'Meara, 13 June 1929

18 Hepburn to J.A. Macpherson, 26 Feb. 1927; HP, Unorganized, 10 Aug. 1927

19 HP, Hepburn to Euler, 6 Feb. 1930; Hepburn to W. Stapleton, 3 Apr. 1930; *STTJ*, 17 Feb., 18 June, 25 July 1930; HP, Blakestock to Hepburn, 16 Apr. 1928

20 Ottawa *Citizen*, Ottawa *Journal*, 2 Dec. 1929; Regina *Leader*, 9 Dec. 1929

21 HP, Hepburn to Ponsford, 1 Mar. 1927; Hepburn to L.M. Bradley, 21 Apr. 1928; Hepburn to E. Lee, 26 Apr. 1928; Hepburn to C. Harris, 16 Feb. 1929; Bradley to Hepburn, 22 Feb. 1927; Hepburn to W.F. Free, Secretary of the Elgin United Farmers, 22 May 1928; Brown to Hepburn, 22 May 1930; Rutherford to Hepburn, 5 Mar. 1930

22 *HCD*, 9 Apr. 1929: 1425; HP, Hepburn to Rutherford, 5 Mar. 1929; Hepburn to Cooper, 5 Mar. 1929

23 *ME*, 27, 29 Apr. 1929; KP, Deachman to Haydon, 29 Apr. 1929; Haydon to Deachman, 30 Apr. 1929

24 See Ronald F. Rennie, *The Tariff in Dairy Products* (Trade Research Committee, Madison 1933); Joseph M. Jones, *Tariff Retaliation: Repercussions of the Hawley-Smoot Tariff* (Philadelphia 1934); Ontario, Dept. of Agriculture, *Annual Report of the Statistics Branch*; G.E. Britnell, *Canadian Agriculture in Peace and War* (Stanford 1962), 64; AO, Dept. of Agriculture, Agricultural Representatives Annual Reports, 1928–30.

25 HP, Dunning to Hepburn, 3 Jan. 1930; W.G. Thompson to Hepburn, 3 Feb.

1930; K.W. McKay to Hepburn, 9 Dec. 1929; Hepburn to R. Deachman, 23 Jan. 1930; Hepburn to W. Clark and others, 25 Mar. 1930; *Globe*, 23 Mar. 1930

26 *HCD*, 11 Mar.: 514; *Globe*, 12 Mar. 1930; *TDS*, 5 Apr. 1930

27 HP, Hepburn to Deachman, 23 Jan. 1930; *TDS*, 5 Apr. 1930; KD, 20 Mar. 1930; *HCD*, 8 May 1930: 1881

28 See H. Blair Neatby, *William Lyon Mackenzie King, The Lonely Heights* (Toronto 1963), 287, 315; KP, Spence to King, 6 Jan. 1930; HP, Hepburn to W.E. Gundy and Wellington Hay, 21 Jan. 1930; KP, Darrach to King, 10 Mar. 1930; King to Darrach, 15 Mar. 1930.

29 *STTJ*, 19 Apr. 1930; London *Free Press*, 30 Apr. 1930; Carty Papers, n.d. n. sig.; Carty Diary, 9 Feb. 1935; HP, Hepburn to W.R. Macdonald, 8 May 1930; AO, Dept. of Agriculture, Agricultural Representatives Annual Reports, 1930; *Farmers' Sun*, May–June 1930. The unsigned report in the Carty Papers was obviously the result of some private investigation. By the time the Tories picked up the story nine months later the tracks had been covered. Although one police officer was prepared to swear it was Mitch, W.H. Kippen, the broker, was prepared to swear it was not. Smith's story was that his companion, a St Thomas friend, thought it would be a lark to give Mitch's name, and was prepared to say that 'If any inconvenience is caused Hepburn he will not hesitate to publicly explain.'

30 *STTJ*, 31 May 1930; HP, Hepburn to Parker, 28 June, 14 July 1930; Hepburn to Deachman, 23, 28 June, 7, 14 July 1930; Hepburn to S.V. Seversen, R.A. McAllister, 9 June 1930; Hepburn to Parker, 9 July 1930

31 *STTJ*, 17, 22 June 1930; Power Papers, Power to J.A. Glen, 2 July 1930; HP, Hepburn to Lapointe, 9 June 1930; Lapointe to Hepburn, 30 June 1930; interview, Colin Campbell; Ferguson Papers, Ferguson to Borden, 6 Aug. 1930; KD, 17 June 1930

32 *STTJ*, 31 May, 21, 24 July 1930; Bennett Papers, Ford to Bennett, 27 May 1930

33 KP, Darrach to King, 2 Jan. 1931; Reid Papers, Mitchell Hepburn File; interview, Colin Campbell; *Winnipeg Free Press*, 24 Dec. 1930

CHAPTER 3: 'A JOSHUA WHO WILL REALLY DO THE TRICK'

1 Dafoe Papers, Gregory to Dafoe, 6 Aug. 1930; KP, Power to King, 9 Jan. 1931; *HCD*, 18 Sept. 1930: 407

2 See Peter Oliver, 'The Ontario Liberal Party in the 1920s: A Study in Political Collapse,' in *Public and Private Persons: The Ontario Political Culture 1914–1934* (Toronto 1975), 128–54.

3 KP, Bowman to King, 28 Apr. 1929; Haydon to King, 17 Sept. 1929

4 CTPA Papers, Martin Quinn to George Lynch-Staunton, 13 Oct. 1933; Carty

Diary, 4 Jan. 1934; Peter Oliver, *G. Howard Ferguson: Ontario Tory* (Toronto 1977), 362

5 KP, Sinclair to King, 4 Dec. 1928; McGuire to Haydon, 5 Nov. 1928; KD, 7 Oct. 1929

6 HP, Young to Hepburn, 10 Feb. 1938; Campbell to Hepburn, 25 Sept. 1930; Martin Papers, interviews, A-16, side 1; *TDS*, 21 Oct. 1930

7 *STTJ*, 24 Oct. 1930; *ME, TDS*, 31 Oct. 1930; KP, Parker to King, 21 Nov. 1930; Martin Papers, interviews, A-16, side 2

8 KP, Parker to King, 3 Nov. 1930; KD, 5 Nov. 1930

9 King invited Martin to tea at Kingsmere and attempted, Martin recalled, 'to dissuade me from actively campaigning on Hepburn's behalf' and said that he did not like Mitch's private life or his drinking friends (Martin Papers, interviews, A-16, side 2).

10 Donnelly Papers, Donnelly to Hepburn, 26 Nov. 1930; AO, Roebuck Papers, Hepburn to Roebuck, 26 Nov. 1930; Southam to Roebuck, 14 Nov. 1930; Roebuck to Southam, 28 Nov. 1930; Roebuck to Deachman, 4 Nov. 1930; Roebuck to Hepburn, 2 Dec. 1930

11 KD, 13 Feb. 1930; Dafoe Papers, Dafoe to Harry Sifton, 6 Dec. 1930; KP, King to Parker, 6 Nov. 1930; Parker to King, 21 Nov.; KD, 25 Nov. 1930; *Globe*, 28 Nov., 4 Dec. 1930

12 KP, Johnson to King, 2 Dec. 1930; Parker to King, 1 Dec. 1930

13 KP, King to Parker, 4 Dec. 1930; King to Johnson, 4 Dec. 1930; Johnson to King, 8 Dec. 1930; King to Johnson, 10 Dec. 1930; King to Sinclair, 11 Dec. 1930; Dafoe Papers, H. Sifton to Dafoe, 8 Dec. 1930

14 KP, King to A. Darrach, 27 Nov. 1930; A. Rogers to King, 11 Dec. 1930; B.H. McCreath to King, 8 Nov. [sic Dec.] 1930; Parker to King, 15 Dec. 1930; Dafoe Papers, H. Sifton to Dafoe, 15 Dec. 1930

15 *ME*, 16 Dec. 1930; *TDS*, 27 Nov., 8 Dec. 1930

16 *Farmers' Sun*, 13 Nov. 1930; Dafoe Papers, H. Sifton to Dafoe, 1 Dec. 1930

17 *Globe*, 18 Dec. 1930

18 *TDS, Globe, TET, ME*, 17, 18 Dec. 1930; *STTJ*, 23 Dec. 1930; HP, Donnelly to Hepburn, 12 Apr. 1934; interview, Colin Campbell

19 *ME, TDS, TET, Globe*, 18 Dec. 1930

20 *Globe*, 28 Nov. 1930; AO, Roebuck Papers, Roebuck to Tweed, 4 Dec. 1930; *Globe*, 13 Dec. 1930; Dafoe Papers, H. Sifton to Dafoe, Thursday [18 Dec. 1930]; *TDS, Globe, ME*, 17–19 Dec. 1930. Sinclair's last-minute withdrawal puzzled many Liberals. See KP, Sinclair to King, 30 Dec. 1930; H. Johnson to King, 18 Feb. 1931; Dafoe Papers, H. Sifton to Dafoe, Thursday [18 Dec. 1930]).

21 Interviews, Colin Campbell, George Fulford (who stated that he signed the paper on Hardy's behalf); Donnelly Papers, Hardy to Donnelly, 17 Sept. 1931; *TDS, Globe, TET, ME*, London *Free Press*, 17–19 Dec. 1930

CHAPTER 4: 'RISE DEAD MEN AND FIGHT'

1 Cited in *STTJ*, 23 Dec. 1930; KP, B.H. McReath to King, 22 Dec. 1930; W. Sinclair to King, 30 Dec. 1930; *ME*, 23 Dec. 1930; *TDS*, 18, 22 Dec. 1930; Dafoe Papers, H. Sifton to Dafoe, 19 Dec. 1930; KP, King to Hepburn, 18, 31 Dec. 1930; KD, 17 Dec. 1930. John Marshall of the Toronto *Star* and other reporters were interviewing Mitch the next morning in his hotel room when King's telegram arrived. Mitch passed it over to them with the comment, 'Well, he finally had to do it' (John Marshall, 'Reflections,' *Shelburne Free Press and Economist*, 2 Apr. 1977).

2 Henry Papers, Ferguson to Henry, 17 Apr. 1931; Henry to Ferguson, 27 Apr. 1931; NAC, Sissons Papers, Henry to C.B. Sissons, 9 Aug. 1921

3 Dafoe Papers, Dafoe to Sifton, 6 Dec. 1930; *ME*, *TDS*, Hamilton *Spectator*, 9 Jan.–12 Feb. 1931; KP, Johnson to King, 20 Dec. 1930; King to Hepburn, 13 Feb. 1931; Roebuck Papers, Roebuck to Hepburn, 13 Jan. [*sic* 13 Feb.], 1931; KP, Power to King, 9 Jan., 10 Feb. 1931; *ME*, 27 Apr. 1931; KD, 25 Apr. 1931

4 Interview, Colin Campbell; *TDS*, *Globe*, 18 Dec. 1930; Dafoe Papers, H. Sifton to Dafoe, Thursday [18 Dec. 1930]; KP, King to Sinclair, 18 Dec. 1930; Sinclair to King, 30 Dec. 1930; Henry Papers, Ferguson to Henry, 26 Feb. 1931; *Canadian Annual Review* 1930–1: 110; *ME*, 2 Mar. 1931

5 For a very thorough study of Beauharnois, see T.D. Regehr, *The Beauharnois Scandal: A Story of Canadian Entrepreneurship and Politics* (Toronto 1990). The fullest account of the ownership and relationship among the private power companies is *Seventh Annual Report of the Power Authority of the State of New York*, 1938. See also R.B. Belfield, 'The Niagara Frontier: The Evolution of Electric Power Systems in New York and Ontario, 1880–1935' (University Microfilms International, PHD thesis, University of Pennsylvania 1981); *Moody's Manual of Investments: Public Utilities*, 1936; John Dales, *Hydroelectricity and Industrial Development: Quebec, 1898–1940* (Cambridge 1953).

6 OH, Minutes, Hydro-Electric Power Commission of Ontario, (hereafter Ontario Hydro), 1928–1930

7 KP, J.H. Spence to King, 12 Jan. 1929; H. Blair Neatby, *William Lyon Mackenzie King, The Lonely Heights 1924–1932* (Toronto 1963), 262; OH, Minutes, Ontario Hydro, 30 May, 28 Oct., 27 Nov. 1929; PC, Roebuck Papers, Memorandum to the Chairman Re: Power Contracts with Quebec Corporations, Hogg and Jeffery, 5 Mar. 1935

8 Houston Standard Publications, *Annual Financial Review (Canada)*, 1930; *ME*, 11 July 1931; *HCD*, 22 May 1930, 2383; Sweezey Papers, Sweezey to Hepburn, 1 May 1930

9 *Globe*, 22 Apr. 1931

10 KP, Hardy to King, 5 May 1931; Murphy Papers, Murphy to Sinclair, 11
   May 1931; Sinclair to Murphy, 22 May 1931. Hardy bought 300
   Beauharnois shares in May 1931 and Spence also owned stock. Mrs Harriet
   Sweezey had also bought 250 shares of MacLaren in June 1929 at $375 a
   share (Sweezey Papers, n.d.).

11 *HCD*, 19 May 1931: 1732; *STTJ*, 29 Apr., 22 May 1931; *Globe*, 22 May
   1931; Gregory Papers, Gregory to Hepburn, 29 May 1931; Henry Papers,
   Memorandum respecting statements made in a paper by M.F.A. Gaby ...
   referring to an address by Mr. Mitchell F. Hepburn, n.d.

12 KP, Rutherford to King, 12 June 1931; King to Hepburn, 10 June, 17 June
   1931; Eva Hepburn to King, 12 June 1931; King to Eva Hepburn, 25 June
   1931; *STTJ*, 22 July 1931; HP, Medical Report, 28 Nov. 1932

13 Canada, House of Commons, Special Committee on the Beauharnois Power
   Project, *Reports and Minutes of Proceedings and Evidence* (1931), 325–6, 823;
   KD, 17 July 1931; Sweezey Papers, Sweezey to Parker, 7 Feb. 1931; Sweezey
   Papers, Memorandum No. 2, 3 Oct. 1931. In the above memorandum
   Sweezey or another Beauharnois officer insisted that they were pressed to
   provide a contribution and believed the $125,000 to Aird was for the party.
   When the matter came before the Commons committee 'it was suggested'
   that Beauharnois should state it was given as a bonus to Aird and if the
   company did so there would be no further inquiries concerning the
   contributions to the Liberals, all this 'in order to vindicate a certain highly
   placed member of the conservative Party in Ontario, as it had been
   suggested in political circles that he personally had benefitted by this
   subscription.' Beauharnois refused. At that point Aird revealed he still had
   the bonds, but the memorandum observes that since Aird 'had apparently
   deposited the bonds, or part of them, in the bank only the day previous to
   his testimony' it appeared that they 'had not been in his hands up to that
   time.' However, fearing the vengeance of the Conservative party, which
   certainly could at any time have ruined the company, Beauharnois instructed
   its attorney to stop a cross-examination which was rapidly breaking down
   Aird's testimony. Aird's letters to J.A. O'Brien of Madawaska suggested that
   he, his father, and J.H. Black were involved in the lobbying. As he wrote on
   23 Aug. 1928, Black had seen Ferguson 'and received his word that he will
   do everything to help us in this scheme. This, of course is the most
   optimistic thing we have ever received and I am highly delighted. As you
   know, the whole matter revolves around the Premier' (PC, Roebuck Papers,
   copy, Aird to O'Brien, 22, 28 Aug. 1928). I am persuaded that the Aird
   money was for the party, and that another $200,000, as charged by others,
   found its way to the Tory campaign fund. That was a small percentage for
   an enterprise of such size and importance. Only the danger of damage to the
   party could explain Manion's wire to Bennett when Sinclair demanded an

investigation: 'ADVISE YOU SEE MR. AIRD. CUT OFF MR. SINCLAIR INVESTIGATION. WILL SEE YOU TUESDAY' (Bennett Papers, 7 Aug. 1931). In addition to the Commons inquiry there was also a Senate inquiry in 1932 and Ontario royal commissions (discussed later) in 1932 and 1934.

14 *Globe*, *TDS*, 28 July, 6, 7, Aug. 1931

15 KP, Hardy to King, 25 July 1931; Parker to King, 28 July 1931; Moore to King, 27 July 1931; Young to King, 14 Aug. 1931; HP, Young to Hepburn, 13 Aug. 1931; Chalmers Papers, Chalmers to J.B. McLean, 25 Aug. 1931

16 Donnelly Papers, Hepburn to Donnelly, 11 Aug. 1931; KD, 1 Sept., 23 Apr. 1931

17 HP, Charles Robertson to Hepburn, 14 Aug. 1931; Murphy Papers, Murphy to Sanderson, 3 Oct. 1932; KP, B.H. McCreath to King, 10 Nov. 1931; *Globe*, 12 Oct. 1931; KP, McCreath to King, 12 Oct. 1931; KD, 12 Oct. 1931

18 London *Free Press*, *ME*, 21, 22 Oct. 1931; HP, Hardy to Hepburn, 23 Nov. 1931; KP, Hardy to King, 20 Nov. 1931

19 HP, *Speeches and Speech Notes*, n.d.; Hardy to Hepburn, 3 Dec. 1931

20 HP, Rutherford to Hepburn, 23 Oct. 1931; AO, Roebuck Papers, Roebuck to Hepburn, 18 Aug., 30 Sept. 1931

21 *ME*, 7 Oct. 1931; *Globe*, 12 Oct. 1931

22 *ME*, 27 Oct. 1931; HP, Hardy to Hepburn, 12 Nov. 1931; KD, 15, 16 Nov. 1931

23 *ME*, 19 Nov. 1931; Power Papers, Johnson to Power, 2, 9 Dec. 1931; HP, Hardy to Hepburn, 20 Nov. 1931; McGuire to Hepburn, 21 Nov. 1931

24 *TDS*, 18 Dec. 1930; KP, McCreath to King, 22 Dec. 1930; HP, Nixon to Hepburn, 24 Nov. 1931; Hardy to Hepburn, 3 Dec. 1931; Drury Papers, Nixon to W. Mackenzie, Feb. 1932, cited in John R. Campbell, 'The Dirt Farmer from Brant: Harry Corwin Nixon 1919–1934' (BA thesis, Wilfrid Laurier University 1980), 66. 'Nixon and I agreed to go with Hepburn if he left it [booze] out of speeches altogether' wrote William Newman, MLA (HP, Newman to C. Foreman, 16 Dec. 1933).

CHAPTER 5: 'I SWING TO THE LEFT'

1 HP, Hepburn to T. McQuesten, 19 May 1932

2 *Canadian Annual Review*, 1932: 690

3 Henry Papers, W.J. Stewart, mayor of Toronto, to Henry, 21 Sept. 1931

4 Ontario, Dept. of Agriculture, *Annual Report*, 1930–2; AO, Dept. of Agriculture, Agricultural Representatives Annual Reports, 1930–1; Canada, Dept. of Agriculture, *The Economic Analyst*, 1929–32, *passim*

5 See James Struthers, *No Fault of Their Own: Unemployment and the Canadian Welfare State 1914–1941* (Toronto 1983), 44.

6 Stewart Bates, *Financial History of Canadian Governments* (Ottawa 1939)

7 AO, Treasury Dept., Series II-3, H.A. Cotnam and W. Campbell, Report to the Provincial Treasurer on Sinking Funds and Debt Retirement ..., 2 Mar. 1936; Henry Papers, Henry to W. Finlayson, 31 Dec. 1931. The correspondence with the banks may be found in AO, Treasury Dept., files 1612–10 and 603/1.

8 *HCD*, 22 Feb. 1932: 384; 3 Mar. 1932: 748; KD, 2 Mar. 1932; House of Commons, Select Committee on Banking and Commerce, Minutes, Reference: Price of Gasoline, 1932

9 *HCD*, 17 Mar. 1932, 1222; KD, 17 Mar. 1932

10 Bennett Papers, Memorandum for the Hon. R.B. Bennett: re Policy Holders Association & Sun Life, 16 Apr. 1931; *Report of the Superintendent of Insurance for Canada ... 1928* (Ottawa 1929), vol. 2: xxxi; Bennett Papers, Finlayson to Bennett, 19, 26 Sept., 9 Oct. 1931; *Journal of Commerce*, Dec. 1931, Jan. 1932

11 Spry Papers, Diary, 6 Oct. 1931; Ferguson Papers, Bennett, wire in code, to Ferguson, 18 Jan. 1932; Ferguson to Bennett, 25 Jan. 1932; interview, Sherwood Walters

12 *HCD*, 14 Mar. 1932: 1102, 1106

13 HP, Parker to Hepburn, 19 Mar. 1932; Young to Hepburn, 24 Mar. 1932; Philpott to Hepburn, 6 Apr. 1932; Donnelly to Hepburn, 6 Apr. 1932; Macdonald to Hepburn, 4 Apr. 1932; Hepburn to Macdonald, 19 Apr. 1932

14 *ME*, 1 Apr. 1932; HP, Hardy to Hepburn, 7 Apr. 1932

15 *ME*, 13 Apr. 1932; Bennett Papers, G. Reid to A.W. Merriam, 13 Apr. 1932; *Hush*, 14 Apr. 1932; KP, Rogers to King, 13 Apr. 1932; King to Rogers, 16 Apr. 1932

16 HP, Johnson to Hepburn, 19 Apr. 1932; KP, Johnson to King, 14 June 1932

17 The account of the election is based on the four city papers, 11–30 May 1932

18 H. Blair Neatby, *William Lyon Mackenzie King: The Prism of Unity 1932–1939* (Toronto 1976), 30; HP, Roebuck to Hepburn, 22 May 1932

19 *Globe, TDS, ME, TET*, 16–30 May 1932; Buckley Papers, MSS Reminiscences, n.d.; *Saturday Night*, 4 June 1932

20 HP, McQuesten to Hepburn, 17 May 1932; Hardy to Hepburn, 31 May 1932

21 *TDS*, 14, 30 June 1932

22 HP, Proctor to Hepburn, 5 July 1932

23 PC, Roebuck Papers, Roebuck to Hepburn, 13 July 1932

24 HP, Hepburn to Hardy, 24 Aug. 1932; LD, 12 Oct. 1932

25 Minutes of the East Lambton Liberal Association, 1932–1933; KP, Hepburn to King, 24 Aug.; King to Hepburn, 29 Aug. 1932; Neatby, *Prism of Unity*, 24; HP, Hepburn to Medd, 13 Oct. 1932 Hepburn to L. McGuinness, 12 Oct. 1932

26 Henry Papers, Henry to Ferguson, 23 Nov. 1931; Ferguson to Henry, 10 Dec. 1931; *TDS, ME*, 3, 4 Feb. 1932

27 Canada, Senate, *Report and Proceedings of the Special Committee ... on the Beauharnois Power Project 1932*, 19; Bennett Papers, Arthur Ford to Bennett, 18 Mar. 1932; HP, Dafoe to Hepburn, 16 Mar. 1932; OHA, Royal Commission to enquire into certain matters appertaining to the Hydro Power Commission of Ontario 1932, *Hearings*, 5 vols.: 920 (Sweezey), 769 (Ferguson); OHA, Royal Commission ... 1932, Special Report for W.N. Tilley re John Aird Jr. by Thorne, Mulholland, 9 May 1932

28 OH, Minutes, Ontario Hydro, 4 Oct. 1929–11 Apr. 1930

29 OH, Minutes, 11 Apr. 1930; Henry Papers, Ferguson to Henry, 10 Dec. 1931

30 *FP*, 26 Sept. 1931; OHA, Inquiry into the Hydro-Electric Power Commission, *Hearings*, 1011; *FP*, 30 July 1932

31 See Forest Macdonald, *Insull* (Chicago 1962).

32 *Farmers' Sun*, 13 Oct. 1932; HP, Harpell to Hepburn, 17 Oct. 1932; KD, 21 Oct. 1932; KP, Hardy to King, 22 Oct. 1932

33 KD, 26, 27 Oct. 1932; KP, Hardy to King, 22 Oct. 1932; HP, Hardy to Hepburn, 22 Oct. 1932; Roebuck to Hepburn, 1 Nov. 1932

34 KD, 2 Nov. 1932; *HCD*, 2 Nov. 1932: 744; 4 Nov. 1932: 845; Malcolm Papers, Malcolm to Wood, 15 Nov. 1932; HP, Hepburn to Roebuck, 3 Nov. 1932; Montreal *Gazette*, 28 Dec. 1932

35 HP, Fraser to Hepburn, 21 June 1932

36 HP, Hepburn to John Godfrey, 18 Feb. 1932; Fraser to Hepburn, 21 June 1932; Dunning Papers, Fraser to Dunning, 21 Dec. 1931

37 KP, McCreath to King, 10, 20 Nov. 1931; Parliament to King, 5 Aug. 1932; Hardy to King, 20 Nov. 1932; HP, Hardy to Hepburn, 28 Nov. 1931; Johnson to Hepburn, 12 Jan. 1932

38 HP, O'Connor to Hepburn, n.d.; AO, Roebuck Papers, Memorandum by Patrick Donnelly, n.d.; HP, McQuesten to Hepburn, 14 Oct. 1932

39 HP, Medical Report, Nov. 1932

40 Donnelly Papers, Hardy to Donnelly, 17 Sept. 1931; KP, Parker to King, 28 July, 4 Dec. 1931; Murphy Papers, Murphy to Sinclair, 11 May 1932; Murphy to M.J. Quinn, 23 Feb. 1932. Five years later Hardy told King that since 1919 he had put up $200,000 for the Liberal party, '25,000 of which went to help Mitch Hepburn chiefly because I knew if he could win Ontario we could make a better showing in the federal house.' He added that he had loaned Spence money to save his seat in the Senate and had never got it back and was suing for recovery (KP, Hardy to King, 20 Aug. 1937).

41 KP, Charles Collins to Hardy, 22 Feb. 1932; Roebuck to King, 7 Dec. 1933, enc. Report of the Ontario Liberal Association Maintenance Fund 1933; HP, Hepburn to McQuesten, 15 Oct. 1931; Hepburn to Mulock, 21 Oct. 1932; KD, 19 Oct. 1932

42 *ME*, 14 Nov. 1932

43 Ibid., 19 Nov. 1932; KD, 17 Nov. 1932; Dewan Papers, Diary, 18 Nov. 1932

44 *ME*, 16 Dec. 1932; *Farmers' Sun*, 22 Dec. 1932
45 HP, McQuesten to Hepburn, 17 Dec. 1932; Hardy to Hepburn, 15 Dec. 1932; Johnson to Hepburn, 29 Nov. 1932; *Farmers' Sun*, 19 Jan. 1933; *TET*, 17 Dec. 1932

CHAPTER 6: 'THE TORIES ON THE RUN'

1 HP, Hardy to Hepburn, 22 Dec. 1932. See G.M. LeFresne, 'The Royal Twenty-Centers: The Department of National Defence and Federal Unemployment Relief 1932–1936' (MA thesis, Royal Military College 1962).
2 *Globe*, 1 Dec. 1932; *Farmers' Sun*, 17 Nov., 1 Dec. 1932; UFO, Minutes of the Annual Meeting, 29–30 Aug. 1932; Gerald L. Caplan, *The Dilemma of Canadian Socialism: The CCF in Ontario* (Toronto 1973)
3 HP, Sinclair to Hepburn, 6 Jan. 1932 [*sic*]. This account is based on the lengthy correspondence between Sinclair, Proctor, and Hepburn in January and February 1933 in the Hepburn Papers.
4 HP, Duncan McArthur to Hepburn, 14 June 1932; *HCD*, 4 Nov. 1922: 865
5 HP, Sinclair to Hepburn, 6, 13 Jan. 1933; Hepburn to Sinclair, 6 Feb. 1933; *ME*, 16, 20 Jan. 1933
6 *Globe*, 24 Jan. 1933; *ME*, 30 Jan. 1933. Mitch received some welcome support from Roosevelt when on 8 March the United States adopted currency expansion. On 19 April Roosevelt approved a program of controlled inflation and the United States went off the gold standard.
7 H. Blair Neatby, *William Lyon Mackenzie King: The Prism of Unity* (Toronto 1976), 34; KP, 3, 8 Feb. 1933; *ME*, 9 Feb. 1933; *Canadian Forum*, 23 Apr. 1933
8 *Globe*, 6 Feb. 1933; HP, Philpott to Hepburn, 28 Nov. 1932; McQuesten to Hepburn, 6 Feb. 1933; Proctor to Sinclair, 17 Mar. 1933; Hepburn to German, 28 Feb. 1933
9 HP, Hardy to Hepburn, 23 Jan. 1933; S.L. Springsteen to Hepburn, 4 Mar. 1933; KP, Johnson to Lambert, 8 Mar. 1933; Chalmers Papers, Chalmers to Col. J.B. MacLean, 2 Mar. 1933
10 HP, Hepburn to Sinclair, 6 Feb. 1933; Sinclair to Proctor, 26 Feb. 1933; Sinclair to Cassidy, 3 Apr. 1933; Grube Papers, Cassidy to Sinclair, 28 Mar. 1933
11 Spry Papers, Diary, 22 Nov., 11 Mar. 1931; Michiel Horn, *The League for Social Reconstruction: Intellectual Origins of the Democratic Left in Canada 1930–1942* (Toronto 1980), 26; *Farmers' Sun*, 12, 19, 26 Jan., 2 Feb. 1933
12 Spry Papers, Diary, 22 Nov. 1931; HP, Spry to Hepburn, 30 Mar. 1933; Hepburn to Massey, 10 Apr. 1933; Hepburn to Nixon, 8 Apr. 1933; Hepburn to Spry, 8 Apr. 1933
13 *Farmers' Sun*, 6 Apr. 1933

14 Caplan, *Dilemma of Canadian Socialism*, 31–2. Caplan was told the story by LeBourdais. There is no evidence in the Hepburn, LeBourdais, or Spry papers. The circumstantial evidence suggests that the meeting was held between 13 and 15 April when Mitch was passing through Toronto on his way to St Thomas. With Mitch were Philpott, Proctor, and probably Johnson, Roebuck, and Nixon. Other than LeBourdais, the CCF contingent is unknown.

15 *Globe*, 17 Apr. 1933; HP, Johnson to Hepburn, 17 Apr. 1933

16 Carty Diary, 8 Feb. 1933; Ferguson Papers, Ferguson to Reta Saunderson, 16 Feb. 1933

17 HP, Johnson to Hepburn, 1 Feb. 1933; Donnelly Papers, Donnelly to Hepburn, 7 Feb. 1933

18 HP, McQuesten to Hepburn, 6 Feb. 1933; Hepburn to Blakelock, 6 Feb. 1933; *Canadian Annual Review*, 1933, 139; Donnelly Papers, Donnelly to Hepburn, 22 Feb. 1933: *ME*, 28 Feb. 1933; HP, Hepburn to Mel Rossie, 28 Feb. 1933

19 George Henry, MSS Memoirs, 218; Henry Papers, Memo to the Attorney General from Registrar of Loan Corporations, 10 Feb. 1933; Bennett Papers, Price to Bennett, 2 Mar. 1933

20 Henry Papers, Henry to Ferguson, 28 Apr. 1933

21 Ibid., Henry to Ferguson, 28 Apr. 1933; Henry to Dr. J.F. Fotheringham, 12 Apr. 1933; Henry to Flavelle, 18 Apr. 1933; *TDS*, *ME*, 6 Apr. 1933; Bennett Papers, Price to Bennett, 24 Mar. 1933; OHA, Inquiry into the Hydro-Electric Power Commission, 1934: 291

22 Angela Bruce Diary, 27 Feb. 1933; *TDS*, *ME*, *TET*, London *Free Press*, Ottawa *Journal*, 4–7 Apr. 1933; *TDS*, 21 Apr. 1933; *ME*, 21 Apr., 15 July 1933; interview, L.R. MacTavish, QC

23 Bennett Papers, Home Smith to Bennett, 14 June [1934]; Henry Papers, E.P. Taylor to Henry, 19 Sept. 1932; *FP*, 2 July 1932; *TDS*, 11 May 1932

24 Henry Papers, W.S. Dingham to Henry, 27 Jan. 1931; Home Smith to Henry, 30 Aug. 1932; Henry to Home Smith, 31 Aug. 1932; Henry to Ferguson, 28 Apr. 1933 (where Henry wrote that 'Home Smith and the Moderation League did what they could to persuade members of the party to desert me'); Bennett Papers, Price to Bennett, 24 Mar. 1933; *Globe*, 4 Apr. 1933

25 Dafoe Papers, Dafoe to Harry Sifton, 7 Apr. 1933; HP, Parker to Hepburn, 6 Apr. 1933; Hepburn to Parker, 8 Apr. 1933; Parker to Hepburn, 10 Apr. 1933

26 HP, Hepburn to Nixon, 12 Mar. 1932; Hepburn to Cross, 30 Mar. 1932; Paul Martin to Hepburn, 14 Feb. 1933; *STTJ*, 7 Feb. 1931; Donnelly Papers, Hepburn to Donnelly, 12 Apr. 1933; HP, Donnelly to Hepburn, 11 Apr. 1933. Years later E.P. Taylor told an interviewer that at some point

Parker had brought Mitch to see him, and Mitch assured him that if Henry brought in beer and wine the Liberals would accept it; Taylor Papers, transcript of interviews; Richard Rohmer, *E.P. Taylor* (Toronto 1978), 68–9

27 HP, Newman to Charles Foreman, 1 Dec. 1933, enclosed in Newman to Johnson, 16 Dec. 1933; Donnelly Papers, Greenwood to Donnelly, 1, 7 May 1933; *ME*, 6 May 1933; *Globe*, 8 May 1933; HP, Hepburn to Tom Murray, 1 May 1933. All the MLAs except Tweed and Sinclair attended, and all but Murray believed the proposal was politically unwise.

28 F.A. Walker, *Catholic Education and Politics in Ontario* (Toronto 1964), 366

29 HP, Hepburn to Frank McCarroll, 19 Apr. 1932; Paul Leduc to Hepburn, 9 Dec. 1932, 16 Jan. 1933; Hepburn to Hardy, 30 Jan. 1933; Quinn to Hepburn, 21 Jan., 3 Feb. 1933; Hepburn to Quinn, 2 Feb. 1933

30 O'Neil Papers, Lynch-Staunton to O'Neil, 28 Feb. 1933; Quinn to McGuire, 26 Apr. 1935; HP, Hepburn to R.R. Crommarty, 10 May 1933; Quinn to Hepburn, 10 Apr. 1933; Quinn to James Day, 31 Jan. 1934, cited in Walker, *Catholic Education*, 385; Carty Papers, Diary, 23 Dec. 1933, 2 Jan. 1934; HP, Dr J.H. McConnell to D.J. McDougald, 11 July 1933

31 HP, Hepburn to James Clark, 28 Mar. 1933; Roebuck to Hepburn, 30 Sept. 1931; Charles Dunlop to Hepburn, 1 July 1933; KP, Parker to King, 25 Oct. 1933

32 HP, A.F. Hely to Hepburn, 5 June 1933. According to Croll, Mitch had promised him a cabinet post as early as the spring of 1933, 'subject to Arthur Hardy's approval' (KD, 28 June 1933). The only biography of Croll is R. Warren James's *People's Senator: The Life and Times of David A. Croll* (Toronto 1991).

33 *ME*, 14 Feb. 1933; HP, Parker to Hepburn, 6 Apr. 1933

34 *TET*, 14 July 1933; AO, Roebuck Papers, Roebuck to J. Haining, 25 July 1933; Roebuck to J.A. Kelly, 25 Nov. 1933

35 KP, William Slater to King, 8 Apr. 1933; HP, Parker to Hepburn, 25 Aug. 1933; HP, Hardy to Hepburn, 22 Aug. 1933

36 HP, Johnson to Hepburn, 29 Nov. 1932; KP, Parker to King, 10 Dec. 1932

37 *ME*, 29 June 1933; *TDS, ME, TET*, 27 July 1933

38 *Globe*, 24 Aug. 1933; *ME*, 8 Sept. 1933

39 HP, Slaght to Hepburn, 29 July 1933; Fraser to Hepburn, 15 Aug. 1933; Hardy to Hepburn, 22 Aug. 1933; Henry Papers, Henry to Ferguson, 3 Oct. 1933

40 HP, Hepburn to King, 19 Oct. 1933; Hepburn to Parker, 19 Oct. 1933; Cameron Papers, Cameron to Crerar, 15 Aug. 1933

41 PC, Roebuck Papers, Roebuck to Hepburn, 27 Sept. 1933

42 *TDS*, 30 Sept. 1933; HP, Hardy to Hepburn, 13 Oct. 1933. Hepburn to Hardy, 1933

43 *Border Cities Star*, 17 Oct. 1933; HP, Johnson to Hepburn, 18 Oct. 1933. It is

not clear from the news story and a column by George McCracken exactly
what Mitch said. There is in the Hepburn Papers a professionally typed
undated speech calling for a radical reform program to prevent more
extreme radical movements. The proposals were for inheritance taxes of 50%
on all estates over $50,000 and 90% over $90,000; income taxes of 50% at
$30,000 and 90% at $70,000; and currency expansion, internal borrowing,
and a massive program of labour-intensive public works. This was roughly
what Mitch advocated (HP, Speeches and Speech Notes).

44 HP, Johnson to Hepburn, 18 Oct. 1933; Ellison Young to Hepburn, 1 Nov.
1933. *Border Cities Star*, 17 Oct. 1933
45 HP, Lewis Duncan to Hepburn, 25 Oct. 1933; Frank Denton to Hepburn, 20
Oct. 1933; Hepburn to Denton, 23 Oct. 1933
46 HP, Parker to Hepburn, 20 Oct. 1933; KP, Johnson to King, 7 Nov. 1933;
Globe, *TDS*, 20 Nov. 1933
47 PC, Roebuck Papers, Johnson to Parker, 26 Sept. 1933; KP, Roebuck to
King, 7 Dec. 1933
48 Donnelly Papers, Roebuck to Donnelly, 14 June 1933
49 KP, Hardy to King, 9 June 1933; King to Hardy, 12 June 1933
50 Massey Papers, Diary, 22 June 1933; KP, Fraser to King, 13 July 1933; HP,
Fraser to Hepburn, 15 Aug. 1933
51 KP, Crerar to King, 2 Nov. 1933; KD, 26 Oct. 1933; Massey Papers, Diary,
26 Oct. 1933; KP, Massey to King, 30 Oct. 1933; LD, 27 Oct. 1933; KP, King
to Johnson, 4 Nov. 1933
52 Murray Papers, Hepburn to Murray, 13 Nov. 1933; KP, Fraser to King, 20
Nov. 1933; Roebuck to King, 7 Dec. 1933; HP, Fraser to Hepburn, 13 Dec.
1933; KP, Johnson to King, 13 Nov. 1933

CHAPTER 7: 'GO OUT AND SLAY THE ASSYRIANS'

1 HP, Hardy to Hepburn, 22 Aug. 1933
2 LD, 19 June 1934; Henry Papers, R. Home Smith to Bennett, 25 May 1934
3 *Globe*, *TDS*, *ME*, *TET*, 5, 6, 8 Jan. 1934; *TDS*, 12 Jan. 1934
4 Roy Greenaway, *The News Game* (Toronto 1966), 177; *TET*, 17 Jan. 1934
5 Henry Papers, Ferguson to Henry, 24 Oct. 1933
6 *ME*, 2 Mar. 1934
7 *TDS*, 20 Mar. 1934; *Globe*, 21 Mar. 1934; *Canadian Annual Review*, 1934: 147
8 Bennett Papers, J. Earl Lawson to Bennett, 4 Nov. 1933; Henry Papers,
Home Smith to Henry, 16 Mar. 1934. See also the unverifiable but suspect
account in Richard Rohmer, *E.P. Taylor* (Toronto 1978), 68–9. Home Smith
was one of the many Tories who tried to remove Henry. As he wrote to
Bennett after the election, 'a few months ago I had him out but I was
double crossed – ask our friend Charlie [McCrea] the debonair or Grattan

O'Leary' (Bennett Papers, Home Smith to Bennett, n.d. [circa 25 June 1934]).

9 *ME, TDS,* 22 Mar. 1934

10 *ME,* 21, 28 Mar. 1934

11 HP, H. Johnson to Hepburn, 7 Apr. 1934. Despite his silence, Mitch was not wavering. 'Alice is quite disappointed as she had hoped that I could at least oppose Beer and Wine by the glass,' Patrick Dewan, the provincial candidate in Oxford, noted in his diary after asking Mitch if he had any freedom (Dewan Papers, Diary, 8 Apr. 1934).

12 *TDS,* 23 Apr. 1934; *ME,* 25, 30 Apr. 1934; KP, Darrach to King, 11 June 1934; AO, Roebuck Papers, Roebuck to W.M. Southam, 2 Apr. 1934

13 Henry Papers, Henry to Ferguson, 9 Feb., 10 May 1934; *ME,* 14, 22 July 1933; *ME,* 26 Apr. 1934; Henry Papers, Henry to Bennett, 22 Mar. 1934; *TDS,* 7 Apr. 1934; *TET,* 6 Apr. 1934. The increase in relief expenditures in 1934, despite improving conditions, almost doubled in per capita terms, or as a percentage of 1930 income, and was greater than in any province but Saskatchewan. See *Report of the Royal Commission on Dominion-Provincial Relations* (Ottawa 1939), vol. 3, *passim.*

14 Henry Papers, Ferguson to Henry, 24 Oct. 1934; Home Smith to Henry, 16 Mar. 1934; Memorandum on Organization in Western Ontario, 3 Apr. 1934

15 *TET,* 24 May 1934; *ME,* 2, 17 June, 24 Apr. 1934

16 *TET,* 11 June 1934; Bennett Papers, 349299, press release, 18 June 1934; Home Smith to Bennett, 4 June 1934. These and other pamphlets are in the Archives of Ontario.

17 Robert Caygeon, 'Hepburn, Liberal St. George,' *Saturday Night,* 11 Nov. 1933; Bennett Papers, n.d., n.sig., 349257; Hepburn Papers, A.M. Orpen to Hepburn, n.d. (presumably written after the election when the facts were discovered, and it was revealed that Williams paid the bill from a secret bank account); Carty Diary, 4, 5, 7 Jan. 1934

18 OH, Minutes, 6 Dec. 1933. For the correspondence with Sims & Stransky, see OHA, Meighen Law Suit File.

19 The fourteen reports are in OHA, Meighen Law Suit File; HP, Stewart Lyon to Hepburn, 17 Oct. 1934

20 Philpott later told King that Hepburn had told him that 'he already had a plentiful supply of funds from Quebec sources' and that he believed in 1934 'he had made a cut and dried bargain. His part was to block the St. Lawrence waterway plan until Quebec interests had safely disposed of their own actual and potential surplus' (KP, Philpott to King, 19 Dec. 1937). With Mitch intimating that he would review, and perhaps cancel, the Quebec contracts, his version seems implausible.

21 LD, 19 Jan., 5 Feb., 7 Mar., 19 Apr., 17 May, 1934

22 AO, Roebuck Papers, enc. Parker to Roebuck, 23 July 1934. Despite the tension, Vincent Massey did assist Mitch in cultivating Liberals who had not

been drawn to the provincial party. In May he was a host at luncheon with
W.L. Grant, A.E. Ames, George Cottrell, B.K. Sandwell, Newton Rowell,
and others. 'The party, which I planned very carefully, as regards places at
the table, initiation of subjects by myself and one or two others, etc., was a
great success. Hepburn made a distinctly favourable impression, and I think
he liked the group asked to meet him' (Massey Papers, Diary, 11 May 1934).

23 PC, Roebuck Papers, Johnson to Parker, 26 Sept. 1933; Carty Diary, 4 Jan.
1934. Ralph Hyman of the *Mail and Empire*, who accompanied Mitch
during the campaign and claimed to be invested with the power to deny
Mitch a drink until after his speeches, told me that initially the campaign
was run on a shoe-string. One day, when they were at a restaurant in either
Kingston or Belleville, Harry Johnson raced in with a cheque – 'We're in,
the breweries have come through.'

24 *Globe*, 25 Apr. 1934; Ferguson Papers, Ferguson to Reta Saunderson, 16
May 1934

25 PC, Roebuck Papers, Roebuck to A.A. Campbell, 5 Jan. 1934; HP, Hepburn
to Johnson, 6 Feb. 1934 (where Mitch unenthusiastically asked Johnson to
go through the 1930 convention resolutions and see 'if you can find anything
worthwhile'); *ME*, 8 Mar. 1934

26 PC, Roebuck Papers, Roebuck to McQuesten, 28 Apr. 1934; Roebuck to
Campbell, 5 Jan. 1934; *ME*, 28 May 1934

27 *ME*, 6 June 1934; HP, enc., Johnson to Hepburn, 10 Apr. 1934. Greenaway,
News Game, 178

28 KP, Hardy to King, 29 Aug. 1934; Greenaway, *News Game*, 179; interview,
William Shields. Mitch did get good press from the reporters, even in
newspapers such as the *Mail and Empire* that were scathing in their
editorials. Atkinson applauded his swing to the left, and editorially
supported the party although he found it difficult to endorse the leader. As
early as 1932, Colonel Jaffray of the *Globe* had decided to support the
provincial Liberals, although he believed that despite his ability, Mitch was
too 'inclined to speak twice while he thought once' (KP, H. Johnson to King,
9 Nov. 1932). Henry's beer and wine decision eased the consciences of the
two temperance publishers.

29 HP, Hardy to Hepburn, 17 Apr. 1934; KP, King to Hepburn, 24 May 1934.
Mitch seems not to have kept the letter.

30 HP, H. Holton to Hepburn, 16 Mar. 1934; Campbell to Hepburn, 4 Apr. 1934

31 *TDS*, 18 June 1934; PC, Roebuck Papers, J. German to Roebuck, 16-18 July,
enc. J.H. Gardner to German, 12 July and Paul Martin to German, 7 July
1936. There were 7,800 Italian voters in Toronto ridings, and another 10,000
elsewhere, with the heaviest concentrations in Windsor, Hamilton, Niagara
Falls, and Welland. (NAC, Progressive Conservative Party Papers, York
South File, J.E. Lawson to J.M. Robb, 5 May 1939).

32 AO, Roebuck Papers, Roebuck to F.L. Hutchinson, 22 Jan. 1934; *TET*, 14
    July 1933, 10 May 1934
33 L. Frost Papers, Frost to J.W. Morden, 10 Aug. 1834; Reid Papers, Colin
    Campbell interview, 29–30 June 1932; interview, Colin Campbell; Henry
    Papers, Clysdale to Henry, 1 June 1934
34 HP, Fraser to Hepburn, 21 May 1934; interview, Odette Ouimet (née
    Lapointe)
35 HP, Fraser to Hepburn, 21 May 1934; interview, George Fulford; AO, Liquor
    Control Board Inquiry Report, 28 June 1935, Unprinted Sessional Papers,
    No. 51, 1936: 39
36 Reid Papers, Colin Campbell interview; HP, Fraser to Hepburn, 21 May
    1934; Henry Papers, Clysdale to Henry, 1 June 1934; Henry to Clysdale, 8
    June 1934; Bennett Papers, Bennett to Henry, 22 May 1934; Henry Papers,
    Memorandum to the Prime Minister, 28 May 1934. There were 5,022 men in
    the DND camps in June in thirteen different ridings, including York West,
    Kingston, and Norfolk, that had military bases. The DND prohibited political
    speeches in the camps, and Bennett's shifting and other devices managed to
    reduce the number of eligible voters to 1,429. The vote was almost equally
    split (D. Hist., 113.302009, Colonel D.W.B. Spry to Brigadier T.B.
    Anderson, 12 June 1934, and *passim*; KP, Heenan to King, 21 May 1934).
    There were probably about 30,000 men in the board camps and settlers
    camps in twenty-five ridings throughout the Shield.
37 Henry Papers, Home Smith to Henry, 26 Apr. 1934; Henry to Home Smith,
    27 Apr. 1934; Home Smith to Henry, 14 May 1934; Clysdale to Henry, 1
    June 1934
38 KP, Johnson to King, 7 Nov. 1933; UFO, Minute Books, 31 May 1934.
    Macphail ceased to be a member of the CCF when the UFO withdrew, and
    Philpott resigned from the party.
39 *ME*, 22 May 1934; CCF Papers, Secretary's Report for the Provincial Council
    Meeting, 18 Aug. 1934
40 Spry Papers, Annual Report of the Executive Committee of the CCF.
    (Ontario Section) 1934; *Saturday Night*, 25 Aug. 1934; Manion Papers, D.M.
    Hogarth to Manion, 4 July 1934; Bennett Papers, W.H. Price to Bennett, 9
    Mar. 1933. In Oshawa the CCF candidate, Charles Millard, said he had been
    offered $500 by another party, and there was widespread suspicion and some
    evidence that the local CCF clubs had taken money from another party. See
    (J.A. Pendergest, 'Labour and Politics in Oshawa and District 1928–1943'
    (MA thesis, Queen's University 1973); Glen Papers, Herbert Orloff to Glen,
    11 Aug. 1934
41 HP, H.H. Hyland to Hepburn, 15, 18 Aug. 1934. Mitch denied any
    knowledge of the arrangement in August when Hyland, who had been paid
    only $85, asked that a brand of Scotch, for which he had somehow become

an agent, be listed. His request was rejected although he had promised to contribute some of his commission to the party (*TDS*, 19 June 1934; *HCD*, 22 Sept. 1934: 4207).

42 Pouliot Papers, Pouliot to B. Lemant, 21 June 1934; *Le Droit*, 8 June 1934; HP, Hepburn to A.D. Roberts, 19 Apr. 1934; KD, 11 Apr., 30 May, 7 June 1934; *ME*, June 8, 1934. Grattan O'Leary, in *Maclean's*, commented that King's speech at the luncheon 'was a notable exercise in restraint, something extra-ordinary in a statesman whose talent·for exuberant praise is one of his principal characteristics' (1 Aug. 1934).

43 Henry Papers, Home Smith to Henry, 14 May 1934; *STTJ*, 13 June 1934; HP, W.H. Kippen to Hepburn, 9 Aug. 1934

44 *TET*, 15 June 1934; O'Brien Papers, O'Brien to McNeil, 1 Apr. 1934; McNally to O'Brien, 2 Apr. 1934; HP, Quinn to V. Foley, 8 May, enc. in Foley to Hepburn, 9 May 1934; CTPA Papers, Quinn to parish chairmen, 2, 12 Apr., 23, 29 May 1934. For the fullest account of the deliberations and negotiations see F.A. Walker, *Catholic Education and Politics in Ontario* (Toronto 1964), 387. See also the correspondence in the Archdiocesan Archives of Toronto and Kingston and the diocese of London, as well as the papers of the CTPA.

45 Bennett Papers, Home Smith to Bennett, 11 June 1934; *TET*, 15 June 1934; Henry Papers, Henry to D. Spence, MP, 15 June 1934; *TDS*, 18 June 1934

46 *TDS*, *ME*, *TET*, 18 June 1934

47 Carty Diary, 19 June 1934; *STTJ*, *TDS*, 19 June 1934

48 Bennett Papers, Bennett to Home Smith, 11 May 1934; Home Smith to Bennett, 4, 11 June 1934; W.H. Price to Bennett, 11 June 1934; Henry Papers, Home Smith to Henry, 25 May 1934; *Globe*, 16–18 June 1934; *STTJ*, 19 June 1934

49 Bennett Papers, J. Earl Lawson to Bennett, 15 June 1934

50 HP, Hardy to Hepburn, 28 May 1934. The turnout in twenty-five urban ridings in the province increased from 49 to 65 per cent, and in Toronto from 40 to 65 per cent. In fifteen northern ridings the total vote increased from 138,422 to 204,591. Contemporaries noted a large increase in the number of young people and women voting, particularly Roman Catholic women.

51 Murray Papers, Oliver Bedard to Murray, 22 June 1934; LD, 20 June 1934; KP, King, wire, to Hepburn, 19 June 1934; KD, 19, 21 June 1934. The account of the election is based on the *TDS*, *ME*, *Globe*, *TET*, Ottawa *Citizen*, *Border Cities Star*, Sudbury *Star*, Hamilton *Spectator*, *STTJ*, 19–21 June 1934.

CHAPTER 8: 'THE TERRIBLE DESCENT FROM MOWAT AND BLAKE'

1 *TDS*, 23–26 June 1934; *ME*, Ottawa *Citizen*, *Le Droit*, 25 June 1934; *Jack Canuck*, 27 Sept. 1934

2 KD, 21 June 1934

3 Ibid, 25 June 1933; KP, King to Hepburn, 12 July 1934

4 O'Brien Papers, Murphy to Quinn, 17 Aug. 1934; Murphy Papers, Dewan to Murphy, 3, 5 Sept. 1934; Murphy to Dewan, 4 Sept. 1934; KD, 27 June 1934. Mitch persuaded Earl Hutchinson to exchange his seat for the chairmanship of the Workmen's Compensation Board to enable Heenan to run in Kenora.

5 HP, I Bradette to Hepburn, 26 June 1934; LD, 20 Aug. 1934; KD, 25–26 June 1934; interview, Ralph Hyman

6 HP, Fulford to Hepburn, 3 July 1934; Crerar to Hepburn, 21 June 1934; copy, Roebuck to E.J. Wallwork, 29 June 1934

7 Bruce Diary, 6, 8 July 1934; Bruce Papers, Bruce to Bennett, 7 July 1934; Bruce to Henry, 9 July 1934; Bennett Papers, Bruce to Bennett, 12 July 1934; Bennett to Bruce, 10 Aug. 1934; Bruce Diary, 10 July 1934; Henry Borden, ed., *Letters to Limbo* (Toronto 1971), 109. For several years Mitch had argued that the functions of the lieutenant-governor could be performed by the chief justice during the Depression, but did not advocate abolishing the office. Henry had also been concerned about the cost of Chorley Park when Bruce was appointed in 1932, as was Herbert Bruce himself. Mitch did threaten to 'freeze out' the lieutenant-governor, if necessary (*ME*, 26 May 1933; Bruce Papers, Bruce to McGibbon, 30 Oct. 1932).

8 *FP*, 18 Aug. 1934. Roebuck and McQuesten served on the Hydro Commission without salary, whereas their predecessors had received $10,000 a year. With a salary of $10,000, Odette replaced two liquor commissioners each of whom had been paid $12,000.

9 HP, Drury to Hepburn, 27 June 1934; Bennett Papers, R.C. Mathews to Bennett, 21 July 1934; Borden to Ross, 22 June 1934; *ME*, 19 Oct. 1934. On the Drew dismissal, see the correspondence in the Hepburn, Roebuck, and Drew papers in the Ontario Archives.

10 *Globe*, 24 July 1934

11 *ME, TDS, Globe, TET*, 16–18 Aug. 1934; T.W. Crossen, 'The Political Career of Attorney General Arthur Roebuck, 1934–1937' (MA thesis, University of Waterloo 1973)

12 Bennett Papers, Bennett to R.A. Reid, 7 Aug. 1934; Dafoe Papers, Colquhoun to Dafoe, 30 Aug. 1934.

13 Bruce Diary, 18 July 1934. It is extremely difficult to be precise on the number of people dismissed since classifications differ for inside and outside workers, civil servants and public employees, temporary, seasonal, and permanent employees, and employees of Hydro, the LCBO, hospitals, the attorney general's department, prisons and reformatories. One set of figures compiled for Hepburn by Foster's office indicated that between 11 July 1934 and 18 Apr. 1935, 1,067 employees of all kinds had resigned or been dismissed and 839 were hired (AO, Civil Service Commission, C-6, Foster,

Memorandum for the Prime Minister, 29 Feb. 1936). See also a number of memoranda, monthly reports and compilations in c-5 and c-6. A statement in the legislature on 11 March 1935 cited figures prepared by Foster that 1,330 had resigned or been dismissed, but no indication was given as to how many were rehired or replaced (*JLAO*, 1935: 44).

14 HP, Hardy to Hepburn, 17, 29 Aug. 1934; Hepburn to Hardy, 22 Aug. 1934. The drivers were offered jobs at the Guelph reformatory (*ME*, 14 Aug. 1934).

15 HP, Gardhouse to Hepburn, 13 Aug. 1934; KP, Hardy to King, 3 Sept. 1934. At the LCBO, 481 were dismissed and 265 were hired. In Toronto, at least, members or defeated candidates indicated who should be fired and hired (Malcolm Papers, Arnold Smith to Malcolm, 5 Feb. 1935).

16 PC, Roebuck Papers, anon. to Wilfrid Heighington, 15 Sept. 1934; HP, Hepburn to B. Hurwitz, 19 July 1935. Many of the new appointments inevitably failed to meet the requirements of the Public Service Act, always more honoured in the breach than in the observance. Hepburn told Foster and the provincial auditor to approve all recommendations because the act would be changed (and it was) to increase ministerial discretion and strip away the camouflage (HP, Hepburn, to G.A. Brown, 31 July 1934; AO, orders-in-council, 17 Jan. 1935; *SO*, 25 Geo. v, ch. 58).

17 Interview, Ralph Hyman; KD, 26, 29 June, 28 July 1934; *FP*, 1 Sept. 1934

18 *New Commonwealth*, 22 Dec. 1934; *ME*, 9 Aug. 1934; HP, Hepburn to O'Connor, 5 Mar. 1937. On at least one of Mitch's alleged interventions, see the correspondence and testimony on the Hotel Dennis case involving Mitch's distant cousin, Nina Osborne (HP, Osborne File, 1937); *JLAO*, 1937, Appendix 1: 230).

19 *TDS*, 18, 25, 26 Oct. 1934; *ME*, 9, 10 Aug., 23, 29, 30 Oct. 1934; HP, Odette to Hepburn, 20 Oct. 1934; *Canadian Annual Review*, 1934: 182

20 HP, J. Boylen to Hepburn, 3 Aug. 1934; *TDS*, 10 July, 14 Nov. 1934

21 Pierre Berton, *The Dionne Years: A Thirties Melodrama* (Toronto 1977), 74; *TDS*, 27, 28 July 1934

22 Bennett Papers, R.C. Matthews to Bennett, 3 Aug. 1934

23 HP, Cromie to Hepburn, 6 Nov. 1934; Hepburn to Cromie, 16 Nov. 1934; *TDS*, 31 July, 1 Aug. 1934; Bennett Papers, H. Hereford to R. Finlayson, 9, 12 Aug. 1934, enclosing notes of the meetings 30–31 July 1934; HP, G.G. McGeer to Hepburn, 13 Aug. 1934; Hepburn to McGeer, 15 Oct. 1934. The $40 million may have been a reference to the June 1934 amendment to the Dominion Notes Act which permitted a currency expansion of $52.5 million, although again only about 5 per cent went into circulation and the trend of bank loans continued downward.

24 *Globe*, 11 Aug. 1934; *ME*, 13 Aug. 1934; *FP*, 18 Aug. 1934; *Canadian Annual Review*, 1935: 360

25 *Globe, ME, TDS,* 25, 27, 28 Aug. 1934; *Financial Times,* 31 Aug. 1934
(which noted that Nova Scotia and Montreal, 'bankers to the province,' had
been unaware that a deal was being negotiated); AO, Treasury Dept., Series
II-I, File 1604/9; HP, J.H. Gundy to Hepburn, 25 Aug. 1934; LD, 25, 28 Aug.
1934

26 *TDS,* 13 Sept. 1934; *FP,* 1 Sept. 1934; Bennett Papers, Bennett to Price, 28
Aug. 1934

27 Bennett Papers, Dominion-Provincial Meeting on Relief, 30–31 July 1934,
121763. When Mitch returned Bennett agreed provisionally to advance a
grant of $750,000 a month, but categorically refused to consider paying the
$5.4 million Mitch claimed Henry had spent on pre-election projects;
whatever assurances Wesley Gordon had given Henry that Ottawa would
pick up part of the $15 million bill, the expenditures had been turned down
(NAC, Dept. of Labour, v. 200, file 617.1.5, W.M. Dickson, Memorandum
for the Minister, 24 Aug. 1934); *Globe, TDS,* 21 Aug. 1934

28 Manion Papers, Manion to Hepburn, 3 Aug. 1934; HP, Hardy to Hepburn,
25 Aug. 1934; Bennett Papers, Matthews to Bennett, 3 Aug. 1934

29 *TDS, Globe,* 14, 17 June, 2 Aug. 1934; *TET, Border Cities Star,* 2 Aug.
1934; *Saturday Night,* 11 Aug. 1934; *Globe,* 11 Aug. 1934; KP, W. Murdoch
to King, 17 Oct. 1935. On Liberal relief policy, see James Struthers, 'How
Much Is Enough? Creating a Social Minimum in Ontario, 1930–44,'
Canadian Historical Review (Mar. 1991), 39–83.

30 The 1934 Hydro investigation under justices Latchford and Smith
condemned the Abitibi contract, described the settlement as a gift to the
bondholders, and found the conduct of Meighen and Henry to be improper.
With Slaght as prosecutor and the two judges openly hostile, there was some
truth in Meighen's description of it as 'a political inquisition' (Bennett
Papers, Meighen to Bennett, 23 July, 3 Aug. 1934; *Globe,* 27 Mar. 1935).
The liquor inquiry did not uncover a formal tollgate, but did reveal that
friends at court were more than helpful in getting brands listed, and that the
board and the stores were an arm of the Tory party. Inefficiency, patronage,
and generous expense accounts were the most damaging revelations to come
from the inquiries into the T&NO, the Ontario Air Service, and the Niagara
Parks Commission. The reports are summarized in *Canadian Annual Review,*
1934: 188.

31 Manion Papers, Home Smith to Manion, 25 July, 2 Aug. 1934; HP, Hepburn
to Manion, 18 Jan. 1935

32 Mitch's offer of help troubled King, for it suggested 'some thought he might
have re campaign funds. I did not like that – we must get away from that
curse now altogether' (KD, 26 June 1934). Even King and Hardy admitted
there was no cabinet material in Ontario except Dunning, whom King
distrusted, 'save Euler who is selfish & single-tracked. Eliot[t], he thinks wd.

break down. Malcolm already broken down, Moore not to be trusted, wd. intrigue, Sanderson ditto as a bankrupt' (KD, 27 Nov. 1934). The Chateau Laurier barber aroused King's suspicions when he reported that Mitch 'had kept questioning him of my health, to be sure it was better, almost as if he did not wish to believe it so' (ibid., 22 Aug. 1934).

33 LD, 26, 27, 29 June, 10, 14 July 1934; KP, King to Fraser, Hepburn et al., 16 July 1934; King to Elliott, 17 July 1934

34 KP, Fraser to King, 17 July 1934; Massey to King, 28 July 1934

35 LD, 30 July 1934; KD, 28 July 1934

36 KP, Massey to King, 28 July 1934; KD, 3 Aug. 1934; LD, 25 July 1934 (where Mitch agreed to financial support)

37 KD, 3, 4 Aug. 1934; Lambert Papers, vol. 13, E.G. Long, financial records

38 TDS, ME, Globe, STTJ, 20 Aug.–25 Sept. 1934

39 Ottawa Journal, 17 Sept. 1934; London Free Press, 22 Sept. 1934; Winnipeg Free Press, 22 Sept. 1934; LD, 5 Sept. 1934

40 HP, Hepburn to Fraser, 22 Aug. 1934; LD, 20 Aug. 1934

41 KP, Johnson to King, 25 July 1934; King to Slaght, 17 July 1934; Slaght to King, 27 July 1934; KD, 29 June, 28 July 1934; Manion Papers, Hepburn to Manion, 18 Jan. 1935

42 See the Heenan-Gordon correspondence in the Hepburn Papers and Manion Papers (Trans Canada Highway File); Bennett Papers, Gordon to Bennett, 4 Dec. 1934; TDS, 16 Nov., 15 Dec. 1934.

43 Dunn Papers, Dunn to Wright, 12 Nov. 1935; Wright to Dunn, 17, 29 Nov. 1934; HP, Wright to Hepburn, 15 Nov. 1934; Hepburn to Wright, 22 Nov. 1934; I.A. Humphries, CONFIDENTIAL Memorandum to: The Honorable the Attorney General, Nov. 24, 1934; Roebuck to Hepburn, n.d.; Dunn to Hepburn, 13 Aug. 1941. The reorganization is fully and critically treated by Duncan McDowall in Steel at the Sault (Toronto 1984), 142, who believes that Hepburn was unaware of Dunn's involvement. I find that difficult to imagine.

44 AO, orders-in-council, 11, 25 Sept. 1934. See also H.V. Nelles, The Politics of Development: Forests, Mines and Hydro-Electric Power in Ontario, 1849–1941 (Toronto 1974), 454; R.S. Lambert and P. Pross, Renewing Nature's Wealth (Toronto 1967), 336.

45 The correspondence, reports of OPP inspectors, and summary memoranda may be found in AO, Dept. of Labour, Series VIII-1, Manpower Services Division, General Subject Files and Series II-1, vol. 12, Strikes, Bushworkers, 1934. See also D. Hist. 161.009 (063), A.F. Reames, CO, O Division to OC Military District No. 1, 6 Oct., 6 Nov. 1934.

46 TDS, 9 Oct., 6 Nov. 1934; TET, 1 Nov. 1934.

47 TDS, 6 Nov., 17 Oct. 1934; LD, 23 Oct. 1934; HP, A.M. Orpen file, 1934, n.d., s.sig.

48 *TDS, Globe, Border Cities Star*, 13, 14, 21–30 Aug. 1934; *Globe*, 5 Sept., 10–11 Oct., 2 Nov. 1934; *FP*, 20 Oct. 1934

49 *TDS*, 15 June, 12 July, 25 Aug., 1 Sept., 1 Oct. 1934; *Globe*, 4 Sept. 1934. For the minutes of meetings between Roebuck and representatives of labour and industry concerning the codes, see AO, Dept. of Labour, Series VIII-1, vol. 28.

50 HP, Burton to Hepburn, 2 Aug. 1934, *TET*, 16 Oct. 1934; *TDS, ME*, 6 Nov. 1934; *TDS*, 28 Nov. 1934

51 HP, Blakelock to Hepburn, 15 Oct. 1934; *ME*, 24 Oct. 1934

52 HP, Hardy to Hepburn, 27 Nov. 1934; *Globe, ME, TDS*, 27–29 Nov. 1934; Bruce Journal, 3 Apr. 1935; KD, 1 Dec. 1934

53 HP, Hepburn to Bennett, 3 Dec. 1934; Bennett Papers, Gordon to Bennett, 4 Dec. 1934; *TDS*, 3, 5 Dec. 1934; KD, 1 Dec. 1934

54 AO, Roebuck Papers, Roebuck to King, 1 Oct. 1934; *FP*, 18 Aug. 1934; HP, Hardy to Hepburn, 27 Nov. 1934; KD, 1 Dec. 1934

55 KD, 24, 27 Nov. 1934; Manion Papers, Manion to Hogarth, 4 Dec. 1934; confidential interview; Bruce Journal, Feb. 1935; *TET*, 11 Jan. 1935. The Tories attempted to check on Mitch's escapades in the Caribbean but Manion was disappointed when his contact in Bermuda came up with nothing more than a golf game and a luncheon (NAC, Manion Papers, Manion to E.P. Tucker, 10 Feb. 1935; Tucker to Manion, 19 Feb. 1935).

CHAPTER 9: 'A STRUGGLE AGAINST FEUDALISM'

1 Bruce Journal, Feb. 1935; Bennett Papers, Bruce to Bennett, 30 Jan., 1935; Bruce Diary, 18, 19, Feb. 1935

2 HP, Rossie to Hepburn, 9 Feb. 1935; Massey Diary, 20 Feb. 1935; *TDS, Globe, ME*, 20, 21 Feb. 1935

3 AO, Treasury Dept., Series II-1, Box 3, Chester Walters, Memorandum re Hydro Electric Power Commission, 29 Mar. 1935; HP, Lyon to Hepburn, 10 Nov. 1934

4 The interest rate was usually between 5 and 6%, although in some cases it was as high as 8%. Tax arrears were generally above 30% and in much of suburban Toronto over 40%. *Globe*, 24 Jan. 1936; HP, Municipal Indebtedness Files, *passim*

5 Towers Papers, Memoranda, 12 Feb. 1935; Bennett Papers, Bennett, wire, to Hepburn, 5 Feb. 1935; Hepburn to Bennett, 7 Feb. 1935; HP, Cottrell to Hepburn, 4 Feb. 1935, and enclosure; *Globe*, 5 Feb. 1935; *FP*, 16 Feb. 1935

6 Bruce Journal, 14 Feb. 1935; Massey Diary, 13 Feb. 1935; HP, Cottrell to Hepburn, 18 Feb. 1935

7 Bruce Journal, Feb. 1935; Price Papers, Bennett to Price, 5 Feb. 1935; interviews: Hugh Brown, Sherwood Walters. Walter's analysis of the

Agricultural Development Board, for example, found that it owed the Treasury $5,300,000, was owed $9,000,000 in arrears of principal and interest, was losing money on every outstanding loan, and had five hundred repossessed farms for sale. In August, with federal money available under the Canadian Farm Loan Act, the board was shut down (HP, Memorandum to the Prime Minister, 4 Apr. 1935; Comptroller of the ADB, Memorandum for Chester Walters, 22 Aug. 1935; Elmhirst to A. Robertson, 23 Aug. 1935).

8 *TDS*, *Globe*, *ME*, 3 Apr. 1935

9 AO, Roebuck Papers, C.J. Foster to Roebuck, 26 July 1935. The news of Roebuck's appointment immediately threatened to lower the value of Beauharnois bonds. R.O. Sweezey (whose firm owned four million) phoned Mitch and was relieved to hear that 'the silly talk about the Beauharnois contract is all the imagination of the troublemakers' but asked Mitch to send a letter he might show investment dealers. Mitch used the phone (HP, Sweezey to Hepburn, 8 Aug. 1934, on which is a pencilled note: 'Mr. Hepburn telephoned Mr. Sweezey').

10 *Globe*, 11 Dec. 1934; *New Commonwealth*, 15 Dec. 1934

11 AO, Commissions and Committees, Proceedings of the Select Committee Investigating Hydro Power Contracts and Hydro Administration (hereafter Committee Investigating Hydro), 1144 (Jeffery)

12 AO, Committee Investigating Hydro, 1146, 1135 (a text of Roebuck's speech is in PC, Roebuck Papers). By February 1935 Hydro was paying for 260,000 hp of Gatineau 25-cycle power, 129,000 hp from Beauharnois, and 40,000 from MacLaren (at a cost of $5.5 million) in addition to 96,000 from Ottawa Valley on the Quebec side of Chats Falls. In July 1935 it was contracted to receive an additional 27,000 from MacLaren; in Oct. 1935 an additional 67,000 from Beauharnois; in 1936 another 33,000 from MacLaren and 54,000 from Beauharnois. The total cost when all contracts were fulfilled was $8,077,500, excluding Ottawa Valley. The transmission lines and storage facilities at Leaside could handle between 400,000 and 450,000 hp and a second system was estimated to cost about $16 million.

13 Roebuck relied on the legal advice of Lewis Duncan (PC, Roebuck Papers, Duncan to T.R. Harrison, 4 Apr. 1935; Duncan to B.K. Sandwell, 11 Apr. 1935).

14 *ME*, 1 Mar. 1935; Committee Investigating Hydro, 1440 (Hepburn); interview, Ralph Hyman; Bruce Diary, 10 Apr. 1935; LD, 2 Mar. 1935; AO, Committee Investigating Hydro, 518 (Roebuck); *TDS*, 2 Mar. 1935; Globe 5 Mar. 1935

15 *Financial Counsel*, 5, 14 Mar. 1935; *TDS*, 4 Mar. 1935; HP, R.W. Gouinlock, President, Investment Dealers' Association, to Hepburn, 6 Mar. 1935; D.H. Logan, Canadian Bankers' Association, to Hepburn, 1 Apr. 1935. The cancellation of the contracts seriously affected Canadian credit in London,

(see Magrath Papers, Borden to Charles Magrath, 13 Dec. 1935; Towers
Papers, Memoranda 1935–1939, Memorandum of Conversation with Sir
Edward Peacock in London, Nov. 1936).

16 AO, Roebuck Papers, W.F. Ryan to S. Lyon, 18 Oct. 1934; Zolf papers,
Jeffery and Long to Lyon, 28 Nov. 1934; AO, Committee Investigating
Hydro, 1144 (Jeffery); 1274 (Hogg); AO, Roebuck Papers, Memorandum, 27
May 1938, Comments upon the Niagara System Load and Capacity Graph
used by Mr. Roebuck in his speech to the Legislature commencing 27 Feb.
1935. The commission managed both sides of the river, but there was the
danger that deliveries from the Quebec side could be cut off or the sluices
opened. Chat's had a capacity of 96,000 on each side, but the normal
generation was little more than half.

17 *TDS*, 4 Mar. 1935; Beauharnois Papers, Ward Wright to Loring Christie, 8,
12, Mar. 1935; *FP*, 23 Mar. 1935; *Financial Counsel*, 14 Mar. 1935; *New
York Times*, 10 Mar. 1935

18 HP, E.G. Mackenzie to Elmhirst, 12 Mar. 1935; Beauharnois Papers, Wright
to Christie, 12 Mar. 1935. The long, undated, hand-scrawled memorandum
presumably prepared for Roebuck's proposal to cabinet is in AO, Roebuck
Papers, File HEPC Niagara System 1935. The text of Roebuck's radio
addresses were printed in Hydro's *The Bulletin*, May 1935. Roebuck never
relented in his attacks on the contracts and the necessity of cancellation. But
privately he wanted to appear more conciliatory. In a long meeting with
Ward Wright on 4 April he explained that the major reason for the
cancellation was that 'once he got into the bond mortgages he found that no
amendment of the contracts was possible without the consent of the
bondholders, and that this would involve such time and expense, that he
deemed it advisable to simply cancel the contracts and start afresh.' He
admitted that Hydro needed power, however, 'but they expected the Power
Companies to assist them in this.' Concluding their discussion, Roebuck
promised to send for Wright again when they knew what their requirements
were and 'hoped it would be possible to cooperate on a satisfactory basis to
both the Commission and the Company' (Beauharnois Papers, Wright to
L. Christie, 4 Apr. 1935).

19 *SO*, 25 Geo V, ch. 53; *FP*, 23 Mar. 1935

20 Beauharnois Papers, Circular, Confidential, For Clients Only, 8 Apr. 1935;
Globe, 4 Apr. 1935; Bennett Papers, *passim*, 349711; KD, 6 Apr. 1935; Dafoe
Papers, Sifton to Roebuck, 3 Apr., enc. in Sifton to Dafoe, 8 Apr. 1935;
Borden Papers, Borden to Dafoe, 15 Apr. 1935; Chalmers Papers, Chalmers
to Col. J.B. McLean, 4 Apr. 1935; *Globe*, 9 Apr. 1935

21 HP, Press Gallery File, 1936, n.d., press statement; AO, Committee
Investigating Hydro, 1440 (Hepburn); 250 (Lyon); Montreal *Gazette*, 6 Apr.
1935; Taschereau Papers, Taschereau to Hepburn, 3 Apr. 1935; Hepburn to

Taschereau, 3 Apr. 1935. Months later, Taschereau issued a press statement in which he said: 'I ignore what passed at Toronto, not having been present at the conference, but I am authorized by Hon. Mr. Scott to say that he was not instructed to make such a threat, and at no time did he make it. It is quite possible that he said that public opinion was much aroused in Quebec, that good neighbourhood was endangered, and that retaliation would be possible, but again I ignore if Mr. Scott used such language.' He also admitted that he knew there was talk of opening the sluice gates at Chat's Falls, but said the government was not party to it and could not have prevented it (*GM*, 19 Dec. 1936). As quoted in *La Presse* (19 Dec. 1935), Taschereau did admit that he had said that public opinion might force him to take 'quelque action draconnienne.'

22 Bruce Journal, 10 Apr. 1935

23 AO, Committee Investigating Hydro, 273 (Lyon); 518 (Roebuck); 1274 (Hogg); *TDS*, *ME*, 9–12 Apr. 1935. Roebuck certainly looked back in pride: 'In the Parliament Buildings I was ringed around with enemies, bent on my destruction. The cancellation would not have taken place had I not jammed it through' (*GM*, 24 Sept. 1937).

24 According to Dr McQuibban, Roebuck was also the 'best hated man in the house, absolutely without a friend' (Bruce Journal, 3 Apr. 1935). Mitch announced the new regulations in the fight against the financial racketeers in October soon after John Godfrey was appointed (*Globe*, 10 Oct. 1935) The real estate industry had apparently asked for tighter regulations and Mitch established an advisory board under M.C. Zimmerman, a Liberal fund-raiser (*TET*, 16 Apr. 1935).

25 AO, Dept. of Labour, Series VIII-1, vol. 28, Series I-1, vol. 15; HP, Memorandum to the Prime Minister, 16 Feb. 1935; HP, R.L. Sargant to Roebuck, copy, 29 Mar. 1935. The best study of the IDA is Mark Cox, 'The Limits of Reform: Industrial Regulation and Management Rights in Ontario, 1930–7,' *Canadian Historical Review* (Dec. 1987), 552–75.

26 *Globe*, 4 Apr. 1935; HP, Parker to Hepburn; Burton to Hepburn, n.d. [circa 8 Apr. 1935]

27 *TDS*, *ME*, *Globe*, 15–17 Apr. 1935. The housing provisions were included in An Act Respecting Unemployment Relief (*SO*, 25 Geo. V, ch. 71, s.9, ss3). F.W. Nicholls, a housing specialist, told W.C. Clark of the Department of Finance that 'I am familiar with most modernization and rehabilitation acts which have been passed to date, but I unhesitatingly say that this is the finest piece of legislature [*sic*] ever enacted for this purpose, in fact it is the only workable act in existence' (NAC, Dept. of Finance, vol. 3433, Bank of Canada File 1934-40, Memorandum for W.C. Clark, 27 Jan. 1936).

28 HP, Hepburn to Senator George Graham, 1 Feb. 1935

29 An Act respecting Mental Hospitals and Schools, *SO* 25 Geo. V, ch. 39; AO,

Dept of Health, Series 15-B, Box 39, Circular to all provincial doctors from Dr B.T. McGhie, 1 Aug. 1935

30 *Globe*, 11 Apr. 1935; *ME*, 11 Apr. 1935; *GM*, 6 Jan. 1978

31 KD, 25 June 1935; Kidd Papers, Kidd to Quinn, 27 Sept. 1935; O'Neil Papers, Kidd to McGuigan, 27 Dec. 1934; Murphy Papers, Murphy to Quinn, 10 Sept. 1935; Murphy to Rodolphe Lemieux, 10 Jan. 1935; Memorandum Plot No. 1, Plot No. 2; KD, 1 Dec. 1935. Hepburn denied that he had seen Stanley (KD, 11 Mar. 1935)

32 O'Brien Papers, O'Brien to Bishop D.D. O'Connor, 15 Dec. 1935; O'Brien to Archbishop Guillaume Forbes, 17 Dec. 1935; McGuigan Papers, Quinn to E.C. Desormeaux, 18 Feb. 1937; O'Brien Papers, Quinn to O'Brien, 31 Dec. 1934; O'Brien to Quinn, 2 Jan. 1935; Quinn to O'Brien, 11 Jan. 1935

33 HP, Some Points by a Delegation which Waited on Cabinet, 22 Jan. 1935, n.d. n.sig.; CTPA Papers, Quinn to J.A. McNevin, 8 Oct. 1937; *TDS*, *TET*, *Globe*, 23 Jan. 1935

34 *TDS*, 23 Jan. 1935; *TET*, 14 Feb. 1935; *The Gospel Witness*, 7 Mar. 1935; AO, Dept. of Education, D-3, F.H. Saunders to Simpson, 26 Feb. 1935 and enc.

35 CTPA Papers, Quinn to J.A. McNevin, 8 Oct. 1937; W. Scott to Quinn, 23 Jan., 23 Feb. 1939; O'Brien Papers, Quinn to O'Brien, 7 Feb. 1935

36 McGuigan Papers, Mgr. F.A. Carroll to Quinn, 7 Mar. 1935; Quinn to Carroll, 11 Mar. 1935; O'Brien Papers, Quinn to O'Brien, 30 Mar. 1935; Murphy Papers, Murphy to Quinn, 1 Apr. 1935; HP, Quinn to Hepburn, 10 Apr. 1935; *Globe*, 12 Apr., 4 May 1935

37 *ME*, 16 Mar. 1935; *ME*, 12 Apr. 1935; Bruce Journal, 3 Apr. 1935

38 OH, Minutes, 13 Apr. 1935; *Globe*, 3 May 1935; Beauharnois Papers, Memorandum, meeting, 2 May 1935

39 Beauharnois Papers, Note on Tactics, n. sig [Loring Christie], 12 Apr. 1935; Bennett Papers, Loring Christie, NOTES ON NATIONAL EMERGENCY, 11 Apr. 1935; *TDS*, 9 May 1935; Beauharnois Papers, Wright to R.A.C. Henry, 1 June 1935; HP, Lyon to Hepburn, 17, 23 Apr., 27 May 1935; OH, Minutes, 4 June 1935

40 *Globe* 9 Apr. 1935; HP, Hepburn to Odette, 1 Feb. 1935

41 AO, Treasury Dept., Series II-1, Box 24, File: Loans Proposed 1612/9, J. Gordon Weir to Walters, 2 May 1935

42 Towers Papers, Towers to Walters, 25 Apr. 1939; Walters to Towers, 26 Apr. 1939, enc. Walters to Towers, 4 May 1935; Towers to Walters, 4 May 1939; BCA, Proceedings of the National Finance Committee, 9 Dec. 1936, Z-3; *JLAO*, 1939, Appendix 2, Report, Minutes and Proceedings of the Standing Committee on Public Accounts, 24 Apr. 1939, 325

43 Among the guests on the expedition organized by Jack Bickell and Ben Smith were the secretary of state for New York, the president of American

Airlines, and the head of the Reconstruction Finance Corporation in Washington (*Globe*, Ottawa *Journal*, 6 June 1935).

44 Montreal *Gazette*, 10 June 1935; AO, Treasury Dept., Series II-1, Box 55, File 1-87, Bulletin Service, the Financial News Bureau, 10 June, 11:15 a.m.

45 *Globe, TDS, ME*, 11–15 June 1935; HP, Hepburn to E.N. Rhodes, 12 June 1935; Bennett to Hepburn, 12 June 1935

46 *TDS*, 17 June 1935; *Globe*, 18 June 1935

47 *TDS*, 17 June 1935; Bennett Papers, White to Bennett, 19 June 1935; Bennett to White, 20 June 1935. Bennett told King that White and the banks were perfectly correct in supporting Hepburn (KD, 19 June 1935).

48 AO, Drew Papers, Memorandum, n.d., n.sig.; HP, C. Sifton to Hepburn, 20 June 1935. The general distribution was: mining companies, $5 million; banks, $5 million; insurance companies, $2 million; manufacturing and commercial, $1.7 million; department and chain stores, $900,000 (of which $500,000 was by Eaton's); unknown dealers, $2.4 million; Workmen's Compensation Board, $500,000; Ontario Savings Offices, $586,000; sundry, $1.7 million (AO, Treasury Dept., Series II-1, Box 13, File 1604/10).

49 Bennett Papers, 28 Aug. 1935, n.sig, 336683

50 Financial Post, *Business Year Book*, 1935–7 *passim*; AO, Dept. of Labour, Series I-1, vol. 8, H.C. Hudson to Roger Irwin, 13 Apr. 1935; *Labour Gazette*, Jan. 1936; NAC, Dept. of Labour, Acc 70/382, Box 86, File: Relief Confidential, tables dated 12 June 1936; HP, E.A. Horton to Hepburn, 22 Dec. 1937

51 *TDS, Globe, ME*, 2 Apr.–10 May 1935. The strike is discussed in Alan Young, 'Organized Labour in Welland-Crowland: The Formative Years,' (Honours thesis, Sir Wilfrid Laurier University 1978).

52 *TET*, 11 July 1935; *Sudbury Star*, 13 July 1935; Ontario, Dept. of Labour, *Annual Report*, 1936; *Globe*, 10 July 1935

53 HP, D.B. Harkness to Hepburn, 15 July 1935; Hepburn to R.H. Cooper, 19 July 1935; N.H. Wark to D.B. Harkness, 19 July 1935; Hepburn to M.D. Bogart, 23 July 1935; N.H. Wark to D.B. Harkness, 29 July 1935; Windsor *Star*, 24 June–31 July 1935

54 AO, Ministry of Community and Social Services (formerly Dept. of Public Welfare) Series II-3, Box 1, Circular, 26 July 1935; HP, H.A. Cotnam, Memorandum for Chester Walters, 7 Aug. 1935; *TDS, Globe, ME*, 29 July–2 Aug. 1935

55 HP, Walters to Hepburn, 30 July 1935; H.L. Cummings to Hepburn, 31 July, 6 Aug. 1935; Roger Irwin to Hepburn, 22 July 1935; R. Smith to Hepburn, 10 Aug. 1935; AO, Treasury Dept., Series II-1, Box 48, File 13G, R. Irwin to D.B. Harkness, 1 Aug. 1935; H.L. Cummings to Walters, 2 Aug. 1935; Cummings to Hepburn, 9 Aug. 1935

56 See the text of a radio address and data on farm placements in HP, Unemployment Relief file, 1935; *New Commonwealth*, 3, 10 Aug. 1935.

57 Carty Diary, 31 July 1935; Windsor *Star*, 31 July 1935; *TDS*, Windsor *Star*,
   London *Free Press*, 21–30 Aug. 1935; AO, Ministry of Community and
   Social Services, Series II-3, Box 1, Circular, D.B. Harkness, 29 Aug. 1935. A
   36-page memorandum from Cummings to Hepburn (HP) on 6 August
   outlined the enormous difficulties in even a gradual implementation of the
   policy, and warned of the likely bankruptcy of more municipalities.
   Implementation was further delayed until the King government determined
   the level of support it would give to the provinces.
58 HP, Dr G.C. Brink, Medical Report, 11 Mar. 1935
59 Murphy Papers, Murphy to Lemieux, 29 Jan. 1935; Bruce Diary, 2 Feb.
   1935; interviews, confidential
60 *TDS*, 18, 23 May 1935.
61 Roy Greenaway, *The News Game*, (Toronto 1966) 179; William A. Shields to
   the author, 2 Feb. 1984; *Globe*, 18 June 1935; London *Free Press*, 6 Aug.
   1935; *TDS*, 3, 6 Aug. 1935; HP, Hepburn to Roebuck, 25 Sept. 1935;
   Windsor *Star*, 16 Oct. 1935

CHAPTER 10: 'A BIG BLACK *X* AGAINST HIS NAME'

1 *ME*, 14 Aug. 1935
2 LD, 7, 19 Dec. 1934
3 KD, 12 Dec. 1934; HP, Hepburn to Cromie, 16 Nov. 1934; *ME*, 29 Jan. 1935
4 HP, Hepburn to Hardy, 18 Jan., 1 Feb. 1935; Hardy to Hepburn, 23 Jan., 6
   Feb. 1935; LD, 7 Feb. 1935
5 Interview, Colin Campbell; LD, 12 Feb., 2, 4, 8, Mar. 1935; KD, 11 Mar.
   1935 When Henry resigned he left unpaid bills on the Abitibi Canyon
   project of over $6 million, the largest of which was Dominion Construction
   for over $3 million, followed by Canadian General Electric for $1.6 million.
   The negotiations between Hydro and the companies were long and involved,
   and Hepburn ultimately intervened. An intriguing letter from a John McGill
   to Hepburn suggested that the settlement was in part political: 'Burn this as
   soon as you read same. Harry McLean has been a good friend of ours you
   know and is prepared to go the limit if treated half decent, nothing small
   about this man. We had a very pleasant visit at Peter's [Heenan] house on
   Rosemarie. Peter knows how things are and the "nigger in the fence".' An
   order-in-council of 23 March authorized payment of only $2 million to
   Dominion, and the details remain a mystery. CGE got the full amount
   claimed, with some last-minute negotiations adding $25,000, the amount the
   company contributed to the 1935 campaign fund (HP, N. Rowell to Hepburn
   16 Jan. 1935; McGill to Hepburn, 17, 23, Jan. 1935; Memorandum for
   Prime Minister File, 'Memorandum – See Roebuck and Lyon regarding
   financial statement Abitibi claims. Suggest some action during this coming

week.' M.F.H. 1 Feb. 1935; A.C. Dyment to Hepburn, 9 Apr. 1935).

6 KD, 20 Mar. 1935

7 LD, 23 Apr., 10 May 1935; KD, 10 May 1935. When O'Connor planned a
   world cruise for 1935 there had been panic in Ottawa until Mitch persuaded
   O'Connor to remain and 'assist the party during the coming Federal General
   Election' (LD, 12 Jan. 1935; KP, Hardy to King, 10 Jan. 1935; HP, Hepburn
   to Hardy, 18 Jan. 1935).

8 LD, 16 May, 9, 11 Sept. 1935; KD, 31 May, 9, 11, Sept. 1935; Dafoe Papers,
   Grant Dexter to Dafoe, 3 Sept. 1935. For details of the subscriptions, see
   Lambert Papers, vol. 13. The financing of the party is discussed in Reginald
   Whitaker, *The Government Party* (Toronto 1977), 53.

9 Roy Greenaway, *The News Game* (Toronto 1966), 180. Mitch apparently
   knew of E.P. Taylor's 'tied hotels' and the government turned a blind eye to
   the breweries' practice of buying soft drink companies, giving the products
   names identical to their own, and advertising the soft drinks on giant
   billboards to circumvent the prohibition against advertising (HP, P.A.
   Mancross to Hepburn, 18 May 1935). The 1934 act restoring beer parlours
   denied a licence to a hotel 'in which any brewer ... had any interest ...
   whether such interest is direct or indirect.' When the act was proclaimed, the
   Brewing Corporation still had six old hotels on its hands, and E.P. Taylor
   was anxious to develop a chain of hotels. In a conversation with Taylor,
   Mitch apparently raised no objection. Mohawk Investments was
   incorporated in August 1934. Each hotel in the chain was incorporated, all
   the stock was held by Mohawk, and by the fall of 1935 Taylor and Mohawk
   owned twenty-one hotels and were about to buy six more. Although Taylor
   denied he owned the hotels, there was unquestionably at least an indirect
   relationship. When the matter became public after the federal election, Mitch
   only suspended the licences until the hotels could be sold. The iniquitous
   tied hotels, he assured reporters, were a thing of the past, but the *FP* mused
   editorially that it 'may be that the whole story has not been told ... that
   there was more "politics" in the suspension of the hotel licenses and the
   early restoration of most of them than appears on the surface' (HP, Arnold
   Smith to Hepburn, 25 Oct. 1935; *ME*, 24 Oct., 2 Nov. 1935; *Globe*, 25 Oct.,
   2 Nov. 1935; *FP*, 16 Nov. 1935).

10 HP, Hepburn to King, 31 Aug. 1935 (copied to Bickell); King to Hepburn, 2
   Sept. 1935; LD, 12, 21, 26 Sept., 1, 4 Oct. 1935; Vancouver *Sun*, 30 Sept.
   1935. In May O'Connor had asked King for some commitment on the gold
   tax, but King replied that he 'could & would give nothing in the way of
   undertakings' (KD, 31 May 1935).

11 LD, 2 Mar., 13, 20, 26 Sept. 1935; *FP*, 10 Nov. 1934; KD, 17 Jan. 1941.
   Mitch told Duff Pattullo, with some exaggeration, that 'It is needless for me
   to point out that it was friends of our Government who financed the Federal

candidates from Quebec to British Columbia' (Pattullo Papers, Hepburn to Pattullo, 27 July 1937). When Pattullo reported Mitch's claim to him, King dismissed it: 'That so far as Hepburn was concerned, we had helped to really finance his travelling expenses, that the campaign fund had been collected by others. As a matter of fact, it was the Federal government committee. I did not tell him but the facts were that I did not want Hepburn to help us in the campaign. He did us more harm than good in some places' (KD, 17 Jan. 1941).

12 HP, Hepburn to Hardy, 11 July 1935; KP, W. Fraser to King, 11 July 1935; Lambert Papers, Fraser to E. Long, 18 July 1935; LD, 10 July 1935; Dafoe Papers, Lambert to Dafoe, 17 July 1935

13 KD, 26 June 1935

14 LD, 12 July 1935; Claxton Papers, Claxton to Massey, 30 Sept. 1935; Claxton to McDermott, 30 Sept. 1935; Claxton to McDermott, 10 Oct. 1935

15 Power Papers, Johnson to Power, 6 Aug. 1935; Power to Johnson, 14 Aug. 1935

16 Bennett Papers, n.sig., 28 Aug. 1935, 336683. The same document found its way to R.A.C. Henry of Beauharnois.

17 The account of the campaign is based on the *Globe*, *TDS*, *ME*, *TET*, Ottawa *Citizen*, *Winnipeg Free Press*, Regina *Leader-Post*, Edmonton *Bulletin*, Halifax *Herald*, Vancouver *Sun* and *Province* from 5 Aug.–15 Oct. 1935.

18 Hepburn tried to press King into a more positive position on monetary reform. 'You stand alone as the head of the only party that unanimously approves the principle of a publicly owned national bank,' he reminded King, and he assured a sceptic that King believed in fundamental monetary reform (KP, Hepburn to King, 31 Aug. 1935; HP, Hepburn to King, 24 Sept. 1935; Hepburn to R.H. Babbage, 26 Aug. 1935).

19 KP, King to Hepburn, 6 Aug. 1935; *Globe*, *TDS*, 9 Oct. 1935

20 *TDS*, 3 Sept. 1935; KP, Mr. Hepburn's Broadcast Tuesday Night, 8 Oct., 1935

21 During the provincial election earlier in the summer the Alberta Liberal leader had asked Mitch to help stem the Social Credit tide. 'This Province is particularly interested in Monetary Reform, and the war which you have waged in Ontario has made a tremendous appeal to our people' (HP, W.M. Houson to Hepburn, 22 June 1935). The tour was arranged by the national office in cooperation with the western organizations.

22 HP, Hepburn to King, 31 Aug. 1935; King to Hepburn, 2 Sept. 1935; Elmhirst to Harry Johnson, 11 Sept. 1935; John Miller, chief inspector, CPR, to Elmhirst, 30 Aug. 1935

23 HP, Hepburn to Johnson, 4 Sept. 1935; Elmhirst to Johnson, 5 Sept. 1935

24 HP, Elmhirst to Johnson, 11 Sept. 1935; Edmonton *Bulletin*, 16 Sept. 1935; editorial, Moose Jaw *Times-Herald*, reprinted in Windsor *Star*, 19 Sept. 1935

25 *Winnipeg Free Press*, 4 Sept. 1935; Vancouver *Province*, 11 Sept. 1935;
    Moose Jaw *Times-Herald*, quoted in Windsor *Star*, 19 Sept. 1935; Edmonton
    Bulletin, 16 Sept. 1935
26 Vancouver *Sun*, 7 Sept. 1935; HP, McGeer to Hepburn, 3 May 1935; J.A.
    Campbell to Hepburn, 14 Sept. 1935; Vancouver *Province*, 11, 12 Sept. 1935
27 HP, Pouliot to Hepburn, 29 July 1935; Power to Lambert, 30 Aug. 1935;
    Pouliot Papers, Elmhirst to Pouliot, 18 Sept. 1935; Johnson to Pouliot, 7
    Sept. 1935; *Le Devoir*, *TDS*, 1 Oct. 1935. Mitch was urged to campaign in
    New Brunswick before the election was called, and Lambert advised against
    it. His campaign was an enormous success (LD, 20 June 1935; HP, Angus
    Macdonald to Hepburn, 18 Oct. 1935; Colin Mackenzie to Hepburn, 16 Oct.
    1935; *TDS*, 24 Sept., 27 Sept. 1935).
28 Massey, Diary, 1 Sept., 1935; KP, Memoranda and Notes, Dominion of
    Canada, Federal Elections, Oct. 1935, Liberal Publicity Campaign; Manion
    Papers, Hogarth to Manion, 10 Oct. 1935; Anthony W.E. Rasporitch, 'A
    Boston Yankee in Prince Arthur's Landing: C.D. Howe and His
    Constituency,' *Canada: An Historical Magazine* (Winter 1973), 28
29 *Globe*, 10 Oct. 1935; HP, King to Hepburn, 3 Oct. 1935; Dunning Papers,
    Dunning to E.A. Macdonald, 21 Aug. 1935; Manion Papers, Manion to
    Hogarth, 2 Sept. 1935
30 HP, Roebuck to Hepburn, 14 Oct. 1935; Honoré Mercier to Hepburn, 15
    Oct. 1935; Angus Macdonald to Hepburn, 18 Oct. 1935; A.T. Whitaker to
    Hepburn, 15 Oct. 1935; Colin Mackenzie to Hepburn, 16 Oct. 1935
31 *ME*, 16 Oct. 1935; KD, 17 Oct. 1935. As early as February 1935 King was
    worried about Slaght and, with Roebuck thinking of running federally, told
    Lambert that 'R's candidature would help solve problem of H. and Federal
    Cabinet and also of Slaght' (LD, 16 Feb. 1935).
32 KD, 17 19, 21 Oct.; interviews, confidential; Bennett Papers, R. Reid to
    Bennett, 4 Aug. 1934
33 KD, 19, 21 Oct. 1935
34 KD, 22 Oct. 1935; KP, Hepburn to King, 21 Oct. 1935; King to Hepburn, 22
    Oct. 1935; interviews, Colin Campbell, Harry Nixon
35 KD, 21–23 Oct. 1935; *TDS*, 25 Oct. 1935; AO, Maclean Hunter Papers,
    Dexter to Floyd Chalmers, 27 Oct. 1937. See also Frederick W. Gibson,
    'The Cabinet of 1935,' in F. Gibson, ed., *Cabinet Formation and Bicultural
    Relations*, vol. 6 of Studies of the Royal Commission on Bilingualism and
    Biculturalism, (Ottawa 1970).
36 OHA, Lyon to Hepburn, 29 Apr. 1935; Minutes, Special Engineering
    Committee, 11 July 1935; HP, Report on Power Supplies in Southern
    Ontario, enclosed in W. LaCrosse and W.F. Ryan to Lyon, 29 July 1935;
    Ryan to Hepburn, 20 Sept. 1935; OH, Minutes, 2 Aug., 19 Sept. 1935.
    According to Sweezey, Hydro compelled Niagara Hudson to agree to supply

power 'on pain of having Ontario condemn and take over the Canadian Niagara Power Plant' (Roosevelt Papers, OF 156, CONFIDENTIAL MEMORANDUM TO THE PRESIDENT ... Frank P. Walsh, 10 July 1936).

37 AO, Roebuck Papers, Hogg to Lyon, 18 Sept. 1935, Ryan to Lyon, 23 Sept., 2 Oct. 1935; OHA, Memorandum, Hogg, The Problem of Quebec Power, 15 Oct. 1935 (Roebuck's underlining); AO, Roebuck Papers, Lyon to Roebuck, 16 Oct. 1935, enclosing Hogg's 15 Oct. report

38 OH, Minutes, 18 Oct. 1935; HP, Lyon to Hepburn, 18 Oct. 1935; *ME*, 19 Oct. 1935; OHA, J.D[iblee], Memorandum for Filing, 20 Oct. 1935; Don Carlos to Hogg, 21 Oct. 1935; J.D[iblee] to Hogg, 22 Oct. 1935

39 Hydro had also secured the legal opinion from Louis St Laurent that Quebec did not have the constitutional power to close the border to exports (OHA, Lewis Duncan to T.S. Lyon, 17 July 1935 enclosing Louis St. Laurent to Duncan, 4 July 1935).

40 Committee Investigating Hydro, 509 (Roebuck), 296 (Lyon), 947 (R.A.C. Henry); OH, Minutes, 3 Oct. 1935, enc. Jeffery to Lyon, 28 Sept. 1935; Gatineau Papers, 763, File 705, Memorandum, Gordon Gale, 27 Sept. 1935

41 Taschereau Papers, Ralston to Taschereau, 16 Nov. 1935; Taschereau to H. Nixon, 16 Nov. 1935; Ralston to Taschereau, 26 Nov. 1935; Taschereau to Ralston, 26 Nov. 1935; OHA, Lyon to the Commissioners, 29 Oct. 1935, enclosing a lengthy memorandum from Gatineau outlining its preferred position; Lyon to Hogg, 23 Oct. 1935; Lyon to Gale, 25 Oct. 1935; Graustein [unsigned] to the commission, 30 Oct. 1935; Gale to Lyon, 13 Dec. 1935; Beauharnois Papers, Memorandum Re Suggested Negotiations with Hydro-Electric Power Commission [n.d., n.sig]; Henry to Norris, 27 Jan. 1936, enclosing Memorandum Re Beauharnois Development, 23 Jan. 1936; H.J. Symington to Nixon, 13 Nov. 1935. Mitch had also received a letter from the Quebec Power Companies Security Committee insisting that all parties should make comparable sacrifices and assuring him that the bondholders would be 'willing to accept a reasonable reduction in interest, providing some method of safeguarding the principal can be found' (HP, J.H. Lumbar and I.E. Weldon to Hepburn, 22 Oct. 1935).

42 HP, Taschereau to Hepburn, 12 Mar. 1935; Hepburn to Taschereau, 18 Mar. 1935. Bennett and Taschereau did meet the producers in 1934, and Bennett promised federal action if requested by the two provinces. Hepburn was not at the meeting, but told Bennett that Ontario 'will support federal action ... with details of application open to consideration and approval' (Bennett Papers, Hepburn to Bennett, 7 Nov. 1934; HP, draft press release, 24 Oct. 1934; *New York Times*, 23–24 Oct. 1934). See also B.L. Vigod, *Quebec before Duplessis: The Political Career of Louis-Alexandre Taschereau* (Montreal 1980), 181–7.

43 HP, Graustein to Hepburn, 31 Aug. 1935; Vining to Hepburn, Oct. 23, 1935; *JLAO*, 1941, Appendix No. 1, Final Report and Proceedings of the Select

Committee of the Legislative Assembly appointed to inquire into the Administration of the Department of Lands and Forests (hereafter *JLAO*, Timber Inquiry), 1172 (Vining); HP, Heenan to Hepburn, Oct. 29, 1935, enclosing Memorandum for Rundle, Macdonnell, and MacKelcan, 18 Oct. 1935

44 HP, Hepburn to Ralston, 30 Oct. 1935; Graustein to Hepburn, 4 Nov. 1935, enclosing Graustein to Frank Knox, 4 Nov. 1935; Rowell to Hepburn, 1 Nov. 1935; Taschereau to Hepburn, 7 Nov. 1935; *Globe*, 2, 7 Nov. 1935; *JLAO*, Timbert Inquiry, 1198 (Vining).

45 *Globe*, 24 Oct. 1935; LD, 4 Nov. 1935; *New Commonwealth*, 16 Nov. 1935. Dunning wanted to force the issue in Ontario, but King had no desire to confront Hepburn and found Dunning a seat in Prince Edward Island after the sitting member accepted a sinecure in Fisheries, (KD, 10 Dec. 1935; Dafoe Papers, Dexter to Dafoe, 17 Dec. 1935; Carty Diary, 9 June 1937).

46 *Globe*, 5–6 Nov. 1935; Windsor *Star*, 5, 9 Nov. 1935; HP, Hardy to Hepburn, Nov. 7, 1935; KD, Nov. 5, 1935; HP, Hepburn to Macdonald, 6 Nov. 1935

47 HP, O'Connor to Elmhirst, 18 Nov. 1935

48 AO, Roebuck Papers, R.A.C. Henry to Lyon, 4 Nov. 1935; Roebuck to Lyon, 5 Nov. 1935; Symington to Roebuck, 23 Nov. 1935; Roebuck to Symington, 30 Novemer 1935; HP, Symington to Hepburn, 30 Nov. 1935; HP, Symington to Hepburn, 30 Nov. 1935. Ralston informed Taschereau on 29 November that Mitch intended to proclaim the acts on his return, but admitted that there were 'so many rumours that it is hopeless to guess what are well-founded and what are spurious' (Taschereau Papers). There was considerable truth in the conclusion reached by Henry, the general manager of Beauharnois, that the companies did want to find a compromise 'but we were given very scant consideration chiefly I think because Roebuck seemed to be determined to leave no stone unturned to actually cancel the contracts' (McGrath Papers, Henry to McGrath, 16 Feb. 1940).

49 *Globe*, *TDS*, *ME*, 7 Dec. 1935; AO, Committee Investigating Hydro, 947 (Henry); Bruce Diary, 6 Dec. 1935

50 HP, R.B. Baxter to Hepburn, 19 Dec. 1935; Henry to Hepburn, 18 Dec. 1935; OHA, Gale to the commission, 18 Dec. 1935; OH, Minutes, 17, 19 Dec. 1935; AO, Committee Investigating Hydro, 199 (Lyon), 554 (Roebuck); Beauharnois Papers, Henry to John Norris, 17, 21 Dec. 1935; Gatineau Papers, Minute Book, 18 Dec. 1935; Taschereau Papers, H.J. Symington to Taschereau, 22 Jan. 1936

51 AO, Committee Investigating Hydro, 553 (Roebuck); *TDS*, 23 Dec. 1935; AO, Roebuck Papers, Duncan to Roebuck, 8 Dec. 1935; McGrath Papers, Borden to McGrath, 13 Dec. 1935; KD, 27 Oct. 1936

52 The opening remarks and committee reports are published in *Dominion*

Provincial Conferences 1927–1935–1941 (Ottawa 1951). Two secretaries kept a record of the finance committee meetings (NAC, Federal Provincial Conferences, Series 3, vol. 64) which were later edited into a final version (HP, Box 233). The two do not always agree, and I have tried to reconstruct the debate using both versions. For the Ontario briefs, see AO, Treasury Dept., Series II-1, Box 46.

53 Dafoe Papers, T. Crerar to Dafoe, 17 Dec. 1935

54 KD, 10 Dec. 1935. By 1934 the federal government collected 72 per cent of the taxes on metal mines.

55 Bennett Papers, Hepburn to Bennett, 30 Oct. 1934; Supreme Court of Canada, Factums of the Attorney General of the Province of Ontario [on the New Deal cases]. The proposals for amendment and patriation are in NAC, Federal-Provincial Conferences, Series 3, vol. 601 (a), Memorandum submitted by the Attorney General of Ontario, Amendment of the British North America Act, The Written Constitution, n.d.

56 KD, 13 Dec. 1935

57 Chalmers Papers, Memorandum, 14 Dec. 1935; *FP*, 21 Dec. 1935; KD, 13, 19 Dec. 1935; *Globe*, 20 Dec. 1935 Chalmer's analysis owed much to Grant Dexter who wrote that 'King's choice of Dunning was deliberate and for clearly discernible reasons. King actually wants Rogers as his successor. It was a choice between left and right wing liberalism. Dunning stood for the right wing; Hepburn for the left. King chose deliberately to put the boots to Mitch ... Mitch and Charlie [Dunning] see each other as rivals for the Federal leadership and Charlie, rightly, has stressed the contrast between himself and the radicalism of Mitch. But Mitch will now veer off and seek to become the leader of left wing liberalism. He may succeed and in a big way. He will have a number of active allies in the Federal cabinet – Ian Mackenzie and Jimmy Gardiner if he comes to Ottawa, for another ... Gerry McGeer may get in on the recount and he will go for Mitch sure.' Monetary policy, added Dexter, will be the first 'field of combat' (AO, Maclean Hunter Papers, Dexter to Chalmers, 27 Oct. 1937).

CHAPTER 11: 'THEN SEND US DOWN TO DEFEAT'

1 Carty Diary, 30 Jan., 6, 24 Feb. 1936; London *Free Press*, *Globe*, 11–15 Feb. 1936

2 According to Mrs Bruce, an earlier draft had been much more specific in its reference to separate schools (Bruce Diary, 11 Feb. 1936).

3 HP, J.T. White to Hepburn, 30 Nov. 1934; *TDS*, 13 May 1935; *Globe*, 15 Jan. 1936

4 Bruce Diary, 3, 14 Jan. 1936; Bennett Papers, Bennett to H. Napier Moore, 17 Dec. 1936

5 The tax was to be collected by Ottawa, as agreed at the December conference, and based on the federal schedule. Ontario allowed the federal tax paid to be deducted from taxable income, and Walters soon complained that the high federal rates left little room for the province. 'It will thus be seen that in what is in fact a strictly provincial field of taxation,' he protested, 'the Dominion reaps while the province can only glean' (BCA, *RD* 162, 2 B. 440, Proceedings of the National Finance Committee, 11 Dec. 1936).

6 HP, Gundy to Hepburn, 18 Mar. 1936

7 *Globe*, 27 Mar. 1936. By 1937 the Succession Duty Branch had a list of 3,414 estates to be investigated with a total value of $1.3 billion. The collection 'target' for 1937 was $10 million and by August over $4 million had been collected, with the Robert Laidlaw estate, which had closed in 1929, leading with an additional $1.8 million (AO, Treasury Dept., Series II-2, Box 63, File 16J). By the end of 1936 the government had acquired about 40 per cent of the outstanding bonds, most of the remainder being in England where they were held for investment only (BCA, RD 162, 2 B. 440, Proceedings of the National Finance Committee, Dec. 11, 1936).

8 Jacob Finkelman and Bora Laskin, 'The Industrial Standards Act of Ontario and its Administration,' *Publications of the Industrial Law Research Council* (July 1936), 1–16

9 *JLAO*, Timber Inquiry, 125, 131 (Heenan), 1212 (Vining). On the Gaefell plan negotiations, see *ME*, 16–19 Oct., 21, 23 Dec. 1935, 22 Feb. 1936; *FP*, 4 Apr. 1936.

10 *JLAO*, Timber Inquiry, 215 (Heenan); *TDS*, 20 Dec. 1935, 26 Feb. 1936; *ME*, 24 Feb. 1936. See H.V. Nelles, *Politics of Development* (Toronto 1974), 454–6; R.S. Lambert and P. Pross, *Renewing Nature's Wealth* (Toronto 1967), 339–40; B.L. Vigod, *Quebec before Duplessis: The Political Career of Louis-Alexandre Taschereau* (Montreal 1986), 180.

11 McGuigan Papers, Quinn to O'Brien, 25 Oct. 1935; Quinn to O'Connor, 28 Oct. 1935. Quinn to McGuigan, 7 Nov. 1935; Quinn to O'Brien, 4 Dec. 1935; O'Brien Papers, McGuigan to O'Brien, Feast of Christ the King, [24 Nov.] 1935. In his letter to O'Connor, designed for Mitch's eye, Quinn stated that McArthur was 'the greatest cause of uneasiness amongst our people closest in touch with the situation.' During their first meeting, said Quinn, 'I regarded his attitude as definitely unfriendly and he certainly advanced arguments in opposition to us that were never thought of even by the Orangemen.'

12 McGuigan Papers, Quinn to McGuigan, 13 Dec. 1935; O'Brien Papers, Quinn to O'Brien, 3 Jan. 1936; Quinn to O'Brien, 11 Jan. 1936; *TDS*, 5 Nov., 11 Dec. 1935; *ME*, 12 Dec. 1935. From Florida, Mitch, Slaght and O'Connor wired their congratulations to McBride.

13 HP, Quinn to Robert Kerr, 7 Feb. 1936. *TDS*, 10–11 Feb. 1936; HP, Ivers
    Kell to Knowles, 10 Feb. 1936, enclosing Ross's filed story; Hepburn to
    Quinn, 21 Feb. 1936; McGuigan Papers, McGuigan to Heenan, n.d.
14 HP, Hepburn to E.M. Macdonald, 5 Mar. 1936. Only Croll, Leduc, and
    Heenan were enthusiastically behind Mitch according to the Windsor *Star*
    (25 Mar. 1936), which often got its stories from Croll.
15 *TDS, ME*, 25, 26, 28 Feb. 1936; Kidd Papers, Quinn to Bishop John T
    Kidd, 15 Feb. 1936; *Le Droit*, 17 Mar. 1936; ACFEO Papers, C2/69/7, L. Scott
    to E. Cloutier, ed., *Le Droit*, 17 Mar.; Quinn to Scott, 19 Mar. 1936. At one
    point the government had drafted and printed Bill 52 and then with the
    apparent help of the police recovered and destroyed all copies. No trace of
    Bill 52 has been found. The front page was reproduced in the *ME* (26 Feb.)
    and the bill apparently authorized municipalities to levy a 3.5% tax on
    corporation income for schools.
16 *TDS, ME*, 21–25 Mar., 31 Mar., 2 Apr. 1936; McGuigan Papers,
    Memorandum, n.d. n.sig.; Kidd Papers, Quinn to J.A. McNevin, 8 Oct.
    1937; McGuigan Papers, Quinn to McGuigan, 1 Feb. 1937. The *ME* (4
    Apr.) reported that McArthur had threatened to resign during the drafting.
17 *ME, TDS*, 4 Apr. 1936
18 Toronto Board of Education, Minutes 6 Apr. 1936
19 The amendments removed the explicit reference to Bell and the CPR as
    widely held companies that would fall under section 33b and raised the
    subsidiary provision from 25 to 50 per cent (the original draft is in AO, Dept.
    of the Provincial Secretary, Office of the Clerk of the Legislature, Box 307).
20 HP, Memorandum for the Prime Minister, W.R.R.P[arker], 8 Apr. 1936;
    confidential interview
21 The detailed data on those on relief are not always consistent and the
    definitions sometimes change. The best sources, from which the above figures
    have been compiled, are to be found in a large number of memoranda and
    tables in NAC, Dept. of Labour, Acc 70/382, Boxes 66–80. See also Ontario,
    Annual Report of the Department of Public Welfare, 1935–1937. Until 1935,
    according to a federal government report, the data were not complete: 'It is
    only in the last eighteen months that every person [in Ontario] in receipt of
    relief has been reported by the municipalities so that the numbers may
    appear to be higher although not actually had the municipalities reported in
    the same manner as previously' (NAC, Dept. of Labour, Acc 70/382, Box 68,
    Progress Report – Mr. Baldwin, Dominion Unemployment Relief as related
    to Economic and Employment Tendencies in Ottawa, Oct. 31, 1936). The
    estimates of farmers receiving relief are taken from slightly different data in
    NAC, Dept. of Labour, Acc 70/382, Box 66; National Employment
    Commission, Registration – Sept. 1936, Farm Relief, Province of Ontario
    (where only 2.5% were regarded as genuine farmers in the agricultural

counties); and NAC, Dept. of Labour, Acc. 70/382, Box 71, Memorandum Re Relief in Ontario, 7 June 1937.

22 AO, Treasury Dept., Series II-1, Box 43, Croll to F.F. Berry, City Clerk, Hamilton, 6 Feb. 1936; *Globe*, 4 Feb., 18 Mar. 1936

23 HP, Rogers to Hepburn, 1 Apr. 1936; KD, 27, 30, 31 Mar., 1, 8 Apr. 1936: *HCD*, 3 Apr. 1936, 1787; *ME*, 3 Apr. 1936

24 NAC, Dept. of Labour, Acc 70/382, Box 67, Watson Sellar, Memorandum for the Minister: Re Relief Costs in Ontario, 9 Sept. 1936

25 *TDS*, *Globe*, *ME*, 29 June–10 July 1936; HP, A.P. Gow to Hepburn, 10 July 1936; D. Hist., 161.009 (063), R.E. Mercer to Officer Commanding, Military District No. 1, 6 July 1936

26 *TDS*, *Globe*, 9–11 July 1936

27 AO, Attorney General, 4-02, File 6.3, J. Sedgwick to Leduc, 13 July 1936; Leduc to Board of Police Commissioners, 13 July 1936; *TDS*, 7 Dec. 1936; Cohen Papers, Cohen to Hepburn, 31 July, 5 Aug. 1936; Hepburn to Cohen, 4 Aug. 1936

28 Manion Papers, Hogarth to Manion, 22 June 1934

29 Ibid., A.A. Allan to Manion, 20 Nov. 1935. The most persistent rumours concerned no other than 'Boss' Ferguson, who, Hogarth assured Angela Bruce, 'is still after it' (Bruce Diary, 5 Jan. 1936). A move to draft Ferguson fizzled out at the convention.

30 *TDS*, 19, 21 May 1936

31 Ontario Progressive Conservative Association Papers, Proceedings of the Liberal-Conservative Association of Ontario, 27–28 May 1936; *TDS*, *ME*, *Globe*, 26–29 May 1936

32 *TDS*, 12, 19, 23, 30 June 1936; *Globe*, 18 June, 1 Oct. 1936

33 NAC, Drew Papers, George Wardrope to Rowe, 14 Aug. 1936, enclosed in Mel Jack to Drew, 18 Aug. 1936

34 *TDS*, 12, 13 June, 3 July 1936; *Globe*, 7, 16 Sept. 1936; London *Free Press*, 29 May 1936

35 Carty Diary, 8 May 1936; *TDS*, *TET*, 6 May 1936; *Globe*, 13 July 1936

36 KD, 6, 28 Jan. 1937. Hill, a prominent Orangeman, had held the riding by 418 votes in 1934.

37 *Globe*, 7 Nov. 1936; HP, East Hastings By-election, Manifesto, 5 Dec. 1936

38 HP, A.L. McDougall to C.F. Stammeras, 14 Nov. 1936; *JLAO*, 1937: 181–2; L. Frost Papers, Frost to George White, 14 Dec. 1936; Frost to E.F. Reid, 28 Nov. 1936

39 The account of the election has been taken from the Toronto press, 7 Nov.–10 Dec. 1936. The Drew Papers in the NAC (File 623) contain handouts, posters, cartoons, and the 25 November press release cited. The campaign had its moments. When Mitch commented that when Drew was securities commissioner high-pressure stock salesmen operated out of hotel

rooms, Drew replied that Mitch was 'more of an authority on the occupants of hotel rooms than I am' (*GM*, 1 Dec. 1936).

40 For the Plainfield speech see *GM*, 27 Nov. and the *Star*, 27, 28 Nov. 1936. No other report included the words cited by the *Star*. Drew had affidavits from an Anglican minister, a lawyer, a reeve and others on the platform denying that he had said anything resembling the *Star* report. The Liberals' affidavits, Drew claimed, were from two of 'the most rabid Catholic families' and a boy whose father had a road contract and was threatened with dismissal (NAC, Drew Papers, Drew to Arthur Meighen, 12 Dec. 1936). The issue came up in the House in March 1937 when Drew again denied he made the statement and stated that of the six reporters present only the *Star* reported it. Mitch replied there were three reporters present, but McTaggert of the *Globe* had taken his story from a Tory organizer, presumably from a press release, before the speech. William Shields, then a Queen's Park reporter, stated that Farley Faulkner and Eric Hutton of the *Star* were there and swore the report was accurate (interview, William Shields). Drew was apparently convinced that Mitch seriously thought of replacing King who, it was rumoured in Drew's circles at least, would retire after he returned from the coronation (NAC, Drew Papers, Drew to Dr H.O. Hewitt, 28 Dec. 1936).

41 Bruce Diary, 1 Dec. 1936; LD, 21 Dec. 1936, where O'Connor states the election cost $33,000.

42 *TDS*, 10 Dec. 1936; HP, W. Bulmer, Memorandum for ... Hepburn, 22 Dec. 1936; Hepburn to G.W. Jones, 16 Dec. 1936; L. Frost Papers, Frost to H.S. Pritchard, 11 Feb. 1937; *STTJ*, 10, 11 Dec. 1936. Actually the Tories slipped in the lightly populated north, and gained in the south. In Mayo, where there were no Catholics among the 260 voters, the Tories fell from 60 to 49% of the vote, a tribute perhaps to material inducements rather than religious convictions. Father F.J. Brennan reported to Archbishop O'Brien that reports that seven or eight hundred Catholics failed to vote were false; his information was that 85 to 95% voted, and voted Liberal. O'Brien undertook his own investigation and concluded that almost 100% voted Liberal, and asked Bishop Kidd to convey that information to Hepburn (O'Brien Papers, Brennan to O'Brien, 10 Mar. 1937; O'Brien to Kidd, 21 Mar. 1937).

43 NAC, Federal-Provincial Conferences, Series F, vol. 73, Proceedings of the Permanent Committee on Financial Questions of the Dominion-Provincial Conference, Ottawa, 13–14 Jan. 1936

44 KD, 6 Aug. 1937; KP, Memorandum, For Mr. King, E.A.P., 31 Jan. 1936; HP, Hepburn to E.M. Macdonald, 5 Mar. 1936; NAC, Privy Council Office, vol. 1332, Report of the Minister of Justice, approved 31 Mar. 1936

45 LD, 19 Mar., 18, 19 Apr. 1936; Bruce Journal, 18, 19 Apr. 1936

46 KD, 30 Apr., 1 May 1936

47 Ibid, 1, 2, 22, 28, 29 Apr. 1936; H. Blair Neatby, *William Lyon Mackenzie King: Prism of Unity, 1932–1939* (Toronto 1976), 162–4
48 *TET*, 6 May 1936; LD, 28 May, 4, 12 June, 12 Aug., 9 Sept. 1936
49 KP, Lambert to Hepburn, 5 Nov. 1936; Hepburn to Lambert, 12 Nov. 1936; LD, 16, 20 Nov., 7, 21 Dec. 1936; *TET*, Windsor *Star*, 8 Jan. 1937

CHAPTER 12: 'A MUCH DIVIDED CROWD'

1 In the majority decision on the appeal, Mr Justice Masten stated that the determination of the legislative powers of the dominion or the province could not be withdrawn from the judiciary and that a province could not destroy a right over which it had no jurisdiction and then protect its action by denying injured parties access to the courts (*Ottawa Valley Power Co.* v. *Hydro-Electric Power Commission* (1936) OR 265–97
2 See Brian J. Young, 'C. George McCullagh and the Leadership League' (MA thesis, Queen's University 1964); J.C. Furness, 'Canada's Wonder Boy,' *Saturday Night* (22 Jan. 1938); Pierre Berton, 'The Amazing Career of George McCullagh,' *MacLean's*, 15 Jan. 1949.
3 Bruce Diary, 18 Oct. 1936; KD, 6 Jan. 1937; *Globe*, 29 Sept. 1936
4 *Saturday Night*, 24 Oct. 1936; E.A. Beeder, 'The Toronto Press,' *Canadian Forum*, 31 Oct. 1936
5 There were reports that O'Connor had a financial interest in the paper, and Harry Johnson boasted that Mitch had been 'the principal factor in getting McC in the newspaper business.' McCullagh categorically denied that either had been involved (LD, 20–21 Nov. 1936; *GM*, 30 Nov. 1936; Mackenzie Papers, C. Burns to Mackenzie, 26 Oct. 1936).
6 *Globe*, 3 Nov. 1936; *GM*, 23 Nov. 1936; KP, McCullagh to King, 17 Nov. 1936; King to McCullagh, 20 Nov. 1936; KD, 19 Nov. 1936
7 Sir Anthony Jenkinson, *Where Seldom a Gun is Heard* (London 1937), 218; R.E. Knowles, 'President and Publisher,' *Saturday Night*, 14 Nov. 1936
8 *GM*, 23 Nov. 1936; KP, McCullagh to King, 5 Dec. 1936; KD, 6 Jan. 1937; Bruce Diary, 29 Nov. 1936
9 *GM*, 3 June 1938; *STTJ*, 15 Dec. 1936; Beauharnois Papers, Reille Thompson to C.S. Bagg, 28 Dec. 1936; AO, Committee Investigating Hydro, 590 (Roebuck); AO, Roebuck Papers, Box 43, 'The Story' (notes for what appears to be his testimony before the select committee)
10 *GM*, 17, 18 Dec. 1936
11 *TET*, 17–20 Dec. 1936; *Financial Times*, 18, 25 Dec. 1936; *GM*, 19, 30 Dec. 1936; *GM*, 6, 19 Jan. 1937; OHA, W.N. Tilley to W.G. Hanna, 30 Dec. 1936; *FP*, 2 Jan. 1937
12 Bruce Diary, 6 Jan. 1937; AO, Roebuck Papers, Robertson to Roebuck, 14 Jan. 1936; SO, 1937, ch. 62: 59, 58

13 Roosevelt Papers, Press Conference no. 105, 14 Mar. 1934 (reference courtesy Blair Neatby); OH, Minutes, 18 July 1934; HP, Lyon to Hepburn, 14 Apr. 1936. The King government had agreed to such a diversion in 1925, but the US Senate had rejected the convention in 1931.

14 Bennett Papers, Hepburn to Bennett, 13 Aug. 1934; Bennett to Hepburn, 29 Aug. 1934; OH, Minutes, 14 Sept. 1934

15 Lyon to Skelton, 16 Nov. 1935; Skelton to Lyon, 15 Feb. 1936, *Correspondence and Documents Relating to St. Lawrence Deep Waterway Treat 1932, Niagara Convention 1929, and Ogoki River and Kenogami River (Lake) Projects and Export of Electrical Power* (Ottawa 1938) (hereafter *Correspondence re St. Lawrence*); HP, Lyon to Hepburn, 14 Apr., 21 May 1936; OH, Minutes, 28 Feb., 11 May 1936

16 Roosevelt Papers, OF 156, Walsh to Roosevelt, 10 July 1936, enclosing CONFIDENTIAL MEMORANDA TO THE PRESIDENT On Matters Relating to Negotiations Touching Development of the Great Lakes–St. Lawrence Basin, 10 July 1936. Walsh was also concerned that Hydro was hostage to Niagara Hudson because of the interchange of power at Niagara and Niagara Hudson's agreement to supply emergency power. Lyon had told him, 'Your President may be defeated next year, in which case the private companies on your side will have everything in their hands. We cannot take any position which ties us up with the prospects of public development on your side.'

17 Roosevelt Papers, OF 156, Walsh to Roosevelt, 12 Dec. 1936; PSF 185, John Hickerson, Memorandum for Judge Moore, 14 Dec. 1936; KD, 4 Dec. 1936

18 Norman Armour to Cordell Hull, 5 Jan. 1937, *Foreign Relations of the United States*, 1927, vol. 2, 168; KP, King to Hepburn, 8 Jan. 1937. The solution, Armour told Hull, was for King to take a firm stand 'in favour of finding some solution acceptable to both sides' and, if necessary, be willing to 'bear a greater burden of the cost so far as Canada is concerned.'

19 KP, Precis of Correspondence with Ontario Government respecting Niagara-Ogoki and Long Lake (Albany River System) Diversions – St. Lawrence Waterway, prepared by L.C. Christie, Aug. 18, 1937 (includes a record of the 14 Jan. meeting)

20 KD, 6, 28 Jan. 1937; *TDS*, 9 Jan. 1936; *GM*, 16 Jan. 1937; KP, Hepburn to King, 16 Jan. 1937

21 Bruce Diary, 18 Jan. 1937; KD, 28 Jan. 1937

22 *GM*, 19, 21 Jan. 1937. Ottawa Valley had issued a statement on 18 January denying that it had ever refused to negotiate and stating that, despite the likelihood of winning in court, it was still ready to negotiate (*GM*, 19 Jan. 1937).

23 OH, Minutes, 7 Jan. 1937; AO, Committee Investigating Hydro, 1313 (Hogg)

24 HP, Kirby to Hepburn, 21 Jan. 1937

25 Ibid., Hogg to Hepburn, Nixon to Hepburn, 21 Jan. 1937

26 Ibid., Hepburn, wire, to Elmhirst, 20 Jan. 1937; *GM*, 22 Jan. 1937; OHA, Nixon to Symington, 30 Jan. 1937

27 OHA, Nixon to Lyon, 1 Feb. 1937; AO, Committee Investigating Hydro, 328 (Lyon); HP, Lyon to Nixon, 5 Feb. 1937; Hepburn to O'Connor, 10 Feb. 1937; Dafoe Papers, Symington to Dafoe, 8 Mar. 1937

28 HP, Hepburn to O'Connor, 10, 26 Feb. 1937; Hepburn to T. Hayes, 5 Mar. 1937

29 Windsor *Star*, 9 Mar. 1937; London *Free Press*, 11 Mar. 1937; AO, Dept. of Labour, Series 1-1, vol. 12, Memoranda for Croll, 26 Feb. 1937, n. sig.

30 AO, McPhail Papers, McPhail to E.A. Olsen, 8 Jan. 1937; HP, Hepburn to Curran, 10 Feb. 1937; D.W.H. McDougall to Hepburn, 12 Feb. 1937. The account here differs from that of Duncan McDowall, *Steel at the Sault*, (Toronto 1984), 160 and N.V. Nelles, *The Politics of Development* (Toronto 1974), 431–4. McDowall writes that without waiting for McDougall's 'unbiased expert opinion' Hepburn made the decision on the 'rather incestuous advice' of Curran, while Nelles comments that Dunn 'in effect dictated' the decision. Both scholars appear to have overlooked McDougall's 12 February letter, on which the decision was based, and cited instead his later formal report which Mitch had requested for use in the House. McDougall, in fact, recommended a higher bounty (HP, Memorandum, D.H. McDougall, 3 Mar. 1937). McDowall also writes that Dunn made his concrete proposal in Arizona where Mitch 'had joined Dunn and Beaverbrook to have a grand time riding horses, flying dangerous planes ... and shooting craps with Sam·Goldwyn and other magnates of Hollywood.' Actually Dunn had gone on from the Hayes ranch to join Beaverbrook in Palm Springs.

31 *GM*, 5, 6 9 Mar.; *Sault Star*, 29 May 1937; HP, 1937, File: Dr Roberts; HP, Hepburn to J.C. Shipley, 28 July 1937. Realizing that Hepburn had a file which included evidence of influence-peddling in liquor and fishing licences and timber leases, and farming out medical contracts he had secured, Roberts later declared that his attack had been based on 'erroneous information.'

32 *TDS*, 25 Feb. 1937; *FP*, 3 Apr. 1937

33 HP, Dafoe to Hepburn, 4 Feb. 1937; Windsor Municipal Archives, Herman Papers, Croll to Lum Clark, 4 Jan. 1937; HP, German to Hepburn, 19 Dec. 1936, enclosing German to Croll, 8 Dec. 1936 and Croll to German, 9 Dec. 1936. The unsigned and undated report of Dafoe's accusations were given to Hepburn on six pages of journalist's copy paper. Dafoe charged that Croll was taking a cut of all contracts, including Dafoe's radio contracts (HP, Memorandum, Dionne Quintuplets). Dafoe repeated the accusations to Angela Bruce; he told her that although 'he had not enough evidence to go

into a court of law, he knew that Croll had got $17,000 for the picture "The Country Doctor".' Joseph Sedgwick, he added, was 'his go between ...' (Bruce Journal, 29 Sept. 1937) Croll refused to turn over the contracts, despite the efforts of the official guardian and the courts, and later claimed to have destroyed them when he went overseas in 1941. However, when Sedgwick, who was dismissed with Croll and Roebuck in April, immediately attempted to act for the contracting companies, Croll approved and promised to bring the contracts to Toronto 'which I will turn over to you, to be held for my order' (HP, Dionne Quintuplets File, Percy Wilson to Hepburn, 7 Sept. 1937 and enclosures; AO, Sedgwick Papers, Croll to Sedgwick, 19 May 1937; Pierre Berton details the attempts to secure the documents in *The Dionne Years: A Thirties Melodrama* [Toronto 1977] 146–7).

34 *GM, TDS,* 10 Mar. 1937; *FP,* 13 Mar. 1937

35 AO, Ontario Securities Commission, Scrapbook, *passim*; KP, Meighen to King, 16 Mar. 1937; Lapointe to King, 17 Apr. 1937; Meighen Papers, Gordon to Meighen, 28 Feb. 1937

36 *TDS,* 3 Feb. 1937

37 ACFEO Papers C2/69/6, Memorandum. n.d.nig. (noted as Senator Coté, 5 Apr. 1935) [*sic* 1936]; McGuigan Papers, Gerald Kelly, Chairman, Toronto Separate School Board, to E.F. Henderson, 30 May 1936; Circular, E.F. Henderson, Re Amendment to Assessment Act, 28 Aug. 1936; Toronto, Board of Education, Minutes of the Finance Committee, 31 Aug. 1937

38 *Dillon* v. *Catelli Food Products et al.: Re Assessment Act,* (1937), DLR, 353–409; McGuigan Papers, MEMORANDUM RE ASSESSMENT ACT AMENDMENT – 1936 and JUDGEMENT OF ONTARIO COURT OF APPEAL, n.d., n.sig.

39 McGuigan Papers, Quinn to McGuigan, 1, 22 Feb. 1937; HP, Quinn to Hepburn, 22 Feb. 1937; HP, Hepburn to O'Connor, 26 Feb. 1937; McGuigan Papers, G. Kelly to McGuigan, 30 May 1936; CTPA Papers, Minutes of a meeting of the Executive Committee ... 6 Mar. 1937; O'Brien Papers, Edmond Cloutier to McGuigan, 2 Sept. 1938. The third member of the committee was Father F.J. Brennan, editor of the *Catholic Record* of London. Murphy was a moderate who believed that any legislation which resulted in the arbitrary division of taxes derived from non-Catholics was contrary to the 1863 Scott Act and would meet with justifiable opposition. As he wrote Bishop Kidd: 'If, owing to the complexity of modern business, it is impossible for Separate School Supporters to receive taxation from all property represented by shares in corporations, I feel the loss must be theirs, for Catholics could not claim a share of property which could not be identified' (Kidd Papers, Murphy to Kidd, 1 Aug. 1937; HP, Murphy to Leduc, 11 Aug. 1937).

40 *GM,* 23, 24 Mar. 1937; Windsor *Star,* 24 Mar. 1937; Richard Alway, 'A "Silent Issue": Mitchell Hepburn, Separate School Taxation and the Ontario

Election of 1937,' in Michael Cross and R. Bothwell, eds., *Policy by Other Means: Essays in Honour of C.P. Stacey* (Toronto 1972), 208, 218, n17; Kidd Papers, Quinn to Murphy, 7 Sept. 1937

41 *GM, TDS*, 24, 25 Mar. 1937; HP, Ellis to Hepburn, n.d.

42 In fiscal 1936–7, Cox had a licence to export over 15 per cent of the pulpwood exported (*JLAO*, 1937: 146). Cox dropped the charges against Eileen Flanagan, stating that as mayor he had to assume responsibility for cuts in teachers' salaries which, he claimed, was the reason she attacked him. After some difficulty in getting the necessary doctors' signatures, she was admitted to the Whitby hospital (Carty Diary, 3 Mar. 1937; LD, 11 Feb. 1937; *TDS*, 9 Feb. 1937; 19, 24 *GM*, 19, 24 Mar. 1937).

43 Dewan Papers, Dewan to C. Murphy, 25 Apr. 1935; *GM*, 20 Feb. 1937; LD, 11 Feb. 1937; J.P. Bertrand, 'Timber Wolves' (unpublished MSS, n.d.)

44 Carty Diary, 8 Nov. 1935; KD, 6 Jan., 4 Mar. 1937; Bruce Diary, 1 Feb. 1937

45 LD, 16 Feb., 1 Mar. 1935; KD, 6 Jan. 1937

CHAPTER 13: 'IF NECESSARY WE'LL RAISE AN ARMY TO DO IT'

1 See Harvey A. Levenstein, *Communism, Anticommunism and the CIO* (Wesport 1981); Roger Keeran, *The Communist Party and the Auto Workers Union* (Bloomington 1980); Ivan Avakumovic, *The Communist Party in Canada* (Toronto 1975); Irving M. Abella, *Nationalism, Communism, and Canadian Labour: The CIO, the Communist Party, and the Canadian Congress of Labour* (Toronto 1973); John Manley, 'Communists and Auto Workers: The Struggle for Industrial Unionism in the Canadian Automobile Industry, 1925–1936,' *Labour/Le Travail* (Spring 1986), 105–33.

2 AO, Ontario Provincial Police (OPP), E-96, File 12:2, D.C. Draper to the Commissioner, 31 Jan. 1936: D. Hist, 161.009 (D63), monthly reports, 6 May, 5 Sept. 1936; Buck Papers, interviews conducted by Max Reynolds with Tim Buck, 596; Ralph Ellis, 'The Unionization of a Mill Town: Cornwall in 1936,' *The Register: The McGill History Journal* (Mar. 1981), 83–101; HP, Report re Conferences and Meetings held by the Committee for Industrial Organization during Oct. and Nov. 1936 at Pittsburgh, Pa., Detroit, Mich., and Indianapolis, Ind., n.d., n.sig., stamped 'Secret and Confidential'

3 Sidney Fine, *Sit-down: The General Motors Strike of 1936–1937* (Ann Arbor 1969), 213; Claude E. Hoffman, *Sit-Down in Anderson: UAW Local 663, Anderson, Indiana* (Detroit 1968)

4 *FP*, 13 Feb. 1937

5 The standard account of the Oshawa strike is Irving M. Abella, 'Oshawa 1937,' in Abella, ed., *On Strike: Six Key Labour Struggles in Canada 1919–1949* (Toronto 1974). An extremely useful account is J.A. Pendergest,

'Labour and Politics in Oshawa and District 1928–1943' (MA thesis, Queen's University 1973), which makes excellent use of the since destroyed *Oshawa Times*. Like Pendergest and Abella, Colin Read made extensive use of the *Times* and also interviewed many of the participants ('The Oshawa Strike of 1937,' graduate research paper, University of Toronto 1969). There is some uncertainty about who called Detroit. William Gelech, the instigator of the move to get an organizer, was apparently the leader of one of the CP cells (Pendergest, 'Labour and Politics in Oshawa,' 136). Buck says the call went from Salsberg (Buck Papers, interview ... with Tim Buck, 628).

6 On Thompson's role in the Anderson strike, see Fine, *Sit-down* and Hoffman, *Sit-Down in Anderson*.

7 Duart Snow, 'The Holmes Foundry Strike of Mar. 1937: We'll give their jobs to white men,' *Ontario History* (Mar. 1977), 3–31; H.C. Blank, 'Industrial Relations in Sarnia: The Holmes Factory Strike in 1937' (MA thesis, University of Western Ontario 1974). Those arrested were defended by Jacob Cohen, who advised the American parent not to press charges against the strike-breakers because it would inevitably raise the question of the legality of the sit-down (Cohen Papers, Cohen to Amalgamated Federation..., 18 Mar. 1937; Cohen to Roebuck, 18 Mar. 1937).

8 *GM*, 5, 8, 15 Mar. 1937; HP, Transcript of the speeches given at the United Automobile Workers Meeting held ... Windsor, n.d. (date stamped 9 Mar. 1937).

9 HP, Hepburn to Ian Mackenzie, 25 Feb. 1937; Crerar to Hepburn, 4, 5 Mar. 1937; Hepburn to Roebuck, 26 Feb. 1937

10 AO, OPP, E-105, File 1:8; Read, 'Oshawa Strike,' 8 (citing Hall interview); *HCD*, 24: 2114; 30: 2294, Mar. 1937; Lapointe Papers, Nixon to Lapointe, 30 Mar. 1937; *New York Times*, 27 Mar. 1937; *GM*, 24, 26 Mar., 1 Apr. 1937; KD, 16, 23 Mar. 1937

11 HP, Notes of Meeting, 18, 23 Mar. 1937. There is in the Hepburn Papers a summary of each meeting between GM and the employees. Although the titles vary they are cited here as Notes of Meeting. There is no formal indication of their origin, although it is likely they were drafted by GM.

12 Keeran, *Communist Party*, 148; HP, Memorandum for Ministers File, Strictly Private and Confidential, 15 Mar., 1937; C.R. Magone, Memorandum for the ... Prime Minister, 31 Mar. 1937; Abella, 'Oshawa,' 100, citing Thompson to Abella, 19 Feb. 1968; Lapointe Papers, Verbatim and Unedited Report of an Address by Mr. Fred Hall, 25 Mar. 1937, enclosed in Nixon to Lapointe, 30 Mar. 1937; HP, Notes of Meeting, 25 Mar. 1937

13 HP, Notes of Meeting, 31 Mar. 1937

14 *GM*, 1, 2 Apr. 1937

15 HP, Notes of Meeting, 2 Apr. 1937 (incorrectly dated by Abella as 1 Apr.); HP, Notes of Meeting, 5 Apr. 1937. In many later interviews Croll said that

when he left on vacation everything had been settled. 'Hepburn left me entirely alone to deal with that strike,' he told the Ontario Historical Studies interviewer. 'He never interfered ... He let me handle it my own way and I had the strike settled. Done and finished when they decided for some reason they didn't like it. I'm talking not so much [about] the General Motors who were ready to go along with it, but I refer to pressure from other groups. They realized that this could be a forerunner of something else that would come along; they convinced him that I was no longer useful, that I would get him into trouble with the business community generally and that I had assisted the C.I.O. to get a foothold in this province.' In another interview many years ago, Croll stated: 'I had some conversations with him [Hepburn] in the course of the strike when I reported to him from time to time as to how the strike was going on and what steps would be taken to bring about a settlement and my recollection's very clear that I had a settlement arranged for and satisfactory from all points of view where the union would be recognized. And it was just on the verge of that when this whole business blew up' (CBC Wednesday Night). Croll's recollections do not appear to fit the facts. Mitch left on 27 March, for example, and it was not until 31 March that Croll intervened.

16 AO, Dept. of Labour, Series I-I, vol. 12, File, Memos 1935–1937, Roger Irwin, Memorandum to H.C. Nixon, Acting Minister of Labour, 6 Apr. 1937; HP, Notes of Meeting, 6 Apr. 1937. The record of the meeting would not seem to support Abella's statement that GM agreed 'to negotiate all the union's demands and to recognize Millard as the representative of Local 222' ('Oshawa,' 102). Like Croll, Irwin had a very selective memory. A few weeks after the strike he wrote that before his departure Croll had settled the critical issue of union recognition. 'Four days after negotiations began, the Labour Department was able to predict settlement before nightfall. Mitchell Frederick Hepburn ... returned that day from a post-Parliament holiday in Miami and demonstrated an immediate interest in the situation. That night the government official upon the Oshawa scene reported that an unexplainable monkey-wrench had been tossed into the settlement machine. General Motors was refusing to recognize the local' ('The Battle of Oshawa,' *The Nation*, 1 May 1937: 503–4). Irwin neglected to point out that GM had refused to recognize the UAW from the outset, and that he had predicted a strike before Mitch returned. Abella dates the Irwin memo 7 April and builds his scenario around his dating: 'Thwarted by the federal Liberals, Hepburn was kept fully informed of the situation in Oshawa and when a settlement favourable to the CIO seemed imminent, Hepburn suddenly ended a Florida vacation and hurried back to Toronto. Nor was it too surprising that on the day Hepburn returned, General Motors once again changed its stand and refused to negotiate with Millard as long as he was "a repre-

sentative of the CIO." With Hepburn's return, the worst was not expected at Queen's Park.' It was then, states Abella, that Irwin sent his 6 April memo (*Nationalism, Communism*, 12).

17 HP, Hepburn to G. Fulford, 9 Apr. 1937; *GM*, 8 Apr. 1937

18 HP, Notes of Meeting, 7 Apr. 1937. Pendergest ('Labour and Politics,' 148) states that Millard told him that 'Hugh Thompson had been in favour of a strike and he had been the man most responsible for setting a deadline for strike action.' Arthur Scheltz, financial secretary of the union, told Read that Detroit had refused permission to strike, but Charles Millard insisted Thompson received 'tacit approval' (Read, 'Oshawa Strike,' n25). Abella states that what he sees as 'a hardening of the company's position' was the result of the return of Mitch Hepburn to Toronto that afternoon. Presumably citing an interview with Fine, he writes that at the afternoon meeting Highfield and Chappell told Fine that 'Hepburn had phoned Chappell and had urged the company to take a firm stand against recognition of the CIO. Naturally with the Premier's promise of "total support" the company refused to reconsider its position. At the meeting with the union that evening, Chappell broke off negotiations with the statement that the GM position was firm, and there was nothing left to discuss. The union now had no alternative to strike' (Abella, 'Oshawa 1937,' 102). Contemporary evidence does not lend much support to Abella's view. GM's position had not changed from the outset and, as even Fine indicated, the committee kept introducing new elements at each of the April meetings. There is no evidence of a meeting with GM that evening in Pendergest or Read. Mitch may well have phoned Chappell on his return, but it was clear from the outset that GM would not recognize the CIO union.

19 HP, R.H.E.[Elmhirst], Memorandum for the Prime Minister, 8 Apr. 1937; Hepburn to Lapointe, Lapointe to Hepburn, 8 Apr. 1937; KD, 8 Apr. 1937; Lapointe Papers, MacBrien to Lapointe, 8 Apr. 1937; MacBrien to Officer Commanding, Toronto, 9 Apr. 1937

20 *GM, TET*, 9 Apr. 1937

21 *New York Times*, 9 Apr. 1937; Chalmers Papers, Memorandum to Horace Hunter, 9 Dec. 1937; Hunter to J.B. Maclean, 12 Apr. 1937; *GM*, 9 Apr. 1937. The *Times* had a reporter in Oshawa and I have relied on it as much as possible because the Toronto papers were actors in the drama. One *Globe* reporter was ordered to rewrite a story because 'you couldn't have done a better job if you had been working for the C.I.O' (Brian J. Young, 'George McCullagh and the Leadership League' [MA thesis, Queen's University 1964], 40). Atkinson assigned his top reporters, Roy Greenaway and Frederick Griffin, to Oshawa and, Greenaway remarked, 'As far as we were concerned, it was war at Oshawa and the ground was mined' (Roy Greenaway, *The News Game* [Toronto 1966], 182).

22 *GM, TET, TDS,* 19 Apr. 1937; HP, Verbatim and Unedited ... Report of
    Address by Hugh Thompson, 8 Apr. 1937
23 Roebuck's secretary, who had accompanied him on his working holiday,
    confirmed that Hepburn had been trying to reach him (interview, Lorne
    McTavish). Differing accounts of the discussion were given by Hepburn and
    Roebuck in their testimony before the 1938 Hydro inquiry (AO, Committee
    Investigating Hydro, 641, 1449.) The unreliability of many 'recollections' is
    amply demonstrated by Roebuck's reconstruction of his part in the Oshawa
    strike in a letter to David Croll complaining that he was only mentioned
    twice in Ross Harkness's book on Atkinson (NAC, Roebuck Papers, 3 July
    1963).
24 *New York Times, TDS, GM,* 10 Apr. 1937; HP, W.C. Killing to Hepburn, 9
    Apr. 1937; Killing to the Commissioner, OPP, 10 Apr. 1937; AO, OPP, E-105,
    File 1:7, Sergeant G.E. MacKay, Memorandum for the Chief Inspector, 13
    Apr. 1937; PC, Conant Papers, MSS autobiography
25 *TDS, GM, TET,* 12 Apr. 1937. An agent reported that at a meeting of the
    'BOLSHEVIST-COMMUNIST PARTY' on 10 April the decision was made to retain
    Cohen (AO, OPP, E-105, File 1:1, n.d., Secret and Confidential, J.L. Cohen).
    However, Cohen later sent his bill for $2,450 to the UAW in Detroit (Cohen
    Papers, File 2609, G.F. Addes to Cohen, 10 May 1937). Cohen was widely
    suspected of being a communist, but not formally a member of the party.
    Tim Buck stated categorically that he was 'a Communist' (Buck Papers,
    interview ... with Tim Buck, 723).
26 *GM, TDS,* 13 Apr. 1937
27 HP, I.A. Humphries, Memorandum for the Prime Minister, 13 Apr. 1937;
    Hepburn, wire, to Lapointe, 13 Apr. 1937; Chalmers Papers, Hunter to J.B.
    Maclean, 12 Apr. 1937; *Daily Clarion,* 15, 16 Apr. 1937
28 RCMP Papers, RCMP Headquarters, Weekly Summary, Report on
    Revolutionary Organizations and Agitation in Canada, No. 851, 14 Apr.
    and, No. 852, 21 Apr. 1937 (secured under the Access to Information Act)
    contain the names of about a dozen communists working in Oshawa, but all
    names other than Sam Scarlett are blacked out); AO, OPP, E-105, File 1:7,
    Sergeant G.E. MacKay, Memorandum for the Chief Inspector, 15 Apr.
    1937; Cohen Papers, Cohen to J. O'Hamley, 13 Apr. 1937; WSU, Thompson
    Papers, M. Montgomery to Thompson, 13 Apr. 1937; *FP,* 8 May 1937
29 HP, Lapointe to Hepburn, 13 Apr. 1937; W. Harmer, Local 222, wire to
    Hepburn, 13 Apr. 1937; Hepburn, wire, to King, 13 Apr. 1937; King, wire,
    to Hepburn, 13 Apr. 1937; KD, 13 Apr. 1937; Ottawa *Citizen,* 15 Apr. 1937;
    GM, 14 Apr. 1937
30 *GM, TDS, TET,* Windsor *Star,* 12–14 Apr. 1937; HP, Hepburn to Croll and
    Roebuck, 14 Apr. 1937; Croll to Hepburn, 14 Apr. 1937; Roebuck to
    Hepburn, 14 Apr. 1937

31 HP, Hardy to Hepburn, 18 Apr. 1937; Bruce Diary, 14 Apr. 1937; KD, 14 Apr. 1937; Dafoe Papers, Crerar to Dafoe, 17 Apr. 1937

32 KD, 14 Apr. 1937; HP, Lapointe, wire, to Hepburn, 6:27 p.m., 14 Apr. 1937

33 *GM*, 15 Apr. 1937; KP, Mackenzie, wire, to King, 14 Apr. 1937; KD, 15 Apr. 1937; *TET*, 15 Apr. 1937; LD, 16 Apr. 1937

34 *GM*, *TDS*, *TET*, 15, 16 Apr. 1937; Lapointe Papers, Hepburn, wire, to Lapointe, 15 Apr. 1937. Williams obviously gave Mitch a somewhat misleading version of a telegram received by the Officer Commanding the RCMP in Toronto on 9 April from MacBrien stating that while providing assistance 'should occasion arise, yet it is anxious that our action should be in support rather than taking initiatives in any action that may become necessary. Our force should be kept in the background as much as possible. It is not intended these instructions should prevent closest cooperation if need arises' (Lapointe Papers, MacBrien to Officer Commanding, R.C.M.P., Toronto, 9 Apr. 1937). The total number of special constables officially recruited appears to have been 244, many of whom were veterans and some were students. (Ministry of the Solicitor General, W.K. Wellstead to Todd Harris, 12 June 1987. I am indebted to Peter Oliver and Todd Harris for a copy of the list of recruits.) The constables were to be given uniforms but no weapons and paid $25 a week. An order-in-council on 1 June reconstituted the force as the OPP reserve force with pay of $100 a year or $100 a month if called out.

35 HP, Statement by W.H. Moore, 19 Apr. 1937; *TET*, 19 Apr. 1937, Cohen Papers, Hepburn, wire, to Millard, 15, 19 Apr. 1937. Although Abella attributes Mitch's invitation to the Detroit decision, that decision was reached at night *after* Moore's trip to Toronto (*New York Times*, 16 Apr. 1937).

36 *New York Times*, *GM*, *TDS*, 15–17 Apr. 1937; HP, Cohen, wire, to Hepburn, 12.55 a.m., 17 Apr. 1937; HP, McIntyre to Doug Oliver, 17 Apr. 1937

37 HP, Notes of Meeting, 17 Apr. 1937; *New York Times*, *GM*, *TDS*, 19 Apr. 1937; Abella, 'On Strike,' 116ff

38 *New York Times*, 19 Apr. 1937; Addes Papers, Minutes, Special Meeting of the General Executive Board of the International Union, United Automobile Workers of America, 19–23 Apr. 1937; Thompson Papers, Martin, wire, to Thompson, 20 Apr. 1937

39 AO, OPP, E-105, File 1:7, Sergeant George MacKay, Memorandum for the Chief Inspector, C.I.B. 18, 20 Apr. enclosing informant's reports 16, 18 Apr. 1937; *New York Times*, *GM*, *TDS*, *TET*, 20, 21 Apr. 1937

40 *New York Times*, *GM*, *TDS*, *TET*, 20, 21 Apr. 1937; HP, Hepburn, wire, to McLaughlin, 20 Apr. 1937; Cohen Papers, Cohen, wire, to Martin, 20 Apr. 1937. While there were rumours in Oshawa that a delegation had visited Mitch, no one on the street seemed to know for sure, but the report

apparently convinced the union leaders to capitulate and empower Millard to meet GM as soon as possible (AO, OPP, E-105, File 1:7, Sergeant George MacKay, Memorandum for Chief Inspector, C.I.B., 22 Apr., enclosing informant's report, 21 Apr. 1937).

41 HP, Notes of Meeting, 21 Apr. 1937; *GM, TDS*, 23 Apr. 1937; HP, Memorandum on Oshawa Strike Situation, 22 Apr. 1937; McIntyre, wire, to Doug Oliver, Queen's Park, 3.58 p.m., 22 Apr. 1937; n.d., n. sig, draft document concerning Kramer. The only Kramer I have been able to identify is Charles Kramer, a leading UAW organizer and a veteran of Anderson.

42 HP, Memorandum of the agreement ... between General Motors ... and The Employees of the Company ..., n.d. The agreement was signed by Millard, E.E. Bathe, vice-president, and F.H. Day, as well as GM, and was initialled 'OK' by JLC. Within a few days similar agreements were signed with GM employees in Windsor and St Catharines.

43 Underhill Papers, Forsey to Underhill, 22 Apr. 1937; HP, A.R. Mosher to Hepburn, 24 Apr. 1937; *New York Times*, 24 Apr. 1937

44 *GM, TDS*, 26 Apr. 1937; HP, Hepburn, wire, to Crerar, 23 Apr. 1937

45 KD, 6 Nov. 1937; McCullagh to R.H. McMaster, 18 Jan. 1943, cited in Young, 'George McCullagh and the Leadership League,' 47

46 *New York Times, GM, TDS*, 19, 20 Apr. 1937; *New Commonwealth*, 24 Apr. 1937; Windsor *Star*, 20, 21 Apr. 1937

47 HP, John Knox to Hepburn, 16 Apr. 1937; Thompson Papers, J.G. Munro to Thompson, 15 Apr. 1937; *New York Times, GM*, 19 Apr. 1937. AO, Dept. of Mines, Main Office, Leduc, vol. 2, Mining Companies 1937–1938, Knox to Leduc, 22 Apr. 1937. Police reports may be found in AO, OPP, E-105 Files 1:1 and 1:7 as well as the Hepburn Papers. Abella cites a number of police reports between 13 and 16 April which now cannot be located in the Hepburn Papers (Abella, 'Oshawa,' n58). The report on George Anderson is contained in AO, OPP, E-105 File 1:7, J.H. MacBrien, RCMP, to the Commissioner, OPP, 2 Apr. 1937. See also L.S. MacDowell '*Remember Kirkland Lake': The History and Effects of the Kirkland Lake Gold Miners' Strike, 1941–1942* (Toronto 1983), 60–4.

48 Windsor *Star*, 21 Apr. 1937. The document was a message from the chief inspector of the OPP relaying a phone report from Inspector Creasey on the Sunday meeting in Timmins (HP, Memorandum for the Commissioner of Police: Re Labour Situation, 19 Apr. 1937). Mitch made no attempt to blame the downward volatility of gold mining stocks in April on the CIO, nor did McCullagh or the miners. As everyone knew, by the spring of 1937 the international gold market was jittery, for it had long been oversold, particularly for junior stocks. A panic in Johannesburg had quickly spread to New York and Toronto before Roosevelt denied on 9 April that he planned to cut the price of gold. But the market soon moved lower again and the shares fell

sharply on 17 April and again on the 19th amid rumours that Roosevelt planned to tax foreign gold. Prices rose on 21 April before collapsing on the New York and London markets a week later. There would appear to be no plausible basis for Abella's comment that 'The Fears of Hepburn and the mine owners ... were underscored by a major gold-stock collapse on the Toronto Stock Exchange on Monday, April 19 – a collapse due largely to the rumours of CIO activities in the gold fields' (Abella, 'Oshawa,' 117). Indeed, the *Monetary Times* (24 Apr. 1937) reported that mining executives 'seemed to be very little upset regarding the possibility' of strikes.

49   KD, 6 Jan. 1938
50   *GM*, *TDS*, 17 Apr. 1937. Following his private appeal to Rowe, Mitch had publicly commended the Tories 'for refraining from criticizing the government in this crisis.' Political expediency should be set aside, he added, and 'when it becomes obvious that there is anyone better able to deal with this situation I will be glad to step aside and render every assistance' (*TDS*, *TET*, 13 Apr. 1937).
51   Bruce Journal, 'The Strike Trouble of April 1937,' n.d.; HP, Birdsall to Hepburn, 25 Apr. 1937. Mrs Bruce noted, 'Drew is strong for a National Government. Ontario and Quebec National, and Canada is well controlled.'
52   Bruce Journal, 'The Strike Trouble'
53   NAC, Drew Papers, Drew to Rowe, 26 Apr. 1937
54   Bruce Journal, 'The Strike Trouble.' Earl Rowe recalled these events on two different occasions: in a memorandum written for Irving Abella (used in 'On Strike' but since lost) on which some of the above has been based, and in an interview for the Ontario Historical Studies Series. In his OHSS interview Rowe stated that he rejected Mitch's proposal at once. 'I can't accept it. It's just out and out beyond. I'm not capable of accepting it because I'm not smart enough to do something I don't believe in.' He did admit that he went to Ottawa, however, 'and revealed it in confidence to R.B. Bennett after I had already refused it.'
55   Bruce Journal, 'The Strike Trouble'; LD, 30 Apr. 1937. Bennett later stated that he had categorically rejected the proposal. 'Frankly, I have never been able to understand how that could be possible unless a convention were called to deal with the matter,' he wrote Bruce (Bennett Papers, Bennett to Bruce, 23 June 1938).
56   NAC, Drew Papers, Drew to Rowe, 30 Apr. 1938. The later controversy was generated during the leadership campaign when Rowe, the Frosts and others, in their attempt to stop Drew, charged that he had resigned because of Rowe's refusal to agree to a coalition. Drew insisted that he had broken with the party over its position on the CIO and that he had not accepted the statement drawn up at the Albany Club meeting by the Frost brothers, later released by Rowe in his 5 May speech at Arthur, which he wanted to deliver

before making Drew's resignation public (see NAC, Drew Papers, Memorandum 10-16 Nov. 1938; E.J. Young to Drew, 26 Aug., Drew to Young, 2 Sept. 1938; L. Frost Papers, Frost to W.S. Frost, 26 Apr. 1937; Bennett Papers, Drew to Bennett, 3 Mar., 22 June 1938; Bennett to Drew, 18 June, 14 July 1938). The evidence clearly supports Drew's position that he resigned over the CIO and that he had every reason to believe that the coalition door had not been closed on 30 April when he resigned. In a letter of 2 May accepting Drew's resignation, Rowe wrote, 'It was with deep regret that I received your letter of May 1 [sic] asking me to accept your resignation as Organizer of our party in Ont. until such time as we are in agreement on matters of policy' (NAC, Drew Papers, Rowe to Drew, 2 May 1937).

57 LD, 1, 3 May 1938; GM, TDS, TET, 1–6 May 1937; Montreal Gazette, 4 May 1938; Saturday Night, 15 May 1937. Except for his one meeting with Rowe, Hepburn does not appear to have been involved in any of the discussions with the Conservatives, and Drew stated he had not seen Hepburn since the East Hastings by-election (TDS, TET, 7 May 1937). Mitch later stated that many people in both parties favoured the idea. 'Personally I was not convinced of the need for such a coalition, but I listened to the men who were pressing for such action' (TDS, TET, 3 Dec. 1938). Rowe's reply that Drew 'was the only Conservative who even suggested to me that I should seriously consider it' suggests, if true, that he did not talk to many leading provincial Conservatives (GM, 6 Dec. 1938). The Star claimed to have information from a man high in the councils of the Conservative party that the coalition was master-minded by 'at least one prominent Conservative Toronto financier-industrialist and a small but powerful group of mine owners and executives from both political parties' (5 May 1937).

CHAPTER 14: 'IT IS THE "FELLOWS" THAT COUNT'

1 HP, Lyon to Hepburn, 14 Apr. 1937; KD, 6 Jan., 4 Mar. 1937; Pattullo Papers, Hepburn to Pattullo, 27 July 1937
2 Roosevelt Papers, OF 156, Frank Walsh, Memorandum in Re: Great Lakes–St. Lawrence Treaty, 18 Feb. 1937; USNA, Dept. of State, H.C. Hengstler, Consul General, Toronto, to J.F. Simmons, 15 June 1938
3 Roosevelt Papers, OF 156, Frank Walsh Memorandum to the President in Re: Great Lakes–St. Lawrence Treaty, 20 Feb. 1937; OHA, Engineering Reports, 29 Jan., 13 Feb. 1937; Christie Papers, Memorandum, Pickering to King, 16 Feb. 1937; KD, 24 Feb. 1937; KP, Precis of Correspondence [L.C. Christie], Memorandum, J.T. Johnson, 24 Feb. 1937; NAC, Dept. of External Affairs, D1, vol 91, 734, Notes for Conference with Premier M.F. Hepburn, 24 Feb. 1937 re St. Lawrence and Niagara Treaties

4 KD, 4, 5 Mar. 1937; USNA, Dept. of State, C8, 800.1 Memorandum of
   Interview [Armour and King], 22 Mar. 1937.
5 HP, Lyon to Hepburn, 5 Mar. 1937; OHA, Lyon to Ryan, 17 Apr. 1937
6 AO, Roebuck Papers, Roebuck to Hepburn, draft, Apr. 1937; Roebuck to
   Hepburn, 16, 19 Apr. 1937; KP, Roebuck to King, 22 Apr. 1937
7 OHA, Engineering Report, 18 June 1937; HP, R.A. Jeffery, Summary of my
   statements to Premier Hepburn regarding Hydro matters during my
   interview with him on 8 June 1937.
8 Bruce Journal, Mar. 1938. McCullagh made the same statement in an
   editorial after the election (*GM*, 18 Dec. 1937).
9 Roosevelt Papers, OF 156, Frank Walsh, Memorandum for the President in
   Re: Urgent Need of Ontario for Niagara and St. Lawrence Power, 1 Apr.
   937, Gatineau Papers, Memorandum, Gordon Gale to Mr. Simpson 19 June
   1937; OHA, *Beauharnois Power Corporation*, Thompson, Martin & Company,
   7 June 1937. Main Johnson of the *Star* stated that 'someone who ought to
   know had told me back in the month of May that there was a very direct
   deal on between Hepburn and Beauharnois...' (Main Johnson Papers,
   Autobiographical Essays, 29 Oct. 1937). Without additional transmission
   and switching facilities, Hydro could only carry an additional 70,000 h.p.
   from Quebec (Beauharnois Papers, General Manager to Collateral Trust
   Bond Committee, 5 Nov. 1937). There was a surprising increase in the bid
   for Beauharnois 5 1/2% bonds from $54.50 on 30 March to $71 on 6 April
   for reasons I have not been able to determine. They then fell back to $54.50
   by the middle of May.
10 *Beauharnois Light, Heat and Power Co. Ltd.* v. *The Hydro-Electric Power
   Commission*, OR (1937), 796, 820; HP, Lyon to Hepburn, 22 Oct. 1937; *GM*,
   23 June 1937; AO, Committee to Investigate Hydro, 135 (Lyon)
11 Hamilton *Spectator*, 14, 28 June 1937; *TDS*, 26 June 1937; Windsor *Star*, 30
   June 1937; Gatineau Papers, Pitfield & Co., Memorandum, All Branches –
   Not for Bulletin Boards or Press, 9 July 1937; Bruce Diary, 22 July 1937;
   Correspondence re St. Lawrence, Nixon to Rinfret, 21 July 1937
12 Gatineau Papers, Gale to Mr. Simpson, 16 Sept. 1937. There is no hard
   evidence that an agreement had been reached before the election. Hogg
   denied that he had been involved in any negotiations prior to his
   appointment as chairman after the election (*The Bulletin*, Feb. 1938: 60).
   George Montgomery and R.A.C. Henry of Beauharnois made similar
   denials. When in Toronto after the court decision, Henry said he expected
   some proposal from the government but left empty-handed and on his way
   to London to the Judicial Committee (HP, Memorandum re Hydro
   Negotiations, 1937, n.d., n. sig. [Henry]; Memorandum re Beauharnois
   Negotiation, n.d., n. sig. [Montgomery]). Roebuck later stated that he had
   stumbled into a room he believed to be Croll's in the Royal York late in

June and saw Henry with Hogg and Bethune Smith. This was denied by Henry and Hogg before the select committee. The man in question was Kenney of MacLarens, for whom Smith was a solicitor, who had come to discuss the sale of more power. Lyon believed the deal was made late in June when Henry visited Toronto 'and discussed the matter with a member of the government.' Henry denied it on oath (Committee Investigating Hydro, 201 [Lyon]). Before the 1938 select committee inquiry Hepburn stated, 'I had no thought of any deal with Beauharnois. I take very sharp issue with that statement. Your charge is that I communicated with Beauharnois during the course of the election. I did nothing of the kind directly or indirectly. I am under oath, and I hope you will take my word in that regard.' Mitch wore his oath lightly, but his statement that he had not been in touch with Beauharnois 'during the course of the election' was probably true (1482).

13 *TDS, GM,* Windsor *Star, TET,* 4 June 1937; KP, Peter Sims to King, 13 July 1937; L. McCarthy to King, 12 July 1937

14 KD, 14 Oct. 1937; *GM,* 5 June 1937. McCullagh told King he was not responsible for Hepburn's statement and later told Ian Mackenzie that he opposed the attack on Ottawa (KD, 6 Nov. 1937; Mackenzie to King, 28 July 1937).

15 Carty Diary, 8 June 1937

16 Pattullo Papers, Hepburn to Pattullo, 27 July 1937; KP, Mackenzie to King, 28 July 1937. King later said that Mitch had told him 'he should not have mentioned my name; that it was the Government that he had in mind; the lack of co-operation from my Ontario colleagues. That where he blamed me was that I had not made them do something that they ought to have done' (KD, 22 Oct. 1937).

17 *FP,* 5, 19 June 1937; Windsor *Star,* 4 June 1937; *Maclean's,* 15 July 1937; KD, 7 Jan. 1937; Chalmers Papers, Report on Meeting with Arthur D. Purvis, Montreal, 20 May 1937

18 KD, 4 June 1937; KP, Memorandum for the Prime Minister, 4 June 1937

19 Conrad Black, *Duplessis* (Toronto 1977), 170; Montreal *Gazette, Le Devoir,* 5 June 1937; Montreal *Star,* 4 June 1937; *L'Unité,* 10 June 1937; KP, Tweedsmuir to King, 14 June 1937

20 HP, Daniel Gillmore to Hepburn, 10 July 1937; Hepburn to Gillmore, 26 July 1937; Pattullo Papers, Hepburn to Pattullo, 27 July 1937; KP, Mackenzie to King, 28 July 1937

21 *Saturday Night,* 12 June 1937

22 Bruce Diary, 28 June, 13 July 1937; Manion Papers, Hogarth to Rowe, 5 July 1937, enclosed in Hogarth to Manion, 20 Jan. 1939; L. Frost Papers, L. Frost to C. Frost, 29 July 1937; Drew Papers, H.O. Howitt to Drew, 2 July 1937

23 *Maclean's*, 15 July 1937; *GM*, 10 June 1937; *GM*, 19, 20, 21 May 1937; KD, 6 Jan. 1937. After a long talk with McCullagh, Ian Mackenzie sent King a somewhat different, and internally inconsistent, rendering of his coalition manoeuvres. 'As a result of certain incidents which came to light with reference to Mr. Hepburn and which are in the possession of Mr. Atkinson of the Toronto Star and also leading Conservatives Mr. McCullagh personally approached Mr. George Drew in order to have some alternative in the event of Hepburn's collapse. Drew at that time refused any consideration of a coalition Government although he stated he was not any supporter of Rowe. Mr. Hepburn was thoroughly familiar with the details of the approaches made to Drew. Evidently Drew consented to nominate five Conservatives for coalition in the provincial party' (KP, Mackenzie to King, 28 July 1938).

24 HP, J. O'Brien to Hepburn, 19 June 1937

25 Bennett Papers, Drew to Bennett, 3 Mar. 1938; Bennett to Drew, 18 June 1938

26 HP, Hepburn to W.G. Nixon, 3 May 1937; McCullagh Papers, McCullagh to Eddie Wooliver, 2 June 1937; KD, 28 July 1937

27 Bruce Diary, 22 July 1937; KP, Memorandum, E.A. Pickering to King, 23 July 1937; *GM*, 13 Aug. 1937; AO, Treasury Dept., Series II-2, Box 57, File 15E, Asst. Solicitor under Succession Duty Act, Memorandum for C.S. Walters, 12 Oct. 1937

28 Douglas Cruickshank and G.S. Kealey, 'Strikes in Canada 1891–1950,' *Labour/Le Travailleur* (Fall 1987), 138; *Labour Gazette*, Mar. 1938, 247; Bennett Papers, Drew to Bennett, 3 Mar. 1938. Although many of the strikes were for union recognition, most had multiple causes. While CIO organizers may not have been responsible for the largest number of strikes, they appear to have been responsible for most of the long ones, accounting perhaps for as much as 75% of the days lost.

29 NAC, CCF Papers, Spry to Lewis, 9 Dec. 1936; AO, OPP, E-105, File 1:1, General Report of Bolshevik-Communist Party and C.I.O. Activities, 28 May 1937. Of the twenty-three Canadians present at a 25 May meeting of CIO organizers, seventeen can be readily identified as members of the CP and four cannot be identified.

30 *GM*, 17 Sept. 1937; *TDS*, 10 Sept., 12 May 1937

31 *STTJ*, 2 Oct. 1937

32 *GM*, 23 Sept. 1937; AO, Conant Papers, Speech Material, n.d.; *GM*, *TET*, 27 Sept. 1937

33 King had replied to Nixon's 21 July letter on 7 September pointing out that since the Americans were determined to tie the northern diversion to the St Lawrence there was no point in forwarding their request to Washington. Mitch was then in Kapuskasing, and Nixon sent the letter to Lyon at the

commission. Nixon claimed not to have told Mitch about the letter until a week after the election. The Conservatives later argued that the letter was proof that Mitch had talked of the northern diversions during the campaign when he was fully aware that the Americans would not agree (*Correspondence relating to Kenogami River (Long Lake) Project and Export of Electrical Power* [Ottawa 1938], King to Nixon, 7 Sept. 1937, cited in Hepburn to King, 25 Feb. 1938; Nixon to Hepburn, 14 Oct. 1937).

34 *TDS*, 16 Sept. 1937; *GM*, 5 Oct. 1937; *Foreign Relations of the United States, 1937*, vol. 2: 173, Armour to the Secretary of State, 2 Nov. 1937; *GM*, 21 Aug. 1937; *TET*, 28 Sept., 1 Oct. 1937; *Free Press*, 31 Aug. 1937

35 *Time*, 20 Sept. 1937; AO, Roebuck Papers, G.N. Gordon to Roebuck, 22 Feb. 1943. Radio was used extensively. Both parties took over eleven hours on the CBC and an estimated 275 hours on private radio, compared to 125 in the 1935 federal election. The experience persuaded the CBC that it should review the whole question of political broadcasting because 'there was so much repetition of argument that the public became surfeited and indifferent' (CBC/25F, File 11-40-1-7, General Manager, Circular Letter, 2 Dec. 1937).

36 HP, Hepburn to Odette, 14 Sept. 1937; OA, Conant Papers, M. Hood to J.C. Anderson, 27 Oct. 1927; HP, Birdsall to Hepburn, 25 Aug. 1937; *STTJ*, 9 Sept. 1937

37 LD, 16 May 1935; KD, 6 July 1937; HP, J.D. Mansfield to Hepburn, 29 July 1937; AO, Ferguson Papers, Dafoe to Ferguson, 4 Aug. 1937; HP, Dunn to Hepburn, 4 Aug. 1937; Bruce Diary, 8 Sept. 1937; HP, Colin Brookes to Hepburn, 25 Sept. 1937; *GM*, 25 Sept. 1937

38 King makes frequent references in his diary to Beauharnois contributions which he takes as fact although he had no evidence. The CCF failed to find any evidence that American anti-CIO interests contributed to the Liberal campaign (NAC, CCF Papers, E.B. Jolliffe to David Lewis, 21 Sept. 1937; Lewis to Jolliffe, 26 Sept. 1937).

39 Conant spent $7,000 in Oshawa. The losing Liberal candidate spent $7,700 in East Simcoe, a large sum he said because there was so much money flowing in the contest between Rowe and Simpson in neighbouring Simcoe Centre that the epidemic spread across the border. (Conant Papers, Mangan to Conant, 16 Oct. 1937; HP, Tanner to Hepburn, 3 Nov. 1937); Manion Papers, Hogarth to Manion, 20 Jan. 1939.

40 *TDS*, 5 Oct. 1937; McCullagh Papers, McCullagh to Wooliver, 28 Aug. 1937; *GM*, 5 Oct. 1937. McCullagh's radio addresses were printed in the *GM*, 4 Oct. 1937. The incessant Tory charges that 'Sell Em' Ben Smith and 'Buy Em' George McCullagh were running the government finally drove McCullagh to use the radio to mock the accusations and declare that the CIO was the central issue in the campaign.

41 KP, W.J.T.[Turnbull], Memorandum for Mr. King, 11 June 1937; Hardy to
    King, 13 July 1937; Mulock to King, 15 July 1937; H.D. Angus to Lambert,
    2 July 1937; *TDS*, 15 July 1937; KD, 15 July 1937; KP, Memorandum, E.A.
    Pickering to King, 26 July 1937; KD, 27 July 1937; KP, Mackenzie to King,
    28 July 1937; KD, 28 July 1937; Ottawa *Citizen*, 13 Aug. 1937; KP, King to
    Sir William Mulock, 16 Aug. 1937
42 *TDS, GM, TET*, 1 Oct. 1937; *STTJ*, 2 Oct. 1937
43 KD, 30 Sept., 2–6 Oct. 1937; *GM*, 29 Sept., 5 Oct. 1937. Main Johnson of the
    Star was with King when Rogers arrived at Kingsmere. He felt that Rogers's
    resentment confirmed the rumours 'of a split in the Federal cabinet and of
    machinations by Gardiner against King. Mr. King did not admit such a
    revolt but it was plainly to be inferred from what Mr. Rogers and Mr. King
    said. Mr. King seemed quite prepared for the fact that he was facing a
    divided support in Ottawa as well as trouble in separate provinces' (Main
    Johnson Papers, Autobiographical Essays, 7 Oct. 1937). Gardiner's claim that
    a *Globe* reporter had not been at the meeting led King to exclaim 'a
    damnable bit of business.' The *Globe* story was by-lined, while the similarity
    of those in the *Star* and the *TET* suggested they came from the same source.
    The full report in the Kingston *Whig-Standard* (1 Oct.) is perhaps the most
    accurate. Gardiner argued that it was impossible for the federal government
    to keep CIO organizers out because only one province had requested it and
    they could enter Canada – and then Ontario – through another province.
    However, he continued, (as paraphrased in the report): 'Mr. Hepburn may
    have been impetuous but his impetuosity had assured there were no filled
    graves in Canada from the CIO troubles, no lawlessness and no men lying
    maimed in hospitals as had been the case in the United States.'
44 L. Frost Papers, Frost File, Transcript of a speech over C.R.T.C., 1 Oct.
    1937; Windsor *Star*, 2 Oct. 1937
45 Rowe's Arthur speech was published in pamphlet form as 'The Path to
    Industrial Peace.' On the genesis of the policy, see L. Frost Papers (Subject
    Correspondence, A Series), where a text is noted, 'This was written by
    C.G.F. and L.M.F. and then refined by party leadership.'
46 Manion Papers, Hogarth to Rowe, 5 July 1937 enclosed in Hogarth to
    Manion, Jan. 20, 1939; *GM*, 27 Sept. 1937; Bennett Papers, Senator Iva
    Fallis, Peterborough, to Bennett, 11, 31 Aug. 1937
47 Bennett Papers, J.F. Belford to Bennett, 1 Dec. 1937; Manion Papers,
    Hogarth to Manion, 20 Jan. 1939; F.K. Morrow of Loblaws headed the
    finance committee with Hogarth, six Toronto Tories, and R.R. Evans of
    Hamilton as members. Cecil Frost was the campaign chairman (C. Frost
    Papers, B-77-025, vol. 1, 'Provincial Campaign Committee').
48 Underhill Papers, Spry to Underhill, 25 Oct. 1937; CCF Papers, Lewis to
    Eugene Forsey, 21 Sept. 1937

49 *New Commonwealth*, 29 May 1937; NAC, CCF Papers, vol. 54, 'Speakers Notes'; AO, OPP, E-105, File 1:1, General Report ..., 25 May, 8, 18, 21, 25 June, 7 July 1937; *GM*, 18 June 1937; *New Commonwealth*, 2 Oct. 1937; NAC, CCF Papers, Jolliffe to Lewis, 22 Sept. 1937; Lewis to Woodsworth, 29 Sept. 1937.

50 Kidd Papers, Murphy to Leduc, 11 Aug. enc. in Murphy to Kidd, 11 Aug. 1937; O'Brien Papers, Quinn to O'Brien, 6 Apr. 1937; Quinn to McGuigan, 29 June, enc. in Quinn to O'Brien, 29 June 1937

51 O'Brien Papers, O'Brien to Quinn, 5 Aug. 1937; McGuigan Papers, Circular, 'To Parish Priests,' 7 Aug. 1937; O'Brien Papers, Quinn to O'Brien, 10 Aug. 1937; HP, Murphy to Hepburn, 11 Aug. 1937; 'Decisions of the Plenary Meeting of the Hierarchy of Ontario held at Ottawa on September 2, 1937', in M.J. Quinn, *The Frustration of the Lay Catholic Effort in Ontario, The Catholic Primary School* (Toronto 1943), 27

52 L. Frost Papers, Subject Correspondence, Box 10, Circular, H.B. Fetterley, Co-chairman, Legislative Committee, 'To Be Read in Open Lodge,' 9 June 1937; *TET*, 16 Sept. 1937; *TDS*, 7 Sept. 1937

53 Kidd Papers, Kidd to McGuigan, 17 Sept. 1937; O'Brien Papers, O'Brien to McGuigan, Sept. 17, 1937; McGuigan Papers, Quinn to Murphy, 22 Sept. 1937; Murphy to Hepburn, 25 Sept. enc. in Murphy to Kidd, 27 Sept. 1937

54 O'Brien Papers, enc. in H.J. Hanley to O'Brien, 1 Oct. 1937; C. Frost Papers, John Robb to C.G. Frost, 11 Oct. 1937; Frost to Robb, 8 Nov. 1937; L. Frost Papers, L. Frost to Father Butler, 4 Nov. 1937

55 *GM*, 4 Oct. 1937; KD, 2 Oct. 1937

56 Conant Papers, Memorandum Re Hepburn Meeting Oshawa Armouries, 4, 5 Oct. 1937; *GM*, *TDS*, 6 Oct. 1937

57 *STTS*, 7 Oct. 1937. There is no doubt about increased Liberal strength in almost every industrial riding except Oshawa. The Liberal vote was sharply up in the urban polls in Brantford, Kitchener, Niagara Falls, Peterborough, Waterloo, and Hamilton. In Oshawa it fell from 61.7 to 37.5 per cent, as the CCF increased its popular vote from 13 to 30 per cent. Communist candidates with 25,000 votes polled a significant vote in nine ridings, including Cochrane South and Sudbury. If two heavily Catholic polls in Waterloo were a fair indication, the Catholic vote remained solid. In 1929, 328 voted Tory and 102 Liberal; in 1934, 433 Liberal and 87 Tory; and in 1937, 446 Liberal and 25 Tory (HP, W.J. Motz to Day, Ferguson, Wilson & Kelly, 22 June 1934).

58 KD, 7 Oct. 1937. Most contemporaries, including King, attributed the Liberal victory in large part to the war against the CIO. Alex Hall, the mayor of Oshawa, offered the interesting observation that the Tories were defeated by a Tory platform, with Mitch's nationalism and anti-Americanism recalling that of Macdonald. Cecil Frost agreed: 'we were technically right

and popularly wrong; accordingly thousands of Conservatives throughout the Province quite mistakenly decided to put their country before their Party and vote against Rowe' (C. Frost Papers, Hall to Frost, 25 Oct. 1937; Frost to Hall, 6 Nov. 1937).

CHAPTER 15: 'WE ARE READY FOR THE FIGHT'

1 KP, King to Bruce, 29 Sept. 1937; King to Hepburn, Oct. 8, 1937; Hepburn to King, 12 Oct. 1937. Hepburn had stated in the legislature on 25 March that appropriations for Chorley Park would end on 31 October when Bruce's term expired (London *Free Press*, 26 Mar. 1937). See Colin Read and Donald Forster, '"Opera Bouffe": Mackenzie King, Mitch Hepburn, the Appointment of the Lieutenant-Governor, and the Closing of Government House, Toronto, 1937,' *Ontario History* (December 1977), 239–56.
2 KD, 13 Oct. 1937; KP, F. Sanderson to King, 20 Oct. 1937, enc. Memorandum of my conversation with Premier M.F. Hepburn in Toronto at Queen's Park, Wednesday morning, 13 Oct. 1937 between eleven and twelve; Bruce Papers, Personal and Confidential, n.d., n.sig; Bennett Papers, Bruce to Bennett, 9 July 1938
3 KD, 14 Oct. 1937; KP, Hepburn, wire, to King, 18 Oct. 1937; KD, 19 Oct. 1937; KD, Handwritten, 21 Oct. describing events on 22 Oct. 1937; typewritten, 22 Oct. 1937; Bruce Journal, 'Autumn of 1937 and Mr. Hepburn'
4 Bruce Journal, 'Autumn of 1937 and Mr. Hepburn'; KP, Bruce to Tweedsmuir, 27 Oct. 1937, enc. in Tweedsmuir to King, 27 Oct. 1937; King to Tweedsmuir, 29 Oct. 1937; Bruce Papers, Tweedsmuir to Bruce, 30 Oct. 1937; KP, Tweedsmuir to King, 30 Oct. 1937; KD, 29 Nov. 1937; KP, W.E. Rundle to King, 16 Nov. 1937; Bruce to King, 16 Nov. 1937; Bruce Diary, 15 Nov. 1937
5 KD, 10–23 Nov. 1937; Bruce Papers, Bruce to Tweedsmuir, 10 Dec. 1937; KD, 13, 14 Oct. 1937
6 HP, Hepburn to Lyon, 21 Oct. 1937; Memorandum re Beauharnois Negotiations, Geo. H. Montgomery, n.d.; Memorandum re Hydro Negotiations, R.A.C. Henry; AO, Committee Investigating Hydro, 975 (Montgomery), 991 (Wright); Gatineau Papers, Memo Re Directors' Meeting, 22 Oct. 1937 (Montgomery of Beauharnois was also a Gatineau director and offered to leave the meeting but was asked to remain).
7 OHA, Memorandum Respecting the Limitation in the use of Quebec Power Imposed by the Leaside Transformer Station, 22 Apr. 1938; Beauharnois Papers, Henry to Collateral Trust Bond Committee, 5 Nov., 12 Dec. 1937
8 Roosevelt Papers, OF 156, Leland Olds to Roosevelt, 4 Aug. 1939, enc. Memorandum Summarizing Federal Power Commission Staff Exhibit Data

Showing Private Power Tie-ups Across the United States-Canadian Border. Shawinigan had a substantial interest in MLHP and owned 20% of Saguenay, which was 53% owned by Alcan. The Aluminum Company of America was a major shareholder in Niagara Hudson, in International Power Securities (a utility holding company on whose board sat Aldred of Shawinigan), and through the associated Mellon interests had an important position in International Paper and Power, the owner of Gatineau (see *Seventh Annual Report of the Power Authority of the State of New York* [1938]).

9 KD, 11 Aug., 29 Nov. 1937; Shawinigan Papers, Minute Book, 21 Apr. 1937; Robert Rumilly, *Maurice Duplessis et son temps* (Montreal 1973), I: 349. The export of power was governed by the 1907 Electricity and Fluid Exportation Act which prohibited the export of power without cabinet approval. The practice had been to renew all licences automatically, but no new permits had been approved for many years.

10 Roosevelt Papers, OF 156, Olds to Roosevelt, 16 Dec. 1937, enc. Memorandum to the President In Re: St. Lawrence Treaty-Ontario-Quebec Plans for Export of Power to the United States, 16 Dec. 1937; HP, Hogg to Hepburn, 20 Nov. 1937; KD, 22, 25, 26 Nov. 1937; KP, E.A. Pickering, Memorandum for the Prime Minister, 29 Nov. 1937

11 KD, 29 Nov. 1937

12 KD, 6 Jan. 1938; *GM*, 11 Dec. 1937

13 *GM*, *TDS*, 10, 11, 14 Dec. 1937; Montreal *Gazette*, *GM*, 14–17 Dec. 1937; KD, 16 Dec. 1937; Roosevelt Papers, PSF 93, Armour to Cordell Hull, 17 Dec. 1937

14 *GM*, *TDS*, *Gazette*, 17, 18 Dec. 1937

15 KD, 17 Dec. 1937; *GM*, Montreal *Gazette*, 18 Dec. 1937

16 KP, Hepburn to King, 18 Dec. 1937; *TDS*, 18 Dec. 1937; KD, 18, 19 Dec. 1937; KD, manuscript version, 19 Dec. 1937; *GM*, 20, 21 Dec. 1937; NAC, Dept. of External Affairs, D1, vol. 739, file 116, Secret and Personal, St. Lawrence Seaway Political Implications, 3 Feb. 1940, n.sig (where Skelton comments, after Mitch had agreed to go ahead with the St Lawrence in the fall of 1939 that 'our alibi to Mr. Roosevelt against action is gone'); KD, 20, 21 Dec. 1937; HP, Duplessis to Hepburn, 28 Dec. 1937. Although no agreement existed, Ottawa had certainly accepted the twinning of the two without protest. As Armour reminded Hull, 'Dr. Skelton on more than one occasion told me that the well-known desire of Hepburn to secure further power at Niagara ... would he felt, perhaps be the strongest lever or argument in inducing Mr. Hepburn eventually to accept the treaty' (Roosevelt Papers, PSF 93, Armour to Hull, 18 Dec. 1937).

17 HP, Hepburn to W. Euler, 21 Jan. 1938; *Correspondence and Documents*, 15–16, 51–56, W.A. Riddell to Hull, 27 Jan. 1938; Hepburn to King, 14 Feb., King to Hepburn, 22 Feb. 1938; *Correspondence Relating to Kenogami*

(Long Lake) Project and Export of Electrical Power, 5–8, Hepburn to King, 25 Feb. 1938; King to Hepburn, 1 Mar. 1938

18 KP, Mulock to King, 22 Dec. 1937; KD, 1, 2, 11 Feb. 1938.

19 KP, Memoranda and Notes, Confidential Memorandum for the Prime Minister [E.A. Pickering], 23 Feb. 1938; HP, Slaght to Hepburn, 11 Mar. 1938; *HCD*, 10 Mar. 1938: 1191, 21 Mar. 1938: 1564

20 Roosevelt Papers, OF 136, Frank Walsh, Confidential Memorandum to the President ..., 10 July 1936; Walsh to Roosevelt, 27 July 1936; PSF 185, Leland Olds to Roosevelt, 16 Dec. 1937; USNA, Dept. of State, 711.42157 SA 29/1623, Frank Walsh, Memorandum to the President In Re: Great Lakes–St. Lawrence Treaty, 15 Feb. 1938; *Correspondence Relating to Kenogami River*, Hull to Marler, 17 Mar. 1938; Memorandum, Department of State to the Canadian Minister to the United States, 17 Mar. 1938

21 KD, 21, 22 Mar. 1938; *GM*, 22 Mar. 1938; HP, Slaght to Hepburn, 24 Mar. 1938

22 *GM*, 18 Dec. 1837; 3, 18, 24, 26 Mar., 7 Apr. 1938; *JLAO*, 1939, Appendix No. 1, Reports of the Majority and Minority Groups of the Select Committee appointed by the Legislative Assembly during the Session of 1938 to inquire into certain contracts with Quebec Power Companies

23 R.S. Lambert and P. Pross, *Renewing Nature's Wealth* (Toronto 1967), 339; *JLAO*, 1938, 77; ibid., 1941, Appendix No. 1, 'Final report and Proceedings of the Select Committee of the Legislative Assembly appointed to inquire into the Administration of the Department of Lands and Forests'; HP, G.D. Conant, Memorandum to the Honourable Prime Minister: re Lake Sulphite Co. Ltd., 28 Feb. 1937; Sweezey to Hepburn, 5 May 1937; *GM*, 26 Feb., 2 Mar. 1938; AO, Dept. of Labour, Series II-1, vol. 19, J. Nixon, OPP, Report re industrial unrest, 20 Dec. 1937

24 HP, Nixon to Hepburn, 10 Dec. 1937; AO, Dept. of Agriculture, Pasteurization; HP, Allan Brown to Hepburn, 23 Dec. 1937; *GM*, 16 Feb. 1938; HP, Hepburn to A. McLaghlan, 26 Apr. 1938

25 *Budget Address ... March 19, 1938* (Toronto 1938); *GM*, 23 Mar. 1938; Towers Papers, Memoranda, Visit to Toronto, 21–24 Apr. 1938, 27 Apr. 1938

26 *GM*, 6, 7 Apr. 1938; *JLAO*, 1938: 136; Hamilton *Spectator*, 14 Feb. 1938; *GM*, 21 Mar. 1938

27 KP, Skelton to King, 20 Apr. 1937. The best study of the Rowell Sirois Commission is D.M. Fransen, '"Unscrewing the Unscrewable": The Rowell-Sirois Commission, the Ottawa Bureaucracy, and Public Finance Reform 1935–1941' (PHD thesis, University of Toronto 1984).

28 *GM*, 10 Mar. 1937; *TET*, 17 Aug. 1937; HP, McLarty to Hepburn, 18 Sept. 1937

29 Royal Commission on Dominion Provincial Relations, Report of Proceedings, 366; *GM*, 30 Nov., 4 Dec., 1937; AO, Treasury Dept., Series II-1, Box 73, Lang to Walters, 10 Dec. 1937

30 *GM*, *TDS*, 10, 11 Dec. 1937; KD, 10 Dec. 1937
31 *Gazette*, *GM*, *TDS*, 14–17 Dec. 1937; Rumilly, *Duplessis*, 1, 405–6, 445–7
32 *Gazette*, *GM*, 11 Jan. 1938; HP, Hepburn to Duplessis, 14 Feb. 1938.
33 KP, Hepburn to King, 25 Nov. 1937; *Gazette*, 17 Dec. 1937; *TDS*, 11, 25 Jan. 1938; HP, Hepburn to Duplessis, 24 Jan. 1938; H. Blair Neatby, *William Lyon Mackenzie King: Prism of Unity* (Toronto 1976), 348, n.64; HP, Hepburn to Duplessis, 14 Feb. 1938; Dafoe Papers, Dafoe to G. Ferguson, 23, 30 Jan. 1938; *TDS*, 18, 24 June 1938
34 *GM*, 10, 17 Feb. 1938; *TDS*, 16 Feb. 1938; Rogers Papers, Rogers to Cross, 15 Feb. 1938; Statement by Hon. Norman Rogers, Minister of Labour, 12 Mar. 1938; *GM*, 15 Mar. 1938
35 MacKay Papers, MacKay to Mrs MacKay, 22 Apr. 1938; *GM*, 21 Apr. 1938
36 *Winnipeg Free Press*, 26 Apr., 3 May 1938; MacKay Papers, MacKay to Mrs MacKay, 30 Apr. 1938. Angus Papers, MSS Autobiography, 262. The working papers are in AO, Treasury Dept., Series II-1 (boxes 48, 73) and VI-1, Box 2.
37 *Statement by the Government of Ontario to the Royal Commission on Dominion-Provincial Relations. Book 1. Prime Minister's Statement (Apr. 1938)*; MacKay Papers, MacKay to Mrs MacKay, 3 May 1938. Much of the opening statement might be compared with W.H. Moore, *The Definite National Purpose* (Toronto 1933), particularly ch. 8, and Moore's attack on Bennett's marketing bill (*HCD*, 1934: 2384, 3098) and on Dunning's 1937 budget (*HCD*, 1937: 1656).
38 *Winnipeg Free Press*, 3 May 1938; *GM*, *TDS*, 4 May 1938; Mackay Papers, MacKay to Mrs MacKay, 3 May 1938
39 *Statement by the Government of Ontario*, Book II. General statement; Royal Commission on Dominion-Provincial Relations, *Report of Proceedings*, vol. 14; *Winnipeg Free Press*, 5 May 1938.
40 MacKay Papers, MacKay to Mrs MacKay, 8 May, 15 May 1938; Wilfrid Eggleston, *While I Still Remember* (Toronto 1968), 239. A good summary of the Ontario position is Christopher Armstrong, *The Politics of Federalism* (Toronto 1981), 213.

CHAPTER 16: 'SOMETHING IN THE WIND'

1 Dafoe Papers, Crerar to Dafoe, 18 Dec. 1937; KD, 6 Jan. 1938
2 KP, Philpott to King, 19 Dec. 1937; LD, 13 Mar. 1938; KD, 17 Mar., 25 Apr. 1938
3 KD, 26 Apr. 1938
4 Ibid., 29 Apr., 2, 3, 4 May 1938; LD, 4, 5 May 1938. Arthur Hardy, the sixty-six year-old senator, was afraid to take the initiative because he was afraid Mitch would go after his estate when he died (LD, 5 May 1938).

5 *Canadian Liberal Monthly* (May 1938), 8; KD, 18 May 1938
6 KP, Hepburn to Crerar, 30 May 1938; James Struthers, *No Fault of Their Own: Unemployment and the Canadian Welfare State 1914–1941* (Toronto 1983), 188; H. Blair Neatby, *William Lyon Mackenzie King: The Prism of Unity* (Toronto 1976), 250; *GM*, 15, 27, 28 July 1939
7 KP, Hepburn to Dunning, 15 June 1935; Dunning to Hepburn, 18 June 1938; *GM*, 18 July 1938; HP, Hepburn to King, 29 June 1938; Alex Skelton to Hepburn, 8 July, 12 Aug., Hepburn to Skelton, 13 July, 19 Aug. 1938; MacKay Papers, Skelton to MacKay, 22 July 1938
8 *GM*, 22 June 1938; *Le Soleil*, 11 July 1938; *TDS*, 16 July 1938; KP, Confidential Memorandum for the Prime Minister [E.A. Pickering], 14 July 1938
9 *GM*, 20 July 1938; *Winnipeg Free Press*, 20 July 1938; Edmonton *Journal*, July 1938; *TDS*, 28 July 1938; *GM*, 29 July 1938; Vancouver *Sun*, 1, 3 Aug. 1938
10 *TET*, 8 Aug. 1938; *GM*, *TDS*, 11, 12 Aug. 1938
11 Carty Diary, 12 Aug. 1938; *STTJ*, *GM*, *TET*, 7, 12, 13 Aug. 1938
12 HP, McGuinness to Hepburn, 18 Aug. 1938; Chalmers Papers, Memorandum [of a conversation with Dunn], 13 May 1938; LD, 12 Aug. 1938. 'He seems to visualize Hepburn as a possible leader of a new national government for Canada,' Chalmers noted, 'but I think he does not realize the degree to which Hepburn is a purely local politician who had done nothing to gain for himself any prestige or respect in the provinces outside of Ontario.'
13 *TDS*, 18 Aug. 1938; KD, 18 Aug. 1938
14 Roosevelt Library, Berle Papers, Memorandum for the President in Re: Proposed Next Step to Secure St. Lawrence Treaty, 11 Apr. 1938, n. sig. [Leland Olds]; *Correspondence and Documents* ..., 43, Hull to Marler, 28 May 1938; HP, King to Hepburn, 31 May 1938
15 *GM*, *TDS*, 19 Aug. 1938; KP, Memorandum for the P.M., 19 Aug. 1938. Roosevelt's 'revelations' were based on the information and speculation in the 1937 report of the New York State Power Authority. Roosevelt did not mention any names, but in his discussion with King – 'Will make first start to-day, and do[go]on, bit by bit, bringing out disclosure,' King noted – referred to the Niagara Hudson Co. and the Aluminum Company (KD, 18 Aug. 1938). King was delighted. As he informed the governor general, 'I have not the least doubt that Hepburn has become the instrument of the privately owned power companies in the United States and Canada to help them maintain their monopoly' (KP, King to Tweedsmuir, 25 Aug. 1938).
16 KP, Hepburn to King, 19 Aug. 1938; *TDS*, *GM*, 19 Aug. 1938
17 Chalmers Papers, Memorandum, Notes Re Mr. Hepburn, 19 Aug. 1938; Memorandum [Hogg], 23 Dec. 1937. Chalmers could find no evidence that Mitch was allied to the private power interests.
18 LD, 23 June 1938; *GM*, 20, 22 Aug. 1938

19 *Correspondence and Documents...* 45, King to Hepburn, 30 Aug. 1938; Hepburn to King, 21 Sept. 1938

20 Chalmers Papers, Memorandum [conversation with Hogg], 23 Dec. 1937; Roosevelt Papers, OF 156, Memorandum with Reference to the Canadian Situation and the St. Lawrence Treaty, 1 Sept. 1938. n. sig. [hand-written notation, 'Hon. Frank Walsh']

21 *TDS*, 16 Mar. 1938; *GM*, 17 Mar. 1938; Chalmers Papers, Memorandum, Hepburn and Money, 19 Aug. 1938; *TDS*, 14 Nov. 1938; *GM*, 12 Dec. 1938; Campbell Papers, Box 2, Folder 3, draft speech. n.d.; comment by Colin Campbell on a *Globe* editorial, 17 June 1938, n.d.

22 KD, 20 Aug. 1938; LD, 17 Aug. 1938; *GM*, 10 Oct. 1938; Waterloo *Chronicle*, 25 Oct. 8 Nov. 1938; Kitchener *Daily Record*, 11, 15 Nov. 1938; Galt *Daily Reporter*, 15 Nov. 1938; KD, 15 Nov. 1938; LD, 1938 *passim*

23 HP, Dunn to Hepburn, 5 Nov. 1938; Dunn Papers, Dunn to Duplessis, 5 Nov. 1938; KD, 5 Jan. 1939

24 Dafoe Papers, Dafoe to Ferguson, 17 Nov. 1938

25 KD, 21, 29 Nov., 8, 13 Dec. 1938; 18 Jan. 1939; *GM*, 15 Dec. 1938. When Mitch released a slightly different version of their discussion to the press, King forced Gardiner to issue a stronger and more specific statement than Gardiner would have liked. King's collapse in September and a month-long Caribbean vacation in October, attributed by Neatby to his inability to cope with domestic and international problems, encouraged the suspicion that he might resign. There were many who shared Brooke Claxton's opinion that King did not 'seem to have the strength and courage to pull the country together and there is no one in sight likely to do it' (Neatby, *Prism of Unity*, 288; Claxton Papers, Claxton to Arnold Toynbee, 30 Dec. 1938).

26 KD, 21, 29 Nov., 8 Dec. 1938; *GM*, 14 Dec. 1938. Mitch told the Carty brothers that he had concluded that King would fight the next election and advised Gardiner that he would 'seriously consider withdrawing from public life rather than disrupt the Liberal party' but could not 'stretch' his 'conscience to support King' (Carty Diary, 12 Dec. 1938).

27 KP, Davis to Gardiner, 10 Dec. 1938

28 LD, 2 Dec. 1938; KD, 2, 5 Dec. 1938. Mitch denied any knowledge of Johnson's mission (LD, 22 Dec. 1938).

29 KD, 8 Dec. 1938

30 Ibid.; HP, Cox to Hepburn, 24 Dec. 1938. I have found no evidence of a plot to defeat Howe.

31 The fullest text of Rogers's speech is the report from Port Arthur (KP, 210482) and of Howe's in Howe Papers (vol. 147); Fort William *Times-Journal*, 10, 12, 13 Dec. 1938. Privately and publicly Mitch demanded that Rogers prove the conspiracy charge. In a draft letter, apparently never sent, Rogers wrote: 'Whether the parties to this attempt included this person or

that person is a matter of secondary importance. I may say, however, that when I spoke at Port Arthur I did so with full knowledge that a person who is known to enjoy your confidence and assumed to speak for you indicated that Mr. Duplessis could guarantee a stated number of seats in the province of Quebec as a part of the plan to secure a new Leader of the Liberal Party before the next election.' Presumably he was referring to Johnson (Rogers Papers, Rogers to Hepburn, draft, 27 Feb. 1938).

32 *GM*, 12 Dec. 1938
33 KD, 8, 12 Dec. 1938; *GM*, *TDS*, 12, 13 Dec. 1938. King's statement is printed in full in *Canadian Liberal Monthly* (Dec. 1938), 5.
34 Carty Diary, 12 Dec. 1938; Windsor *Star*, *TDS*, 13 Dec. 1938
35 HP, Addresses 1942, 'Present Day Problems,' 15 Dec. 1938; *TDS*, *GM*, *TET*, 16 Dec. 1938; Main Johnson Papers, Autobiographical Essays, 30 Dec. 1938; KD, Dec. 17, 1938; Carty Diary, 24 Dec. 1938; *TET*, 20 Dec. 1938
36 KD, 13, 15 Dec. 1938
37 KD, 17, 18 Dec. 1938; LD, 12 Dec. 1938
38 LD, 18 Dec. 1938; the resolution, signed by F.G. Sanderson, chairman of the resolutions committee, is in KP, J4, vol. 192, 135112; KD, 19, 20 Dec. 1938; interview, W.A. Taylor; KP, King to Taylor, 19 Dec. 1938. Slaght was among those who did not attend and did not sign later as King requested (KP, J4, 135121).
39 *Maclean's*, 15 Jan. 1939; LD, 19 Dec. 1938; KD, 21 Dec. 1938; *TET*, 19 Dec. 1938
40 LD, 22 Dec.; KD, 21, 22 Dec. 1938; Carty Diary, 24 Dec. 1938. In his 20 December diary entry Lambert stated: 'Bill Taylor told me about Fraser & Gray going to see Hepburn & bringing back 3 conditions. (1) Two new cabinet ministers (2) Rogers' retirement (3) Johnson a Senator.' There is some inconsistency here. Gray and Fraser had arrived on 20 December, spent the night at Bannockburn, and returned to Ottawa on the afternoon of 21 December. They phoned King at once, but he refused to see them. 'Told them I wanted to be in a position to say I had taken no part in any of this' (KD, 21 Dec. 1938).
41 KD, Gordon to King, 6 June, 13 Dec. 1938; Dafoe Papers, Dafoe to G. Ferguson, 11 Oct. 1938; KD, 7 Dec. 1938
42 *TDS*, *GM*, 16–20 Dec. 1938; KD, 17 Dec. 1938, 7 Jan. 1939. *TDS*, 24 Feb. 1939. The discussion of the succession continued after Mitch left for Australia. Lambert recorded (LD, 10 Jan.) that 'Bill Chisholm phoned from Toronto re H. Nixon for leadership & said he was ready to take over.'
43 *GM*, 19 Sept., 6 Oct. 1938
44 *TDS*, 2 Sept. 1938. personal interviews, William Shields, Paul Martin
45 Carty Diary, 30 July 1936; Sir Anthony Jenkinson, *Where Seldom a Gun Is Heard* (London 1937), 215; *Saturday Night*, Dec., 1937; HP, Sandwell to

Hepburn, 17 Dec. 1937; Bruce Journal, Mar. 1938. McCullagh was there and talked to Jenkinson; Heenan was presumably the minister.

46 Manion Papers, Manion to Hogarth, 9 Mar. 1936; HP, Gordon Best to Hepburn, 28 July 1942; HP, Wooliver to Hepburn, n.d.; NAC, Drew Papers, Drew to John Bassett, 13 Feb. 1942

47 Personal interviews, confidential; KD, 5 June 1939, 7 Jan. 1939

48 HP, F.C. Crawford to Hepburn, 20 Oct. 1934 (recommending Imperial, Inco, and Stelco, among others, for 'the purpose you have in mind'); McCullagh Papers, McCullagh to Hepburn, 29 Jan. 1937; *Monetary Times*, 26 Apr., 30 Dec. 1937; HP, Hepburn to Sparks, 19 Feb. 1938; USNA, Dept. of State 842.00/548 – 1/2, David Key to J.F. Hickerson, 2 Feb. 1939, enc. Memorandum, Jan. 30, 1939, 'Additional Information concerning rumours that Mr. Hepburn has enriched himself'

49 Carty Diary, 15 Oct. 1935; Elgin County Land Records; interviews, William Tapsell, Eva Hepburn; *STTJ*, 7 Aug. 1937, 12 Oct. 1940; Carty Diary, 8 May 1936; HP, Hepburn to T. Crerar, 30 May 1938; Carty Diary, 17 May 1937

CHAPTER 17: 'A FAMOUS MAN OF THE EMPIRE'

1 Interview, Colin Campbell; *GM, TDS*, 16, 17 Dec. 1938

2 Sydney *Morning Herald*, 24 Jan. 1939; HP, H. Miles Cox to Hepburn, 1 Sept. 1939; interview, confidential. The ticketing and itinerary records are in AO, Treasury Dept., Series II-1, Boxes 31–2. Press clippings are in HP, Box 297.

3 London *Free Press, GM*, 24 Feb. 1939

4 *STTJ*, 15–28 Oct. 1925; London *Free Press*, 27 Jan. 1927; HP, Hepburn to A. Conley, 10 Dec. 1926; Hepburn to A.W. Graham, 8 Feb. 1927; *TDS*, 1 Oct. 1936; Carty Diary, 14 Sept. 1936

5 *TDS*, 19 Jan. 1938; *GM*, 19 Jan., 29 Sept., 27, 29 Oct. 1938

6 Sydney *Morning Herald*, 24 Jan. 1939; *GM*, 4, 21 Feb. 1939; interview, Colin Campbell. The conclusion reached by the editor of the proceedings was that 'Canada was shown to be generally negative in her attitude towards British Commonwealth relations' (H.V. Hodson, *The British Commonwealth and the Future: Proceedings of the Second Unofficial Conference on British Commonwealth Relations, Sydney 3rd–17th Sept., 1938* [London 1939], 62).

7 London *Free Press, TDS, GM*, 24 Feb. 1939; Ontario Progressive Conservative Party Papers, Gordon Reid to John Robb, 1 Mar. 1939

8 KD, 27 Feb. 1939; Manion Papers, Hogarth to Manion, 31 Jan. 1939; HP, Hepburn to O'Connor, 6, 16 Mar. 1939; Bruce Papers, McCullagh to Bruce, 24 Apr. 1939; Bruce to B. Baxter, Bruce to Bennett, July 13, 1939; Brian J. Young, 'George McCullagh and the Leadership League' (MA thesis, Queen's University 1964), 201–26

9 ACFEO Papers, C2/70/4, Circular letter ... 12 Mar. 1940; Cloutier et al. to McGuigan, 2 Sept. 1938; HP, In the Matter of the Roman Catholic Separate Schools of Ontario, 7 Mar. 1938; HP, Adelard, Quinn, and Brennan to Hepburn, 30 Mar. 1938; CTPA Papers, Quinn to W. Scott, 29 Mar. 1938; J.A. McNevin to James Day, 14 Apr. 1938; M.J. Quinn, *The Frustration of the Lay Catholic Effort in Ontario* (Toronto 1943), 23; F.A. Walker, *Catholic Education and Politics in Ontario* (Toronto 1964), 464

10 CTPA Papers, Quinn to Scott, 25 Jan. 1939; O'Brien Papers, Brennan to O'Brien, 10 Mar. 1939; AO, Dept. of Labour, Series 1-1, vol. 23, A.H. Murphy et al. to Hepburn, 25 Mar. 1939; Brennan to Hippel, 13 Apr. 1939 (where Brennan states that the committee had received 'Very Favourable' responses from 8 ministers and 26 members of caucus and 'Favourable' from 4 ministers and 22 members, with the remainder of caucus prepared to give 'favourable consideration' to the legislation when they had seen it); O'Brien Papers, Brennan to O'Brien, 4 Apr., 4 May 1939; CTPA Papers, Brennan to D.A. Casey, 28 Apr. 1939; ACFEO Papers, Murphy et al., Circular letter ... 12 Mar. 1940

11 HP, Hepburn to O'Connor, 25 Mar. 1939; *GM*, 4, 5, 27 Apr. 1939

12 Underhill was the subject of a more extended denunciation late in the session when George Drew cited a passage from a speech given in 1935 in which he said Canadians should make it clear that 'the poppies blooming in Flanders Fields have no further interest for us' and if the call came again to participate in a British war 'the simplest answer is to thumb our noses at them.' Drew insisted the time had come to stop such disloyal statements. Mitch promised that if the University of Toronto did nothing to discipline Underhill and others, 'then I shall consult with the law officers of the house, and with the honourable the leader of the opposition, and devise some means of dealing with them   some means, I'm confident, that would meet with the approval of every loyal member of this House.' However, when Colonel Hunter's motion for Underhill's dismissal came before the legislature, Mitch had it withdrawn, as he did another motion by Drew and Glass for an inquiry into organizations 'which are seeking to destroy our democratic institutions.' Despite his rhetoric, Mitch made no attempt to force the university to discipline Underhill, who made his peace with the president and the board. Not one member of the House had supported Underhill and Gratton O'Leary told Dafoe that there was not 'a paper in Ontario (which must include the *Journal*) that will stand up for freedom of speech if Hepburn attacks the Universities' (*GM*, Apr. 14, 15, 28, 1939; Dafoe Papers, Dafoe to G. Ferguson, Apr. 16, 1939). The incident is fully discussed in Douglas Francis, *Frank H. Underhill: Intellectual Provocateur* (Toronto 1986), 109–14.

13 KD, 20 Mar. 1939; H. Blair Neatby, *William Lyon Mackenzie King: The Prism of Unity* (Toronto 1976), 297

14 *JLAO*, 20, 23 Mar. 1939; *GM*, *TDS*, 24 Mar. 1939; HP, Dunn to Hepburn, 25 May 1939

15 HP, Hepburn to O'Connor, 16, 25 Mar. 1939; *Saturday Night*, 15 Apr. 1939; LD, 17 Mar. 1939; Manion Papers, H. Price to Manion, 25 Apr. 1939; *Saturday Night*, 29 Aug. 1939. During the session, Drew often dropped in to Mitch's office for a drink with Colin Campbell the bartender (OHSS, interview, Colin Campbell).

16 Manion Papers, Hepburn to Manion, 29 May 1939; *TDS*, *GM*, 22, 23 May 1939; KD, 22 May 1939; *GM*, 30 May 1939

17 LD, 16, 17 Jan. 1939; KD, 18 Jan. 1939

18 KD, 18 Jan. 1939; USNA, Dept. of State, 842.00/548 – 1/2, David Key to John Hickerson, 2 Feb. 1939, enc. Memorandum, Liberal Caucus of January 18th, 28 Jan. 1939

19 KD, 7, 18, 23 Jan. 1939

20 AO, Roebuck Papers, N. McLarty to Roebuck, 21 Jan. 1943; LD, 30 Mar., 3, 8, 11, 13, 19, 20, 24, 26, 27 Apr., 3 May 1939; *Canadian Liberal Monthly*, Apr. 1939. However, Lambert did appoint an organizer and set up a federal office in Ontario. The man chosen was Bart Sullivan, ironically the director of travel and publicity in the Ontario government (*TDS*, 5 July 1939).

21 LD, 23, 25 May 1939; KD, 5, 6 June 1939

22 USNA, Dept. of State, Box 84, File 800, Warwick Perkins, US Consulate, Toronto, Memorandum, 6 June 1939, Premier Hepburn's Plans for the Future; 842.00/533, Herbert C. Hengsler to the Secretary of State, 6 July 1939; Memorandum, 6 July 1939, Conversation between Mr. F.C. Mears, parliamentary correspondent Montreal *Gazette* and Mr. Key; HP, C.O. Knowles to Hepburn, 5 July 1939; *GM*, 29 June 1939; LD, 4 July 1939; HP, Hepburn to T. Wayling, 4 July 1939

23 Manion Papers, Manion to Drew, 31 Mar., 12 June, 3 Aug. 1939; Drew to Manion, 5 Apr. 1939; Dafoe Papers, Dafoe to G. Ferguson, 15 Apr. 1939

24 Manion Papers, Manion to C.G. Dunn, 14 July 1939; *GM*, 11, 12 July 1939; Windsor *Star*, 11 July 1939; Manion Papers, Hogarth to Manion, 18 July 1939; Dunn Papers, Dunn to Duplessis, 19 July 1939; LD, 24 Mar., 3 Apr., 14 June 1939; *TDS*, 20 July 1939. In his first major speech of the pre-campaign at Rimouski, with Duplessis providing a motorcycle escort, Manion stated that 'I believe I can get along better with Mr. Hepburn and Duplessis than he [King] has done' (*TDS*, 10, 11 July 1939).

25 KD, 19 Jan. 1939; Roosevelt Papers, OF 156, Roper to the Secretary of State, Subject: St. Lawrence Waterway project,' conversation with Prime Minister Mackenzie King, 28 June 1939, enclosed in Hull to Roosevelt, 15 July 1939; Roosevelt Papers, PSF 35, Roosevelt to Roper, 10 July 1939

26 KP, King to Crerar, 10 July 1939; Crerar to King, 25 July 1939; KD, 20, 26 July, 11 Aug. 1939

27 KD, 26 July, 8 Aug. 1939; LD, 8, 9 Aug. 1939; *TDS*, 9 Aug. 1939

CHAPTER 18: 'THE CLOVEN HOOF OF THE GANG'

1 KD, 31 Aug. 1939; *GM*, 1 Sept. 1939; *HCD*, 9 Sept. 1939; 65; HP, Hepburn to Lapointe, 11 Sept. 1939; HP, Hepburn to Thomas Wayling, 5 Sept. 1939

2 KP, Col. K. Stuart, Record of Conversation with the Premier and Attorney General of Ontario Regarding the Subject of Civil Security, 20 Apr. 1939; HP, Assistant Chief Engineer, to Hogg, 20 Apr. 1939; KP, J.C. MacNeill, Memorandum for the Minister of Justice, 31 Aug. 1939; HP, Mackenzie to Conant, 31 Aug. 1939

3 *GM*, 2 Sept. 1939; HP, Hepburn to King, 5 Sept. 1939; KD, 5 Sept. 1939; *GM*, 6 Sept. 1939; HP, Conant to Mackenzie, 11 Sept. 1939. The fear of a torpedo attack had been aroused by the discovery in a Chicago restaurant of a drawing of a torpedo with floats and instructions how it could be used to destroy a hydro plant similar to Queenston (KP, Col. K. Stuart, Record of Conversation ..., 20 Apr. 1939).

4 AO, Drew Papers, Drew to Hepburn, 1 Sept. 1939; *GM*, *TDS*, 20–23, 29 Sept. 1939; *GM*, 28 July, 15 Sept. 1939; Manion Papers, Memorandum, 20 Sept. 1939; L. Frost Papers, Frost to A.W.R. Sinclair, 23 Sept. 1939; HP, Hepburn to E.J. Krause, 23 Sept. 1939. The *Star* (19 Jan. 1940) claimed that in September 1939 only three members were prepared to back Mitch in some form of anti-King statement.

5 KD, 28 Sept. 1938; KP, Slaght to King, 9 Sept. 1939; KD, 9–12, 15, 28 Sept. 1939; KP, Hardy to King, 30 Sept.; King to Hardy, 2 Oct. 1939

6 HP, Hepburn to Wayling, 5 Sept. 1939. Bill Avery, one of Mitch's physicians, had seen the 'hot box' in Chicago and became its avid promoter in Ontario. Those infected with gonorrhea were placed in the casket-like box, with a hole for the head, and endured temperatures of 106+ F. for eight to ten hours. There were the inevitable rumours that Mitch had been in the box (confidential interview). There are four versions of the meeting which differ in emphasis not substance: King's (KD, 3 Oct. 1939); Hepburn's (Lambert Papers, Memorandum, Confidential [Jack Hambleton] to Mr. Brown [*TDS*]); Drew's (NAC, Drew Papers, Memorandum, Extremely Confidential, 4 Oct. 1939); and the official minutes kept by Heeney (KP, C114601, Memorandum, For File: Re: Meeting of Cabinet with representatives of the Ontario Legislature, 3 Oct. 1939).

7 Lambert Papers, H. Hindmarsh to Lambert, 6 Oct. 1939; KP, Lambert to King, 7 Oct. 1939; KD, 10 Oct. 1939; LD, 11 Oct. 1939

8 Chalmers Papers, Memorandum, 21 Nov. 1939; *GM*, *TET*, 23–25 Nov. 1936

9 HP, Rogers to Hepburn, 14 Oct., 4 Dec.; Hepburn to Rogers, 18 Oct., 5 Dec. 1939; Lapointe to McQuesten, 17 Oct. 1939; *GM*, 24 Oct. 1939; KP, Conant

to Lapointe, 17 Nov. 1939; Commissioner S.T. Wood, Memorandum ... for the Minister of Justice, 20, 22 Nov. 1939; AO, Treasury Dept., Series II-2, Box 72, C. Fraser Elliott to Walters, 13 Sept. 1939; KP, Hepburn to King, 1 Dec. 1939; HP, King to Hepburn, 17 Oct., 15 Nov.; Hepburn to King, 28 Oct., 4 Dec. 1939; KD, 21 Dec. 1939

10 GM, TDS, 11, 17 Jan. 1939; Manion Papers, Drew to Manion, 15 Jan. 1940; Manion to Drew, 16 Jan. 1940; *Saturday Night*, 27 Jan. 1940

11 GM, TDS, 19 Jan. 1940; *JLAO*, 18 Jan. 1940: 20; KD, 16 Jan. 1941; KP, W. Ross Macdonald to King 6 Feb. 1940; TDS, 12 Feb. 1940. In his interview with the OHSS, Farquhar Oliver stated that Drew was proposing a motion of censure when Mitch interrupted to say he would do it 'and so they immediately took the proposed vote of censure across from Mr. Drew to Mr. Hepburn's desk.' There is no confirming evidence. Drew seems to have been unaware of Mitch's intentions, but did believe that his condemnation of King was responsible for the resolution (Manion Papers, Karl Homuth to Manion, 20 Jan. 1939; NAC, Drew Papers, Drew to H. Howitt, 5 Feb. 1940).

12 KD, 18, 19, 22 Jan. 1940. King later concluded that Mitch had, in fact, wanted to be defeated. 'Had the resolution been defeated, he would there and then joined up with Drew for national government and gone to the country before our Parliament met. That chance was spoiled by members of his own government and following voting with him to the extent they did, and enabling the resolution to follow, thereby averting dissolution' (KD, 12 Mar. 1940).

13 KD, 24, 25, 26 Jan. 1940; GM, Ottawa *Citizen*, 30 Jan. 1940

14 GM, TDS, 11 Jan. – 15 Feb. 1940

15 KP, Sullivan to Lambert, 11 Feb. 1940; LD, 14 Feb. 1940; Manion Papers, Manion to J.A. Clark, 22 Jan. 1940; Price to Manion, 25 Jan. 1940; Howard A. Naugler, 'R.J. Manion and the Conservative Party, 1938–1940 (MA thesis, Queen's University, 1966), 270, citing interview with Richard Bell; Bruce Journal, 'The Election of 1940'; Dexter Papers, Memo – 27 Jan. 1940; Manion Papers, Manion to Hepburn, 7 Feb. 1940; Bruce Papers, Bruce to McCullagh, 24 Feb. 1940; McCullagh to Bruce, 4 Mar. 1940; Ottawa *Citizen*, Windsor *Star*, 1 Mar. 1940

16 GM, Ottawa *Citizen*, 5 Mar. 1940; HP, W.R. Davies to Hepburn, 5 Mar. 1940. Gary Evans states that Colonel John Cooper, acting commissioner in Grierson's absence and a Tory, had realized the political value of the film and persuaded Famous Players not to show it in Ontario until after the election. When he informed Hepburn that Walter Turnbull, King's secretary, demanded that the film be shown, Mitch intervened. Evans based his account on interviews with Turnbull and Ross McLean of the film board. See *John Grierson and the National Film Board: The Politics of Wartime Propaganda* (Toronto 1984), 71. To justify his position, Mitch later produced an advertisement from a Vancouver paper urging readers to see the film described as

'a graphic record of accomplishment which is, in great part, the work of our British Columbia Minister, Ian Mackenzie' (Windsor *Star*, 7 Mar. 1940). On the censoring of opposition speeches, see *HCD*, 13 June 1940: 755; Manion Papers, Anthony Adamson to Manion, 29 Feb. 1940, enclosing the text of his censored broadcast. King was forced to issue a press statement on 18 March denying that the government was in any way responsible.

17 *GM, TDS, STTJ*, 6–13 Mar. 1940; HP, W.H. Stringer, Memorandum for the Attorney General, 11 Feb. 1940

18 Ottawa *Citizen*, 7 Mar. 1940; Bennett Papers, MacLeod to Bennett, 9 Mar. 1940; KD, 8 Mar. 1940; *TDS*, 7 Mar. 1940

19 *TDS*, 11, 12, 14 Mar. 1940; *GM*, 12 Mar. 1940; *STTJ*, 14 Mar. 1940; Windsor *Star*, 11 Mar. 1940; *GM*, 12 Mar. 1940

20 KD, 11, 12 Mar. 1940. There is no evidence that Mitch had contacted Matthews; it is more likely that Nixon had done so. On 11 March, Nixon spoke to Lambert 're possibilities of cabinet meeting tomorrow & consequent appeals to Lt. Gov.' (LD, 11 Mar. 1940).

21 *GM, TDS*, 12, 13 Mar. 1940

22 *TS*, 13, 14 Mar.; *GM*, 13, 14 Mar. 1940; Personal File 1; Conant Papers, Conant to Hepburn, Mar. 14, 1940; see also Ross Harkness, *Atkinson of the Star* (Toronto 1963), 330–1). Before cabinet on 13 March, Mitch asked the *Star* reporter point blank to name the cabinet minister he quoted, but Hambleton refused. Mitch brought a *Telegram* reporter to cabinet and stated: 'We want to say on our honor that none of us have given this interview to the Toronto *Star*. Is that correct, gentlemen?' Each minister in turn agreed. There is an interesting telegram from G.N. Gordon to King on 13 March in KP: 'Am informed from fairly close quarters Hepburn has taken the pledge promised to resign upon request of Nixon who is to succeed him and who is to discontinue criticisms not approved by Nixon.' Eric Cross claimed that he and Simpson persuaded Nixon to return on the understanding that the ministers were free to support King (CBC interview, Eric Cross).

23 *GM*, 25 Jan. 1940; KP, B. Sullivan to Lambert, 11 Feb., 6 Mar. 1940; *GM*, 28 Mar. 1940; Manion papers, List of Subscriptions over $1,000, 22 Apr. 1940; Manion to Hepburn, 27 Mar. 1940

24 LD, 27 Mar., 1, 3 Apr. 1940; KD, 27 Mar., 2 Apr. 1940; *TDS*, 29 Mar.–4 Apr. 1940; AO, Dept. of Labour, G.N. Gordon to Hipel, 27 Mar. 1940; KP, Mulock to W. Turnbull, 3 Apr. 1940; *GM*, 3 Apr. 1940; *Saturday Night*, 27 Apr. 1940

CHAPTER 19: 'WITH BLOOD IN MY EYE'

1 Manion Papers, Hepburn to Manion, 1 Apr. 1940; CBC interview, Eric Cross
2 *GM*, 22 May 1940; KD, 22, 23 May 1940

3 KP, Davies to King, 22 May 1940; KD, 29, 30 May 1940

4 *GM*, 21, 22 May, 10 June 1940; Kitchener *Daily Record*, 25, 27, 31 May, 4,
   8, 10 June 1940; HP, Robinson and Dalgleish to Hepburn, 17 June 1940;
   GM, 27, 28, 31 May, 4, 21, 27 June 1940; Judith Robinson, 'Who Is
   "CALLING CANADA"?', *Liberty*, 31 Aug. 1940, 4; PCO, Minutes, Cabinet War
   Committee, 3, 5, 7, 29 June, 9 July 1940; KD, 3, 4, 6, 27 June 1940; *HCD*, 27
   June 1940: 1183; 2 July 1940: 1245. On 1 November 1939 Mitch, with
   Meighen and ten other prominent Torontonians, attended a dinner hosted
   by McCullagh to hear Colonel Carter, a British tank expert then in Canada,
   discuss the critical importance of tanks. During the discussion, wrote one of
   those present, Mitch had said that he had 'viewed the uncensored motion
   pictures of the German advance in Poland … the effectiveness and the
   irresistibility of the German tanks in action was spectacular, so much so,
   that permission to show the pictures in the theatres of Ontario had been
   refused because of the possible adverse effect it might have upon recruiting if
   the recruits should feel that they would be sent against such a totally
   impossible situation.' Mitch also said that he had discussed the production
   of tanks with the head of one automobile company, who stated that it would
   take eighteen months to get into tank production (Dexter Papers,
   C.S.[ifton?] to Victor Sifton, 2 Nov. 1939). Mitch added to the criticism
   when he announced on 3 June that at the request of theatre managers, he
   had agreed to eliminate scenes of Mackenzie King at the opening of
   Parliament. The managers, he claimed, had reported that King's appearance
   provoked noisy anti-King demonstrations. 'We have always endeavoured to
   avoid matters of a controversial nature on our screens,' said J.J. Fitzgerald
   of Famous Players, 'and we felt it was in the best interests of our patrons to
   eliminate this item' (*GM*, 4 June 1940).

5 *TDS*, 7 Dec. 1939; KP, Memorandum Re: Defence of Canada Regulations,
   23 May 1940; William Kaplan, *The Jehovah's Witnesses and the Fight for
   Civil Rights* (Toronto 1989), 33; *HCD*, 20 May 1940: 2–29, 23 May, 153, 4
   June 1940: 533. On CP activities generally see the RCMP reports reprinted in
   G.S. Kealey and R. Whitaker, eds., *R.C.M.P. Security Bulletins: The War
   Series, 1939–1941* (St John's 1989).

6 KP, Hepburn to King, 21 May 1940; King to Hepburn, 22, 23 May 1940; OA,
   Treasury Dept., Series II-2, Box 75, Conant to Rogers, 20, 22, May, 5 June
   1940; PCO, Minutes, Cabinet War Committee, 22 May 1940; KD, 22, 23 May
   1940; *HCD*, 22 May 1940: 118; 23 May 1940: 192; *GM*, 5 June 1940

7 *GM*, *TDS*, *TET*, 11–15 June 1940; *HCD*, 13 June 1940: 760–1; PCO, Minutes,
   Cabinet War Committee, 14 June 1940; AO, Treasury Dept., Series II-2, Box
   75, Power to Conant, 20 June; Conant to Power, 22 June 1940; press release,
   27 June 1940; *GM*, 11 July 1940; KD, 22 May 1940; L. Frost Papers, Frost
   to Drew; 12 June 1940. When Commissioner Stringer was asked to reveal his

information to the RCMP, he refused without the approval of the premier (*HCD*, 14 June 1940: 782).

8 HP, E.F. Stevens to Hepburn, 23 Apr. 1940; *GM*, 15 June 1940; KD, 15 June 1940

9 *TDS*, 26, 27 June 1940; *GM*, 9, 19 July 1940; *STTJ*, 10 July 1940; Frederick Edwards, 'Watch Mitchell Hepburn,' *Liberty*, 21 Dec. 1940, 4–6

10 HP, Hepburn to Aemillius Jarvis, 16 Oct. 1939; Hepburn to H. Miles Cox, 12 Oct. 1940; Hepburn to James Murdoch, 3 Dec. 1940; Hepburn to Ralston, draft, 14 Aug. 1940; Bickell to Hepburn , 4 Sept. 1940; Campbell to Hepburn, 15 Sept. 1940; OHSS interview, Colin Campbell. Mitch was still hoping for a posting to England through Bickell and Beaverbrook in August 1942, but his hopes were dashed when Bickell finished his work and returned to Toronto (*GM*, *TDS*, 11–14 Aug. 1942).

11 HP, Hepburn to Neil McLean, 26 July 1940; *GM*, 26, 31 July, 2, 3 Oct. 1940; *TDS*, 25, 26 July 1940; *Report of the Commissioner of the Ontario Provincial Police*, 1940, 1941; HP, Addresses and Speeches, A Report on the War Activities of the Departments of the Hepburn Government, n.d. [Oct. 1942].

12 *GM*, 24 Oct., 3, 6 Dec. 1940; *TDS*, 3 Dec. 1940; Politicus, 'Mitchell Hepburn, the New Appeaser,' *Saturday Night*, 19 Oct. 1940: 14; HP, Hepburn to Lapointe, 4 Dec. 1940.

13 CBC interview, Eric Cross; PC, Dewan Papers, Diary, 1940 *passim*; AO, Drew Papers, Drew to Hepburn, draft, 4 Oct. 1940; NAC, Drew Papers, Drew to Gordon Graydon, 30 Nov. 1940; C. Frost Papers, Drew to C. Frost, 25 June 1940; KP, 31 Jan. 1942. Senior civil servants recalled that Mitch seldom came to the buildings in the early 1940s and they were frequently summoned to the King Edward (personal interview, Lorne McTavish).

14 KD, 5, 19 July 1940; KP, Howe to King, 19 Aug. 1940; KP, Memorandum to the Right Honourable Mackenzie King re Ontario, n.d. [Dec. 1940] (an archivist has dated it December 1940, but from internal evidence it was probably written late in the fall); LD, 6 Dec. 1940

15 KP, Norman Lambert, Memorandum to the Right Honourable Mackenzie King re Ontario, n.d.; *GM*, 19, 27 July, 20 Aug. 1940; AO, Dept. of Labour, Series I-1, vol. 31, McLarty to N. Hipel, 16 May 1940

16 KD, 14 Jan. 1941, 19 Sept. 1940. See D.M. Fransen, '"Unscrewing the Unscrewable": The Rowell-Sirois Commission, the Ottawa Bureaucracy, and Public Finance Reform 1935–1941' (PHD thesis, University of Toronto 1984), 401, and Christopher Armstrong, *The Politics of Federalism* (Toronto 1981), 219. Briefly, the report recommended that the provinces surrender access to the direct tax fields in return for federal responsibility for unemployment insurance, assumption of provincial debts, and National Adjustment Grants, which would give every province the capacity to provide services at a national average level with taxes at the national average level.

17 Dafoe Papers, Dexter to Dafoe, 17 Oct. 1940; *Report of the Royal Commission on Dominion-Provincial Relations* (Ottawa, 1940), Book II: 82, 96–97. The estimates for Ontario were given by McQuesten at the January 1941 conference (*Dominion-Provincial Conference, Tuesday, January 14, 1941 and Wednesday, January 15, 1941* (Ottawa 1941), 75).

18 Dafoe Papers, Dexter to Dafoe, 25 Oct. 1940; KD, 22 Oct. 1940

19 NAC, Dept. of Finance, vol. 108, Special Cabinet Committee on Dominion-Provincial Relations Report and Emergency Measures (Finance and Economic), 25 Oct. 1940; Report of the Cabinet Sub- Committee Appointed to consider the Report of the Royal Commission on Dominion-Provincial Relations, 30 Oct. 1940; *GM*, 7 Nov. 1940; KP, Hepburn to King, 8 Nov. 1940; KD, 14 Jan. 1941

20 KP, Lambert, Memorandum for the … Prime Minister, n.d.; KD, 14 Jan. 1941; *TDS*, 15 Nov. 1941; KP, Heeney, Memorandum for the Prime Minister, 16 Nov. 1940. With Drew also refusing to take a position, the *Star* (28 Nov. 1940) floated the story that Mitch planned another coalition on the issue. As usual, King believed it and told Roebuck Mitch would 'form a national government with Drew' and use the conference as a springboard for an election. 'The cry will be "On to Ottawa" for a national government there afterward' (KD, Dec. 6, 1940). 'The subject is not under discussion,' Drew wrote to Gordon Graydon, 'and I can see no possible reason why it should be under discussion. It does not seem to me that the arguments which apply in support of National Government in Ottawa have any similar bearing upon the subject of coalition in the province' (NAC, Drew Papers, 30 Nov. 1940).

21 KD, 13 Dec. 1940; Dafoe Papers, Dexter to Dafoe, 26 Dec. 1940

22 *Dominion-Provincial Conference … 1941*, 1–10; Dafoe Papers, Crerar to Dafoe, 16 Jan. 1941

23 HP, Hepburn to Power, 7 Jan. 1941; *Dominion-Provincial Conference … 1941*, 10–16 and passim; Dafoe Papers, Crerar to Dafoe, 16 Jan. 1941.

24 Dafoe Papers, Crerar to Dafoe, 16 Jan. 1941; *Dominion-Provincial Conference … 1941*, 66, 101; KD, 16 Jan. 1941; KP, A.L.M. [Macdonald], n.d. (an archivist has dated the note 16 Jan., but it almost certainly should be 15 Jan. before the conference broke up).

25 *GM*, 20 Jan. 1941; KD, 20 Jan. 1941; *GM*, 21 Jan. 1941; LD, 19 Jan. 1941. Mitch seemed unaware that about a third of the additional financial requirements, or about $500 million, had in fact come from currency expansion and that economists were convinced that with the country nearing full employment, further expansion would be inflationary, see A.F.W. Plumptre, *Mobilizing Canada's Resources for War* (Toronto 1941), 213; J. Douglas Gibson, 'Financing the War', in J.F. Parkinson, *Canadian War Economics* (Toronto 1941), 33–46. Mitch's statement on finance won Aberhart's approval. What Canada needed, he wrote, was less constitutional

change than the creation of a National Finance Commission which would control monetary and fiscal policy, for productive and counter-cyclical purposes, remove the banks' power to issue notes, and place them firmly under the control of the NFC and the Bank of Canada (HP, Aberhart to Hepburn, 14 Feb. 1941). Mitch agreed that 'only by the recasting of our monetary system can this democracy survive,' but added that his position was 'more difficult in view of the fact that Toronto is the centre for entrenched finance for the Dominion, and the Press, generally speaking, are very hostile' (HP, Hepburn to Aberhart, 18 Feb. 1941).

26 *TDS*, 28 Jan. 1941

27 C. Frost Papers, A.R. Douglas, Memorandum, n.d. [Jan. 1941]; C. Frost, Memoranda for the President and the Leader, Jan. 1941; NAC, Drew Papers, Drew to G.K. Fraser, 26 Jan. 1941; *TDS*, 20 Feb. 1941, 22 Jan. 1941

28 *GM*, 6, 7, 11, 18 Jan., 8 Feb., 20 June 1941; Dafoe Papers, B.T. Richardson to Dafoe, 6 Jan. 1941; K.W. Taylor, 'The War-time Control of Prices,' in Parkinson, *Canadian War Economics*, 128–149. Data on farm production and prices may be found in *A Conspectus of the Province of Ontario* (Toronto 1941).

29 C. Frost Papers, L. Frost to Drew, 25 Nov. 1941; NAC, Drew Papers, Alex Mckenzie to Col. B.O. Hooper, 14 Jan. 1941

30 *GM*, *TDS*, 26 Feb. 1941

31 *GM*, 14 Feb., 15 Mar. 1941. The numbers on relief had fallen to 76,000 in February from over 200,000 a year earlier (NAC, Dept. of Labour, vol. 614, Report No. 139, May 1942, Direct Relief on February 1942 and February 1941).

32 PCO, Minutes, Cabinet War Committee, 28 Jan. 1941; KD, 26 Mar. 1941; J.L. Granatstein, *Canada's War* (Toronto 1975), 172; Denis Smith, *Gentle Patriot: A Political Biography of Walter Gordon* (Edmonton 1973), 22

33 *GM*, 30 Apr. 1941; Ilsley Papers, Hepburn to Ilsley, 8 May 1941; HP, Hepburn to Ilsley, 14 May 1941; NAC, Dept. of Finance, vol. 2698, Memorandum: Re Mr. Hepburn's objection to 15 percent tax on non-residents, W.L.T. [Turnbull] 15 May; HP, Hepburn to King, 19, 21 May 1941; King to Hepburn, 26 May 1941; Hepburn to King, 28 May 1941

34 KD, 30 May 1941; HP, King to Hepburn, 30 May 1941; *GM*, 21, 31 May 1941

35 KD, 4, 5 June 1941

36 Dafoe Papers, R. Fowler to Dafoe, 10 Apr. 1941; KD, 8 Mar. 1941; *GM*, 11 June, 28 May 1941

37 OHSS interview, Farquhar Oliver, 5; C. Frost Papers, Frost to Drew, 5 Sept. 1941; NAC, Drew Papers, Kennedy to Drew, 12 Sept. 1941 The consensus at the meeting of the Conservative executive committee on 13 September 1941 was that Hepburn's 'stock is high just now' and that nothing should be done to give him an excuse to have an election (AO, Latimer Papers, Minutes ...).

38 KD, 26–31 July 1941; PCO, Minutes, Cabinet War Committee, 28, 29, 31 July
    1941
39 *GM*, 11 Aug., 11, 12 Sept. 1941; Chatham *Daily News*, 10 Sept. 1941; HP,
    Conant to Hepburn, 10 Sept. 1941; Memorandum to Peter Heenan, n.sig.,
    10 Sept. 1941; A.S. Wilson, C.I.B., Industrial Unrest at Campbell Soup
    Factory ... 14–15 Sept. 1941; Hardy to Hepburn, 11 Sept. 1941
40 *GM*, 12, 13 Sept. 1941; HP, Hepburn to Howe, 12, 16 Sept. 1941; Howe to
    Hepburn, 13 Sept. 1941; Conant to Hepburn, 15 Sept. 1941
41 The standard account of the strike is L.S. MacDowell, *Remember Kirkland
    Lake: The History and Effects of the Kirkland Lake Gold Miners' Strike,
    1941–42* (Toronto 1983), 160, 207.
42 *GM*, 23-26 Sept. 1941; KP, Memorandum for the Prime Minister, W.J.T.
    [Turnbull], 25 Sept. 1941; Ottawa *Citizen*, 26 Sept. 1941. The text of
    Hepburn's speeches are in a scrapbook at Bannockburn.

CHAPTER 20: 'SOMEBODY ELSE'S WAR'

1 KD, 14 Nov. 1941, 22 Jan. 1942; Dexter Papers, Dafoe to Dexter, 15 Mar.
   1942. J.L. Granatstein, *Canada's War* (Toronto 1975), is the best account of
   King's manoeuvres.
2 *TDS*, 9 Jan. 1942; KD, 9 Jan. 1942; *GM*, 22 Jan. 1942
3 Dafoe Papers, Crerar to Dafoe, 31 Jan. 1942; HP, L.B. Spencer to Hepburn,
   23 Jan. 1942; *GM*, *TDS*, 28–30 Jan. 1942. A day after Meighen opened his
   campaign on 9 January, the Committee for Total War held its inaugural
   meeting in Toronto and demanded conscription. Contrary to what many
   suspected, Mitch had not been involved, but he did admit to a fellow
   conscriptionist that he was greatly interested 'in the movement launched by
   our friend Jim Murdoch which seems to be doing good' (HP, Hepburn to
   C.H. Carlisle, 14 Jan. 1942). Arthur Slaght told Robert Laurier that Mitch
   would be taking Drew to Welland and 'they might announce the formation
   of a national government there' (KD, 31 Jan. 1942).
4 *GM*, *TDS*, 2–7 Feb. 1942; *Le Devoir*, 27 Jan. 1942. The texts of his radio
   addresses are in HP, Personal, MU 4940. Following a phone call from
   McCullagh, Meighen had sent him some thoughts on the approach Mitch
   should take in speaking for him in the by-election (Meighen Papers,
   Memorandum, n.d., 131801).
5 KD, 29, 30 Jan. 1942; KP, McLarty to King, 4 Feb. 1942; *GM*, 6 Feb. 1942;
   KD, 5 Feb. 1942
6 *TDS*, 3-4 Feb. 1942. The fullest account of York South is J.L. Granatstein,
   'The York South By-Election of February 9, 1942: A Turning Point in
   Canadian Politics,' *Canadian Historical Review* (June 1967), 142–158.
7 *TDS*, 31 Jan. 1942; *GM*, 7 Feb. 1942; KD, 4 Feb. 1942; Granatstein,

Canada's War, 157; J. Gardiner Papers, T.H. Wood to Gardiner, 2 Feb. 1942, with enclosure; HP, Wright to Hepburn, 4 Feb. 1942. I am indebted to J.L. Granatstein for the Wood letter which he obtained before the Gardiner Papers were closed. Mitch had spent a week in August with Slaght and others as the guests of Arthur Schmon, the manager of Ontario Paper which was owned by Colonel R. McCormick, publisher of the anti-British *Chicago Tribune*.

8 KD, 31 Jan., 4 Feb. 1942; *TDS*, 6 Feb. 1942; HP, Nixon to Hepburn, 6 Feb. 1942

9 KD, 2, 9 Feb. 1942; OHSS interview, Edward Jolliffe; Roger Graham, *Arthur Meighen* (Toronto 1965), 3: 84; LD, 18, 19 Jan., 24 Feb. 1942; Dafoe Papers, Dexter to Dafoe, 20 Jan. 1942. Gallup had run a small poll and found that Noseworthy would win 53 per cent of the vote (KP, R.K. Taylor to W. Turnbull, 17 Feb. 1942). Howe told a disbelieving King that 'they are betting 3 to 2 against Meighen winning in Toronto' (KD, 9 Feb. 1942). York South had been solidly Conservative since 1911, and appeared to be one of the safest in Ontario. However, it was also the strongest CCF riding in the province in 1935 and 1940. The key to the CCF success, wrote Claxton, would be 'to get the vote to the poll' (Claxton to G. Ferguson, 3 Feb. 1942).

10 LD, 12 Feb. 1942; *GM*, *TDS*, 10 Feb. 1942; KD, 9, 10 Feb. 1942

11 Windsor *Daily Star*, 10 Feb. 1942, for the fullest account of his speech in Chatham: Ottawa *Citizen*, 12 Feb. 1942; *New York Times*, 11 Feb. 1942; *HCD*, 11 Feb. 1942: 511; KP, Secretary of State for External Affairs to Leighton McCarthy, n.d.; Pierpont Morgan to King, 14 Feb. 1942; G.H. Lash to King, 23 Feb. 1942; *TDS*, *GM*, *New York Times*, 13, 14 Feb. 1942; *Winnipeg Free Press*, 17 Feb. 1942; KD, 14 Feb. 1942. In fact, the engagement was at best a marginal success. The total damage was one transport and sub-chaser sunk, four ships damaged, and eighteen planes destroyed. See S.E. Morison, *The Rising Sun in the Pacific 1931–April 1942* (Boston 1965), 261.

12 *TDS*, *GM*, 11, 17 Feb. 1942; Dafoe Papers, Sifton to Dafoe, 13 Mar. 1942; KD, 10 Feb., 19 Mar. 1942

13 AO, Legislative Assembly Papers, Legislation 1942, Conant to Hepburn, 14, 27 Jan. 1942

14 AO, Treasury Dept., Series II-3, Report of a Conference ... at Parliament Buildings, Ottawa, 30 Sept. 1941; NAC, Dept. of Finance, vol. 754, File 222-Q-7-1, Ilsley to Hepburn, 1 Nov. 1941; Walters to W. Gordon, 2, 14 Jan. 1942; Gordon to Walters, 6 Jan. 1942

15 *Budget Address delivered by the Hon. Mitchell F. Hepburn ...* (Toronto 1942); *GM*, 3, 6, 16 Apr. 1942

16 *GM*, *TDS*, 24 Mar.–20 Apr. 1942; *Maclean's*, 15 May 1942. On the assistance given to Eaton see HP, Eaton to Hepburn, 16, 18 July 1942; Conant Papers, Hogarth to Conant, 22 Dec. 1942; KD, 31 July 1942.

17 *GM, TDS*, 16 Apr. 1942
18 HP, Hepburn to D.E. Maidenburg, 17 Apr. 1942; *GM*, 27 Apr. 1942; KD, 1 May 1942; KP, Howe to King, 2 May 1942
19 HP, Hepburn to John Krause, 27 Feb. 1942; *GM*, 16 July 1942; HP, Hepburn to Slaght, 22 July 1942
20 PCO, Minutes, Cabinet War Committee, 3 Jan. 1942; *Maclean's*, 15 Sept. 1942; HP, A.W. McIntyre to Hepburn, 17 Oct. 1942
21 NAC, Dept. of Labour, file 614.02: II-7, Allan W. Mitchell, Memorandum of meeting with Mr. Marsh ... January 16, 1942; KP, Heenan, wire, to A. MacNamara, 5 Feb.; NAC, Dept. of External Affairs, vol. 3004, File 3464-G-40, HLK[Keenleyside], Memorandum for Mr. Robertson, Japanese Labour in Ontario, 4 Feb. 1942; KD, N.A. Robertson, Memorandum for the Prime Minister, n.d., enc. HLK, Memorandum for the Prime Minister, Movement of Japanese from British Columbia, 6 Feb. On the evacuation and dispersal, see P. Roy, J.L. Granatstein, M. Iino, and H. Takamura, *Mutual Hostages* (Toronto 1990), ch. 6.
22 NAC, Dept. of Labour, Mitchell to Heenan, 28 Feb., 7 Mar. and Heenan to Mitchell, 5 Mar. 1942; Minutes of: Meeting with Mr. Macnamara ... 19 March, 1942; Ottawa *Citizen*, 18 Mar. 1942; PAO, Dept. of Labour, Series II-1, Memorandum respecting proposed agreement ... 1 April, 1942. *Report of the Department of Labour on the Administration of Japanese Affairs in Canada 1942–1944* (Ottawa Aug. 1944). In addition there were 750 interned in northern Ontario by October 1942.
23 *GM*, 14 Mar. 1942; HP, Taylor to Hepburn, 15 Mar. 1942; Hepburn to Nelson Spencer, 2 Apr. 1942; Yatabe to Hepburn, 24 June 1942
24 On the opposition, see the correspondence in HP, Private 1942, 'Japanese'; HP, Dewan to W. M. Foreman, 18, 19 Sept. 1942; Toronto did remove the ban and seven hundred entered the city, but in April 1943 council imposed the ban again for all but compassionate cases.
25 AO, Treasury Dept., Series II-1, Box 34, Nixon to Walters, 13 Mar. 1942, enclosing O. Mitchell to H.J. Symington, 7 Mar. 1942; HP, H.J. Symington to O. Mitchell, 17 Mar. 1942; Houck to Hepburn, 13 Mar. 1942; OHA, Memorandum, Des Joachims, telephone conversation between Dr. Hogg and Premier Hepburn, 28 Apr. 1942; Memorandum, Ottawa River Power Development, 29 Apr. 1942; Memorandum, Ottawa River Power Sites, Dr. Hogg's Account of his Meeting in Quebec on 6 May 1942; Memorandum, Eastern Ontario Power Resources, 16 June 1942; HP, A.K. MacMillan to Hepburn, 29 June 1942; *Re Ontario-Quebec Ottawa River Power Agreement: Correspondence Between Hon. G.D. Conant, Premier of Ontario, and Dr. T.H. Hogg, Chairman, Hydro-Electric Power Commission of Ontario Including Report of Dr. Hogg* (Toronto 1943); L. Frost Papers, Frost to Drew, 8 Oct. 1942

26 KD, 1 May 1942; KP, Howe to King, 2 May, enc. Secret, Memo of Discussions between Ontario Cabinet Ministers at Meeting of April 30th; LD, 5 May 1942. There is no record of the caucus to which Lambert referred.

27 KD, 28 Apr. 1942; KP, Howe to King, 2 May 1942; Granatstein, *Canada's War*, 228

28 Angus Macdonald Papers, Diary, 28 Apr. 1942, cited in Granatstein, *Canada's War*, 229; Dexter Papers, Memorandum, 16 June 1942; *STTJ*, 31 July 1942; *GM*, 12 June, 18, 24, 25 July, 8 Aug. 1942

29 KD, 8, 17 July 1942; *HCD*, 15 July 1942: 4265

30 See Reg Whitaker, 'Official Repression of Communism during World War II,' *Labour/Le Travail* (Spring 1986), 135–166; Ivan Avakumovic, *The Communist Party in Canada – a History* (Toronto 1973), 148; HP, Hepburn to F.M. Macdonnell, 19 June 1942; *GM*, 23 June 1942.

31 Buck Papers, interview with Max Reynolds, pp. 687, 706 (for slightly different versions of what appears to be the same meeting). A CIPO poll in October indicated that support for release was 57 to 43% outside Quebec and 62 to 38% in Ontario. In Quebec, it was 80 to 20% against release (*TDS*, 17 Oct. 1942).

32 *GM*, 17 July 1942; HP, W.T. Lawson to Hepburn, 27 July 1942; KD, 25 July 1942

33 HP, Hepburn to W. Rayfield, 5 Oct. 1942; KD, 29 Sept. 1942; HP, Hepburn to St Laurent, 3 Oct. 1942; Hepburn to King, 5 Oct. 1942; St Laurent to Hepburn, 7 Oct. 1942. Hepburn's 'minority influence' allegation struck home and King warned one back-bencher that 'our Quebec friends had been through a difficult place, and to expect the government to remove a ban on Communism would be almost too much for them' (KD, 25 July 1942).

34 *TDS*, 22 Sept., 14 Oct. 1942; AO, Drew Papers, Memorandum, 22 Sept. 1942, HMR[obbins]; NAC, Drew Papers, Drew to L. Frost, 26 Sept. 1942

35 L. Frost Papers, Frost to Drew, 29 July 1942

36 *Public Opinion Quarterly* (Summer 1942), 42; (Summer 1943), 326; (Winter 1942), 656; Ramsay Cook, *The Politics of John W. Dafoe and the Free Press* (Toronto 1953), 269; Alvin Finkel, *The Social Credit Phenomenon in Alberta* (Toronto 1989), 79

37 HP, Aberhart to Hepburn, 30 July 1942; Aberhart Papers, E.G. Hansell to Aberhart, 30 May 1942; Aberhart to Mrs J.W. Maynard, St Thomas, 3 July 1942; Maynard to Aberhart, 9 July 1942; David R. Elliott and Iris Miller, *Bible Bill: A Biography of William Aberhart* (Edmonton 1987), 302

38 Bruce Papers, Bruce, draft, to Hepburn, 6 Aug. 1942; Herbert A. Bruce, *Varied Operations* (Toronto 1958), 285–6. Bruce had won Toronto Parkdale in the 1940 election and was a fervent supporter of Meighen, to whom he had offered his seat after York South, and of conscription. With J.M.

Macdonnell attempting to refashion the Conservative party, Les Frost attempted to persuade Drew that there was no time and the prospect of revising the party was 'doubtful ... The only practical solution that I can think of is that there should be a union between provincial Liberals and Conservatives ... I believe that such a government should appeal to the people at once, form a completely new party organization which would take the place of both the Liberal and Conservative organizations; at once make advances to the people in Manitoba and British Columbia. Take say Bracken as Dominion leader and start at once organizing for a new state of affairs in Ottawa' (L. Frost Papers, Frost to Drew, 15, 19 July 1942).

39 HP, Aberhart to Hepburn, 28 Sept. 1942; Hepburn to Aberhart, 6 Oct. 1942. Aberhart wrote an almost identical letter to Drew on 28 Sept. to which Drew replied on 8 Oct. 'I assure you that the absence of any definite word from me does not suggest any change in the conviction I expressed to you when we met in Toronto last summer. On the other hand it has been very difficult for me to achieve the results which we both agree are necessary. It is not only the question of Party Politics which enters into the broad problem. There are also questions of sectionalism as well as racialism ... Mr. Hepburn has been away but I will no doubt hear him on his return (Aberhart Papers, Drew to Aberhart, 8 Oct. 1942).

40 GM, TDS, 17 Oct. 1942; TDS, 24 Oct. 1942

41 GM, TDS, TET, 22 Oct. 1942; TDS, TET, 29 Oct. 1942; OHSS interview, Farquhar Oliver; Neil McKenty, Mitch Hepburn (Toronto 1967), 261; KD, 26 Oct. 1942; Conant Papers, Conant to Hepburn, 22 Oct. 1942; KD, 22 Oct. 1942. In a CBC interview, Mrs Conant stated that at her husband's request she returned to Queen's Park the next day and begged Mitch to stay in office.

CHAPTER 21: 'THE HEPBURN JITTERS'

1 GM, 5 Nov. 1942; KD, 26 Oct. 1942; Duff letter in the Public Record Office (DO 35/857) courtesy of J.L. Granatstein

2 Larry Zolf Papers, notes on interview with Gordon Sinclair; AO, Roebuck Papers, Report re Oakwood Hotel, n.d., n.sig. A leaf from a day book suggests the report may have been submitted in December 1941. Whatever truth there was in the report, there is no doubt Mitch was being watched.

3 AO, Roebuck Papers, Roebuck to G.N. Gordon, 26 Oct. 1942; KD, 17 Dec. 1942; Maclean's, 15 Nov. 1942

4 KD, 23 Sept., 15, 16, 21 Oct. 1942; PCO, Minutes, Cabinet War Committee, 19 Nov. 1941; 8 May, 17 July, 9, 14 Oct. 1942

5 Winnipeg Free Press, 23, 26 Oct. 1942; Ralston Papers, Ralston to Stuart Ralston, 2 Nov. 1942; GM, 27 Oct. 1942; Maclean's, 15 Nov. 1942

6 *GM*, *TDS*, 22–24 Oct. 1942; KD, 22, 26 Oct. 1942; KP, King to McLarty, 23, 29 Oct. 1942; Osgoode Society interview, Lorne MacTavish; confidential interviews

7 *GM*, 5 Nov., 29 Oct. 1942; KD, 29 Oct. 1942. The text of Hepburn's statement is in HP, Private, 1942.

8 HP, Hepburn to E.J. Anderson, 18 Nov. 1942 (*GM*, *TDS*, 10–19 Feb. 1943)

9 *GM*, *TDS*, *TET*, 26, 27 Nov. 1942; KP, Hardy to King, 27 Nov. 1942; Nixon to King, 20 Dec. 1942; KD, 17 Dec. 1942, where Cross reported that Mitch swayed many members who otherwise would have favoured an immediate convention.

10 McCullagh Papers, Memorandum, R.A. Farquharson to McCullagh, 24 Dec. 1942

11 KP, Memorandum for the Prime Minister, W.J. T[Turnbull], 21 Jan. 1943, enclosing Campbell to Turnbull, 21 Jan. 1943

12 AO, Roebuck Papers, circular letter, 18 Jan., 4 Feb. 1943; Roebuck to McLarty, 29 Jan. 1943; AO, Roebuck Papers, Roebuck to G.N. Gordon, 12 Feb. 1943; Roebuck to B.A.P. Brickenden, 18 Feb. 1943; LD, 18 Jan. 1943

13 *GM*, 5, 11, 17, 25 Dec. 1942; HP, O.J. Silverthorne to Hepburn, 28 Dec. 1942; Hepburn, wire, to Power and Grierson and replies, 28 Dec. 1942. The picture had been made for the Americans, but was released in Canada at once. Mitch was still head of the Motion Picture Bureau.

14 John Kendle, *John Bracken* (Toronto 1979); HP, Hepburn to Bracken, 17 Nov. 1942; *GM*, 5 Dec. 1942, 2 Feb. 1943; *STTJ*, 4, 5 Feb., 5 Mar. 1943; USNA, State Department, 842.00/683, Lewis Clark to the Secretary of State, 9 Mar. 1943. Bracken also entered the ephemeral discussions of a wild-eyed scheme to form a national coalition of anti-King forces. Although Mitch had not answered his letters, Aberhart persisted in his attempt to get him to take the lead. On 10 November he invited him to address the conferences he planned in mid-December to begin the campaign for a new social order after the war. Mitch replied that because of the 'disturbed political situation and the prospect of a session' he could not attend, but he apparently authorized a Conservative friend, Kenneth MacLaren, a Toronto investment dealer, to meet Aberhart during a western trip. After talking to Aberhart for two hours and meeting the cabinet, MacLaren wrote Mitch that there 'is now no doubt in my mind that the time for action has come. People from Coast to Coast are crying out for leadership and it will be criminal if we don't give it to them.' On his return, MacLaren continued, 'I expect to be authorized to convene a meeting between yourself, Cardin, Aberhart and Bracken. In this connection it might be well for you to wire or phone Bracken that I shall call on him in Winnipeg ... Suffice it to say your friend Bill is right behind any organized and constructive movement along the lines we have been discussing and he says Bracken will be also. Hence my desire to get an

expression of opinion from Bracken. With you four on common ground surely we can push forward from there and nothing can stop you.' Whatever the substance of the scheme, it died stillborn. Bracken's election as leader in December killed any prospect of his participation, and it was difficult to see how three conscriptionists could link up with Cardin, who had resigned in May 1942 when the cabinet forced King to remove the limiting clause from the National Resources Mobilization Act.

15 KD, 11 Aug., 14 Sept., 5 Oct., 2, 12, 17, 19 Nov., 10, 14–16 Dec. 1943; *GM*, 17 Dec. 1943; *GM*, 20 Jan. 1943; KD, 28 Jan. 1943

16 *STTJ*, 13 Feb. 1943; *GM*, 10 Feb. 1943

17 *GM*, 12 Feb. 1943. This account is based on a report from Ken Cragg (*GM*, *TDS*, 19 Feb. 1943). It is more or less confirmed by the Nixon call (KD, 13 Feb. 1943). Sherwood Walters recalled that his father mentioned the incident to him and claimed that he persuaded Conant, and perhaps others, to reject Hepburn's proposal (interview, Sherwood Walters). Tom McQuesten was likely the minister who called the evening meeting.

18 Interview, Mrs Conant; Conant Papers, Gordon to Conant, 9 Feb. 1943; AO, Roebuck Papers, Gordon to Roebuck, 9, 22 Feb. enc. Gordon to Conant, 22 Feb. 43; *GM*, *TDS*, 20, 22 Feb. 1943; HP, Conant to Hepburn, Hepburn to Conant, 3 Mar. 1943; KD, 4, 27 Mar. 1943. His latest girl friend, a demanding young woman in her early twenties who loved the fast life, had transferred to the motion picture branch in the summer of 1941. She was unceremoniously dismissed a few weeks after Mitch left.

19 *Report of the Fifty-Ninth Annual Convention of the Trades & Labor Congress of Canada*, Aug. 1943, 14; G.M. Grube, 'Legislating for Labor,' *Canadian Forum* (May 1943), 30–1; *TDS*, 7 Apr. 1943; David Millar, 'Shapes of Power: The Ontario Labour Relations Board, 1944 to 1950' (PHD thesis, York University 1980)

20 KD, 27 Mar. 1943; AO, Roebuck Papers, Roebuck to G.N. Gordon, 12 Feb.; Gordon to Roebuck, 4 Mar. 1943

21 KP, Roebuck to King, 5 Apr. 1943; Ottawa *Citizen*, 27 Apr. 1943; KP, Memorandum, W.J. Turnbull to King, 6 May 1943; AO, Roebuck Papers, Roebuck to Gordon, 6 May 1943

22 *GM*, *TDS*, 28 Apr.–1 May 1943; KD, 30 Apr., 2 May [incorrectly dated 3 May], 1943

23 *GM*, *TET*, 3, 4 May 1943; KD, 11, 13 May 1943; *TDS*, 12 May 1943; *GM*, 28 May 1943

24 KD, 27 Mar. 1943; *TDS*, 28 July 1942; USNA, Dept. of State, 842.00/701, Lewis Clark to the Secretary of State, 24 July 1943. Mitch categorically denied a report in the *Telegram* that he had kept the Liberal war chest of between $500,000 and $750,000 in his own hands (*TET*, 23, 24 Mar. 1943).

25 AO, Drew Papers, Proceedings, Organization Meeting of Progressive Conservative Association of Ontario, 3 July 1943; *GM*, 30, 31 July 1943. The best study of the 22 Points is Bill Summers, 'George Drew's Twenty-Two Point Platform' (Graduate Research Paper, York University 1975) which was based in part on interviews with contemporaries.

26 *GM*, 31 May 1943; L. Frost Papers, Frost to Drew, 26 June 1943; NAC, PC Party Papers, Bell to Mackenzie, 5 July 1943. 'Canada: Changes in Party Fortunes,' *The Round Table* (Dec. 1943), 71. St Laurent's speech is in HCD, 5 July 1943: 4338. King's support in Ontario had fallen to 32 per cent in August, six points behind the Tories and five ahead of the CCF (*TDS*, 3 June 1943).

27 *TDS*, 26 Apr. 1943; *GM*, 11 June 1943; Carty Diary, 27 July 1943; KP, Maybank to King, 13 Aug. 1943; Gerald L. Caplan, *The Dilemma of Canadian Socialism* (Toronto 1973), 100

28 KP, A. St Clair Gordon to King, 23 June 1943; KD, 23, 26 Feb., 3, 12, 18 Mar. 1943; KP, George Hoadley to Turnbull, 30 Sept. 1943; Maybank to King, 13 Aug. 1943; KD, 7 Sept. 1943

29 *STTJ*, 30 July, 3 Aug. 1943. The *Times-Journal* supported Drew but gave Mitch good coverage. He lost only seven polls, winning St Thomas easily, but his rural support fell off badly.

30 KD, 1 Aug. 1943; Dewan Papers, Dewan to P.F. Purdom, 10 Aug. 1943. There was a consensus that as many as two-thirds of those who did not vote across the province were Liberals (USNA, State Department 842.00/704, Lewis Clark to the Secretary of State, 11 Aug. 1943). Clark also emphasized the importance of federal issues.

31 KP, Maybank to King, 13 Aug. 1943. KD, 4 Aug. 1943; *GM*, *STTJ*, 5 Aug. 1943; KP, H[enry], for the Prime Minister, 9 Aug. 1943. Senator Bench later told King that Drew had offered four seats to the Liberals, including Hepburn and Gordon, and there were other rumours to that effect (KD, 6 Oct. 1944).

CHAPTER 21: 'MORE JOY IN HEAVEN'

1 *GM*, 17 Nov. 1943; *GM*, 15 Jan. 1944; *TET*, 15 Mar. 1944. Exports of beer increased from 240,666 gallons in 1940 to 7.5 million in 1943 and six million in 1944. The value of beer production also increased significantly (Dominion Bureau of Statistics, *Breweries*, 1960).

2 *GM*, 14 Dec. 1943

3 Port Arthur *News-Chronicle*, 15 Aug. 1944; KD, 6 Oct. 1944

4 KD, 6 Oct. 1944; *GM*, 10 Aug. 1944; *GM*, 27 July 1944

5 *GM*, 4 Oct. 1944; *TDS*, 7 Oct. 1944; KP, Mills to King, 10 Oct. 1944

6 KD, 4, 6 Oct. 1944

7 KP, Bench to King, 10 Oct. 1944. King was not certain about the sinner. When Bench told him that Mitch had given up drinking 'for the past year; has been living on his farm, and looks and acts in great shape,' King was not convinced. 'Personally I wish I could believe him but I do not feel he is ever to be trusted. However, the Ontario field is their own, and the thing to do now is to make sure of the return of the Liberals in the federal field' (KD, 6 Oct. 1944).

8 KP, Nixon to King, 12 Oct. 1944, enclosing the text of his speech

9 McQuesten Papers, Dunn to McQuesten, 18 Oct. 1944

10 GM, TDS, 7 Dec. 1944; Ontario Liberal News, Jan. 1945; KD, 6 Dec. 1944; Maclean's, 15 Jan. 1945

11 CCF Papers, Provincial Council Meeting, 10 Sept. 1944

12 KP, Slaght to King, 7 Mar. 1945; LD, 19 Feb. 1945; Gerald L. Caplan, The Dilemma of Canadian Socialism (Toronto 1973), 151, citing interviews with Jolliffe and others. Jolliffe later said that Mitch and Nixon had come to him to ask 'how do we get Drew out and form a coalition government? Well, I had to turn that down too' (OHSS interview).

13 KD, 23 Jan. 1945; LD, 19 Feb. 1945

14 AO, Debates of the Legislative Assembly, verbatim transcript, 27 Feb.–22 Mar. Mitch's argument was clearly supported by Rule 114 (Alex C. Lewis, Parliamentary Procedure in Ontario [Toronto 1940], 70).

15 GM, 3 Apr. 1945; KP, Slaght to King, 7 Mar. 1945; GM, 2 Mar. 1945; Debates, verbatim transcript, 6 Mar. 1945: 776; KD, 3 Apr. 1945

16 KD, 22, 23 Mar., 12 Apr., 19 Feb. 1945; KP, Hepburn, wire, to King, 13 Apr. 1945; KD, 14, 16 Apr. 1945

17 NAC, Drew Papers, Drew to McCullagh, 30 Nov. 1943; L. Frost Papers, transcript, Meeting of the Ontario Progressive Conservative Party, 12 May 1945

18 NAC, Drew Papers, Drew to McCullagh, 30 Nov. 1943; David Lewis Papers, copy, Drew to J.G. Johnston, 3 Nov. 1943; GM, 15 May 1945; TET, 18 May 1945. See Caplan, Dilemma of Canadian Socialism, 134–65; David Lewis, The Good Fight (Toronto 1981), 288–319; Irving Abella, Nationalism, Communism and Canadian Labour: The CIO, the Communist Party and the Canadian Congress of Labour (Toronto 1973), 67–85.

19 TDS, GM, 25 May–5 June 1945. Jolliffe had known of Dempster's work for eighteen months (Lewis Papers, transcript, Jolliffe interview). For a discussion of the Gestapo charges, which still need a fuller examination, see Caplan, Dilemma of Canadian Socialism, 168–88; Lewis, The Good Fight, 261–87 (which uses material from the Drew Papers); AO, Commissions and Committees, Series B-107 and Report of Royal Commission appointed May 28, 1945 to Investigate Charges Made by Mr. E.B. Jolliffe … It is difficult to prove that the Gestapo charge boomeranged, but most contemporaries felt that it had.

20 *TDS*, *GM*, 24 Apr., 13 May 1945
21 *TDS*, 5, 10 May 1945; *STTJ*, 17 May 1945
22 KD, 19 Apr. 1945; *STTJ*, 1 June 1945; KP, Roebuck to King, 27 Apr. 1945; KP, Roebuck to King, 16, 23 May 1945; W.J. Turnbull, Memorandum for the Prime Minister, 28 May 1945
23 *Canadian Tribune*, 16 Dec. 1944, 17, 31 Mar., 21, 28 Apr., 5 May, 2 June 1945; *GM*, 2 Apr. 1945; *TDS*, 24 Apr. 1945; Communist Party of Canada Papers, Correspondence Series, transcript, Tim Buck, radio address, 9 May 1945. Arthur Slaght told King that Mitch 'has been personally attracted by MacLeod ... and that in a Provincial election that Party would nominate and run candidates in ridings where they believed they would do the most harm to the CCF.' In return, Mitch would not make a serious effort to oppose MacLeod, Salsberg, and one or two other LPP candidates (KP, Slaght to King, 7 Mar. 1945). As it turned out, the LPP could only have defeated the CCF in a handful of ridings if every LPP or Labour voter would otherwise have voted CCF.
24 *GM*, 19, 20 May 1945
25 *STTJ*, 28 Apr., 18, 30 May, 2 June 1945
26 King did win fifty-three of the sixty-five Quebec seats. In Ontario he received 40% of the popular vote and won thirty-four of the eighty-two seats, including every riding with a significant Franco-Ontarian vote. The CCF fell to 14% federally and did not elect a member.
27 *STTJ*, 5 June 1945; KD, 4, 5 June 1945
28 KP, Hazel Monteith, St Thomas, to King, n.d.; *STTJ*, 18 Oct., 3, 7, 10 Nov. 1951, 14 June 1948, *GM*, 1 Nov. 1951; interviews, Paul Martin, Ralph Hyman
29 Interviews, William Tapsell, Peter Hepburn; *STTJ*, 5 Jan. 1953
30 *STTJ*, 7 May 1949, 5, 8, Jan. 1953; St Thomas courthouse, Records of the Surrogate Court of the County of Elgin, will dated 10 June 1942 and audit file; interviews, Colin Campbell, George Ponsford, confidential. Bannockburn was assessed at $100,000; property in St Thomas and London, $48,000; cattle, $50,000; farm and gravel equipment, cars and trucks, $35,000.

CHAPTER 23: 'IF ONLY'

1 Martin Papers, interview A-16-2
2 Paul Roazen, '"As If" and Politics,' *Political Psychology* (Oct. 1983), 690. Roazen would probably say that Mitch was a person who satisfied Helen Deustch's psychoanalytic concept of one who behaved 'as if they possessed a fully felt emotional life' whose 'morality, ideals, beliefs are also mere shadow phenomena. They are ready for anything good or bad, if they are given examples to follow, and they are generally apt to join social, ethical or religious groups in order to give substance to their shadow existence by

identification' (p. 687).

3 L.L. Golden, 'What Makes Mitch Hepburn Tick?' *Winnipeg Free Press Magazine*, 16 May 1942

4 Alan Brinkley, *Forces of Protest: Huey Long, Father Coughlin and the Great Depression* (New York 1982), 282

Bibliography of Primary Sources

The research for this book began many years ago. Some of the private collections may now be in public institutions, and some of the collections have been reorganized. However, I have left the references as they were at the time of my research. I understood that the small collection of private Hepburn Papers, then restricted, were to be grouped with the major collection of his papers as premier (RG 3) and I have not distinguished between them. The material before 1934 has come largely from the private collection, which is not to be confused with those labelled 'private' in RG 3. There are four collections of Roebuck Papers. The main collection is in the Archives of Ontario. However, when Larry Zolf, a student of mine who might have written this book, was working on a study of Hepburn he secured some papers from Roebuck which are now found in the Zolf Papers (NAC) or in his possession (PC). A small collection, recently placed in the NAC, contains material on Roebuck's career in the Senate. Some of George Drew's papers are in the Archives of Ontario (RG 3). The major collection in the NAC is closed to researchers, but Edward Drew kindly allowed me very limited access. Claude Bissell permitted me to use Vincent Massey's diary but not his papers. When his biography was completed the papers were transferred from Massey College to the University of Toronto Archives and closed. I was unable to secure the late Norman Ward's permission to use the James Gardiner Papers in Saskatoon.

Institutional

NATIONAL ARCHIVES OF CANADA (NAC)
Angus, Henry; Bell, Richard; Bennett, R.B.; Borden, Robert; Cameron, A.K.;
    Claxton, Brooke; Cohen, Jacob; Christie, Loring; Dafoe, J.W.; Drew,
    George; Dunn, Sir James; Ilsley, James; King, W.L.M.; Lapointe, Ernest;
    Lewis, David; MacKay, R.A.; Mackenzie, Ian; Magrath, Charles; Manion,
    Robert; Malcolm, James; Martin, Paul; Meighen, Arthur; Murphy, Charles;
    Pouliot, J-F.; Progressive Conservative Party of Canada; Ralston, J.L.; Reid,
    Escott; Roebuck, Arthur; Sissons, C.B.; Spry, Graham; Taylor, E.P.;
    Underhill, F.H.; Zolf, Larry

DIRECTORATE OF HISTORY, NATIONAL DEFENCE HEADQUARTERS,
DEPARTMENT OF NATIONAL DEFENCE (D. HIST.)
161.009 (D63) – Correspondence and Reports on Communist Activities ...
162.009(D8) – Unemployment Relief ...
325,009(D290) – Subversion Propaganda ...

ARCHIVES OF ONTARIO
Conant, Gordon; Dafoe, Dr R.A.; Drew, George; Drury, E.C.; Ferguson, G.
    Howard; Henry, George; Hepburn, Mitchell F.; Latimer, Hugh; Maclean
    Hunter; McPhail, J.A.; McQuesten, Thomas; Murray, Thomas; Price,
    William; Roebuck, Arthur; Sedgwick, Joseph

BRITISH COLUMBIA ARCHIVES AND RECORDS SERVICES
Pattullo, Dufferin

NATIONAL ARCHIVES OF QUEBEC
Taschereau, L-A.

PROVINCIAL ARCHIVES OF ALBERTA
Aberhart, William

PROVINCIAL ARCHIVES OF MANITOBA
Bracken, John

QUEEN'S UNIVERSITY ARCHIVES
Bruce, Herbert; Campbell, Colin; Co-operative Commonwealth Federation
    (Ontario); Crerar, Thomas; Dexter, Grant; Dunning, Charles; Glen, Andrew;
    Gregory, W.D.; Grube, George; Lambert, Norman; Power, Charles; Rogers,
    Norman; Sweezey, Robert.

UNIVERSITY OF OTTAWA, CENTRE DE RECHERCHE EN CIVILISATION CANADIENNE-FRANÇAISE
L'Association Canadienne-Française d'Education d'Ontario (ACFEO)
UNIVERSITY OF TORONTO ARCHIVES
Cassidy, H.M.; Massey, Vincent: Diary (previously held in Massey College)

TRENT UNIVERSITY ARCHIVES
Frost, C.G.; Frost, Leslie M.; Ontario Progressive Conservative Association

UNIVERSITY OF WESTERN ONTARIO: REGIONAL HISTORY COLLECTION
Carty, Edmund; East Lambert Liberal Association, Minutes, 1908–1934; Gray, Ross

YORK UNIVERSITY ARCHIVES
Buck, Tim

WAYNE STATE UNIVERSITY ARCHIVES: ARCHIVES OF LABOR HISTORY (WSU)
Addes, George; Thompson, Hugh; United Automobile Workers

FRANKLIN D. ROOSEVELT LIBRARY: HYDE PARK
Berle, Adolph A. Jr.; Roosevelt, F.D.R.

DIOCESAN ARCHIVES
Kidd, Bishop John T. (London); McGuigan, Archbishop James J. (Toronto); McNally, Bishop J.T. (Hamilton); McNeil, Archbishop Neil (Toronto); O'Brien, Archbishop M.J. (Kingston)

METROPOLITAN TORONTO REFERENCE LIBRARY
Buckley, James; Johnson, Main

COMMUNIST PARTY OF CANADA: TORONTO
Communist Party

METROPOLITAN TORONTO SEPARATE SCHOOL BOARD
Catholic Taxpayers Association

ONTARIO HYDRO ARCHIVES
Cooke, J.R.; Ontario Hydro Electric Commission

ONTARIO HYDRO ELECTRIC COMMISSION: HEAD OFFICE
Minutes, Ontario Hydro Electric Commission

HYDRO-QUÉBEC ARCHIVES, MONTREAL
Beauharnois Light, Heat and Power; Gatineau Power; Shawinigan Power

WINDSOR MUNICIPAL ARCHIVES
Herman, H.F.

UNITED CO-OPERATIVES OF ONTARIO
United Farmers Papers

Private Collections

Bruce, Angela (Toronto); Chalmers, Floyd (Toronto); Dewan, Paul (Wood-stock); Donnelly, Patrick (Toronto); Fulton, James (St Thomas); McCullagh, George; Roebuck, Arthur (Larry Zolf)

Government Record Collections

NATIONAL ARCHIVES OF CANADA
RG 2 – Privy Council Office
RG 9 – Militia and Defence
RG 17 – Department of Agriculture
RG 19 – Department of Finance
RG 18 – Royal Canadian Mounted Police
RG 24 – Department of National Defence
RG 25 – Department of External Affairs
RG 27 – Department of Labour
RG 41 – Canadian Broadcasting Corporation
RG 47 – Federal-Provincial Conferences

ARCHIVES OF ONTARIO
RG 4 – Attorney-General
RG 6 – Treasury Department
RG 7 – Department of Labour
RG 8 – Provincial Secretary
RG 10 – Department of Health
RG 13 – Department of Mines
RG 16 – Department of Agriculture
RG 18 – Commissions and Committees
RG 23 – Ontario Provincial Police Papers
RG 29 – Ministry of Community and Social Services (formerly Department of Public Welfare)
RG 36 – Liquor Licensing Board of Ontario

RG 47 – Ministry of Culture and Communications
RG 70 – Ontario Securities Commission
RG 33 – Ministry of the Solicitor General

BANK OF CANADA ARCHIVES, OTTAWA
Research Department Files; Towers, Graham

UNITED STATES NATIONAL ARCHIVES (USNA)
RG 84 – Department of State

Interviews

The names of those I have interviewed or consulted, as well as those interviewed by others, are too extensive to be listed. Transcripts of the Ontario Historical Studies Series Interviews are generally available with permission of the editors. Transcripts of the interviews for a CBC Wednesday Night documentary on Hepburn in my possession and taped transcripts for a TV documentary I prepared on Hepburn will be deposited in the York University Archives. Transcripts of interviews by the Osgoode Society may be examined with permission of the society.

Picture Credits

National Archives of Canada: A ten-year-old (C 31027); Conservative election cartoon, p. 141 (C 9117)

City of Toronto Archives, Globe and Mail collection: Leaders of the liberal oppositions (28827); Slaght and O'Connor (33123); Roebuck's version of Hydro supply and demand (36008); Croll, Roebuck, and children (36466); 'There is no road too rough' (37487); 'There you have the promise of one' (37489); A cast of two (37483); The result, 6 Oct. 1937 (47215); Election night on Talbot Street (47213); Queen's Park, 17 April 1937 (44196)

Archives of Ontario: Croll, Dafoe, and the Quints (S 801); 'The Quints at Queen's Park' (RG 3, Series A-14-a, Box 14, Drew, Folder 1); 'Look! An International Victim' (Hepburn Papers)

York University Archives, from the Toronto *Telegram*: 'One issue emerges of transcendent importance – HEPBURNISM'; 'The invitation ... and the welcome!' cartoon on p. 180

John T. Saywell: Bannockburn (courtesy of Peter Hepburn); With Barney and King; Winter on Lake Laurier; Road to victory 1937; Sketches of a premier (courtesy of Peter Hepburn); Mitch and Duplessis; Birthdays, the beauty of nature, and 'pressure from millionaires' (courtesy of Peter Hepburn); Three reasons for returning; Beyond politics

Toronto *Star*: 'Sweeping back the sea' (16 April 1937), cartoon on p. 313

Globe and Mail: 'The Prodigal' (3 March 1945), cartoon on p. 517

Index